T0296739

Soft Numerical Computing in Uncertain Dynamic Systems

Soft Numerical Computing in Uncertain Dynamic Systems

Prof. Tofigh Allahviranloo
Faculty of Engineering and Natural Sciences, Bahcesehir University, Istanbul, Turkey

Prof. Witold Pedrycz
Department of Electrical and Computer Engineering, University of Alberta, Canada

Academic Press is an imprint of Elsevier
125 London Wall, London EC2Y 5AS, United Kingdom
525 B Street, Suite 1650, San Diego, CA 92101, United States
50 Hampshire Street, 5th Floor, Cambridge, MA 02139, United States
The Boulevard, Langford Lane, Kidlington, Oxford OX5 1GB, United Kingdom

Library of Congress Cataloging-in-Publication Data
A catalog record for this book is available from the Library of Congress

British Library Cataloguing-in-Publication Data
A catalogue record for this book is available from the British Library

ISBN: 978-0-12-822855-5

For information on all Academic Press publications
visit our website at https://www.elsevier.com/books-and-journals

Publisher: Mara Conner
Editorial Project Manager: Rachel Pomery
Production Project Manager: Swapna Srinivasan
Cover Designer: Victoria Pearson

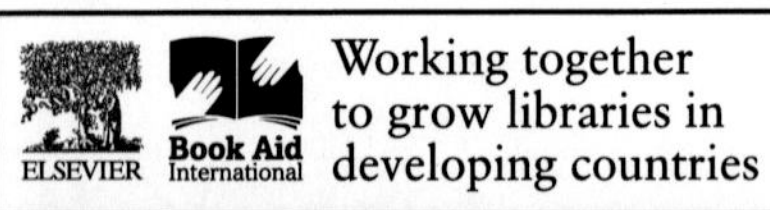
ELSEVIER
Book Aid International
Working together to grow libraries in developing countries
www.elsevier.com • www.bookaid.org

Typeset by SPi Global, India

Dedication

This book is dedicated to the scientific society.

Contents

Preface

This book contains a wealth of useful information to identify dynamic systems and differential equations under uncertainty. By studying this book, you can get acquainted with various kinds of ambiguous information and learn how to use it efficiently in dynamic systems. A careful examination of fuzzy differential equations from a numerical point of view has been carried out. For this purpose, numerical and semianalytical methods have been investigated to solve these equations. The development of solutions in the presence of complex data has been proposed. In addition, a thorough error analysis of solutions has been delivered. Interesting applications of these systems in engineering and biology have also been reported.

Tofigh Allahviranloo
Istanbul
Witold Pedrycz
Edmonton

Chapter 1

Introduction

1.1 Introduction

Uncertainty is an intrinsic component of knowledge, and yet in an age of controversial expertise, many fear their audience's reaction if they publicly communicate their uncertainty about what they know. Experimental research is widely dispersed in many disciplines. These interdisciplinary overview structures and summaries of current practice and research in the field are a combination of a statistical and psychological perspective. They inform us of a framework for communicating uncertainty in which we identify three uncertainties—facts, numbers, and science—and two levels of uncertainty: direct and indirect. Examining current practices provides a scale of nine expressions of direct uncertainty. We discuss attempts to decode indirect uncertainty in terms of the quality of the underlying evidence.

We review the limited literature on the impact of epistemological uncertainty on cognition, affect, trust, and decision-making. While there is evidence that epistemic uncertainty does not necessarily have a negative effect on the audience, its impact can vary between individuals and formats of communication. Case studies in economic statistics and climate change illustrate the framework for action. In this

Soft Numerical Computing in Uncertain Dynamic Systems. https://doi.org/10.1016/B978-0-12-822855-5.00001-X

important, by consulting with regard to future researchers we conclude but so far neglected field.

When we know that we actually live in uncertainty, we must admit that uncertainty lives with us and may be involved with any of our real-life problems. When the mind is in a state of uncertainty, it gives the slightest motivation to each side. Either you allow uncertainty to stop, hinder, or paralyze you, or you use it to inspire you to take up opportunities, seek out excitement, and achieve growth. Eventually, it all comes down to perspective and focus. Choose to focus on growth instead of stagnation. Choose to focus on possibilities instead of limitations. Choose to focus on elevating instead of staying the same.

> *It is very important to know that we cannot distinguish the exact answers to many of our real questions. This attitude of mind—this attitude of uncertainty—is critical to the scientists, and it is the attitude of the mind that the students must first acquire. Instead of trying to fight uncertainty, our duty is to figure out how we can embrace it. Because in uncertainty there is also the growth, the possibilities, and the life you want. The students should know that uncertainty creates an environment for us to grow our ability and to learn more.*
>
> **Richard P. Feynman**

The mathematical truth has a validity independent of place, personality, or human authority. Proving a mathematical theorem may have been a very romantic part of the mathematician's personal life, but one cannot expect to use it to discover his/her race, gender, or temperament itself. Truth cannot be explained or evaluated only in terms of false or true. Sometimes it is almost right, or sometimes it is probably wrong. Most of the time, the answer is given by personal feelings, for example, "I hope it's true" or "I think so." This is why a mathematician should consider the linguistic propositions in mathematical logic, which is an entrance for uncertainty in mathematics. In fact, uncertainty has a history in human civilization, and humanity has long been thinking about controlling and exploiting this kind of information.

The theory of probability can be considered as one of the cases of uncertainty. Dice gambling was the beginning of what is now called the theory of probability. In the 16th century, there was no way to quantify luck. If someone rolled two sixes during a game of dice, people thought it was just good luck. That means we can measure an event and exactly how lucky or unlucky we are—to work.

One of the most ancient and obscure concepts is the word "luck." Gambling and dice have had important roles in developing the theory of probability. In the 15th century, Cardano (2016) was one of the most well-known figures in formal algebraic activity. In *The Game of Chance*, he gave his first analysis of the rules of luck, and solved such problems numerically. In 1657, Huygens wrote the first book on probability, *On the Calculation of Chances*. This book arguably marks the real birth of probability. The theory of probability was started mathematically by Blaise Pascal and Pierre de Fermat in the 17th century, who sought to solve mathematical problems in certain gambling issues. Its translation was done in 1714 (Huygens, 1714).

The concept of "expected value" is now a key part of economics and finance: by calculating the expected value of an investment, we can work out how much it is worth to each party. This is defined as the proportion of times in a game such as a coin-tossing such that each side would win on average if the game were repeatedly played to completion. Since the 17th century, the theory of probability has been continuously formulated and applied in various disciplines. Today, it is important in most areas of engineering and tool management, and is even used in medicine, ethics, law, and other areas.

In classical logic, the values "true" and "false" or the numbers "zero" and "one" are the values for making a decision in binary logic. However, these will not work well in multivalued logic with a set of degrees of truth. Another aspect of uncertainty appears in multivalued logic. This is nonclassical logic similar to classical logic in that it embodies the truth-function principle; that is, the truth of a compound sentence is determined by the truth values of its component sentences.

Multivalued logic uses its truth degrees as technical tools for choosing particular suitable applications. It is a challenging philosophical problem to discuss the (possible, nontechnical) nature of such "truth degrees" or "truth values."

In this logic, there are propositional variables together with connectives, truth degree constants, and object constants, in the case of propositional languages and functional symbols, as well as quantifiers.

The first person to speak of ambiguity was Planck (1937). He published an article on the analysis of logic called ambiguity in the journal of *Science*. He did not mention a fuzzy word, but in fact explained the fuzzy logic that, of course, was provided by the universe; science and philosophy were ignored (Robitaille, 2007).

Eventually, in 1965, Professor L.A. Zadeh, by using fuzziness as one type of uncertainty, developed a new way to accept this idea (Zadeh, 1965). He published an article entitled "Fuzzy Sets" in the journal *Information and Control*, which used a new fuzzy logic for the sets. Zadeh considered the fuzzy name for these sets to divert it from binary logic. The emergence of this science opened up a new way of solving problems with vague values and reality-based modeling, and scientists used it to model ambiguity as part of the system.

As a practical example, in the literature of artificial intelligence and uncertainty modeling, there has long been a misunderstanding about the role of fuzzy set theory and multivalued logic. The recurrent question is whether there is a mathematical meaning to the performance of a compound calculation and the validity of the rules between exceptions. This confusion, despite some early philosophers' warnings, encompasses early developments in probable logic. Regarding this fact, three main points can be identified.

First, it shows that the root of the differences lies in the uneasy confusion between the hierarchy of beliefs and what logicians call "degrees of truth." The latter are usually composites, while the former is not. This claim is first shown by spurring the argument of noncompeting belief embedded in the standard proposition account. It seems that a copy of all or nothing of the theory is not possible. This framework is then expanded to discuss the case of fuzzy logic vs the grading theory. Next, it has been shown that any belief in the idea that combinability is accepted is at worst a fall into a Boolean truth task and at best a weak tool. Finally, some claims about the possibility of the theory of possibility being combinatory are rejected, thus illuminating the pervasive confusion between axioms of possibility theory and the underlying fuzzy set connections. Section 1.1 provides an introduction to uncertain dynamic systems.

1.1.1 Introduction to uncertain dynamic systems

The modeling of these systems is used to describe and predict the interaction over time between several uncertain components of a phenomenon that is viewed as a system. This focuses on the mechanism of how uncertain components and systems evolve over time. While many communication researchers have linked theories to uncertain dynamic processes that unfold over time, few have applied mathematical modeling techniques and none has applied soft numerical computing languages to represent formally the theories proposed. The uncertain dynamic systems allow communication researchers to explore the gap between conceptual and linguistic phenomena as dynamic and formally studied phenomena.

Uncertain dynamic systems in many academic fields have a rich history stemming from uncertain mathematics and physics, prior to their entrance into the life, social, and behavioral sciences. In the field of communication, they have already been used for a number of important research questions. Communication researchers are aware of their many benefits as data collection and analytical techniques become more accessible. Dynamic systems can be of use not only in analyzing data and testing hypotheses, but also in designing and developing theories.

The main issue here is the definition of an uncertain dynamic system. Why is it called a dynamic system, and what is its main concept?

An examination of each of the so-called components of dynamic system modeling can help clarify its meaning. The dynamic component shows that time is incorporated as a fundamental element of the model. In traditional static models, time is often overlooked, and this may impair the influence of the variables studied. In dynamic models, time is applied to the underlying data structure and understanding of how a fundamental process is formed. In some uncertain dynamic system models, uncertain and accurate data are organized by time as a sequence of repeated observations of time-varying variables called time-series data. The data is assumed to be serial dependent, meaning that individual data points are not conceived independently of each other, but each data value is affected by previous values.

Generally speaking, in dynamic models, time variable always plays a crucial role in the distribution of response time in model formulation and prediction. Dynamic system models assume that the current states of a system are dependent on past states. This is generally reflected in formal models using differential operators or differential equations with system feedback or lag terms. Within a dynamic system, the interactions are treated in an orderly manner, following rules that can be identified and defined. While systems are orderly, they behave in complex ways that make it difficult for researchers to describe them with natural verbal language. Changing one component can lead to a larger change throughout the system. A central question of any dynamic system is how it maintains stability or resistance to change over time.

Systems vary in their stability, and the following factors may affect this stability:

- how likely the system is to change states;
- the amount of expected variability within the system across time; and
- how it responds to small disturbances.

The uncertain dynamic system modeling component indicates that dynamic relationships between uncertain components of a system are executed as formal mathematical equations with uncertainty and/or using soft computing languages. Broadly speaking, modeling methods can be distinguished as mathematical/computational and statistical. In general, mathematical models express theoretical structures and relationships as explicit mathematical relationships, and make specific and detailed claims. This is in contrast to the more common theological theories in the social and behavioral sciences, which can provide rich descriptions of phenomena to generate hypotheses in which may be ambiguous and able to make equally accurate and specific testable predictions such as formal models.

It is clear that computational models are based on mathematical models. They typically implement mathematical models using computer resources and rely on computers to develop, simulate, and test complex systems. Mathematical models differ from statistical models, which are more familiar to communication researchers. Statistical models are general analytical tools that researchers use to test specific hypotheses. The models themselves may provide support or a theoretical prediction, but the statistical model is not a formal representation of the theory itself. In comparison, a mathematical or computational model is a formal representation of the theory's arguments, and how the model works directly shows what the theory predicts, and can be used for testing against experimental data. Mathematical/computational models and statistical models can be seen as the ends of a spectrum, and a variety of models fall between these two types. More specifically, uncertain dynamic systems models commonly have the following three main elements to describe how a system generally behaves.

- First, the state of the system in an uncertain environment, which represents all the system information at a determined moment in time. In this case, time and the state-space in uncertain dynamic system models may be either discrete or continuous. If time is indexed as a series of equally spaced points with unique sequential values, then it is discrete. In contrast, uncertain differential equations are used when time is treated as continuous. In this case, the variables are not indexed using specific units of time in the same manner. In general, the defined uncertain differential equation for the continuous case of time has an uncertain continuous solution that can be determined and illustrated in a discrete-time series.
- Second, the uncertainty state-space of the system, which represents all possible system states that can occur. In this case, the models may be either linear or nonlinear in the relationships they situate between variables. That is, the relationships between model uncertain parameters are explained by either linear or nonlinear functions, and even in linear cases, the model may not produce a linear output. This is because the behavior of the system predicted by the linear model can be nonlinear due to the influence of previous system states.
- Third, the state-transition function, which describes how the uncertainty state of the system changes over time. Here, the models may be stochastic or as any other cases of uncertainty. In each model, a future uncertain system state can be fully determined with complete uncertain knowledge of current system states. In a stochastic model, a future uncertain system cannot be exactly predicted, but only probabilistically determined. This formally reflects some fundamental uncertainty, imprecision, or unpredictability of a system by including an uncertain random variable or variables. The coefficients in the model can be considered as either time-invariant or time-variant. In other words, this suggests that as a process unfolds over time, the formal relationship between components in a system either does or does not change.

As far as we know, many systems in the applied sciences like medicine, economics, management, engineering, finance, and some parts of psychology work with data combined with uncertainty and ambiguities like those mentioned in the above data. The concept of uncertainty is highlighted and has long been of use, particularly in the most important areas of decision-making that are involved with our lives and problems. This is because without the right and true making of a decision, life may go in the wrong direction. As an additional illustration, a logical decision should be made in the field of indeterminacy or in the real-life environment that is formed and combined by undetermined concepts and data.

Modeling, analyzing, and solving real-life problems are the key challenges facing us. For instance, in medical science most of a patient's problems are dynamic, because they are changing over time and their behaviors are dependent on time passing. For example, nowadays cancer is a common disease and as time passes, cancer grows. Modeling and solving cancer-related problems, and analyzing and simulating solutions, are very helpful and important tasks.

1.1.2 History

Dynamic systems conceptually have long been part of some theories of social scientists. James' (1890) "stream of consciousness" emphasizes the dynamic changes in attention and thinking, while Levine's field theory (1939) explicitly uses the concepts of physics in describing dynamic interactions between the person and their environment. Early research in cybernetics has shown in detail how systems can be self-regulated through feedback, and many examples are explicitly derived from human behavior (Weiner, 1961 cited in Latta and Patten, 1978). While cybernetic ideas have been presented mathematically, many social scientists only emphasized the broader conceptual framework.

Some reasons why dynamic systems models have lagged behind social and behavioral science and theories are the lack of research and resources, and the absence of performing the appropriate data analyses in relation to capable computer technologies. Before 1950, computer simulations of dynamic processes started with system dynamics modeling and, during the 1980s, when sufficiently powerful computer technologies became more available, modeling efforts in the social and behavioral sciences began to grow in popularity. Certainly, cognitive models based on simulated and real experimental data are now increasingly popular and the whole field of cognitive science is moving toward a dynamic research paradigm. Further information about uncertain information can be found in the book by Allahviranloo (2020).

A book entitled *Uncertain Dynamic Systems*, authored by Schweppe (1973), is the only one that deals with subject matter similar to the one mentioned here. The book concerns dynamics, estimation theory, statistical hypothesis testing, and system analysis. This book is designed to help the reader make certain statements about dynamic systems when uncertainty exists in a system's input and output, and in the nature of the system itself. The methods of interest are applicable to large-scale, multivariable systems. The problems of and interactions among modeling, analysis, and design are considered. Emphasis is placed on techniques that can be implemented on a computer.

In general, there is a huge difference between the abovementioned book and this book, because in our book, the numerical simulations of the solutions obtained by numerical methods are discussed in detail. *Uncertain Dynamic Systems* does not discuss the numerical solutions, convergence, and consistency, although it mentions theoretical analysis of uncertain dynamic systems.

Another relevant book is *Extremal Fuzzy Dynamic Systems*, written by Sirbiladze (2013). Sirbiladze presents a new approach to the study of dynamic systems with weak structures. The book's approach differs from those of other publications by considering time as a source of fuzzy uncertainty in dynamic systems. *Extremal Fuzzy Dynamic Systems* progresses systematically by covering the theoretical aspects first before tackling the applications. In the application section, a software library is described, which contains discrete EFDS identification methods elaborated during fundamental research of the book.

The uncertainty mentioned in *Extremal Fuzzy Dynamic Systems* is very limited, and involves only fuzzy sets; the models are fuzzy models with fuzzy inputs and outputs. In addition, the author does not discuss several other types of uncertainty and numerical simulations that we consider in this volume. To the best of our knowledge and at the time of writing, there is no other book with our book title and subject matter, making this volume completely original.

Fuzzy Dynamic Systems was published by de Barros et al. (2017). It presents an introduction to fuzzy dynamic systems, both continuous and discrete. To study the dynamic case, the concepts of fuzzy derivative and fuzzy integral are presented. Several kinds of derivatives are explored, and several types of fuzzy differential equations are consequently studied. The discrete case is studied by means of an interactive process. All cases are illustrated using the Malthusian model.

It is known that uncertainty can appear as fuzziness; the topic of fuzzy dynamic systems has recently gained more interest and many researchers have worked on the topic both theoretically and numerically. A system of fuzzy differential equations is utilized for the purpose of modeling problems in the fields of engineering, biology, and physics among others. Differential equations have been unable to predict all the possible forms of arrhythmia, leading to failure to detect numerous disturbances by cardiologists. As an application of fuzzy differential equations in biomedical science, fuzzy differential equations are promising in terms of anticipating the nuances of each category of arrhythmia (different run lengths of premature ventricular contraction), contributing to the efficient diagnosis of heart abnormalities.

Another aspect of a dynamic system can occur as fuzzy fractional differential equations. It differentiates different materials and processes in many applied sciences like electrical circuits, biology, biomechanics, electrochemistry, electromagnetic processes, and others, and is widely recognized to predict accurately by using fractional differential operators in accordance with their memory and hereditary properties. For complex phenomena, the modeling and its results in diverse widespread fields of science and engineering are very complicated, and to achieve accuracy, the only powerful tool suitable is fractional calculus. This is not only a very important and productive topic, but also represents a new point of view on how to construct and apply a certain type of nonlocal operator to real-world problems.

1.1.3 STRUCTURE OF THE BOOK

The structure of this monograph is planned as follows. Chapter 2 covers the concepts of uncertain sets. In this chapter, we define, introduce, and explain types of uncertainties. The concept of uncertainty can come in many forms, such as an unspecified set, the expected amount or interval of data, random data, or a combination of all of these. A different perspective can be described as a membership function called fuzzy data and a combination of membership functions, probability, and distribution.

In Chapter 3, operators like distance, derivative, and ranking on fuzzy sets are considered. One of the most important operations on fuzzy sets is the difference. It may seem strange that we call it difference and not by subtract; this is because the subtraction of two sets of ordered pairs or functions cannot be defined properly, and here we define it by the Hukuhara difference.

This concept is a key operator to define the derivative of a fuzzy function. In advance, the combination of distributive function and fuzzy membership function and its combination with other uncertain sets are defined as advanced combined uncertain sets. Soft computing on the last type of uncertainty is a very different and new discussion topic. Sometimes this operation does not have a formal form of computing and should be done by expert systems. We will therefore need to discuss uncertain inferences and logical decisions to reach the results for the calculations.

Chapter 4 covers the concept of the continuous numerical solution, which means that the solution of the numerical method approximates the exact solution functionally. For instance, the Taylor method is one method that works with an arbitrary order of differentiability under uncertainty. Another functional numerical method is variational iteration. To explain this method, we need to discuss the weakly and strongly uncertain nonlinear equation cases. Variational iteration is the most effective and convenient method for both weakly and strongly uncertain nonlinear equations. This method has been shown to solve effectively, easily, and accurately a large class of nonlinear problems with components converging rapidly to accurate solutions.

Chapter 5 discusses Euler's method and other finite difference methods, such as Runge–Kutta's method, and predictor and corrector methods to solve the problem numerically. It is more appropriate to use the prefix "uncertain" for all of these methods. Because the modeling of the methods under uncertainty will be almost different. Since the definition of difference has two cases, the derivative of an uncertain function is defined in two cases as well. Now considering the order of differentiability or differential equations with high order, the cases for the uncertain differential equations have several types. In each of several cases, we discuss the details for convergence theorems and consistency, and stability as well. Stability is one of the most important concepts in dynamic systems, especially in uncertain cases. Several types of stability are considered in detail.

Chapter 6 discusses fractional operators, which have been much highlighted over the past decade, and which have many applications in real-world problems. Different materials and processes in many applied sciences like electrical circuits, biology, biomechanics, electrochemistry, electromagnetic processes, and others are widely recognized to be predicted effectively by using fractional differential operators in accordance with their memory and hereditary properties. For complex phenomena, the modeling and its results in diverse widespread fields of science and engineering are very complicated, and to achieve accuracy, the only powerful tool suitable is fractional calculus. This is not only a very important and productive topic, but also represents a new point of view on how to construct and apply a certain type of nonlocal operator to real-world problems. Since the uncertainty in our real environment and data plays an important role, this causes us to discuss the uncertainty in the mentioned topics.

Finally, in Chapter 7, we discuss partial differential equations with uncertainty. As far as we know, many real-world problems in engineering science relate to partial differential equations, such as wave equations, heat equations, heat and mass transferring, etc. All of the related equations work with uncertain information like fuzzy, interval, and any others that we mentioned earlier. Since most of the numerical methods for solving these types of equations are finite difference methods, we will investigate further new uncertain finite difference methods for solving these equations. These methods are connected to some linear systems and in this case, we will be involved with uncertain linear systems.

As similar to other equations, the numerical solutions of these equations need to prove convergence, stability, and consistency. We will therefore consider these properties theoretically as well. On this topic, the operator of a derivative as a partial derivative can be an uncertain operator, and this is why, when starting this subject, we have to illustrate the uncertain operators of the partial derivative.

References

Allahviranloo, T., 2020. Uncertain Information and Linear Systems, Studies in Systems, Decision and Control. Springer.

Cardano, G., 2016. The Book of Game of Chance: The 16th-Century Treatise on Probability. Mathematical Association of America (Chapter 1).

de Barros, L.C., Bassanezi, R.C., Lodwick, W.A., 2017. A First Course in Fuzzy Logic, Fuzzy Dynamical Systems, and Biomathematics—Theory and Applications. Studies in Fuzziness and Soft Computing, vol. 347. Springer. ISBN 978-3-662-53322-2, pp. 1–295.

Huygens, C., 1714. The Value of Chances in Games of Fortune. English translation. https://math.dartmouth.edu/~doyle/docs/huygens/huygens.pdf.

James, W., 1890. The Principles of Psychology. Henry Holt, New York, NY.

Latta, R.M., Patten, R.L., 1978. A test of Weiner's attribution theory inertial motivation hypothesis. J. Pers. 46, 383–399.

Robitaille, P.-M., 2007. Max Karl Ernst Ludwig Planck: (1858–1947). Prog. Phys 4, 117–121.

Schweppe, F.C., 1973. Uncertain Dynamic Systems. Prentice Hall, Englewood Cliffs, NJ.

Sirbiladze, G., 2013. Extremal fuzzy dynamic systems—theory and applications. In: IFSR International Series in Systems Science and Systems Engineering, Springer.

Zadeh, L.A., 1965. Fuzzy sets. Inf. Control. 8 (3), 338–353.

Chapter 2

Uncertain sets

2.1 Short introduction to this chapter

Let us start with a quote from Richard P. Feynman, the American physicist:

I think that when we know that we actually do live in uncertainty, then we ought to admit it; it is of great value to realize that we do not know the answers to different questions. This attitude of mind—this attitude of uncertainty—is vital to the scientist, and it is this attitude of mind which the student must first acquire.

In this chapter, several types of uncertainties are discussed. First, an uncertain set is defined, and it is considered as a membership function. Second, a special case of the membership function appears as an interval; it is then defined and explained. Under some conditions, a fuzzy set can be defined as uncertain data. After explaining these data, a combination of membership function and distributive function as Z-sets will be discussed. All these uncertain data are evaluated completely and calculations on them are evaluated properly.

Soft Numerical Computing in Uncertain Dynamic Systems. https://doi.org/10.1016/B978-0-12-822855-5.00002-1

2.2 Textual short outline

Any uncertainty space is formed by uncertain variables and an uncertain variable to be completed by measurable space. To define a measurable space, we need to define a measurable set. A measurable set is an extended set with measures. It means any member of the set has a measure. The measures for the members come from a measurable function. The measures have their own rules and these rules define an algebra. We therefore have to work with a space of measurable functions and these can be called membership functions, because normally the measures can play the role of memberships for the members of the set. To continue the discussion, distributive functions, sigma algebra, and Borel sets should be discussed.

2.3 Measures

As we mentioned, to define the measure we have to define a measurable space. For defining a measurable space we need to have a measurable set. Mathematically and essentially, the uncertainty theory is an alternative theory of measure in a measurable space, and this is why uncertainty theory should be discussed on a measurable space. In this section we are not going to discuss the preliminary definitions in-depth, because more and sufficient results can be found in many other books that discuss them thoroughly (Allahviranloo, 2020; Liu, 2015).

2.3.1 Measurable space

A set, $\mathbb{S}$, with a nonempty collection, $\mathbb{C}$, of subsets of $\mathbb{S}$, $(\mathbb{S}, \mathbb{C})$, is called a measurable space if it satisfies the following two conditions:

1. For $A, B \in \mathbb{C}$ then $A - B = A \cap B^c \in \mathbb{C}$.
2. For any $\{A_i\}_{i=1}^{\infty} \in \mathbb{C}$ then $\bigcup_{i=1}^{\infty} A_i \in \mathbb{C}$.

The members of this collection $\mathbb{C}$ are called **measurable sets.**

Based on the definition, several properties of the measurable sets are immediately obvious:

1. The empty set $\emptyset \in \mathbb{C}$ is a measurable set and $(\mathbb{S}, \mathbb{C})$ is a measurable space, because it satisfies two of the conditions.
2. If A and B are two measurable sets then $A \cap B$, $A \cup B$ and $A - B$ are measurable sets. The proofs are clear. First, suppose we want to prove that $A - B$ is a measurable set. Since $A, B \in \mathfrak{c}$, then based on the first condition $A - B \in \mathbb{C}$ and it is exactly the first condition of the definition. Now, to prove that $A \cap B \in \mathbb{C}$, we

use $A \cap B = A - (A - B)$ and clearly it is already proved. Finally, for proving the union $A \cup B$, using the second property of the definition on the sequence $A, B, \varnothing$, $\varnothing$, ... our assertion is finalized.

3. For $\{A_i\}_{i=1}^{\infty}$ measurable sets the $\bigcap_{i=1}^{n} A_i$ is a measurable set. It is clear because $A_1 \cap A_2 \cap A_3 \cap \ldots = A_1 - \{(A_1 - A_2) \cup (A_1 - A_3) \cup (A_1 - A_4) \cup \ldots\}$ and $\{(A_1 - A_i)\}_{i=1}^{\infty}$, and their unions are measurable, therefore the proof is completed.

Note: Measurable sets are closed under taking countable intersections and unions operators.

2.3.2 Examples

The spaces $(\mathbb{S}, \mathbb{C} = \{\varnothing\})$, $(\mathbb{S}, \mathbb{C} = \{All\,subsets of\,\mathbb{S}\})$.

Now, let $(\mathbb{S}, \mathbb{C})$ be a measurable space. A **measure** on this space consists of a nonempty subset, $\mathcal{M}$, of $\mathbb{C}$, together with a mapping $\mu : \mathcal{M} \to R^+$ satisfying the following two conditions:

1. For any $A \in \mathcal{M}$ and $\mathbb{C} \ni B \subset A$, we have $B \in \mathcal{M}$.
2. Let $A = \bigcup_{i=1}^{\infty} A_i$ for all disjoint $\{A_i\}_{i=1}^{\infty} \in \mathcal{M}$, then:

$$A \in \mathcal{M} \Leftrightarrow \sum_{i=1}^{\infty} \mu(A_i) \to \mu(A)$$

Each type of measurable space is defined by its own measure: probability space is defined by probability measure, uncertainty space is defined by uncertainty measure, and fuzzy space can be defined by fuzzy measure. In fact, the measures play the role of membership for the member of a set belonging to $\mathbb{C}$ of the measurable space. Suppose that $(\mathbb{U}, \mathbb{C})$ is an uncertain space and μ is the degree of uncertainty of members of a set $\mathcal{M}$. This concept points out that the members of every set that belongs to uncertainty space have a membership degree in the set. These membership degrees satisfy the two abovementioned properties.

2.4 Uncertain sets and variables

Uncertain variables are tools to model the data in an indeterminacy field that cannot be predicted exactly, such as throwing coins, tossing dice, playing poker, stock pricing, marketing and market demand, and lifetime.

What is the answer to this question, which person is beautiful? Apparently, the answer depends on one's personality and varies by different ones. It is clear that we have an uncertain variable regarding beautiful people. The membership of everyone in this set is called a membership degree. The membership degree can be considered as a real number from the interval [0, 1].

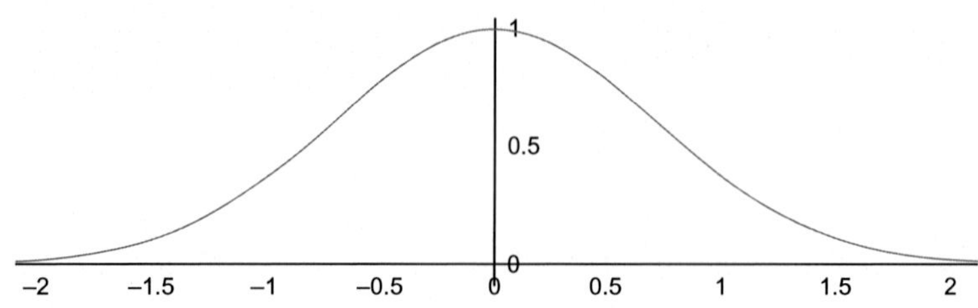

Fig. 2.1 Gaussian membership function on $[a_1, a_2] = [-2, 2]$.

Indeed, an uncertain set is formed by ordered pairs such that the second component is the membership degree of the first one. Graphically, these ordered pairs lie on the function and this function is called the membership function. Sometimes the uncertain set takes the role of an uncertain variable. It depends on the situation. For instance, to consider an uncertain function requires an uncertain variable, and is indeed a measurable set and has a membership function. In the following, several uncertain sets and variables are plotted and modeled mathematically.

- Gaussian form membership function on $[a_1, a_2]$ (Fig. 2.1)

$$f_1(x) = \begin{cases} 0, & x \le a_1 \\ e^{-x^2}, & a_1 \le x \le a_2 \\ 0, & x \ge a_2 \end{cases}$$

- Triangular form membership function on $[a_1, a_2]$

$$f_2(x) = \begin{cases} 0, & x \le a_1 \\ \dfrac{x - a_1}{\overline{a} - a_1}, & a_1 \le x < \overline{a} \\ 1, & x = \overline{a} \\ \dfrac{a_2 - x}{a_2 - \overline{a}}, & \overline{a} < x \le a_2 \\ 0, & x \ge a_2 \end{cases}$$

If we suppose that $a_1 = -2, \overline{a} = 1, a_2 = 2$, the figure is Fig. 2.2.

- Trapezoidal form membership function on $[a_1, a_2]$

$$f_2(x) = \begin{cases} 0, & x \le a_1 \\ \dfrac{x - a_1}{\overline{a} - a_1}, & a_1 \le x < a' \\ 1, & a' \le x \le a'' \\ \dfrac{a_2 - x}{a_2 - \overline{a}}, & a'' < x \le a_2 \\ 0, & x \ge a_2 \end{cases}$$

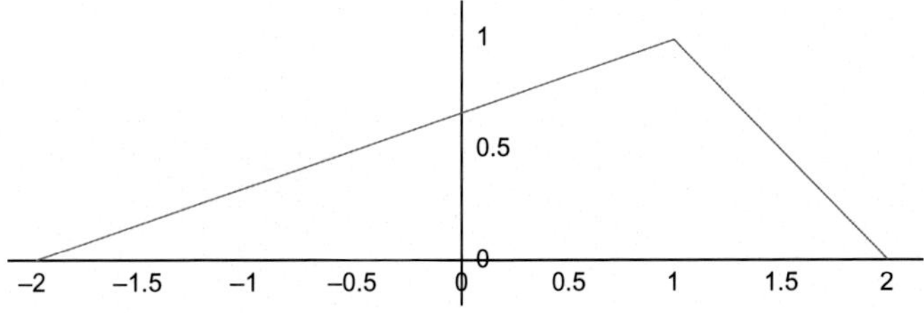

Fig. 2.2 Triangular membership function.

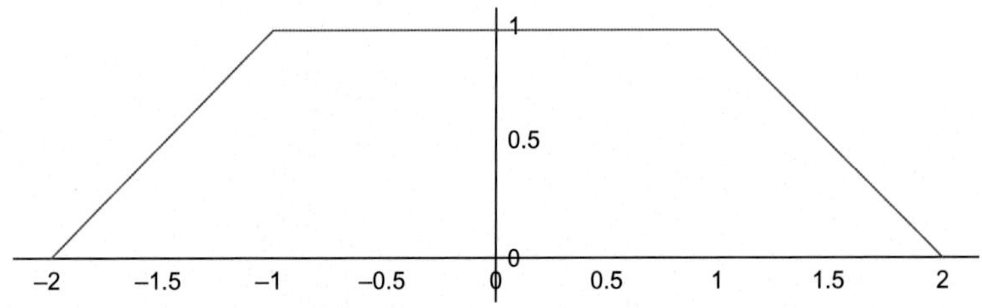

Fig. 2.3 Trapezoidal membership function.

If we suppose that $a_1 = -2$, $a' = -1$, $a'' = 1$, $a_2 = 2$, the figure is Fig. 2.3.

Consider the following function. In this figure $x(t) \in [0, 1] \subseteq R^+$; the variable x is an uncertain variable and can be chosen from uncertainty space (Fig. 2.4).

2.4.1 Examples

$$x_1(t) = t,\ x_2(t) = kt^n, k, n \in R^+,\ x_3(t) = \exp(t), \ldots$$

2.4.1.1 *Zigzag uncertain variable*

This example is the shape of zigzag uncertain variables. Suppose we are talking about the tallness of five children, everyone shorter than 1 m is not called as a tall child, but all children with tallness between 1 and 1.20 m can be called tall. The children with tallness between 1.20 and 1.30 are called almost tall and the rest more than 1.30 m are called completely tall. The children with tallness 1.20–1.30 are almost tall and the rest more than 1.30 m are completely tall (Fig. 2.5).

$$x(t) = \begin{cases} 0, & t \leq 1 \\ \dfrac{t-40}{30}, & 1 < t \leq 1.20 \\ \dfrac{t-60}{10}, & 1.20 < t \leq 1.30 \\ 1, & 1.30 < t \end{cases}$$

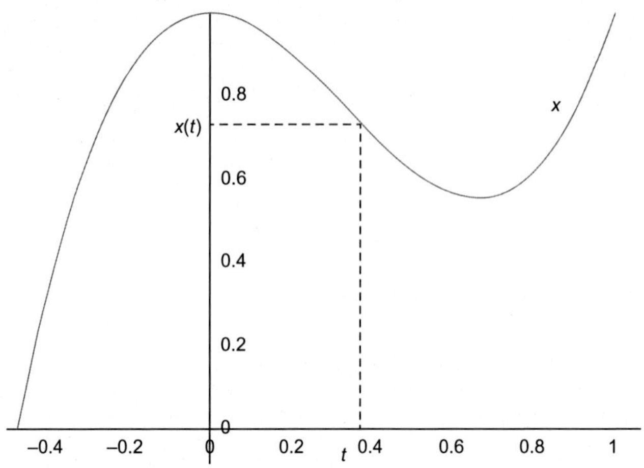

Fig. 2.4 Uncertain variable.

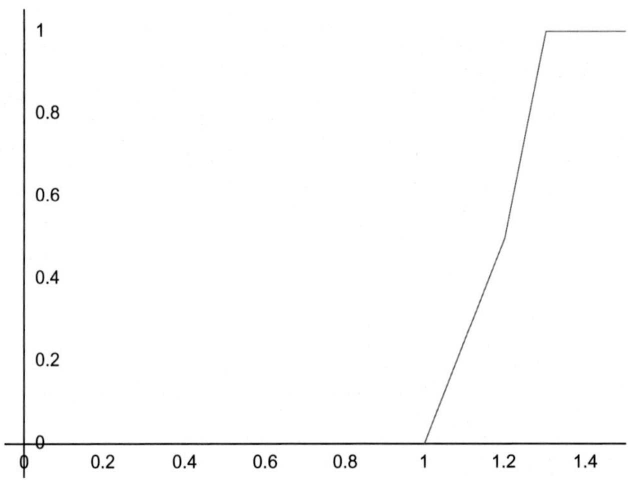

Fig. 2.5 The set of tall children as an uncertain variable.

2.4.2 Experimental uncertain variables

The following membership function is for an experimental uncertain variable with the following figure.

$$x(t) = \begin{cases} 0, & t \le t_1 \\ \theta, & t = t_i + \theta(t_{i+1} - t_i) \\ 1, & t_n < t \end{cases}$$

where $1 \le i \le n-1$, $0 < \theta \le 1$ (Fig. 2.6).

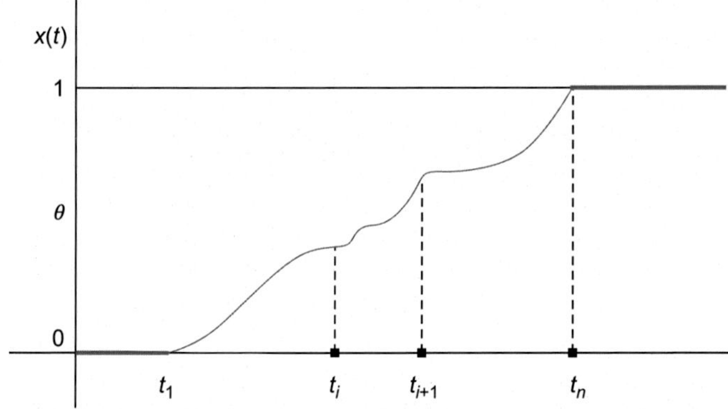

Fig. 2.6 An experimental uncertain variable.

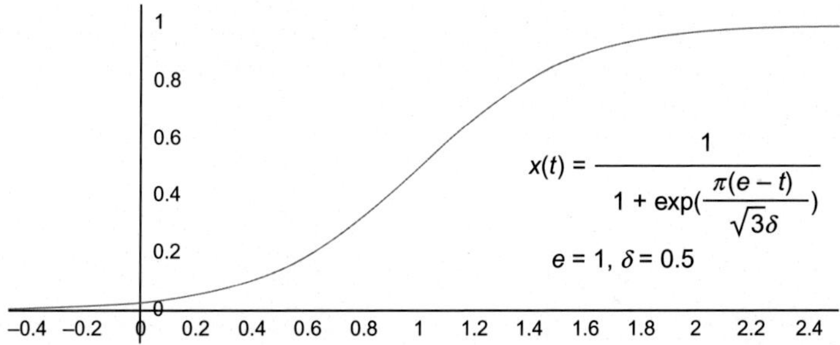

Fig. 2.7 An experimental uncertain variable.

Or another case of an experimental uncertain variable (Fig. 2.7):

$$x(t) = \frac{1}{1 + \exp\left(\frac{\pi(e-t)}{\sqrt{3}\delta}\right)}, \quad e, \delta \in R^+ x \in R$$

Note. We now have enough information about the uncertainty and uncertain sets and variables. One of the uncertainty cases is fuzzy sets. Like other uncertain sets, the fuzzy set is a set of ordered pairs (the member and its membership). It is a membership function as well and its structures and forms are the same as the structures and forms of uncertain sets (see Figs. 2.1–2.3).

2.4.3 Membership function

For a fuzzy set (uncertain set), A, the membership of its elements, $x \in A$, has a membership degree, $A(x) \in [0, 1]$. If the degree is 0, the member does not belong to the set and if the degree is 1, the member belongs to the set completely.

This is why any real set is a special case of an uncertain set and has the characteristic degree and function. In this case, the range of the membership degree is $\{0,1\}$. It is obvious than the set A is a fuzzy set and

$$A=\{(x,A(x))\,|\,A(x)\in[0,1],\ x\in A\}$$

This set is called the membership function.

In this concept, if x belongs to the uncertain set with the membership degree $A(x)$, at the same time it does not belong to the set with $1-A(x)$ membership degree. In the following section, we discuss fuzzy numbers and their properties.

2.5 Fuzzy numbers and their properties

First of all, we should know why we need a fuzzy number and why it is important: because we need to make computations and rank the fuzzy sets. This is why fuzzy sets must have some additional properties. We shall now explain their graphical and mathematical forms and computations. First of all, we should define a fuzzy set as a fuzzy number.

2.5.1 Definition of a fuzzy number

A fuzzy membership function $A:R\to[0,1]$ is called a fuzzy number if it has the following conditions:

1. A is normal. This means there is at least a real member x_0 such that $A(x_0)=1$.
2. A is fuzzy convex. This means for two arbitrary real points x_1, x_2 and $\lambda\in[0,1]$, we have:

$$A(\lambda x_1+(1-\lambda)x_2)\geq\min\{A(x_1),A(x_2)\}$$

3. A, is upper-semicontinuous. This means that if we increase its value at a certain point x_0 to $f(x_0)+\epsilon$ (for some positive constant ϵ), then the result is upper-semicontinuous; if we decrease its value to $f(x_0)-\epsilon$, then the result is lower-semicontinuous.
4. The closure of the set $\text{Supp}(A)=\{x\in R|\ A(x)>0\}$, as a support set, is a compact set.

As an example, the triangular, trapezoidal fuzzy sets are fuzzy numbers.

The definition of a fuzzy number can be defined as other forms: parametric and level-wise.

2.5.2 Level-wise form of a fuzzy number

The level-wise membership function is, in fact, an inverse function of the membership function that proposes an interval-valued function. In fact, any level in the

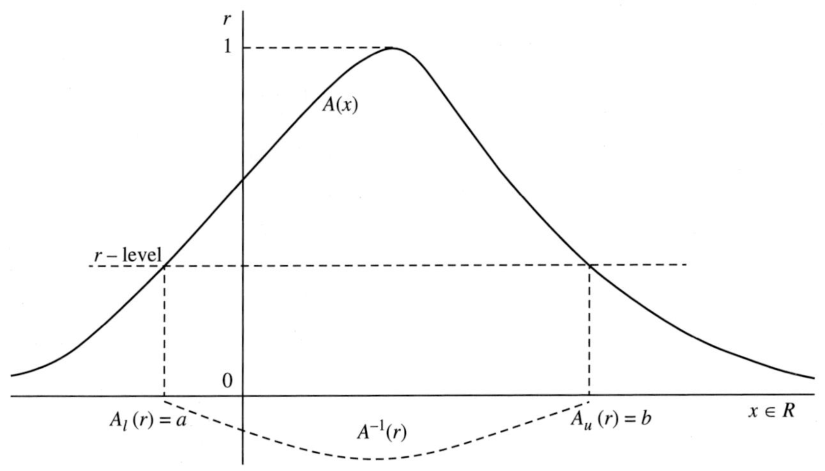

Fig. 2.8 Level-wise form of a fuzzy set.

vertical axis gives us an interval in the horizontal axis. For example, consider one of the following triangular membership functions (Fig. 2.8).

In this figure, all real numbers in the interval $[a, b]$ have a degree of membership greater than or equal to the value of "r-level" in the fuzzy set A, i.e.,

$$\forall x \in [a, b],\ A(x) \geq r,\ 0 \leq r \leq 1$$

Then the r-cut or r-level set of the membership function can be defined as follows:

$$A^{-1}(r) = \{x \in R |\, A(x) \geq r\} = [a, b] = [A_l(r), A_u(r)] := A[r],\ 0 \leq r \leq 1$$

Based on the inequality property in the set, $A[r]$, $A(x) \geq r$, it is clear that the membership function, $A(x)$, can be obtained by:

$$A(x) = \sup\{0 \leq r \leq 1\ |x \in A^{-1}(r)\},\ x \in R$$

This means that there is a one-to-one map between two functions: the membership function $A^{-1}(r)$ and the level-wise membership function $A(x)$.

Fig. 2.9 shows that for each interval there is a degree or level, and vice versa. In fact, it can be claimed that:

$$\text{Domain of } A(x) = \bigcup_{0 \leq r \leq 1} [A_l(r), A_u(r)]$$

Now, in general, a fuzzy set A in level-wise form can be shown as follows:

$$A[r] = [A_l(r), A_u(r)],\ \ 0 \leq r \leq 1$$

Another form of the definition in Section 2.5.1 can be defined as follows.

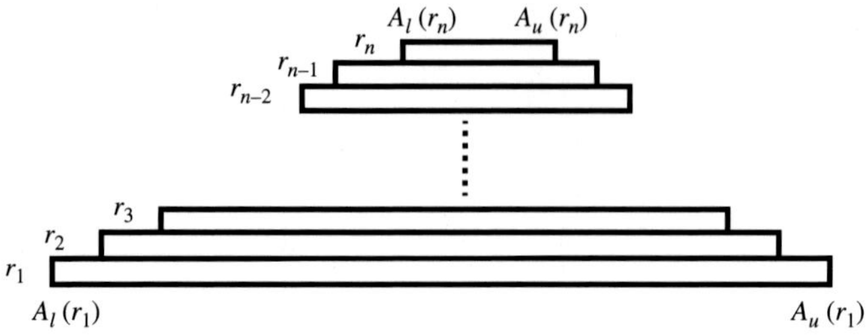

Fig. 2.9 One-to-one corresponding.

2.5.3 Definition of a fuzzy number in level-wise form

A fuzzy membership function $A: R \rightarrow [0, 1]$ is called a fuzzy number if its level-wise form $A[r] = [A_l(r), A_u(r)]$ is a compact interval for any $0 \leq r \leq 1$.

Another form of Definition 2.5.3 is called a stacking theorem and can be defined as follows.

2.5.4 Definition of a fuzzy number in level-wise form

Sufficient and necessary conditions for $A^{-1}(r) = A[r]$ to be a level-wise membership function of a fuzzy number are as follows (Fig. 2.10):

i. (Nesting property) For any two r-levels, r_1, r_2
If $r_1 \leq r_2$ then $A[r_1] \supseteq A[r_2]$

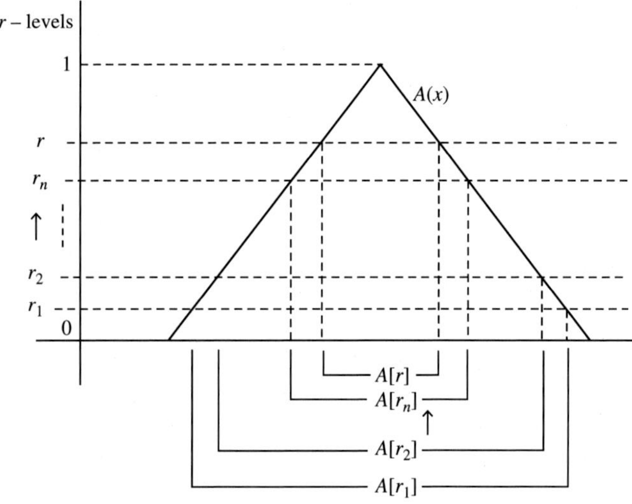

Fig. 2.10 Two conditions in Definition in Section 2.5.4.

ii. For any monotone increasing sequence of levels, $0<r_1<r_2<\ldots<r_n<1$,

$$(\text{if})\ \{r_n\}_n \nearrow \mathrm{r}, \text{then}\ \mathrm{A}[\mathrm{r_n}] \rightarrow \mathrm{A}[\mathrm{r}],\quad \text{for any}\ 0 \leq \mathrm{r} \leq 1$$

2.5.4.1 *A singleton fuzzy number*

A real number "a" is called a singleton fuzzy number if:

$$a[r] = [a_l(r), a_u(r)] = [a, a]$$

It means in the membership function the membership degree at "a" is 1 and at other values is zero. $a_l(r) = a_u(r) = a$.

Based on this definition, we have the same for fuzzy zero number or origin and $a_l(r) = a_u(r) = 0$.

2.5.5 Definition of a fuzzy number in parametric form

Any fuzzy number, A, has the parametric form $A(r) = (A_l(r), A_u(r))$ for any $0 \leq r \leq 1$, if and only if:

- **i.** $A_l(r) \leq A_u(r)$;
- **ii.** $A_l(r)$ is an increasing and left continuous function on $(0, 1]$ and right continuous at 0 with respect to r; and
- **iii.** $A_u(r)$ is a decreasing and left continuous function on $(0, 1]$ and right continuous at 0 with respect to r.

Note that, in items (ii) and (iii), both functions can be bounded.

In both forms of fuzzy numbers—level-wise form and parametric form—both functions, lower, $A_l(r)$, and upper, $A_u(r)$, are the same. But the differences can be listed as follows:

1. In level-wise form, the values of both functions for any arbitrary but fixed r are real numbers. But in parametric form, they take the role of a function with respect to r.
2. In level-wise form, the level is an interval for any arbitrary but fixed r. However, in parametric form, it is a couple of functions with respect to r.

Now we are going to introduce other forms of a fuzzy number in linear, nonlinear cases. The following figure shows that it does not matter which fuzzy number we consider for analyzing.

Indeed, a membership function that corresponds to a fuzzy number is a piece-wise function. For example:

$$A_1(x)=\begin{cases} x, & 0\le x\le 1 \\ 2-x, & 1\le x\le 2 \\ 0, & \text{otherwise} \end{cases}$$

$$A_2(x)=\begin{cases} 1-|x|, & -1\le x\le 1 \\ 0, & \text{otherwise} \end{cases}$$

$$A_3(x)=\begin{cases} |x|, & -1\le x\le 1 \\ 0, & \text{otherwise} \end{cases}$$

$$A_4(x)=\begin{cases} \sqrt{x}, & -1\le x\le 1 \\ 1, & \text{otherwise} \end{cases}$$

In general form, the function can be shown as follows:

$$A(x)=\begin{cases} L\left(\dfrac{x-a}{b-a}\right), & a\le x\le b \\ 1, & b\le x\le c \\ R\left(\dfrac{d-x}{d-c}\right), & c\le x\le d \\ 0, & \text{otherwise} \end{cases}$$

where $L, R:[0,1]\longrightarrow[0,1]$ are two nondecreasing shape functions and

$$R(0)=L(0)=0,\ R(1)=L(1)=1.$$

To obtain the level-wise or parametric forms of the fuzzy number in the general form, the relations are:

$$A_l(r)=a+(b-a)L^{-1}(r),$$

$$A_u(r)=d-(d-c)R^{-1}(r),\ r\in[0,1]$$

Clearly, if the functions L and R are linear, then we will have trapezoidal and triangular membership functions as fuzzy numbers. If they are nonlinear, then they will appear as curves that look trapezoidal or triangular.

The general form of a fuzzy number in linear or nonlinear cases can be shown in Fig. 2.11.

2.5.6 Nonlinear fuzzy number

For instance, in the following cases, the fuzzy numbers do not have any linear lower and upper functions.

$$L(x)=\frac{1}{1+x^2},\ R(x)=\frac{1}{1+2|x|},\ \alpha=3,\ \beta=2,\ m=4$$

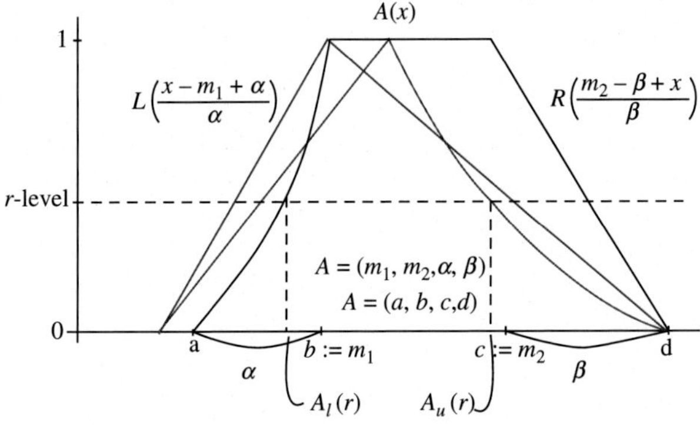

Fig. 2.11 General form of a fuzzy number.

Then the membership function is:

$$A(x) = \begin{cases} L\left(\dfrac{4-x}{3}\right) = \dfrac{1}{1+\left(\dfrac{4-x}{3}\right)^2}, & x \leq 4 \\ R\left(\dfrac{x-4}{2}\right) = \dfrac{1}{1+2\left|\dfrac{x-4}{2}\right|}, & 4 \leq x \\ 0, & \text{otherwise} \end{cases}$$

The figure of this membership function is as shown in Fig. 2.12. Generally, the r-level set of a fuzzy set A is:

$$A[r] = [A_l(r), A_u(r)] = \left[a + (b-a)L^{-1}(r), d - (d-c)R^{-1}(r)\right]$$

Note that members of an r-level set as an interval are included in the membership function with membership degree or uncertain measure, r.

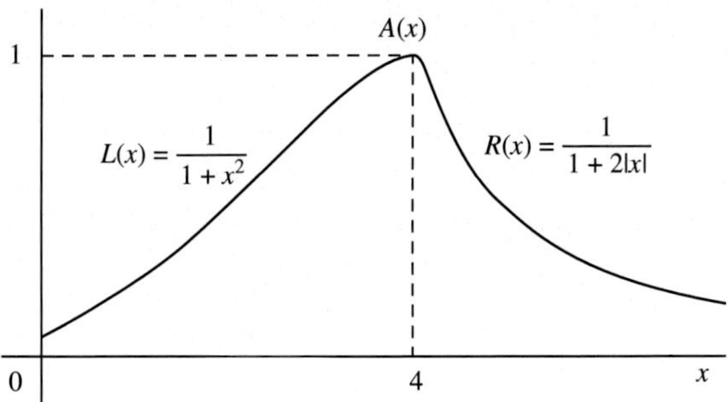

Fig. 2.12 Nonlinear fuzzy number.

2.5.7 Trapezoidal fuzzy number

The general level-wise or parametric forms are:

$$A_l(r) = b - (b-a)L^{-1}(r),$$

$$A_u(r) = c + (d-c)R^{-1}(r), \quad r \in [0, 1]$$

where, in the linear case, the left and right functions can be replaced by linear functions like $R(r) = L(r) = r$ or others.

Now suppose that $b-a=\alpha$, $d-c=\beta$, $b=m_1$, $c=m_2$ then the membership function will be:

$$A(x) = \begin{cases} L\left(\dfrac{m_1 - x}{\alpha}\right), & m_1 - \alpha \le x \le m_1 \\ R\left(\dfrac{x - m_2}{\beta}\right), & m_2 \le x \le m_2 + \beta \\ 1, & m_1 \le x \le m_2 \\ 0, & \text{otherwise} \end{cases}$$

where α, β are left and right spreads, and m_1, m_2 are cores of a trapezoidal fuzzy number.

$$A_l(r) = m_1 - \alpha L^{-1}(r),$$

$$A_u(r) = m_2 + \beta R^{-1}(r), \quad r \in [0, 1]$$

The formal formats to show this number can be written as:

$$A = (a, b, c, d) := A = (m_1, m_2, \alpha, \beta) := A[r] = [A_l(r), A_u(r)] := A(r) = (A_l(r), A_u(r))$$

Note that these formats are only for presenting the fuzzy number and each one has its own properties and calculations. The calculations on them will be explained in the next sections.

The r-level set of a trapezoidal fuzzy set $A = (a, b, c, d)$ is:

$$A[r] = [A_l(r), A_u(r)] = [b + (b-a)(r-1), c + (d-c)(1-r)]$$

2.5.8 Triangular fuzzy number

The only difference of triangular fuzzy number from trapezoidal is the number of the cores in membership functions. In the trapezoidal, if the cores are the same, i.e., $m_1 = m_2 = m$, then it will be a triangular fuzzy number. The general level-wise or parametric forms are:

$$A_l(r) = b - (b-a)L^{-1}(r),$$

$$A_u(r) = b + (c-b)R^{-1}(r), \quad r \in [0, 1]$$

where in the linear case, the left and right functions can be replaced by linear functions like $R(r) = L(r) = r$ or others.

Now suppose that $b - a = \alpha,\ c - b = \beta,\ b = m$ then the membership function will be as follows:

$$A(x) = \begin{cases} L\left(\dfrac{x - m + \alpha}{\alpha}\right), & m - \alpha \le x \le m \\ R\left(\dfrac{m + \beta - x}{\beta}\right), & m \le x \le m + \beta \\ 0, & \text{otherwise} \end{cases}$$

where α, β are left and right spreads, and m is the core of a triangular fuzzy number.

$$A_l(r) = m - \alpha L^{-1}(r),$$

$$A_u(r) = m + \beta R^{-1}(r),\ \ r \in [0, 1]$$

The formal formats to show this number can be written as follows:

$$A = (a, b, c) := A = (m, \alpha, \beta) := A[r] = [A_l(r), A_u(r)] := A(r) = (A_l(r), A_u(r))$$

The r-level set of a triangular fuzzy set $A = (a, b, c)$ is:

$$A[r] = [A_l(r), A_u(r)] = [b + (b - a)(r - 1), b + (c - b)(1 - r)]$$

For both formats of the r-level sets of triangular and trapezoidal fuzzy numbers, the lower and upper functions can be obtained practically as follows.

Consider the following figure of fuzzy set A. First, the line segment between two points A and B is defined as:

$$\frac{y - y_A}{x - x_A} = \frac{y_B - y_A}{x_B - x_A} \Rightarrow y = \frac{1}{\alpha}(x - m + \alpha)$$

Then, after finding the equation of the line, we have this system:

$$y = \frac{1}{\alpha}(x - m + \alpha)\ \ \&\ \ y = r$$

So:

$$r = \frac{1}{\alpha}(x - m + \alpha)$$

The inverse is a reflective function on $x = r$ and it is as follows:

$$A_l(r) = x = m + \alpha(r - 1)$$

The same procedure will be true for points B and C. Then it will be obtained as follows:

$$\frac{y - y_B}{x - x_B} = \frac{y_C - y_B}{x_C - x_B} \Rightarrow y = \frac{1}{\beta}(m - x) + 1$$

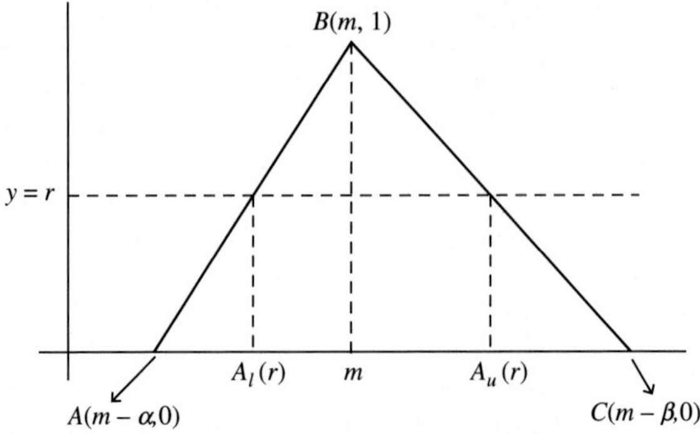

Fig. 2.13 Fuzzy number in triangular form.

Again we will have:

$$r = \frac{1}{\beta}(m - x) + 1$$

and the inverse function will be $A_u(r)$ (Fig. 2.13):

$$A_u(r) = m + \beta(1 - r)$$

2.5.9 Operations on level-wise form of fuzzy numbers

In this section, the main calculations on fuzzy sets in parametric or level-wise form are going to be defined and discussed. Since the concept of the difference is different and needs more attention, so this operation will be discussed more, because here the subtraction has the meaning of difference between two sets or two functions.

Before the discussion on the operations, we need some explanations. It should be noted that the fuzziness will be growing under these operators. It means, for two arbitrary fuzzy numbers A and B, and a continuous measurable function like $f \in \{\oplus, \odot, \oslash\}$, the fuzziness of A and fuzziness of B are less than or equal to the fuzziness of $f(A,B)$. One of the concepts of the fuzziness is the diameter of a fuzzy number. The diameter of an interval in level-wise form of a fuzzy number can be known as fuzziness of A in any level of r.

$$\text{Fuzz}(A_r) = \text{diam}([A_l(r), A_u(r)]) = A_u(r) - A_l(r), \ \ 0 \le r \le 1$$

Now it is proven that:

$$Fuzz(A_r) \le Fuzz\left(f(A,B)_r\right) \ \& \ Fuzz(B_r) \le Fuzz\left(f(A,B)_r\right)$$

and also:

$$C = f(A, B) \Rightarrow C[r] = f(A[r], B[r])$$

This means that if the function f is continuous and measurable, then:

$$\textit{if } A \oplus B = C \text{ then } A[r] + B[r] = C[r],$$

$$\textit{if } A \odot B = C \text{ then } A[r] + B[r] = C[r],$$

$$\textit{if } A \oslash B = C \text{ then } A[r] + B[r] = C[r].$$

Now we can discuss the operators separately.

2.5.9.1 *Summation*

For any two arbitrary fuzzy numbers A and B and any arbitrary but fixed $0 \le r \le 1$, if $A \oplus B = C$, we have:

$$C[r] = [C_l(r), C_u(r)] = A[r] + B[r] = [A_l(r), A_u(r)] + [B_l(r), B_u(r)]$$

Then:

$$C_l(r) = A_l(r) + B_l(r), \;\; C_u(r) = A_u(r) + B_u(r)$$

2.5.9.1.1 Example

Suppose that:

$$A = [r - 1, 1 - r], B = [r, 2 - r^2],$$

To compute the summation $A \oplus B = C$ we need the following:

$$A_l(r) = r - 1, A_u(r) = 1 - r, B_l(r) = r, B_u(r) = 2 - r^2$$

So, $C_l(r) = 2r - 1$, $C_u(r) = 3 - r - r^2$. Fig. 2.14 shows the summation of two fuzzy numbers in the example.

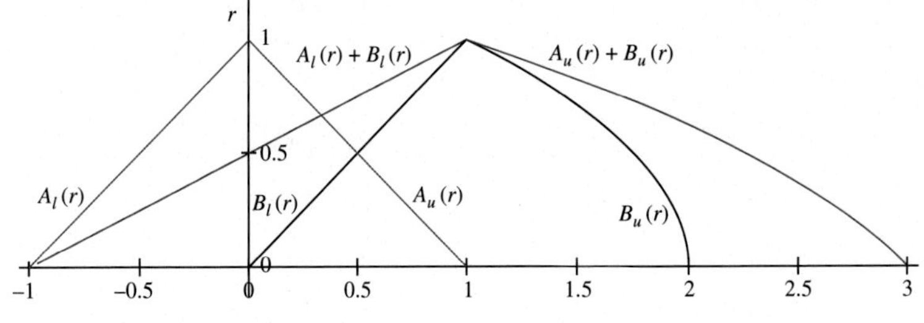

Fig. 2.14 Summation.

As can be seen, we have:

$$A_u(r) - A_l(r) = \text{Fuzz}(A_r) \leq \text{Fuzz}(A \oplus B)_r = C_u(r) - C_l(r)$$

and

$$B_u(r) - B_l(r) = Fuzz(B_r) \leq Fuzz(A \oplus B)_r = C_u(r) - C_l(r)$$

for all levels.

2.5.9.2 Multiplication

For any two arbitrary fuzzy numbers A and B and any arbitrary but fixed $0 \leq r \leq 1$, if $A \odot B = C$, we have:

$$C[r] = [C_l(r), C_u(r)] = A[r] \cdot B[r] = [A_l(r), A_u(r)] \cdot [B_l(r), B_u(r)]$$

Then:

$$C_l(r) = \min\{A_l(r) \cdot B_l(r), A_l(r) \cdot B_u(r), A_u(r) \cdot B_l(r), A_u(r) \cdot B_u(r)\},$$
$$C_u(r) = \max\{A_l(r) \cdot B_l(r), A_l(r) \cdot B_u(r), A_u(r) \cdot B_l(r), A_u(r) \cdot B_u(r)\}$$

In the previous example:

$$C_l(r) = \min\{(r-1) \cdot r, (r-1) \cdot (2-r^2), (1-r) \cdot r, (1-r) \cdot (2-r^2)\},$$
$$C_u(r) = \max\{(r-1) \cdot r, (r-1) \cdot (2-r^2), (1-r) \cdot r, (1-r) \cdot (2-r^2)\}$$

We can see that:

$$C_l(r) = (r-1)(2-r^2), \; C_u(r) = (1-r)(2-r^2)$$

Fig. 2.15 shows the multiplication of two fuzzy numbers in the example. For more illustration, see Allahviranloo (2020).

2.5.9.3 Difference

The difference of two fuzzy numbers is indeed the difference of two membership functions. Two different differences in the sense of standard and nonstandard cases will be discussed in level-wise form.

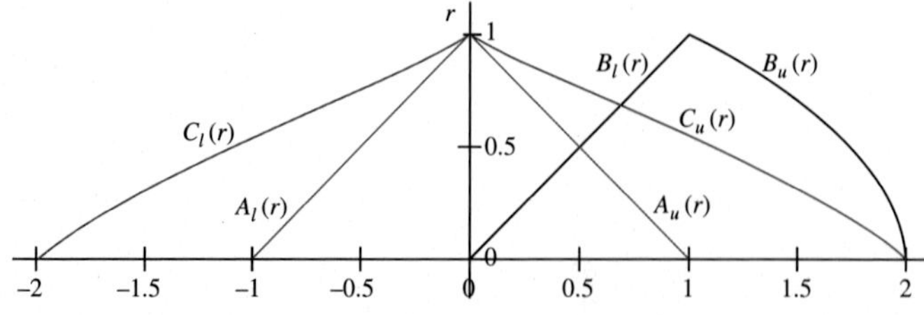

Fig. 2.15 Multiplication.

First of all, we should consider the multiplying a membership function by a scalar in level-wise form. Suppose that $\lambda \in R$ is a scalar. Then in triple form of fuzzy number:

$$\lambda \odot A = \lambda \cdot (a, b, c) = \begin{cases} (\lambda a, \lambda b, \lambda c), & \lambda \geq 0 \\ (\lambda c, \lambda b, \lambda a), & \lambda < 0 \end{cases}$$

and in level-wise form of fuzzy number:

$$\lambda A[r] = \begin{cases} [\lambda A_l(r), \lambda A_u(r)], & \lambda \geq 0 \\ [\lambda A_u(r), \lambda A_l(r)], & \lambda < 0 \end{cases}$$

For any $0 \leq r \leq 1$.

The concept of scalar multiplication is the same as the multiplication of the scalar to each member of the interval. It means:

$$A[r] = [A_l(r), A_u(r)] = \{z_t \mid z_t = A_l(r) + t(A_u(r) - A_l(r)), 0 \leq t \leq 1\}$$

For any $0 \leq r \leq 1$.

So, in r-level:

$$\lambda A[r] = \{\lambda z_t \mid 0 \leq t \leq 1\} = \begin{cases} [\lambda A_l(r), \lambda A_u(r)], & \lambda \geq 0 \\ [\lambda A_u(r), \lambda A_l(r)], & \lambda < 0 \end{cases}$$

For instance, if we consider one of the previous fuzzy numbers like:

$$A[r] = [A_l(r), A_u(r)] = [r, 2 - r^2]$$

and $\lambda = -1$, then:

$$(-1)A[r] = [-A_u(r), -A_l(r)] = [r^2 - 2, -r]$$

For more illustration, see Fig. 2.16.

For using this scalar multiplication in the definition of the difference of two fuzzy numbers, let $A[r] = [A_l(r), A_u(r)]$ and $B[r] = [B(r), B_u(r)]$ be two fuzzy numbers in level-wise form. In this case the difference is defined as follows:

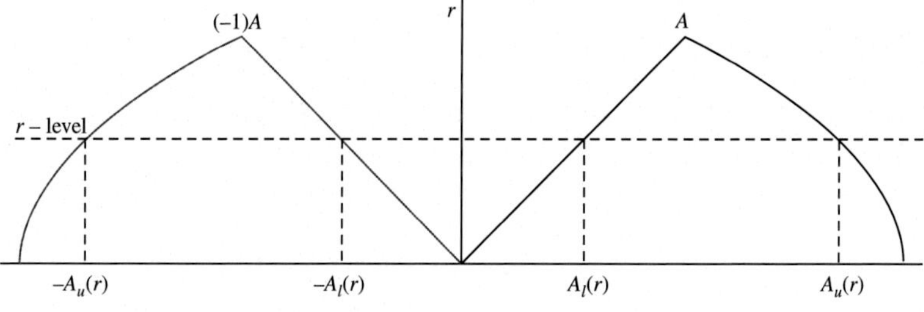

Fig. 2.16 Multiplication of (−1).

$$A[r]-B[r]=A[r]+(-1)B[r]=$$
$$=[A_l(r),A_u(r)]+(-1)\,[B_l(r),B_u(r)]$$
$$=[A_l(r),A_u(r)]+[-B_u(r),\ -B_l(r)]$$
$$=[A_l(r)-B_u(r),B_u(r)-A_l(r)]$$

Or in the format of convex combination, for any arbitrary but fixed $0\le r\le 1$:

$$A[r]=\{z_t'|\,z_t'=A_l(r)+t(A_u(r)-A_l(r)),0\le t\le 1\}$$
$$B[r]=\{z_t''\,|\,z_t''=B_l(r)+t(B_u(r)-B_l(r)),0\le t\le 1\}$$
$$A[r]-B[r]=\{z_t'-z_t''\,|\,0\le t\le 1\}=[A_l(r)-B_u(r),B_u(r)-A_l(r)]$$

In this definition:

$$A\ominus(-1)\odot A\neq 0,$$

because, based on the definition, the result is a symmetric interval centered at zero and it is always a nonzero interval.

$$A[r]-A[r]=[A_l(r)-A_u(r),A_u(r)-A_l(r)]\neq 0=[0,0]$$

Note that the symmetric interval centered at zero is called a zero interval. This comes from the concept of equivalency class. If we consider an equivalency class of zero as a set of all symmetric intervals centered at zero, then all of the members of the class are known as a zero interval. Moreover:

$$\text{Fuzz}(A_r)\le\text{Fuzz}((\lambda\odot A)_r),\ \ 0\le r\le 1.$$

2.5.9.4 Hukuhara difference

Suppose that A and B are two fuzzy numbers in level-wise form. The Hukuhara difference of $A\ominus_H B$ is defined as follows:

$$\exists C; A\ominus_H B=C\Leftrightarrow A=B\oplus C$$

It is clear that the existence of the difference is conditional and depends on the existence of fuzzy number C.

Note. For the existence of H-difference, A, B, and C must all be fuzzy numbers. This means that if the fuzzy set B can be transformed by C then it will fall into A.

Now considering $A=B\oplus C$, and the level-wise form of both sides of the equation, we have:

$$A[r]=B[r]+C[r]$$

$$[A_l(r), A_u(r)] = [B_l(r), B_u(r)] + [C_l(r), C_u(r)] = [B_l(r) + C_l(r), B_u(r) + C_u(r)]$$

$$A_l(r) = B_l(r) + C_l(r), A_u(r) = B_u(r) + C_u(r)$$

Finally:

$$C_l(r) = A_l(r) - B_l(r), C_u(r) = A_u(r) - B_u(r)$$

The level-wise form of the Hukuhara difference, or H-difference, is defined as subtractions of two endpoints of two intervals, respectively.

$$[(A \ominus_H B)_l(r), (A \ominus_H B)_u(r)] = [C_l(r), C_u(r)] = [A_l(r) - B_l(r), A_u(r) - B_u(r)]$$

Note that the difference:

$$A \ominus_H B \neq A \oplus (-1) \odot B,$$

because in level-wise form the differences between intervals in both sides are not the same.

$$(A \ominus_H B)[r] = [A_l(r) - B_l(r), A_u(r) - B_u(r)]$$
$$\neq [A_l(r) - B_u(r), B_u(r) - A_l(r)] = (A \oplus (-1) \odot B)[r]$$

2.5.9.4.1 Example

Consider the following two fuzzy numbers in parametric forms:

$$A[r] = [A_l(r), A_u(r)] = [2r, 4 - 2r], B[r] = [B_l(r), B_u(r)] = [r - 1, 1 - r],$$

Now to obtain $A \ominus_H B = C$:

$$C_l(r) = r + 1, \ C_u(r) = 3 - r$$

So the Hukuhara difference in parametric form is:

$$C[r] = [r + 1, 3 - r]$$

Fig. 2.17 shows the H-difference.

As can be seen in the figure, and based on the definition of H-difference:

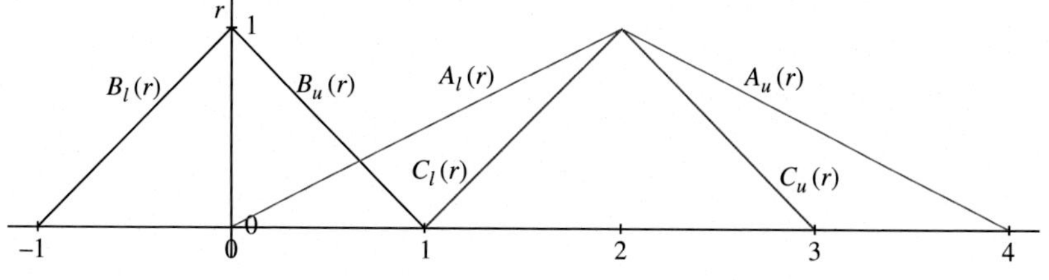

Fig. 2.17 $A \ominus_H B$.

$$A_u(r) - A_l(r) = \text{Fuzz}(A_r) \geq \text{Fuzz}(A \ominus_H B)_r = C_u(r) - C_l(r)$$

and

$$B_u(r) - B_l(r) = \text{Fuzz}(B_r) \leq A_u(r) - A_l(r) = \text{Fuzz}(A_r)$$

because the difference C is a shift for extending of B to be into A.

We shall now find some sufficient conditions for the existence of H-difference. To this purpose, let us consider:

$$A_r = (A_{1,r}, A_{2,r}, A_{3,r}),\ B_r = (B_{1,r}, B_{2,r}, B_{3,r}),\ C_r = (C_{1,r}, C_{2,r}, C_{3,r})$$

where:

$$A_{1,r} \leq A_{2,r} \leq A_{3,r},\ B_{1,r} \leq B_{2,r} \leq B_{3,r},\ \text{and}\ B_{1,r} \leq B_{2,r} \leq B_{3,r}$$

are representation of fuzzy numbers in triple forms for each level r.

This means in each level the intervals are satisfying the conditions of a real interval.

Lemma The sufficient condition for the existence of the H-difference $A \ominus_H B = C$ is:

$$\text{Fuzz}(B_r) = B_{3,r} - B_{1,r} \leq \min\{A_{2,r} - A_{1,r}, A_{3,r} - A_{2,r}\}$$

To show $A = B \oplus C$ with condition $C_{1,r} \leq C_{2,r} \leq C_{3,r}$, our assertion for the existence is only proving $C_{1,r} \leq C_{2,r} \leq C_{3,r}$ or $A_{1,r} - B_{1,r} \leq A_{2,r} - B_{2,r} \leq A_{3,r} - B_{3,r}$. Because:

$$A = B \oplus C \Leftrightarrow A_{1,r} = B_{1,r} + C_{1,r}, A_{2,r} = B_{2,r} + C_{2,r}, A_{3,r} = B_{3,r} + C_{3,r}$$

To show $A_{1,r} - B_{1,r} \leq A_{3,r} - B_{3,r}$ it is enough to show $B_{3,r} - B_{1,r} \leq A_{3,r} - A_{1,r}$. In the first case suppose that $\min\{A_{2,r} - A_{1,r}, A_{3,r} - A_{2,r}\} = A_{2,r} - A_{1,r} > 0$. Now we have $B_{3,r} - B_{1,r} \leq A_{2,r} - A_{1,r} \leq A_{3,r} - A_{1,r}$ and the proof is completed.

In the second case, suppose that $\min\{A_{2,r} - A_{1,r}, A_{3,r} - A_{2,r}\} = A_{3,r} - A_{2,r} > 0$. Now we have $B_{3,r} - B_{1,r} \leq A_{3,r} - A_{2,r} \leq A_{3,r} - A_{1,r}$ and the proof is also completed.

To show $A_{1,r} - B_{1,r} \leq A_{2,r} - B_{2,r}$ it is enough to show $B_{2,r} - B_{1,r} \leq A_{2,r} - A_{1,r}$. In the first case, suppose that $\min\{A_{2,r} - A_{1,r}, A_{3,r} - A_{2,r}\} = A_{2,r} - A_{1,r} > 0$. Now we have $B_{2,r} - B_{1,r} \leq B_{3,r} - B_{1,r} \leq A_{2,r} - A_{1,r}$ and the proof is completed. In the second case, suppose that $\min\{A_{2,r} - A_{1,r}, A_{3,r} - A_{2,r}\} = A_{3,r} - A_{2,r} > 0$. Now we have $B_{2,r} - B_{1,r} \leq B_{3,r} - B_{1,r} \leq A_{3,r} - A_{2,r} \leq A_{2,r} - A_{1,r}$ and the proof is also completed.

To show $A_{2,r} - B_{2,r} \leq A_{3,r} - B_{3,r}$ it is enough to show $B_{3,r} - B_{2,r} \leq A_{3,r} - A_{2,r}$. In the first case, suppose that $\min\{A_{2,r} - A_{1,r}, A_{3,r} - A_{2,r}\} = A_{2,r} - A_{1,r} > 0$. Now we have $B_{3,r} - B_{2,r} \leq B_{3,r} - B_{1,r} \leq A_{2,r} - A_{1,r} \leq A_{3,r} - A_{2,r}$ and the proof is completed. In the second case, suppose that $\min\{A_{2,r} - A_{1,r}, A_{3,r} - A_{2,r}\} = A_{3,r} - A_{2,r} > 0$. Now we have $B_{3,r} - B_{2,r} \leq B_{3,r} - B_{1,r} \leq A_{3,r} - A_{2,r}$ and the proof is also completed.

2.5.9.4.2 Example

As we mentioned, the existence of the difference is conditional. Now in this example, we will see that it does not always exist. Suppose that in $A \ominus_H B$:

$$\text{Fuzz}(B_r) = B_{3,r} - B_{1,r} > \min\{A_{2,r} - A_{1,r}, A_{3,r} - A_{2,r}\}$$

For instance, $A[r] = [1-r, r-1]$ and $B[r] = [2-r, r-2]$, now:

$$(A \ominus_H B)[r] = [A_l(r) - B_l(r), A_u(r) - B_u(r)] = [-1, -3]$$

As we can see, it is not an interval and for any r. So the difference does not exist.

2.5.9.5 Generalized Hukuhara difference

In this case, we can define the difference in another way. Suppose that we want to try $B \ominus_H A = (-1)C$ and the difference C may exist. Considering the level-wise forms of two sides:

$$(B \ominus_H A)[r] = [B_l(r) - A_l(r), B_u(r) - A_u(r)] = ((-1)C)[r] = [-C_u(r), -C_l(r)]$$

we have:

$$B_l(r) - A_l(r) = -C_u(r), \; B_u(r) - A_u(r) = -C_l(r)$$

or:

$$A_l(r) - B_l(r) = C_u(r), \; A_u(r) - B_u(r) = C_l(r)$$

In general:

$$\left[(B \ominus_H A)_l(r), (B \ominus_H A)_u(r)\right] = [C_l(r), C_u(r)] = [A_u(r) - B_u(r), A_l(r) - B_l(r)]$$
$$:= \ominus(-1)\left[(A \ominus_H B)_l(r), (A \ominus_H B)_u(r)\right]$$

Now to define an almost right definition for the difference, we have two cases to consider.

$$A \ominus_{gH} B = C \Leftrightarrow \begin{cases} i) & A = B \oplus C \\ & \text{or} \\ ii) & B = A \oplus (-1)C \end{cases}$$

The generalized Hukuhara difference is defined in two cases. If the case (i) exists, so there is no need to consider the case (ii). Otherwise we will need the second case. The relation between the two cases can be explained as follows:

- In case (i):

$$A \ominus_H B = C$$

- In case (ii):

$$B\ominus_H A=(-1)C$$

The relationship is:

$$(A\ominus_{gH}B)_i[r]:=\ominus(-1)\left((A\ominus_{gH}B)_{ii}[r]\right)$$

In the case that both exist, then $C=(-1)C$ and it is concluded that both types of the difference are the same and equal (Abbasi and Allahviranloo, 2018).

2.5.9.5.1 The level-wise form of generalized difference

As we found, the level-wise form in case (i) is:

$$\left[(A\ominus_{gH}B)_l(r),\ (A\ominus_{gH}B)_u(r)\right]=[C_l(r),C_u(r)]$$
$$=[A_l(r)-B_l(r),A_u(r)-B_u(r)]$$

and in case (ii) it is as follows:

$$\left[(B\ominus_{gH}A)_l(r),\ (B\ominus_{gH}A)_u(r)\right]=[C_l(r),C_u(r)]$$
$$=[A_u(r)-B_u(r),A_l(r)-B_l(r)]$$

So to define the endpoints of the difference:

$$C_l(r)=\min\{A_l(r)-B_l(r),A_u(r)-B_u(r)\}$$
$$C_u(r)=\max\{A_l(r)-B_l(r),A_u(r)-B_u(r)\}$$

To show two cases at the same time, we use gH-difference notation and define it in the following form:

$$(A\ominus_{gH}B)[r]=$$
$$=[\min\{A_l(r)-B_l(r),A_u(r)-B_u(r)\},\ \max\{A_l(r)-B_l(r),A_u(r)-B_u(r)\}]$$

2.5.9.5.2 Some properties of *gH*-difference

It should be noted that all of the following properties can be proved in level-wise form easily.

1. If the gH-difference exists it is unique.
2. $A\ominus_{gH}A=0$.
3. If $A\ominus_{gH}B$ exists in case (i) then $B\ominus_{gH}A$ exists in case (ii) and vice versa.
4. In both cases $(A\oplus B)\ominus_{gH}B=A$. (It is easy to show in level-wise form.)
5. If $A\ominus_{gH}B$ and $B\ominus_{gH}A$ exist then $0\ominus_{gH}(A\ominus_{gH}B)=B\ominus_{gH}A$.
6. If $A\ominus_{gH}B=B\ominus_{gH}A=C$ if and only if $C=-C$ and $A=B$.

The difference even in the gH-difference case may not exist. It can be, for example, that the gH-difference of two fuzzy numbers is not always a fuzzy number.

2.5.9.5.3 Example

This example shows that the generalized Hukuhara difference does not exist for each arbitrary level of difference.

Suppose that one of the numbers is triangular and another one is in trapezoidal forms. $A=(0,2,4)$ or in parametric form $A[r]=[2r,4-2r]$ and $B=(0,1,2,3)$ or in parametric form $B[r]=[r,3-r]$.

In case (i):

$$\left(A\ominus_{gH}B\right)[r]=[r,1-r]$$

If $r=1$, the difference is as $[1,0]$, which is not an interval.

In case (ii):

$$\left(A\ominus_{gH}B\right)[r]=[1-r,r]$$

If $r=0$, the difference is as $[1,0]$ that is not an interval. So as we see the gH-difference does not exist for all $r\in[0,1]$.

Note. In all methods in this book, we will suppose that the gH-difference always exists.

Some other properties of gH-difference are now shown, considering one of the ordering methods of fuzzy numbers.

Generally, there are many methods to order or rank the fuzzy numbers. The most useful one is partial ordering, in the case of level-wise form. To define this, consider two fuzzy numbers A and B.

2.5.9.6 Partial ordering

For two fuzzy numbers $A,B\in\mathbb{F}_R$, we call $\preccurlyeq$ a partial order notation and $A\preccurlyeq B$ if and only if $A_l(r)\leq B_l(r)$ and $A_u(r)\leq B_u(r)$.

We also have the same definition for the strict inequality, $A\prec B$ if and only if $A_l(r)<B_l(r)$ and $A_u(r)<B_u(r)$.

For any $r\in[0,1]$.

2.5.9.6.1 Some properties of partial ordering

1. If $A\preccurlyeq B$ then $-B\preccurlyeq -A$.
2. If $A\preccurlyeq B$ and $B\preccurlyeq A$ then $A=B$.

To prove the properties, we use the level-wise form and they are very clear. For instance, we prove the first property:

$A\preccurlyeq B$ if and only if $A_l(r)\leq B_l(r)$ and $A_u(r)\leq B_u(r)$

$-B \preccurlyeq -A$ if and only if $-B_l(r) \leq -A_l(r)$ and $-B_u(r) \leq -A_u(r)$

So the proof is completed. The second one is obtained in a similar way.

2.5.9.6.2 Absolute value of a fuzzy number

The absolute value of a fuzzy number A is defined as follows:

$$|A| = \begin{cases} A, & A \succcurlyeq 0 \\ -A, & A \prec 0 \end{cases}$$

where 0 fuzzy number is called a singleton fuzzy zero number.

2.5.9.6.3 Some properties of partial ordering in *gH*-difference

1. If $A \preccurlyeq B$ then $A \ominus_{gH} B \preccurlyeq 0$.
2. If $A \succcurlyeq B$ then $A \ominus_{gH} B \succcurlyeq 0$.

They are very easy to prove in level-wise form.

2.5.9.7 Approximately generalized Hukuhara difference

In the case that the gH-difference does not exist or $(A \ominus_{gH} B)[r]$ do not define a fuzzy number for any $r \in [0,1]$, we can use the nested property of the fuzzy numbers and define a proper fuzzy number as a difference. We call this approximately gH-difference, denoted by $\ominus_g$, and it is defined in level-wise form as follows:

$$(A \ominus_g B)[r] = cl\left(\bigcup_{\beta \geq r} (A \ominus_{gH} B)[\beta]\right), \quad r \in [0, 1]$$

If the gH-difference $(A \ominus_{gH} B)[\beta]$ exists or defines a proper fuzzy number for any $\beta \in [0,1]$, then $(A \ominus_g B)[r]$ is exactly the same as the gH-difference $(A \ominus_{gH} B)[r]$ and it is exactly the same as the $(A \ominus_H B)[r]$ Hukuhara difference, where:

$$(A \ominus_g B)[r] = \left[\inf_{\beta \geq r} \min\{A_l(\beta) - B_l(\beta), A_u(\beta) - B_u(\beta)\},\ \sup_{\beta \geq r} \max\{A_l(\beta) - B_l(\beta), A_u(\beta) - B_u(\beta)\}\right]$$

Proposition g.1 For any two fuzzy numbers, $A, B \in R_F$, the two of $A \ominus_g B$ and $B \ominus_g A$ exist for any $r \in [0,1]$ and $A \ominus_g B = -(B \ominus_g A)$ where:

$$(A \ominus_g B)[r] = [D_l(r), D_u(r)]$$

$$D_l(r) = \inf\{\{A_l(\beta) - B_l(\beta) \mid \beta \geq r\} \cup \{A_u(\beta) - B_u(\beta) \mid \beta \geq r\}\}$$

$$D_u(r) = \sup\{\{A_l(\beta) - B_l(\beta) \mid \beta \geq r\} \cup \{A_u(\beta) - B_u(\beta) \mid \beta \geq r\}\}$$

It should be noted that in the case of finite numbers of level or discretized levels, the abovementioned interval is the same as the gH-difference.

$$(A\ominus_g B)[r] = [D_l(r), D_u(r)]$$

$$D_l(r) = \min\{A_l(r) - B_l(r), A_u(r) - B_u(r)\}$$

$$D_u(r) = \max\{A_l(r) - B_l(r), A_u(r) - B_u(r)\}]$$

Proposition g.2 For any two fuzzy numbers, $A, B \in R_F$, $A\ominus_g B$ always exists or is a fuzzy number, because it satisfies the conditions of fuzzy numbers.

$$\inf_{\beta\geq r} \min\{A_l(\beta) - B_l(\beta), A_u(\beta) - B_u(\beta)\} \leq \sup_{\beta\geq r} \max\{A_l(\beta) - B_l(\beta), A_u(\beta) - B_u(\beta)\}$$

1. $\inf_{\beta\geq r} \min\{A_l(\beta) - B_l(\beta), A_u(\beta) - B_u(\beta)\}$ *is nondecreasing, left continuous, and bounded function for any* r $\in$ *[0,1].*
2. $\sup_{\beta\geq r} \max\{A_l(\beta) - B_l(\beta), A_u(\beta) - B_u(\beta)\}$ *is nonincreasing, left continuous, and bounded function for any* r $\in$ *[0,1].*

2.5.9.7.1 Some properties of *g*-difference

For any two fuzzy numbers A, $B \in R_F$:

1. $A\ominus_g B = A\ominus_{gH} B$ subject to $A\ominus_{gH} B$ exists.
2. $A\ominus_g A = 0$.
3. $(A\oplus B)\ominus_g B = A$.
4. $0\ominus_g(A\ominus_g B) = B\ominus_g A$.
5. $A\ominus_g B = B\ominus_g A = C$ if and only if $C = -C$, the immediate conclusion is $C = 0$ and $A = B$. In conclusion:

$$A\ominus_g B = B\ominus_g A \Leftrightarrow A = B$$

All the properties can be proved very easily based on the definition of the g-difference in level-wise form.

Let us consider some examples when the gH-difference does not exist, while the g-difference exists.

2.5.9.7.2 Example

Consider two trapezoidal fuzzy numbers as follows:

$$A = (0, 2, 2, 4), \quad B = (0, 1, 2, 3)$$

where:

$$A_l(\beta) = 2\beta, \ A_u(\beta) = 4 - 2\beta, \ B_l(\beta) = \beta, \ B_u(\beta) = 3 - \beta$$

and:

$$\inf_{\beta \geq r} \min\{A_l(\beta) - B_l(\beta), A_u(\beta) - B_u(\beta)\} = \inf_{\beta \geq r} \min\{\beta, 1 - \beta\} = 0$$

$$\sup_{\beta \geq r} \max\{A_l(\beta) - B_l(\beta), A_u(\beta) - B_u(\beta)\} = \sup_{\beta \geq r} \max\{\beta, 1 - \beta\} = 1$$

So the g-difference is:

$$(A \ominus_g B)[r] = [0, 1]$$

The corresponding trapezoidal fuzzy number of g-difference is $(a, b, c, d) = (0, 0, 1, 1)$.

In the next example, we will see that the gH-difference does not exist.

2.5.9.7.3 Example

Consider two trapezoidal fuzzy numbers as follows:

$$A = (2, 3, 5, 6), \ \ B = (0, 4, 4, 8)$$

where:

$$A_l(\beta) = 2 + \beta, \ \ A_u(\beta) = 6 - \beta, \ \ B_l(\beta) = 4\beta, \ \ B_u(\beta) = 8 - 4\beta$$

and:

$$\inf_{\beta \geq r} \min\{A_l(\beta) - B_l(\beta), A_u(\beta) - B_u(\beta)\} = \inf_{\beta \geq r} \min\{2 - 3\beta, -2 + 3\beta\}$$

$$\sup_{\beta \geq r} \max\{A_l(\beta) - B_l(\beta), A_u(\beta) - B_u(\beta)\} = \sup_{\beta \geq r} \max\{2 - 3\beta, -2 + 3\beta\}$$

Based on the definition of gH-difference, we cannot claim that:

$$\min\{2 - 3r, \ -2 + 3r\} \leq \max\{2 - 3r, \ -2 + 3r\}$$

for any $r \in [0, 1]$. Because:

$$A_u(r) - B_u(r) = -(A_l(r) - B_l(r))$$

and:

If $A_l(r) - B_l(r) \geq 0$ then $A_u(r) - B_u(r) \leq A_l(r) - B_l(r)$ then

$$\min\{A_l(r) - B_l(r), A_u(r) - B_u(r)\} = A_u(r) - B_u(r)$$

$$\max\{A_l(r) - B_l(r), A_u(r) - B_u(r)\} = A_l(r) - B_l(r)$$

If $A_l(r) - B_l(r) < 0$ then $A_u(r) - B_u(r) > A_l(r) - B_l(r)$ then

$$\min\{A_l(r) - B_l(r), A_u(r) - B_u(r)\} = A_l(r) - B_l(r)$$

$$\max\{A_l(r) - B_l(r), A_u(r) - B_u(r)\} = A_u(r) - B_u(r)$$

Now here for $0 \le r \le \frac{2}{3}$:

$$\min\{A_l(r) - B_l(r), A_u(r) - B_u(r)\} = -2 + 3r$$

$$\max\{A_l(r) - B_l(r), A_u(r) - B_u(r)\} = 2 - 3r$$

and otherwise for $\frac{2}{3} < r \le 1$:

$$\min\{A_l(r) - B_l(r), A_u(r) - B_u(r)\} = 2 - 3r$$

$$\max\{A_l(r) - B_l(r), A_u(r) - B_u(r)\} = -2 + 3r$$

Then the gH-difference does not exist.

However, the g-difference is as for $0 \le r \le 0.32$:

$$(A \ominus_g B)[r] = \left[\frac{100}{32}r - 2, \frac{-100}{32}r + 2\right]$$

and for $0.32 < r \le 1$:

$$(A \ominus_g B)[r] = [-1, 1]$$

2.5.9.8 Generalized division

Now like generalized difference, for any two arbitrary fuzzy numbers, A and B, the generalized division can be defined as follows:

$$A \oslash_g B = C \Leftrightarrow \begin{cases} i) & A = B \odot C \\ & \text{or} \\ ii) & B = A \odot C^{-1} \end{cases}$$

It is clear that if both cases are true then $A = B \odot C = A \odot C^{-1} \odot C$ and in this case the only option is $C^{-1} \odot C = C \odot C^{-1} = \{1\}$, where 1 is a singleton fuzzy number or a real scalar, and C is also a nonzero real scalar.

The generalized division in the level-wise or interval form can be defined as follows:

$$A[r]/B[r] = C[r] \Leftrightarrow \begin{cases} i) & A[r] = B[r] \cdot C[r] \\ & \text{or} \\ ii) & B[r] = A[r] \cdot C^{-1}[r] \end{cases}$$

where $C^{-1}[r] := \left[\frac{1}{C_u(r)}, \frac{1}{C_l(r)}\right]$ and does not contain zero for all $r \in [0, 1]$.

In case (i):

$$[A_l(r), A_u(r)] = [B_l(r), B_u(r)] \cdot [C_l(r), C_u(r)]$$

and indeed:

$$[C_l(r), C_u(r)] = [A_l(r), A_u(r)]/[B_l(r), B_u(r)]$$

then:

$$C_l(r) = \min\left\{\frac{A_l(r)}{B_l(r)}, \frac{A_l(r)}{B_u(r)}, \frac{A_u(r)}{B_l(r)}, \frac{A_u(r)}{B_u(r)}\right\},$$

$$C_u(r) = \max\left\{\frac{A_l(r)}{B_l(r)}, \frac{A_l(r)}{B_u(r)}, \frac{A_u(r)}{B_l(r)}, \frac{A_u(r)}{B_u(r)}\right\}$$

Subject to $0 \notin [B_l(r), B_u(r)]$, it means $B_u(r) < 0$, *or* $0 < B_l(r)$ for all $r \in [0, 1]$.

In case (ii):

$$[B_l(r), B_u(r)] = [A_l(r), A_u(r)] \cdot \left[\frac{1}{C_u(r)}, \frac{1}{C_l(r)}\right]$$

and indeed:

$$\left[\frac{1}{C_u(r)}, \frac{1}{C_l(r)}\right] = [B_l(r), B_u(r)]/[A_l(r), A_u(r)]$$

so:

$$\frac{1}{C_u(r)} = \min\left\{\frac{B_l(r)}{A_l(r)}, \frac{B_l(r)}{A_u(r)}, \frac{B_u(r)}{A_l(r)}, \frac{B_u(r)}{A_u(r)}\right\},$$

$$\frac{1}{C_l(r)} = \max\left\{\frac{B_l(r)}{A_l(r)}, \frac{B_l(r)}{A_u(r)}, \frac{B_u(r)}{A_l(r)}, \frac{B_u(r)}{A_u(r)}\right\}$$

In fact, similar to the two cases of generalized difference, two endpoints changed the roles.

$$C_u(r) = \min\left\{\frac{A_l(r)}{B_l(r)}, \frac{A_l(r)}{B_u(r)}, \frac{A_u(r)}{B_l(r)}, \frac{A_u(r)}{B_u(r)}\right\},$$

$$C_l(r) = \max\left\{\frac{A_l(r)}{B_l(r)}, \frac{A_l(r)}{B_u(r)}, \frac{A_u(r)}{B_l(r)}, \frac{A_u(r)}{B_u(r)}\right\}$$

Remark The following results in both cases of division are easy to investigate.

If $A_l(r) > 0$, $B_l(r) > 0$ then $C_l(r) = \frac{A_l(r)}{B_u(r)}, C_u(r) = \frac{A_u(r)}{B_l(r)}$

If $A_u(r) < 0$, $B_u(r) < 0$ then $C_l(r) = \frac{A_u(r)}{B_l(r)}, C_l(r) = \frac{A_l(r)}{B_u(r)}$

In general, if:

$$C_l(r) = \frac{A_i(r)}{B_i(r)}, C_u(r) = \frac{A_j(r)}{B_j(r)}, i, j \in \{l, u\}$$

then the adequate condition to reach $C_l(r) \leq C_u(r)$ is:

$$A_i(r) \cdot B_j(r) \leq A_j(r) \cdot B_i(r), i, j \in \{l, u\} \text{ for all } r \in [0, 1]$$

and $C_l(r)$ and $C_u(r)$ must be left as continuous increasing and decreasing functions, respectively.

2.5.9.8.1 Some properties of division

It should be noted that all the following properties can be proved in level-wise form easily. Suppose that A and B are fuzzy numbers and 1 is $\{1\}$.

1. If $0 \notin A[r], \forall r \in [0,1]$ then $A \oslash_g A = 1$.
2. If $0 \notin B[r], \forall r \in [0,1]$ then $A \odot B \oslash_g B = A$.
3. If $0 \notin A[r], \forall r \in [0,1]$ then $1 \oslash_g A = A^{-1}$ and $1 \oslash_g A^{-1} = A$.
4. If $A \oslash B$ exists, then either $B \odot (A \oslash_g B) = A$ or $A \odot (A \oslash_g B)^{-1} = B$ and both equalities hold if and only if $A \oslash_g B$ is a real number.

Note. In all methods in this book, we will suppose that the division always exists.

2.5.9.8.2 Examples

Here we explain the generalized division based on its level-wise definition.

Suppose that $A[r] = [1+2r, 7-4r]$ and $B[r] = [-3+r, -1-r]$, now according to case (i):

$$A[r]/B[r] = C[r] \Leftrightarrow A[r] = B[r] \cdot C[r]$$

and is $C[r] = \left[\frac{7-4r}{-3+r}, \frac{1+2r}{-1-r}\right]$.

Suppose that $A[r] = [-7+2r-4-r]$ and $B[r] = [12+5r, -4-3r]$, now according to case (ii):

$$A[r]/B[r] = C[r] \Leftrightarrow B[r] = A[r] \cdot C^{-1}[r]$$

and is $C[r] = \left[\frac{-7+2r}{-12+5r}, \frac{-5+r}{11-5r}\right]$.

In some cases the g-division does not exist. For instance, consider:

$$A[r] = [1+0.5r, 5-3.5r] \text{ and } B[r] = [-4+2r, -1-r]$$

In this case, as with the g-difference, we have to define an approximate g-division as follows.

2.5.9.9 *Approximately generalized division*

In the case that the g-division does not exist or $(A \oslash_{Ag} B)[r]$ does not define a fuzzy number for any $r \in [0,1]$, we can use the nested property of the fuzzy numbers and define a proper fuzzy number as a division. We call this approximately g-division, denoted by $\oslash_{Ag}$, and it is defined in level-wise form as follows:

$$(A \oslash_{Ag} B)[r] = cl\left(\bigcup_{\beta \geq r} (A \oslash_g B)[\beta]\right), \quad r \in [0, 1]$$

If the g-division $(A \oslash_g B)[\beta]$ exists or defines a proper fuzzy number for any $\beta \in [0,1]$, then $(A \oslash_{Ag} B)[r]$ is exactly the same as the gH-difference $(A \oslash_g B)[r]$ subject to $0 \notin B[r]$, for any $r \in [0,1]$.

Suppose that $A \oslash_{Ag} B = C$ on a discrete partition $0 \leq r_0 \leq r_1 \leq \cdots \leq r_n \leq 1$ of $[0,1]$. A discretize version of $A \oslash_{Ag} B = C$ is obtained using:

$$A[r_i]/B[r_i] = W[r_i] = [W_{l,i}, W_{u,i}], 0 \leq i \leq 1$$

and $C_{l,\ n} = W_{l,\ n}$, $C_{u,\ n} = W_{u,\ n}$ also for $i = n-1, \ldots, 0$

$$C_{l,i} = \min\{C_{l,i+1}, W_{l,i}\}$$

$$C_{u,i} = \max\{C_{u,i+1}, W_{u,i}\}$$

2.5.9.9.1 Example

Suppose that $A[r] = [1+0.5r, 5-3.5r]$ and $B[r] = [-4+2r, -1-r]$. The g-division $A \oslash_g B = \left[\frac{5-3.5r}{-4+2r}, \frac{1+0.5r}{-1-r}\right]$ does not define a proper fuzzy number for any $r \in [0,1]$. However, using the Ag-division, the result is as $A \oslash_{Ag} B = \left[\frac{5-3.5r}{-4+2r}, -0.75\right]$.

2.5.10 Piece-wise membership function

Sometimes the lower and upper functions are piece-wise. For instance:

$$A_1(r) = x_1 + (x_2 - x_1)L_1^{-1}(r), \quad r \in [x_1, x_2],$$

$$A_2(r) = x_2 + (x_3 - x_2)L_2^{-1}(r), \quad r \in [x_2, x_3],$$

$$A_3(r) = x_4 - (x_4 - x_3)R_1^{-1}(r), \quad r \in [x_3, x_4],$$

$$A_4(r) = x_5 - (x_5 - x_4)R_2^{-1}(r), \quad r \in [x_4, x_5].$$

More information about these computations and those operators are in (Bede and Gal, 2005; Stefanini, 2010) (Fig. 2.18).

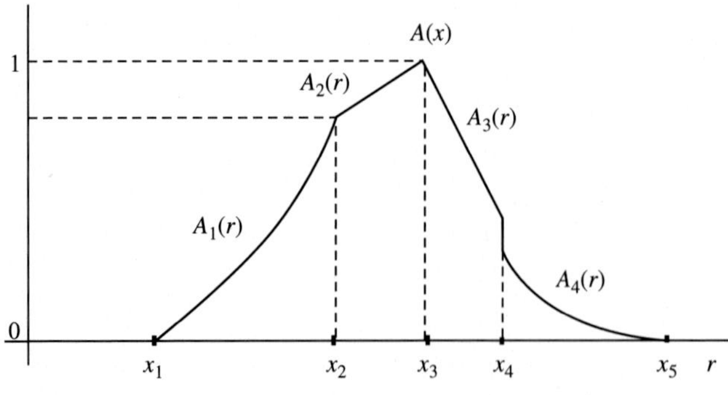

Fig. 2.18 Multifunctional membership function.

2.5.11 Some properties of addition and scalar product on fuzzy numbers

In this section, we need to consider and prove the following properties. Here it is supposed that the zero fuzzy number is a singleton fuzzy number. In general, a singleton fuzzy number is defined as follows.

2.5.11.1 Definition—singleton fuzzy number

A fuzzy number like a is called a singleton fuzzy number if the membership degree of a is one and the membership degrees for the other members are zero. See the following figure.

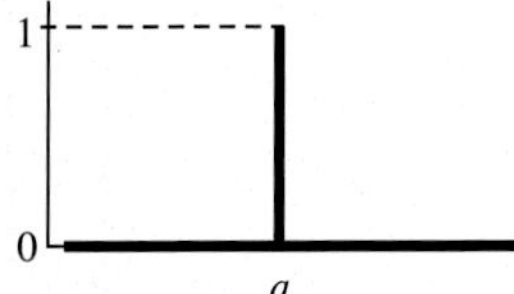

Singleton fuzzy number.

Some of the scalar product and addition properties on fuzzy numbers are as follows. For all properties $0, A \in F_R$ are singleton zero number and any fuzzy number, respectively, of which F_R is the set of all fuzzy numbers, those are defined on real numbers.

1. $0 \oplus A = A \oplus 0$.
2. There is no inverse with respect to $\oplus$. It means $A \oplus (-1)A \neq 0$.
3. For two arbitrary real numbers $a, b \in R$ in which $a \cdot b \geq 0$:

$$(a+b)A = a \odot A \oplus b \odot A$$

4. For any $\lambda \in R$ and $A, B \in R_F$:

$$\lambda \odot (A \oplus B) = \lambda \odot A \oplus \lambda \odot B$$

5. For any $\lambda, \mu \in R$ and $A \in R_F$:

$$\lambda \odot (\mu \odot A) = (\lambda \cdot \mu) \odot A$$

All of the abovementioned properties can be proved very easily by using the computations in level-wise form.

2.6 Advanced uncertainties and their properties

In this section, we first introduce a broad version of uncertainty called "pseudo-octagonal" uncertain sets. Special cases are then discussed as "pseudo-triangular" and "trapezoidal."

The motivation is that, in most of the social sciences, the use of uncertainty in triangular and trapezoidal forms may not usually be used sufficiently to measure the characteristics of personal beliefs and beliefs that lead to the fragment. It is common information that can be further expressed from four different points of view in the real line. Thus, even unspecified trapezoidal collections cannot be sufficiently plausible to show such cases from social science measurements. Therefore, in order to fill this gap in the uncertainty literature, the concept of a pseudo-octagonal uncertain set is introduced. The second part of this section is about introducing other uncertain advanced collections and combining them together. The idea was put forward by Professor Lotfi A. Zadeh as "Z-numbers." Here we will also talk about Z-process improvements. All this information is also explained in Abbasi et al. (2018), Abbasi and Allahviranloo (2018), Alive et al. (2016), Allahviranloo and Ezadi (2019), and Zadeh (2011).

2.6.1 PSEUDO-OCTAGONAL SETS

An uncertain set, A, is called a pseudo-octagonal uncertain set if its membership function $A(x)$ is as follows (Abbasi and Allahviranloo, 2018):

$$A(x) = \begin{cases} l_{1,A}(x), & a_1 \le x \le a_2 \\ \frac{1}{2}, & a_2 \le x \le a_3 \\ l_{2,A}(x), & a_3 \le x \le \underline{a} \\ 1, & \underline{a} \le x \le \overline{a} \\ r_{2,A}(x), & \overline{a} \le x \le a_4 \\ \frac{1}{2}, & a_4 \le x \le a_5 \\ r_{1,A}(x), & a_5 \le x \le a_6 \\ 0, & \text{otherwise} \end{cases}$$

This uncertain set is denoted by:

$$A = \left(a_1, a_2, a_3, \underline{a}, \overline{a}, a_4, a_5, a_6, (l_{1,A}(x), l_{2,A}(x)), (r_{2,A}(x), r_{1,A}(x)) \right)$$

where the pair of functions $(l_{1,\ A}(x), l_{2,\ A}(x))$ contains two nondecreasing functions and $(r_{2,\ A}(x), r_{1,\ A}(x))$ contains two nonincreasing functions.

This presentation of an uncertain set is more general and without 0.5-level it is changed to the normal pseudo-trapezoidal and trapezoidal fuzzy numbers. In the case of $\underline{a} = \overline{a}$, it is an exactly triangular fuzzy number.

The level-wise form or r-level of a pseudo-octagonal uncertain set is defined as follows:

$$A[r] = \left(\bigcup_{r \in \left(0, \frac{1}{2}\right]} r\left[l_{1,A}^{-1}(r), r_{1,A}^{-1}(r)\right] \right) \bigcup [a_2, a_3] \bigcup [a_4, a_5] \bigcup \left(\bigcup_{r \in \left[\frac{1}{2}, 1\right]} r\left[l_{2,A}^{-1}(r), r_{2,A}^{-1}(r)\right] \right)$$

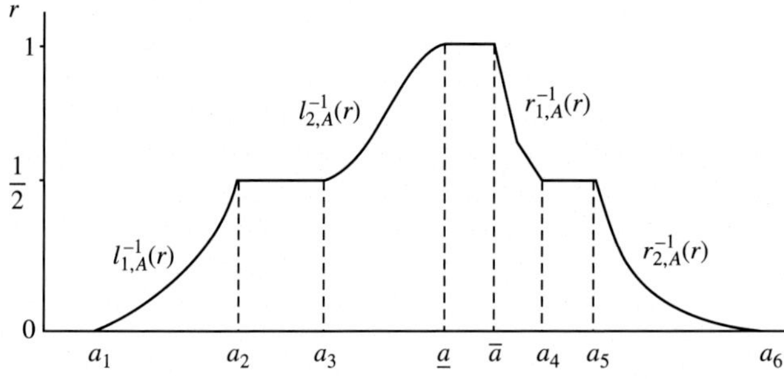

Fig. 2.19 Pseudo-octagonal uncertain set.

Note 1. If $[l_{1,A}^{-1}(r), r_{1,A}^{-1}(r)]$ and $[l_{2,A}^{-1}(r), r_{2,A}^{-1}(r)]$ are not linear, the set is called pseudo-octagonal (see Fig. 2.19).

Note 2. It is clear that if $a_2 = a_3$ and $a_4 = a_5$, then the set is a pseudo-trapezoidal uncertain set.

Note 3. If $[l_{1,A}^{-1}(r), r_{1,A}^{-1}(r)]$ and $[l_{2,A}^{-1}(r), r_{2,A}^{-1}(r)]$ are linear, the set is called octagonal (see Fig. 2.20).

Note 4. Clearly, if $a_2 = a_3$ and $a_4 = a_5$, then the set is a trapezoidal fuzzy set.

The arithmetic on these uncertain sets is not exactly similar to the normal fuzzy numbers, but generally, they have similar rules. To explain, we consider two of these uncertain sets as follows:

$$A = (a_1, a_2, a_3, \underline{a}, \overline{a}, a_4, a_5, a_6, (l_{1,A}(x), l_{2,A}(x)), (r_{2,A}(x), r_{1,A}(x)))$$

$$B = \left(b_1, b_2, b_3, \underline{b}, \overline{b}, b_4, b_5, b_6, (l_{1,B}(x), l_{2,B}(x)), (r_{2,B}(x), r_{1,B}(x))\right)$$

The operations on these sets are now explained in level-wise form of the uncertain sets. Consider:

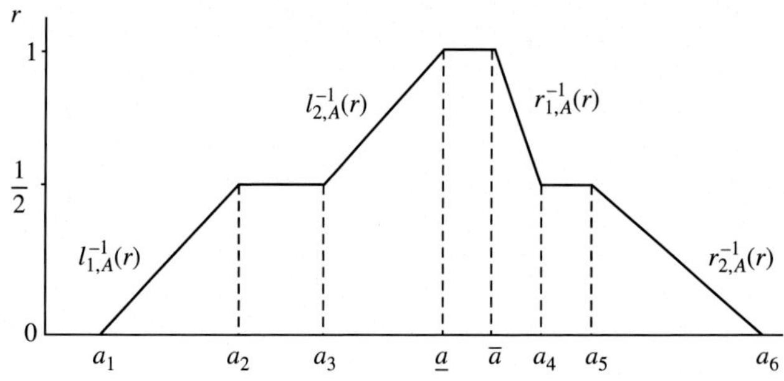

Fig. 2.20 Octagonal uncertain set.

$$A[r]=\left(\bigcup_{r\in\left(0,\frac{1}{2}\right]} r\left[l_{1,A}^{-1}(r),r_{1,A}^{-1}(r)\right]\right)\bigcup[a_2,a_3]\bigcup[a_4,a_5]\bigcup\left(\bigcup_{r\in\left[\frac{1}{2},1\right]} r\left[l_{2,A}^{-1}(r),r_{2,A}^{-1}(r)\right]\right)$$

$$B[r]=\left(\bigcup_{r\in\left(0,\frac{1}{2}\right]} r\left[l_{1,B}^{-1}(r),r_{1,B}^{-1}(r)\right]\right)\bigcup[b_2,b_3]\bigcup[b_4,b_5]\bigcup\left(\bigcup_{r\in\left[\frac{1}{2},1\right]} r\left[l_{2,B}^{-1}(r),r_{2,B}^{-1}(r)\right]\right)$$

The general form of computations like $\circledast\in\{\oplus,\ominus,\odot,\oslash\}$ between these uncertain sets can be displayed as the following general form.

$$(A\circledast B)[r]=\left(\bigcup_{r\in\left(0,\frac{1}{2}\right]} r(A_1\circledast B_1)[r]\right)\bigcup\left[\underline{l},\overline{l}\right]\bigcup\left[\underline{r},\overline{r}\right]\bigcup\left(\bigcup_{r\in\left[\frac{1}{2},1\right]} r(A_2\circledast B_2)[r]\right)$$

where:

$$a=\frac{\underline{a}+\overline{a}}{2},\quad b=\frac{\underline{b}+\overline{b}}{2}$$

For instance, in the case of **addition** $\oplus$, we have:

$$\underline{l}=\frac{a+b}{2}+\frac{a_2+b_2}{2},\quad \overline{l}=\frac{a+b}{2}+\frac{a_3+b_3}{2}$$

$$\underline{r}=\frac{a+b}{2}+\frac{a_4+b_4}{2},\quad \overline{r}=\frac{a+b}{2}+\frac{a_5+b_5}{2}$$

and:

$$(A_1\oplus B_1)[r]=\left[\frac{a+b}{2}+\left(\frac{l_{1,A}^{-1}(r)+l_{1,B}^{-1}(r)}{2}\right),\frac{a+b}{2}+\left(\frac{r_{1,A}^{-1}(r)+r_{1,B}^{-1}(r)}{2}\right)\right]$$

$$(A_2\oplus B_2)[r]=\left[\frac{a+b}{2}+\left(\frac{l_{2,A}^{-1}(r)+l_{2,B}^{-1}(r)}{2}\right),\frac{a+b}{2}+\left(\frac{r_{2,A}^{-1}(r)+r_{2,B}^{-1}(r)}{2}\right)\right]$$

In the case of **difference** $\ominus$:

$$\underline{l}=\frac{a-3b}{2}+\frac{a_2+b_2}{2},\quad \overline{l}=\frac{a-3b}{2}+\frac{a_3+b_3}{2}$$

$$\underline{r}=\frac{a-3b}{2}+\frac{a_4+b_4}{2},\quad \overline{r}=\frac{a-3b}{2}+\frac{a_5+b_5}{2}$$

and:

$$(A_1 \ominus B_1)(r) = \left[\frac{a-3b}{2} + \left(\frac{l_{1,A}^{-1}(r) + l_{1,B}^{-1}(r)}{2}\right), \frac{a-3b}{2} + \left(\frac{r_{1,A}^{-1}(r) + r_{1,B}^{-1}(r)}{2}\right)\right]$$

$$(A_2 \ominus B_2)[r] = \left[\frac{a-3b}{2} + \left(\frac{l_{2,A}^{-1}(r) + l_{2,B}^{-1}(r)}{2}\right), \frac{a-3b}{2} + \left(\frac{r_{2,A}^{-1}(r) + r_{2,B}^{-1}(r)}{2}\right)\right]$$

In the other cases of multiplication and division, the relations are discussed conditionally and depend on the signs of a and b.

In the case of **multiplication** $\odot$:

Case 1 If $a \geq 0$, $b \geq 0$:

$$\underline{l} = \frac{b}{2}a_2 + \frac{a}{2}b_2,\ \bar{l} = \frac{b}{2}a_3 + \frac{a}{2}b_3,\ \underline{r} = \frac{b}{2}a_4 + \frac{a}{2}b_4,\ \bar{r} = \frac{b}{2}a_5 + \frac{a}{2}b_5$$

$$(A_1 \odot B_1)[r] = \left[\frac{b}{2}l_{1,A}^{-1}(r) + \frac{a}{2}l_{1,B}^{-1}(r), \frac{b}{2}r_{1,A}^{-1}(r) + \frac{a}{2}r_{1,B}^{-1}(r)\right]$$

$$(A_2 \odot B_2)[r] = \left[\frac{b}{2}l_{2,A}^{-1}(r) + \frac{a}{2}l_{2,B}^{-1}(r), \frac{b}{2}r_{2,A}^{-1}(r) + \frac{a}{2}r_{2,B}^{-1}(r)\right]$$

Case 2 If $a \geq 0$, $b \leq 0$:

$$\underline{l} = \frac{b}{2}a_5 + \frac{a}{2}b_2,\ \bar{l} = \frac{b}{2}a_4 + \frac{a}{2}b_3,\ \underline{r} = \frac{b}{2}a_3 + \frac{a}{2}b_4,\ \bar{r} = \frac{b}{2}a_2 + \frac{a}{2}b_5$$

$$(A_1 \odot B_1)[r] = \left[\frac{b}{2}r_{1,A}^{-1}(r) + \frac{a}{2}l_{1,B}^{-1}(r), \frac{b}{2}l_{1,A}^{-1}(r) + \frac{a}{2}r_{1,B}^{-1}(r)\right]$$

$$(A_2 \odot B_2)[r] = \left[\frac{b}{2}r_{2,A}^{-1}(r) + \frac{a}{2}l_{2,B}^{-1}(r), \frac{b}{2}l_{2,A}^{-1}(r) + \frac{a}{2}r_{2,B}^{-1}(r)\right]$$

Case 3 If $a \leq 0$, $b \leq 0$:

$$\underline{l} = \frac{b}{2}a_5 + \frac{a}{2}b_5,\ \bar{l} = \frac{b}{2}a_4 + \frac{a}{2}b_4,\ \underline{r} = \frac{b}{2}a_3 + \frac{a}{2}b_3,\ \bar{r} = \frac{b}{2}a_2 + \frac{a}{2}b_2$$

$$(A_1 \odot B_1)[r] = \left[\frac{b}{2}r_{1,A}^{-1}(r) + \frac{a}{2}r_{1,B}^{-1}(r), \frac{b}{2}l_{1,A}^{-1}(r) + \frac{a}{2}l_{1,B}^{-1}(r)\right]$$

$$(A_2 \odot B_2)[r] = \left[\frac{b}{2}r_{2,A}^{-1}(r) + \frac{a}{2}r_{2,B}^{-1}(r), \frac{b}{2}l_{2,A}^{-1}(r) + \frac{a}{2}l_{2,B}^{-1}(r)\right]$$

Case 4 If $a \leq 0$, $b \geq 0$:

$$\underline{l} = \frac{b}{2}a_2 + \frac{a}{2}b_5,\ \bar{l} = \frac{b}{2}a_3 + \frac{a}{2}b_4,\ \underline{r} = \frac{b}{2}a_4 + \frac{a}{2}b_3,\ \bar{r} = \frac{b}{2}a_5 + \frac{a}{2}b_2$$

$$(A_1 \odot B_1)[r] = \left[\frac{b}{2} l_{1,A}^{-1}(r) + \frac{a}{2} r_{1,B}^{-1}(r), \frac{b}{2} r_{1,A}^{-1}(r) + \frac{a}{2} l_{1,B}^{-1}(r)\right]$$

$$(A_2 \odot B_2)[r] = \left[\frac{b}{2} l_{2,A}^{-1}(r) + \frac{a}{2} r_{2,B}^{-1}(r), \frac{b}{2} r_{2,A}^{-1}(r) + \frac{a}{2} l_{2,B}^{-1}(r)\right]$$

In the case of **multiplication** $\oslash$, we consider that $\frac{A}{B} = A \odot B^{-1}$, so first introduce the B^{-1} in level-wise form as follows:

$$B^{-1}[r] = \left(\bigcup_{r \in (0, \frac{1}{2}]} r\left(\left[\frac{1}{b^2} l_{1,B^{-1}}^{-1}(r), \frac{1}{b^2} r_{1,B^{-1}}^{-1}(r)\right]\right)\right) \bigcup \left[\frac{1}{b^2} b_2, \frac{1}{b^2} b_3\right]$$

$$\bigcup \left[\frac{1}{b^2} b_4, \frac{1}{b^2} b_5\right] \bigcup \left(\bigcup_{r \in [\frac{1}{2}, 1]} r\left(\left[\frac{1}{b^2} l_{2,B^{-1}}^{-1}(r), \frac{1}{b^2} r_{2,B^{-1}}^{-1}(r)\right]\right)\right)$$

$$(A \odot B^{-1})[r] = \left(\bigcup_{r \in (0, \frac{1}{2}]} r(A_1 \cdot B_1^{-1})[r]\right) \bigcup [\underline{l}, \overline{l}] \bigcup [\underline{r}, \overline{r}] \bigcup \left(\bigcup_{r \in [\frac{1}{2}, 1]} r(A_2 \cdot B_2^{-1})[r]\right)$$

Now, as in the multiplication case, we should consider the previous four cases, because it is indeed a multiplication by an inverse. Here, it should be mentioned that b is not zero, $b \neq 0$.

Case 1 If $a \geq 0$, $b > 0$:

$$\underline{l} = \frac{1}{2b} a_2 + \frac{a}{2b^2} b_2,\ \overline{l} = \frac{1}{2b} a_3 + \frac{a}{2b^2} b_3,\ \underline{r} = \frac{1}{2b} a_4 + \frac{a}{2b^2} b_4,\ \overline{r} = \frac{1}{2b} a_5 + \frac{a}{2b^2} b_5$$

$$(A_1 \odot B_1^{-1})[\alpha] = \left[\frac{1}{2b} l_{1,A}^{-1}(\alpha) + \frac{a}{2b^2} l_{1,B}^{-1}(\alpha), \frac{1}{2b} r_{1,A}^{-1}(\alpha) + \frac{a}{2b^2} r_{1,B}^{-1}(\alpha)\right]$$

$$(A_2 \odot B_2^{-1})[\alpha] = \left[\frac{1}{2b} l_{2,A}^{-1}(\alpha) + \frac{a}{2b^2} l_{2,B}^{-1}(\alpha), \frac{1}{2b} r_{2,A}^{-1}(\alpha) + \frac{a}{2b^2} r_{2,B}^{-1}(\alpha)\right]$$

Case 2 If $a \geq 0$, $b < 0$:

$$\underline{l} = \frac{1}{2b} a_5 + \frac{a}{2b^2} b_2,\ \overline{l} = \frac{1}{2b} a_4 + \frac{a}{2b^2} b_3,\ \underline{r} = \frac{1}{2b} a_3 + \frac{a}{2b^2} b_4,\ \overline{r} = \frac{1}{2b} a_2 + \frac{a}{2b^2} b_5$$

$$(A_1 \odot B_1^{-1})[\alpha] = \left[\frac{1}{2b} r_{1,A}^{-1}(\alpha) + \frac{a}{2b^2} l_{1,B}^{-1}(\alpha), \frac{1}{2b} l_{1,A}^{-1}(\alpha) + \frac{a}{2b^2} r_{1,B}^{-1}(\alpha)\right]$$

$$(A_2 \odot B_2^{-1})[\alpha] = \left[\frac{1}{2b} r_{2,A}^{-1}(\alpha) + \frac{a}{2b^2} l_{2,B}^{-1}(\alpha), \frac{1}{2b} l_{2,A}^{-1}(\alpha) + \frac{a}{2b^2} r_{2,B}^{-1}(\alpha)\right]$$

Case 3 If $a \leq 0,\ b < 0$:

$$\underline{l} = \frac{1}{2b}a_5 + \frac{a}{2b^2}b_5,\ \bar{l} = \frac{1}{2b}a_4 + \frac{a}{2b^2}b_4,\ \underline{r} = \frac{1}{2b}a_3 + \frac{a}{2b^2}b_3,\ \bar{r} = \frac{1}{2b}a_2 + \frac{a}{2b^2}b_2$$

$$\left(A_1 \odot B_1^{-1}\right)[\alpha] = \left[\frac{1}{2b}r_{1,A}^{-1}(\alpha) + \frac{a}{2b^2}r_{1,B}^{-1}(\alpha),\ \frac{1}{2b}l_{1,A}^{-1}(\alpha) + \frac{a}{2b^2}l_{1,B}^{-1}(\alpha)\right]$$

$$\left(A_2 \odot B_2^{-1}\right)[\alpha] = \left[\frac{1}{2b}r_{2,A}^{-1}(\alpha) + \frac{a}{2b^2}r_{2,B}^{-1}(\alpha),\ \frac{1}{2b}l_{2,A}^{-1}(\alpha) + \frac{a}{2b^2}l_{2,B}^{-1}(\alpha)\right]$$

Case 4 If $a \leq 0,\ b > 0$:

$$\underline{l} = \frac{1}{2b}a_2 + \frac{a}{2b^2}b_5,\ \bar{l} = \frac{1}{2b}a_3 + \frac{a}{2b^2}b_4,\ \underline{r} = \frac{1}{2b}a_4 + \frac{a}{2b^2}b_3,\ \bar{r} = \frac{1}{2b}a_5 + \frac{a}{2b^2}b_2$$

$$\left(A_1 \odot B_1^{-1}\right)[\alpha] = \left[\frac{1}{2b}l_{1,A}^{-1}(\alpha) + \frac{a}{2b^2}r_{1,B}^{-1}(\alpha),\ \frac{1}{2b}r_{1,A}^{-1}(\alpha) + \frac{a}{2b^2}l_{1,B}^{-1}(\alpha)\right]$$

$$\left(A_2 \odot B_2^{-1}\right)[\alpha] = \left[\frac{1}{2b}l_{2,A}^{-1}(\alpha) + \frac{a}{2b^2}r_{2,B}^{-1}(\alpha),\ \frac{1}{2b}r_{2,A}^{-1}(\alpha) + \frac{a}{2b^2}l_{2,B}^{-1}(\alpha)\right]$$

2.6.2 *Z*-PROCESS

At this point, we are interested in expanding the concept of advanced uncertain sets, and we need to explain the benefits and motivations of these sets. In decision science, one who wants to decide on an object must be based on its information. We all know that information about us is linguistic and unclear. This information must be reliable and useful for its usefulness and applicability; it must be mathematically modeled for rational decisions.

For example, I may say:

"I'll be at home for about 20 minutes."

Or another example, we can almost predict the economic situation of the country in about 5 years, and any other similarly complex proposition about other matters.

It is easy to say that is obviously not easy to deal with, and decision-making has complexity problems. In fact, mathematical decision-making uses a lot of words or language computations. In some cases, the occurrence of some uncertain information is conditional and may depend on another occurrence. Lotfi A. Zadeh was a scientist who introduced and discussed this information as the Z-process. Here we explain these sets and those advanced cases.

Basically, in phrases that we use in logical inferences with uncertainty, the ambiguities with reliability do have very strong support in decision-making in comparison with other phrases without any reliability.

2.6.2.1 Definition—Z-process

A Z-process introduces another type of uncertainty and is shown by an ordered pair of two linguistic uncertain variables, A and B. It is denoted as $Z=(A,B)$. The first component, A, is the membership function or any uncertain restriction, $R(X)$, on the values of real valued uncertain universe set, X, and the second component, B, is a probability measure of reliability and it mentions certainty of the first component (Zadeh, 2011).

Note that the type of uncertain restriction depends on the type of uncertain set, X. For instance, if X is a random variable then the probability distribution plays the role of a probabilistic restriction on X.

Mathematically, the relation is defined as follows:

$$\text{Probability}(X\,is\,A)=B$$

Here, the restriction Probability(X *is* A) is referred to as a possibility restriction or constraint, with A playing the role of the possibility distribution of X. In other words, the restriction $R(X)$ is X is A.

Indeed it can be explained as the membership degree of some value of X, which satisfies the restriction and is exactly the possibility measure of the values.

$$R(X):X\,\text{is}\,A\rightarrow\text{Poss}(x=X)=A(x)$$

where $A(x)$ is the membership degree of x in A. To complete the discussion, a probabilistic restriction is expressed as:

$$R(X):X\,\text{is probability}\,p_x$$

where X is a random variable and here p_X is the probability density function of X. So:

$$\text{Probability}(X\,is\,A)=B\rightarrow\int_R A(x)p_X(x)\text{d}x\,\text{is}\,B$$

In fact, $\int_R\mu_X(x)p_X(x)\text{d}x$ is the probability measure.

In general, the ordered triple (X,A,B) is referred to as a Z-valuation that is equivalent to an assignment statement, X is (A,B). Basically, uncertain computation is a computation system in which the objects are not the computation of variable values but are constraints on the values of variables. For convenience, the value of X is referred to as X, realizing that if we are talking precisely, A is not an X value but a limit on the values that X can use. The second component, B, is called certainty, and is close to the concepts of sureness, confidence, reliability, strength of belief, probability, possibility, etc. When X is a random variable, certainty may be equated to probability. Informally, B, may be interpreted as a response to the question: "How sure are you that X is A?" Typically, A and B are perception-based and are described in natural language.

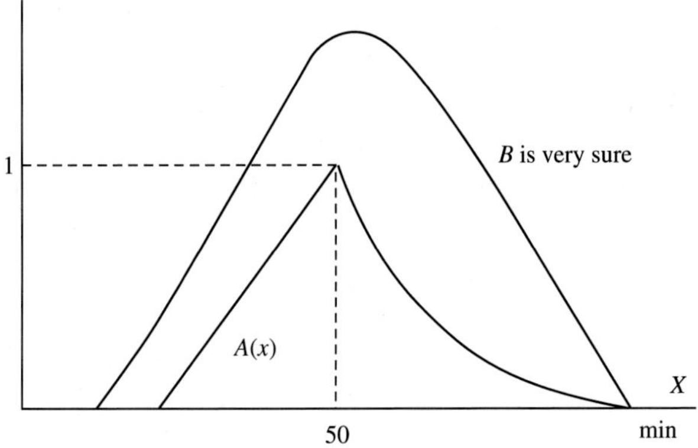

Fig. 2.21 $Z=(A, B)=$(about 50 minutes, very sure).

2.6.2.2 Example

Consider the following Z-process:

$$Z=(A, B)=(\text{about 50 minutes, very sure})$$

In the example "about 50 min" is a restriction in the role of uncertain set and "very sure" plays the role of reliability of the "about 50 min" as another uncertain set. We can consider the process as "*I am very sure that he will arrive about 50 minutes later*" (Fig. 2.21).

In fact, a Z-number or process may be viewed as a summary of probability distribution that is not known. It is important to note that in day-to-day decisions, most decisions are based on summary information. Viewing a Z-process as a summary is consistent with this fact. In applications for decision analysis, a fundamental problem that arises is the ranking of Z-numbers.

2.6.2.3 Example

Is (approximately 80, probably) more than (approximately 80, very likely)? Or (approximately 100, very likely) more than (approximately 90, surely)? Are these meaningful questions? It seems that the relations of probability distribution p_X and B can be explained immediately. For instance, if $Z=(A,B)$ is a Z-process, its complement can be described as $Z^c=(A^c,B^c)$ where A^c is the complement of A and B^c plays the role of complement of B. For example, consider the previous example, if:

$$Z=(A, B)=(\text{about 50 minutes, very sure})$$

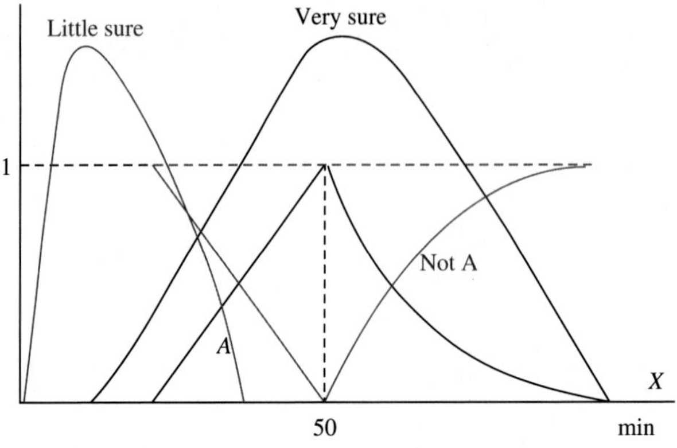

Fig. 2.22 $Z^c = (A^c, B^c) =$ (not about 50 minutes, unsure).

then:

$$Z^c = (A^c, B^c) = (\text{Not about 50 minutes, little sure})$$

In graphical form, it can be shown as in Fig. 2.22.

2.6.3 Computations on Z-Numbers

First, we should determine the meaning of a fuzzy number. In the Z-process like $Z=(A,B)$, the first component, A, is a fuzzy set with the reliability B, and there is no need to be a fuzzy number. But in the case that A is a fuzzy number with the reliability of B, then the Z-process is called a Z-number.

Calculating this information is not as easy as we think. Therefore, it is intended to simplify a particular case of this information. To this end, the summarization of the Z-number can be demonstrated as follows:

$$Z = (A, B) = (A(x), P_{R_X}(x)) \text{ or } Z = (A, P_{R_X}).$$

where:

$$\text{Poss}(x = X) = A(x)$$

$$\text{Probability}(X \text{ is } A) = B$$

And we say probability distribution, p_X, is not known and what is known is restriction on p_X, which is demonstrated as follows:

$$\int_R A(x) p_X(x) \mathrm{d}x \text{ is } B$$

Now suppose that $A(x)$ and $B(y)$ are two membership functions of two fuzzy numbers and P_{R_X} and P_{R_Y} are two independent probability density functions on two universe uncertain sets on X and Y, respectively.

Consider the following two Z-numbers:

$$Z_X = (A_1, P_{R_X}),\ Z_Y = (A_2, P_{R_Y}),$$

such that:

$$P_{R_X} = \int_R A_1(x)p_X(x)\mathrm{d}x,\ P_{R_Y} = \int_R A_2(y)p_Y(y)\mathrm{d}y$$

and:

$$\int_R p_X(x)\mathrm{d}x = 1,\ \int_R p_Y(y)\mathrm{d}y = 1$$

For the compatibility of two components of an uncertain set, we should have the following relations:

$$\int_R x p_X(x)\mathrm{d}x = \frac{\int_R x\mu_X(x)\mathrm{d}x}{\int_R \mu_X(x)\mathrm{d}x}$$

$$\int_R y p_Y(y)\mathrm{d}y = \frac{\int_R y\mu_Y(y)\mathrm{d}y}{\int_R \mu_Y(y)\mathrm{d}y}$$

Suppose an arbitrary operation, like $\circledast \in \{\oplus, \ominus, \odot, \oslash\}$. The calculations on the two abovementioned Z-numbers can be defined as:

$$Z_X \circledast Z_Y = (A_1 \circledast A_2, P_{R_X} \circledast P_{R_Y}) = (A_1 \circledast A_2, P_{R_X \circledast R_Y})$$

It should be mentioned that the binary operation $\circledast$ whose operands are membership functions is different from the binary operation $\circledast$ whose operands are probability density functions. Actually $P_{R_X} \circledast P_{R_Y}$ is the convulsion of two probability density functions P_{R_X} and P_{R_Y} and it is very difficult to follow. It is exactly dependent on the meaning of extension of uncertainty under the operation $\circledast$. It means that the uncertainty of $Z_X \circledast Z_Y$ should be increased in comparison of operands uncertainties and increasing the uncertainty is related to not only the first part, but also the second part. So to extend the uncertainty and evaluation of the extension, if-then rules are suggested.

Considering the previous concepts, we have:

$$Z_X = (A_1, P_{R_X}),\ Z_Y = (A_2, P_{R_Y}),$$

then:

$$Z_X = \left(A_1, \int_R A_1(x)p_X(x)\mathrm{d}x\right),\ Z_Y = \left(A_2, \int_R A_2(y)p_Y(y)\mathrm{d}y\right),$$

In general form, based on Zadeh's extension principle, two of the components do have membership functions and those can be defined as follows:

$$(A_1 \circledast A_2)(t) = \sup_{t=r*s} \min\{A_1(r), A_2(s)\},$$

and the probability distribution of $P_{R_X \circledast RY}$ is referred to as a convolution of P_{R_X} and P_{R_Y}.

$$P_{R_X \circledast R_Y}(t) = \int_R (A_1 \circledast A_2)(t) p_{X*Y}(t)\mathrm{d}t$$

2.6.3.1 Summation of two Z-numbers

If we suppose that the operation is summation:

$$Z_X \oplus Z_Y = (A_1 \oplus A_2, P_{R_X \oplus R_Y})$$

The first component is the summation of two membership functions of two fuzzy numbers and it can be investigated by using Zadeh's extension principle. Then we have:

$$(A_1 \oplus A_2)(t) = \sup_{t=r+s} \min\{A_1(r), A_2(s)\},$$

and the probability distribution of $P_{R_X \oplus RY}$ is:

$$P_{R_X \oplus R_Y}(t) = \int_R (A_1 \oplus A_2)(t) p_{X+Y}(t)\mathrm{d}t,$$

where:

$$p_{X+Y}(t) = \int_R p_X(s) p_Y(t-s)\mathrm{d}s$$

As we can see, the relations are too complicated and the other computations have the same procedure as the summation.

2.6.3.2 Difference of two Z-numbers

Now suppose that the operation is the difference between two Z-numbers:

$$Z_X \ominus_H Z_Y = (A_1 \ominus_H A_2, P_{R_X \ominus R_Y})$$

The probability distribution of $P_{R_X \ominus RY}$ is:

$$P_{R_X \ominus R_Y}(t) = \int_R (A_1 \ominus_H A_2)(t) p_{X-Y}(t) \mathrm{d}t,$$

where:

$$(A_1 \ominus_H A_2)(t) = \sup_{t=r-s} \min\{A_1(r), A_2(s)\},$$

and:

$$p_{X-Y}(t) = \int_R p_X(s) p_Y(s-t) \mathrm{d}s$$

The other computations have the same structures.

2.6.3.3 Multiplication of two Z-numbers

Now suppose that the operation is multiplication:

$$Z_X \odot Z_Y = (A_1 \odot A_2, P_{R_X \odot R_Y})$$

Again, similar to the previous operations, we have:

$$P_{R_X \odot R_Y}(t) = \int_R (A_1 \odot A_2)(t) p_{X \cdot Y}(t) \mathrm{d}t$$

where:

$$(A_1 \odot A_2)(t) = \sup_{t=r \cdot s} \min\{A_1(r), A_2(s)\},$$

and:

$$p_{X \cdot Y}(t) = \int_R p_X(s) p_Y\left(\frac{t}{s}\right) \frac{1}{|s|} \mathrm{d}s$$

2.6.3.4 Division of two Z-numbers

For the division:

$$Z_X \oslash Z_Y = (A_1 \oslash A_2, P_{R_X \oslash R_Y})$$

Again, similar to the previous operations, we have:

$$P_{R_X \oslash R_Y}(t) = \int_R (A_1 \oslash A_2)(t) p_{X/Y}(t) \mathrm{d}t$$

where:

$$(A_1 \oslash A_2)(t) = \sup_{t=r/s} \min\{A_1(r), A_2(s)\},$$

and:

$$p_{X \cdot Y}(t) = \int_R |s| p_X(s) p_Y\left(\frac{s}{t}\right) \mathrm{d}s$$

2.6.3.5 *Level-wise form of a Z-number*

For a Z-number like $Z=(A,B)$ on X, we suppose the two components are compatible and the second component is a continuous and normal probability density function (central limit theorem) associated with A. For instance:

$$N(t;\mu,\sigma) = \frac{1}{\sigma\sqrt{2\pi}} \exp\left(-\frac{(t-\mu)^2}{2\sigma^2}\right), \quad t \in R$$

Clearly, for $\mu=1$, $\sigma=0$, we will have the standard normal probability density function. So instead of the second component we can have $N(t;\mu,\sigma)$.

To explain the level-wise form of a Z-number, the following examples are provided:

I say with high probability that I will be at the airport at about 2 o'clock in the morning.

Or

I say with low probability that I will be at the airport at about 2 o'clock in the morning.

In both phrases, we see high and low probability, and that if the level is close to zero then the probability is low, and in the case of it being close to one, the probability is high.

2.6.3.5.1 High membership degree does have high reliability

We are now able to show two components in level-wise form and we have:

$$Z[r] = (A,N)[r] = [A[r], N[r]], \quad 0 \le r \le 1,$$

where:

$$A[r] = [A_l(r), A_u(r)], N[r] = [N_l(r), N_u(r)], \quad 0 \le r \le 1$$

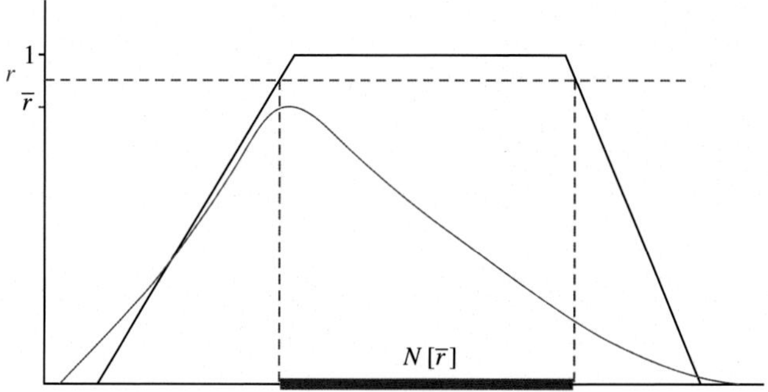

Fig. 2.23 *Z*-number in level-wise form of case 1

The relation between r and $\overline{r} = \text{height}(N)$ can be discussed in two cases.
Case 1 $0 \leq \overline{r} \leq 1$

$$Z[r] = \begin{cases} (A[r], N[r]), & 0 \leq r \leq \overline{r} \\ (A[r], N[\overline{r}]), & \overline{r} \leq r \leq 1 \end{cases}$$

In this case, if $\overline{r} \leq r \leq 1$, the highest level is considered for the elements of $A[r]$ (Fig. 2.23).
Case 2 $\overline{r} > 1$

$$Z[r] = \begin{cases} (A[r], N[r]), & 0 \leq r \leq 1 \\ (A[1], N[r]), & 1 < r \leq \overline{r} \end{cases}$$

This means that the highest level of probabilities are for the elements of $A[1]$ for $1 < r \leq \overline{r}$ (Fig. 2.24).

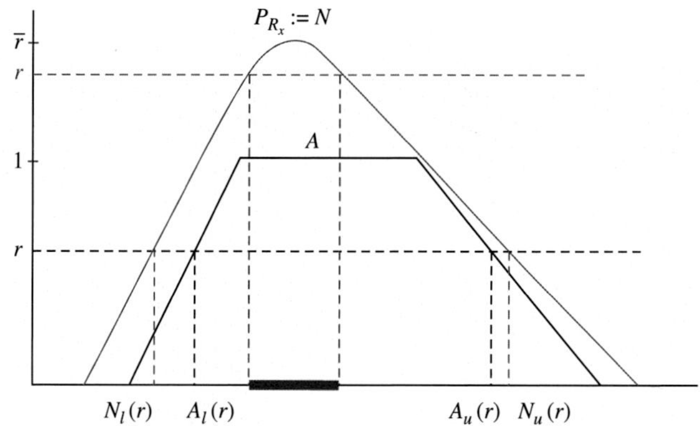

Fig. 2.24 *Z*-number in level-wise form of case 2

2.6.3.5.2 Definition—Level-wise form of a standard Z-number

The level-wise form of the standard Z-number with standard normal probability density function should have the following conditions for any $0 \leq r \leq 1$:

- $A_l(r) \leq A_u(r)$ and $N_l(r) \leq N_u(r)$.
- $A_l(r)$ and $N_l(r)$ are two increasing and left continuous functions on $(0, 1]$ and right continuous at 0 w.r.t. r.
- $A_u(r)$ and $N_u(r)$ are decreasing and left continuous functions on $(0, 1]$ and right continuous at 0 w.r.t. r.
- $\int_{-\infty}^{\text{core}(N)} N_l(r)\mathrm{d}r = \int_{-\infty}^{\text{core}(N)} N_u(r)\mathrm{d}r = \frac{1}{2}$.

Note that for cases (ii) and (iii), both functions can be bounded. The word standard comes from the standard normal probability density function as a second component. Based on this definition, we suppose that the standard normal probability function is a best approximation to part B being the Z-number.

2.6.3.6 *Summation in level-wise form*

For two standard Z-numbers like $Z_1=(A_1,N_1)$, $Z_2=(A_2,N_2)$:

$$(Z_1+Z_2)[r] = Z_1[r] + Z_2[r] = [[A_1[r], N_1[r]] + [A_2[r], N_2[r]]]$$

$$= [A_1[r] + A_2[r], N_1[r] + N_2[r]],$$

$$= [\,[A_{1,l}(r), A_{1,u}(r)] + [A_{2,l}(r), A_{2,u}(r)],\, [N_{1,l}(r), N_{1,u}(r)] + [N_{2,l}(r), N_{2,u}(r)]\,]$$

$$= [[A_{1,l}(r) + A_{2,l}(r), A_{1,u}(r) + A_{2,u}(r)],\, [N_{1,l}(r) + N_{2,l}(r), N_{1,u}(r) + N_{2,u}(r)]\,]]$$

For example:

$$Z_1 = (\text{about 2 o'clock, very sure}), Z_1 = (\text{about 3 o'clock, a little sure})$$

Now the summation is as follows:

$$Z_1 + Z_2 = (\text{about 2 o'clock} + \text{about 3 o'clock, very sure} + \text{a little sure})$$

Usually we can say that:

$$Z_1 + Z_2 = (\text{about 5 o'clock, a little too sure})$$

Now:

$$(\text{a little too sure})[r] = (\text{very sure})[r] + (\text{a little sure})[r]$$

In (a little too sure)[r], if $r \to 1$, the highest probability of a little too sure as a reliability occurs. This means the elements in the support of fuzzy number about 5 o'clock with the membership degree of r do have the degree of r reliability in a little too sure.

2.6.3.7 Scalar multiplication in level-wise form

Suppose that $\lambda \in R$ is a real scalar and $Z=(A,N)$ is a standard normal probability function. We are going to investigate the scalar multiplication in level-wise form.

$$(\lambda Z)[r]=(\lambda A[r],\lambda N[r])=\begin{cases}([\lambda A_l(r),\lambda A_u(r)],[\lambda N_l(r),\lambda N_u(r)]), & \lambda \geq 0\\([\lambda A_u(r),\lambda A_l(r)],[\lambda N_u(r),\lambda N_l(r)]), & \lambda < 0\end{cases}$$

For example:

$$Z=(\text{about } 1,\text{sure}), Z[r]=([1,2-r],\text{sure}[r])$$

Now suppose $\lambda=-1$:

$$(-1)Z=(\text{about }(-1),\text{sure}),((-1)Z)[r]=([r-2,-1],\text{sure}[r])$$

In the Z-number, $(-1)Z$, the reliability "sure" is for the fuzzy set "about(-1)" (see Fig. 2.25).

2.6.3.8 Hukuhara difference in level-wise form

As mentioned earlier, the H-difference and gH-difference between two fuzzy numbers are different from the negative scalar multiplication and here we will have the similar discussions with some generalizations (Allahviranloo and Ezadi, 2019).

Again, suppose two Z-numbers as follows:

$$Z_1=(A_1,N_1),\ Z_2=(A_2,N_2)$$

The H-difference of these two Z-numbers $Z_1 \ominus_H Z_2$ exists and is equal to Z_3 if and only if:

$$\exists Z_3,\ Z_1 \ominus_H Z_2 = Z_3 \Leftrightarrow Z_1 = Z_2 \oplus Z_3$$

where Z_3 is another Z-number. This means the existence of the H-difference depends on Z_3 and it should be a Z-number as well.

Now we can have the following, as mentioned previously:

$$Z_1[r]=(Z_2 \oplus Z_3)[r]=Z_2[r]+Z_3[r]$$

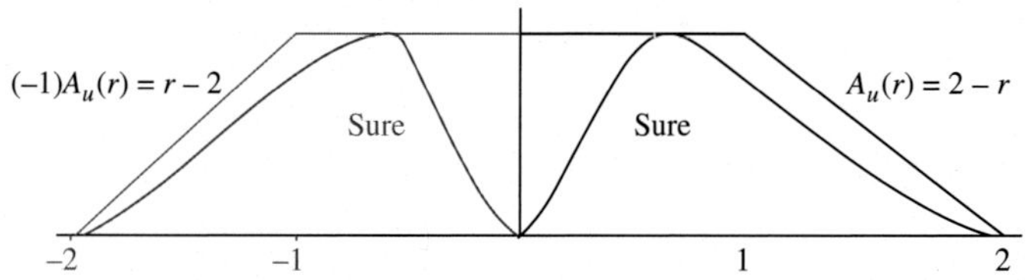

Fig. 2.25 Z and $(-1)Z$ in level-wise form.

$$= [\,[A_{2,l}(r), A_{2,u}(r)] + [A_{3,l}(r), A_{3,u}(r)], [N_{2,l}(r), N_{2,u}(r)] + [N_{3,l}(r), N_{3,u}(r)]\,]$$

$$= [[A_{2,l}(r) + A_{3,l}(r), A_{2,u}(r) + A_{3,u}(r)], [N_{2,l}(r) + N_{3,l}(r), N_{2,u}(r) + N_{3,u}(r)]\,]]$$

so:

$$[A_{1,l}(r), A_{1,u}(r)] = [A_{2,l}(r) + A_{3,l}(r), A_{2,u}(r) + A_{3,u}(r)]$$

$$[N_{1,l}(r), N_{1,u}(r)] = [N_{2,l}(r) + N_{3,l}(r), N_{2,u}(r) + N_{3,u}(r)]]$$

then:

$$A_{3,l}(r) = A_{1,l}(r) - A_{2,l}(r),\ A_{3,u}(r) = A_{1,u}(r) - A_{2,u}(r),$$

$$N_{3,l}(r) = N_{1,l}(r) - N_{2,l}(r),\ N_{3,u}(r) = N_{1,u}(r) - N_{2,u}(r)$$

and:

$$[[A_{3,l}(r), A_{3,u}(r)], [N_{3,l}(r), N_{3,u}(r)]] =$$

$$= [[A_{1,l}(r) - A_{2,l}(r), A_{1,u}(r) - A_{2,u}(r)], [N_{1,l}(r) - N_{2,l}(r), N_{1,u}(r) - N_{2,u}(r)]]$$

The conditions for the existence of the Hukuhara difference are as follows:

- $A_{3,l}\ (r) \leq A_{3,u}\ (r)$ and $N_{3,l}\ (r) \leq N_{3,u}\ (r)$.
- $A_{3,l}\ (r)$ and $N_{3,l}\ (r)$ are two increasing and left continuous functions on $(0, 1]$ and right continuous at 0 w.r.t. r.
- $A_{3,\,u}(r)$ and $N_{3,\,u}(r)$ are decreasing and left continuous functions on $(0, 1]$ and right continuous at 0 w.r.t. r.
- $\int_{-\infty}^{\text{core}(N)} N_{3,l}(r)\text{d}r = \int_{-\infty}^{\text{core}(N)} N_{3,u}(r)\text{d}r = \frac{1}{2}$.

For any $0 \leq r \leq 1$.

As we observe that the conditions are very difficult to satisfy, in cases where at least one of the conditions does not work, we are going to consider the H-difference as $Z_2 \ominus_H Z_1 = (-1)Z_3$. If this one is true then we are going to define the generalized Hukuhara difference.

2.6.3.9 Generalized Hukuhara difference in level-wise form

In this case, we can define the difference in another way. Suppose that we want to try $Z_2 \ominus_H Z_1 = (-1)Z_3$ and let the difference Z_3 exist. Considering the level-wise forms of two sides:

$$(Z_2 \ominus_H Z_1)[r] = [[A_{2,l}(r) - A_{1,l}(r), A_{2,u}(r) - A_{1,u}(r)], [N_{2,l}(r) - N_{1,l}(r), N_{2,u}(r) - N_{1,u}(r)]]$$

$$= ((-1)Z_3)[r] = [[-A_{3,u}(r),\ -A_{3,l}(r)], [-N_{3,u}(r),\ -N_{3,l}(r)]]$$

Then we have:

$$[A_{2,l}(r) - A_{1,l}(r), A_{2,u}(r) - A_{1,u}(r)] = [-A_{3,u}(r),\ -A_{3,l}(r)],$$
$$[N_{2,l}(r) - N_{1,l}(r), N_{2,u}(r) - N_{1,u}(r)] = [-N_{3,u}(r),\ -N_{3,l}(r)]$$

Immediately:

$$A_{2,l}(r) - A_{1,l}(r) = -A_{3,u}(r), A_{2,u}(r) - A_{1,u}(r) = -A_{3,l}(r)$$
$$N_{2,l}(r) - N_{1,l}(r) = -N_{3,u}(r), N_{2,u}(r) - N_{1,u}(r) = -N_{3,l}(r)$$

and here:

$$[[A_{3,l}(r), A_{3,u}(r)], [N_{3,l}(r), N_{3,u}(r)]] =$$
$$= [[A_{1,u}(r) - A_{2,u}(r), A_{1,l}(r) - A_{2,l}(r)], [N_{1,u}(r) - N_{2,u}(r), N_{1,l}(r) - N_{2,l}(r)]]$$

In comparison with previous results, the only difference is interchanging the endpoints of the intervals.

So the generalized Hukuhara difference is shown by $\ominus_{gH}$ and defined in two cases.

- In case (i):

$$Z_1 \ominus_{gH} Z_2 = Z_3 \Leftrightarrow Z_1 = Z_2 \oplus Z_3$$

and the level-wise form is as follows:

$$[[A_{3,l}(r), A_{3,u}(r)], [N_{3,l}(r), N_{3,u}(r)]] =$$
$$= [[A_{1,l}(r) - A_{2,l}(r), A_{1,u}(r) - A_{2,u}(r)], [N_{1,l}(r) - N_{2,l}(r), N_{1,u}(r) - N_{2,u}(r)]]$$

- In case (ii):

$$Z_2 \ominus_{gH} Z_1 = (-1)Z_3 \Leftrightarrow Z_2 = Z_1 \oplus (-1)Z_3$$

and the level-wise form is as follows:

$$[[A_{3,l}(r), A_{3,u}(r)], [N_{3,l}(r), N_{3,u}(r)]] =$$
$$= [[A_{1,u}(r) - A_{2,u}(r), A_{1,l}(r) - A_{2,l}(r)], [N_{1,u}(r) - N_{2,u}(r), N_{1,l}(r) - N_{2,l}(r)]]$$

If case (i) exists, there is no need to consider case (ii). Otherwise we will need the second case. The relation between the two cases can be explained as follows:

$$(Z_1 \ominus_{gH} Z_2)_i [r] = \ominus(-1)\left((Z_2 \ominus_{gH} Z_1)_{ii} [r]\right)$$

If both cases exist, then $Z_3=(-1)Z_3$ and it is concluded that both types of difference are the same and equal.

Considering the two cases, to define the endpoints of the generalized Hukuhara difference:

$$A_{3,l}(r)=\min\{A_{1,u}(r)-A_{2,u}(r),A_{1,l}(r)-A_{2,l}(r)\}$$

$$A_{3,u}(r)=\max\{A_{1,u}(r)-A_{2,u}(r),A_{1,l}(r)-A_{2,l}(r)\}$$

$$N_{3,l}(r)=\min\{N_{1,u}(r)-N_{2,u}(r),N_{1,l}(r)-N_{2,l}(r)\}$$

$$N_{3,u}(r)=\max\{N_{1,u}(r)-N_{2,u}(r),N_{1,l}(r)-N_{2,l}(r)\}$$

$$A_3[r]=\left[\min\{A_{1,u}(r)-A_{2,u}(r),A_{1,l}(r)-A_{2,l}(r)\},\ \max\{A_{1,u}(r)-A_{2,u}(r),A_{1,l}(r)-A_{2,l}(r)\}\right]$$

$$N_3[r]=\left[\min\{N_{1,u}(r)-N_{2,u}(r),N_{1,l}(r)-N_{2,l}(r)\},\ \max\{N_{1,u}(r)-N_{2,u}(r),N_{1,l}(r)-N_{2,l}(r)\}\right]$$

2.6.3.10 Some properties of generalized Hukuhara

It should be noted that all of the following properties can be proved in level-wise form easily.

1. If the gH-difference exists, it is unique.
2. $Z\ominus_{gH}Z=0$.
3. If $Z_1\ominus_{gH}Z_2$ exists in case (i), then $Z_2\ominus_{gH}Z_1$ exists in case (ii) and vice versa.
4. In both cases $(Z_1\oplus Z_2)\ominus_{gH}Z_2=Z_1$. (It is easy to show in level-wise form.)
5. If $Z_1\ominus_{gH}Z_2$ and $Z_2\ominus_{gH}Z_1$ exist, then $0\ominus_{gH}(Z_1\ominus_{gH}Z_2)=Z_2\ominus_{gH}Z_1$.
6. If $Z_1\ominus_{gH}Z_2=Z_2\ominus_{gH}Z_1=Z$ if and only if $Z=-Z$ and $Z_1=Z_2$.

Note. The difference even in the gH-difference case may not exist. It can be said that the gH-difference of two Z-numbers are not always a Z-number.

For instance, item 4 in level-wise form can be explained as follows:

$$(Z_1[r]\oplus Z_2[r])\ominus_{gH}Z_2[r]=$$

$$=((A_1[r],N_1[r])\oplus(A_2[r],N_2[r]))\ominus_{gH}(A_2[r],N_2[r])$$

$$\begin{aligned}&=([A_{1,l}(r)+A_{2,l}(r),A_{1,u}(r)+A_{2,u}(r)],[N_{1,l}(r)+N_{2,l}(r),N_{1,u}(r)+N_{2,u}(r)])\\&\quad-([A_{2,l}(r),A_{2,u}(r)],[N_{2,l}(r),N_{2,u}(r)])\\&=([A_{1,l}(r),A_{1,u}(r)],[N_{1,l}(r),N_{1,u}(r)])\end{aligned}$$

Subtracting component-wise, the right-hand side is achieved very easily.

References

Abbasi, F., Allahviranloo, T., 2018. New operations on pseudo-octagonal fuzzy numbers and its application. Soft Comput. 22, 3077–3095.

Abbasi, F., Allahviranloo, T., Abbasbandy, S., 2018. A new attitude coupled with the basic fuzzy thinking to distance between two fuzzy numbers. Iran. J. Fuzzy Syst. 22, 3077–3095.

Alive, R.A., Huseynov, O.H., Serdaroglu, R., 2016. Ranking of Z-numbers, and its application in decision making. Int. J. Inform. Technol. Dec. Mak. 15, 1503.

Allahviranloo, T., 2020. Uncertain information and linear systems. In: Studies in Systems, Decision and Control. vol. 254. Springer.

Allahviranloo, T., Ezadi, S., 2019. Z-advanced number processes. Inform. Sci. 480, 130–143.

Bede, B., Gal, S.G., 2005. Generalizations of the differentiability of fuzzy-number-valued functions with applications to fuzzy differential equations. Fuzzy Set Syst. 151, 581–599.

Liu, B., 2015. Uncertain Theory. Springer-Verlag, Berlin.

Stefanini, L., 2010. A generalization of Hukuhara difference and division for interval and fuzzy arithmetic. Fuzzy Set Syst. 161, 1564–1584.

Zadeh, L.A., 2011. A note on Z-numbers. Inform. Sci. 181, 2923–2932.

Further reading

Allahviranloo, T., Perfilieva, I., Abbasi, F., 2018. A new attitude coupled with fuzzy thinking for solving fuzzy equations. Soft Comput. 22, 3077–3095.

Chapter 3

Soft computing with uncertain sets

3.1 Introduction

The aims of this chapter are considering any operators such as differentials, and integral operators on fuzzy numbers. As we know, the distance between two fuzzy numbers is defined as a function and indeed can be known as a type of operator. We will discuss different types of distances of fuzzy numbers, several ranking methods, and expected value and lengths functions.

Basically, the operators in this chapter are real and the functions and sets as operands are considered as fuzzy and uncertain sets. In the previous chapter, the main four calculating operators $\{\oplus, \ominus, \odot, \oslash\}$ were explained and applied on fuzzy numbers. In this chapter, first, we will discuss the distance between two arbitrary uncertain sets. To explain it, some concepts are considered, such as the expected value in uncertainty.

Soft Numerical Computing in Uncertain Dynamic Systems. https://doi.org/10.1016/B978-0-12-822855-5.00003-3

3.2 Expected value

The concept of expected value can be found in a similar way but it depends on the measure of an uncertain set. For a measurable fuzzy set $A \in \mathcal{M}$ with probability measure, we know that $A^c \in \mathcal{M}$, which is a complement fuzzy set of $A \in \mathcal{M}$.

Suppose that:

$$\sup_x A(x), \quad \sup_{\sim x} A(x)$$

are the supremum membership of an element x and not x in fuzzy set A. The following concept is noted as relation and connection of x and A.

$$\text{Mid}\{x \in A\} = \frac{1}{2}(\sup_x A(x) + 1 - \sup_{\sim x} A(x))$$

Let y be an uncertain variable, then for any relation like $y = x$, $y \leq x$ and $y \geq x$ we have:

$$\text{Mid}\{y = x\} = \frac{1}{2}\left(\sup_{y=x} A(y) + 1 - \sup_{y \neq x} A(y)\right):$$

$$\text{Mid}\{y \leq x\} = \frac{1}{2}\left(\sup_{y \leq x} A(y) + 1 - \sup_{y > x} A(y)\right):$$

$$\text{Mid}\{y \geq x\} = \frac{1}{2}\left(\sup_{y \geq x} A(y) + 1 - \sup_{y < x} A(y)\right):$$

Consider the second one:

$$\text{Mid}\{y \leq x\} = \frac{1}{2}\sup_{y \leq x} A(y) + \frac{1}{2} - \frac{1}{2}\sup_{y > x} A(y)$$

Since A is a fuzzy number, so if we consider a point like x_0 such that $A(x_0) = 1$ then we obviously will have:

$$\text{Mid}\{y \leq x\} = \begin{cases} \frac{1}{2}\sup_{y \leq x} A(y), & x \leq x_0 \\ 1 - \frac{1}{2}\sup_{y > x} A(y), & x > x_0 \end{cases}$$

and it can be considered in another case:

$$\text{Mid}\{y \geq x\} = \begin{cases} 1 - \frac{1}{2}\sup_{y \leq x} A(y), & x \leq x_0 \\ \frac{1}{2}\sup_{y > x} A(y), & x > x_0 \end{cases}$$

Based on the middle functions the expected value is defined as follows:

$$E(y \geq x) = x_0 + \frac{1}{2}\int_{x_0}^{+\infty} \sup_{y \geq x} A(y) \mathrm{d}x - \frac{1}{2}\int_{-\infty}^{x_0} \sup_{y < x} A(y) \mathrm{d}x$$

On the other hand:

$$E(y \leq x) = x_0 + \frac{1}{2}\int_{x_0}^{+\infty} \sup_{y \leq x} A(y)\mathrm{d}x - \frac{1}{2}\int_{-\infty}^{x_0} \sup_{y > x} A(y)\mathrm{d}x$$

Now we can evaluate the following cases:

- If $y \geq x$ then $\sup_{y \geq x} A(y) = A(x)$ for $x \geq x_0$ and $\sup_{y < x} A(y) = A(x)$ for $\leq x_0$.
- If $y \leq x$ then $\sup_{y \leq x} A(y) = A(x)$ for $x \geq x_0$ and $\sup_{y > x} A(y) = A(x)$ for $\leq x_0$.

Then in each case the expected value is defined as:

$$E(A) = x_0 + \frac{1}{2}\int_{x_0}^{+\infty} A(x)\mathrm{d}x - \frac{1}{2}\int_{-\infty}^{x_0} A(x)\mathrm{d}x$$

RemarkIn accordance with the linearity of the integral the expected value is also linear. This means that for two uncertain sets A and B and two real numbers a and b:

$$E(aA + bB) = aE(A) + bE(B)$$

Because:

$$E(aA + bB) = x_0 + \frac{1}{2}\int_{x_0}^{+\infty} (aA + bB)(x)\mathrm{d}x - \frac{1}{2}\int_{-\infty}^{x_0} (aA + bB)(x)\mathrm{d}x$$

then:

$$E(aA + bB) = a\left[x_0 + \frac{1}{2}\int_{x_0}^{+\infty} A(x)\mathrm{d}x - \frac{1}{2}\int_{-\infty}^{x_0} A(x)\mathrm{d}x\right]$$
$$+ b\left[x_0 + \frac{1}{2}\int_{x_0}^{+\infty} B(x)\mathrm{d}x - \frac{1}{2}\int_{-\infty}^{x_0} B(x)\mathrm{d}x\right] = aE(A) + bE(B)$$

Now let us consider the level-wise form of a fuzzy set A. The expected value in this format can be displayed as:

$$E(A) = \frac{1}{2}\int_0^1 (\inf A[r] + \sup A[r])\mathrm{d}r$$

$$= \frac{1}{2}\int_0^1 (A_l(r) + A_u(r))\mathrm{d}r$$

In the case of a triangular fuzzy set, $A = (A_1, A_2, A_3)$, which the components are three ordered points in the support of the fuzzy number:

$$A_l(r) + A_u(r) = A_2 + (A_2 - A_1)(r - 1) + A_2 + (A_3 - A_2)(1 - r)$$

and the expected value is:

$$E(A) = \frac{1}{2}\int_0^1 (A_2 + (A_2 - A_1)(r-1) + A_2 + (A_3 - A_2)(1-r))dr$$
$$= \frac{A_1 + 2A_2 + A_3}{4}$$

For any Trapezoidal uncertain set, $A = (A_1, A_2, A_3, A_4)$, with:

$$A_l(r) + A_u(r) = A_2 + (A_2 - A_1)(r-1) + A_3 + (A_4 - A_3)(1-r)$$

Again, the components are three ordered points in support of the fuzzy number. The expected value is:

$$E(A) = \frac{1}{2}\int_0^1 (A_2 + (A_2 - A_1)(r-1) + A_3 + (A_4 - A_3)(1-r))dr$$
$$= \frac{A_1 + A_2 + A_3 + A_4}{4}$$

For more explanation, see Liu (2015) and Allahviranloo (2020).

3.3 Distance of two fuzzy numbers

In this section, we will discuss the several types of distances between two arbitrary fuzzy numbers. Basically, the distance is a type of operator from the space all fuzzy numbers to the set of real numbers. If we suppose that the $\mathbb{F}_R$ is the set of all fuzzy numbers, then:

$$D : \mathbb{F}_R \times \mathbb{F}_R \to R$$

Clearly, this operator should have some conditions or properties such as following.

For any arbitrary fuzzy numbers A, B, C, and D:

- $D(A,B) > 0$
- $D(A,B) = 0 \Leftrightarrow A = B$
- $D(A \oplus C, B \oplus C) = D(A,C)$
- $D(A \oplus B, C \oplus D) \leq D(A,C) + D(B,D)$
- $D(\lambda A, \lambda B) = |\lambda| D(A,B), \quad \lambda \in R$

The first distance is evaluated by the concept of expected value that was discussed in the previous section. For two fuzzy numbers A and B, the absolute value of Hukuhara difference $A \ominus_H B$ can define a distance. Now the distance is defined using expected value of $|A \ominus_H B|$ as:

$$D(A,B) = E(|A \ominus_H B|)$$

The concept of absolute value means that the members are considered as nonnegative values. Based on the definition of expected value, the distance can be expressed as:

$$D(A,B)=E(|A\ominus_H B|)$$

$$=\frac{1}{2}\int_0^{+\infty}\left(\sup_{|y|\geq x}|A\ominus_H B|(y)+1-\sup_{|y|<x}|A\ominus_H B|(y)\right)\mathrm{d}x$$

If we consider $|A\ominus_H B|=C$ the distance can be written as:

$$D(A,B)=E(|A\ominus_H B|)=E(|C|)=\frac{1}{2}\int_0^1(\inf|C|[r]+\sup|C|[r])\mathrm{d}r$$

$$=\frac{1}{2}\int_0^1(|C_l|(r)+|C_u|(r))\mathrm{d}r$$

As an example, consider the following fuzzy numbers in level-wise form:

$$A=[A_l,A_u]=[2r,4-2r],\quad B=[B_l,B_u]=[r-1,1-r]:$$

and:

$$A\ominus_H B=C,\ C_l=A_l-B_l=r+1,\ C_u=A_u-B_u=3-r$$

So the Hukuhara difference in parametric form is:

$$C[r]=[\inf|C|(r),\sup|C|(r)]=[r+1,3-r]$$

The distance is:

$$D(A,B)=E(|C|)=\frac{1}{2}\int_0^1(\inf|C|[r]+\sup|C|[r])\mathrm{d}r=\frac{1}{2}\int_0^1 4\mathrm{d}r=2$$

and in triple form:

$$A\ominus_H B=(0,2,4)\ominus_H(-1,0,1)=(1,2,3)=C=(C_1,C_2,C_3)$$

$$D(A,B)=E(|C|)=\frac{C_1+2C_2+C_3}{4}=2$$

Obviously, for the proposed distance by expected value, all the mentioned above properties are true. Because:

- $E(|A\ominus_H B|)>0$. This property is very clear to prove, because the expected value is always nonnegative and, in the case of zero, is considered as follows.
- $E(|A\ominus_H B|)=0\Leftrightarrow\int_0^1(\inf|A\ominus_H B|[r]+\sup|A\ominus_H B|[r])dr=0\Leftrightarrow\inf|A\ominus_H B|[r]$ $+\sup|A\ominus_H B|[r]=0\Leftrightarrow\inf|A\ominus_H B|[r]=\sup|A\ominus_H B|[r]=0\Leftrightarrow A=B$
- $E(|(A\oplus C)\ominus_H(B\oplus C)|)=E(|A\ominus_H B|)$

To prove this, suppose that:

$$(A \oplus C) \ominus_H (B \oplus C) = M$$

Based on the definition in level-wise form, the left-hand side can be written as:

$$E(|\, (A \oplus C) \ominus_H (B \oplus C)|\,) = \frac{1}{2}\int_0^1 (|\, M_l|\,(r) + |\, M_u|\,(r))\mathrm{d}r$$

where:

$$M_l = (A \oplus C)_l - (B \oplus C)_l = (A \ominus_H B)_l :$$
$$M_u = (A \oplus C)_u - (B \oplus C)_u = (A \ominus_H B)_u$$

Then the proof is completed.

- $E(|\,(A \oplus B) \ominus_H (C \oplus D)|\,) \leq E(|A \ominus_H C\,|) + E(|B \ominus_H D\,|)$

To prove this, again suppose that:

$$(A \oplus B) \ominus_H (C \oplus D) = M$$

Based on the definition in level-wise form, the left-hand side can be written as:

$$E(|\, (A \oplus B) \ominus_H (C \oplus D)|\,) = \frac{1}{2}\int_0^1 (|\, M_l|\,(r) + |\, M_u|\,(r))\mathrm{d}r$$

where:

$$M_l = (A \oplus B)_l - (C \oplus D)_l = (A \ominus_H C)_l + (B \ominus D)_l :$$
$$M_u = (A \oplus B)_u - (C \oplus D)_u = (A \ominus_H C)_u + (B \ominus D)_u$$

so:

$$|M|_l = \left|(A \ominus_H C)_l + (B \ominus D)_l\right| \leq \left|(A \ominus_H C)_l\right| + \left|(B \ominus D)_l\right| :$$
$$|M|_u = \left|(A \ominus_H C)_u + (B \ominus D)_u\right| \leq \left|(A \ominus_H C)_u\right| + \left|(B \ominus D)_u\right|$$

The proof is clear based on the triangular inequality property of absolute value.

- $E(|\,\lambda A \ominus_H \lambda B\,|) = |\lambda| E(|A \ominus_H B\,|), \quad \lambda \in R$

The proof is clear.

For more explanation, see Liu (2015) and Allahviranloo (2020).

3.3.1 *P*-DISTANCE

For two fuzzy numbers A and B, $D_p(A,B) \in R^{\geq 0}$ is defined as follows:

$$D_p(A, B) = \left[\int_0^1 |A_l(r) - B_l(r)|^p \mathrm{d}r + \int_0^1 |A_u(r) - B_u(r)|^p \mathrm{d}r\right]^{\frac{1}{p}},\ p \geq 1.$$

To prove the properties, the first and second ones are trivial. The third property can be proved:

$$D_p(A+C,B+C)=\left[\int_0^1 |A_l(r)+C_l(r)-B_l(r)-C_l(r)|^p \mathrm{d}r \right.$$

$$\left. +\int_0^1 |A_u(r)+C_u(r)-B_u(r)-C_u(r)|^p \mathrm{d}r \right]^{\frac{1}{p}}$$

$$=\left[\int_0^1 |A_l(r)-B_l(r)|^p \mathrm{d}r+\int_0^1 |A_u(r)-B_u(r)|^p \mathrm{d}r\right]^{\frac{1}{p}}=D_p(A,B)$$

The last property is proved easily:

$$D_p(\lambda A,\lambda B)=\left[\int_0^1 |\lambda A_l(r)-\lambda B_l(r)|^p \mathrm{d}r+\int_0^1 |\lambda A_u(r)-\lambda B_u(r)|^p \mathrm{d}r\right]^{\frac{1}{p}}=|\lambda| D_p(A,B)$$

The other properties, we leave for you as exercises.

3.3.2 Hausdorff Distance

Again, for two fuzzy numbers, A and B, $D_H(A,B)\in R^{\geq 0}$ as Hausdorff distance is defined as follows:

$$D_H(A,B)=\sup_{0\leq r\leq 1}\max\{|A_l(r)-B_l(r)|,|A_u(r)-B_u(r)|\}$$

All of the properties can be verified easily. Here, some of the properties are proved as follows:

- $D_H(A\ominus_H B, C\ominus_H D)\leq D_H(A,C)+D_H(B,D)$, subject that $A\ominus_H B$ and $C\ominus_H D$ exist.

To prove it, we have the following relations:

$$|A_l(r)-B_l(r)|\leq \max\{|A_l(r)-B_l(r)|,|A_u(r)-B_u(r)|\}$$

$$|A_u(r)-B_u(r)|\leq \max\{|A_l(r)-B_l(r)|,|A_u(r)-B_u(r)|\}$$

and:

$$|C_l(r)-D_l(r)|\leq \max\{|C_l(r)-D_l(r)|,|C_u(r)-D_u(r)|\}$$

$$|C_u(r)-D_u(r)|\leq \max\{|C_l(r)-D_l(r)|,|C_u(r)-D_u(r)|\}$$

$$|A_l(r)-B_l(r)-C_l(r)+D_l(r)|\leq |A_l(r)-B_l(r)|+|C_l(r)-D_l(r)|\leq$$

$$\max\{|A_l(r)-B_l(r)|,|A_u(r)-B_u(r)|\}+\max\{|C_l(r)-D_l(r)|,|C_u(r)-D_u(r)|\}$$

$$|A_u(r)-B_u(r)-C_u(r)+D_u(r)|\leq |A_u(r)-B_u(r)|+|C_u(r)-D_u(r)|\leq$$

$$\max\{|A_l(r)-B_l(r)|,|A_u(r)-B_u(r)|\}+\max\{|C_l(r)-D_l(r)|,|C_u(r)-D_u(r)|\}$$

so:

$$\max\{|A_l(r)-B_l(r)-C_l(r)+D_l(r)|,|A_u(r)-B_u(r)-C_u(r)+D_u(r)|\}\leq$$
$$\max\{|A_l(r)-B_l(r)|,|A_u(r)-B_u(r)|\}+\max\{|C_l(r)-D_l(r)|,|C_u(r)-D_u(r)|\}$$

then:

$$\begin{aligned}\sup_{0\leq r\leq 1}\max\{|A_l(r)-B_l(r)-C_l(r)+D_l(r)|,|A_u(r)-B_u(r)-C_u(r)+D_u(r)|\}\\ \leq \sup_{0\leq r\leq 1}\max\{|A_l(r)-B_l(r)|,|A_u(r)-B_u(r)|\}\\ +\sup_{0\leq r\leq 1}\max\{|C_l(r)-D_l(r)|,|C_u(r)-D_u(r)|\}\end{aligned}$$

The property is now proved and:

$$D_H(A\ominus_H B, C\ominus_H D)\leq D_H(A,C)+D_H(B,D)$$

- $D_H(A\ominus_{gH}B,0)=D_H(A,B)$

Based on the definition of Hausdorff distance the proof is easy. Because the left-hand side can be written as:

$$\begin{aligned}D_H\left(A\ominus_{gH}B,0\right)&=\sup_{0\leq r\leq 1}\max\{|A_l(r)-B_l(r)-0|,|A_u(r)-B_u(r)-0|\}\\&=\sup_{0\leq r\leq 1}\max\{|A_l(r)-B_l(r)|,|A_u(r)-B_u(r)|\}=D_H(A,B)\end{aligned}$$

- $D_H\left(\lambda\odot A\ominus_{gH}\mu\odot A,0\right)=|\lambda-\mu|D_H(A,0),\ \ A\in\mathbb{F}_R,\lambda,\mu\geq 0.$

To prove the property, in accordance with the property of the distance, the left-hand side can be shown as:

$$D_H\left(\lambda\odot A\ominus_{gH}\mu\odot A,0\right)=D_H(\lambda\odot A,\mu\odot A)$$

Now, considering the definition of the distance:

$$\begin{aligned}D_H(\lambda\odot A,\mu\odot A)&=\sup_{0\leq r\leq 1}\max\{|\lambda A_l(r)-\mu A_l(r)|,|\lambda A_u(r)-\mu A_u(r)|\}\\&=\sup_{0\leq r\leq 1}\max\{|\lambda-\mu|A_l(r),|\lambda-\mu|A_u(r)\}\\&=|\lambda-\mu|\sup_{0\leq r\leq 1}\max\{A_l(r),A_u(r)\}=|\lambda-\mu|D_H(A,0)\end{aligned}$$

The proof is now completed.
For more explanation, see Bede and Gal (2005) and Stefanini and Bede (2009).

3.4 Limit of fuzzy number valued functions

In this section, we are going to display some preliminarily definitions and theorems about fuzzy set number valued functions (Allahviranloo et al., 2015; Gouyandeha et al., 2017).

3.4.1 Definition—Fuzzy set valued function

Any function, like $x(t)$, is called a fuzzy set valued function if it is a fuzzy set for any $t \in R$.

3.4.2 Definition—Fuzzy number valued function

Any function, like $x(t)$, is called a fuzzy number valued function if it is a fuzzy number for any $t \in R$.

3.4.3 Definition—The limit of fuzzy number valued function

Suppose that $x(t)$ is a fuzzy number valued function and is defined from any real interval like $[a, b]$ to $\mathbb{F}_R$. If for any positive ϵ there is a positive δ such that:

$$\forall \epsilon > 0 \, \exists \delta > 0 \, \forall t (|t - t_0| < \delta \Longrightarrow D_H(x(t), L) < \epsilon)$$

where D is the Hausdorff of $x(t)$ and $L \in \mathbb{F}_R$. It is equivalent to the following limit:

$$\lim_{t \to t_0} x(t) = L$$

Note. The limit of a fuzzy number valued function $x(t)$ exists whenever the value L is a fuzzy number not a fuzzy set.

Also if we have:

$$\lim_{t \to t_0} x(t) = x(t_0)$$

Then the function $x(t)$ is called continuous at the point t_0.

It should be noted that the same function is continuous on its real domain $[a, b]$ if it is continuous at all points of the interval.

Now we are going to consider some properties on the limit of a fuzzy number valued function.

3.4.4 Theorem—Limit of summation of functions

Suppose that $x(t), y(t) : [a, b] \to \mathbb{F}_R$ are two fuzzy number valued functions. If:

$$\lim_{t \to t_0} x(t) = L_1, \; \lim_{t \to t_0} y(t) = L_2$$

Such that two values $L_1, L_2 \in \mathbb{F}_R$. Then:

$$\lim_{t \to t_0} [x(t) \oplus y(t)] = L_1 \oplus L_2$$

Proof. For the function $x(t)$:

$$\forall \frac{\epsilon}{2} > 0 \, \exists \delta_1 > 0 \, \forall t \left(|t - t_0| < \delta_1 \Longrightarrow D_H(x(t), L_1) < \frac{\epsilon}{2} \right)$$

Because $\lim_{t\to t_0} x(t) = L_1$. And also for another one, $y(t)$, we have:

$$\forall \frac{\epsilon}{2} > 0 \exists \delta_2 > 0 \forall t\left(|t - t_0| < \delta_2 \Longrightarrow D_H(y(t), L_2) < \frac{\epsilon}{2}\right)$$

Now $|t - t_0| < \delta_1$ and $|t - t_0| < \delta_2$ clearly $|t - t_0| < \min\{\delta_1, \delta_2\} = \delta$. Now for any positive $\frac{\epsilon}{2}$ there is a positive δ and based on the property of the Hausdorff distance:

$$D_H(x(t) \oplus y(t), L_1 \oplus L_2) \le D_H(x(t), L_1) + D_H(y(t), L_2) < \frac{\epsilon}{2} + \frac{\epsilon}{2} = \epsilon$$

So finally, we prove that:

$$\forall \epsilon > 0 \exists \delta > 0 \forall t(|t - t_0| < \delta \Longrightarrow D_H(x(t) \oplus y(t), L_1 \oplus L_2) < \epsilon)$$

The proof is completed.

3.4.5 Theorem—Limit of difference of functions

Considering all assumptions of the previous theorem, we can prove that:

$$\lim_{t\to t_0} \left[x(t) \ominus_{gH} y(t)\right] = L_1 \ominus_{gH} L_2$$

Subject to $L_1 \ominus_{gH} L_2$ existing.

Proof. Suppose that $x(t) \ominus_{gH} y(t) = z(t)$, so, based on the definition of *gH*-difference:

$$x(t) \ominus_{gH} y(t) = z(t) \Leftrightarrow \begin{cases} i) & x(t) = y(t) \oplus z(t) \\ & \text{or} \\ ii) & y(t) = x(t) \oplus (-1)z(t) \end{cases}$$

First, case (i).

- In case (i):

Since $\lim_{t\to t_0} x(t) = L_1$ then $\lim_{t\to t_0} (y(t) \oplus z(t)) = L_1$ and based on the previous theorem we have:

$$\lim_{t\to t_0} (y(t) \oplus z(t)) = \lim_{t\to t_0} y(t) \oplus \lim_{t\to t_0} z(t) = L_1$$

Now it is concluded that:

$$\lim_{t\to t_0} z(t) = L_1 \ominus \lim_{t\to t_0} y(t) = L_1 \ominus L_2$$

- In case (ii):

Since $\lim_{t\to t_0} y(t) = L_2$ then $\lim_{t\to t_0} (x(t) \oplus (-1)z(t)) = L_2$ and again based on the previous theorem we have:

$$\lim_{t\to t_0} (x(t) \oplus (-1)z(t)) = \lim_{t\to t_0} x(t) \oplus (-1) \lim_{t\to t_0} z(t) = L_2$$

Now it is concluded that:

$$L_1 \oplus (-1) \lim_{t \to t_0} z(t) = L_2$$

and based on the second case of the gH-difference:

$$\lim_{t \to t_0} z(t) = L_1 \ominus L_2$$

The proof is completed.

3.4.6 Theorem—Limit of multiplication

Suppose that $x(t) : [a, b] \to \mathbb{F}_R$ is a fuzzy number valued function and $y(t)$ is a nonnegative real function. If:

$$\lim_{t \to t_0} x(t) = L_1, \quad \lim_{t \to t_0} y(t) = L_2$$

Such that the two values $L_1 \in \mathbb{F}_R, L_2 \in R^+$. Then:

$$\lim_{t \to t_0} [x(t) \odot y(t)] = L_1 \odot L_2$$

Proof. To prove it, first we investigate the Hausdorff distance of a fuzzy number valued function $x(t)$ and zero.

$$\begin{aligned} D_H(x(t)0) &= D_H\left(x(t) \ominus_{gH} L_1 \oplus L_1 0\right) \le D_H\left(x(t) \ominus_{gH} L_1, 0\right) + D_H(L_1 0) \\ &= D_H(x(x) L_1) + L_1 < \epsilon + L_1 \end{aligned}$$

The ϵ is any arbitrary positive number and it can be considered as $\epsilon = 1$, so:

$$D_H(x(t), 0) < 1 + L_1$$

For the function $x(t)$ we have the same limit definition as:

$$\forall \epsilon_1 = \frac{\epsilon}{2L_2} > 0 \, \exists \delta_1 > 0 \, \forall t(|t - t_0| < \delta_1 \Longrightarrow D_H(x(t), L_1) < \epsilon_1)$$

The function $y(t)$ is real and a nonnegative function and we have:

$$\forall \epsilon_2 = \frac{\epsilon}{2(1 + L_1)} > 0 \, \exists \delta_2 > 0 \, \forall t(|t - t_0| < \delta_2 \Longrightarrow |y(t) - L_2| < \epsilon_2)$$

By all assumptions we have:

$$D_H(x(t) \odot y(t), L_1 \odot L_2) = D_H\left(x(t) \odot y(t) \ominus_{gH} L_1 \odot L_2, 0\right)$$

$$= D_H\left(x(t) \odot y(t) \ominus_{gH} x(t) \odot L_2 \oplus x(t) \odot L_2 \ominus_{gH} L_1 \odot L_2, 0\right)$$

As we know $y(t)$ and L_2 are nonnegative and let us consider $(y(t) - L_2) \ge 0$. So the following result is immediately concluded.

$$x(t) \odot y(t) \ominus_{gH} x(t) \odot L_2 = x(t) \odot (y(t) - L_2)$$

Considering the level cuts of both sides, it is proved easily.
Moreover:

$$x(t)\odot L_2 \ominus_{gH} L_1 \odot L_2 = \left(x(t)\ominus_{gH} L_1\right)\odot L_2$$

Now the proof is continued as:

$$D_H\left(x(t)\odot y(t)\ominus_{gH} x(t)\odot L_2 \oplus x(t)\odot L_2 \ominus_{gH} L_1 \odot L_2, 0\right) =$$

$$= D_H\left(x(t)\odot(y(t)-L_2)\oplus\left(x(t)\ominus_{gH} L_1\right)\odot L_2, 0\right)$$

$$\leq D_H(x(t)\odot(y(t)-L_2), 0) + D_H\left(\left(x(t)\ominus_{gH} L_1\right)\odot L_2, 0\right)$$

$$= |y(t)-L_2| D_H(x(t), 0) + |L_2| D_H\left(x(t)\ominus_{gH} L_1, 0\right)$$

$$= |y(t)-L_2| D_H(x(t), 0) + |L_2| D_H(x(t), L_1)$$

$$< \frac{\epsilon}{2(1+L_1)}(1+L_1) + |L_2|\frac{\epsilon}{2L_2} = \frac{\epsilon}{2} + \frac{\epsilon}{2} = \epsilon$$

The proof now is completed.

3.4.7 Other properties of limit

Suppose that:

$$\lim_{n\to\infty} x_n = x, \quad \lim_{n\to\infty} y_n = y$$

Such that $x_n, y_n, x, y \in \mathbb{F}_R$, then:

- $\lim_{n\to\infty} D_H(x_n, y_n) = D_H(\lim_{n\to\infty} x_n, \lim_{n\to\infty} y_n) = D_H(x, y)$
- $\lim_{n\to\infty}(c_n \odot x_n) = c \odot x$, where $\lim_{n\to\infty} c_n = c$ and c, c_n are two nonnegative real numbers.

The proof is very clear.

3.5 Fuzzy Riemann integral operator

Suppose that the function $f(t)$ is a fuzzy number valued function, $f(t)\in\mathbb{F}_R$ (Gouyandeha et al., 2017). The Fuzzy Riemann integral is defined as the following summation and denoted by:

$$J = FR\int_a^b f(t)\mathrm{d}t := \oplus \sum_{i=0}^{n} \Delta t_i \odot f(t_i)$$

where $FR\int_a^b f(t)\mathrm{d}t$ is denoted as a fuzzy Riemann integral and $\oplus\sum_{i=0}^{n}\Delta t_i \odot f(t_i)$ points out fuzzy summations of fuzzy numbers $\Delta t_i \odot f(t_i)$ for any $i=0, 1, \ldots, n$. Moreover, $\Delta t_i = t_{i+1} - t_i$ and the set of points $\{a=t_0<t_1<\cdots<t_n=b\}$ is a partition on interval $[a,b]$.

To define the fuzzy Riemann integral, since both sides are fuzzy numbers and for the equality of two fuzzy numbers we use the Hausdorff distance, so:

$$\forall\epsilon>0\,\exists\delta>0\,D_H\left(\oplus\sum_{i=0}^{n}\Delta t_i\odot f(t_i), J\right)<\epsilon$$

Note. The important point is, J should be a fuzzy number not a fuzzy set.

In the level-wise form of integral, it can be displayed as:

$$J[r]=\left(FR\int_a^b f(t)dt\right)[r]:=\left(\oplus\sum_{i=0}^{n}\Delta t_i\odot f(t_i)\right)[r]$$

for any $0\le r\le 1$. Indeed the definition of the Hausdorff distance needs the level-wise form and it can be brought as:

$$\begin{aligned}[J_l(r),J_u(r)]&=\left[\sum_{i=0}^{n}\Delta t_i\cdot f_l(t_i,r),\ \sum_{i=0}^{n}\Delta t_i\cdot f_u(t_i,r)\right]\\&=\left[R\int_a^b f_l(t,r)dt, R\int_a^b f_u(t,r)\mathrm{d}t\right]\end{aligned}$$

On the one hand:

$$\left[\sum_{i=0}^{n}\Delta t_i\cdot f_l(t_i,r),\ \sum_{i=0}^{n}\Delta t_i\cdot f_u(t_i,r)\right]=\sum_{i=0}^{n}\Delta t_i[f_l(t_i,r),f_u(t_i,r)]$$

then:

$$\left[R\int_a^b f_l(t,r)\mathrm{d}t, R\int_a^b f_u(t,r)\mathrm{d}t\right]=R\int_a^b [f_l(t,r),f_u(t,r)]\mathrm{d}t$$

In summary:

$$J_l(r)=R\int_a^b f_l(t,r)\mathrm{d}t=\sum_{i=0}^{n}\Delta t_i\cdot f_l(t_i,r):$$

$$J_u(r)=R\int_a^b f_u(t,r)\mathrm{d}t=\sum_{i=0}^{n}\Delta t_i\cdot f_u(t_i,r)$$

3.5.1 Some properties of fuzzy Riemann integral

- Suppose that the functions $f(t), g(t) \in \mathbb{F}_R$ and are Riemann integrable functions. Then:

$$FR\int_a^b (f(t)\oplus g(t))\mathrm{d}t = \oplus\sum_{i=0}^{n}\Delta t_i \odot (f(t_i)\oplus g(t_i))$$

This property is easy to prove.

- For the previous function and any $c\in[a,b]$:

$$FR\int_a^b f(t)\mathrm{d}t = FR\int_a^c f(t)\mathrm{d}t \oplus FR\int_c^b f(t)\mathrm{d}t$$

To prove the property, since $c\in[a,b]$ the partition for the integral will be as:

$$\{a=t_0<t_1<\cdots<t_k=c<\cdots<t_n=b\},\ \exists k\in\{0,1,\ldots,n\}$$

Now based on the definition:

$$FR\int_a^c f(t)\mathrm{d}t = \oplus\sum_{i=0}^{k}\Delta t_i \odot f(t_i)$$

$$FR\int_c^b f(t)\mathrm{d}t = \oplus\sum_{i=k+1}^{n}\Delta t_i \odot f(t_i)$$

It is clear that:

$$\oplus\sum_{i=0}^{k}\Delta t_i \odot f(t_i) \oplus \sum_{i=k+1}^{n}\Delta t_i \odot f(t_i) = \oplus\sum_{i=0}^{n}\Delta t_i \odot f(t_i)$$

The property is now proved.

- $(-1)FR\int_a^b f(t)\mathrm{d}t = FR\int_b^a f(t)\mathrm{d}t$

3.6 Differential operator

The main discussion of this chapter is related to the differential operator. Generally, a differential operator is a nonlinear operator on its domain, which is defined by a differential expression. Usually the operator is acting on a space of differentiable vector-valued functions. In this section, we suppose that the operand function is a fuzzy number valued function and we shall consider the effect of a derivative operator on it. Basically, the derivative is defined by the rate of changes and here the changes are related to the changes of fuzzy set valued function. In this section we will also consider the first and high order of differentiability of a fuzzy number valued function.

3.6.1 Definition—*gH*-differentiability

As before, suppose that the function $x(t)$ is a fuzzy number valued function and t_0 is an inner point of its domain as an interval like $[a,b]$. So we consider $t_0 \in (a,b)$.

We also suppose that for any small enough number $h \to 0$, $t_0 + h \in (a,b)$.

Now the gH-differential of the $x(t)$ at the point t_0 is denoted by $x_{gH}'(t_0)$ and defined as:

$$x'_{gH}(t_0) = \lim_{h \to 0} \frac{x(t_0 + h) \ominus_{gH} x(t_0)}{h}$$

Subject to the gH-difference $x(t_0 + h) \ominus_{gH} x(t_0)$ exists (Bede and Gal, 2005).

Note. The point is that the gH-differential exists at the point t_0 if $x_{gH}'(t_0)$ is a fuzzy number not a fuzzy set.

The level-wise form of this fuzzy number as a derivative can be explained as the following two cases, because the gH-difference in the definition is defined in two cases. So these two cases are considered separately and in general we can claim and prove that the necessary and sufficient conditions for the gH-differentiability a fuzzy number valued function $x(t)$ are:

In case (i):

$$\left(x'_{i-gH}(t)\right)[r] = \left[x'_l(t_0, r), x'_u(t_0, r)\right]$$

In case (ii):

$$\left(x'_{ii-gH}(t)\right)[r] = \left[x'_u(t_0, r), x'_l(t_0, r)\right]$$

Subject to the functions $x_l'(t_0, r)$ and $x_u'(t_0, r)$ being two real valued differentiable functions with respect to t and uniformly with respect to $r \in [0,1]$. It should be noted that both of the functions are left continuous on $r \in (0,1]$ and right continuous at $r = 0$. Moreover, the following conditions should be satisfied.

- The function $x_l'(t_0, r)$ is nondecreasing and the function $x_u'(t_0, r)$ is nonincreasing as functions of r and, $x_l'(t_0, r) \le x_u'(t_0, r)$. Or:
- The function $x_l'(t_0, r)$ is nonincreasing and the function $x_u'(t_0, r)$ is nondecreasing as functions of r and, $x_u'(t_0, r) \le x_l'(t_0, r)$.
- $(x_{gH}'(t_0))[r] = [\min\{x_l'(t_0, r), x_u'(t_0, r)\}, \max\{x_l'(t_0, r), x_u'(t_0, r)\}]$

3.6.1.1 Example

Let the function $x(t) = \mu \odot t$ be a fuzzy number function, and μ be a fuzzy number and t a real number (Stefanini and Bede, 2009).

Based on the definition of the gH-differentiability we have:

$$x'_{i-gH}(t) = \lim_{h\to 0} \frac{x(t+h)\ominus_{gH}x(t)}{h}$$

Suppose that the gH-difference exists in case (i), it means if we define it as the following:

$$x(t+h)\ominus_{gH}x(t) = (\mu\odot(t+h))\ominus_{gH}\mu\odot t = [\mu\odot t\oplus\mu\odot h]\ominus_{gH}\mu\odot t$$

Considering the properties of the gH-difference:

$$x(t+h)\ominus_{gH}x(t) = (\mu\odot(t+h))\ominus_{gH}\mu\odot t = \mu\odot h$$

Case (i), If $t\geq 0$ then $h>0$ and $x(t+h)=x(t)\oplus\mu\odot h=\mu\odot t\oplus\mu\odot h$. This is exactly the definition of gH-difference in case (i). So, the differential also exists in case (i) and:

$$x'_{i-gH}(t) = \lim_{h\nearrow 0} \frac{\mu\odot h}{h} = \mu$$

In the level-wise form:

$$\left(x'_{i-gH}(t)\right)[r] = [x'_l(t,r), x'_u(t,r)] = [\mu_l(r), \mu_u(r)]$$

Case (ii):
Based on the definition of gH-difference in case (ii):

$$x(t+h)\ominus_{gH}x(t) = (\mu\odot(t+h))\ominus_{gH}\mu\odot t = y(t;h)$$

then:

$$\mu\odot t = (\mu\odot(t+h))\oplus(-1)y(t;h) = (\mu\odot t\oplus\mu\odot h)\oplus(-1)y(t;h)$$

Finally:

$$\mu\odot t = (\mu\odot t\oplus\mu\odot h)\oplus(-1)y(t;h)$$

This is also true if $y(t;h) = \ominus((-1)h)\odot\mu$ and it happens only for $t<0$ and $h<0$: This is investigated by using the level-wise form:

$$(\mu\odot t)_l(r) = \mu_u(r)t$$

and for the right-hand side:

$$((\mu\odot t\oplus\mu\odot h)\oplus(-1)(\ominus((-1)h)\odot\mu))_l(r) =$$

$$((\mu\odot t\oplus\mu\odot h)\ominus(h\odot\mu))_l(r) = \mu_u(r)t$$

Finally, the derivative is as:

$$x'_{i-gH}(t) = \lim_{h\searrow 0} \frac{\ominus((-1)h)\odot\mu}{h} = \ominus((-1)\odot\mu)$$

In the level-wise form:

$$\left(x'_{ii-gH}(t)\right)[r] = [x'_u(t,r), x'_l(t,r)] = [\mu_u(r), \mu_l(r)]$$

3.6.1.2 Example

Suppose the following function:

$$x(t) = \begin{cases} a\left(1 + t^2 \cos\left(\frac{1}{t}\right)\right), & t \neq 0 \\ a, & t = 0 \end{cases}$$

where $a[r] = [r-1, 1-r]$ *or* $a = (-1, 0, 1)$, is a fuzzy number. It is clear that:

$$x(t)[r] = \begin{cases} \left[(r-1)\left(1 + t^2 \cos\left(\frac{1}{t}\right)\right), (1-r)\left(1 + t^2 \cos\left(\frac{1}{t}\right)\right)\right], & t \neq 0 \\ [r-1, 1-r], & t = 0 \end{cases}$$

It can easily be seen that $x(t)$ is gH-differentiable at the point $t=0$ and $x_{gH}'(0) = 0$. But the following H-differences do not exist.

$$x(h) \ominus_H x(0)$$

because there does not exist a $\delta > 0$ such that the H-difference exists for all $h \in (0, \delta)$.

3.6.1.3 Definition—gH-differentiability in level-wise form

For the fuzzy number valued function $x : [a, b] \to \mathbb{F}_R$ and $t_0 \in (a, b)$ with $x_l'(t, r)$ and $x_u'(t, r)$ both differentiable at t_0, the gH-differentiability at the same point is defined in the following cases in level-wise form.

- x is $[i - gH]$-differentiable at t_0 if:

$$x'_{i-gH}(t_0, r) = [x'_l(t_0, r), x'_u(t_0, r)]$$

- x is $[ii - gH]$-differentiable at t_0 if:

$$x'_{ii-gH}(t_0, r) = [x'_u(t_0, r), x'_l(t_0, r)]$$

3.6.1.4 Definition—Switching points of gH-differentiability

We say that a point $t_0 \in (a, b)$ is a switching point for the differentiability of f, if in any neighborhood V of t_0 there exist points $t_1 < t_0 < t_2$ such that:

Type (I), at the point t_1, $x_{i-gH}'(t_0, r)$ hold while $x_{ii-gH}'(t_0, r)$ does not hold and at the point t_2, $x_{ii-gH}'(t_0, r)$ hold while $x_{i-gH}'(t_0, r)$ does not hold; or

Type (II), at the point t_1, $x_{ii-gH}'(t_0, r)$ hold while $x_{i-gH}'(t_0, r)$ does not hold and at the point t_2, $x_{i-gH}'(t_0, r)$ hold while $x_{ii-gH}'(t_0, r)$ does not hold.

In type (II), the left neighborhood of $t_1$is $ii-gH$ differentiability and on the right-hand side it is $i-gH$ differentiable. So on the left-hand side:

$$x'_{ii-gH}(t_1,r)=[x'_u(t_1,r),x'_l(t_1,r)],\ x'_u(t_1,r)\le x'_l(t_1,r)$$

This means:

$$x_u(t_1+h)-x_u(t_1)\le x_l(t_1+h)-x_l(t_1)$$

then:

$$\text{length}[x(t_1+h)]=x_u(t_1+h)-x_l(t_1+h)\le x_u(t_1)-x_l(t_1)=\text{length}[x(t_1)]$$

This means that the length operator is a decreasing one.

Also on the right-hand side:

$$x'_{i-gH}(t_1,r)=[x'_l(t_2,r),x'_u(t_2,r)],\ x'_l(t_2,r)\le x'_u(t_2,r)$$

This means:

$$x_l(t_2+h)-x_l(t_2)\le x_u(t_2+h)-x_u(t_2)$$

then:

$$\text{length}[x(t_2)]=x_u(t_2)-x_l(t_2)\le x_u(t_2+h)-x_l(t_2+h)=\text{length}[x(t_2+h)]$$

On the right-hand side, the length is increasing (see Fig. 3.1).

In type (II), the left neighborhood of $t_1$is $i-gH$ differentiability and on the right-hand side it is $ii-gH$ differentiable (see Fig. 3.2).

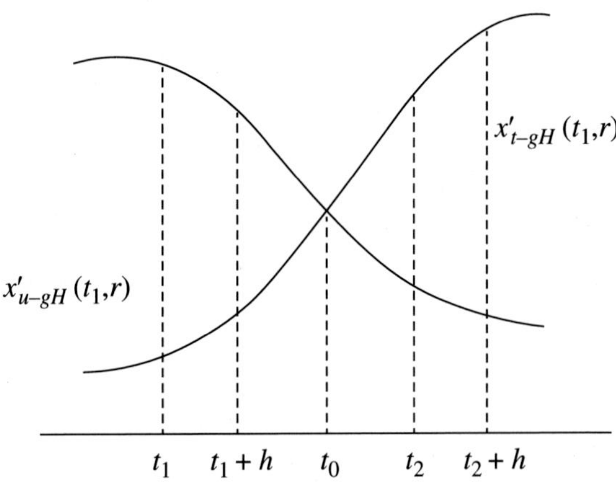

Fig. 3.1 Type II switching point.

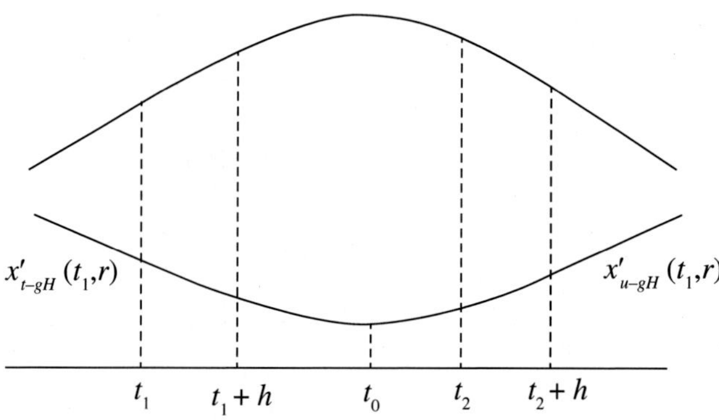

Fig. 3.2 Type I switching point.

3.6.1.4.1 Example

Let us consider the fuzzy set valued function given level-wise for the interval $t \in [0,1]$.

$$x_l(t,r) = te^{-t} + r^2\left(e^{-t^2} + t - te^{-t}\right)$$

$$x_u(t,r) = e^{-t^2} + t + \left(1 - r^2\right)\left(e^t - t + e^{-t^2}\right)$$

The derivatives of two functions are:

$$x_l'(t,r) = (1-t)e^{-t} + r^2\left(1 + (t-1)e^{-t} - 2te^{-t^2}\right)$$

$$x_u'(t,r) = -4te^{-t^2} + e^t - r^2\left(-1 + e^t - 2te^{-t^2}\right)$$

It is easy to see it is not gH-differentiable, because if $r=1$, both are the same as $1-2te^{-t^2}$ and if $r=0$ then:

$$x_l'(t,r) = (1-t)e^{-t}$$

$$x_u'(t,r) = -4te^{-t^2} + e^t$$

and $x_u'(t,r) \leq x_l'(t,r)$.

Fig. 3.3 shows the derivatives in two levels $r=0.0.5$.

3.6.1.5 Proposition—Summation in gH*-differentiability*

For two gH-differentiable fuzzy number valued functions like $x(t)$, $y(t)$ it is clearly proved that if:

$$z(t) = x(t) \oplus y(t)$$

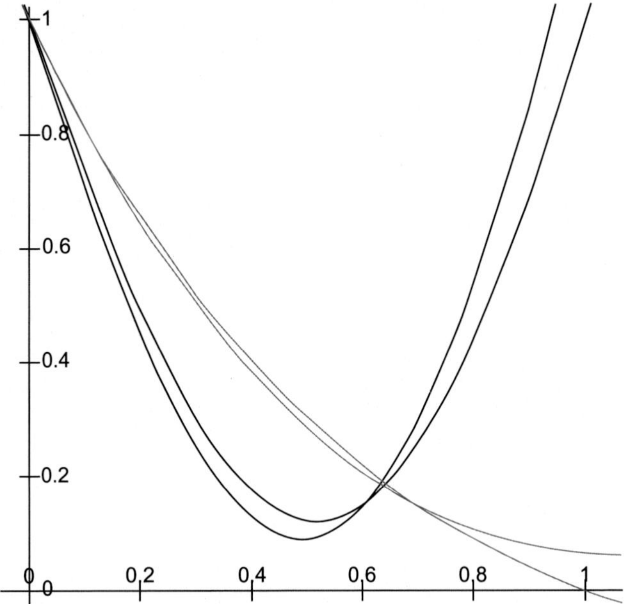

Fig. 3.3 The level-wise form of derivatives for $r=0.0.5$.

then:

$$z'_{i-gH}(t) = x'_{i-gH}(t) \oplus y'_{i-gH}(t)$$

$$z'_{ii-gH}(t) = x'_{ii-gH}(t) \oplus y'_{ii-gH}(t)$$

The proof is clear based on the definition of the differential in each type.

3.6.1.6 Proposition—Difference in gH-differentiability

Again for two *gH*-differentiable fuzzy number valued functions like $x(t)$, $y(t)$, it is clearly proved that if:

$$z(t) = x(t) \ominus_{gH} y(t)$$

then:

$$z'_{i-gH}(t) = x'_{i-gH}(t) \ominus_{gH} y'_{i-gH}(t)$$

$$z'_{ii-gH}(t) = x'_{ii-gH}(t) \ominus_{gH} y'_{ii-gH}(t)$$

These two equations are proved separately as follows in accordance with the definition of gH-difference:

$$z(t)=x(t)\ominus_{gH}y(t)\Leftrightarrow\begin{cases}(i) & x(t)=y(t)\oplus z(t) \text{ or}\\(ii) & z(t)=x(t)\oplus(-1)y(t)\end{cases}$$

First consider case (i), and we know that those differentiabilities are the same.

$$x'_{i-gH}(t)=y'_{i-gH}(t)\oplus z'_{i-gH}(t)$$

$$x'_{ii-gH}(t)=y'_{ii-gH}(t)\oplus z'_{ii-gH}(t)$$

It is concluded that:

$$z'_{i-gH}(t)=x'_{i-gH}(t)\ominus_{gH}y'_{i-gH}(t)$$

$$z'_{ii-gH}(t)=x'_{ii-gH}(t)\ominus_{gH}y'_{ii-gH}(t)$$

Now, in case (ii) we have:

$$z'_{i-gH}(t)=x'_{i-gH}(t)\oplus(-1)y'_{i-gH}(t)$$

$$z'_{ii-gH}(t)=x'_{ii-gH}(t)\oplus(-1)y'_{ii-gH}(t)$$

Because for any real number λ we have:

$$\lambda\left(A\ominus_{i-gH}B\right)=\left(\lambda A\ominus_{i-gH}\lambda B\right)$$

$$\lambda\left(A\ominus_{ii-gH}B\right)=\left(\lambda A\ominus_{ii-gH}\lambda B\right)$$

It can be proved in level-wise form of gH-difference in two cases separately.

3.6.1.7 Proposition—Production in gH-differentiability

Suppose that $x:[a,b]\to\mathbb{F}_R$ is a fuzzy number valued function and it is gH-differentiable on (a,b). Also, let us suppose the function $y:[a,b]\to R$ is a differentiable real function in the same open interval. Then:

$$(x\odot y)'_{gH}(t)=x'_{gH}(t)\odot y(t)\oplus x(t)\odot y'(t)$$

To prove this property, we use the Hausdorff distance.
The left-hand side is as:

$$(x\odot y)'_{gH}(t)=\lim_{h\to 0}\frac{x(t+h)\odot y(t+h)\ominus_{gH}x(t)\odot y(t)}{h}$$

Now considering the distance of two sides of the equation, it is enough to show that the distance intends zero.

$$D_H\left(\frac{x(t+h)\odot y(t+h)\ominus_{gH}x(t)\odot y(t)}{h}, x'_{gH}(t)\odot y(t)\oplus x(t)\odot y'(t)\right)=$$

$$D_H\left(\frac{x(t+h)\odot y(t+h)\ominus_{gH}x(t)\odot y(t+h)\oplus x(t)\odot y(t+h)\ominus_{gH}x(t)\odot y(t)}{h}, x'_{gH}(t)\odot y(t)\oplus x(t)\odot y'(t)\right)$$

$$=D_H\left(\frac{\left(x(t+h)\ominus_{gH}x(t)\right)\odot y(t+h)\oplus x(t)\odot\left(y(t+h)\ominus_{gH}\odot y(t)\right)}{h}, x'_{gH}(t)\odot y(t)\oplus x(t)\odot y'(t)\right)$$

$$\leq D_H\left(\frac{\left(x(t+h)\ominus_{gH}x(t)\right)\odot y(t+h)}{h}, x'_{gH}(t)\odot y(t)\right)$$

$$\oplus D_H\left(\frac{x(t)\odot\left(y(t+h)\ominus_{gH}\odot y(t)\right)}{h}, x(t)\odot y'(t)\right)$$

$$=D_H\left(\frac{\left(x(t+h)\ominus_{gH}x(t)\right)}{h}\odot y(t+h), x'_{gH}(t)\odot y(t)\right)$$

$$\oplus D_H\left(\frac{\left(y(t+h)\ominus_{gH}\odot y(t)\right)}{h}\odot x(t), x(t)\odot y'(t)\right)$$

Now, the limits of the two sides when $h\to 0$ are:

$$\lim_{h\to 0} D_H\left(\frac{x(t+h)\odot y(t+h)\ominus_{gH}x(t)\odot y(t)}{h}, x'_{gH}(t)\odot y(t)\oplus x(t)\odot y'(t)\right)$$

$$=\lim_{h\to 0} D_H\left(\frac{(x(t+h)\ominus_{gH}x(t))}{h}\odot y(t+h), x'_{gH}(t)\odot y(t)\right)$$

$$\oplus\lim_{h\to 0} D_H\left(\frac{(y(t+h)\ominus_{gH}\odot y(t))}{h}\odot x(t), x(t)\odot y'(t)\right)$$

Based on the properties of the limit and distance (as we expressed before) the proof is completed.

$$=D_H\left(\lim_{h\to 0}\frac{x(t+h)\ominus_{gH}x(t)}{h}\odot y(t), x'_{gH}(t)\odot y(t)\right)$$
$$\oplus D_H\left(\lim_{h\to 0}\frac{y(t+h)\ominus_{gH}y(t)}{h}\odot x(t), x(t)\odot y'(t)\right)=0$$

3.6.1.8 Proposition—Composition of gH*-differentiability*

Suppose that $x:[a,b]\to\mathbb{F}_R$ is a fuzzy number valued function and it is *gH*-differentiable at *y*(*t*) on the interval (a,b) (Allahviranloo et al., 2015). Also, let us suppose the function $y:[a,b]\rightarrow R$ is a differentiable real function in the same open interval. Then:

If $y'(t)\geq 0$:

$$(x\,o\,y)'_{i-gH}(t)=y'(t)\odot x'_{i-gH}(y(t)):$$

$$(x\,o\,y)'_{ii-gH}(t)=y'(t)\odot x'_{ii-gH}(y(t)).$$

(if) $y'(t)<0$,

$$(x\,o\,y)'_{i-gH}(t)=y'(t)\odot x'_{ii-gH}(y(t)),$$

$$(x\,o\,y)'_{ii-gH}(t)=y'(t)\odot x'_{i-gH}(y(t)).$$

The proof for two cases can be displayed in level-wise form.

First suppose $y'(t)\geq 0$ and $(x\ o\ y)(t)$ is differentiable in case (i), then for any $r\in[0,1]$ we determine the level-wise form of composite function as:

$$(x\,o\,y)'_{i-gH}(t,r)=\left[(x\,o\,y)'_l(t,r),(x\,o\,y)'_u(t,r)\right]$$

Now the level-wise form of the right-hand side is:

$$\left[y'(t)\cdot x'_l(y(t)),y'(t)\cdot x'_u(y(t))\right]$$

so:

$$(x\,o\,y)'_l(t,r)=y'(t)\cdot x'_l(y(t))$$

$$(x\,o\,y)'_u(t,r)=y'(t)\cdot x'_u(y(t))$$

The proof is completed, and for type (ii) differentiability the same holds. Now for the second case we have a similar process, but the coefficient $y'(t)$ is negative and it will change the endpoints of the intervals in level-wise form:

$$\left[(x\,o\,y)'_l(t,r),(x\,o\,y)'_u(t,r)\right]=\left[y'(t)\cdot x'_u(y(t)),y'(t)\cdot x'_l(y(t))\right]$$

then:

$$(x\,o\,y)'_{i-gH}(t)=y'(t)\odot x'_{ii-gH}(y(t))$$

The same process is used to prove the type (ii) differentiability of the second case.

3.6.1.9 Proposition—Minimum and maximum

For any gH-differentiable fuzzy number function $x(t)$ at the inner point like $c\in(a,b)$, if the function has local minimum or maximum then $x_{gH}{}'(c)=0$.

To prove the proposition, we use the definition of the minimum and maximum value.

The function at the point c has the local maximum value if there is a positive δ and for all t from the neighborhood $|t-c|<\delta$ then $x(t)\preccurlyeq x(c)$. Then $x(t)\ominus_{gH}x(c)\preccurlyeq 0$. On the other hand, for all $t\in(a,c)$, $t-c<0$. Now it can be concluded that:

$$x'_{gH}(t)=\lim_{h\to 0}\frac{x(t)\ominus_{gH}x(c)}{t-c}\succcurlyeq 0$$

All these properties about the partial ordering have been discussed in Chapter 2.

Similarly, the function at the point c has the local minimum value if there is a positive δ and for all t from the neighborhood $|t-c|<\delta$ then $x(c)\preccurlyeq x(t)$. Finally, we have:

$$x'_{gH}(t)=\lim_{h\to 0}\frac{x(t)\ominus_{gH}x(c)}{t-c}\preccurlyeq 0$$

then:

$$x'_{gH}(t)\succcurlyeq 0 \text{ and } x'_{gH}(t)\preccurlyeq 0 \text{ then } x'_{gH}(t)=0$$

3.6.1.10 Definition—Continuous fuzzy number valued function

Consider the fuzzy number valued function $x:[a,b]\to\mathbb{F}_R$. We say the function is continuous at a point like $t_0\in[a,b]$ if for any $\epsilon>0\,\exists\delta>0$ subject to $D_H(x(t),x(t_0))<\epsilon$ whenever x is an arbitrary value from $|x-x_0|<\delta$.

Moreover we say the function is continuous on $[a,b]$ if it is continuous at each point of the interval. Also, another form of definition is level-wise continuity, which means the function as a fuzzy number valued function is continuous if and only if it is continuous in each level.

According the ordering method and the definition of the continuity, it is concluded that if the same function $x(t)$ is continuous on the closed and bounded interval $[a,b]$ then it must attain a maximum and minimum each at least once. So:

$$\forall t\in[a,b]\,\exists t_{\text{Min}}\,\exists t_{\text{Max}}\in[a,b] \text{ s.t. } x(t_{\text{Min}})\preccurlyeq x(t)\preccurlyeq x(t_{\text{Max}})$$

where $\max_{a\le t\le b}x(t)=x(t_{\text{Max}})$ and $\min_{a\le t\le b}x(t)=x(t_{\text{Min}})$.

For more information on this, see Allahviranloo et al. (2015) and Gouyandeha et al. (2017).

3.6.1.11 Proposition

Suppose that the fuzzy number valued function $x:[a,b]\to\mathbb{F}_R$ is continuous and gH-differentiable on (a,b). If $x(a)=x(b)$ then there exists $c\in(a,b)$ such that $x'_{gH}(c)=0$.

To prove the claim, we use $x(a)=x(b)$ and $x(t_{Min})\preccurlyeq x(t)\preccurlyeq x(t_{Max})$. If it is the case that $x(t_{Min})=x(t_{Max})$, it is a constant fuzzy number function and immediately we have $x_{gH}'(c)=0$ for all $t\in[a,b]$. Then it is true to say $x(t_{Min})\prec x(t_{Max})$ and in this case one of the $x(t_{Min})$ and $x(t_{Max})$ do not equal $x(a)=x(b)$. Without loss of the generality, assume that $x(t_{Max})\neq x(a)=x(b)$; the other case is similar and we omit that. Clearly $t_{Max}\in(a,b)$ and the function $x(t)$ is gH-differentiable at t_{Max} so from the previous proposition it does have local minimum and maximum and $x_{gH}'(c)=0$.

3.6.1.12 Proposition—Cauchy's fuzzy mean value theorem

Assume that $x(t)$ is a continuous and gH-differentiable fuzzy number valued function on closed and open intervals, respectively, and $y(t)$ is a real valued continuous and differentiable function on the same intervals. Then there is $c\in(a,b)$ such that:

$$[x(b)\ominus_{gH}x(a)]\odot y'(c)=[y(b)-y(a)]\odot x'_{gH}(c)$$

where the gH-difference exists.

Proof.

Let us consider a new function as follows:

$$\phi(t)=[x(b)\ominus_{gH}x(a)]\odot y(t)\ominus_{gH}[y(b)-y(a)]\odot x(t)$$

This function is continuous because:

Let us consider $x(b)\ominus_{gH}x(a)=k$ and $y(b)-y(a)=l$ so we have:

$$\phi(t)=k\odot y(t)\ominus_{gH}l\odot x(t)$$

Now for any $\epsilon>0\,\exists\delta>0$ if for any t in $|t-t_0|<\delta$ at an arbitrary point t_0 we prove:

$$D_H(\phi(t),\phi(t_0))=D_H\big(k\odot y(t)\ominus_{gH}l\odot x(t),k\odot y(t_0)\ominus_{gH}l\odot x(t_0)\big)$$

Based on the properties of the Hausdorff distance:

$$\leq D_H(k\odot y(t),k\odot y(t_0))+D_H(l\odot x(t),l\odot x(t_0))$$

Based on the definition of Hausdorff distance and definition of absolute value of a fuzzy number we can write:

$$\leq|k||y(t)-y(t_0)|+|l|D_H(x(t),x(t_0))$$

and finally this summation is less than ϵ.

On the other hand $\phi(a)=\phi(b)$, so it is gH-differentiable at the inner point like c and equals zero. Then:

$$\phi'_{gH}(t)=[x(b)\ominus_{gH}x(a)]\odot y'(t)\ominus_{gH}[y(b)-y(a)]\odot x'_{gH}(t)$$

and $\phi_{gH}'(c)=0$, then:

$$[x(b)\ominus_{gH}x(a)]\odot y'(c)\ominus_{gH}[y(b)-y(a)]\odot x'_{gH}(c)=0$$

The proof is completed.

As a corollary, if we take the real function $y(t)=t$ then we will have the fuzzy mean value theorem.

3.6.1.13 Corollary—Fuzzy mean value theorem

Considering all the previous assumptions and $y(t)=t$ we have:

$$[x(b)\ominus_{gH}x(a)]\odot y'(c)=[y(b)-y(a)]\odot x'_{gH}(c)\Longrightarrow$$

$$[x(b)\ominus_{gH}x(a)]=(b-a)\odot x'_{gH}(c)$$

then:

$$x'_{gH}(c)=\frac{x(b)\ominus_{gH}x(a)}{b-a}$$

3.6.1.14 Proposition—Increasing and decreasing function

Let us consider that the fuzzy number valued function $x:[a,b]\to\mathbb{F}_R$ is continuous and gH-differentiable on (a,b). Then:

- If $x_{gH}'(t)\succcurlyeq 0$ for all $t\in(a,b)$ then it is increasing on $[a,b]$.
- If $x_{gH}'(t)\preccurlyeq 0$ for all $t\in(a,b)$ then it is decreasing on $[a,b]$.
- If $x_{gH}'(t)=0$ for all $t\in(a,b)$ then it is constant on $[a,b]$.

For the first case, assume that $x_{gH}'(t)\succcurlyeq 0$ for all $t\in(a,b)$. For any $t_1, t_2\in(a,b),\ t_1<t_2$ there is $c\in(a,b)$ subject to:

$$x'_{gH}(c)=\frac{x(t_2)\ominus_{gH}x(t_1)}{t_2-t_1}$$

It can be concluded that:

$$x(t_2)\ominus_{gH}x(t_1)=x'_{gH}(c)\odot(t_2-t_1)\succcurlyeq 0$$

Then $x(t_2)\succcurlyeq x(t_1)$ and this means that the function is an increasing one. A similar process is introduced to prove the other cases.

3.6.1.15 Proposition—Integral of gH-differentiability

Suppose that the fuzzy number valued function $x:[a,b]\to\mathbb{F}_R$ does not have any switching point in its domain. Then:

$$FR\int_a^b x'_{gH}(t)\mathrm{d}t = x(b)\ominus_{gH}x(a)$$

To prove it, we should consider two cases of gH-differentiability of x.

Case (i), the integrand function is $ii-gH$ differentiable:

$$\left(FR\int_a^b x'_{ii-gH}(t)\mathrm{d}t\right)[r] = R\int_a^b x'_{ii-gH}(t,r)\mathrm{d}t = R\int_a^b \left[x'_u(t,r), x'_l(t,r)\right]\mathrm{d}t$$

$$= \left[R\int_a^b x'_u(t,r)\mathrm{d}t, R\int_a^b x'_l(t,r)\mathrm{d}t\right] = [x_u(b,r)-x_u(a,r), x_l(b,r)-x_l(a,r)]$$

$$= (x(b)\ominus x(a))[r]$$

Then:

$$FR\int_a^b x'_{ii-gH}(t)\mathrm{d}t = \ominus(-1)(x(b)\ominus x(a))$$

or:

$$\ominus(-1)FR\int_a^b x'_{ii-gH}(t)\mathrm{d}t = (x(b)\ominus x(a))$$

The proof for the first case is similar.

If we want to consider two types of differentiability for any arbitrary but fixed t, we will have:

Case (i), $i-gH$

$$x(t) = x(a)\oplus FR\int_a^t x'_{i-gH}(s)\mathrm{d}s$$

Case (ii), $ii-gH$

$$x(t) = x(a)\ominus(-1)FR\int_a^t x'_{ii-gH}(s)\mathrm{d}s$$

3.6.1.16 Proposition—Switching points in integration

Let us suppose that the fuzzy number valued function $x:[a,b]\to\mathbb{F}_R$ is gH-differentiable with n switching points at c_i, $i=1, 2, \ldots, n$, and $a=c_0<c_1<c_2<\cdots<c_n<c_{n+1}=b$. Then:

$$x(b)\ominus_{gH}x(a) = \sum_{i=1}^{n}\left[FR\int_{c_{i-1}}^{c_i} x'_{i-gH}(t)\mathrm{d}t\ominus_{gH}(-1)FR\int_{c_i}^{c_{i+1}} x'_{ii-gH}(t)\mathrm{d}t\right]$$

and also:

$$FR\int_a^b x'_{gH}(t)\mathrm{d}t = \oplus\sum_{i=1}^{n+1} x(c_i)\ominus_{gH}x(c_{i-1})$$

3.6.1.17 High order differentiability

As before, suppose that the function $x(t)$ is a fuzzy number valued function and t_0 is an inner point of its domain as an interval, like $[a,b]$. So we consider $t_0\in(a,b)$.

Also we suppose that for any enough small number $h\rightarrow 0$, $t_0+h\in(a,b)$.

Now the n-th order gH-differential of the $x(t)$ at the point t_0 is denoted by $x_{gH}^{(n)}(t_0)$ and is defined as:

$$x_{gH}^{(n)}(t_0) = \lim_{h\rightarrow 0}\frac{x_{gH}^{(n-1)}(t_0+h)\ominus_{gH}x_{gH}^{(n-1)}(t_0)}{h}$$

Subject to the gH-difference $x_{gH}^{(n-1)}(t_0+h)\ominus_{gH}x_{gH}^{(n-1)}(t_0)$ exists for any order of gH-differentiability or any $n=1, 2, \ldots, m$. Moreover, we have to assume that all the previous derivatives exist and do not have any switching points.

Note. The point is that the n-th order gH-differential exists at the point t_0 if $x_{gH}^{(n)}(t_0)$ is a fuzzy number not a fuzzy set.

The necessary and sufficient conditions for the gH-differentiability as a fuzzy number valued function $x(t)$ are:

In case (i):

$$x_{gH}^{(n)}(t_0,r) = \left[x_l^{(n)}(t_0,r), x_u^{(n)}(t_0,r)\right]$$

In case (ii):

$$x_{gH}^{(n)}(t_0,r) = \left[x_u^{(n)}(t_0,r), x_l^{(n)}(t_0,r)\right]$$

Subject to the functions $x_l^{(n)}(t_0,r)$ and $x_u^{(n)}(t_0,r)$ are two real valued differentiable functions with respect to t and uniformly with respect to $r\in[0,1]$. Note that both of the functions are left continuous on $r\in(0,1]$ and right continuous at $r=0$. Moreover, the following conditions should be satisfied for all n.

- The function $x_l^{(n)}(t_0,r)$ is nondecreasing and the function $x_u^{(n)}(t_0,r)$ is nonincreasing as functions of r and, $x_l^{(n)}(t_0,r)\leq x_u^{(n)}(t_0,r)$. Or:
- $x_{gH}^{(n)}(t_0,r)=[\min\{x_l^{(n)}(t_0,r),x_u^{(n)}(t_0,r)\},\max\{x_l^{(n)}(t_0,r),x_u^{(n)}(t_0,r)\}]$

3.6.1.18 Extended integral relation

Let $x_{gH}^{(n)}(t)$ be a continuous fuzzy number valued function for any $s\in(a,b)$, the following integral equations are valid.

Item 1. Consider $x_{gH}^{(n)}(t)$, $n=1, 2, \ldots, m$ is $(i-gH)$-differentiable and the type of differentiability does not change on (a,b).

$$\left(FR\int_a^s x_{i-gH}^{(n)}(t)\mathrm{d}t\right)[r]=FR\int_a^s \left(x_{i-gH}^{(n)}(t)\right)[r]\mathrm{d}t=$$

$$=\left[R\int_a^s x_l^{(n)}(t,r)\mathrm{d}t, R\int_a^s x_u^{(n)}(t,r)\mathrm{d}t\right]$$

$$=\left[x_l^{(n-1)}(s,r)-x_l^{(n-1)}(a,r), x_u^{(n-1)}(s,r)-x_u^{(n-1)}(a,r)\right]$$

$$=\left[x_l^{(n-1)}(s,r), x_u^{(n-1)}(s,r)\right]-\left[x_l^{(n-1)}(a,r), x_u^{(n-1)}(a,r)\right]$$

$$=\left(x_{i-gH}^{(n-1)}(s)\right)[r]-\left(x_{i-gH}^{(n-1)}(a)\right)[r]$$

Then it is concluded:

$$FR\int_a^s x_{i-gH}^{(n)}(t)\mathrm{d}t=x_{i-gH}^{(n-1)}(s)\ominus x_{i-gH}^{(n-1)}(a)$$

$$x_{i-gH}^{(n-1)}(s)=x_{i-gH}^{(n-1)}(a)\oplus FR\int_a^s x_{i-gH}^{(n)}(t)\mathrm{d}t$$

Item 2. Consider $x_{gH}^{(n)}(t)$, $n=1, 2, \ldots, m$ is $(ii-gH)$-differentiable and the type of differentiability does not change on (a,b).

$$\left(FR\int_a^s x_{ii-gH}^{(n)}(t)\mathrm{d}t\right)[r]=FR\int_a^s x_{ii-gH}^{(n)}(t,r)\mathrm{d}t=$$

$$=\left[R\int_a^s x_u^{(n)}(t,r)\mathrm{d}t, R\int_a^s x_l^{(n)}(t,r)\mathrm{d}t\right]$$

$$=\left[x_u^{(n-1)}(s,r)-x_u^{(n-1)}(a,r), x_l^{(n-1)}(s,r)-x_l^{(n-1)}(a,r)\right]$$

$$=\left[x_u^{(n-1)}(s,r), x_l^{(n-1)}(s,r)\right]-\left[x_u^{(n-1)}(a,r), x_l^{(n-1)}(a,r)\right]$$

$$=x_{ii-gH}^{(n-1)}(s,r)-x_{ii-gH}^{(n-1)}(a,r)$$

Then it is concluded:

$$FR\int_a^s x_{ii-gH}^{(n)}(t)\mathrm{d}t=x_{ii-gH}^{(n-1)}(s)\ominus x_{ii-gH}^{(n-1)}(a)$$

$$x_{ii-gH}^{(n-1)}(s)=x_{ii-gH}^{(n-1)}(a)\oplus FR\int_a^s x_{ii-gH}^{(n)}(t)\mathrm{d}t$$

Item 3. Consider $x_{gH}^{(n)}(t)$ is $(i-gH)$-differentiable and $x_{gH}^{(n-1)}(t)$ is $(ii-gH)$-differentiable, then:

$$\ominus(-1)\left(FR\int_a^s x_{i-gH}^{(n)}(t)\mathrm{d}t\right)[r] = \ominus(-1)FR\int_a^s x_{i-gH}^{(n)}(t,r)\mathrm{d}t$$

$$= \left[R\int_a^s x_u^{(n)}(t,r)\mathrm{d}t, R\int_a^s x_l^{(n)}(t,r)\mathrm{d}t\right]$$

$$= \left[x_u^{(n-1)}(s,r) - x_u^{(n-1)}(a,r), x_l^{(n-1)}(s,r) - x_l^{(n-1)}(a,r)\right]$$

$$= \left[x_u^{(n-1)}(s,r), x_l^{(n-1)}(s,r)\right] - \left[x_u^{(n-1)}(a,r), x_l^{(n-1)}(a,r)\right]$$

$$= x_{ii-gH}^{(n-1)}(s,r) - x_{ii-gH}^{(n-1)}(a,r)$$

Then it is concluded:

$$\ominus(-1)FR\int_a^s x_{i-gH}^{(n)}(t)\mathrm{d}t = x_{ii-gH}^{(n-1)}(s) \ominus x_{ii-gH}^{(n-1)}(a)$$

$$x_{ii-gH}^{(n-1)}(s) = x_{ii-gH}^{(n-1)}(a) \ominus (-1)FR\int_a^s x_{i-gH}^{(n)}(t)\mathrm{d}t$$

Item 4. Consider $x_{gH}^{(n)}(t)$ is $(ii-gH)$-differentiable and $x_{gH}^{(n-1)}(t)$ is $(i-gH)$-differentiable, then:

$$\ominus(-1)\left(FR\int_a^s x_{ii-gH}^{(n)}(t)\mathrm{d}t\right)[r] = \ominus(-1)FR\int_a^s x_{ii-gH}^{(n)}(t,r)\mathrm{d}t$$

$$= \left[R\int_a^s x_l^{(n)}(t,r)\mathrm{d}t, R\int_a^s x_u^{(n)}(t,r)\mathrm{d}t\right]$$

$$= \left[x_l^{(n-1)}(s,r) - x_l^{(n-1)}(a,r), x_u^{(n-1)}(s,r) - x_u^{(n-1)}(a,r)\right]$$

$$= \left[x_l^{(n-1)}(s,r), x_u^{(n-1)}(s,r)\right] - \left[x_l^{(n-1)}(a,r), x_u^{(n-1)}(a,r)\right]$$

$$= x_{i-gH}^{(n-1)}(s,r) - x_{i-gH}^{(n-1)}(a,r)$$

Then it is concluded:

$$\ominus(-1)FR\int_a^s x_{ii-gH}^{(n)}(t)\mathrm{d}t = x_{i-gH}^{(n-1)}(s) \ominus x_{i-gH}^{(n-1)}(a)$$

$$x_{i-gH}^{(n-1)}(s) = x_{i-gH}^{(n-1)}(a) \ominus (-1)FR\int_a^s x_{ii-gH}^{(n)}(t)\mathrm{d}t$$

3.6.1.19 Part-by-part integration

Consider the function $x(t)$ as a gH-differentiable fuzzy number valued function on $[a,b]$ and $y(t)$ as a real valued function on the same interval. Then:

$$\int_a^b x'_{gH}(t)\odot y(t)\mathrm{d}t=(x(b)\odot y(b))\ominus(x(a)\odot y(a))\ominus_{gH}\int_a^b x(t)\odot y'(t)\mathrm{d}t$$

To prove the relation, we use the derivative of the combination of these two functions.

$$(x\odot y)'_{gH}(t)=x'_{gH}(t)\odot y(t)\oplus x(t)\odot y'(t)$$

Integrating both sides with respect to t over the interval $[a,b]$, we will have:

$$\int_a^b (x\odot y)'_{gH}(t)\mathrm{d}t=\int_a^b\left(x'_{gH}(t)\odot y(t)\right)\mathrm{d}t\oplus\int_a^b (x(t)\odot y'(t))\mathrm{d}t$$

The left-hand side can be obtained immediately as:

$$(x(b)\odot y(b))\ominus_H(x(a)\odot y(a))=\int_a^b\left(x'_{gH}(t)\odot y(t)\right)\mathrm{d}t\oplus\int_a^b (x(t)\odot y'(t))\mathrm{d}t$$

Now, based on the definition of the H-difference, the proof is completed.

3.6.1.20 Taylor expansion

Item 1. Let us assume the same continuous fuzzy number valued function and all the derivatives are $(i-gH)$-differentiable for $n=1,2,\ldots,m$ without changing the type of differentiability. Then, based on the previous case, we have the following relation.

$$x(s)=x(a)\oplus FR\int_a^s x^{(1)}_{i-gH}(s_1)\mathrm{d}s_1$$

and:

$$x^{(1)}_{i-gH}(s_1)=x^{(1)}_{i-gH}(a)\oplus FR\int_a^{s_1} x^{(2)}_{i-gH}(s_1)\mathrm{d}s_1$$

Taking the integral of the two sides:

$$FR\int_a^s x^{(1)}_{i-gH}(s_1)\mathrm{d}s_1=FR\int_a^s x^{(1)}_{i-gH}(a)\mathrm{d}s_1\oplus FR\int_a^s FR\int_a^{s_1} x^{(2)}_{i-gH}(s_2)\mathrm{d}s_2\mathrm{d}s_1$$

$$=x^{(1)}_{i-gH}(a)\odot(s-a)\oplus FR\int_a^s\left(\int_a^{s_1} x^{(2)}_{i-gH}(s_2)\mathrm{d}s_2\right)\mathrm{d}s_1$$

On the other hand, the right-hand side is:

$$FR\int_a^s x_{i-gH}^{(1)}(s_1)\mathrm{d}s_1 = x(s)\ominus_H x(a)$$

then:

$$x(s) = x(a)\oplus x_{i-gH}^{(1)}(a)\odot(s-a)\oplus FR\int_a^s\left(\int_a^{s_1} x_{i-gH}^{(2)}(s_2)\mathrm{d}s_2\right)\mathrm{d}s_1$$

Similarly:

$$x_{i-gH}^{(2)}(s_1) = x_{i-gH}^{(2)}(a)\oplus FR\int_a^{s_1} x_{i-gH}^{(3)}(s_1)\mathrm{d}s_1$$

Again, applying the integral operator to the two sides:

$$FR\int_a^{s_1} x_{i-gH}^{(2)}(s_2)\mathrm{d}s_2 = x_{i-gH}^{(2)}(a)\odot(s_1-a)\oplus FR\int_a^{s_1}\left(\int_a^{s_2} x_{i-gH}^{(3)}(s_3)\mathrm{d}s_3\right)\mathrm{d}s_2$$

Now:

$$FR\int_a^s\left(\int_a^{s_1} x_{i-gH}^{(2)}(s_2)\mathrm{d}s_2\right)\mathrm{d}s_1 == x_{i-gH}^{(2)}(a)\odot FR\int_a^s (s_1-a)\mathrm{d}s_1$$
$$\oplus\int_a^s\left(FR\int_a^{s_1}\left(\int_a^{s_2} x_{i-gH}^{(3)}(s_3)ds_3\right)\mathrm{d}s_2\right)\mathrm{d}s_1$$

So by replacement in $x(s)$:

$$x(s) = x(a)\oplus x_{i-gH}^{(1)}(a)\odot(s-a)\oplus x_{i-gH}^{(2)}(a)$$
$$\odot FR\int_a^s (s_1-a)\mathrm{d}s_1\oplus FR\int_a^s\left(FR\int_a^{s_1}\left(\int_a^{s_2} x_{i-gH}^{(3)}(s_3)\mathrm{d}s_3\right)\mathrm{d}s_2\right)\mathrm{d}s_1$$

Since:

$$FR\int_a^s (s_1-a)\mathrm{d}s_1 = \frac{(s-a)^2}{2!}$$

and finally:

$$x(s) = x(a)\oplus x_{i-gH}^{(1)}(a)\odot(s-a)$$
$$\oplus x_{i-gH}^{(2)}(a)\odot\frac{(s-a)^2}{2!}\oplus FR\int_a^s\left(\int_a^{s_1}\left(\int_a^{s_2} x_{i-gH}^{(3)}(s_3)\mathrm{d}s_3\right)\mathrm{d}s_2\right)\mathrm{d}s_1$$

By continuing in the same way, the general expansion is obtained as follows:

$$x(s) = x(a) \oplus x_{i-gH}^{(1)}(a) \odot (s-a)$$

$$\oplus x_{i-gH}^{(2)}(a) \odot \frac{(s-a)^2}{2!} \oplus \cdots \oplus x_{i-gH}^{(m-1)}(a) \odot \frac{(s-a)^{m-1}}{(m-1)!} \oplus R_n(a, s)$$

where $R_n(a,s)$ is noted as a reminder term of the expansion and it is:

$$R_n(a, s) = FR\int_a^s \left(\int_a^{s_1} \cdots \left(\int_a^{s_{n-1}} x_{i-gH}^{(n)}(s_n)\mathrm{d}s_n\right)\mathrm{d}s_{n-1}\cdots\right)\mathrm{d}s_1$$

Item 2. Let us now assume all the derivatives are $(ii-gH)$-differentiable for $n=1, 2, \ldots, m$ without changing the type of differentiability. Then, based on the previous case, we have the following relation:

$$x(s) = x(a) \ominus_H (-1) FR\int_a^s x_{ii-gH}^{(1)}(s_1)\mathrm{d}s_1$$

and:

$$x_{ii-gH}^{(1)}(s_1) = x_{ii-gH}^{(1)}(a) \oplus FR\int_a^{s_1} x_{ii-gH}^{(2)}(s_1)\mathrm{d}s_1$$

Taking the integral of the two sides:

$$FR\int_a^s x_{ii-gH}^{(1)}(s_1)\mathrm{d}s_1 = FR\int_a^s x_{ii-gH}^{(1)}(a)\mathrm{d}s_1 \oplus FR\int_a^s FR\int_a^{s_1} x_{ii-gH}^{(2)}(s_2)\mathrm{d}s_2\mathrm{d}s_1$$

$$= x_{ii-gH}^{(1)}(a) \odot (s-a) \oplus FR\int_a^s \left(\int_a^{s_1} x_{ii-gH}^{(2)}(s_2)\mathrm{d}s_2\right)\mathrm{d}s_1$$

On the other hand, the right-hand side is:

$$\ominus_H (-1) FR\int_a^s x_{ii-gH}^{(1)}(s_1)\mathrm{d}s_1 = x(s) \ominus_H x(a)$$

then:

$$x(s) = x(a) \ominus_H (-1) x_{ii-gH}^{(1)}(a) \odot (s-a) \ominus_H (-1) FR\int_a^s \left(\int_a^{s_1} x_{ii-gH}^{(2)}(s_2)\mathrm{d}s_2\right)\mathrm{d}s_1$$

Similarly:

$$x_{ii-gH}^{(2)}(s_1) = x_{ii-gH}^{(2)}(a) \oplus FR\int_a^{s_1} x_{ii-gH}^{(3)}(s_1)\mathrm{d}s_1$$

Again, applying the integral operator to the two sides:

$$FR\int_a^{s_1} x_{ii-gH}^{(2)}(s_2)ds_2 = x_{ii-gH}^{(2)}(a)\odot(s_1-a)\oplus FR\int_a^{s_1}\left(\int_a^{s_2} x_{ii-gH}^{(3)}(s_3)ds_3\right)ds_2$$

Now:

$$FR\int_a^{s}\left(\int_a^{s_1} x_{ii-gH}^{(2)}(s_2)ds_2\right)ds_1 =$$

$$= x_{ii-gH}^{(2)}(a)\odot FR\int_a^{s}(s_1-a)ds_1\oplus\int_a^{s}\left(FR\int_a^{s_1}\left(\int_a^{s_2} x_{ii-gH}^{(3)}(s_3)ds_3\right)ds_2\right)ds_1$$

So by replacement in $x(s)$:

$$x(s) = x(a)\ominus_H(-1)x_{ii-gH}^{(1)}(a)\odot(s-a)$$

$$\ominus(-1)x_{ii-gH}^{(2)}(a)\odot FR\int_a^{s}(s_1-a)ds_1$$

$$\ominus_H(-1)FR\int_a^{s}\left(FR\int_a^{s_1}\left(\int_a^{s_2} x_{ii-gH}^{(3)}(s_3)ds_3\right)ds_2\right)ds_1$$

Since:

$$FR\int_a^{s}(s_1-a)ds_1 = \frac{(s-a)^2}{2!}$$

finally:

$$x(s) = x(a)\ominus_H(-1)x_{ii-gH}^{(1)}(a)\odot(s-a)\ominus_H(-1)x_{ii-gH}^{(2)}(a)\odot\frac{(s-a)^2}{2!}$$

$$\ominus(-1)FR\int_a^{s}\left(\int_a^{s_1}\left(\int_a^{s_2} x_{ii-gH}^{(3)}(s_3)ds_3\right)ds_2\right)ds_1$$

By continuing in the same way, the general expansion is obtained as follows:

$$x(s) = x(a)\ominus_H(-1)x_{ii-gH}^{(1)}(a)\odot(s-a)\ominus_H(-1)x_{ii-gH}^{(2)}(a)\odot\frac{(s-a)^2}{2!}$$

$$\ominus_H(-1)\cdots\ominus_H(-1)x_{ii-gH}^{(m-1)}(a)\odot\frac{(s-a)^{m-1}}{(m-1)!}\ominus_H(-1)R_n(as)$$

where $R_n(a,s)$ is noted as a reminder term of the expansion and it is:

$$R_n(a,s) = FR\int_a^{s}\left(\int_a^{s_1}\cdots\left(\int_a^{s_{n-1}} x_{ii-gH}^{(n)}(s_n)ds_n\right)ds_{n-1}\cdots\right)ds_1$$

Item 3. Suppose that the same function is $i-gH$ differentiable for $n=2k-1$, $k\in\mathbb{N}$ and it is $ii-gH$ differentiable for $n=2k$, $k\in\mathbb{N}\cup\{0\}$. Now $x(t)$ is $ii-gH$ differentiable and:

$$x(s)=x(a)\ominus_H(-1)FR\int_a^s x_{ii-gH}^{(1)}(s_1)\mathrm{d}s_1$$

According to the hypothesis, $x_{gH}{}'(t)$ is $i-gH$ differentiable and we have:

$$x_{ii-gH}^{(1)}(s)=x_{ii-gH}^{(1)}(a)\ominus_H(-1)FR\int_a^s x_{i-gH}^{(2)}(t)\mathrm{d}t$$

Taking the integral of the two sides:

$$FR\int_a^s x_{ii-gH}^{(1)}(s_1)\mathrm{d}s_1=$$

$$=FR\int_a^s x_{ii-gH}^{(1)}(a)\mathrm{d}s_1\ominus_H(-1)FR\int_a^s FR\int_a^{s_1} x_{ii-gH}^{(2)}(s_2)\mathrm{d}s_2\mathrm{d}s_1$$

$$=x_{ii-gH}^{(1)}(a)\odot(s-a)\ominus_H(-1)FR\int_a^s\left(\int_a^{s_1} x_{ii-gH}^{(2)}(s_2)\mathrm{d}s_2\right)\mathrm{d}s_1$$

so:

$$x(s)=x(a)\ominus_H(-1)x_{ii-gH}^{(1)}(a)\odot(s-a)\oplus FR\int_a^s\left(\int_a^{s_1} x_{ii-gH}^{(2)}(s_2)ds_2\right)\mathrm{d}s_1$$

Similarly:

$$x_{i-gH}^{(2)}(s_1)=x_{i-gH}^{(2)}(a)\ominus_H(-1)FR\int_a^{s_1} x_{ii-gH}^{(3)}(s_1)\mathrm{d}s_1$$

Again, applying the integral operator to the two sides:

$$FR\int_a^{s_1} x_{i-gH}^{(2)}(s_2)\mathrm{d}s_2=$$

$$=x_{i-gH}^{(2)}(a)\odot(s_1-a)\ominus_H(-1)FR\int_a^{s_1}\left(\int_a^{s_2} x_{ii-gH}^{(3)}(s_3)\mathrm{d}s_3\right)\mathrm{d}s_2$$

Now:

$$FR\int_a^s\left(\int_a^{s_1} x_{i-gH}^{(2)}(s_2)\mathrm{d}s_2\right)\mathrm{d}s_1==x_{i-gH}^{(2)}(a)\odot FR\int_a^s(s_1-a)\mathrm{d}s_1$$

$$\ominus(-1)\int_a^s\left(FR\int_a^{s_1}\left(\int_a^{s_2} x_{ii-gH}^{(3)}(s_3)\mathrm{d}s_3\right)\mathrm{d}s_2\right)\mathrm{d}s_1$$

So by replacement in $x(s)$:

$$x(s)=x(a)\ominus(-1)x_{ii-gH}^{(1)}(a)\odot(s-a)$$

$$\oplus x_{i-gH}^{(2)}(a)\odot FR\int_a^s (s_1-a)\mathrm{d}s_1$$

$$\ominus(-1)FR\int_a^s\left(FR\int_a^{s_1}\left(\int_a^{s_2}x_{ii-gH}^{(3)}(s_3)\mathrm{d}s_3\right)\mathrm{d}s_2\right)\mathrm{d}s_1$$

Since:

$$FR\int_a^s (s_1-a)\mathrm{d}s_1=\frac{(s-a)^2}{2!}$$

finally:

$$x(s)=x(a)\ominus_H(-1)x_{ii-gH}^{(1)}(a)\odot(s-a)$$

$$\oplus x_{i-gH}^{(2)}(a)\odot\frac{(s-a)^2}{2!}\ominus_H(-1)FR\int_a^s\left(\int_a^{s_1}\left(\int_a^{s_2}x_{ii-gH}^{(3)}(s_3)\mathrm{d}s_3\right)\mathrm{d}s_2\right)\mathrm{d}s_1$$

By continuing in the same way, the general expansion is obtained as follows:

$$x(s)=x(a)\ominus(-1)x_{ii-gH}^{(1)}(a)\odot(s-a)$$

$$\oplus x_{i-gH}^{(2)}(a)\odot\frac{(s-a)^2}{2!}\ominus_H(-1)\cdots\ominus_H(-1)x_{ii-gH}^{\left(\frac{m-1}{2}\right)}(a)\odot\frac{(s-a)^{\frac{m-1}{2}}}{\left(\frac{m-1}{2}\right)!}\oplus$$

$$x_{i-gH}^{\left(\frac{m}{2}\right)}(a)\odot\frac{(s-a)^{\frac{m}{2}}}{\left(\frac{m}{2}\right)!}\ominus_H(-1)\cdots\ominus_H(-1)R_n(as)$$

where $R_n(a,s)$ is noted as a reminder term of the expansion and it is:

$$R_n(a,s)=FR\int_a^s\left(\int_a^{s_1}\cdots\left(\int_a^{s_{n-1}}x_{i-gH}^{(n)}(s_n)\mathrm{d}s_n\right)\mathrm{d}s_{n-1}\cdots\right)\mathrm{d}s_1$$

Item 4. Suppose that the same function is $i-gH$ differentiable in interval $[a,\xi]$ and ξ is the switching point. Soz:

$$x(\xi)=x(a)\oplus FR\int_a^{\xi}x_{i-gH}^{(1)}(s_1)\mathrm{d}s_1$$

and it is $ii-gH$ differentiable in interval $[\xi,b]$

$$x(s)=x(\xi)\ominus_H(-1)FR\int_{\xi}^{s}x_{ii-gH}^{(1)}(t_1)\mathrm{d}t_1$$

By replacement:

$$x(s)=x(a)\oplus FR\int_{a}^{\xi}x_{i-gH}^{(1)}(s_1)\mathrm{d}s_1\ominus_H(-1)FR\int_{\xi}^{s}x_{ii-gH}^{(1)}(t_1)\mathrm{d}t_1$$

Now we are going to find the first integral on the right-hand side. Let us consider ζ_1 as a switching point for the second gH-derivative. And suppose that $x_{i-gH}^{(1)}$ is $ii--$ gH differentiable on $[a,\zeta_1]$, then the type of differentiability changes and:

$$x_{i-gH}^{(1)}(\zeta_1)=x_{i-gH}^{(1)}(a)\ominus_H(-1)FR\int_{a}^{\zeta_1}x_{ii-gH}^{(2)}(s_2)\mathrm{d}s_2$$

Now for $s_1\in[\zeta_1,\xi]$, $x_{i-gH}^{(1)}$ is $i-gH$ differentiable on$[\zeta_1,\xi]$, then the type of differentiability changes and:

$$x_{i-gH}^{(1)}(s_1)=x_{i-gH}^{(1)}(\zeta_1)\oplus FR\int_{\zeta_1}^{s_1}x_{i-gH}^{(2)}(s_3)\mathrm{d}s_3$$

By substituting:

$$x_{i-gH}^{(1)}(s_1)=x_{i-gH}^{(1)}(a)\ominus_H(-1)FR\int_{a}^{\zeta_1}x_{ii-gH}^{(2)}(s_2)\mathrm{d}s_2\oplus FR\int_{\zeta_1}^{s_1}x_{i-gH}^{(2)}(s_3)\mathrm{d}s_3$$

On the other hand:

$$x_{ii-gH}^{(2)}(s_2)=x_{ii-gH}^{(2)}(a)\oplus FR\int_{\zeta_1}^{s_2}x_{ii-gH}^{(3)}(s_4)\mathrm{d}s_4$$

Using the FR integral on $[a,\zeta_1]$

$$FR\int_{a}^{\zeta_1}x_{ii-gH}^{(2)}(s_2)\mathrm{d}s_2=x_{ii-gH}^{(2)}(a)\odot(\zeta_1-a)\oplus FR\int_{a}^{\zeta_1}\left(\int_{a}^{s_2}x_{ii-gH}^{(3)}(s_4)\mathrm{d}s_4\right)\mathrm{d}s_2$$

and:

$$x_{i-gH}^{(2)}(s_3)=x_{i-gH}^{(2)}(\zeta_1)\oplus FR\int_{\zeta_1}^{s_3}x_{i-gH}^{(3)}(s_5)\mathrm{d}s_5$$

Using the FR integral operator on $[\zeta_1,s_1]$

$$FR\int_{\zeta_1}^{s_1}x_{i-gH}^{(2)}(s_3)\mathrm{d}s_3=x_{i-gH}^{(2)}(\zeta_1)\odot(s_1-\zeta_1)\oplus FR\int_{\zeta_1}^{s_1}\left(\int_{\zeta_1}^{s_3}x_{i-gH}^{(3)}(s_5)\mathrm{d}s_5\right)\mathrm{d}s_3$$

To find $x^{(1)}_{i-gH}(s_1)$, we insert two of last equations in $x^{(1)}_{i-gH}(s_1)$.

$$x^{(1)}_{i-gH}(s_1)=$$

$$=x^{(1)}_{i-gH}(a)\ominus_H(-1)\left(x^{(2)}_{ii-gH}(a)\odot(\zeta_1-a)\oplus FR\int_a^{\zeta_1}\left(\int_a^{s_2}x^{(3)}_{ii-gH}(s_4)\mathrm{d}s_4\right)\mathrm{d}s_2\right)$$

$$\oplus x^{(2)}_{i-gH}(\zeta_1)\odot(s_1-\zeta_1)\oplus FR\int_{\zeta_1}^{s_1}\left(\int_{\zeta_1}^{s_3}x^{(3)}_{i-gH}(s_5)\mathrm{d}s_5\right)\mathrm{d}s_3$$

$$=x^{(1)}_{i-gH}(a)\ominus_H x^{(2)}_{ii-gH}(a)\odot(a-\zeta_1)\oplus x^{(2)}_{i-gH}(\zeta_1)\odot(s_1-\zeta_1)$$

$$\ominus_H(-1)FR\int_a^{\zeta_1}\left(\int_a^{s_2}x^{(3)}_{ii-gH}(s_4)\mathrm{d}s_4\right)\mathrm{d}s_2\oplus FR\int_{\zeta_1}^{s_1}\left(\int_{\zeta_1}^{s_3}x^{(3)}_{i-gH}(s_5)\mathrm{d}s_5\right)\mathrm{d}s_3$$

Using the FR integral operator on $[a,\xi]$:

$$FR\int_a^{\xi}x^{(1)}_{i-gH}(s_1)\mathrm{d}s_1=x^{(1)}_{i-gH}(a)\odot(\xi-a)\ominus x^{(2)}_{ii-gH}(a)\odot(a-\zeta_1)\odot(\xi-a)$$

$$\oplus x^{(2)}_{i-gH}(\zeta_1)\odot\left(\frac{(\xi-\zeta_1)^2}{2}-\frac{(a-\zeta_1)^2}{2}\right)$$

$$\ominus(-1)FR\int_a^{\xi}\left(\int_a^{\zeta_1}\left(\int_a^{s_2}x^{(3)}_{ii-gH}(s_4)\mathrm{d}s_4\right)\mathrm{d}s_2\right)\mathrm{d}s_1$$

$$\oplus FR\int_a^{\xi}\left(\int_{\zeta_1}^{s_1}\left(\int_{\zeta_1}^{s_3}x^{(3)}_{i-gH}(s_5)\mathrm{d}s_5\right)\mathrm{d}s_3\right)\mathrm{d}s_1$$

We have this equation:

$$x(s)=x(a)\oplus FR\int_a^{\xi}x^{(1)}_{i-gH}(s_1)\mathrm{d}s_1\ominus_H(-1)FR\int_{\xi}^{s}x^{(1)}_{ii-gH}(t_1)\mathrm{d}t_1$$

and we obtain the result of the first integral. Now we will express the result of the second integral.

Let us suppose that $x^{(2)}_{i-gH}$ and $x^{(3)}_{i-gH}$ are $ii-gH$ differentiable on $[\xi,b]$, then the type of differentiability changes and:

$$x^{(1)}_{ii-gH}(t_1)=x^{(1)}_{ii-gH}(\xi)\oplus FR\int_{\xi}^{t_1}x^{(2)}_{ii-gH}(t_2)\mathrm{d}t_2$$

and:

$$x^{(2)}_{ii-gH}(t_2)=x^{(2)}_{ii-gH}(\xi)\oplus FR\int_{\xi}^{t_2}x^{(3)}_{ii-gH}(t_3)\mathrm{d}t_3$$

Using the FR integral on $[\xi, t_1]$

$$FR\int_{\xi}^{t_1} x_{ii-gH}^{(2)}(t_2)\mathrm{d}t_2 = x_{ii-gH}^{(2)}(\xi)\odot(t_1-\xi)\oplus FR\int_{\xi}^{t_1}\left(\int_a^{t_2} x_{ii-gH}^{(3)}(t_3)\mathrm{d}t_3\right)\mathrm{d}t_2$$

Substituting in $x_{ii-gH}^{(1)}(t_1)$ we have:

$$x_{ii-gH}^{(1)}(t_1) = x_{ii-gH}^{(1)}(\xi)\oplus x_{ii-gH}^{(2)}(\xi)\odot(t_1-\xi)\oplus FR\int_{\xi}^{t_1}\left(\int_a^{t_2} x_{ii-gH}^{(3)}(t_3)\mathrm{d}t_3\right)\mathrm{d}t_2$$

Using the FR integral operator on $[\xi, s]$:

$$FR\int_{\xi}^{s} x_{ii-gH}^{(1)}(t_1)\mathrm{d}t_1 = x_{ii-gH}^{(1)}(\xi)\odot(s-\xi)\oplus x_{ii-gH}^{(2)}(\xi)\odot\frac{(s-\xi)^2}{2!}$$

$$\oplus FR\int_{\xi}^{s}\left(\int_{\xi}^{t}\left(\int_a^{t_2} x_{ii-gH}^{(3)}(t_3)\mathrm{d}t_3\right)\mathrm{d}t_2\right)\mathrm{d}t_1$$

Now it is the right time to evaluate:

$$x(s) = x(a)\oplus FR\int_a^{\xi} x_{i-gH}^{(1)}(s_1)\mathrm{d}s_1\ominus(-1)FR\int_{\xi}^{s} x_{ii-gH}^{(1)}(t_1)\mathrm{d}t_1$$

$$x(s) = x(a)\oplus x_{i-gH}^{(1)}(a)\odot(\xi-a)\ominus x_{ii-gH}^{(2)}(a)\odot(a-\zeta_1)\odot(\xi-a)$$

$$\oplus x_{i-gH}^{(2)}(\zeta_1)\odot\left(\frac{(\xi-\zeta_1)^2}{2}-\frac{(a-\zeta_1)^2}{2}\right)$$

$$\ominus(-1)FR\int_a^{\xi}\left(\int_a^{\zeta_1}\left(\int_a^{s_2} x_{ii-gH}^{(3)}(s_4)\mathrm{d}s_4\right)\mathrm{d}s_2\right)\mathrm{d}s_1$$

$$\oplus FR\int_a^{\xi}\left(\int_{\zeta_1}^{s_1}\left(\int_{\zeta_1}^{s_3} x_{i-gH}^{(3)}(s_5)\mathrm{d}s_5\right)\mathrm{d}s_3\right)\mathrm{d}s_1$$

$$\ominus(-1)\left(x_{ii-gH}^{(1)}(\xi)\odot(s-\xi)\oplus x_{ii-gH}^{(2)}(\xi)\odot\frac{(s-\xi)^2}{2!}\right.$$

$$\left.\oplus FR\int_{\xi}^{s}\left(\int_{\xi}^{t}\left(\int_a^{t_2} x_{ii-gH}^{(3)}(t_3)\mathrm{d}t_3\right)\mathrm{d}t_2\right)\mathrm{d}t_1\right)$$

3.6.1.20.1 Example

Let us suppose that $x(t) = k\odot\exp(-t), k\in\mathbb{F}_R$ and the point that we want to expand the function around is $a=0$. First, we introduce the derivatives and the type of differentiability.

It is clear that $x(t)$ is $i-gH$ differentiable so we can write the derivatives as follows:

- $x(t) = k\odot\exp(-t)$ is $i-gH$ differentiable;
- $x^{(1)}_{ii-gH}(t) = -k\odot\exp(-t)$ is $ii-gH$ differentiable;
- $x^{(2)}_{i-gH}(t) = k\odot\exp(-t)$ is $i-gH$ differentiable; and
- $x^{(3)}_{ii-gH}(t) = -k\odot\exp(-t)$ is $ii-gH$ differentiable.

It seems that

- $x^{(2n)}_{i-gH}(t) = k\odot\exp(-t)$ is $i-gH$ differentiable for $n\in N\cup\{0\}$ and
- $x^{(2n-1)}_{i-gH}(t) = k\odot\exp(-t)$ is $ii-gH$ differentiable for $n\in N$.

Then the Taylor expansion is:

$$x(t) = x(0)\ominus(-1)t\odot x^{(1)}_{ii-gH}(t)\oplus\frac{t^2}{2!}\odot x^{(2)}_{i-gH}(t)\ominus(-1)\frac{t^3}{3!}\odot x^{(3)}_{ii-gH}(t)\oplus\cdots$$

$$\ominus(-1)\frac{t^{2n-1}}{(2n-1)!}\odot x^{(2n-1)}_{ii-gH}(t)\oplus\frac{t^{2n}}{(2n)!}\odot x^{(2n)}_{i-gH}(t)\oplus\cdots$$

$$x(0) = k,\ x^{(2n-1)}_{ii-gH}(t) = -k\odot\exp(-t),\ x^{(2n)}_{i-gH}(t) = k\odot\exp(-t)$$

By replacement:

$$x(t) = k\ominus t\odot k\odot\exp(-t)\oplus\frac{t^2}{2!}\odot k\odot\exp(-t)\ominus\frac{t^3}{3!}\odot k\odot\exp(-t)\oplus\cdots$$

$$\ominus\frac{t^{2n-1}}{(2n-1)!}\odot k\odot\exp(-t)(t)\oplus\frac{t^{2n}}{(2n)!}\odot k\odot\exp(-t)\oplus\cdots$$

In the next section, we want to express the partial derivative under gH-differential operator. To define it, we need the definition of a two dimensional continuous fuzzy number valued function.

Let us assume that $\mathbb{D}$ is the area of two dimensional points and:

$$\mathbb{D} = \{(t,x)|f(t,x)\in\mathbb{F}_R\}$$

This fuzzy number valued function of two variables is called continuous at the point (t_0, x_0) if for any positive $\epsilon>0$ there exists a positive $\delta>0$ such that:

$$\|(t,x)-(t_0,x_0)\|<\delta\Longrightarrow D_H(f(t,x),f(t_0,x_0))<\epsilon$$

where $\|\cdot\|$ is a Euclidean norm and D_H is the Hausdorff distance.

More explanation may be found in Tofigh Allahviranloo and Ahmadi (2010).

3.6.1.21 gH-*partial differentiability*

The fuzzy number valued function of two variables $f(t,x) \in \mathbb{F}_R$ is called gH-partial differentiable $(gH-p)$ at the point $(t_0,x_0) \in \mathbb{D}$ with respect to t and x and denoted by $\partial_{tgH}f(t_0,x_0)$ and $\partial_{xgH}f(t_0,x_0)$ if:

$$\partial_{tgH}f(t_0,x_0) = \lim_{h\to 0}\frac{f(t_0+h,x_0)\ominus_{gH}f(t_0,x_0)}{h}$$

$$\partial_{xgH}f(t_0,x_0) = \lim_{k\to 0}\frac{f(t_0,x_0+k)\ominus_{gH}f(t_0,x_0)}{k}$$

Provided that both derivatives $\partial_{tgH}f(t_0,x_0)$ and $\partial_{xgH}f(t_0,x_0)$ are fuzzy number valued functions not fuzzy sets.

Another way to introduce partial derivatives is using the distance, and based on the properties of the distance we can show this as:

$$D_H\left(\lim_{h\to 0}\frac{f(t_0+h,x_0)\ominus_{gH}f(t_0,x_0)}{h}, \partial_{tgH}f(t_0,x_0)\right) = 0$$

$$D_H\left(\lim_{k\to 0}\frac{f(t_0,x_0+k)\ominus_{gH}f(t_0,x_0)}{k}, \partial_{xgH}f(t_0,x_0)\right) = 0$$

or:

$$D_H\left(\frac{f(t_0+h,x_0)\ominus_{gH}f(t_0,x_0)}{h}, \partial_{tgH}f(t_0,x_0)\right) \to 0$$

$$D_H\left(\frac{f(t_0,x_0+k)\ominus_{gH}f(t_0,x_0)}{k}, \partial_{xgH}f(t_0,x_0)\right) \to 0$$

3.6.1.21.1 Example

Consider a real and nonnegative differentiable function like $p(t,x)$ and a scalar fuzzy number $u \in \mathbb{F}_R$, then the $gH-p$ derivative for $g(t,x) = p(t,x) \odot u$ with respect to t is $\partial_{xgH}g(t,x) = \partial_x p(t,x) \odot u$.

In accordance with the definition we notice that:

$$g(t,x+k)\ominus_{gH}g(t,x) = p(t,x+k)\odot u \ominus_{gH} p(t,x)\odot u$$

$$= [p(t,x+k) - p(t,x)]\odot u$$

This shows that, considering any sign for $[p(t,x+k) - p(t,x)]$, the gH-difference $g(t,x+k)\ominus_{gH}g(t,x)$ always exists. Dividing both sides by k and using the limit we will have:

$$\lim_{k\to 0}\frac{g(t,x+k)\ominus_{gH}g(t,x)}{k}=\lim_{k\to 0}\frac{[p(t,x+k)-p(t,x)]}{k}\odot u$$

Then $\partial_{xgH}g(t,x)=\partial_x p(t,x)\odot u$.

3.6.1.21.2 Another simple example

Let $f(t,x):\mathbb{D}\to\mathbb{F}_R$ is $gh-p$ differentiable with respect to x and $c\in R^{\geq 0}$ be a nonnegative real number. Then $\partial_{xgH}(c\odot f)(t,x)$ exists and $\partial_{xgH}(c\odot f)(t,x)=c\odot\partial_{xgH}f(t,x)$.

By using the distance and assumptions:

$$D_H\left(\frac{(c\odot f)(t,x+k)\ominus_{gH}(c\odot f)(t,x)}{k},c\odot\partial_{xgH}f(t,x)\right)$$

$$=D_H\left(\frac{c\odot f(t,x+k)\ominus_{gH}c\odot f(t,x)}{k},c\odot\partial_{xgH}f(t,x)\right)$$

$$=cD_H\left(\frac{f(t,x+k)\ominus_{gH}f(t,x)}{k},\partial_{xgH}f(t,x)\right)$$

Now if $k\to 0$, then:

$$cD_H\left(\frac{f(t,x+k)\ominus_{gH}f(t,x)}{k},\partial_{xgH}f(t,x)\right)\to 0$$

then:

$$\partial_{xgH}(c\odot f)(t,x)=c\odot\partial_{xgH}f(t,x)$$

3.6.1.22 Level-wise form of gH*-partial differentiability*

Suppose that the fuzzy number valued function $f(t,x)\in\mathbb{F}_R$ is $gH-p$ differentiable at the point $(t_0,x_0)\in\mathbb{D}$ with respect to t and $f_l(t,x,r), f_u(t,x,r)$ are real valued functions and partial differentiable with respect to t. We say:

- $f(t,x)$ is $(i-gH-p)$ differentiable w.r.t. t at (t_0,x_0) if:

$$\partial_{t,i-gh}f(t_0,x_0,r)=[\partial_t f_l(t,x,r),\partial_t f_u(t,x,r)]$$

- $f(t,x)$ is $(ii-gH-p)$ differentiable w.r.t. t at (t_0,x_0) if:

$$\partial_{t,ii-gh}f(t_0,x_0,r)=[\partial_t f_u(t,x,r),\partial_t f_l(t,x,r)]$$

Note that in each case, the conditions of the definition in level-wise form should be satisfied.

3.6.1.23 *Switching point in* gH*-partial differentiability*

For any fixed ξ_0 we say the point $(\xi_0, x) \in \mathbb{D}$ is a switching point for the gH-differentiability of $f(t,x)$ w.r.t. t, if in any neighborhood V of (t_0, ξ_0) there exist points $(t_1,x) < (\xi_0,x) < (t_2,x)$ for any fixed x such that:

Type I at the point (t_1,x) is $(i-gH-p)$ differentiable and not $(ii-gH-p)$ differentiable and at the point (t_2,x) is $(ii-gH-p)$ differentiable and not $(i-gH-p)$ differentiable.

Type II at the point (t_1,x) is $(ii-gH-p)$ differentiable and not $(i-gH-p)$ differentiable and at the point (t_2,x) is $(i-gH-p)$ differentiable and not $(ii-gH-p)$ differentiable.

3.6.1.23.1 Example

Consider the fuzzy number valued function $f(t,x) : [1,4] \times [0,\pi] \to \mathbb{F}_R$ defined by:

$$f(t,x,r) = [0.7+0.3r,\ 1.8-0.8r]x\sin(t)$$

It is clear that:

$$f_l(t,x,r) = \begin{cases} (0.7+0.3r)x\sin(t), & x\in[1,4],\ t\in\left[0,\dfrac{\pi}{2}\right] \\ (1.8-0.8r)x\sin(t), & x\in[1,4],\ t\in\left[\dfrac{\pi}{2},\pi\right] \end{cases}$$

$$f_u(t,x,r) = \begin{cases} (1.8-0.8r)x\sin(t), & x\in[1,4],\ t\in\left[0,\dfrac{\pi}{2}\right] \\ (0.7+0.3r)x\sin(t), & x\in[1,4],\ t\in\left[\dfrac{\pi}{2},\pi\right] \end{cases}$$

and the differential in level-wise form is:

$$\partial_t f_l(t,x,r) = \begin{cases} (0.7+0.3r)x\cos(t), & x\in[1,4],\ t\in\left[0,\dfrac{\pi}{2}\right] \\ (1.8-0.8r)x\cos(t), & x\in[1,4],\ t\in\left[\dfrac{\pi}{2},\pi\right] \end{cases}$$

$$\partial_t f_u(t,x,r) = \begin{cases} (1.8-0.8r)x\cos(t), & x\in[1,4],\ t\in\left[0,\dfrac{\pi}{2}\right] \\ (0.7+0.3r)x\cos(t), & x\in[1,4],\ t\in\left[\dfrac{\pi}{2},\pi\right] \end{cases}$$

Clearly the function $f(t,x)$ is $(i-gH-p)$ differentiable on $x\in[1,4]$, $t\in\left[0,\frac{\pi}{2}\right]$. At the point $\left(\frac{\pi}{2}, t\right)$ for all $t\in[1,4]$ the derivative is switched to $(ii-gH-p)$ differentiability. So the points $\left(\frac{\pi}{2}, t\right)$ for all $t\in[1,4]$ are switching points to the derivative of $f(t,x)$ (Fig. 3.4).

We will see the switching points in Fig. 3.5 for the derivatives.

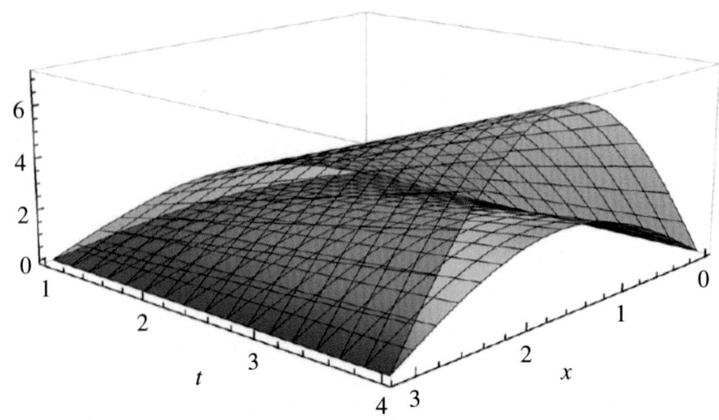

Fig. 3.4 The graph of $f(t, x)$ in level $r=0$.

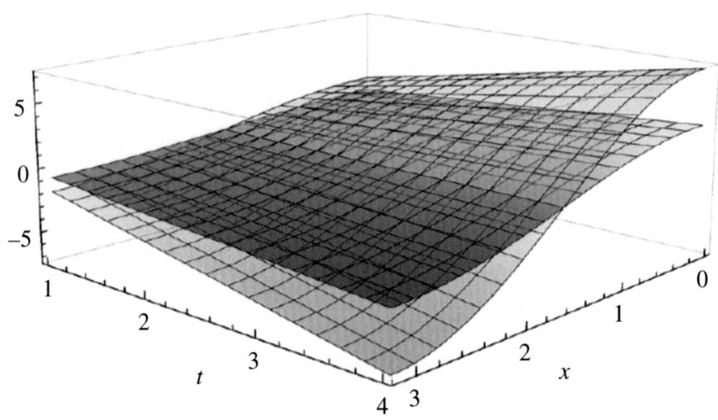

Fig. 3.5 The graph of $f_{gH}'(t, x)$ in level $r=0$.

3.6.1.24 Higher order of gH*-partial differentiability*

Suppose that the fuzzy number valued function $\partial_{tgH}f(t,x)\in\mathbb{F}_R$ is $gH-p$ differentiable at the point $(t_0, x_0)\in\mathbb{D}$ with respect to t and there is no switching point. Moreover, suppose that $\partial_{tt}f_l(t,x,r)$, $\partial_{tt}f_u(t,x,r)$ are real valued functions and partial differentiable with respect to t. We say:

- $\partial_t f(t,x)$ is $(i-gH-p)$ differentiable w.r.t. t at (t_0,x_0) if:

$$\partial_{tt,i-gh}f(t_0,x_0,r)=[\partial_{tt}f_l(t,x,r),\partial_{tt}f_u(t,x,r)]$$

- $\partial_t f(t,x)$ is $(ii-gH-p)$ differentiable w.r.t. t at (t_0,x_0) if:

$$\partial_{tt,ii-gh} f(t_0,x_0,r) = [\partial_{tt} f_u(t,x,r), \partial_{tt} f_l(t,x,r)]$$

Note. In each case the conditions of the definition in level-wise form should be satisfied and the type of gH-partial differentiability for both functions $f(t,x)$ and $\partial_t f(t,x)$ is the same.

3.6.1.25 *Integral relation in* gH*-partial differentiability*

Suppose that the fuzzy number valued function $f(t,x) \in \mathbb{F}_R$ is continuous and $gH-p$ differentiable with respect to t with no switching point in the interval $[a,s]$, then:

$$\int_a^s \partial_{xgH} f(t,x)\mathrm{d}x = f(t,s) \ominus_{gH} f(t,a)$$

According to the lack of switching point and without loss of generality we assume that the function $f(t,x)$ is $(ii-gH-p)$ differentiable (the proof of $(i-gH-p)$ differentiability is similar). So we have:

$$\int_a^s \partial_{xgH} f(t,x,r)\mathrm{d}x = \int_a^s [\partial_t f_u(t,x,r), \partial_t f_l(t,x,r)]\mathrm{d}x$$

$$= [f_u(t,s,r) - f_u(t,a,r), f_l(t,s,r) - f_l(t,a,r)] = f(t,s) \ominus_{gH} f(t,a)$$

3.6.1.26 *Multivariate fuzzy chain rule in* gH*-partial differentiability*

Let $x_i(t)$ be defined on $\mathbb{I}_i := [a,b] \subseteq R, i = 1,2,3$ and be strictly increasing and differentiable functions. Consider U is an open set of R^3 such that $\prod_{i=1}^3 \mathbb{I}_i \subseteq R$. Let us assume that the function $f : U \to \mathbb{F}_R$ is a continuous fuzzy function. Suppose that $\partial_{x_i gH} f : U \to \mathbb{F}_R, i = 1,2,3$ the $gH-p$ derivatives of f exist and are fuzzy continuous functions. Call $x_i := x_i(t)$ and $z := z(t) := f(x_1,x_2,x_3)$. Then $\partial_{tgH} z$ exists and:

$$\partial_{tgH} z = \partial_{x_1 gH} f(x_1,x_2,x_3) \odot \partial_t x_1(t) \oplus \partial_{x_2 gH} f(x_1,x_2,x_3) \odot \partial_t x_2(t)$$

$$\oplus \partial_{x_3 gH} f(x_1,x_2,x_3) \odot \partial_t x_3(t)$$

where $\partial_t x_i(t)$, $i = 1, 2, 3$ are derivatives of $x_i(t)$ with respect to t.

To show the assertion, let $t \in (a,b)$ and $(x_1,x_2,x_3) \in U$ be fixed and $\Delta x_i > 0$, $i = 1$, 2, 3 be small enough. Now set:

$$\alpha_1 = f(x_1 + \Delta x_1, x_2 + \Delta x_2, x_3 + \Delta x_3) \ominus_{gH} f(x_1, x_2 + \Delta x_2, x_3 + \Delta x_3) \in \mathbb{F}_R$$

$$\alpha_2 = f(x_1, x_2 + \Delta x_2, x_3 + \Delta x_3) \ominus_{gH} f(x_1, x_2, x_3 + \Delta x_3) \in \mathbb{F}_R$$

$$\alpha_3 = f(x_1, x_2, x_3 + \Delta x_3) \ominus_{gH} f(x_1, x_2, x_3) \in \mathbb{F}_R$$

So we have:

$$f(x_1+\Delta x_1, x_2+\Delta x_2, x_3+\Delta x_3)\ominus_{gH} f(x_1, x_2, x_3) = \oplus\sum_{i=1}^{3}\alpha_i \in \mathbb{F}_R$$

Since the partial gH-derivative $\partial_{x_i gH} f$ exists, the above gH-differences in α_i exist for $i=1, 2, 3$ when $\Delta x_i \to 0$. Here $\Delta x_i = x_i(t+\Delta t) - x_i(t) := x_i + \Delta x_i$, $i=1, 2, 3$.

Now:

$$\lim_{\Delta t\to 0} D_H\left(\frac{f(x_1+\Delta x_1, x_2+\Delta x_2, x_3+\Delta x_3)\ominus_{gH} f(x_1, x_2, x_3)}{\Delta t}:\right.$$

$$\left.\oplus\sum_{i=1}^{3}\partial_{x_i gH} f(x_1, x_2, x_3)\odot\partial_t x_i(t)\right)$$

$$= \lim_{\Delta t\to 0} D_H\left(\frac{\oplus\sum_{i=1}^{3}\alpha_i}{\Delta t}, \oplus\sum_{i=1}^{3}\partial_{x_i gH} f(x_1, x_2, x_3)\odot\partial_t x_i(t)\right)$$

$$\leq \lim_{\Delta t\to 0} D_H\left(\frac{f(x_1+\Delta x_1, x_2+\Delta x_2, x_3+\Delta x_3)\ominus_{gH} f(x_1, x_2+\Delta x_2, x_3+\Delta x_3)}{\Delta x_1}\odot\frac{\Delta x_1}{\Delta t}:\right.$$

$$\left.\partial_{x_1 gH} f(x_1, x_2, x_3)\odot\partial_t x_1(t)\right)$$

$$+\lim_{\Delta t\to 0} D_H\left(\frac{f(x_1, x_2+\Delta x_2, x_3+\Delta x_3)\ominus_{gH} f(x_1, x_2, x_3+\Delta x_3)}{\Delta x_2}\odot\frac{\Delta x_2}{\Delta t}:\right.$$

$$\left.\partial_{x_2 gH} f(x_1, x_2, x_3)\odot\partial_t x_2(t)\right)$$

$$+\lim_{\Delta t\to 0} D_H\left(\frac{f(x_1, x_2, x_3+\Delta x_3)\ominus_{gH} f(x_1, x_2, x_3)}{\Delta x_3}\odot\frac{\Delta x_3}{\Delta t}:\right.$$

$$\left.\partial_{x_3 gH} f(x_1, x_2, x_3)\odot\partial_t x_3(t)\right)$$

$$\leq \lim_{\Delta t\to 0} D_H\left(\frac{\int_{x_1}^{x_1+\Delta x_1}\partial_{x_1 gH} f(t, x_2+\Delta x_2, x_3+\Delta x_3)dt}{\Delta x_1}\odot\frac{\Delta x_1}{\Delta t}:\right.$$

$$\left.\partial_{x_1 gH} f(x_1, x_2, x_3)\odot\partial_t x_1(t)\right)$$

$$+\lim_{\Delta t\to 0} D_H\left(\frac{\int_{x_2}^{x_2+\Delta x_2}\partial_{x_2gH}f(x_1,t,x_3+\Delta x_3)dt}{\Delta x_2}\odot\frac{\Delta x_2}{\Delta t}:\right.$$

$$\left.\partial_{x_2gH}f(x_1,x_2,x_3)\odot\partial_t x_2(t)\right)$$

$$+\lim_{\Delta t\to 0} D_H\left(\partial_{x_3gH}f(x_1,x_2,x_3)\odot x_3'(t),\partial_{x_3gH}f(x_1,x_2,x_3)\odot\partial_t x_3(t)\right)$$

If the limit operator goes inside the distance then $\lim_{\Delta t\to 0}\frac{\Delta x_i}{\Delta t}=\partial_t x_i(t):=x_3'(t)$. Moreover, in each term the Δx_i is a constant with respect to the integral variable. So:

$$\le \partial_t x_1(t)\lim_{\Delta t\to 0}\frac{1}{\Delta x_1}D_H\left(\int_{x_1}^{x_1+\Delta x_1}\partial_{x_1gH}f(t,x_2+\Delta x_2,x_3+\Delta x_3)\mathrm{d}t,\partial_{x_1gH}f(x_1,x_2,x_3)\right)$$

$$+\partial_t x_2(t)\lim_{\Delta t\to 0}\frac{1}{\Delta x_2}D_H\left(\int_{x_2}^{x_2+\Delta x_2}\partial_{x_2gH}f(x_1,t,x_3+\Delta x_3)\mathrm{d}t,\partial_{x_2gH}f(x_1,x_2,x_3)\right)+0$$

$$\le\frac{\partial_t x_1(t)}{\Delta x_1}\lim_{\Delta t\to 0}\left(\int_{x_1}^{x_1+\Delta x_1}D_H\left(\partial_{x_1gH}f(t,x_2+\Delta x_2,x_3+\Delta x_3),\partial_{x_1gH}f(x_1,x_2,x_3)\right)\mathrm{d}t\right)$$

$$+\frac{\partial_t x_2(t)}{\Delta x_2}\lim_{\Delta t\to 0}\left(\int_{x_2}^{x_2+\Delta x_2}D_H\left(\partial_{x_2gH}f(x_1,t,x_3+\Delta x_3),\partial_{x_2gH}f(x_1,x_2,x_3)\right)\mathrm{d}t\right)$$

$$\le\frac{\partial_t x_1(t)}{\Delta x_1}\lim_{\Delta t\to 0}\left(\sup_{\tau\in[x_1,x_1+\Delta x_1]}D_H\left(\partial_{x_1gH}f(\tau,x_2+\Delta x_2,x_3+\Delta x_3),\partial_{x_1gH}f(x_1,x_2,x_3)\right)\right)\Delta x_1$$

$$+\frac{\partial_t x_2(t)}{\Delta x_2}\lim_{\Delta t\to 0}\left(\sup_{\tau\in[x_1,x_1+\Delta x_1]}D_H\left(\partial_{x_1gH}f(x_1,t,x_3+\Delta x_3),\partial_{x_1gH}f(x_1,x_2,x_3)\right)\right)\Delta x_2\to 0$$

As $\Delta t\to 0$ then all $\Delta x_i\to 0$ and thus $\tau_i\to x_i$ for all $i=1, 2$. Then by continuity of ∂_{x_igH}, two of the terms intend to the zero. The proof is completed.

3.7 The fuzzy Laplace transform operator

In this section we suppose that the Laplace operator acts on a fuzzy number valued function and this is the reason we call it fuzzy Laplace transform (Armand et al., 2019; Salahshour and Allahviranloo, 2013).

As before, let us consider the function f is a fuzzy number valued function and s is a real parameter. The fuzzy Laplace transform is defined as follows:

$$F(s) = L(f(t)) = \int_0^{\infty} e^{-st} \odot f(t)\mathrm{d}t$$

or:

$$F(s) = L(f(t)) = \lim_{\tau \to \infty} \int_0^{\tau} e^{-st} \odot f(t)\mathrm{d}t$$

If we consider the Laplace operator in the level-wise form of $f(t)$ as:

$$L(f(t,r)) = [l(f_l(t,r)), l(f_u(t,r))]$$

then the level-wise form of the Laplace operator is as follows:

$$F(s,r) = \lim_{\tau \to \infty} \int_0^{\tau} e^{-st} \odot f(t,r)\mathrm{d}t$$

and:

$$[F_l(s,r), F_u(s,r)] = \left[\lim_{\tau \to \infty} \int_0^{\tau} e^{-st} f_l(t,r)\mathrm{d}t,\ \lim_{\tau \to \infty} \int_0^{\tau} e^{-st} f_u(t,r)\mathrm{d}t\right]$$

then:

$$F_l(s,r) = \lim_{\tau \to \infty} \int_0^{\tau} e^{-st} f_l(t,r)\mathrm{d}t$$

$$F_u(s,r) = \lim_{\tau \to \infty} \int_0^{\tau} e^{-st} f_u(t,r)\mathrm{d}t$$

To define this operator, the important condition is that the integral must converge to a real number. This means it should be bounded. However, there are some integrals that are not convergent.

3.7.1 EXAMPLE

Suppose the fuzzy number valued function $f(t) = c \odot e^{t^2}, c \in \mathbb{F}_R$. Then:

$$F_l(s,r) = \lim_{\tau \to \infty} \int_0^{\tau} e^{-st} c_l(r) e^{t^2}\mathrm{d}t \to 0$$

$$F_u(s,r) = \lim_{\tau \to \infty} \int_0^{\tau} e^{-st} c_u(r) e^{t^2}\mathrm{d}t \to 0$$

The integral grows without bound for any s as $\tau \to \infty$.

If you remember we defined the absolute value of fuzzy number. Now, in the same way, we can define the absolute value of a fuzzy number valued function.

The absolute value of the same function in level-wise form is defined as:

$$|f(t,r)| = [\min\{|f_l(t,r)|, |f_u(t,r)|\}, \max\{|f_l(t,r)|, |f_u(t,r)|\}]$$

It can be defined in two cases:

Type I. Type 1 absolute value fuzzy number function:

$$|f(t,r)| = [|f_l(t,r)|, |f_u(t,r)|]$$

In other words, if $f_l(t,r) \geq 0$ for all r then f is a type 1 absolute value fuzzy number function.

Type II. Type 2 absolute value function:

$$|f(t,r)| = [|f_u(t,r)|, |f_l(t,r)|]$$

In other words, if $f_u(t,r) < 0$ for all r then f is a type 2 absolute value fuzzy number function.

Moreover, the other conditions of a fuzzy number in level-wise form should be satisfied.

Note. The absolute value of a fuzzy number function is always a positive fuzzy number valued function.ExampleConsider the fuzzy number function $f(t,r) = c[r]e^t$ in the level-wise form where $c[r] = [2+r, 4-r]$. As we know:

$$|f_l(t,r)| = |(2+r)e^t| = (2+r)e^t, |f_u(t,r)| = |(4-r)e^t| = (4-r)e^t$$

and:

$$|f(t,r)| = [(2+r)e^t, (4-r)e^t]$$

Then f is a type 1 absolute value fuzzy number function.

ExampleConsider the fuzzy number function $f(t,r) = c[r]e^t$ in the level-wise form where $c[r] = [-4+r, -2-r]$. As we know:

$$|f_l(t,r)| = |(-4+r)e^t| = (4-r)e^t, |f_u(t,r)| = |(-2-r)e^t| = (r+2)e^t$$

and:

$$|f(t,r)| = [(r+2)e^t, (4-r)e^t]$$

Then f is a type 2 absolute value fuzzy number function.

3.7.2 Definition—Absolutely convergence

The integral operator in the Laplace transformation:

$$F(s) = \lim_{\tau \to \infty} \int_0^{\tau} e^{-st} \odot f(t) \mathrm{d}t$$

Is said to be absolutely convergent if the following exists:

$$\lim_{\tau\to\infty}\int_0^{\tau}|e^{-st}\odot f(t)|dt$$

Considering the level-wise form, both of the following integrals exist.

$$\lim_{\tau\to\infty}\int_0^{\tau}e^{-st}|f_l(t,r)|dt,\ \lim_{\tau\to\infty}\int_0^{\tau}e^{-st}|f_u(t,r)|dt$$

Theoretically, in order to apply the fuzzy Laplace transform to physical problems, it is necessary to involve the inverse transform. If $F(s)=L(f(t))$ is the Laplace transform, the L^{-1} is known as inverse Laplace transform and we have:

$$L^{-1}(F(s))=f(t),\ t\geq 0$$

As with the Laplace transform, the inverse transform is also a linear transform operator. Then, for two fuzzy functions f, g, subject to:

$$L(f(t))=F(s),\ L(g(t))=G(s)$$

then:

$$\begin{aligned}L^{-1}(a\odot F(s)\oplus b\odot G(s))&=a\odot L^{-1}(F(s))\oplus b\odot L^{-1}(G(s))\\&=a\odot f(t)\oplus b\odot g(t)\end{aligned}$$

For any real numbers a, b.

One of the important functions occurring in some electrical systems is the delay, which can be displayed as a unit step function like (Fig. 3.6):

$$u_a(t):=u(t-a)=\begin{cases}1, & t\geq a\\0, & t<a\end{cases}$$

For instance, in an electric circuit for a voltage at a particular time $t=a$. We write such a situation using unit step functions as:

$$V(t)=u(t)-u(t-a)$$

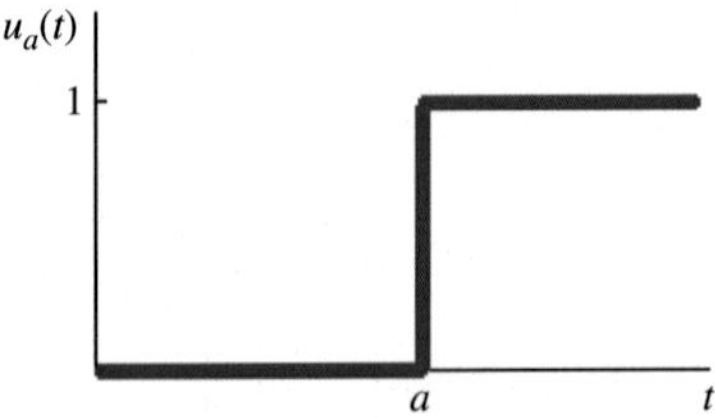

Fig. 3.6 $u_a(t)$.

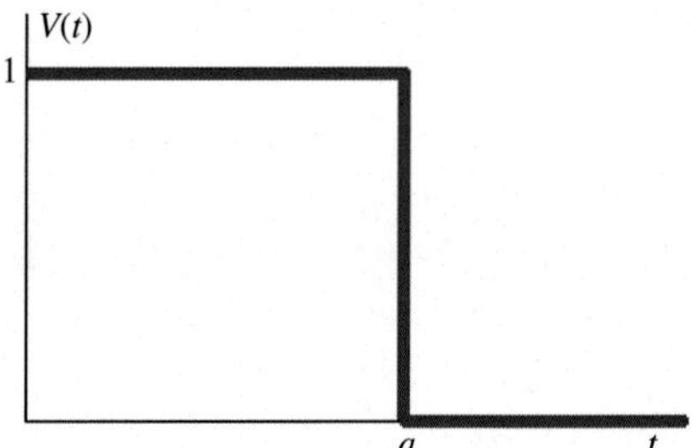

Fig. 3.7 $V(t)$.

It is a shifted unit step. It is clear that $u(t)=u(t-a)=1$ and $V(t)=0$ for $t\geq a\geq 0$ and $u(t)=1$, $u(t-a)=0$ and $V(t)=1$ for $a>t\geq 0$ (Fig. 3.7).

3.7.3 First translation theorem

If $F(s)=L(f(t))$ for $s>a$ then $F(s-a)=L(e^{at}\odot f(t))$ such that a is a real number.

The proof is clear from the definition of Laplace transform:

$$F(s-a)=\int_0^{\infty} e^{-(s-a)t}\odot f(t)\mathrm{d}t=\int_0^{\infty} e^{-st}e^{at}\odot f(t)\mathrm{d}t=L(e^{at}\odot f(t))$$

3.7.4 Second translation theorem

If $F(s)=L(f(t))$ for $s>a\geq 0$ then:

$$e^{as}\odot F(s)=L(u_a(t)\odot f(t-a))$$

According to the definition:

$$L(u_a(t)\odot f(t-a))=\int_0^{\infty} e^{-st}u_a(t)\odot f(t-a)\mathrm{d}t$$

Since $u_a(t)=0$ for $0<t<a$ and $u_a(t)=1$ for $t\geq a$ then:

$$L(u_a(t)\odot f(t-a))=\int_a^{\infty} e^{-st}\odot f(t-a)\mathrm{d}t$$

Let us suppose that $t-a=\tau$

$$\int_a^{\infty} e^{-st}\odot f(t-a)\mathrm{d}t=e^{-sa}\odot\int_a^{\infty} e^{-s\tau}\odot f(\tau)\mathrm{d}\tau=e^{-sa}\odot F(s)$$

Finally:

$$L(u_a(t)\odot f(t-a))=e^{-sa}\odot F(s)$$

3.7.5 Laplace transform on the derivative

In this section we consider the Laplace operator on the gH-derivative of the fuzzy number valued functions, because one of the key operators for this monograph is the derivative of fuzzy functions. Now we work with two operators, entitled Laplace and derivative, on the fuzzy number valued functions.

3.7.5.1 Derivative theorem

Suppose that f and f' are continuous fuzzy number valued on $[0,\infty)$, then:

$$L(f'(t)) = s \odot L(f(t)) \ominus_H f(0)$$

If f is (i)-differentiable:

$$L(f'(t)) = (-1) \odot f(0) \ominus_H (-s \odot L(f(t)))$$

If f is (ii)-differentiable for $s > 0$.

Each part can be proved easily using the level-wise form. For instance, we prove (ii)-differentiability, and the first part is proved in a similar way. The level-wise form of (ii)-differentiability is as:

$$f'(t,r) = \left[f_u'(t,r), f_l'(t,r)\right]$$

then:

$$L(f'(t,r)) = \left[l(f_u'(t,r)), l(f_l'(t,r))\right]$$

On the other hand, the level-wise form of the right-hand side is:

$$[-f_u(0,r) - (-sl(f_u(t,r))),\ -f_l(0,r) - (-sl(f_l(t,r)))] =$$
$$= [sl(f_u(t,r)) - f_u(0,r),\ sl(f_l(t,r)) - f_l(0,r)]$$

so:

$$l(f_u'(t,r)) = sl(f_u(t,r)) - f_u(0,r),\ \ l(f_l'(t,r)) = sl(f_l(t,r)) - f_l(0,r)$$

The proof is completed.

3.7.5.2 High order derivation theorem

Suppose that f, f' and f'' are continuous fuzzy number valued on $[0,\infty)$ (note that for the second derivative the peace-wise differentiability is enough), then:

$$L\left(f''(t)\right) = s^2 \odot L(f(t)) \ominus_H s \odot f(0) \ominus_H f(0)$$

If f and f' are (i)-differentiable:

$$L\left(f''(t)\right) = -f'(0) \ominus_H \left(-s^2\right) \odot L(f(t)) \oplus (-1)s \odot f(0)$$

If f is (i)-differentiable and f' is (ii)-differentiable:

$$L\left(f''(t)\right) = -s \odot f(0) \ominus_H \left(-s^2\right) \odot L(f(t)) \ominus_H f'(0)$$

If f is (ii)-differentiable and f' is (i)-differentiable:

$$L\left(f''(t)\right) = s^2 \odot L(f(t)) \ominus_H s \odot f(0) \oplus (-1)f'(0)$$

If f and f' are (ii)-differentiable.

The proof processes for all four cases are the same and to show the process we just prove the second case. Let f is (i)-differentiable and f' is (ii)-differentiable. The level-wise form of the left-hand side is as:

$$L(f''(t,r)) = [l(f_l''(t,r)), l(f_u''(t,r))]$$

and the right-hand side:

$$\begin{aligned} &\left[-f_u'(0,r), -f_l'(0,r)\right] - \left[-s^2 l(f_u(t,r)), -s^2 l(f_l(t,r))\right] + \left[-sf_u(0,r), -sf_l(0,r)\right] \\ &= \left[-f_u'(0,r) + s^2 l(f_u(t,r)) - sf_u(0,r), -f_l'(0,r) + s^2 l(f_l(t,r)) - sf_l(0,r)\right] \end{aligned}$$

then:

$$l\left(f_l''(t,r)\right) = -f_u'(0,r) + s^2 l(f_u(t,r)) - sf_u(0,r)$$

$$l\left(f_u''(t,r)\right) = -f_l'(0,r) + s^2 l(f_l(t,r)) - sf_l(0,r)$$

The proof is now completed.

3.8 Fuzzy improper integral

Before the discussion of the Fourier transformation, we need to explain the concept of improper integral as a main operator of the Fourier transformation. As we displayed in the previous section the integral over unbounded region of a fuzzy function is referred to as a fuzzy improper integral. In this subsection, we express the double improper integrals and their relation with the derivative. In the following definition, we define the uniformly convergence using the distance.

3.8.1 Definition—Uniform convergence

Let $f(x,t)$ is a continuous fuzzy number valued function on $[a,b]\times[0,\infty)$. Also, suppose that $\int_c^\infty f(x,t)\mathrm{d}t$ convergences (level-wise convergence) for any $x\in[a,b]$. We say $F(x)=\int_c^\infty f(x,t)\mathrm{d}t$ converges uniformly on x if for any positive $\epsilon>0$ there is a number $N(\epsilon)$ that depends on the ϵ such that:

$$D_H\left(F(x), \int_c^d f(x,t)\mathrm{d}t\right) < \epsilon$$

Whenever $d\geq N$ for all $x\in[a,b]$, that is:

$$\sup_{x\in[a,b]} D_H\left(\left(\int_c^d f(x,t)\mathrm{d}t, 0\right)\right) \to 0$$

When $d\to\infty$.

3.8.2 Theorem—Interchanging integrals

Consider that the function $f: R\times R^+ \to \mathbb{F}_R$ is a fuzzy number valued function and its level-wise form is:

$$f(x,t,r)=[f_l(x,t,r), f_u(x,t,r)]$$

Moreover, suppose that:

- $\int_c^\infty f(x,t)\mathrm{d}t$ is convergent for all $x\in[a,\infty]$ and
- $\int_a^\infty f(x,t)\mathrm{d}t$ is convergent for all $\mathrm{t}\in[c,\infty]$.

Then we have:

$$\int_a^\infty \int_c^\infty f(x,t)\mathrm{d}t\mathrm{d}x = \int_c^\infty \int_a^\infty f(x,t)\mathrm{d}x\mathrm{d}t \ \forall a \forall c \in R$$

This is proved easily using the level-wise form.

$$\int_a^\infty \int_c^\infty f(x,t,r)\mathrm{d}t\mathrm{d}x = \left[\int_a^\infty \int_c^\infty f_l(x,t,r)\mathrm{d}t\mathrm{d}x, \int_a^\infty \int_c^\infty f_u(x,t,r)\mathrm{d}t\mathrm{d}x\right]$$

$$= \left[\int_c^\infty \int_a^\infty f_l(x,t,r)\mathrm{d}t\mathrm{d}x, \int_c^\infty \int_a^\infty f_u(x,t,r)\mathrm{d}t\mathrm{d}x\right] = \int_c^\infty \int_a^\infty f(x,t,r)\mathrm{d}x\mathrm{d}t$$

The proof is completed.

3.8.3 THEOREM—INTEGRAL AND DERIVATIVE

Suppose that both functions $f(x,t)$ and $\partial_{xgH}f(x,t)$ are fuzzy continuous in $[a,b]\times[c,\infty)$. Also assume that:

- $F(x)=\int_c^\infty f(x,t)\mathrm{d}t$ converges for all $x\in R$
- $\int_c^\infty \partial_{xgH}f(x,t)\mathrm{d}t$ converges uniformly on $[a,b]$

Then F is gH-differentiable on $[a,b]$ and:

$$F'_{gH}(x)=\int_c^\infty \partial_{xgH}f(x,t)\mathrm{d}t$$

To prove it, we use the distance, and are going to show that:

$$D_H\left(\frac{F(x+h)\ominus_{gH}F(x)}{h},\int_c^\infty \partial_{xgH}f(x,t)\mathrm{d}t\right)\rightarrow 0, h\rightarrow 0$$

To do this, the first part is:

$$\frac{F(x+h)\ominus_{gH}F(x)}{h}=\frac{1}{h}\odot\left(\int_c^\infty f(x+h,t)\mathrm{d}t\ominus_{gH}\int_c^\infty f(x,t)\mathrm{d}t\right)$$

$$=\frac{1}{h}\odot\int_c^\infty \left(f(x+h,t)\ominus_{gH}f(x,t)\right)\mathrm{d}t$$

It can be written as the following equation:

$$f(x+h,t)\ominus_{gH}f(x,t)=\int_x^{x+h}\partial_{\xi gH}f(\xi,t)\mathrm{d}\xi$$

Now by replacing we have:

$$\frac{F(x+h)\ominus_{gH}F(x)}{h}=\frac{1}{h}\odot\int_c^\infty\int_x^{x+h}\partial_{\xi gH}f(\xi,t)\mathrm{d}\xi\mathrm{d}t=$$

$$=\frac{1}{h}\odot\lim_{k\rightarrow\infty}\int_c^k\int_x^{x+h}\partial_{\xi gH}f(\xi,t)\mathrm{d}\xi\mathrm{d}t$$

With uniformly continuity of $\partial_{xgH}f(x,t)$ in $[a,b]\times[c,\infty)$:

$$\forall\epsilon>0\ \exists\delta>0, |x-\xi|<\delta\Longrightarrow D_H\left(\partial_{\xi gH}f(\xi,t)\ominus_{gH}\partial_{xgH}f(x,t),0\right)<\frac{\epsilon}{k-c}$$

The following equation is true because the integral does not depend on the variable ξ and:

$$\int_c^\infty \partial_{xgH} f(x,t)\mathrm{d}t = \frac{1}{h} \odot \int_c^\infty \int_x^{x+h} \partial_{xgH} f(x,t)\mathrm{d}\xi \mathrm{d}t = \frac{1}{h} \odot \lim_{k\to\infty} \int_c^k \int_x^{x+h} \partial_{xgH} f(x,t)\mathrm{d}\xi \mathrm{d}t$$

Finally:

$$D_H\left(\frac{F(x+h)\ominus_{gH}F(x)}{h}, \int_c^\infty \partial_{xgH}f(x,t)\mathrm{d}t\right) =$$

$$= D_H\left(\lim_{k\to\infty}\int_c^k\left(\frac{1}{h}\odot\int_x^{x+h}\left(\partial_{\xi gH}f(\xi,t)\ominus_{gH}\partial_{xgH}f(x,t)\right)\mathrm{d}\xi\right)\mathrm{d}t, 0\right)$$

$$\leq \lim_{k\to\infty}\int_c^k\left(\frac{1}{h}\odot\int_x^{x+h}\left(\frac{\epsilon}{k-c}\right)d\xi\right)\mathrm{d}t = \lim_{k\to\infty}\frac{\epsilon}{k-c}(k-c) = \epsilon$$

The proof is completed.

3.9 Fourier transform operator

In this section, we briefly discuss the fuzzy Fourier transform and will show in the next chapters how this transformation can be used to solve the fuzzy partial differential equation (Gouyandeha et al., 2017).

3.9.1 Definition—Fuzzy Fourier transform

Consider the function $f: R \to \mathbb{F}_R$ is the fuzzy valued function. The fuzzy Fourier transform of *f*(*x*) denoted by $(\mathcal{F}\{f(x)\}: R \to \mathbb{F}_C)$ is given by the following integral:

$$\mathcal{F}\{f(x)\} = \frac{1}{\sqrt{2\pi}}\int_{-\infty}^{\infty} f(x)\odot e^{-iwx}\mathrm{d}x = F(w)$$

Here, $\mathbb{F}_C$ is the set of all fuzzy numbers on complex numbers.

In a classical approach, it would not be possible to use the Fourier transform for a periodic function that cannot be defined in the space of integrable functions on the interval $(-\infty, \infty)$. The use of generalized functions, however, frees us of that restriction and makes it possible to look at the Fourier transform of a periodic function. In the following example, it can be shown that the Fourier series coefficients of a periodic function are sampled values of the Fourier transform of one period of the function.

3.9.2 Example—Fuzzy Fourier transform

Let us consider the following fuzzy set valued function:

$$f(x) = \begin{cases} 0, & -\pi < x < 0 \\ c, & 0 < x < \pi \end{cases}$$

where c is a fuzzy number in level-wise form of:

$$c[r]=[c_l(r),c_u(r)]=[1+r,3-r]$$

So, in order to obtain the Fourier series of the function f, we have:

$$f_N(x)=\frac{a_0}{2}+\sum_{l=0}^{N}\left(\left(a_l\odot\cos\left(\frac{2\pi lx}{P}\right)\right)+\left(b_l\odot\sin\left(\frac{2\pi lx}{P}\right)\right)\right)$$

where:

$$a_l=\frac{2}{P}\int_{-\pi}^{\pi}f(x)\odot\cos\left(\frac{2\pi lx}{P}\right)\mathrm{d}x$$

$$b_l=\frac{2}{P}\int_{-\pi}^{\pi}f(x)\odot\sin\left(\frac{2\pi lx}{P}\right)\mathrm{d}x$$

and $P=2p$ as the period of functions and the integer N is theoretically infinite.

Now we have:

$$a_l=\frac{1}{\pi}\int_{-\pi}^{\pi}f(x)\odot\cos(lx)\mathrm{d}x=0,\ l\neq 0$$

$$b_l=\frac{1}{\pi}\int_{-\pi}^{\pi}f(x)\odot\sin(lx)\mathrm{d}x=c\odot\frac{\left(1+(-1)^{l+1}\right)}{l\pi}$$

Finally:

$$f(x)=\frac{c}{2}\oplus\frac{c}{2}\odot\sum_{l=1}^{\infty}\frac{1}{l}\left(1+(-1)^{l+1}\right)\sin(lx)$$

To test the series, in level-wise form, if you set $r=0$, it is exactly the real one.

3.9.3 Definition—Fuzzy inverse Fourier transform

If $F(w)$ is the fuzzy Fourier transform of $f(x)$, then the fuzzy inverse Fourier transform of $F(w)$ is defined as:

$$\mathcal{F}^{-1}\{F(w)\}=\frac{1}{\sqrt{2\pi}}\int_{-\infty}^{\infty}f(w)\odot e^{-iwx}\mathrm{d}w=f(x)$$

In accordance with the previous discussion on fuzzy integrals, the level-wise form of Fourier transformation is:

$$\mathcal{F}\{f(x,r)\}=\left[\frac{1}{\sqrt{2\pi}}\int_{-\infty}^{\infty}f_l(x,r)e^{-iwx}\mathrm{d}x,\ \frac{1}{\sqrt{2\pi}}\int_{-\infty}^{\infty}f_u(x,r)e^{-iwx}\mathrm{d}x\right]=F(w,r)$$

The endpoints are the real Fourier transforms of the endpoints of:

$$f(x,r)=[f_l(x,r),f_u(x,r)]$$

$$\mathcal{F}(f_l(x,r))=\frac{1}{\sqrt{2\pi}}\int_{-\infty}^{\infty} f_l(x,r)e^{-iwx}\mathrm{d}x, \mathcal{F}(f_u(x,r))=\frac{1}{\sqrt{2\pi}}\int_{-\infty}^{\infty} f_u(x,r)e^{-iwx}\mathrm{d}x$$

and:

$$\mathcal{F}\{f(x,r)\}=[\mathcal{F}(f_l(x,r)),\mathcal{F}(f_u(x,r))]$$

After defining the transformation, the main discussion is the existence of it. The next theorem shows the existence of the fuzzy Fourier transformation. To this end, the concept of a fuzzy absolutely integrable is necessary, and it is explained by the distance as follows:

$$\int_{-\infty}^{\infty} D_H(f(x),0)\mathrm{d}x<\infty$$

3.9.4 Theorem—Existence

Suppose that the fuzzy valued function $f(x)$ is fuzzy absolutely integrable on $(-\infty,\infty)$ the fuzzy Fourier transform $\mathcal{F}\{f(x)\}$ exists.

Using the distance, it will be proved, and:

$$D_H(\mathcal{F}\{f(x)\}0)=D_H\left(\frac{1}{\sqrt{2\pi}}\int_{-\infty}^{\infty} f(w)\odot e^{-iwx}\mathrm{d}w0\right)$$

$$\leq\frac{1}{\sqrt{2\pi}}\int_{-\infty}^{\infty} D_H\left(f(x)\odot e^{-iwx}0\right)\mathrm{d}x\leq\frac{1}{\sqrt{2\pi}}\int_{-\infty}^{\infty} |e^{-iwx}|D_H(f(x)0)\mathrm{d}x$$

Since $|e^{-iwx}|=1$:

$$D_H(\mathcal{F}\{f(x)\},0)\leq\frac{1}{\sqrt{2\pi}}\int_{-\infty}^{\infty} D_H(f(x),0)\mathrm{d}x<\infty$$

The proof is completed.

In the same way, we can show that if $F(w)$ is fuzzy absolutely integrable then the fuzzy inverse Fourier transform $\mathcal{F}^{-1}\{F(w)\}$ exists.

Similar to the fuzzy Laplace transforms, the fuzzy Fourier transformations are linear and this comes from the linearity property of the fuzzy Riemann integral.

Linearity means the image of a linear combination of two functions under this transformation is a linear combination of the images of those functions.

3.9.5 Theorem—Linearity property

Let us consider two functions $f(x)$ and $g(x)$ are fuzzy set valued functions of which the fuzzy Fourier transforms exist. Let a, b be any positive real numbers such that $b \geq a$. Hence, the fuzzy Fourier transform of:

$$a \odot f \oplus b \odot g \text{ and } a \odot f \ominus_{gH} b \odot g$$

exists and:

- $\mathcal{F}\{a \odot f(x) \oplus b \odot g(x)\} = a \odot \mathcal{F}\{f(x)\} \oplus b \odot \mathcal{F}\{g(x)\}$ and
- $\mathcal{F}\left\{a \odot f(x) \ominus_{gH} b \odot g(x)\right\} = a \odot \mathcal{F}\{f(x)\} \ominus_{gH} b \odot \mathcal{F}\{g(x)\}$.

Proof. According to the hypothesis we have $b \geq a > 0$ and the level-wise form, both can be proved by using level-wise form. The level-wise form of the right-hand side:

$$a \odot \mathcal{F}\{f(x,r)\} \oplus b \odot \mathcal{F}\{g(x,r)\} =$$

$$a\left[\frac{1}{\sqrt{2\pi}}\int_{-\infty}^{\infty} f_l(x,r)e^{-iwx}\mathrm{d}x, \frac{1}{\sqrt{2\pi}}\int_{-\infty}^{\infty} f_u(x,r)e^{-iwx}\mathrm{d}x\right]$$

$$+b\left[\frac{1}{\sqrt{2\pi}}\int_{-\infty}^{\infty} g_l(x,r)e^{-iwx}\mathrm{d}x, \frac{1}{\sqrt{2\pi}}\int_{-\infty}^{\infty} g_u(x,r)e^{-iwx}\mathrm{d}x\right] =$$

$$\left[\frac{a+b}{\sqrt{2\pi}}\int_{-\infty}^{\infty} (f_l(x,r)+g_l(x,r))e^{-iwx}\mathrm{d}x, \frac{a+b}{\sqrt{2\pi}}\int_{-\infty}^{\infty} (f_u(x,r)+g_u(x,r))e^{-iwx}\mathrm{d}x\right]$$

$$= \mathcal{F}\{a \odot f(x,r) \oplus b \odot g(x,r)\}$$

Now the poof is completed.

3.9.6 Theorem—Fourier transform of *gH*-derivative

Let $f(x)$ be fuzzy continuous, fuzzy absolutely integrable, and converge to zero as $|x| \rightarrow \infty$. Furthermore, it is fuzzy absolutely integrable on $(-\infty, \infty)$. Then:

$$\mathcal{F}\left\{f'_{gH}(x)\right\} = iw\mathcal{F}\{f(x)\}$$

To prove it, from the definition we have:

$$\mathcal{F}\left\{f'_{gH}(x)\right\} = \frac{1}{\sqrt{2\pi}}\int_{-\infty}^{\infty} f'_{gH}(x) \odot e^{-iwx}\mathrm{d}x$$

Using integrating by part:

$$\mathcal{F}\left\{f'_{gH}(x)\right\} = \frac{1}{\sqrt{2\pi}}\left(f(x) \odot e^{-iwx}\Big|_{-\infty}^{\infty} \ominus_{gH} \int_{-\infty}^{\infty} f(x) \odot e^{-iwx} \mathrm{d}x\right)$$

Since $f(x) \to 0$ as $|x| \to \infty$ then the proof is finished.

References

Allahviranloo, T., 2020. Uncertain information and linear systems. In: Studies in Systems, Decision and Control. vol. 254. Springer.

Allahviranloo, T., Gouyandeh, Z., Armand, A., Hasanoglu, A., 2015. On fuzzy solutions for heat equation based on generalized Hukuhara differentiability. Fuzzy Set. Syst. 265, 1–23.

Armand, A., Allahviranloo, T., Abbasbandy, S., Gouyandeh, Z., 2019. The fuzzy generalized Taylor's expansion with application in fractional differential equations. Iran. J. Fuzzy Syst. 16 (2), 57–72.

Bede, B., Gal, S.G., 2005. Generalizations of the differentiability of fuzzy-number-valued functions with applications to fuzzy differential equations. Fuzzy Set. Syst. 151, 581–599.

Gouyandeha, Z., Allahviranloob, T., Abbasbandyb, S., Armand, A., 2017. A fuzzy solution of heat equation under generalized Hukuhara differentiability by fuzzy Fourier transform. Fuzzy Set. Syst. 309, 81–97.

Liu, B., 2015. Uncertain Theory. Springer-Verlag, Berlin.

Salahshour, S., Allahviranloo, T., 2013. Applications of fuzzy Laplace transforms. Soft Comput. 17, 145–158. https://doi.org/10.1007/s00500-012-0907-4.

Stefanini, L., Bede, B., 2009. Generalized Hukuhara differentiability of interval-valued functions and interval differential equations. Nonlinear Anal. 71, 1311–1328.

Tofigh Allahviranloo, M., Ahmadi, B., 2010. Fuzzy Laplace transforms. Soft Comput. 14, 235–243. https://doi.org/10.1007/s00500-008-0397-6.

Chapter 4

Continuous numerical solutions of uncertain differential equations

4.1 Introduction

In this chapter, we first explain the differential equations under uncertainty. After discussion of uncertain differential equations, they are reviewed as fuzzy differential equations. Several types of fuzzy differential equations will be discussed: first order, high order of differentiability, and system of differential equations. Finally, the uniqueness and existence of the solutions are explained under some conditions and some illustrations of the fuzzy number solution are provided. The uncertainty in differential equations can happen in three cases:

1. The initial values of the differential equation do have uncertainties.
2. Some parameters on the right-hand side function of the model do have some uncertainties.
3. Both of the two abovementioned cases can happen.

Soft Numerical Computing in Uncertain Dynamic Systems. https://doi.org/10.1016/B978-0-12-822855-5.00004-5

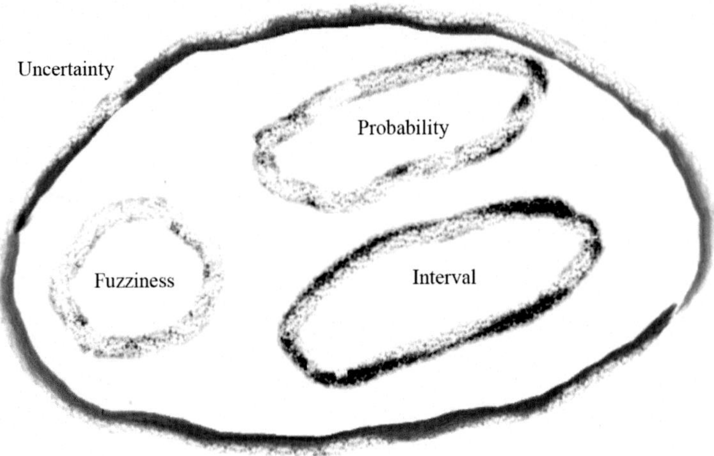

Fig. 4.1 A general illustration of uncertainty.

It should be noted that the uncertainty does contain some other ambiguities like interval-wise, probability, fuzziness, credibility, and confidence, etc. Fig. 4.1 provides a general illustration of the concept of uncertainty.

This is the main reason that we are going to consider fuzziness as a special type of uncertainty and discuss fuzzy differential equations. For more information, see Allahviranloo (2020).

4.2 Uncertain differential equations

Based on the three abovementioned cases, in each case the solution of uncertain differential equation is an uncertain process or a solution with uncertainty. The meaning of uncertain process is that the image of the process belongs to a set of all uncertain sets. The set of uncertain sets contains a measurable set such that is an event. This means it depends on a function like a distributive function corresponding to an uncertain variable, and the members do have membership degree. To define the uncertain differential equation, we need to define some other concepts about uncertainty.

4.2.1 Definition—Uncertain process as a canonical Liu process

An uncertain process C_t is said to be a canonical Liu process if any of the following is the case:

1. All the sample paths (bundle of solutions) even at the initial time $t=0$ are Lipschitz continuous. This means C_t satisfies the Lipschitz condition.

$$D_H(C_{t_i} \ominus_H C_{t_{i+1}}) \leq K|t_i - t_{i+1}|, \ K \in R^{\geq 0}, \ \forall t_i, t_{i+1} \in R$$

2. C_t has stationary and independent increments. This means that for a given $t>0$ and all $s>0$, the increments $C_{s+t} \ominus_H C_t$ are identically distributed uncertain variables and C_{t_0}, $C_{t_1} \ominus_H C_{t_0}$, $C_{t_2} \ominus_H C_{t_1}$, ..., $C_{t_{i+1}} \ominus_H C_{t_i}$ are independent uncertain variables as well.
3. Every increment $C_{s+t} \ominus_H C_t$ is a normal uncertain variable (with normal distributive function) with expected value 0 and variance t^2 whose uncertainty distribution is:

$$\Phi(x) = \left(1 + \exp\left(\frac{-\pi x}{\sqrt{3}t}\right)\right)^{-1}, \ x \in R$$

Remark. It should be noted that here the difference between two uncertain processes is exactly the Hukuhara difference $\ominus_H$ between these two in the fuzzy case. Because in the above we mention that the difference should have a distributive function, which can be a fuzzy membership function, it means that the result of the difference should be a fuzzy variable or, in this case, a fuzzy number.

Example. To complete the concept, for instance, you suppose that $C_0=0$ and C_t has stationary and independent increments and every increment $C_{s+t} \ominus_H C_t$ is a triangular or triangular fuzzy variable, like (at, bt, ct), or exponentially distributed fuzzy variable. Then C_t is an uncertain process and, especially here, is a fuzzy process.

Note. Let us consider that for a canonical or standard C_t as a C process, $\mathrm{d}t$ is an infinitesimal time interval and $\mathrm{d}C_t$ is defined as $\mathrm{d}C_t = C_{t+\mathrm{d}t} \ominus_H C_t$ and it is an uncertain or fuzzy process such that for every t and $\mathrm{d}C_t$ is a normally distributed uncertain or fuzzy variable.

4.2.2 Definition—Liu integral of an uncertain process

Let X_t be an uncertain process and C_t a canonical Liu process. For any partition on the interval $[a,b]$ like $a=t_1<t_2<\cdots<t_{n+1}=b$ and $\Delta = \max_{1\leq i\leq n} |t_{i+1} - t_i|$. Then the uncertain Liu integral of an uncertain process X_t with respect to C_t is defined in the form of a Riemann integral and:

$$\int_a^b X_t \mathrm{d}C_t = \lim_{\Delta\to 0} \oplus \sum_{i=1}^{n} X_{t_i} \odot (C_{t_{i+1}} \ominus_H C_{t_i})$$

As we mentioned before, this integral does exist if the limit exists, and this means that the result of the limit is a fuzzy number. Calling this a Liu integral comes from using his canonical process (Liu, 2015).

4.2.3 Theorem—Chain rule

Before discussing this subject, the same rule has been considered and established on the derivative of fuzzy functions.

Let us consider C_t is a canonical process and the uncertain function $X_t = h(t, C_t)$ is a continuously differentiable function. Then we have the following rule:

$$\mathrm{d}X_t = \frac{\partial h}{\partial t}(t, C_t)\mathrm{d}t \oplus \frac{\partial h}{\partial c}(t, C_t) \odot \mathrm{d}C_t, \quad c := C_t$$

To prove it, since the function $h(t, c)$ is continuously differentiable, so by using the first order Taylor expansion:

$$\Delta X_t = \frac{\partial h}{\partial t}(t, C_t) \odot \Delta t \oplus \frac{\partial h}{\partial c}(t, C_t) \odot \Delta C_t$$

Taking the integral of the two sides on interval $[0, s]$ and changing:

$$\Delta X_t \to \mathrm{d}X_t, \quad \Delta t \to \mathrm{d}t, \quad \Delta C_t \to \mathrm{d}C_t$$

then:

$$\int_0^s \mathrm{d}X_t = \int_0^s \frac{\partial h}{\partial t}(t, C_t)\mathrm{d}t \oplus \int_0^s \frac{\partial h}{\partial c}(t, C_t) \odot \mathrm{d}C_t$$

The right-hand side is:

$$\int_0^s \mathrm{d}X_t = X_s \ominus_H X_0$$

Based on the definition of H-difference, we have:

$$X_s = X_0 \oplus \int_0^s \frac{\partial h}{\partial t}(t, C_t)\mathrm{d}t \oplus \int_0^s \frac{\partial h}{\partial c}(t, C_t) \odot \mathrm{d}C_t$$

for any $s \geq 0$. So this is an uncertain function that satisfies:

$$\mathrm{d}X_t = \frac{\partial h}{\partial t}(t, C_t)\mathrm{d}t \oplus \frac{\partial h}{\partial c}(t, C_t) \odot \mathrm{d}C_t$$

For more illustration, the infinitesimal increment $\mathrm{d}C_t$ may be replaced with the derived C process like:

$$\mathrm{d}Y_t = u_t \mathrm{d}t \oplus v_t \odot \mathrm{d}C_t$$

where $u_t$and v_t are absolutely integrable uncertain or fuzzy processes, so the result can be explained as:

$$\mathrm{d}h(t, Y_t) = \frac{\partial h}{\partial t}(t, Y_t)\mathrm{d}t \oplus \frac{\partial h}{\partial c}(t, Y_t) \odot \mathrm{d}Y_t$$

By replacing, we will obtain:

$$\mathrm{d}h(t,Y_t)=\frac{\partial h}{\partial t}(t,Y_t)\mathrm{d}t\oplus\frac{\partial h}{\partial c}(t,Y_t)\odot(u_t\mathrm{d}t\oplus v_t d\odot C_t)$$

$$\begin{aligned}\mathrm{d}h(t,Y_t)&=\frac{\partial h}{\partial t}(t,Y_t)\mathrm{d}t\oplus\frac{\partial h}{\partial c}(t,Y_t)\odot u_t\mathrm{d}t\oplus\frac{\partial h}{\partial c}(t,Y_t)\odot v_t\odot\mathrm{d}C_t\\&=\frac{\partial h}{\partial c}(t,Y_t)\odot(1\oplus u_t)\mathrm{d}t\oplus\frac{\partial h}{\partial c}(t,Y_t)\odot v_t\odot\mathrm{d}C_t,\ \text{ if } u_t\geq 0\\&=\frac{\partial h}{\partial c}(t,Y_t)\odot w_t\mathrm{d}t\oplus\frac{\partial h}{\partial c}(t,Y_t)\odot v_t\odot\mathrm{d}C_t,\ \ 1\oplus u_t=w_t\end{aligned}$$

This is another form for the $\mathrm{d}X_t$ in chain rule.

As with the integration by parts method for fuzzy number valued functions, which was explained in Chapter 3, here, another version is reviewed for uncertain functions. For more information, see Liu (2015).

4.2.4 Theorem—Integration by parts

For any standard canonical process C_t and absolutely continuous function like $F(t)$, the integration can be written as:

$$\int_0^s F(t)\odot\mathrm{d}C_t=F(s)\odot C_s\ominus_H\int_0^s C_t\odot\mathrm{d}F(t)$$

The proof looks like the previous one in the field of fuzzy sets. It is enough to consider or define $h(t,C_t)=F(t)\odot C_t$ and, using the chain rule, in this case we get:

$$\mathrm{d}(F(t)\odot C_t)=C_t\odot\mathrm{d}F(t)\oplus F(t)\odot\mathrm{d}C_t$$

and easily:

$$F(s)\odot C_s=\int_0^s\mathrm{d}(F(t)\odot C_t)=\int_0^s C_t\odot\mathrm{d}F(t)\oplus\int_0^s F(t)\odot\mathrm{d}C_t$$

The proof is completed.

Now we are going to define the uncertain differential equation as an extension of fuzzy differential equation.

4.2.5 Definition—Uncertain differential equation

We discussed the following equation:

$$\mathrm{d}X_t=\frac{\partial h}{\partial t}(t,C_t)\mathrm{d}t\oplus\frac{\partial h}{\partial c}(t,C_t)\odot\mathrm{d}C_t$$

where $X_t = X_{t+dt} \ominus_H X_t$, $dC_t = C_{t+dt} \ominus_H C_t$ are uncertain processes with normally distributed function or a fuzzy process with the same characters for each t, and dt is an infinitesimal time interval. Now consider that:

$$\frac{\partial h}{\partial t}(t, C_t) := f(t, X_t), \quad \frac{\partial h}{\partial c}(t, C_t) := g(t, X_t)$$

such that f and g are some given functions. Then:

$$dX_t = f(t, X_t)dt \oplus g(t, X_t) \odot dC_t$$

is called an uncertain differential equation or fuzzy differential equation. The solution is the uncertain or fuzzy function X_t that satisfies the main differential equation.

In general, we have:

$$\begin{cases} dX_t = f(t, X_t)dt \oplus g(t, X_t) \odot dC_t \\ dX_t = X_{t+dt} \ominus_H X_t \text{ does have distributive function or membership function} \\ dC_t = C_{t+dt} \ominus_H C_t \text{ does have distributive function or membership function} \\ f(t, X_t) \text{ is an uncertain function} \\ g(t, X_t) \text{ is an uncertain function} \end{cases}$$

This uncertain differential equation is equivalent to the uncertain integral equation like:

$$X_s = X_0 \oplus \int_0^s f(t, X_t)dt \oplus \int_0^s g(t, X_t) \odot dC_t$$

Clearly, this solution is a Liu process as well.

Example. Let consider C_t is a standard canonical process and:

$$dX_t = adt \oplus b \odot dC_t$$

where a is drift coefficient and b is diffusion constant. The solution can be obtained as the following form:

$$X_t = at \oplus b \odot dC_t$$

because:

$$\int_0^s dX_t = \int_0^s adt \oplus \int_0^s b \odot dC_t$$

then:

$$X_s = as \oplus b \odot dC_s, \quad X_0 = 0$$

for any s including t. In other words:

$$X_{t+dt} = a(t+dt) \oplus b \odot dC_{t+dt}$$

and:

$$X_{t+\mathrm{d}t}\ominus_H X_t = a(t+\mathrm{d}t)\oplus b\odot \mathrm{d}C_{t+\mathrm{d}t}\ominus_H at\ominus_H b\odot \mathrm{d}C_t = a\mathrm{d}t\oplus b\odot \mathrm{d}C_t$$

This means the solutions satisfies the equation. More information can be found in Yao (2016).

4.2.6 Remark

Suppose that $f(t,X_t)$ and $g(t,X_t)$ are linear functions as follows:

$$f(t,X_t) = u_{1t}\odot X_t\oplus u_{2t},\ \ g(t,X_t) = v_{1t}\odot X_t\oplus v_{2t}$$

where $u_{1t},\ u_{2t},\ v_{1t},\ v_{2t}$ are uncertain functions. Then the uncertain differential equation:

$$\mathrm{d}X_t = (u_{1t}\odot X_t\oplus u_{2t})\mathrm{d}t\oplus(v_{1t}\odot X_t\oplus v_{2t})\odot \mathrm{d}C_t$$

does have the solution as follows:

$$X_t = U_t\odot V_t$$

where:

$$U_t = \exp\left(\left(\int_0^t u_{1s}\mathrm{d}s\oplus\int_0^t v_{1s}\odot \mathrm{d}C_s\right)\right),$$

$$V_t = X_0\oplus\int_0^t \left(u_{2s}\oslash_g U_s\right)\mathrm{d}s\oplus\int_0^t\left(v_{2s}\oslash_g U_s\right)\odot \mathrm{d}C_s$$

We suppose that the generalized divisions exist.

To show the assertion, we know that:

$$\mathrm{d}U_t = u_{1t}\odot U_t\mathrm{d}t\oplus v_{1t}\odot U_t\odot \mathrm{d}C_t,$$

$$\mathrm{d}V_t = \left(u_{2t}\oslash_g U_t\right)\mathrm{d}t\oplus\left(v_{2t}\oslash_g U_t\right)\odot \mathrm{d}C_t$$

Now, using the chain rule, we have:

$$X_t = U_t\odot V_t \Rightarrow \mathrm{d}X_t = U_t\odot \mathrm{d}V_t\oplus V_t\odot \mathrm{d}U_t$$

So, by substituting:

$$\mathrm{d}X_t = U_t\odot\left(\left(u_{2t}\oslash_g U_t\right)\mathrm{d}t\oplus\left(v_{2t}\oslash_g U_t\right)\odot \mathrm{d}C_t\right)$$

$$\oplus V_t\odot(u_{1t}\odot U_t\mathrm{d}t\oplus v_{1t}\odot U_t\odot \mathrm{d}C_t)$$

and based on the properties of the generalized division and distributive property, it can be displayed as:

$$\mathrm{d}X_t = (u_{2t}\mathrm{d}t \oplus v_{2t} \odot \mathrm{d}C_t) \oplus (u_{1t} \odot U_t \odot V_t \mathrm{d}t \oplus v_{1t} \odot U_t \odot V_t \odot \mathrm{d}C_t)$$

Subject to $u_{1t} \odot U_t \odot V_t$ and $v_{1t} \odot U_t \odot V_t$ are fuzzy numbers. Then:

$$\mathrm{d}X_t = (u_{2t}\mathrm{d}t \oplus v_{2t} \odot \mathrm{d}C_t) \oplus (u_{1t} \odot X_t \mathrm{d}t \oplus v_{1t} \odot X_t \odot \mathrm{d}C_t)$$

$$= (u_{1t} \odot X_t \oplus u_{2t})\mathrm{d}t \oplus (v_{1t} \odot X_t \oplus v_{2t}) \odot \mathrm{d}C_t$$

The proof is completed.

Example. Consider that $f(t,X_t) = u_t$ and $g(t,X_t) = v_t$ then the uncertain differential equation is linear and we have:

$$\mathrm{d}X_t = u_t \mathrm{d}t \oplus v_t \odot \mathrm{d}C_t$$

then:

$$U_t = \exp\left(\left(\int_0^t 0\mathrm{d}s \oplus \int_0^t 0 \odot \mathrm{d}C_s\right)\right) = 1$$

$$V_t = X_0 \oplus \int_0^t u_s \mathrm{d}s \oplus \int_0^t v_s \odot \mathrm{d}C_s$$

so the solution is:

$$X_t = X_0 \oplus \int_0^t u_s \mathrm{d}s \oplus \int_0^t v_s \odot \mathrm{d}C_s$$

subject to these two integrals being fuzzy number valued functions.

Considering the uncertain differential equation, the left-hand side can be transformed to a derivative of an uncertain function and the left-hand side is another uncertain function. Another type of this equation is a fuzzy differential equations (Yao, 2016).

4.3 Fuzzy differential equations

In this section, we first discuss the existence and uniqueness of the solution of these equations. To this end, we need to introduce the fuzzy differential equation.

These equations can be divided into several forms, considering the order and type of differentiability. The general forms of the models can be displayed as a system modeled by differential equations (see Fig. 4.2).

This model can be expressed in the following cases:

- One of the components of the input vector is a fuzzy number and the system does not have any fuzzy parameter. Then the output contains at least a fuzzy number component.

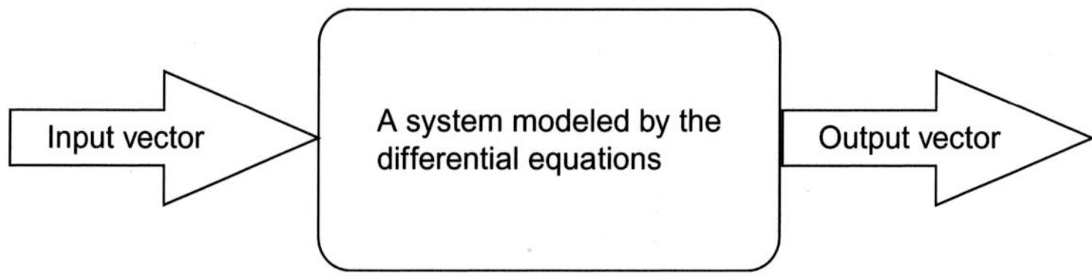

Fig. 4.2 General form of a system modeled by differential equations.

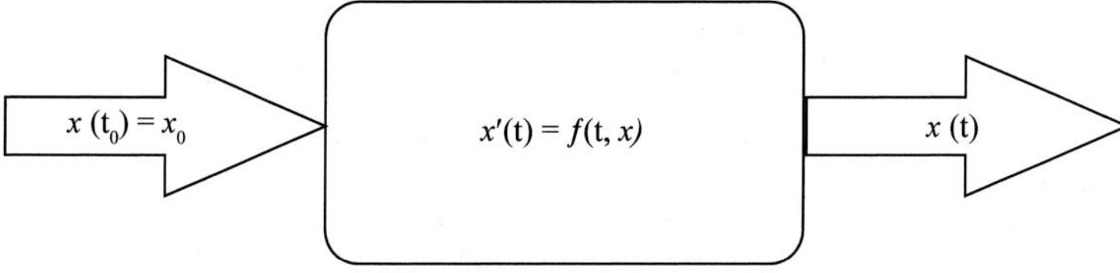

Fig. 4.3 A first order differential equation.

- The input vector is a real vector without any fuzzy components and the main system does have some fuzzy parameters. Then the output contains at least a fuzzy number component.
- One of the components of the input vector is a fuzzy number and the main system does have some fuzzy parameters. Then the output contains at least a fuzzy number component.

For the following first order fuzzy differential equation like (Fig. 4.3):

$$x'_{gH}(t) = f(tx),\ \ x(t_0) = x_0,\ \ t_0 \leq t \leq T$$

This model can be expressed in the following cases:

- The initial value x_0 is a fuzzy number and the system $f(t,x)$ does not have any fuzzy parameter. Then the output $x(t)$ is a fuzzy number.
- The initial value x_0 is a real number and the system $f(t,x)$ does have some fuzzy parameters. Then the output $x(t)$ is a fuzzy number.
- The initial value x_0 is a fuzzy number and the system $f(t,x)$ does have some fuzzy parameters. Then the output $x(t)$ is a fuzzy number.

Sometimes, the main system is a high order differential equation with several initial values (Fig. 4.4).

For this fuzzy differential equation, we also have the same cases.

Now let us consider that the initial value of the first order fuzzy differential equation is a fuzzy number:

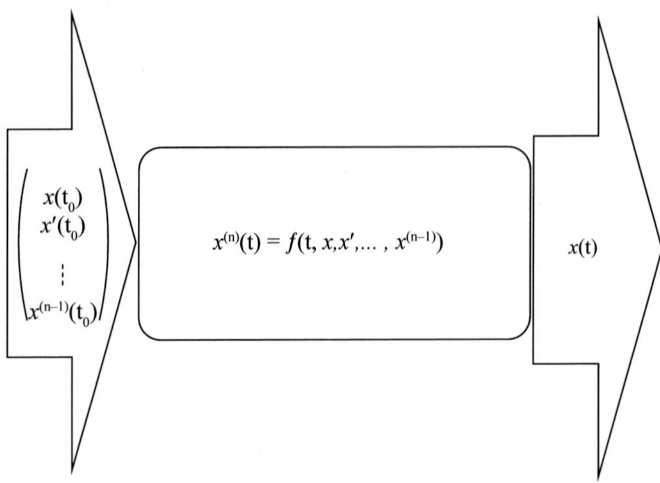

Fig. 4.4 A high order differential equation.

$$x'_{gH}(t) = f(t,x),\ \ x(t_0) = x_0 \in \mathbb{F}_R$$

The solution set of the equation can be defined as:

$$D = \{(t,x) | t_0 \le t \le T,\ \ -\infty < x < \infty,\ \ T{:=}\text{real constant}\}$$

This is called a fuzzy initial value problem.

Considering the fuzzy gH-differential of the left-hand side as:

$$x'_{gH}(t) = \lim_{h \to 0} \frac{x(t+h) \ominus_{gH} x(t)}{h}$$

subject to the gH-difference $x(t+h)\ominus_{gH}x(t)$ existing.

As we discussed in Chapter 3, the level-wise form of this fuzzy number as a derivative can be explained as the following two cases.

In case (i):

$$\left(x'_{gH}(t)\right)[r] = \left[x'_l(t,r), x'_u(t,r)\right]$$

In case (ii):

$$\left(x'_{gH}(t)\right)[r] = \left[x'_u(t,r), x'_l(t,r)\right]$$

subject to the functions $x_l'(t_0,r)$ and $x_u'(t_0,r)$ being two real valued differentiable functions with respect to t and uniformly with respect to $r \in [0,1]$. Moreover, they have all the properties of the fuzzy number valued for the fuzzy derivative.

Now if we consider the level-wise form of the equations:
In case (i), $x_{i-gH}(t,r)$ is known as $i-gH$-solution and

$$x'_{i-gH}(t,r)=\left[x'_l(t,r),x'_u(t,r)\right]=\left[f_l(t,r),f_u(t,r)\right]$$

$$\left[x_l(t_0,r),x_u(t_0,r)\right]=\left[x_{l,0}(r),x_{u,0}(r)\right]$$

In case (ii), $x_{ii-gH}(t,r)$ is known as $ii-gH$-solution and:

$$x'_{ii-gH}(t,r)=\left[x'_u(t,r),x'_l(t,r)\right]=\left[f_l(t,r),f_u(t,r)\right]$$

$$\left[x_l(t_0,r),x_u(t_0,r)\right]=\left[x_{l,0}(r),x_{u,0}(r)\right]$$

then in case (i), $x_{i-gH}(t,r)$ is known as the $i-gH$-solution and:

$$\begin{cases} x'_l(t,r)=f_l(t,r), \\ x_l(t_0,r)=x_{l,0}(r) \end{cases}$$

$$\begin{cases} x'_u(t,r)=f_u(t,r), \\ x_u(t_0,r)=x_{u,0}(r) \end{cases}$$

for $t_0\le t\le T$.

In case (ii), $x_{ii-gH}(t,r)$ is known as the $ii-gH$-solution and:

$$\begin{cases} x'_u(t,r)=f_l(t,r), \\ x_l(t_0,r)=x_{l,0}(r) \end{cases}$$

$$\begin{cases} x'_l(t,r)=f_u(t,r), \\ x_u(t_0,r)=x_{u,0}(r) \end{cases}$$

for $t_0\le t\le T$. Indeed, in case (ii) we will have the system of two real first order differential equations, and solving this system is sometimes more difficult. In both cases:

$$\begin{aligned} f_l(t,r)&:=f_l(t,x_l(t,r),x_u(t,r)) \\ &= \min\{f(t,u)|u\in[x_l(t,r),x_u(t,r)]\}, \end{aligned}$$

$$\begin{aligned} f_u(t,r)&:=f_l(t,x_l(t,r),x_u(t,r)) \\ &= \max\{f(t,u)|u\in[x_l(t,r),x_u(t,r)]\},\ 0\le r\le 1. \end{aligned}$$

Essentially, this is an embedding method for transforming the fuzzy differential equation to two real differential equations for any arbitrary but fixed level. This embeds it to the shape of a convex cone. Why a convex cone? Because every non-negative multiplier of a fuzzy number valued function belongs to the cone. Basically, to ensure that the solutions of two real differential equations are the fuzzy solution of the fuzzy original model for all levels, a characteristic theorem should be considered

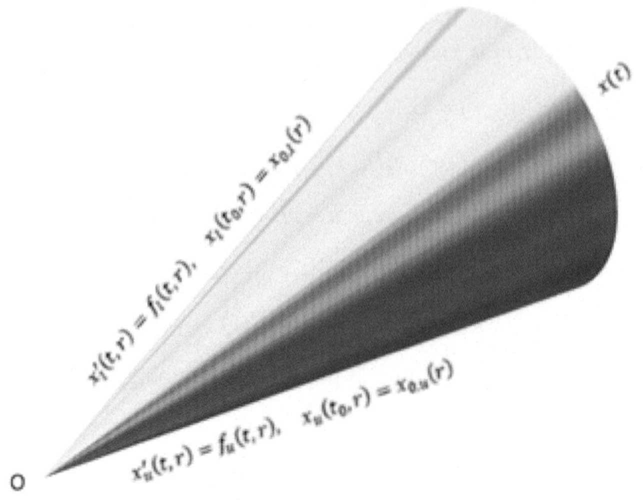

Fig. 4.5 The convex cone in embedding method.

and proved (see Fig. 4.5) (Bede and Gal, 2005; Bede et al., 2007; Gouyandeha et al., 2017; Stefanini and Bede, 2009).

To express the equivalency of the fuzzy differential equation and two real differential equations in the cone, we need to prove a characteristic theorem.

Characteristic theorem

If the function $f:[t_0,T]\times\mathbb{F}_R\rightarrow\mathbb{F}_R$ is a continuous and fuzzy number valued function and gH-differentiable that satisfies the following fuzzy differential equation:

$$x'_{gH}(t)=f(t,x),\;\; x(t_0)=x_0\in\mathbb{F}_R$$

and also suppose the following conditions:

- $f(t,x(t),r)=[f_l(t,x_l(t,r),x_u(t,r)),f_u(t,x_l(t,r),x_u(t,r))]$
- $f_l(t,x_l(t,r),x_u(t,r))$ and $f_u(t,x_l(t,r),x_u(t,r))$ are equicontinuous. it means, for any $\epsilon>0$ and any $(t,u,v)\in[t_0,T]\times R^2$ if $\|(t,u,v)-(t,u_1,v_1)\|<\delta$ we have the following inequalities for $\forall r\in[0,1]$:

$$|f_l(t,x_l(t,r),x_u(t,r))-f_l(t,x_l(t,r),x_u(t,r))|<\epsilon$$

$$|f_l(t,x_l(t,r),x_u(t,r))-f_u(t,x_l(t,r),x_u(t,r))|<\epsilon$$

$$|f_u(t,x_l(t,r),x_u(t,r))-f_l(t,x_l(t,r),x_u(t,r))|<\epsilon$$

$$|f_u(t,x_l(t,r),x_u(t,r))-f_u(t,x_l(t,r),x_u(t,r))|<\epsilon$$

- $f_l(t, x_l(t,r), x_u(t,r))$ and $f_u(t, x_l(t,r), x_u(t,r))$ are uniformly bounded on any bounded set.
- Lipschitz property. There exists $L > 0$ such that:

$$|f_l(t,u_1,v_1,r) - f_l(t,u_2,v_2,r)| < L\max\{|u_1-u_2|, |v_1-v_2|\}$$

$$|f_l(t,u_1,v_1,r) - f_u(t,u_2,v_2,r)| < L\max\{|u_1-u_2|, |v_1-v_2|\}$$

$$|f_u(t,u_1,v_1,r) - f_l(t,u_2,v_2,r)| < L\max\{|u_1-u_2|, |v_1-v_2|\}$$

$$|f_u(t,u_1,v_1,r) - f_u(t,u_2,v_2,r)| < L\max\{|u_1-u_2|, |v_1-v_2|\}$$

for any $r \in [0,1]$.

Then the fuzzy differential equation is equivalent to the each of following real differential equations in the cone:

$$\begin{cases} x_l'(t,r) = f_l(t,r) \\ x_l(t_0,r) = x_{l,0}(r) \end{cases}, \quad \begin{cases} x_u'(t,r) = f_u(t,r) \\ x_u(t_0,r) = x_{u,0}(r) \end{cases}$$

$$\begin{cases} x_u'(t,r) = f_l(t,r) \\ x_l(t_0,r) = x_{l,0}(r) \end{cases}, \quad \begin{cases} x_l'(t,r) = f_u(t,r), \\ x_u(t_0,r) = x_{u,0}(r) \end{cases}$$

Proof. The equicontinuity implies the continuity of the function f. From the Lipschitz property, it is ensured that:

$$\begin{aligned} \sup_r \max\{&|f_l(t,x_l(t,r),x_u(t,r)) - f_l(t,y_l(t,r),y_u(t,r))|, |f_u(t,x_l(t,r),x_u(t,r)) \\ &- f_u(t,y_l(t,r),y_u(t,r))|\} \\ &\le \sup_r \max\{|x_l(t,r)-y_l(t,r)|, |x_u(t,r)-y_u(t,r)|\} \end{aligned}$$

This means that:

$$D_H(f(t,x(t)), f(t,y(t))) \le D_H(x(t), y(t))$$

By the continuity of f, from the Lipschitz condition and the boundedness condition, it is concluded that the fuzzy differential equation has a unique solution and it is gH-differentiable and so the functions $x_l(t,r)$ and $x_u(t,r)$ are differentiable and it is concluded that $(x_l(t,r), x_u(t,r))$ can be the solution of one of the real equations. Conversely, let us assume that $x_l(t,r)$ and $x_u(t,r)$ are the solutions of one of the real equations for any fixed r. (They exist and are unique because of the Lipschitz condition.) On the other hand, since $x(t)$ is gH-differentiable, then $[x_l(t,r), x_u(t,r)]$ is the unique solution of the fuzzy differential equation. The proof is completed.

We start our conversation with an easy example.

Example. Consider:

$$x'_{gH}(t) = \lambda \odot x(t), \ x(t_0) = x_0 \in \mathbb{F}_R, \ \lambda \geq 0$$

This is a simple fuzzy initial value problem. It means the initial value is a fuzzy number. It is clear that this problem does have an $i-gH$ solution, and to find it we must solve the following initial value problems:

$$\begin{cases} x'_l(t,r) = \lambda x_l(t,r), \\ x_l(t_0,r) = x_{l,0}(r) \end{cases}$$

and the solution is $x_l(t) = x_{0,l}(r)\exp(\lambda t)$. Also, for the upper solution, the same procedure is used and the solution is $x_u(t) = x_{0,u}(r)\exp(\lambda t)$ for the following upper differential equation in level-wise form:

$$\begin{cases} x'_u(t,r) = \lambda x_u(t,r), \\ x_u(t_0,r) = x_{u,0}(r) \end{cases}$$

The $i-gH$-solution is:

$$x_{i-gH}(t,r) = [x_{l,0}(r)\exp(\lambda t), x_{u,0}(r)\exp(\lambda t)]$$

Note. In this example, suppose that the constant $\lambda < 0$ is negative, then the problem has the $ii-gH$ solution because the end points of the derivative in level-wise form can interchange. To find that, we have to solve a system of first order differential equations, such as:

$$\begin{cases} x'_l(t,r) = \lambda x_u(t,r), \\ x_l(t_0,r) = x_{l,0}(r) \end{cases}, \quad \begin{cases} x'_u(t,r) = \lambda x_l(t,r), \\ x_u(t_0,r) = x_{u,0}(r) \end{cases}$$

Let us consider the differential operator is noted by:

$$Dx(t) := x'(t) \text{ and } D^2x(t) := x''(t),$$

then:

$$Dx_l(t,r) = \lambda x_u(t,r), \ Dx_u(t,r) = \lambda x_l(t,r)$$

by the second order operator:

$$D^2x_l(t,r) = \lambda Dx_u(t,r) = \lambda^2 x_l(t,r),$$

$$D^2x_u(t,r) = \lambda Dx_l(t,r) = \lambda^2 x_u(t,r)$$

By using the characteristic polynomial for each equation and finding the roots, the solution of each second order differential equation will be found:

$$r^2 - \lambda^2 = 0 \Rightarrow r = -\lambda, +\lambda$$

and the solutions are:

$$x_l(t,r) = A\exp(-\lambda t) + B\exp(\lambda t)$$

$$x_u(t,r) = C\exp(-\lambda t) + D\exp(\lambda t)$$

subject to:

$$x_l(t_0,r) = x_{l,0}(r),\ \ x_u(t_0,r) = x_{u,0}(r)$$

We have two equations with four unknowns, and need two other equations. To this end, we can use the derivative of these equations as other initial values of the second order differential equations:

$$Dx_l(t,r) = (-\lambda)A\exp(-\lambda t) + \lambda B\exp(\lambda t),\ \ Dx_l(t_0,r) = \lambda x_{u,0}(r)$$

$$Dx_u(t,r) = (-\lambda)C\exp(-\lambda t) + \lambda D\exp(\lambda t),\ \ Dx_u(t_0,r) = \lambda x_{l,0}(r)$$

Now, considering the initial values $x_l(t_0,r)=x_{l,0}(r)$, $x_u(t_0,r)=x_{u,0}(r)$ in the solutions:

$$A\exp(-\lambda t_0) + B\exp(\lambda t_0) = x_{l,0}(r),\ \ C\exp(-\lambda t) + D\exp(\lambda t) = x_{u,0}(r)$$

On the other hand:

$$-A\exp(-\lambda t_0) + B\exp(\lambda t_0) = x_{u,0}(r),\ \ -C\exp(-\lambda t_0) + D\exp(\lambda t_0) = x_{l,0}(r)$$

By solving these four equations, the unknown constants A, B, C, D will be found as follows:

$$A = \exp(\lambda t_0)x_{l,0}(r) - \left(\frac{x_{l,0}(r)+x_{u,0}(r)}{2}\right),\ \ B = \exp(-\lambda t_0)\left(\frac{x_{l,0}(r)+x_{u,0}(r)}{2}\right)$$

$$C = \left(\frac{x_{l,0}(r)+x_{u,0}(r)}{2}\right) - \exp(\lambda t_0)x_{l,0}(r),\ \ D = \exp(-\lambda t_0)\left(\frac{x_{l,0}(r)+x_{u,0}(r)}{2}\right)$$

Indeed $A = -C$, $B = D$.

Finally, the solutions are:

$$x_l(t,r) = A\exp(-\lambda t) + B\exp(\lambda t)$$

$$x_u(t,r) = C\exp(-\lambda t) + D\exp(\lambda t)$$

where:

$$A = \exp(\lambda t_0)x_{l,0}(r) - \left(\frac{x_{l,0}(r)+x_{u,0}(r)}{2}\right),\ \ B = \exp(-\lambda t_0)\left(\frac{x_{l,0}(r)+x_{u,0}(r)}{2}\right)$$

$$C = \left(\frac{x_{l,0}(r)+x_{u,0}(r)}{2}\right) - \exp(\lambda t_0)x_{l,0}(r),\ \ D = \exp(-\lambda t_0)\left(\frac{x_{l,0}(r)+x_{u,0}(r)}{2}\right)$$

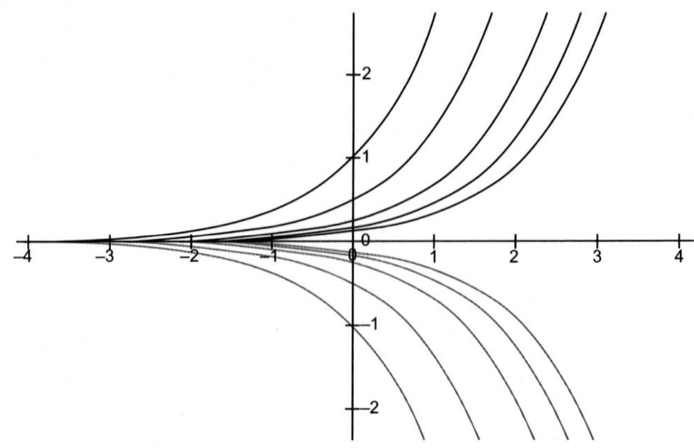

Fig. 4.6 $ii-gH$ solution for $\lambda=-1$.

It is clear that for a larger value of λ, the first term of the solutions vanishes and the second term intends infinity.

To simplify, let us suppose that $t_0=0$. In this case:

$$A=\frac{x_{l,0}(r)-x_{u,0}(r)}{2}=-C,\ B=D=\frac{x_{l,0}(r)+x_{u,0}(r)}{2}$$

For more illustration, consider $[x_{l,\,0}(r), x_{u,\,0}(r)]=[r-1, 1-r]$ and for $\lambda=-1$, we have the solutions as:

$$x_l(t,r)=(1-r)\exp(t),\ x_u(t,r)=(r-1)\exp(t)$$

The $ii-gH$ solution is (Fig. 4.6):

$$x_{ii-gH}(t,r)=[(1-r)\exp(t),(r-1)\exp(t)]$$

The $i-gH$-solution for $\lambda=1$ is (Fig. 4.7):

$$x_{i-gH}(t,r)=[(r-1)\exp(t),(1-r)\exp(t)]$$

Having analyzed the fuzzy initial value problem above, it is now time to mention the existence and uniqueness of the solutions.

4.3.1 Theorem—Existence and uniqueness

Let us assume that the following conditions hold for fuzzy differential equations:

$$x'_{gH}(t)=f(t,x),\ x(t_0)=x_0\in\mathbb{F}_R$$

1. The function $f: I_1\times I_2\to\mathbb{F}_R$ is continuous where I_1 is a closed interval, contains the initial value x_0, and I_2 is any other area such that f is bounded on it.

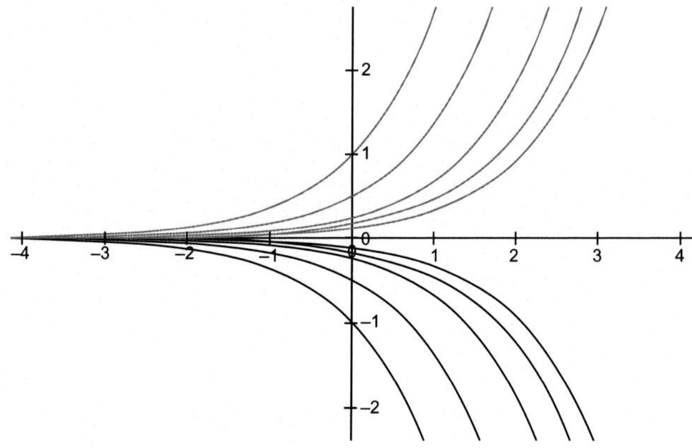

Fig. 4.7 $i-gH$ solution for $\lambda=1$.

2. The function f is bounded. This means $\exists M<0, D_H(f(t,x),0)\leq M, \forall(t,x)\in I_1\times I_2$.
3. The real function $g:I_1\times I_3\rightarrow R$ such that $g(t,u)\equiv 0$ is bounded on $I_1\times I_3$, $\exists M_1>0, 0\leq g(t,u)\leq M_1, \forall(t,u)\in I_1\times I_3$ where I_3 is another closed interval and contains u. Moreover, $g(t,u)$ is nondecreasing in u and its corresponding initial value problem:

$$u'(t)=g(t,u(t)),\ u(t_0)=0$$

has only the solution $u(t)\equiv 0$ on I_1.

4. Also:

$$D_H(f(t,x),f(t,y))\leq g(t,|x-y|),\ \forall(t,x)\forall(t,y)\in I_1\times I_2,\ x,y\in I_3$$

Then the fuzzy initial value problem has two $(i-gH)$-solution $x_{i-gH}(t)$ and $(ii-gH)$-solution $x_{ii-gH}(t)$, and the following successive iterations converge to these two solutions:

$$x_{i,n+1}(t)=x_{i,0}\oplus\int_{t_0}^{t}f(t,x_{i,n}(z))\mathrm{d}z,\ x_{i,0}(t)=x_0$$

and:

$$x_{ii,n+1}(t)=x_{ii,0}\ominus_H(-1)\odot\int_{t_0}^{t}f(tx_{ii,n}(z))\mathrm{d}z,\ x_{ii,0}(t)=x_0$$

Proof. We only prove the $(ii-gH)$ solution and other ones are similar:

$$D_H(x_{ii,n+1}(t),x_{ii,0})\leq\int_{t_0}^{t}f(t,x_{ii,n}(z),0)\mathrm{d}z$$

In addition, by the properties of Hausdorff distance, we have:

$$D_H(x_{ii,1}(t), x_{ii,0}(t)) = D_H\left(x_{ii,1}(t), x_{ii,1}(t) \oplus (-1) \odot \int_{t_0}^{t} f(t, x_{ii,0}(z))\mathrm{d}z\right)$$

$$= D_H\left(\int_{t_0}^{t} f(t, x_{ii,n}(z))\mathrm{d}z, 0\right) \leq \int_{t_0}^{t} D_H(f(t, x_{ii,n}(z)), 0)\mathrm{d}z$$

Continuing by properties of the distance again:

$$D_H(x_{ii,n+1}(t), x_{ii,n}(t)) = D_H(x_0 \ominus x_{ii,n+1}(t), x_0 \ominus x_{ii,n}(t))$$

$$= D_H\left((-1) \odot \int_{t_0}^{t} f(t, x_{ii,n}(z))\mathrm{d}z, (-1) \odot \int_{t_0}^{t} f(t, x_{ii,n-1}(z))\mathrm{d}z\right)$$

$$\leq \int_{t_0}^{t} D_H(f(t, x_{ii,n}(z)), f(t, x_{ii,n-1}(z)))\mathrm{d}z$$

For two points like t, $t+h$ around the initial value t_0, we observe that:

$$x_{ii,n+1}(t) \ominus_H x_{ii,n+1}(t+h) = (-1) \odot \int_{t}^{t+h} f(tx_{ii,n}(z))\mathrm{d}z$$

because:

$$x_{ii,n+1}(t+h) \oplus (-1) \odot \int_{t_0}^{t+h} f(t, x_{ii,n}(z))\mathrm{d}z =$$

$$= x_0 \ominus_H (-1) \odot \int_{t_0}^{t+h} f(tx_{ii,n}(z))\mathrm{d}z \oplus (-1) \odot \int_{t}^{t+h} f(tx_{ii,n}(z))\mathrm{d}z$$

$$= x_0 \ominus_H (-1) \odot \int_{t_0}^{t+h} f(tx_{ii,n}(z))\mathrm{d}z \oplus$$

$$(-1) \odot \int_{t_0}^{t+h} f(tx_{ii,n}(z))\mathrm{d}z \ominus_H (-1) \odot \int_{t_0}^{t} f(tx_{ii,n}(z))\mathrm{d}z$$

$$= x_0 \ominus_H (-1) \odot \int_{t_0}^{t} f(tx_{ii,n}(z))\mathrm{d}z = x_{ii,n+1}(t)$$

then:

$$x_{ii,n+1}(t) \ominus_H x_{ii,n+1}(t+h) = (-1) \odot \int_{t}^{t+h} f(tx_{ii,n}(z))\mathrm{d}z$$

Multiplying by $\frac{1}{-h}$ and passing to limit with $h \searrow 0$, we have:

$$\lim_{h \searrow 0} \frac{x_{ii,n+1}(t) \ominus_H x_{ii,n+1}(t+h)}{-h} = \lim_{h \searrow 0} \frac{1}{h} \odot \int_{t}^{t+h} f(tx_{ii,n}(z))\mathrm{d}z$$

Now, the distance between this derivative and the right-hand side of differential equation is:

$$D_H\left(\frac{1}{h}\odot\int_t^{t+h} f(t,x_{ii,n}(z))\mathrm{d}z, f(t,x_{ii,n}(t))\right) =$$

$$= D_H\left(\frac{1}{h}\odot\int_t^{t+h} f(t,x_{ii,n}(z))\mathrm{d}z, \frac{1}{h}\odot\int_t^{t+h} f(t,x_{ii,n}(t))\mathrm{d}z\right)$$

$$\leq \frac{1}{h}\odot\int_t^{t+h} D_H(f(t,x_{ii,n}(z)), f(t,x_{ii,n}(t)))\mathrm{d}z \leq \sup_{|z-t|\leq h} D_H(f(t,x_{ii,n}(z)), f(t,x_{ii,n}(t)))$$

Finally:

$$\lim_{h\searrow 0}\frac{x_{ii,n+1}(t)\ominus_H x_{ii,n+1}(t+h)}{-h} = f(tx_{ii,n}(t))$$

We have the same relation from the left-hand side and:

$$x_{ii,n+1}(t-h)\ominus_H x_{ii,n+1}(t) = (-1)\odot\int_{t-h}^{t} f(tx_{ii,n}(z))\mathrm{d}z$$

and:

$$\lim_{h\searrow 0}\frac{x_{ii,n+1}(t-h)\ominus_H x_{ii,n+1}(t)}{-h} = f(tx_{ii,n}(t))$$

Now we claim that the $x_{ii,\ n+1}(t)$ is the $ii-gH$ differentiable of:

$$x'_{ii,n+1} = f(t, x_{ii,n}(t))$$

for all points in a closed interval around initial value.

Now the following relations allow us to prove the existence of $ii-gH$ solution:

$$x'_{ii,n+1} = f(t,x_{ii,n}(t)),\ D_H(x_{ii,n+1}(t), x_{ii,0}) \leq \int_{t_0}^{t} f(t,x_{ii,n}(z),0)\mathrm{d}z$$

$$D_H(x_{ii,1}(t), x_{ii,0}(t)) \leq \int_{t_0}^{t} D_H(f(t,x_{ii,n}(z)),0)\mathrm{d}z$$

$$D_H(x_{ii,n+1}(t), x_{ii,n}(t)) \leq \int_{t_0}^{t} D_H(f(t,x_{ii,n}(z)), f(t,x_{ii,n-1}(z)))\mathrm{d}z$$

4.3.2 Fuzzy differential equations—Variation of constants

First of all, let us analyze a modeling problem as fuzzy differential equations in the following forms:

$$x'(t) = -\lambda\odot x(t),\ x'(t)\oplus\lambda\odot x(t) = 0$$

With fuzzy information, these two fuzzy differential equations are different. Because the zero on the right-hand side is basically a membership function, we can call it a forcing term. So:

$$x'(t) \oplus \lambda \odot x(t) = \sigma(t), \quad x'(t) = -\lambda \odot x(t) \oplus \sigma(t)$$

Now these two different differential equations with the same fuzzy initial value $x(t_0) = x_0$ do have different results.

To extend our discussion, let us consider the following fuzzy initial value problem:

$$\begin{cases} x'(t) = a(t) \odot x(t) \oplus b(t) \\ x(t_0) = x_0 \end{cases}$$

where $a(t) \in R, x_0 \in \mathbb{F}_R$ and also $b(t) \in \mathbb{F}_R \forall t$.

In general, this problem is not equivalent to the following problems:

$$\begin{cases} x'(t) \oplus (-a(t)) \odot x(t) = b(t) \\ x(t_0) = x_0 \end{cases}$$

and:

$$\begin{cases} x'(t) \oplus (-b(t)) = a(t) \odot x(t) \\ x(t_0) = x_0 \end{cases}$$

Moreover, these last two problems are not equivalent.

For instance, suppose that the first and second problems have a common solution, then we will have:

$$a(t) \odot x(t) \oplus b(t) \oplus (-a(t)) \odot x(t) = b(t)$$

This causes:

$$a(t) \odot x(t) \oplus (-a(t)) \odot x(t) = 0$$

and it shows that the solution $x(t)$ is a real valued function. This means that these two problems are not equivalent with a fuzzy (but not real) initial value.

Now the question is: which of the above problems should be considered as the fuzzy linear differential equation? Let us remark that in real-world applications, usually a dynamical system under uncertainty is modeled by fuzzification of the crisp (partial) differential equations of the system. So, depending on how we write these three crisp problems and then how we also fuzzify them, we get three different results. This is in contradiction to one of the main requirements of a model, which is that the behavior of the solution should reflect the real behavior of a system and not a particular form of an equation. These three problems are equivalent in the real case but they are inequivalent in the fuzzy case. Then we will provide their solutions at the same time and any of the solutions of these problems can be chosen in modeling the real behavior of a dynamic system under uncertainty. In the following theorem, we present the solution of fuzzy differential equations with variation of constants (Allahviranloo and Chehlabi, 2015; Bede and Gal, 2005; Bede et al., 2007; Chehlabi and Allahviranloo, 2018; Stefanini and Bede, 2009).

4.3.3 Theorem—Existence of the solution

Let consider two functions:

$$x_1(t) = \exp\left(\int_{t_0}^{t} a(z)\mathrm{d}z\right) \odot \left(x_0 \oplus \int_{t_0}^{t} b(z) \odot \exp\left(-\int_{t_0}^{z} a(u)\mathrm{d}u\right)\mathrm{d}z\right)$$

and:

$$x_2(t) = \exp\left(\int_{t_0}^{t} a(z)\mathrm{d}z\right) \odot \left(x_0 \ominus_H \int_{t_0}^{t} (-b(z)) \odot \exp\left(-\int_{t_0}^{z} a(u)\mathrm{d}u\right)\mathrm{d}z\right)$$

provided that the H-difference:

$$x_0 \ominus_H \int_{t_0}^{t} (-b(z)) \odot \exp\left(-\int_{t_0}^{z} a(u)\mathrm{d}u\right)\mathrm{d}z$$

exists. Now the conditions for the solutions are listed as follows:

1. If $a(t) > 0 \, \forall t \in (t_0, t_1)$ then x_1 (i)-differentiable and it is a solution of:

$$\begin{cases} x'(t) = a(t) \odot x(t) \oplus b(t) \\ x(t_0) = x_0 \end{cases}$$

in the same interval.

2. If $a(t) < 0$ and the H-difference $x_0 \ominus \int_{t_0}^{t} (-b(z)) \odot \exp(-\int_{t_0}^{z} a(u)\mathrm{d}u)\mathrm{d}z$ exists for $\forall t \in (t_0, t_1)$ then x_1 (ii)-differentiable and it is a solution of the same problem in (1) in the same interval.
3. If $a(t) < 0$ and $x_1(t+h) \ominus_H x_1(t)$ and $x_1(t) \ominus_H x_1(t-h)$ exist for $\forall t \in (t_0, t_1)$ then x_1 (i)-differentiable and it is a solution of:

$$\begin{cases} x'(t) \oplus (-a(t)) \odot x(t) = b(t) \\ x(t_0) = x_0 \end{cases}$$

in the same interval.

4. If $a(t) < 0$ and $x_1(t) \ominus_H x_1(t-h)$ and $x_1(t-h) \ominus_H x_1(t)$ exist for $\forall t \in (t_0, t_1)$ then x_1 (ii)-differentiable and it is a solution of:

$$\begin{cases} x'(t)\oplus(-b(t)) = a(t)\odot x(t) \\ x(t_0) = x_0 \end{cases}$$

in the same interval.

5. If $a(t)>0$ and the H-difference $x_0\ominus\int_{t_0}^{t}(-b(z))\odot\exp(-\int_{t_0}^{z}a(u)du)dz$ exists for $\forall t\in(t_0,t_1)$ and $x_2(t+h)\ominus_H x_2(t)$ and $x_2(t)\ominus_H x_2(t-h)$ exist for $\forall t\in(t_0,t_1)$ then x_2 is the solution of:

$$\begin{cases} x'(t)\oplus(-b(t)) = a(t)\odot x(t) \\ x(t_0) = x_0 \end{cases}$$

in the same interval.

6. If $a(t)>0$ and the H-difference $x_0\ominus\int_{t_0}^{t}(-b(z))\odot\exp(-\int_{t_0}^{z}a(u)du)dz$ for $\forall t\in(t_0, t_1)$ and $x_2(t-h)\ominus_H x_2(t)$ and $x_2(t-h)\ominus_H x_2(t)$ exist for $\forall t\in(t_0,t_1)$ then x_2 is the solution of:

$$\begin{cases} x'(t)\oplus(-a(t))\odot x(t) = b(t) \\ x(t_0) = x_0 \end{cases}$$

in the same interval (Allahviranloo et al., 2015; Gouyandeha et al., 2017).

Proof. First suppose that the following term of x_1 is (i)-differentiable and its differential is:

$$\left(x_0\oplus\int_{t_0}^{t} b(z)\odot\exp\left(-\int_{t_0}^{z} a(u)du\right)dz\right)' = b(t)\odot\exp\left(-\int_{t_0}^{t} a(u)du\right)$$

and also in the second term of x_2 if the H-difference:

$$x_0\ominus\int_{t_0}^{t}(-b(z))\odot\exp\left(-\int_{t_0}^{z} a(u)du\right)dz$$

exists then x_2 is (ii)-differentiable and:

$$\left(x_0\ominus\int_{t_0}^{t}(-b(z))\odot\exp\left(-\int_{t_0}^{z} a(u)du\right)dz\right)' = b(t)\odot\exp\left(-\int_{t_0}^{t} a(u)du\right)$$

Case 1. Now in the first case, $a(t)>0\,\forall t\in(t_0,t_1)$ then $\exp(\int_{t_0}^{t}a(z)dz)$ is positive as well. So, $(\exp(\int_{t_0}^{t}a(z)dz))' = a(t)>0$.

Now:

$$x_1'(t) = \left(\exp\left(\int_{t_0}^{t} a(z)dz\right)\odot\left(x_0\oplus\int_{t_0}^{t} b(z)\odot\exp\left(-\int_{t_0}^{z} a(u)du\right)dz\right)\right)'$$

$$= \left(\exp\left(\left(\int_{t_0}^{t} a(z)\mathrm{d}z\right)\right)'\odot\left(x_0\oplus\int_{t_0}^{t} b(z)\odot\exp\left(-\int_{t_0}^{z} a(u)\mathrm{d}u\right)\mathrm{d}z\right)\right.$$

$$\oplus\left(x_0\oplus\int_{t_0}^{t} b(z)\odot\exp\left(-\int_{t_0}^{z} a(u)\mathrm{d}u\right)dz\right)'\odot\exp\left(\int_{t_0}^{t} a(z)\mathrm{d}z\right)$$

By substituting:

$$x_1'(t) = a(t)\odot\left(x_0\oplus\int_{t_0}^{t} b(z)\odot\exp\left(-\int_{t_0}^{z} a(u)\mathrm{d}u\right)\mathrm{d}z\right)$$

$$\oplus\left(b(t)\odot\exp\left(-\int_{t_0}^{t} a(u)\mathrm{d}u\right)\right)\odot\exp\left(\int_{t_0}^{t} a(z)\mathrm{d}z\right) = a(t)\odot x_1(t)\oplus b(t)$$

this means that x_1 is the solution of:

$$\begin{cases} x'(t) = a(t)\odot x(t)\oplus b(t) \\ x(t_0) = x_0 \end{cases}$$

Case 2. For this section, we have $a(t) < 0\,\forall t\in(t_0,t_1)$ then $\exp(\int_{t_0}^{t} a(z)\mathrm{d}z)$ is again positive. So $(\exp(\int_{t_0}^{t} a(z)\mathrm{d}z))' = a(t) < 0$.

Now x_2' is (ii)-differentiable and stated as:

$$x_2'(t) = \left(\exp\left(\int_{t_0}^{t} a(z)\mathrm{d}z\right)\odot\left(x_0\ominus_H\int_{t_0}^{t} (-b(z))\odot\exp\left(-\int_{t_0}^{z} a(u)\mathrm{d}u\right)\mathrm{d}z\right)\right)'$$

$$= \left(\exp\left(\int_{t_0}^{t} a(z)\mathrm{d}z\right)\right)'\odot\left(x_0\ominus_H\int_{t_0}^{t} (-b(z))\odot\exp\left(-\int_{t_0}^{z} a(u)\mathrm{d}u\right)\mathrm{d}z\right)$$

$$\oplus\exp\left(\int_{t_0}^{t} a(z)\mathrm{d}z\right)\odot\left(x_0\ominus_H\int_{t_0}^{t} (-b(z))\odot\exp\left(-\int_{t_0}^{z} a(u)\mathrm{d}u\right)\mathrm{d}z\right)'$$

By substituting:

$$x_2'(t) = a(t)\odot\left(x_0\ominus_H\int_{t_0}^{t} (-b(z))\odot\exp\left(-\int_{t_0}^{z} a(u)\mathrm{d}u\right)\mathrm{d}z\right)$$

$$\oplus\exp\left(\int_{t_0}^{t} a(z)\mathrm{d}z\right)\odot\left(b(t)\odot\exp\left(-\int_{t_0}^{t} a(u)\mathrm{d}u\right)\right) = a(t)\odot x_1(t)\oplus b(t)$$

Case 3. We have $a(t) < 0$ and $x_1(t+h)\ominus_H x_1(t)$ and $x_1(t)\ominus_H x_1(t-h)$ exist for $\forall t\in(t_0,t_1)$ and:

$$x_1'(t) = \left(\exp\left(\int_{t_0}^{t} a(z)\mathrm{dz}\right) \odot \left(x_0 \oplus \int_{t_0}^{t} b(z) \odot \exp\left(-\int_{t_0}^{z} a(u)\mathrm{d}u\right)\mathrm{dz}\right)\right)'$$

$$= \exp\left(\int_{t_0}^{t} a(z)\mathrm{dz}\right) \odot \left(x_0 \oplus \int_{t_0}^{t} b(z) \odot \exp\left(-\int_{t_0}^{z} a(u)\mathrm{d}u\right)\mathrm{dz}\right)'$$

$$\ominus_H \left((-1)\exp\left(\int_{t_0}^{t} a(z)\mathrm{dz}\right)\right)' \odot \left(x_0 \oplus \int_{t_0}^{t} b(z) \odot \exp\left(-\int_{t_0}^{z} a(u)\mathrm{d}u\right)\mathrm{dz}\right)$$

By substituting:

$$x_1'(t) = \exp\left(\int_{t_0}^{t} a(z)\mathrm{dz}\right) \odot \left(b(t) \odot \exp\left(-\int_{t_0}^{t} a(u)\mathrm{d}u\right)\right)$$

$$\ominus_H (-1)a(t) \odot \left(x_0 \oplus \int_{t_0}^{t} b(z) \odot \exp\left(-\int_{t_0}^{z} a(u)\mathrm{d}u\right)\mathrm{dz}\right)$$

$$= b(t) \ominus_H (-1)a(t) \odot x_1(t)$$

this means that x_1 is the solution of:

$$\begin{cases} x'(t) \oplus (-a(t)) \odot x(t) = b(t) \\ x(t_0) = x_0 \end{cases}$$

The other cases can be proved similarly.

Example. Let us consider an example to investigate the behavior of the (ii)-differentiable solution. Suppose that:

$$x'(t) = (-1) \odot x(t) \oplus t, \ x(0) = (1, 2, 3)$$

The initial value in level-wise form is as $x(0,r) = [r+1, 3-r]$. Since the following H-difference exists:

$$x_0 \ominus_H \int_0^t (-z) \odot \exp(z)\mathrm{dz}, \ \forall t \in (0, \infty)$$

the (ii)-solution x_2 is:

$$x_2(t) = \exp(-t) \odot \left((1, 2, 3) \ominus_H \int_0^t (-z) \odot \exp(z)\mathrm{dz}\right)$$

$$= (t-1) \odot 1 \oplus (2\exp(-t), 3\exp(-t), 4\exp(-t))$$

where 1 is a singleton fuzzy number. For more illustration, the level-wise form of $(2\exp(-t), 3\exp(-t), 4\exp(-t))$ is $[r+2, 4-r]\exp(-t)$.

The (ii)-differentiable solution is:

$$x_2(t) = [(t+r+1)\exp(-t), (t+5-r)\exp(-t)]$$

For instance, in the levels $r=0$, 1, the solutions are plotted in Fig. 4.8.

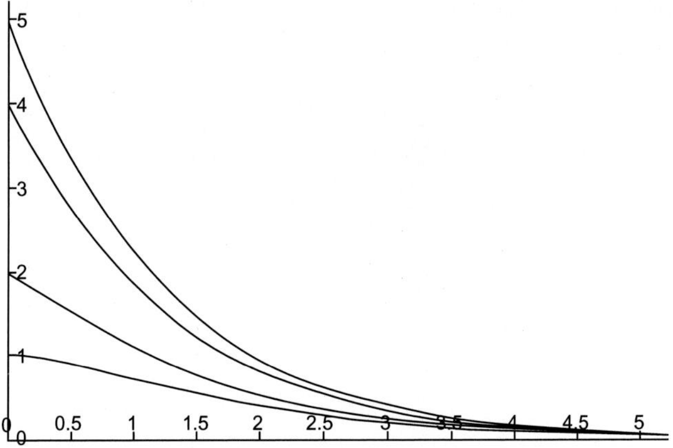

Fig. 4.8 The solution in the levels $r=0$, 1.

Based on our discussions in Chapter 3 on the diameter of (ii)-solutions, the same conclusion is seen here, and the diameter is decreasing.

In the next section, we shall discuss the function entitled length function. After defining this operator, we will use this concept for solving and analyzing fuzzy differential equations with first order.

4.3.4 Length function

First of all, the length, sometimes called the diameter, of the fuzzy function was used for analysis of type 1 and type 2 solutions of fuzzy differential equations. Indeed, in Chapter 3 we pointed out the diameter and here it is explained more with the title of length function.

4.3.4.1 Definition—Length function

The length function of a fuzzy number is a function $l:\mathbb{F}_R \to S$ in which S is the space of continuous functions like $f:[0,1]\to R$. The length is defined as:

$$l(A,r)=A_u(r)-A_l(r),\ \ \forall r\in[0,1].$$

4.3.4.2 Nonlinear property

Generally, the length function is not a linear function and this means that if $\lambda,\mu\in R$ and $A,B\in\mathbb{F}_R$ and $C=\lambda\odot A\oplus\mu\odot B$, $D=\lambda\odot A\ominus_H\mu\odot B$ subject to the H-difference exists, then:

$$l(C,r)=|\lambda|l(A,r)+|\mu|l(B,r)$$

$$l(D,r)=|\lambda|l(A,r)-|\mu|l(B,r)$$

The proof is easy to check and it is expressed by the signs of the coefficients. Let us here consider that $\lambda \geq 0$ and $\mu < 0$. In this case, for all levels $r \in [0,1]$, we have:

$$\begin{aligned} l(C,r) &= l(\lambda \odot A \oplus \mu \odot B, r) \\ &= (\lambda \odot A \oplus \mu \odot B)_u(r) - (\lambda \odot A \oplus \mu \odot B)_l(r) \\ &= \lambda A_u(r) + \mu B_l(r) - \lambda A_l(r) - \mu B_u(r) \\ &= \lambda (A_u(r) - A_l(r)) + (-\mu)(B_u(r) - B_l(r)) \\ &= \lambda l(A,r) + (-\mu) l(B,r) \\ l(D,r) &= l(\lambda \odot A \ominus_H \mu \odot B, r) \\ &= (\lambda \odot A \ominus_H \mu \odot B)_u(r) - (\lambda \odot A \ominus_H \mu \odot B)_l(r) \\ &= \lambda A_u(r) - \mu B_l(r) - \lambda A_l(r) + \mu B_u(r) \\ &= \lambda (A_u(r) - A_l(r)) - (-\mu)(B_u(r) - B_l(r)) \\ &= \lambda l(A,r) - (-\mu) l(B,r) \end{aligned}$$

The proof for the other cases of the coefficients are similar to this case (Allahviranloo and Chehlabi, 2015; Chehlabi and Allahviranloo, 2018).

4.3.4.3 *Theorem—Nonlinear property of fuzzy functions*

Suppose that $f, g : [a,b] \to \mathbb{F}_R$ are two fuzzy number valued functions. In addition, consider that for all $t \in [a,b]$ the function $w(t) = \lambda \odot f(t) \ominus_H \mu \odot g(t)$ exists for some values of $\lambda, \mu \in R$. Moreover, suppose that $l(f(t),r)$ and $l(g(t),r)$ are linearly independent. Then:

$$l(f(t),r) - l(g(t),r) = l(\lambda \odot f(t) \ominus_H \mu \odot g(t), r) \Leftrightarrow |\lambda| = |\mu| = 1$$

Proof. For the first case, consider $w(t) = \lambda \odot f(t) \ominus_H \mu \odot g(t)$ exists subject to $|\lambda| = |\mu| = 1$. Now from the previous theorem it is clear that:

$$l(w(t),r) = l(f(t),r) - l(g(t),r), \quad \forall t \in [a,b] \forall r \in [0,1]$$

Conversely, if $l(w(t),r) = l(f(t),r) - l(g(t),r)$ and from the previous theorem:

$$l(w(t),r) = l(\lambda \odot f(t) \ominus_H \mu \odot g(t), r) = |\lambda| l(f(t),r) - |\mu| l(g(t),r)$$

so:

$$|\lambda| l(f(t),r) - |\mu| l(g(t),r) = l(f(t),r) - l(g(t),r)$$

and:

$$(|\lambda| - 1) l(f(t),r) - (|\mu| - 1) l(g(t),r) = 0$$

based on the linearly independent property, $|\lambda| = |\mu| = 1$. The proof is completed.

4.3.4.4 Remark

As a conclusion, let us consider the function:

$$h(t) = \lambda' \odot f(t) \oplus \mu' \odot g(t), \lambda', \mu' \in R, \ \lambda' \cdot \mu' \neq 0.$$

If $l(f(t), r)$ and $l(g(t), r)$ are linear independent with respect to t, r then it is clear that $l(h(t), r)$ and $l(g(t), r)$ are linear independent with respect to t, r as well. If we suppose that $\lambda' \neq 0$ then we have:

$$f(t) = \lambda \odot h(t) \ominus_H \mu \odot g(t), \ \lambda = \frac{1}{\lambda'}, \ \mu = \frac{1}{\mu'}$$

Therefore, based on the previous theorem, we find:

$$l(f(t), r) = l(h(t), r) - l(g(t), r) \Leftrightarrow |\lambda| = |\mu| = 1$$

This means:

$$l(h(t), r) = l(f(t), r) + l(g(t), r), \ \Leftrightarrow |\lambda'| = |\mu'| = 1$$

for all $\forall t \in [a, b] \forall r \in [0, 1]$.

4.3.4.5 Remark—Differentiability and length

Based on the discussion in Chapter 3, the type of the gH-differentiability can be described by the length operator. As we mentioned before, in the case of type (ii) gH-differentiability the length of the function is decreasing and in type (i) gH-differentiability the length of the function is increasing.

Because for a fuzzy number valued function like $f(t)$ the gH-derivative at the point t in the level-wise form is defined as:

$$f'_{gH}(t) = \lim_{h \to 0} \frac{f(t+h) \ominus_{gH} f(t)}{h}$$

subject to the gH-difference $f(t+h) \ominus_{gH} f(t)$ existing, the necessary and sufficient conditions for the gH-differentiability fuzzy number valued function $f(t)$ are:

In case (i):

$$\left(f'_{i-gH}(t)\right)[r] = \left[f'_l(t, r), f'_u(t, r)\right]$$

In case (ii):

$$\left(f'_{ii-gH}(t)\right)[r] = \left[f'_u(t, r), f'_l(t, r)\right]$$

subject to the functions $f_l'(t, r)$ and $f_u'(t, r)$ being two real valued differentiable functions with respect to t and uniformly with respect to $r \in [0, 1]$. It should be noted that both the functions are left continuous on $r \in (0, 1]$ and right continuous at $r = 0$. Moreover, the following conditions should be satisfied:

- The function $f_l'(t,r)$ is nondecreasing and the function $f_u'(t,r)$ is nonincreasing as functions of r and, $f_l'(t,r) \leq f_u'(t,r)$. Or,
- The function $f_l'(t,r)$ is nonincreasing and the function $f_u'(t,r)$ is nondecreasing as functions of r and, $f_u'(t,r) \leq f_l'(t,r)$.

And:

$$\left(f'_{gH}(t)\right)[r] = \left[\min\{f_l'(t,r), f_u'(t,r)\}, \max\{f_l'(t,r), f_u'(t,r)\}\right]$$

Now, considering the definition of the length function and the abovementioned level-wise form of two types of derivative, we have:

In case (i):

$$l\left(f'_{i-gH}(t), r\right) = f_u'(t,r) - f_l'(t,r) = l'(f(t), r)$$

In case (ii):

$$l\left(f'_{ii-gH}(t), r\right) = f_l'(t,r) - f_u'(t,r) = -l'(f(t), r)$$

4.3.4.6 Theorem—Nonlinear property of fuzzy functions

Let us consider $f, g : (a, b) \to \mathbb{F}_R$ to be differentiable in the sense of (i) or (ii) on (a,b). If the H-difference $\lambda \odot f(t) \ominus_H \mu \odot g(t)$ exists for any $t \in (a,b)$ and some $\lambda, \mu \in R$ then the function $w(t) = \lambda \odot f(t) \ominus_H \mu \odot g(t)$ is differentiable and precisely:

1. If f is $i-gH$ differentiable and g is $ii-gH$ differentiable then w is $i-gH$ differentiable.
2. If f is $ii-gH$ differentiable and g is $i-gH$ differentiable then w is $ii-gH$ differentiable.

In addition, we have:

$$w'_{gH}(t) = \lambda \odot f'_{gH}(t) \ominus_H \mu \odot g'_{gH}(t), \ \forall t \in (a, b)$$

Proof. For simplicity, we set $F(t) = \lambda \odot f(t)$ and $G(t) = \mu \odot g(t)$. It is clear that the functions F and G are differentiable in the same differentiability concept of functions f and g, respectively, and also:

$$F'_{gH}(t) = \lambda \odot f'_{gH}(t), \ G'_{gH}(t) = \mu \odot g'_{gH}(t).$$

Using the length function, we have:

$$l(w(t)) = l(F(t) \ominus_H G(t)) = l(F(t)) - l(G(t))$$

Then in case (1), we have:

$$l\left(F'_{i-gH}(t)\right)=l'(F(t)),\ l\left(G'_{i-gH}(t)\right)=-l'(G(t))$$

and:

$$l'(w(t))=l'(F(t))-l'(G(t))=l\left(F'_{i-gH}(t)\right)+l\left(G'_{i-gH}(t)\right)\geq 0$$

which means w is $i-gH$ differentiable and:

$$\begin{aligned} w'(t,r)=(F\ominus_H G)'(t,r) &= \left[F'_l(t,r)-G'_l(t,r), F'_u(t,r)-G'_u(t,r)\right] \\ &= F'(t,r)-G'(t,r) \end{aligned}$$

In case (2), we have:

$$l\left(F'_{i-gH}(t)\right)=-l'(F(t)),\ l\left(G'_{i-gH}(t)\right)=l'(G(t))$$

and:

$$l'(w(t))=l'(F(t))-l'(G(t))=-\left(l\left(F'_{i-gH}(t)\right)+l\left(G'_{i-gH}(t)\right)\right)\leq 0$$

which means w is $ii-gH$ differentiable and:

$$\begin{aligned} w'(t,r)=(F\ominus_H G)'(t,r) &= \left[F'_u(t,r)-G'_u(t,r), F'_l(t,r)-G'_l(t,r)\right] \\ &= F'(t,r)-G'(t,r) \end{aligned}$$

The proof is now completed.

4.3.4.7 *Theorem—Derivative of integral equation*

Let $f:(a,b)\rightarrow \mathbb{F}_R$ be continuous. In this case:

a. The function $F(t)=\int_a^t f(x)\mathrm{d}x$ is $i-gH$ differentiable and $F'(t)=f(t)$.
b. The function $G(t)=\int_t^b f(x)\mathrm{d}x$ is $ii-gH$ differentiable and $G'(t)=(-1)\odot f(t)$.

Proof. We directly go through the details of the case (b). Using the length function:

$$l(G(t),r)=\int_t^b f_u(x,r)\mathrm{d}x-\int_t^b f_l(x,r)\mathrm{d}x,\ \forall r\in[0,1]$$

so:

$$G_u(t,r)-G_l(t,r)=\int_t^b f_u(x,r)\mathrm{d}x-\int_t^b f_l(x,r)\mathrm{d}x$$

then:

$$G_u(t,r) - \int_t^b f_u(x,r)\mathrm{d}x = G_l(t,r) - \int_t^b f_l(x,r)\mathrm{d}x$$

Taking the differential, we get:

$$G_u'(t,r) + f_u(t,r) = G_l'(t,r) + f_l(t,r)$$

Finally:

$$G_u'(t,r) - G_l'(t,r) = f_l(t,r) - f_u(t,r) = -l(f(t,r)) \le 0$$

This means that the function $G(t)$ is $ii - gH$ differentiable and:

$$l(G'(t)) = -l(f(t))$$

and about its derivative we can handle it by level-wise form:

$$[G_l(t,r), G_u(t,r)] = \left[\int_t^b f_l(x,r)\mathrm{d}x,\ \int_t^b f_u(x,r)\mathrm{d}x\right]$$

then:

$$G_{gH}'(t,r) = \left[\min\left\{G_l'(t,r), G_u'(t,r)\right\}, \max\left\{G_l'(t,r), G_u'(t,r)\right\}\right]$$

where:

$$G_l'(t,r) = -f_l(t,r),\ \ G_u'(t,r) = -f_u(t,r)$$

Finally:

$$G_{gH}'(t,r) = [-f_u(t,r),\ -f_l(t,r)] = -[f_l(t,r), f_u(t,r)] = -f(t,r)$$

for all $\forall r \in [0,1]$. Then:

$$G_{gH}'(t) = (-1) \odot f(t)$$

4.3.4.8 *The length function—Fuzzy differential equations*

In this section, we consider the first order fuzzy differential equations with a fuzzy initial value. Now let us assume the following fuzzy differential equation:

$$x_{gH}'(t) = f(tx(t)),\ \ t \in I = [0\infty],\ x(0) = x_0$$

where $f: I \times \mathbb{F}_R \to \mathbb{F}_R$ is a continuous fuzzy number valued mapping and $x_0 \in \mathbb{F}_R$ is a fuzzy number.

As we mentioned in Chapter 3, if we want to consider two types of differentiability, we will have:

Case (i): $i-gH$

$$x(t)=x_0\oplus FR\int_a^t x'_{i-gH}(s)\mathrm{d}s=x_0\oplus FR\int_a^t f(s,x(s))\mathrm{d}s$$

Case (ii): $ii-gH$

$$x(t)=x_0\ominus_H(-1)FR\int_a^t x'_{ii-gH}(s)\mathrm{d}s=x_0\ominus_H(-1)FR\int_a^t f(sx(s))\mathrm{d}s$$

If the gH-differentiable fuzzy function $x:I\rightarrow\mathbb{F}_R$ is $i-gH$ ($ii-gH$) differentiable and satisfies the fuzzy differential equation, it is called $i-$solution (ii-solution) of the fuzzy differential equation, respectively.

Here again let us consider the following fuzzy initial value problem with variation of constants:

$$\begin{cases} x'_{gH}(t)=a(t)\odot x(t)\oplus b(t) \\ x(t_0)=x_0 \end{cases}$$

where $a(t)\in R, x_0\in\mathbb{F}_R$ and also $b(t)\in\mathbb{F}_R\forall t$. Using the length function, we will find all the existing solutions of the above problem.

In the first case, we consider $a(t)<0$ with ii-differentiability. This means that:

$$x'_{ii-gH}(t,r)=\left[x'_l(t,r),x'_u(t,r)\right]$$

and

$$l(x'(t),r)=l(a(t)x(t),r)+l(b(t),r)$$

It is concluded:

$$x'_l(t,r)-x'_u(t,r)=a(t)x_l(t,r)-a(t)x_u(t,r)+l(b(t),r)$$

then:

$$x'_l(t,r)-a(t)x_l(t,r)=x'_u(t,r)-a(t)x_u(t,r)+l(b(t),r)$$

Let us consider the right-hand side as:

$$\mu(t)=x'_u(t,r)-a(t)x_u(t,r)+l(b(t),r)$$

Finally we have:

$$x'_l(t,r)-a(t)x_l(t,r)=\mu(t)$$

To find the solution, we use integrating factor method and:

$$x_l(t,r)=\exp\left(\int_{t_0}^t a(u)\mathrm{d}u\right)\cdot\left(x_{l,0}(r)+\int_{t_0}^t \mu(u)\cdot\exp\left(-\int_{t_0}^u a(v)\mathrm{d}v\right)\mathrm{d}u\right)$$

Using the value of μ, we can find:

$$x_l(t,r)=\exp\left(\int_{t_0}^{t}a(u)\mathrm{d}u\right)\left(x_{l,0}(r)+x_u(t,r)\exp\left(-\int_{t_0}^{t}a(u)\mathrm{d}u\right)-x_{u,0}(r)\right.$$
$$\left.+\int_{t_0}^{t}l(b(u),r)\cdot\exp\left(-\int_{t_0}^{u}a(v)\mathrm{d}v\right)\mathrm{d}u\right)$$

The same procedure can be applied for the upper level-wise solution. Then:

$$x_u'(t,r)-a(t)x_u(t,r)=x_l'(t,r)-a(t)x_l(t,r)-l(b(t),r)$$

Let us consider the right-hand side as:

$$\mu(t)=x_l'(t,r)-a(t)x_l(t,r)-l(b(t),r)$$

Finally, we have:

$$x_u'(t,r)-a(t)x_u(t,r)=\mu(t)$$

To find the solution, we use the integrating factor method and:

$$x_u(t,r)=\exp\left(\int_{t_0}^{t}a(u)\mathrm{d}u\right)\cdot\left(x_{u,0}(r)+\int_{t_0}^{t}\mu(u)\cdot\exp\left(-\int_{t_0}^{u}a(v)\mathrm{d}v\right)\mathrm{d}u\right)$$

Using the value of μ, we can find:

$$x_u(t,r)=\exp\left(\int_{t_0}^{t}a(u)\mathrm{d}u\right)\left(x_{u,0}(r)+x_l(t,r)\exp\left(-\int_{t_0}^{t}a(u)\mathrm{d}u\right)-x_{l,0}(r)\right.$$
$$\left.-\int_{t_0}^{t}l(b(u),r)\cdot\exp\left(-\int_{t_0}^{u}a(v)\mathrm{d}v\right)\mathrm{d}u\right)$$

Now we can obtain the length of $x(t)$ as:

$$l(x(t),r)=x_u(t,r)-x_l(t,r)$$
$$=\exp\left(\int_{t_0}^{t}a(u)\mathrm{d}u\right)\left(l(x_0,r)-l\left(\int_{t_0}^{t}b(u)\cdot\exp\left(-\int_{t_0}^{u}a(v)\mathrm{d}v\right)\mathrm{d}u\right)\right)$$

The function $b(u)\cdot\exp(-\int_{t_0}^{u}a(v)\mathrm{d}v)\mathrm{d}u$ is continuous and its integral $\int_{t_0}^{t}b(u)\cdot\exp(-\int_{t_0}^{u}a(v)\mathrm{d}v)\mathrm{d}u$ is $i-gH$ differentiable, therefore its length $l(\int_{t_0}^{t}b(u)\cdot\exp(-\int_{t_0}^{u}a(v)\mathrm{d}v)\mathrm{d}u)$ is an increasing function of variable t. On the other hand $l(x_0,r)$ is not dependent on t, so the solution is described by the initial value x_0 and $\int_{t_0}^{t}b(u)\cdot\exp(-\int_{t_0}^{u}a(v)\mathrm{d}v)\mathrm{d}u$ as follows:

$$x(t)=\exp\left(\int_{t_0}^{t}a(u)\mathrm{d}u\right)\cdot\left(\lambda\odot x_0\ominus_H\mu\odot\int_{t_0}^{t}b(u)\cdot\exp\left(-\int_{t_0}^{u}a(v)\mathrm{d}v\right)\mathrm{d}u\right)$$

where $\lambda,\ \mu\in\{-1,1\}$ and the H-difference exists.

Note that all integrations are fuzzy Riemann integrations.

Now we can explain the solution with different values of λ and μ such that the different solutions satisfy all the conditions of theorem 4.3.3. For instance, based on initial conditions $\lambda=1$ then for any $\mu\in\{-1,1\}$ with $a(t)<0$. So considering the second case of theorem 4.3.3, the solution function $x(t)$ is $ii-gH$ differentiable.

In general, we can consider the following equation:

$$x'(t)=a(t)\odot x(t)\oplus(-\mu)\odot b(t)$$

such that for two values of $\mu\in\{-1,1\}$ we have different equations with different solutions as follows:

$$x(t)=\exp\left(\int_{t_0}^{t}a(u)\mathrm{d}u\right)\cdot\left(x_0\oplus\mu\odot\int_{t_0}^{t}b(u)\cdot\exp\left(-\int_{t_0}^{u}a(v)\mathrm{d}v\right)\mathrm{d}u\right)$$

$$x(t)=\exp\left(\int_{t_0}^{t}a(u)\mathrm{d}u\right)\cdot\left(x_0\ominus_H\mu\odot\int_{t_0}^{t}b(u)\cdot\exp\left(-\int_{t_0}^{u}a(v)\mathrm{d}v\right)\mathrm{d}u\right)$$

In case $\mu=-1$

$$x(t)=\exp\left(\int_{t_0}^{t}a(u)\mathrm{d}u\right)\cdot\left(x_0\ominus_H(-1)\odot\int_{t_0}^{t}b(u)\cdot\exp\left(-\int_{t_0}^{u}a(v)\mathrm{d}v\right)\mathrm{d}u\right)$$

is $ii-gH$ differentiable.

Generally, by choosing the different values of μ and two signs of $a(t)$, we will find the same solutions in theorem 4.3.3 (Allahviranloo and Chehlabi, 2015; Chehlabi and Allahviranloo, 2018).

Example. Let us assume the linear first order differential equation:

$$x'(t)=\sin t\odot x(t)\oplus\gamma\odot\sin t, x(0)=\gamma=(-1,0,1), t\in[0,2\pi]$$

In this example, $a(t)=\sin t$, which is nonnegative in $t\in[0,\pi]$ and it is nonpositive in the interval $t\in[\pi,2\pi]$. Then the $i-$solution can be obtained by the following functions with respect to the sign of $a(t)$:

$$x_{i,1}(t)=\exp\left(\int_0^t\sin u\mathrm{d}u\right)\odot\left(\gamma\oplus\int_0^t\sin u\exp\left(-\int_0^u\sin v\mathrm{d}v\right)\odot\gamma\mathrm{d}u\right)$$
$$=(2\exp(1-\cos t)-1)\odot\gamma,\ 0\le t\le\pi.$$

Figs. 4.9 and 4.10 are the i-solutions of the problem.and:

$$x_{i,2}(t)=\exp\left(-\int_\pi^t\sin u\mathrm{d}u\right)\odot\left(\gamma\oplus\int_\pi^t\sin u\exp\left(\int_\pi^u\sin v\mathrm{d}v\right)\odot\gamma\mathrm{d}u\right)$$
$$=(2\exp(1+\cos t)-1)\odot\gamma,\ \pi\le t\le 2\pi.$$

is the i-solution $x_{i,\,2}$ in $\pi\le t\le 2\pi$.

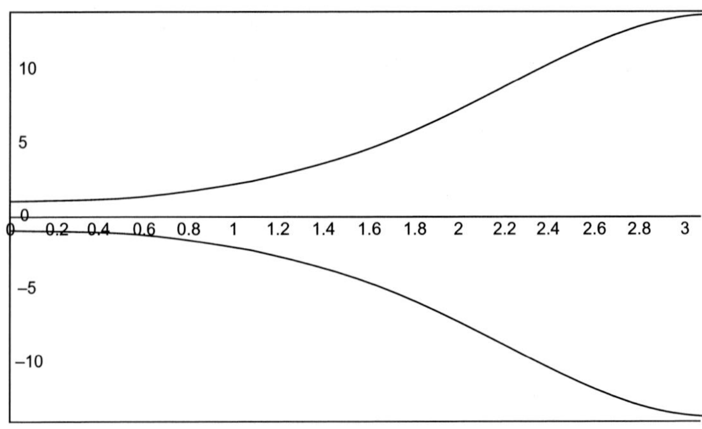

Fig. 4.9 The *i*-solution $x_{i,\ 1}$ in $0 \leq t \leq \pi$.

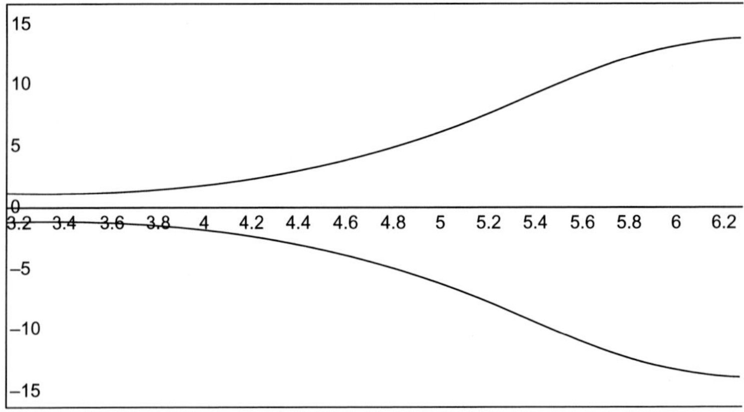

Fig. 4.10 the *i*-solution $x_{i,\ 2}$ in $\pi \leq t \leq 2\pi$.

To find the *ii*-solutions with assumption of the existence of the following *H*-differences:

$$\gamma \ominus_H (-1) \odot \int_0^t \sin u \exp\left(\int_0^u \sin v dv\right) \odot \gamma du$$

and:

$$\gamma \ominus_H (-1) \odot \int_\pi^t \sin u \exp\left(-\int_0^u \sin v dv\right) \odot \gamma du$$

we have *ii*-solution with $a(t) \geq 0$:

$$x_{ii,1}(t) = \exp\left(\int_0^t \sin u du\right) \odot \left(\gamma \ominus_H (-1) \odot \int_0^t \sin u \exp\left(\int_0^u \sin v dv\right) \odot \gamma du\right)$$

$$= (2\exp(\cos t - 1) - 1) \odot \gamma, \ 0 \leq t \leq \arccos(1 - \ln 2).$$

We have *ii*-solution with $a(t) < 0$,

$$x_{ii,2}(t) = \exp\left(\int_0^t \sin u du\right) \odot \left(\gamma \ominus_H (-1) \odot \int_0^t \sin u \exp\left(-\int_0^u \sin v dv\right) \odot \gamma du\right)$$

$$= (2\exp(-\cos t - 1) - 1) \odot \gamma, \ \pi \leq t \leq 2\pi - \arccos(\ln 2 - 1).$$

These are shown in Figs. 4.11 and 4.12, respectively.

Example. Now let us consider other cases of the previous example as the following forms:

$$x'(t) \oplus (-1) \sin t \odot x(t) = \gamma \odot \sin t, \ x(0) = \gamma = (-1, 0, 1), t \in [0, 2\pi]$$

$$x'(t) \oplus (-1) \gamma \odot \sin t = \sin t \odot x(t), \ x(0) = \gamma = (-1, 0, 1), t \in [0, 2\pi]$$

Again, using the solution formula, we can find the solution in the form of:

$$x(t) = \exp\left(\int_0^t \sin u du\right) \cdot \left(\gamma \oplus \mu \odot \int_0^t \gamma \odot \sin u \cdot \exp\left(-\int_0^u \sin v dv\right) du\right)$$

$$x(t) = \exp\left(\int_0^t \sin u du\right) \cdot \left(\gamma \ominus_H \mu \odot \int_0^t \gamma \odot \sin u \cdot \exp\left(-\int_0^u \sin v dv\right) du\right)$$

such that $\mu \in \{-1, 1\}$.

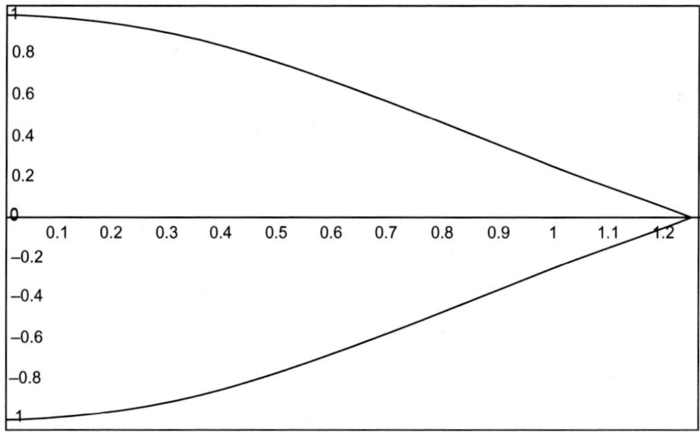

Fig. 4.11 *ii*-solution $x_{ii,\,1}(t)$ with $a(t) \geq 0$.

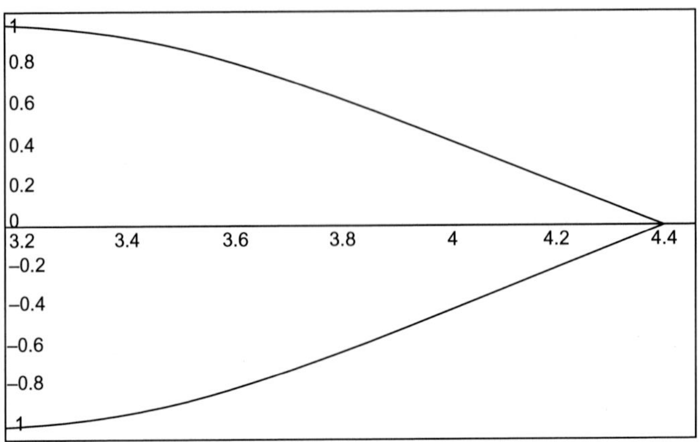

Fig. 4.12 *ii*-solution $x_{ii,\,1}(t)$ with $a(t) < 0$.

Example. Consider the following equation:

$$x'(t) \oplus (-1) \odot (1, 2, 3)t = x(t), \ \ x(0) = (2, 3, 4)$$

Here $a(t) = 1$ and:

$$h(t) = (2, 3, 4) \oplus \int_0^t b(u) \cdot \exp\left(-\int_0^u \mathrm{d}v\right) \mathrm{d}u$$

$$= (2, 3, 4) \oplus \int_0^t (u, 2u, 3u) \odot \exp(-u) \mathrm{d}u$$

$$= (2, 3, 4) \oplus \int_0^t (u \cdot \cosh(u) - 3u \cdot \sinh(u), 2u \cdot \cosh(u) - 2u \cdot \sinh(u), 3u \cdot \cosh(u) - u \cdot \sinh(u)) \mathrm{d}u$$

and the *ii*-solution is in $(0, \ln 2)$,

$$x_{ii,1}(t) = h(t) \cosh t \ominus_H (-1) h(t) \sinh t$$

$$x_{i,1}(t) = (5\exp(t) - 2\exp(-t) - 3t - 1, 5\exp(t) - 2t - 2, 5\exp(t) - 2\exp(-t) - t - 3)$$

Fig. 4.13 shows the *ii*-solution of the example.

4.3.5 Fuzzy differential equations—Laplace transform

In this section, we are going to use the Laplace transform to solve the fuzzy differential equations. It is clear that these transformations can be used for any order of differentiability of equations. First, we apply them for the first order and then we will use them for the high order of differentiability.

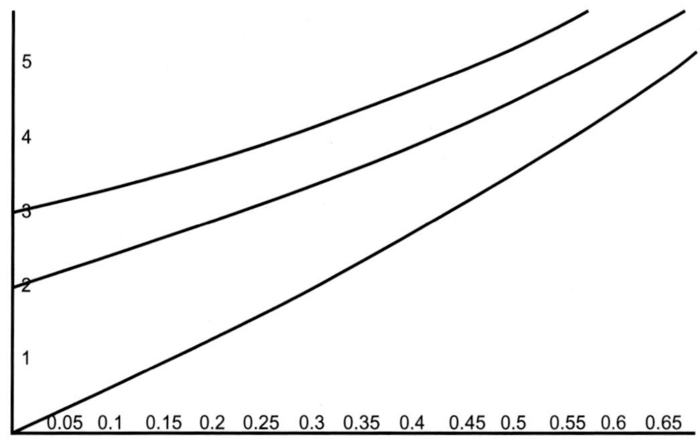

Fig. 4.13 *ii*-solution of the example.

Now consider the following differential equation with fuzzy initial value problem:

$$x'_{gH}(t) = f(tx(t)),\ x(0) = x_0 \in \mathbb{F}_R,\ t \in [0T],\ T \in R$$

where the function $f : R^{\geq 0} \times \mathbb{F}_R \to \mathbb{F}_R$ is a continuous fuzzy mapping. The strategy is using the Laplace transform for two sides of the differential equation and initial value. So:

$$L\left(x'_{gH}(t)\right) = L(f(tx(t)))$$

In the solving procedure, we should consider the types of differentiability. So the cases are as follows:

Case 1. Suppose that the solution function is *i*-differentiable so the derivative in level-wise form is:

$$x'_{i-gH}(t,r) = \left[x'_l(t,r), x'_u(t,r)\right]$$

Also suppose that x and x' are continuous fuzzy number valued on $[0, \infty)$, then:

$$L\left(x'_{gH}(t)\right) = s \odot L(x(t)) \ominus_H x(0)$$

then:

$$l\left(x'_{i-gH}(t,r)\right) = \left[l\left(x'_l(t,r)\right), l\left(x'_u(t,r)\right)\right]$$

and:

$$l\left(x'_u(t,r)\right) = l(f_u(t,x(t),r)) = sl(x_u(t,r)) - x_u(0,r),$$

$$l\left(x'_l(t,r)\right) = l(f_l(t,x(t),r)) = sl(x_l(t,r)) - x_l(0,r).$$

By assuming the right-hand sides as new functions and using the inverse Laplace, the solutions can be found as:

$$l\left(x_l'(t,r)\right) = H_1(s,r),\ \ l\left(x_u'(t,r)\right) = K_1(s,r)$$

then:

$$x_l'(t,r) = l^{-1}(H_1(s,r)),\ \ x_u'(t,r) = l^{-1}(K_1(s,r))$$

Case 2. Suppose that the solution function is *ii*-differentiable so the derivative in level-wise form is:

$$x'_{ii-gH}(t,r) = \left[x_u'(t,r), x_l'(t,r)\right]$$

Also suppose that x and x' are continuous fuzzy number valued on $[0,\infty)$, then:

$$L(x'(t)) = (-1) \odot x(0) \ominus_H (-s \odot L(x(t)))$$

then:

$$l\left(x'_{ii-gH}(t,r)\right) = \left[l\left(x_u'(t,r)\right), l\left(x_l'(t,r)\right)\right]$$

and:

$$l\left(x_u'(t,r)\right) = l(f_l(t,x(t),r)) = -x_u(0,r) - (-sl(x_u(t,r))),$$

$$l\left(x_l'(t,r)\right) = l(f_u(t,x(t),r)) = -x_l(0,r) - (-sl(x_l(t,r))).$$

By assuming the right-hand sides as new functions and using the inverse Laplace, the solutions can be found as:

$$l\left(x_l'(t,r)\right) = H_2(s,r),\ \ l\left(x_u'(t,r)\right) = K_2(s,r)$$

then:

$$x_l'(t,r) = l^{-1}(H_2(s,r)),\ \ x_u'(t,r) = l^{-1}(K_2(s,r))$$

Example. Consider the following fuzzy initial value problem:

$$x'_{gH}(t) = -x(t),\ \ x(0) = x_0 \in \mathbb{F}_R,\ \ t \in [0T],\ \ T \in R$$

Now:

$$L\left(x'_{gH}(t)\right) = L(-x(t)),$$

$$L\left(x'_{gH}(t)\right) = \int_0^{\infty} e^{-st} \odot x'_{gH}(t)\mathrm{d}t$$

In the case of *i*-differentiability we have:

$$L\left(x'_{gH}(t)\right) = s \odot L(x(t)) \ominus_H x(0)$$

therefore:

$$-L(x(t)) = s \odot L(x(t)) \ominus_H x(0)$$

since:

$$-x(t,r) = f(t, x(t), r) = [-x_u(t,r), -x_l(t,r)]$$

Then in level-wise form:

$$-l(x_u(t,r)) = sl(x_l(t,r)) - x_l(0,r)$$

$$-l(x_l(t,r)) = sl(x_u(t,r)) - x_u(0,r)$$

or:

$$l(x_u(t,r)) = x_l(0,r) - sl(x_l(t,r))$$

$$l(x_l(t,r)) = x_u(0,r) - sl(x_u(t,r))$$

Hence the solution can be found as:

$$l(x_l(t,r)) = x_l(0,r)\left(\frac{s}{s^2-1}\right) - x_u(0,r)\left(\frac{-1}{s^2-1}\right)$$

$$l(x_u(t,r)) = x_u(0,r)\left(\frac{s}{s^2-1}\right) - x_l(0,r)\left(\frac{-1}{s^2-1}\right)$$

Thus:

$$x_l(t,r) = x_l(0,r)l^{-1}\left(\frac{s}{s^2-1}\right) - x_u(0,r)l^{-1}\left(\frac{-1}{s^2-1}\right)$$

$$x_u(t,r) = x_u(0,r)l^{-1}\left(\frac{s}{s^2-1}\right) - x_l(0,r)l^{-1}\left(\frac{-1}{s^2-1}\right)$$

Finally:

$$x_l(t,r) = \exp(-t)\left(\frac{x_l(0,r)+x_u(0,r)}{2}\right) + \exp(t)\left(\frac{x_l(0,r)-x_u(0,r)}{2}\right)$$

$$x_u(t,r) = \exp(-t)\left(\frac{x_l(0,r)+x_u(0,r)}{2}\right) + \exp(t)\left(\frac{x_u(0,r)-x_l(0,r)}{2}\right)$$

It should be noted that these solutions are the same as the solutions plotted in Figs. 4.5 and 4.6.

In the case of *ii*-differentiability, we have:

$$L\left(x'_{gH}(t)\right) = (-1) \odot x(0) \ominus_H (-s \odot L(x(t)))$$

therefore:

$$-L(x(t)) = (-1) \odot x(0) \ominus_H (-s \odot L(x(t)))$$

since:

$$-x(t,r)=f(t,x(t),r)=[-x_u(t,r),\ -x_l(t,r)]$$

Then in level-wise form:

$$-l(x_l(t,r))=sl(x_l(t,r))-x_l(0,r)$$

$$-l(x_u(t,r))=sl(x_u(t,r))-x_u(0,r)$$

or:

$$l(x_l(t,r))=x_l(0,r)-sl(x_l(t,r))$$

$$l(x_u(t,r))=x_u(0,r)-sl(x_u(t,r))$$

Hence the solution can be found as:

$$l(x_l(t,r))=x_l(0,r)\left(\frac{1}{1+s}\right)$$

$$l(x_u(t,r))=x_u(0,r)\left(\frac{1}{1+s}\right)$$

Thus:

$$x_l(t,r)=x_l(0,r)l^{-1}\left(\frac{1}{1+s}\right)$$

$$x_u(t,r)=x_u(0,r)l^{-1}\left(\frac{1}{1+s}\right)$$

Finally:

$$x_l(t,r)=\exp(-t)x_l(0,r)$$

$$x_u(t,r)=\exp(-t)x_u(0,r)$$

Now the solution can be displayed for any initial value (Salahshour and Allahviranloo, 2013; Tofigh Allahviranloo, 2010).

4.3.6 Fuzzy differential equations—Second order

In this section, we will discuss the fuzzy differential equations with order of two differentiability. The higher orders do have a similar procedure to discuss. It is apparent that in these equations we should explain the type of differentiability for any order of differentials separately. Now consider the following general form of second order fuzzy differential equations with fuzzy initial values:

$$\begin{cases} x''_{gH}(t) = f\left(t, x(t), x'_{gH}(t)\right) \\ x(t_0) = x_0 \in \mathbb{F}_R \\ x^{gH\prime}(t_0) = x_1 \in \mathbb{F}_R \end{cases}$$

where the function $f : [0, T] \times \mathbb{F}_R \times \mathbb{F}_R \to \mathbb{F}_R$ is a fuzzy number valued and continuous function. Here the functions x, x', x'' are also fuzzy number valued and continuous ones. It is clear that in accordance with the type of differentiability we will have several differential equations. The function x can be in two forms of differentiability and also x', for more illustration, in the level-wise form for $0 \le r \le 1$.

Case I. Both functions x, x' are $i-gH$ differentiable:

$$x'_{i-gH}(t,r) = \left[x'_l(t,r), x'_u(t,r)\right], \ x''_{i-gH}(t,r) = \left[x''_l(t,r), x''_u(t,r)\right]$$

$$\begin{cases} x''_{i-gH}(t,r) = f\left(t, x(t), x'_{i-gH}(t), r\right) \\ x(t_0,r) = x_0(r) \\ x'_{i-gH}(t_0,r) = x_1(r) \end{cases}$$

and:

$$\begin{cases} x''_l(t,r) = f_l\left(t, x(t), x'_{i-gH}(t), r\right) \\ x_l(t_0,r) = x_{l,0} \\ x'_l(t_0,r) = x_{l,1} \end{cases} \quad \begin{cases} x''_u(t,r) = f_u\left(t, x(t), x'_{i-gH}(t), r\right) \\ x_u(t_0,r) = x_{u,0} \\ x'_u(t_0,r) = x_{u,1} \end{cases}$$

where:

$$f_l\left(t, x(t), x'_{i-gH}(t), r\right) = \min\left\{f(t,u,u') \mid u \in [x_l(t,r), x_u(t,r)], u' \in \left[x'_l(t,r), x'_u(t,r)\right]\right\}$$

$$f_u\left(t, x(t), x'_{i-gH}(t), r\right) = \max\left\{f(t,u,u') \mid u \in [x_l(t,r), x_u(t,r)], u' \in \left[x'_l(t,r), x'_u(t,r)\right]\right\}$$

Case II. The function x is $i-gH$ differentiable and $x'$is $ii-gH$ differentiable:

$$x'_{i-gH}(t,r) = \left[x'_l(t,r), x'_u(t,r)\right], \ x''_{ii-gH}(t,r) = \left[x''_u(t,r), x''_l(t,r)\right]$$

$$\begin{cases} x''_{ii-gH}(t,r) = f\left(t, x(t), x'_{i-gH}(t), r\right) \\ x(t_0,r) = x_0(r) \\ x'_{i-gH}(t_0,r) = x_1(r) \end{cases}$$

and:

$$\begin{cases} x''_u(t,r) = f_l\left(t, x(t), x'_{i-gH}(t), r\right) \\ x_l(t_0,r) = x_{l,0} \\ x'_l(t_0,r) = x_{l,1} \end{cases} \quad \begin{cases} x''_l(t,r) = f_u\left(t, x(t), x'_{i-gH}(t), r\right) \\ x_u(t_0,r) = x_{u,0} \\ x'_u(t_0,r) = x_{u,1} \end{cases}$$

Case III. The function x is $ii-gH$ differentiable and $x'$is $i-gH$ differentiable:

$$x'_{ii-gH}(t,r)=\left[x'_u(t,r),x'_l(t,r)\right],\ x''_{i-gH}(t,r)=\left[x''_l(t,r),x''_u(t,r)\right]$$

$$\begin{cases} x''_{i-gH}(t,r)=f\left(t,x(t),x'_{ii-gH}(t),r\right) \\ x(t_0,r)=x_0(r) \\ x'_{ii-gH}(t_0,r)=x_1(r) \end{cases}$$

and:

$$\begin{cases} x''_l(t,r)=f_l\left(t,x(t),x'_{ii-gH}(t),r\right) \\ x_l(t_0,r)=x_{l,0} \\ x'_u(t_0,r)=x_{u,1} \end{cases} \quad \begin{cases} x''_u(t,r)=f_u\left(t,x(t),x'_{ii-gH}(t),r\right) \\ x_u(t_0,r)=x_{u,0} \\ x'_l(t_0,r)=x_{l,1} \end{cases}$$

Case IV. Both functions x, x' are $ii-gH$ differentiable:

$$x'_{ii-gH}(t,r)=\left[x'_u(t,r),x'_l(t,r)\right],\ x''_{ii-gH}(t,r)=\left[x''_u(t,r),x''_l(t,r)\right]$$

$$\begin{cases} x''_{ii-gH}(t,r)=f\left(t,x(t),x'_{ii-gH}(t),r\right) \\ x(t_0,r)=x_0(r) \\ x'_{ii-gH}(t_0,r)=x_1(r) \end{cases}$$

and:

$$\begin{cases} x''_u(t,r)=f_l\left(t,x(t),x'_{ii-gH}(t),r\right) \\ x_l(t_0,r)=x_{l,0} \\ x'_u(t_0,r)=x_{l,1} \end{cases} \quad \begin{cases} x''_l(t,r)=f_u\left(t,x(t),x'_{ii-gH}(t),r\right) \\ x_u(t_0,r)=x_{u,0} \\ x'_l(t_0,r)=x_{u,1} \end{cases}$$

Now based on the characteristic theorem, the equations in each of the five cases are equivalent to:

$$\begin{cases} x''_{gH}(t)=f\left(t,x(t),x'_{gH}(t)\right) \\ x(t_0)=x_0\in\mathbb{F}_R \\ x'_{gH}(t_0)=x_1\in\mathbb{F}_R \end{cases}$$

As we know, the problems in these cases can be solved by any method, and here we are going to use the Laplace transform to solve them.

Example. Consider the following second order fuzzy differential equation:

$$\begin{cases} x''_{gH}(tr)=\sigma_0(r),\sigma_0(r)=[r-1\ \ 1-r] \\ x(0r)=\sigma_0(r) \\ x'_{gH}(0r)=\sigma_0(r) \end{cases}$$

Case I. Both functions x, x' are $i-gH$ differentiable:

$$L\left(x''_{gH}(t)\right)=s^2\odot L(x(t))\ominus_H s\odot x(0)\ominus_H x(0)=L(\sigma_0)=\frac{\sigma_0}{s}$$

and:

$$s^2 \odot L(x(t)) \ominus_H s \odot \sigma_0 \ominus_H \sigma_0 = \frac{\sigma_0}{s}$$

in the level-wise form:

$$s^2 l(x_l(t,r)) - s\sigma_{l,0}(r) - \sigma_{l,0}(r) = \frac{\sigma_{l,0}(r)}{s}$$

$$s^2 l(x_u(t,r)) - s\sigma_{u,0}(r) - \sigma_{u,0}(r) = \frac{\sigma_{u,0}(r)}{s}$$

Finally, after using inverse Laplace:

$$x_l(t,r) = \sigma_{l,0}(r)\left(\frac{s^2}{2} + s + 1\right)$$

$$x_u(t,r) = \sigma_{u,0}(r)\left(\frac{s^2}{2} + s + 1\right)$$

where $\sigma_{l,\ 0}(r) = r - 1$ and $\sigma_{u,\ 0}(r) = 1 - r$.

Case II. The function x is $i-gH$ differentiable and $x'$is $ii-gH$ differentiable. Then by taking the Laplace transform and:

$$L\left(x''_{gH}(t)\right) = (-1) \odot x'_{gH}(0) \ominus_H (-s^2) \odot L(x(t)) \oplus (-1)s \odot x(0)$$

$$L\left(x''_{gH}(t)\right) = (-1) \odot \sigma_0 \ominus_H (-s^2) \odot L(x(t)) \oplus (-1)s \odot \sigma_0 = \frac{\sigma_0}{s}$$

in the level-wise form we will have:

$$-\sigma_{u,0}(r) + s^2 l(x_u(t,r)) - s\sigma_{u,0}(r) = \frac{\sigma_{l,0}(r)}{s}$$

$$-\sigma_{l,0}(r) + s^2 l(x_l(t,r)) - s\sigma_{l,0}(r) = \frac{\sigma_{u,0}(r)}{s}$$

Finally, after using inverse Laplace, the solutions are defined on $(0, 1)$ as follows:

$$x_l(t,r) = \sigma_{l,0}(r)\left(-\frac{s^2}{2} + s + 1\right)$$

$$x_u(t,r) = \sigma_{u,0}(r)\left(-\frac{s^2}{2} + s + 1\right)$$

Case III. The function x is $ii-gH$ differentiable and $x'$is $i-gH$ differentiable:

$$L\left(x''_{gH}(t)\right) = -s \odot \sigma_0 \ominus_H (-s^2) \odot L(x(t)) \ominus_H \sigma_0$$

$$-s \odot \sigma_0 \ominus_H (-s^2) \odot L(x(t)) \ominus_H \sigma_0 = \frac{\sigma_0}{s}$$

In the level-wise form we will have:

$$-s\sigma_{u,0}(r)+s^2 l(x_u(t,r))-\sigma_{l,0}(r)=\frac{\sigma_{l,0}(r)}{s}$$

$$-s\sigma_{l,0}(r)+s^2 l(x_l(t,r))-\sigma_{u,0}(r)=\frac{\sigma_{u,0}(r)}{s}$$

Finally, after using inverse Laplace, the solutions are defined on $(0,\sqrt{3}-1)$ as follows:

$$x_l(t,r)=\sigma_{l,0}(r)\left(-\frac{s^2}{2}-s+1\right)$$

$$x_u(t,r)=\sigma_{u,0}(r)\left(-\frac{s^2}{2}-s+1\right)$$

Case IV. Both functions x, x' are $ii-gH$ differentiable:

$$L\left(x''_{gH}(t)\right)=s^2\odot L(x(t))\ominus_H s\odot x(0)\oplus(-1)\odot x'_{gH}(0)$$

and we have:

$$s^2\odot L(x(t))\ominus_H s\odot\sigma_0\oplus(-1)\odot\sigma_0=\frac{\sigma_0}{s}$$

In the level-wise form we will have:

$$s^2 l(x_l(t,r))-s\sigma_{l,0}(r)-\sigma_{u,0}(r)=\frac{\sigma_{l,0}(r)}{s}$$

$$s^2 l(x_u(t,r))-s\sigma_{u,0}(r)-\sigma_{l,0}(r)=\frac{\sigma_{u,0}(r)}{s}$$

Finally, after using inverse Laplace, the solutions are defined on $(0,1)$ as follows:

$$x_l(t,r)=\sigma_{l,0}(r)\left(\frac{s^2}{2}-s+1\right)$$

$$x_u(t,r)=\sigma_{u,0}(r)\left(\frac{s^2}{2}-s+1\right)$$

Example. Consider the following second order fuzzy differential equation:

$$\begin{cases} x''_{gH}(tr)\oplus x(t)=\sigma_0(r),\sigma_0(r)=[r2-r] \\ x(0r)=[r-1\ \ 1-r] \\ x'_{gH}(0r)=[r-1\ \ 1-r] \end{cases}$$

Case I. Both functions x, x' are $i-gH$ differentiable. Applying the Laplace transform, we get:

$$s^2 \odot L(x(t)) \ominus_H s \odot x(0) \ominus_H x'_{gH}(0) + L(x(t)) = \frac{\sigma_0}{s}$$

Similar to the previous example, the solutions in level-wise form are:

$$x_l(t,r) = r(1+\sin t) - \sin t - \cos t$$

$$x_u(t,r) = (2-r)(1+\sin t) - \sin t - \cos t$$

The solution x in level-wise form is a fuzzy number valued function and is shown in Fig. 4.14.

The solution x in level-wise form is not $i-gH$ differentiable and is shown in Fig. 4.15. This is because:

$$x_l'(t,r) = (r-1)\cos t + \sin t$$

$$x_u'(t,r) = (1-r)\cos t + \sin t$$

and $x_l'(t,r) \nleq x_u'(t,r)$ in all points of the domain and, as we see in the figure, there is a switching point at which the type of differentiability is changed. Based on our previous discussions and definitions, this type of differentiability is called $ii-gH$ differentiability.

So in general, there is no solution for this case.

Case II. The function x is $i-gH$ differentiable and $x'$is $ii-gH$ differentiable. Then by taking the Laplace transform and:

$$(-1) \odot \sigma_0 \ominus_H (-s^2) \odot L(x(t)) \oplus (-1) s \odot \sigma_0 \oplus L(x(t)) = \frac{\sigma_0}{s}$$

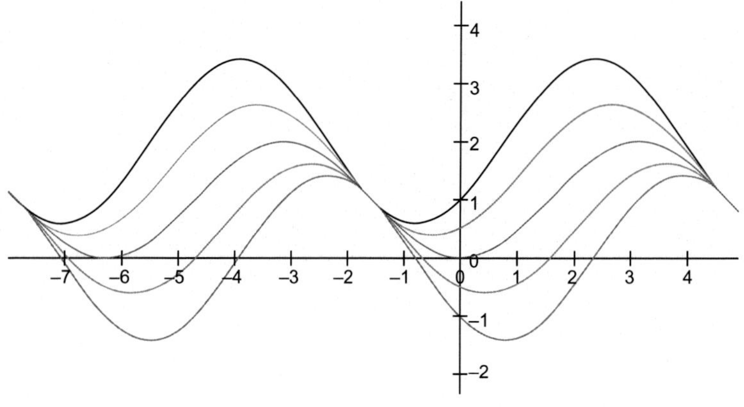

Fig. 4.14 The *i*-solution *x*.

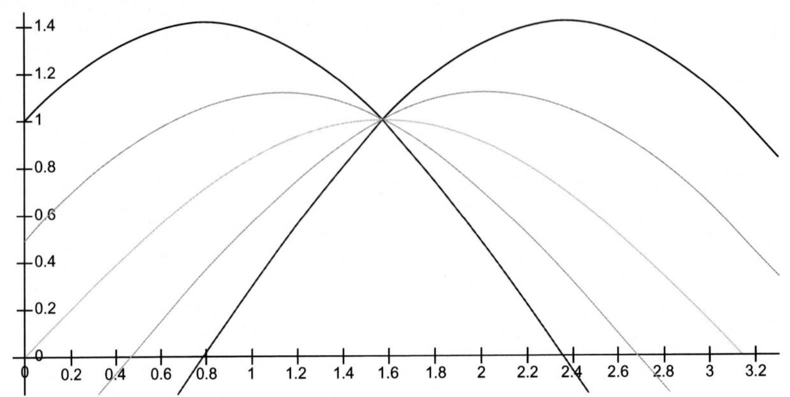

Fig. 4.15 $ii-gH$ differentiability of the solution.

Similar to the previous case, the solution in level-wise form is:

$$x_l(t,r) = r(1+\sinh t) - \sinh t - \cos t$$

$$x_u(t,r) = (2-r)(1+\sinh t) - \sinh t - \cos t$$

In this case, x is $i-gH$ differentiable. Fig. 4.16 shows us the behavior of x'. It is clear that the lower and upper functions continue regularly without interchanging.

In addition, the x' is $ii-gH$ differentiable because x'' satisfies the definition of type 2 differentiability.

Therefore, the solutions are acceptable.

Case III. The function x is $ii-gH$ differentiable and x' is $i-gH$ differentiable. Then by taking the Laplace transform and:

$$(-1)\odot\sigma_0\ominus_H(-s^2)\odot L(x(t))\ominus_H\sigma_0\oplus L(x(t)) = \frac{\sigma_0}{s}$$

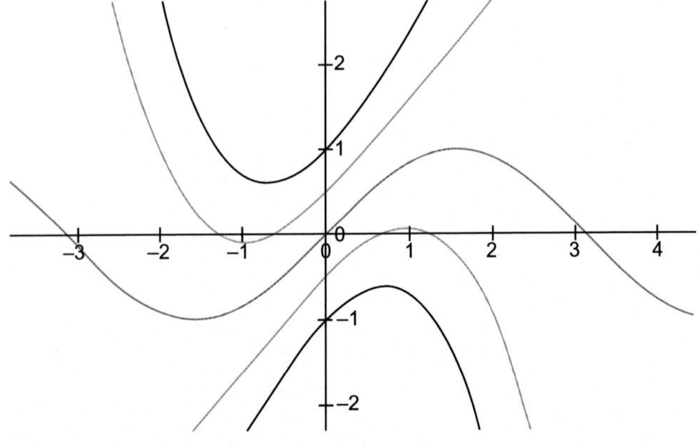

Fig. 4.16 $i-gH$ differentiability of the solution: x'.

similar to the previous case, the solution in level-wise form is:

$$x_l(t,r) = r(1-\sinh t) + \sinh t - \cos t$$

$$x_u(t,r) = (2-r)(1-\sinh t) + \sinh t - \cos t$$

wIfweconsiderthederivativesofthesolution,itis$ii-gH$differentiableandinlevel-wise formthereisinterchangingoftheendpointsoftheintervalanditlookslikeFig.4.16,butthelower andupperfunctionsarechanged.Inaddition,ithappensforthex'',andthismeans$x'$is$ii-gH$ differentiabletoo.Therefore,thesolutionisnotacceptable.

Case IV. Both functions x, x' are $ii-gH$ differentiable.

Then by taking the Laplace transform and:

$$(-1)\odot\sigma_0\oplus s^2\odot L(x(t))\ominus_H s\odot\sigma_0\oplus L(x(t)) = \frac{\sigma_0}{s}$$

similar to the previous case, the solution in level-wise form is:

$$x_l(t,r) = r(1-\sin t) + \sin t - \cos t$$

$$x_u(t,r) = (2-r)(1-\sin t) + \sin t - \cos t$$

If we consider the derivatives of the solution, it is $ii-gH$ differentiable in $\left(0,\frac{\pi}{2}\right)$ and in level-wise form there is interchanging of the end points of the interval and it looks like Fig. 4.15, but the lower and upper functions are changed. In addition, it happens for the x'', and this means x' is $ii-gH$ differentiable too and looks like Fig. 4.17. Therefore, the solution is not acceptable at any point of the domain (Salahshour and Allahviranloo, 2013).

4.3.7 Fuzzy differential equations—Variational iteration method

The aim of this section is introducing the fuzzy variational iteration method to solve the fuzzy differential equations. This method is one of the semianalytical methods and approximates the fuzzy solution functionally with many conditions. Indeed it is

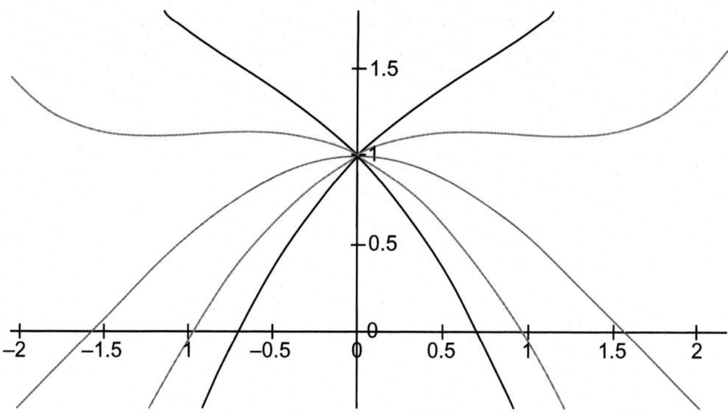

Fig. 4.17 $ii-gH$ differentiability of the x'.

conditional and all the derivatives should exist. After discussion on the method, the convergence and error are also investigated. Here a nonlinear fuzzy differential equation is defined as follows in general form (Allahviranloo and Abbasbandy, 2014):

$$Lx(t) \oplus Nx(t) \ominus_{gH} g(t) = 0, \quad t \geq 0$$

where L is a linear operator and is denoted by $L = \frac{d^m}{dt^m}$ and N is a nonlinear operator and g is a known fuzzy function. The fuzzy initial values are:

$$x^{(k)}(0) = c_k \in \mathbb{F}_R, \quad k = 0, 1, \ldots, m-1$$

subject to all the derivatives existing, i.e., being fuzzy numbers. In addition, the zero number on the right-hand side is a singleton fuzzy number.

We know the solution of any fuzzy differential equation is the solution of a corresponding fuzzy integral equation, such as the following form:

Case 1.

$$x_{n+1}(t) = x_n(t) \oplus \int_0^t \{\lambda(\tau) \odot (Lx(\tau) \oplus Nx(\tau) \ominus_{gH} g(\tau))\} d\tau, \quad n \geq 0$$

if $\frac{d^m}{dt^m} x(t)$ is $i-gH$ differentiable, and:

Case 2.

$$x_{n+1}(t) = x_n(t) \ominus_H (-1) \odot \int_0^t \{\lambda(\tau) \odot (Lx(\tau) \oplus Nx(\tau) \ominus_{gH} g(\tau))\} d\tau, \quad n \geq 0$$

if $\frac{d^m}{dt^m} x(t)$ is $ii-gH$ differentiable.

In both equations the multiplier λ is a general Lagrange multiplier, which can be identified optimally via variational theory and considering limited variations for the function x, it means $\delta x(t) = 0$. So after obtaining the optimal multiplier λ, using the initial value x_0, the successive approximations $x_n(t)$, $n \geq 1$ will be obtained as a sequence. It is clear that we should show that the sequence does have terms converging to the solution of the fuzzy differential equation:

$$\lim_{n \to \infty} x_n(t) = x(t)$$

On the other hand, to have a solution with restricted or limited variations we need to denote that the variations of the nonlinear term are also limited. So, we have to consider that $\delta Nx(t) = 0$. By this condition, the new successive iteration method with limited variations in two cases are:

Case 1.

$$\delta x_{n+1}(t) = \delta x_n(t) \oplus \delta \int_0^t \{\lambda(\tau) \odot (Lx(\tau) \ominus_{gH} g(\tau))\} d\tau, \quad n \geq 0$$

if $\frac{d^m}{dt^m} x(t)$ is $i-gH$ differentiable, and:

Case 2.

$$\delta x_{n+1}(t) = \delta x_n(t) \ominus_H (-1) \odot \delta \int_0^t \{\lambda(\tau) \odot (Lx(\tau) \ominus_{gH} g(\tau))\} d\tau, \ n \geq 0$$

if $\frac{d^m}{dt^m}x(t)$ is $ii-gH$ differentiable. Since the function g is a known one and independent of x, so the variations on it are meaningless. Then, two cases are simplified to the following cases:

Case 1.

$$\delta x_{n+1}(t) = \delta x_n(t) \oplus \delta \int_0^t \{\lambda(\tau) \odot L x_n(\tau)\} d\tau, \ n \geq 0$$

if $\frac{d^m}{dt^m}x(t)$ is $i-gH$ differentiable, and:

Case 2.

$$\delta x_{n+1}(t) = \delta x_n(t) \ominus_H (-1) \odot \delta \int_0^t \{\lambda(\tau) \odot L x_n(\tau)\} d\tau, \ n \geq 0$$

if $\frac{d^m}{dt^m}x(t)$ is $ii-gH$ differentiable.

It should be noted that the multiplier λ depends on τ and even t, and it will be found ultimately based on these variables. As we know, the linear operator is $L = \frac{d^m}{dt^m}$ and by replacing, we will have:

Case 1.

$$\delta x_{n+1}(t) = \delta x_n(t) \oplus \delta \int_0^t \left\{\lambda(\tau) \odot \frac{d^m}{dt^m} x_n(\tau)\right\} d\tau, \ n \geq 0$$

if $\frac{d^m}{dt^m}x(t)$ is $i-gH$ differentiable, and:

Case 2.

$$\delta x_{n+1}(t) = \delta x_n(t) \ominus_H (-1) \odot \delta \int_0^t \left\{\lambda(\tau) \odot \frac{d^m}{dt^m} x_n(\tau)\right\} d\tau, \ n \geq 0$$

if $\frac{d^m}{dt^m}x(t)$ is $ii-gH$ differentiable.

In two cases, using the part-by-part integration (Chapter 3):

$$\int_0^t \left\{\lambda(\tau) \odot \frac{d^m}{dt^m} x_n(\tau)\right\} d\tau = \lambda(t) \odot \frac{d^{m-1}}{dt^{m-1}} x_n(t) \ominus_{gH} \int_0^t \left\{\lambda'(\tau) \odot \frac{d^{m-1}}{dt^{m-1}} x_n(\tau)\right\} d\tau$$

we have:

Case 1.

$$\delta x_{n+1}(t) = \delta x_n(t) \oplus \delta \left[\lambda(t) \odot \frac{d^{m-1}}{dt^{m-1}} x_n(t) \ominus_{gH} \int_0^t \left\{\lambda'(\tau) \odot \frac{d^{m-1}}{dt^{m-1}} x_n(\tau)\right\} d\tau\right]$$

if all derivatives are $i-gH$ differentiable, and:

Case 2.

$$\delta x_{n+1}(t)=\delta x_n(t)\ominus_H(-1)\delta\left[\lambda(t)\odot\frac{d^{m-1}}{dt^{m-1}}x_n(t)\ominus_{gH}\int_0^t\left\{\lambda'(\tau)\odot\frac{d^{m-1}}{dt^{m-1}}x_n(\tau)\right\}d\tau\right]$$

if all derivatives are $ii-gH$ differentiable.

Continuing by this integration again:

$$\int_0^t\left\{\lambda'(\tau)\odot\frac{d^{m-1}}{dt^{m-1}}x_n(\tau)\right\}d\tau=\lambda'(t)\odot\frac{d^{m-2}}{dt^{m-2}}x_n(t)\ominus_{gH}\int_0^t\left\{\lambda''(\tau)\odot\frac{d^{m-2}}{dt^{m-2}}x_n(\tau)\right\}d\tau$$

and finally by considering that:

$$\delta x_{n+1}(t)=0,$$

and all the gH-differences exist in two cases, it is concluded that the following successive iteration method is found:

Case 1.

$$0=\delta x_n(t)\oplus\delta\left[\lambda\odot\frac{d^{m-1}}{dt^{m-1}}x_n(t)\oplus\lambda'\odot\frac{d^{m-2}}{dt^{m-2}}x_n(t)\oplus\cdots\oplus\lambda^{(m-1)}x_n(t)\right]\oplus\int_0^t\lambda^{(m)}\odot\delta x_n(\tau)d\tau$$

if all derivatives are $i-gH$ differentiable, and:

Case 2.

$$0=\delta x_n(t)\ominus_H(-1)\delta\left[\lambda\odot\frac{d^{m-1}}{dt^{m-1}}x_n(t)\oplus\lambda'\odot\frac{d^{m-2}}{dt^{m-2}}x_n(t)\oplus\cdots\oplus\lambda^{(m-1)}x_n(t)\right]\oplus\int_0^t\lambda^{(m)}\odot\delta x_n(\tau)d\tau$$

if all derivatives are $ii-gH$ differentiable.

In two cases, by comparing two sides of the equalities:

Case 1.

$$1+\lambda^{(m-1)}=0,\ \lambda^{(m)}=0,\ \lambda=\lambda'=\cdots=\lambda^{(m-1)}=0$$

Case 2.

Note. In this case, the multiplier λ C

$$1+\lambda^{(m-1)}=0,\ \lambda^{(m)}=0,\ \lambda=\lambda'=\cdots=\lambda^{(m-1)}=0$$

otherwise the abovementioned relations are not true easily.

Because in level-wise form of case (2), the relations are:

$$0=\delta x_{n,l}(t)+\delta\left[\lambda\frac{d^{m-1}}{dt^{m-1}}x_{n,u}(t)+\lambda'\frac{d^{m-2}}{dt^{m-2}}x_{n,u}(t)+\cdots+\lambda^{(m-1)}x_{n,u}(t)\right]$$
$$+\int_0^t\lambda^{(m)}\delta x_{n,u}(\tau)d\tau$$

$$0=\delta x_{n,u}(t)+\delta\left[\lambda\frac{d^{m-1}}{dt^{m-1}}x_{n,l}(t)+\lambda'\frac{d^{m-2}}{dt^{m-2}}x_{n,l}(t)+\cdots+\lambda^{(m-1)}x_{n,l}(t)\right]+\int_0^t\lambda^{(m)}\delta x_{n,l}(\tau)d\tau$$

then there is only one way to have this quality, and it is $x_{n,\ l}(t)=x_{n,\ u}(t)=0$ and:

$$\lambda=\lambda'=\cdots=\lambda^{(m-1)}=\lambda^{(m)}=0$$

Now we discuss only case (1). In this case, by considering the relations, the multiplier can be found as:

$$\lambda(t,\tau)=\frac{(-1)^m}{(m-1)!}(\tau-t)^{m-1},\ 0<t<\tau<T.$$

So our successive iterates relation is:

$$x_{n+1}(t)=x_n(t)\oplus\int_0^t\left\{\frac{(-1)^m}{(m-1)!}(\tau-t)^{m-1}\odot\left(Lx_n(\tau)\oplus Nx_n(\tau)\ominus_{gH}g(\tau)\right)\right\}d\tau$$

for $n\geq 0$. Now define an operator like A as follows:

$$A[x]=\int_0^t\left\{\frac{(-1)^m}{(m-1)!}(\tau-t)^{m-1}\odot\left(Lx(\tau)\oplus Nx(\tau)\ominus_{gH}g(\tau)\right)\right\}d\tau$$

Then another sequence with components v_n is defined:

$$v_0=x_0,\ \ v_1=A[x_0],\ldots,v_{n+1}=A[v_0\oplus v_1\oplus\cdots\oplus v_n]$$

where:

$$v_0(t)=c_0\oplus\sum_{k=1}^{m}\frac{c_k\odot t^k}{k!}$$

$$v_{n+1}(t)=\int_0^t\left\{\frac{(-1)^m}{(m-1)!}(\tau-t)^{m-1}\odot\left(\frac{d^m}{dt^m}[v_0\oplus v_1\oplus\cdots\oplus v_n](\tau)\oplus N[v_0\oplus v_1\oplus\cdots\oplus v_n]\ominus_{gH}g(\tau)\right)\right\}d\tau$$

Finally:

$$x(t)=\lim_{n\to\infty}x_n(t)=\sum_{n=0}^{\infty}v_n\Leftrightarrow\lim_{n\to\infty}D_H\left(x_n(t),\sum_{n=0}^{\infty}v_n\right)=\lim_{n\to\infty}D_H(x_n(t),x(t))=0$$

Existence and convergence. Now the convergence of the method should be considered. To explain it, we have to show that the series solution $\sum_{n=0}^{\infty}v_n(t)$ such that the terms are obtained from:

$$v_{n+1}(t)=\int_0^t\left\{\frac{(-1)^m}{(m-1)!}(\tau-t)^{m-1}\odot\left(\frac{d^m}{dt^m}[v_0\oplus v_1\oplus\cdots\oplus v_n](\tau)\oplus N[v_0\oplus v_1\oplus\cdots\oplus v_n]\ominus_{gH}g(\tau)\right)\right\}d\tau$$

and satisfies the following inequality:

$$D_H(v_{n+1},0) \le \gamma D_H(v_n,0), \ 0 < \exists\gamma < 1$$

converging to the exact solution $x(t)$.

To show the assertion, first we define the sequence $\{s_n\}_{n=0}^{\infty}$ as:

$$s_0 = v_0, \ s_1 = v_0 \oplus v_1, \ldots, s_n = v_0 \oplus v_1 \oplus \cdots \oplus v_n$$

$$D_H(s_{n+1},s_n) = D_H(v_{n+1},0) \le \gamma D_H(v_n,0) \le \gamma^2 D_H(v_{n-1},0) \le \cdots \le \gamma^{n+1} D_H(v_0,0)$$

For any $j \le n \in N$, we have:

$$D_H(s_n,s_j) \le D_H(s_n,s_{n-1}) + D_H(s_{n-1},s_{n-2}) + \cdots + D_H(s_{j+1},s_j)$$

$$\le \gamma^n D(v_0,0) + \gamma^{n-1} D_H(v_0,0) + \cdots + \gamma^{j+1} D_H(v_0,0) = \frac{1-\gamma^{n-j}}{1-\gamma}\gamma^{j+1} D_H(v_0,0)$$

Since $0 < \gamma < 1$, we get:

$$\lim_{n,j\to\infty} D_H(s_n,s_j) = 0$$

Therefore, the sequence $\{s_n\}_{n=0}^{\infty}$ is a Cauchy sequence in the normed space. In the same way, we can show that:

$$D_H\left(x(t), \sum_{k=0}^{j} v_k\right) \le \frac{1-\gamma^{n-1}}{1-\gamma}\gamma^{j+1} D_H(v_0,0) \le \frac{1}{1-\gamma}\gamma^{j+1} D_H(v_0,0)$$

Now the proof is completed.

Example. Consider the following fuzzy Duffing's differential equation:

$$x''(t) \oplus 3 \odot x(t) \ominus_H 2 \odot (x(t))^3 = \cos t \cdot \sin 2t, \ t \ge 0$$

$$x(0,r) = [r-1, 1-r], \ x'(0,r) = [r, 2-r], \ r \in [0, 1]$$

Now the initial approximate guesses:

$$v_0(t,r) = (r-1+rt, 1-r+(2-r)t)$$

The successive iterated relation for $m=2$ is formed as:

$$x_{n+1}(t) = x_n(t) \oplus \int_0^t \left\{(\tau - t) \odot \left(x''(t) \oplus 3 \odot x(t) \ominus_H 2 \odot (x(t))^3 \ominus_H \cos t \cdot \sin 2t\right)\right\} d\tau$$

In order to find it, we have to use the Maclaurin series expansions of $\sin t$ and $\cos t$:

$$\cos t = 1 - \frac{t^2}{2} + \frac{t^{24}}{24} - \frac{t^6}{720}, \ \cos t = 2t - \frac{4t^3}{3} + \frac{4t^5}{15}$$

If the H-differences exist, after replacing the Maclaurin series expansions in the abovementioned iterated relation, the solution can be approximated (Allahviranloo and Abbasbandy, 2014).

4.3.8 Fuzzy differential equations—Legendre differential equation

In this section, first the fuzzy generalized power series method, in which the coefficients are fuzzy numbers, is introduced and then the conditions of the uniqueness of the solution and its convergence for the fuzzy differential equation are investigated. Then, using the fuzzy generalized power series method, the fuzzy Legendre differential equation is considered as a case study, and finally, for further illustration, some related examples are solved. For more discussion on the subject, we need to introduce some properties of one of the types of ranking of fuzzy numbers and fuzzy sequences that we are going to use in this section.

The ranking that we use is defined as level-wise form.

Level-wise ranking. For instance, consider two fuzzy numbers $A,B\in\mathbb{F}_R$, if we say $A\preccurlyeq(\prec)B$ it means $A_l(r)\leq(<)B_l(r)$ and $A_u(r)\leq(<)B_u(r)$. Also for a real scalar $k\in R$, $k\preccurlyeq(\prec)A$, it means that $k\leq(<)A_l(r)$ and $k\leq(<)A_u(r)$. We talked about the following properties earlier, and we shall use them in this section.

1. $(\ominus_H)^k$ means $\underbrace{\ominus_H\cdots\ominus_H}_{k}$ and $(\ominus_H)^k=\begin{cases}\oplus, & k=2n\\ \ominus_H, & k=2n+1\end{cases}$
2. $(\ominus_H A)^k=\oplus A^k,\quad k=2n,\ n\in N\cup\{0\}$
3. $(\ominus_H A)^k=\ominus_H A^k,\quad k=2n+1,\ n\in N\cup\{0\}$
4. $(\ominus_H)^k A=\oplus A,\quad k=2n,\ n\in N\cup\{0\}$
5. $(\ominus_H)^k A=\ominus_H A,\quad k=2n+1,\ n\in N\cup\{0\}$
6. For two nonnegative real numbers $\lambda_1,\ \lambda_2\in R$, then:

$$\ominus_H(-1)\lambda_1\odot A\oplus(-1)\lambda_2\odot A=\begin{cases}\ominus_H(-1)(\lambda_1-\lambda_2)\odot A, & \lambda_1-\lambda_2\geq 0\\ \ominus_H(\lambda_1-\lambda_2)\odot A, & \lambda_1-\lambda_2<0\end{cases}$$

The proofs of the items are very easy, as was pointed out in Chapter 2. Here we prove item 6. It can be proved in level-wise form very easily.

In the first case, $\lambda_1-\lambda_2\geq 0$, then we have the following relations in level-wise form:

$$(\ominus_H(-1)\lambda_1\odot A\oplus(-1)\lambda_2\odot A)[r]=(\ominus_H(-1)\lambda_1\odot A)[r]+((-1)\lambda_2\odot A)[r]$$
$$=\ominus_H(-1)[\lambda_1A_l(r),\lambda_1A_u(r)]+[-\lambda_2A_u(r),\ -\lambda_2A_l(r)]$$
$$=[\lambda_1A_u(r),\lambda_1A_l(r)]+[-\lambda_2A_u(r),\ -\lambda_2A_l(r)]=[(\lambda_1-\lambda_2)A_u(r),(\lambda_1-\lambda_2)A_l(r)]$$
$$=\ominus_H(-1)(\lambda_1-\lambda_2)\odot A[r]$$

In the second case, $\lambda_1 - \lambda_2 < 0$:

$$(\ominus_H(-1)\lambda_1 \odot A \oplus (-1)\lambda_2 \odot A)[r] = \cdots = [(\lambda_1 - \lambda_2)A_u(r), (\lambda_1 - \lambda_2)A_l(r)]$$
$$= (\lambda_1 - \lambda_2)[A_u(r), A_l(r)] = \ominus_H(\lambda_1 - \lambda_2)[A_l(r), A_u(r)] = \ominus_H(\lambda_1 - \lambda_2)\odot A[r]$$

As discussed under generalized division in Chapter 2, some of this division will be used in this section.

Note. In all methods in this book, we will suppose that the division always exists.

1. If $0 < A_l(r) \le A_u(r)$ and $B_l(r) \le B_u(r) < 0$ then:

$$\begin{cases} A_l(r)B_l(r) \ge A_u(r)B_u(r) \Rightarrow C_l(r) = \dfrac{A_u(r)}{B_l(r)}, \ C_u(r) = \dfrac{A_l(r)}{B_u(r)} \\ A_l(r)B_l(r) \le A_u(r)B_u(r) \Rightarrow C_l(r) = \dfrac{A_l(r)}{B_u(r)}, \ C_u(r) = \dfrac{A_u(r)}{B_l(r)} \end{cases}$$

2. If $0 < A_l(r) \le A_u(r)$ and $0 < B_l(r) \le B_u(r)$ then:

$$\begin{cases} A_l(r)B_u(r) \le A_u(r)B_l(r) \Rightarrow C_l(r) = \dfrac{A_l(r)}{B_l(r)}, \ C_u(r) = \dfrac{A_u(r)}{B_u(r)} \\ A_l(r)B_u(r) \ge A_u(r)B_u(r) \Rightarrow C_l(r) = \dfrac{A_u(r)}{B_u(r)}, \ C_u(r) = \dfrac{A_l(r)}{B_l(r)} \end{cases}$$

3. If $A_l(r) \le A_u(r) < 0$ and $B_l(r) \le B_u(r) < 0$ then:

$$\begin{cases} A_u(r)B_l(r) \le A_l(r)B_u(r) \Rightarrow C_l(r) = \dfrac{A_u(r)}{B_u(r)}, \ C_u(r) = \dfrac{A_l(r)}{B_l(r)} \\ A_u(r)B_l(r) \ge A_l(r)B_u(r) \Rightarrow C_l(r) = \dfrac{A_l(r)}{B_l(r)}, \ C_u(r) = \dfrac{A_u(r)}{B_u(r)} \end{cases}$$

4. If $A_l(r) \le A_u(r) < 0$ and $0 < B_l(r) \le B_u(r)$ then:

$$\begin{cases} A_l(r)B_l(r) \le A_u(r)B_u(r) \Rightarrow C_l(r) = \dfrac{A_l(r)}{B_u(r)}, \ C_u(r) = \dfrac{A_u(r)}{B_l(r)} \\ A_l(r)B_l(r) \ge A_u(r)B_u(r) \Rightarrow C_l(r) = \dfrac{A_u(r)}{B_l(r)}, \ C_u(r) = \dfrac{A_l(r)}{B_u(r)} \end{cases}$$

If $A_l(r) \le 0$, $A_u(r) \ge 0$ and $B_l(r) \le B_u(r) < 0$ then:

$$C_l(r) = \frac{A_u(r)}{B_l(r)}, \ C_u(r) = \frac{A_l(r)}{B_l(r)}.$$

If $A_l(r) \le 0$, $A_u(r) \ge 0$ and $0 < B_l(r) \le B_u(r)$ then:

$$C_l(r) = \frac{A_l(r)}{B_u(r)}, \ C_u(r) = \frac{A_u(r)}{B_u(r)}.$$

4.3.8.1 Definition—Power series with fuzzy coefficients

The following series with fuzzy coefficients and fuzzy operations is called the fuzzy power series:

$$x(t) = \sum_{n=0}^{\infty} a_n \odot (t - t_0)^n, \ \forall t \in R, \ \exists t_0 \in R$$

where the radius of convergence ρ is defined as $\rho = \lim_{n\to\infty} \frac{a_n(0)}{a_{n+1}(0)}$ provided that the limit exists and is a fuzzy number, and also the division exists for two fuzzy numbers $a_n(0)$, $a_{n+1}(0)$.

Note. We assume here that $\rho > 0$ and $x(t)$ and its derivatives are defined in $|x - x_0| < \rho$.

The level-wise form of the series is:

$$x(t,r) = [x_l(t,r), x_u(t,r)],$$

where:

$$x_l(t,r) = \begin{cases} \sum_{n=0}^{\infty} a_{n,l}(r)(t-t_0)^n, & t \geq t_0 \\ \sum_{n:even} a_{n,l}(r)(t-t_0)^n + \sum_{n:odd} a_{n,u}(r)(t-t_0)^n, & t < t_0 \end{cases}$$

$$x_u(t,r) = \begin{cases} \sum_{n=0}^{\infty} a_{n,u}(r)(t-t_0)^n, & t \geq t_0 \\ \sum_{n:even} a_{n,u}(r)(t-t_0)^n + \sum_{n:odd} a_{n,l}(r)(t-t_0)^n, & t < t_0 \end{cases}$$

Therefore, considering the above level-wise functions, the form of the series with fuzzy operators should be as the following form:

$$x(t) = \sum_{n:\text{even}} a_n \odot (t - t_0)^n \ominus_H (-1) \odot \sum_{n:\text{odd}} a_n \odot (t - t_0)^n, \ t < t_0$$

If we want to consider the gH-derivative of the fuzzy series, we need to define the derivatives of the $x_l(t,r)$ and $x_u(t,r)$:

$$x_l'(t,r) = \begin{cases} \sum_{n=1}^{\infty} n a_{n,l}(r)(t-t_0)^{n-1}, & t \geq t_0 \\ \sum_{n:even} a_{n,u}(r)(t-t_0)^{n-1} + \sum_{n:odd} a_{n,l}(r)(t-t_0)^{n-1}, & t < t_0 \end{cases}$$

$$x_u'(t,r) = \begin{cases} \sum_{n=1}^{\infty} n a_{n,u}(r)(t-t_0)^{n-1}, & t \geq t_0 \\ \sum_{n:even} a_{n,l}(r)(t-t_0)^{n-1} + \sum_{n:odd} a_{n,u}(r)(t-t_0)^{n-1}, & t < t_0 \end{cases}$$

and now:

$$x_{gH}'(t,r) = \left[\min\left\{x_l'(t,r), x_u'(t,r)\right\}, \max\left\{x_l'(t,r), x_u'(t,r)\right\}\right]$$

and:

$$x_{gH}'(t) = \sum_{n=1}^{\infty} n \odot a_n \odot (t-t_0)^{n-1}$$

In the fuzzy series $f(x)$ the coefficient is fined by $a_n = \frac{x_{gH}^{(n)}(t_0)}{n!}$ subject to the nth derivatives existing, which means all of them are fuzzy numbers.

Now based on the nature of the gH-differentiability, two types of differentiability appear here again:

$$x_{i-gH}'(t) = \sum_{n=1}^{\infty} n \odot a_n \odot (t-t_0)^{n-1}$$

$$x_{ii-gH}'(t) = \ominus_H(-1) \sum_{n=1}^{\infty} n \odot a_n \odot (x-x_0)^{n-1}$$

And the level-wise form is:

$$x_{i-gH}'(t,r) = \left[x_l'(t,r), x_u'(t,r)\right]$$

$$x_{ii-gH}'(t,r) = \left[x_u'(t,r), x_l'(t,r)\right]$$

4.3.8.2 Some properties of fuzzy series

Fuzzy sequence. Let $u: Z^+ \to \mathbb{F}_R$ (Z^+ means set of positive integer numbers) is a fuzzy number valued function. $u := \{u_n\}$ is a fuzzy sequence if for all $n \in N$, $u_n \in \mathbb{F}_R$.

Bounded sequence. Suppose that $k \in \mathbb{F}_R$ and $k \succ 0$:

1. k is a fuzzy lower bound of the fuzzy sequence $\{u_n\}$ if for all $n \in N \cup \{0\}$, $k \preccurlyeq u_n$.
2. k is a fuzzy upper bound of the fuzzy sequence $\{u_n\}$ if for all $n \in N \cup \{0\}$, $k \succcurlyeq u_n$.

Convergence. An infinite fuzzy series $\sum_{n=1}^{\infty} u_n$ with positive terms is convergent if and only if its fuzzy sequence of partial sums has a fuzzy upper bound.

Fuzzy comparison test. Suppose that $\sum_{n=1}^{\infty} u_n$ and $\sum_{n=1}^{\infty} v_n$ are two fuzzy series with positive terms such that for all $n \in N$, $u_n \succcurlyeq v_n$ then:

1. If the fuzzy series $\sum_{n=1}^{\infty} u_n$ is convergent, then the fuzzy series $\sum_{n=1}^{\infty} v_n$ is also convergent.
2. If the fuzzy series $\sum_{n=1}^{\infty} u_n$ is divergent, then the fuzzy series $\sum_{n=1}^{\infty} v_n$ is also divergent.

Two of the properties can be proved easily by the definition of convergence.

4.3.8.3 Fuzzy calculated operations

Let us suppose that:

$$x(t) = \sum_{n=0}^{\infty} a_n \odot (t - t_0)^n, \ y(t) = \sum_{n=0}^{\infty} b_n \odot (t - t_0)^n$$

such that $f(x)$ is a fuzzy series and $g(x)$ is a real one and for both the radius of convergence is positive. We know that:

$$x(t) = \sum_{n=0}^{\infty} a_n \odot (t - t_0)^n, \ t \geq t_0$$

$$x(t) = \sum_{n:\text{even}} a_n \odot (t - t_0)^n \ominus_H (-1) \odot \sum_{n:\text{odd}} a_n \odot (t - t_0)^n, \ t < t_0$$

Here, four fuzzy calculated operations of these two series are going to be explained. The sign of coefficients and also $x - x_0$ are considered necessary to obtain a fuzzy number valued series as a result.

Summation.

- If $t \geq t_0$:

$$x(t) \oplus y(t) = \sum_{n=0}^{\infty} (a_n \oplus b_n) \odot (t - t_0)^n$$

- If $t < t_0$:

$$x(t) \oplus y(t) = \sum_{n:\text{even}}^{\infty} (a_n \oplus b_n) \odot (t - t_0)^n \ominus_H (-1)$$

$$\odot \sum_{n:\text{odd}} (a_n \oplus b_n) \odot (t - t_0)^n$$

Production.

- If $t \geq t_0$:

$$x(t) \odot y(t) = \sum_{n:\text{even}}^{\infty} \sum_{k=0, b_{n-k} \geq 0}^{n} (a_k \odot b_{n-k}) \odot (t - t_0)^n \ominus_H (-1)$$

$$\odot \sum_{n:\text{odd}}^{\infty} \sum_{k=0, b_{n-k} \geq 0}^{n} (a_k \odot b_{n-k}) \odot (t - t_0)^n$$

- If t$<t_0$:

$$x(t)\odot t(t)=\sum_{n:\text{even}}^{\infty}\sum_{k=0,b_{n-k}\geq 0}^{n}(a_k\odot b_{n-k})\odot(t-t_0)^n\ominus_H(-1)$$

$$\odot\sum_{n:\text{odd}}^{\infty}\sum_{k=0,b_{n-k}\geq 0}^{n}(a_k\odot b_{n-k})\odot(t-t_0)^n$$

$$\ominus_H(-1)\sum_{n:\text{even}}^{\infty}\sum_{k=0,b_{n-k}<0}^{n}(a_k\odot b_{n-k})\odot(t-t_0)^n$$

$$\oplus\sum_{n:\text{odd}}^{\infty}\sum_{k=0,b_{n-k}<0}^{n}(a_k\odot b_{n-k})\odot(t-t_0)^n$$

Difference.

- If $t\geq t_0$:

$$x(t)\ominus_{gH}y(t)=\sum_{n=0}^{\infty}(a_n\ominus_{gH}b_n)\odot(t-t_0)^n$$

This case is explained as two other cases, because the gH-difference is defined in two cases: i-difference and ii-difference:

Case i-difference:

$$x(t)=y(t)\oplus\sum_{n=0}^{\infty}(a_n\ominus_H b_n)\odot(t-t_0)^n$$

Case ii-difference:

$$y(t)=x(t)\oplus(-1)\sum_{n=0}^{\infty}(a_n\ominus_H b_n)\odot(t-t_0)^n$$

- If $t<t_0$:

$$x(t)\ominus_{gH}y(t)=\sum_{n=0}^{\infty}(a_n\ominus_{gH}b_n)\odot(t-t_0)^n$$

This case is also explained as two other cases:

Case i-difference:

$$x(t)=y(t)\oplus\sum_{n:\text{even}}^{\infty}(a_n\ominus_H b_n)\odot(t-t_0)^n$$

$$\ominus_H(-1)\odot\sum_{n:\text{odd}}^{\infty}(a_n\ominus_H b_n)\odot(t-t_0)^n$$

Case *ii*-difference:

$$y(t) = x(t) \oplus (-1) \left\{ \sum_{n:\text{even}}^{\infty} (a_n \ominus_H b_n) \odot (t - t_0)^n \ominus_H (-1) \odot \sum_{n:\text{odd}}^{\infty} (a_n \ominus_H b_n) \odot (t - t_0)^n \right\}$$

$$= x(t) \oplus (-1) \sum_{n:\text{even}}^{\infty} (a_n \ominus_H b_n) \odot (t - t_0)^n \ominus_H \sum_{n:\text{odd}}^{\infty} (a_n \ominus_H b_n) \odot (t - t_0)^n$$

All can be proved very easily by using the level-wise forms of the two sides of the equations.

4.3.8.4 Fuzzy power series method for solving Legendre's equation

First of all, we are going to consider the general form of the fuzzy second order differential equations and Legendre's equations:

$$\begin{cases} x''_{gH}(t) = f\left(t, x(t), x'_{gH}(t)\right) \\ x(t_0) = x_0 \in \mathbb{F}_R \\ x'_{gH}(t_0) = x_1 \in \mathbb{F}_R \end{cases}$$

To find the fuzzy power series solution we use the following procedure step by step.

1. The model has the fuzzy power series solution in the form of:

$$x(t) = \sum_{n=0}^{\infty} a_n \odot (t - t_0)^n$$

2. As we mentioned before, we obtain the $x'(t)$, $x''(t)$.
3. Fuzzy arithmetic operations such as production, summation, and difference are calculated according to the previous discussions.
4. The fuzzy series solution and its derivatives as obtained series are replaced in the fuzzy differential equation.
5. We claimed that:

$$\sum_{n=0}^{\infty} a_n \odot (t - t_0)^n = 0 \Leftrightarrow \forall n \, a_n = 0$$

and also the fuzzy coefficients are determined. It is confirmed that they are fuzzy numbers.

6. The fuzzy series solutions are now found.

Now let us consider the fuzzy Legendre's equation as follows:

$$(1-t^2)\odot x''_{gH}(t)-2t\odot x'_{gH}(t)\oplus\varphi(\varphi+1)\odot x(t)=0$$

subject to:

$$x(0)=x_0\in\mathbb{F}_R,\ x'_{gH}(0)=x_1\in\mathbb{F}_R,\ \varphi\in N\cup\{0\}$$

Since the functions $\frac{2t}{1-t^2}$ and $\frac{\varphi(\varphi+1)}{1-t^2}$ are analytical functions at $x_0=0$, then the fuzzy series solution is a unique solution in the form of:

$$x(t)=\sum_{n=0}^{\infty}a_n\odot(t-t_0)^n$$

To solve the problem, first we consider that x, x' are $i-gH$ differentiable. In this case, we have:

$$x'_l(t,r)=\begin{cases}\sum_{n=0}^{\infty}na_{n,l}(r)(t-t_0)^{n-1}, & t\geq t_0\\ \sum_{n:even}a_{n,u}(r)(t-t_0)^{n-1}+\sum_{n:odd}a_{n,l}(r)(t-t_0)^{n-1}, & t<t_0\end{cases}$$

$$x'_u(t,r)=\begin{cases}\sum_{n=0}^{\infty}na_{n,u}(r)(t-t_0)^{n-1}, & t\geq t_0\\ \sum_{n:even}a_{n,l}(r)(t-t_0)^{n-1}+\sum_{n:odd}a_{n,u}(r)(t-t_0)^{n-1}, & t<t_0\end{cases}$$

and now:

$$x'_{gH}(t,r)=\left[\min\{x'_l(t,r),x'_u(t,r)\},\ \max\{x'_l(t,r),x'_u(t,r)\}\right]$$

and:

$$x'_{gH}(t)=\oplus\sum_{n=0}^{\infty}n\odot a_n\odot(t-t_0)^{n-1}$$

In this case, the coefficients are:

$$a_2=\ominus_H\frac{\varphi(\varphi+1)}{2}\odot a_0,\ a_3=\ominus_H\frac{(\varphi+2)(\varphi-1)}{2}\odot a_1$$

and:

$$a_{n+2}=\ominus_H\frac{(\varphi-n)(n+\varphi+1)}{(n+2)(n+1)}\odot a_1,\ n=2,3,\ldots$$

Finally, the solution is:

$$x(t) = a_0 \odot \left(1 \ominus_H \frac{\varphi(\varphi+1)}{2!} x^2 \oplus \frac{(\varphi+2)\varphi(\varphi+1)(\varphi+3)}{4!} x^4 \ominus_H \cdots \right) \oplus$$

$$\oplus a_1 \odot \left(x \ominus_H \frac{(\varphi-1)(\varphi+2)}{3!} x^3 \oplus \frac{(\varphi-3)(\varphi-1)(\varphi+2)(\varphi+4)}{5!} x^5 \ominus_H \cdots \right)$$

Example. Consider the following fuzzy second order differential equation with the fuzzy series centered about 0:

$$x''_{gH}(t) \ominus_{gH} 3 \odot x'_{gH}(t) \oplus 2 \odot x(t) = 0, \;\; x(0) = (2, 4, 7), x'(0) = (3, 6, 10.5)$$

The fuzzy series solution is:

$$x(t) = \sum_{n=0}^{\infty} a_n \odot t^n$$

Suppose that x, x' are $i-gH$ differentiable. So:

$$x'_{i-gH}(t) = \sum_{n=1}^{\infty} n a_n \odot t^{n-1}, \;\; x''_{i-gH}(t) = \sum_{n=2}^{\infty} n(n-1) a_n \odot t^{n-2}$$

By substituting in the equation, we have:

$$x(0) = a_0 = (2, 4, 7), \;\; x'_{i-gH}(0) = a_1 = (3, 6, 10.5)$$

$$\sum_{n=2}^{\infty} n(n-1) a_n \odot t^{n-2} \ominus_{gH} 3 \odot \sum_{n=1}^{\infty} n a_n \odot t^{n-1} \oplus 2 \odot \sum_{n=0}^{\infty} a_n \odot t^n = 0$$

and we know that:

$$\sum_{n=2}^{\infty} n(n-1) a_n \odot t^{n-2} = \sum_{n=0}^{\infty} (n+1)(n+2) a_{n+2} \odot t^n$$

$$\sum_{n=1}^{\infty} n a_n \odot t^{n-1} = \sum_{n=0}^{\infty} (n+1) a_{n+1} \odot t^n$$

Finally:

$$\sum_{n=0}^{\infty} \left((n+1)(n+2) a_{n+2} \ominus_{gH} 3 \odot (n+1) a_{n+1} \oplus 2 \odot a_n \right) \odot t^n = 0$$

Then we obtain:

$$a_{n+2} = \frac{3(n+1) \odot a_{n+1} \ominus_H 2 \odot a_n}{(n+1)(n+2)}, \;\; n = 0, 1, \ldots$$

The fuzzy series solution is:

$$x(t) = (2,4,7)\odot\left(1\ominus_H x^2\ominus_H x^3\ominus_H \frac{14}{24}x^4\ominus_H \frac{30}{120}x^5\ominus_H\cdots\right)\oplus$$

$$(3,6,10.5)\odot\left(x\oplus\frac{3}{2}x^3\oplus\frac{15}{24}x^4\oplus\frac{31}{120}x^5\oplus\cdots\right)$$

Example. Consider the following fuzzy second order differential equation with the fuzzy series centered about 0:

$$x''_{gH}(t)\oplus 5\odot x'_{gH}(t)\oplus 6\odot x(t) = 0,\ x(0) = (1,3,4),\ x'_{gH}(0) = (-10,\ -7.5,\ -2.5)$$

The fuzzy series solution is:

$$x(t) = \sum_{n=0}^{\infty} a_n\odot t^n$$

Suppose that x, x' are $i-gH$ differentiable. So:

$$x'_{ii-gH}(t) = \ominus_H(-1)\sum_{n=1}^{\infty} na_n\odot t^{n-1},$$

$$x''_{ii-gH}(t) = \ominus_H(-1)\sum_{n=2}^{\infty} n(n-1)a_n\odot t^{n-2}$$

Using the same procedure, we have the solution in the form of:

$$x(t) = (1,3,4)\odot\left(1\ominus_H\frac{6}{2}x^2\oplus\frac{30}{6}x^3\oplus\frac{114}{24}x^4\ominus_H\cdots\right)\oplus$$

$$(-10,\ -7.5,\ -2.5)\odot\left(\ominus_H(-1)x\ominus_H\frac{5}{2}x^2\ominus_H(-1)\frac{19}{6}x^3\ominus_H\frac{5}{24}x^4\oplus\cdots\right)$$

4.3.9 Linear systems of fuzzy differential equations

In this section, we will discuss the fuzzy linear system of differential equations of the form:

$$x'_{1_{gH}}(t) = a_{11}(t)\odot x_1(t)\oplus\cdots\oplus a_{1n}(t)\odot x_n(t)\oplus f_1(t)$$

$$x'_{2_{gH}}(t) = a_{21}(t)\odot x_1(t)\oplus\cdots\oplus a_{2n}(t)\odot x_n(t)\oplus f_2(t)$$

$$\vdots$$

$$x'_{n_{gH}}(t) = a_{n1}(t)\odot x_1(t)\oplus\cdots\oplus a_{nn}(t)\odot x_n(t)\oplus f_n(t)$$

such that the functions $a_{ij}(t)$, $i, j = 1, \ldots, n$ are real functions and $f_i(t)$, $i = 1, \ldots, n$ are fuzzy number valued functions.

In the compact form of the system, we have:

$$\boldsymbol{x}'_{gH}(t) = \boldsymbol{A}(\boldsymbol{t}) \odot \boldsymbol{x}(\boldsymbol{t}) \oplus \boldsymbol{f}(\boldsymbol{t}), \boldsymbol{x}(\boldsymbol{t_0}) = \boldsymbol{x_0}$$

where:

$$\boldsymbol{x}(\boldsymbol{t}) = \begin{pmatrix} x_1(t) \\ \vdots \\ x_n(t) \end{pmatrix}, \; \boldsymbol{A}(\boldsymbol{t}) = \begin{pmatrix} a_{11}(t) \cdots a_{1n}(t) \\ \vdots \quad \ddots \quad \vdots \\ a_{n1}(t) \cdots a_{nn}(t) \end{pmatrix}, \; \boldsymbol{f}(\boldsymbol{t}) = \begin{pmatrix} f_1(t) \\ \vdots \\ f_n(t) \end{pmatrix}$$

such that $\boldsymbol{f}(\boldsymbol{t})$ is a fuzzy vector number. Indeed, this system is called a nonhomogeneous fuzzy system and in the case that the vector $\boldsymbol{f}(\boldsymbol{t}) = 0$, then it is called a homogeneous fuzzy system. In addition, if the coefficient matrix $\boldsymbol{A}(\boldsymbol{t})$ is a real constant matrix $\boldsymbol{A}$, then the system is called a fuzzy linear system of differential equations with constant coefficients. It is clear that each equation of this system needs the initial values. The fuzzy initial values are as:

$$x_1(t_0) = A_1, \; x_2(t_0) = A_2, \ldots, x_n(t_0) = A_n$$

where:

$$A_1, A_2, \ldots, A_n \in \mathbb{F}_R$$

Our discussions will be illustrated in two parts, the first for the homogeneous and the second for nonhomogeneous systems.

4.3.9.1 Homogeneous fuzzy linear differential systems

Now consider the following special case of the system with constant coefficient matrix:

$$\boldsymbol{x}'_{gH}(t) = \boldsymbol{A} \odot \boldsymbol{x}(\boldsymbol{t})$$

where:

$$\boldsymbol{A} = \begin{pmatrix} a_{11} \cdots a_{1n} \\ \vdots \quad \ddots \quad \vdots \\ a_{n1} \cdots a_{nn} \end{pmatrix}$$

with the fuzzy initial values:

$$\boldsymbol{x}'_{gH}(t) = \begin{pmatrix} x'_1(t) \\ \vdots \\ x'_n(t) \end{pmatrix}, \; \boldsymbol{x}(0) = \begin{pmatrix} x_{1,0} \\ \vdots \\ x_{n,0} \end{pmatrix}, \; x_{i,0} \in \mathbb{F}_R, \; i = 1, \ldots, n$$

It is clear that the solution vector is:

$$\boldsymbol{x}(\boldsymbol{t}) = \boldsymbol{e}^{\boldsymbol{At}}\boldsymbol{x}_0$$

where:

$$\begin{pmatrix} x_1(t) \\ \vdots \\ x_n(t) \end{pmatrix} = \begin{pmatrix} e^{a_{11}t} \dots e^{a_{1n}t} \\ \vdots \quad \ddots \quad \vdots \\ e^{a_{n1}t} \dots e^{a_{nn}t} \end{pmatrix} \begin{pmatrix} x_{1,0} \\ \vdots \\ x_{n,0} \end{pmatrix}$$

Clearly we can check that this satisfies the system and initial condition. Then it is a solution, and for the uniqueness, suppose that the vector function $\boldsymbol{y}(\boldsymbol{t})$ is an arbitrary solution of the system. The following vector function can be defined by $\boldsymbol{y}(\boldsymbol{t})$:

$$\boldsymbol{Z}(\boldsymbol{t}) = \boldsymbol{e}^{-\boldsymbol{At}}\boldsymbol{y}(\boldsymbol{t}),\ \boldsymbol{Z}'_{\boldsymbol{gH}}(\boldsymbol{t}) = \boldsymbol{e}^{-\boldsymbol{At}}\boldsymbol{y}'_{\boldsymbol{gH}}(\boldsymbol{t}) \oplus (-1)\boldsymbol{A}\boldsymbol{e}^{-\boldsymbol{At}}\boldsymbol{y}(\boldsymbol{t}) = 0$$

So the vector fuzzy number valued function $\boldsymbol{Z}(\boldsymbol{t})$ is a constant one and at the initial point is $\boldsymbol{Z}(\boldsymbol{0}) = \boldsymbol{y}(\boldsymbol{0}) = \boldsymbol{x}_0$, hence $\boldsymbol{Z}(\boldsymbol{t}) = \boldsymbol{x}_0$ there for any arbitrary solution $\boldsymbol{y}(\boldsymbol{t})$ is given by $\boldsymbol{y}(\boldsymbol{t}) = \boldsymbol{x}(\boldsymbol{t}) = \boldsymbol{e}^{\boldsymbol{At}} \odot \boldsymbol{x}_0$.

Example—Bimathematic two-compartment model

A two-compartment fuzzy model for drug absorption and circulation through the gastrointestinal tract and blood has been formulated in the beginning. In Fig. 4.18, the first compartment corresponds to the gastrointestinal tract and after that, the drug diffuses into the second compartment, blood.

Let $c_1(t)$ and $c_2(t)$ denote the fuzzy valued of concentration of drug in stomach or gastrointestinal tract and blood stream compartments, respectively. If c_0 is the fuzzy initial concentration of drug dosage, then the general fuzzy model describing the rate of change in oral drug administration is given as:

$$\begin{cases} c'_{1_{gH}}(t) = (-1)k_1 \odot c_1(t), & c_1(0) = c_0 \\ c'_{2_{gH}}(t) = k_1 \odot c_1(t) \oplus (-1)c_2(t), & c_2(0) = 0 \end{cases}$$

where $c_0 \in \mathbb{F}_R$ and k_1, k_e are positive real constants such that they show the rate constant from one compartment to another and the clearance constant. The coefficient

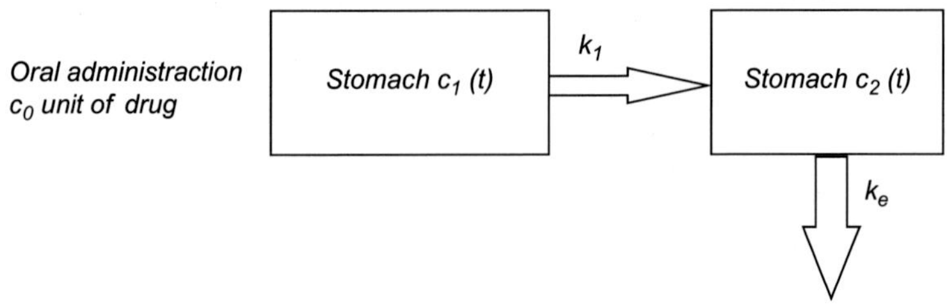

Fig. 4.18 Drug administration through the stomach and blood.

matrix is:

$$A = \begin{pmatrix} -k_1 & 0 \\ k_1 & -k_e \end{pmatrix}$$

and the compact form of the system is:

$$\begin{pmatrix} c'_{1_{gH}} \\ c'_{2_{gH}} \end{pmatrix} = \begin{pmatrix} -k_1 & 0 \\ k_1 & -k_e \end{pmatrix} \begin{pmatrix} c_1(t) \\ c_2(t) \end{pmatrix}$$

So the solution can be computed as:

$$\boldsymbol{c}(\boldsymbol{t}) = \boldsymbol{e}^{\boldsymbol{A}\boldsymbol{t}} \boldsymbol{c}_0$$

$$\begin{pmatrix} c_1(t) \\ c_2(t) \end{pmatrix} = \begin{pmatrix} e^{-k_1 t} & 0 \\ e^{k_1 t} & e^{-k_e t} \end{pmatrix} \begin{pmatrix} c_0 \\ 0 \end{pmatrix}$$

then:

$$c_1(t) = c_0 \odot e^{-k_1 t}, \; c_2(t) = \frac{c_0 \odot k_1}{k_1 - k_e} \left(e^{-k_e t} - e^{-k_1 t} \right)$$

Example—Biomathematic three-compartment model

The blood flow in the cardiovascular system is one directional, so the drug administration through venous blood can be shown by the following pattern (see Fig. 4.19).

Consider that the amount of drug flow toward tissue by arterial blood is at the rate of k_b and from tissue compartment to the venous blood at the rate ofk_t. Moreover, the clearance rate of drug from the blood is k_e. Consider $c_1(t)$, $c_2(t)$, and $c_3(t)$ denote the concentration of drug in the arterial blood, tissue, and venous blood compartment, respectively. If c_0 is the fuzzy initial value of drug, then the mathematical model of the drug concentration with respect to this compartment is:

$$\begin{cases} c'_{1_{gH}}(t) = (-1)k_b \odot c_1(t), & c_1(0) = c_0 \\ c'_{2_{gH}}(t) = k_b \odot c_1(t) \oplus (-1)k_t \odot c_2(t), & c_2(0) = 0 \\ c'_{3_{gH}}(t) = k_t \odot c_2(t) \oplus (-1)k_e \odot c_3(t), & c_2(0) = 0 \end{cases}$$

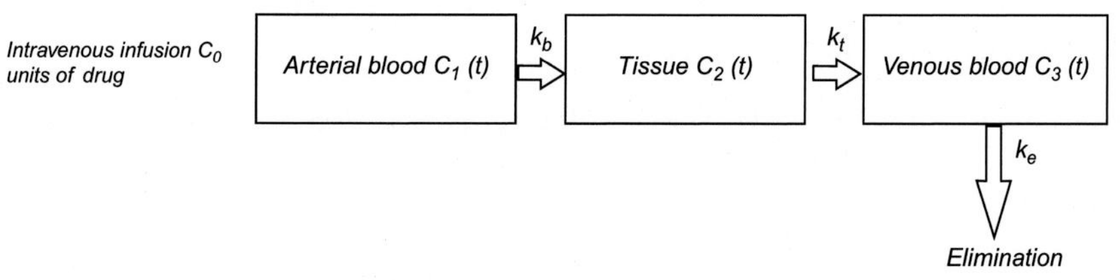

Fig. 4.19 Drug administration through arterial blood and tissue and venous blood.

The matrix and the vector solution are:

$$A = \begin{pmatrix} -k_b & 0 & 0 \\ k_b & -k_t & 0 \\ 0 & k_t & -k_e \end{pmatrix}, \quad c(t) = \begin{pmatrix} c_1(t) \\ c_2(t) \\ c_3(t) \end{pmatrix}$$

Then, using the same procedure, the solution is:

$$c_1(t) = c_0 \odot e^{-k_b t}$$

$$c_2(t) = \frac{c_0 \odot k_b t}{k_b - k_t}\left(e^{-k_t t} - e^{-k_b t}\right)$$

$$c_3(t) = \frac{c_0 \odot k_b k_t e^{-(k_b + k_e + k_t)t}}{(k_b - k_e)(k_b - k_t)(k_e - k_t)}$$

$$\left(k_b e^{(k_b + k_e)t} - k_b e^{(k_b + k_t)t} - k_e e^{(k_b + k_e)t} + k_e e^{(k_e + k_t)t} + k_t e^{(k_b + k_e)t} - k_t e^{(k_e + k_t)t}\right)$$

4.3.9.2 Nonhomogeneous fuzzy linear differential systems

In this section, the following nonhomogeneous fuzzy system of first order linear fuzzy differential equation with real constant coefficients will be solved:

$$\boldsymbol{x}'_{gH}(t) = \boldsymbol{A}(\boldsymbol{t}) \odot \boldsymbol{x}(\boldsymbol{t}) \oplus \boldsymbol{f}(\boldsymbol{t}), \quad \boldsymbol{x}(\boldsymbol{t_0}) = \boldsymbol{x_0} \in \mathbb{F}_R^n$$

Considering the definition of gH-difference, this equation is equivalent to the following equation:

$$\boldsymbol{x}'_{gH}(t) \ominus_{gH} \boldsymbol{A}(\boldsymbol{t}) \odot \boldsymbol{x}(\boldsymbol{t}) = \boldsymbol{f}(\boldsymbol{t})$$

Multiplying both sides of the equation by $e^{-At} \geq 0$, we have:

$$e^{-\boldsymbol{A}t} \odot \boldsymbol{x}'_{gH}(t) \ominus_{gH} e^{-\boldsymbol{A}t} \boldsymbol{A}(\boldsymbol{t}) \odot \boldsymbol{x}(\boldsymbol{t}) = e^{-\boldsymbol{A}t} \odot \boldsymbol{f}(\boldsymbol{t})$$

Based on the gH-derivative of composite of two fuzzy functions, the left-hand side can be considered in the form of:

$$\left(e^{-\boldsymbol{A}t} \odot \boldsymbol{x}(\boldsymbol{t})\right)'_{gH} = (-1) e^{-\boldsymbol{A}t} \boldsymbol{A}(\boldsymbol{t}) \odot \boldsymbol{x}(\boldsymbol{t}) \oplus e^{-\boldsymbol{A}t} \odot \boldsymbol{x}'_{gH}(t)$$

since $0 \ominus_{ii-gH} U = (-1)U$. So:

$$\left(e^{-\boldsymbol{A}t} \odot \boldsymbol{x}(\boldsymbol{t})\right)'_{gH} = \ominus_{gH} e^{-\boldsymbol{A}t} \boldsymbol{A}(\boldsymbol{t}) \odot \boldsymbol{x}(\boldsymbol{t}) \oplus e^{-\boldsymbol{A}t} \odot \boldsymbol{x}'_{gH}(t)$$

Finally, we have:

$$\left(e^{-\boldsymbol{A}t} \odot \boldsymbol{x}(\boldsymbol{t})\right)'_{gH} = e^{-\boldsymbol{A}t} \odot \boldsymbol{f}(\boldsymbol{t})$$

As we discussed before, based on two types of differentiability we have two types of solution as well:

- If $\boldsymbol{x}(\boldsymbol{t})$ is *i*-differentiable:

$$\boldsymbol{x}(\boldsymbol{t}) = e^{\boldsymbol{A}(t-t_0)} \odot \boldsymbol{x}(t_0) \oplus \int_{t_0}^{t} e^{\boldsymbol{A}(t-u)} \boldsymbol{f}(u) \mathrm{d}u$$

- If $\boldsymbol{x}(\boldsymbol{t})$ is *ii*-differentiable:

$$\boldsymbol{x}(\boldsymbol{t}) = e^{\boldsymbol{A}(t-t_0)} \odot \boldsymbol{x}(t_0) \ominus_H (-1) \int_{t_0}^{t} e^{\boldsymbol{A}(t-u)} \boldsymbol{f}(u) \mathrm{d}u$$

Example—Biomathematic two-compartment model

In this model, just two compartments—the tissues and bloodstream—were identified. The mathematical model to describe this is governed by the system of two differential equations such that each equation describes the rate of change of drug concentration with respect to time (see Fig. 4.20). We assume that a drug is ingested at a given rate u such that u is a fuzzy function.

Consider that $c_1(t)$ and $c_2(t)$ denote the concentration of drug in the compartments, the bloodstream and the tissue, respectively:

$$\begin{cases} c'_{1_{gH}}(t) \oplus k_b \odot c_1(t) = u(t), & c_1(0) = 0 \\ c'_{2_{gH}}(t) \oplus k_t \odot c_2(t) = k_b \odot c_1(t), & c_2(0) = 0 \end{cases}$$

where k_b is the rate constants from the bloodstream. In the following case, we illustrate the use of the fuzzy Laplace transform for solving the metabolism model.

The drug lidocaine is used in the treatment of irregular heartbeat. Now assume that $u(t) = (1.9, 2, 2.2) \odot \delta(t)$ mg of lidocaine is injected into the bloodstream and then move into the tissue of the heart, where $\delta(t)$ is Kronecker delta function. If $c_1(t)$ describes the amount of lidocaine in the bloodstream and $c_2(t)$ evaluates the amount of drug in the tissue, then:

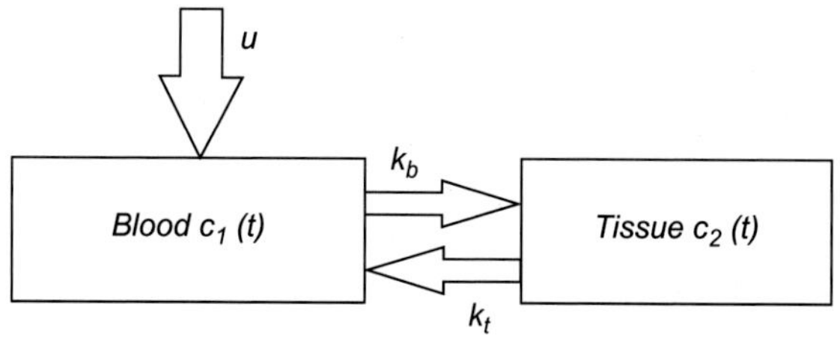

Fig. 4.20 Drug administration through blood and tissue.

$$\begin{cases} c'_{1_{gH}}(t) \oplus c_1(t) = (1.9, 2, 2.2) \odot \delta(t), & c_1(0) = 0 \\ c'_{2_{gH}}(t) \oplus c_2(t) = c_1(t), & c_2(0) = 0 \end{cases}$$

As we stated in Chapter 3, taking the Laplace transform of both sides of the equations in the system, we have:

$$\begin{cases} L\left(c'_{1_{gH}}(t)\right) \oplus L(c_1(t)) = (1.9, 2, 2.2) \odot L(\delta(t)), \\ L\left(c'_{2_{gH}}(t)\right) \oplus L(c_2(t)) = L(c_1(t)), \end{cases}$$

Let us consider that:

$$L(c_1(t)) = C_1(s), \ L(c_2(t)) = C_2(s)$$

$$L\left(c'_{1_{gH}}(t)\right) = s \odot L(c_1(t)) \ominus_{gH} x(0) = s \odot C_1(s)$$

$$L\left(c'_{2_{gH}}(t)\right) = s \odot L(c_2(t)) \ominus_{gH} x(0) = s \odot C_2(s)$$

so the systems is as follows:

$$\begin{cases} s \odot C_1(s) \oplus C_1(s) = (1.9, 2, 2.2), \\ s \odot C_2(s) \oplus C_2(s) = C_1(s), \end{cases}$$

The solutions are:

$$C_1(s) = \frac{(1.9, 2, 2.2)}{s+1}, \ C_1(s) = \frac{(1.9, 2, 2.2)}{(s+1)^2}$$

Now, using the inverse Laplace, the solution of original fuzzy systems is found as follows (Fig. 4.21):

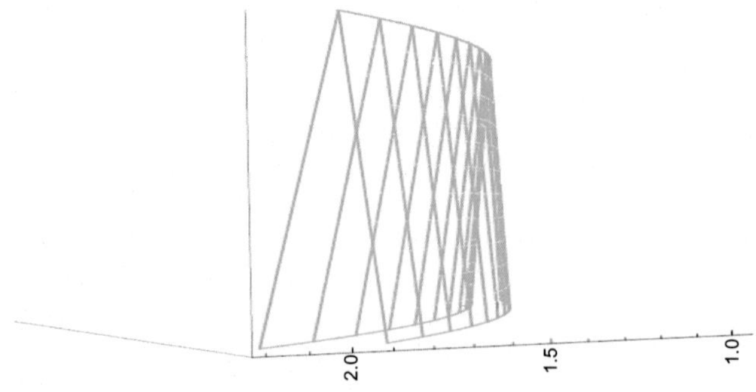

Fig. 4.21 The solution $c_1(t)$.

$$c_1(t) = L^{-1}\left(\frac{(1.9, 2, 2.2)}{s+1}\right) = (1.9, 2, 2.2)\odot L^{-1}\left(\frac{1}{s+1}\right) = (1.9, 2, 2.2)\odot e^{-t}$$

$$c_2(t) = L^{-1}\left(\frac{(1.9, 2, 2.2)}{(s+1)^2}\right) = (1.9, 2, 2.2)\odot L^{-1}\left(\frac{1}{(s+1)^2}\right) = (1.9, 2, 2.2)\odot te^{-t}$$

4.3.9.3 Reduction of a second order fuzzy differential equations to a system of first order equations

The second order linear differential equation:

$$x''_{gH}(t)\oplus a_1(t)\odot x'_{gH}(t)\oplus a_2(t)\odot x(t) = f(t),$$

with the initial values:

$$x(t_0) = A_1,\ x'_{gH}(t_0) = A_2$$

where the initial values are two fuzzy numbers. To reduce the second order differential equation to the system of first order differential equation, we assume that:

$$x(t) = y_1(t),\ x'_{gH}(t) = y_2(t)$$

so:

$$y'_{1_{gH}}(t) = x'_{gH}(t) = y_2(t)$$

$$y'_{2_{gH}}(t) = x''_{gH}(t) = f(t)\ominus_{gH} a_1(t)\odot x'_{gH}(t)\ominus_{gH} a_2(t)\odot x(t)$$

By substituting the relations in the last one:

$$y'_{2_{gH}}(t) = f(t)\ominus_{gH} a_1(t)\odot y_2(t)\ominus_{gH} a_2(t)\odot y_1(t)$$

We then arrive at the following system of fuzzy first order differential equations:

$$\begin{cases} y'_{1_{gH}}(t) = y_2(t), & y_1(t_0) = A_1 \\ y'_{2_{gH}}(t) = f(t)\ominus_{gH} a_1(t)\odot y_2(t)\ominus_{gH} a_2(t)\odot y_1(t), & y_2(t_0) = A_2 \end{cases}$$

Note that the types of differentiability of $x(t)$ and $y_1(t)$ and also $x_{gH}'(t)$ and $y_2(t)$ are the same.

Example—Fuzzy forced harmonic oscillator problem

Consider the following fuzzy second order differential equation that is denoted as a forced harmonic oscillator problem:

$$x''_{gH}(t)\oplus x(t) = f(t),\ x(0) = x_0 \in \mathbb{F}_R,\ x'_{gH}(0) = x_1 \in \mathbb{F}_R$$

By using the same procedure, it is concluded that:

$$\begin{cases} y'_{1_{gH}}(t) = y_2(t), & y_1(t_0) = x_0 \\ y'_{2_{gH}}(t) = f(t) \ominus_{gH} y_1(t), & y_2(t_0) = x_1 \end{cases}$$

in the matrix form:

$$\boldsymbol{A} = \begin{pmatrix} 0 & 1 \\ -1 & 0 \end{pmatrix}, \ \boldsymbol{b}(t) = \begin{pmatrix} 0 \\ f(t) \end{pmatrix}, \ \boldsymbol{y}(0) = \begin{pmatrix} x_0 \\ x_1 \end{pmatrix}$$

and:

$$e^{At} = \begin{pmatrix} \cos t & \sin t \\ -\sin t & \cos t \end{pmatrix}, \ e^{-At} = \begin{pmatrix} \cos t & -\sin t \\ \sin t & \cos t \end{pmatrix}$$

The i-differentiable solution is:

$$\boldsymbol{y}(t) = \left(e^{At} \boldsymbol{x}_0 \oplus e^{At} \int_0^t e^{-A\tau} \boldsymbol{b}(\tau) d\tau \right)$$

In another form:

$$\begin{pmatrix} y_1(t) \\ y_2(t) \end{pmatrix} = \begin{pmatrix} \cos t & \sin t \\ -\sin t & \cos t \end{pmatrix} \begin{pmatrix} x_0 \\ x_1 \end{pmatrix} \oplus \begin{pmatrix} \cos t & \sin t \\ -\sin t & \cos t \end{pmatrix} \int_0^t \begin{pmatrix} \cos \tau & -\sin \tau \\ \sin \tau & \cos \tau \end{pmatrix} \begin{pmatrix} 0 \\ f(\tau) \end{pmatrix} d\tau$$

and:

$$y_1(t) = x(t) = x_0 \cos t \oplus x_1 \sin t \oplus \int_0^t f(\tau) \sin(t-\tau) d\tau$$

So the fuzzy i-differentiable solution is:

$$x(t) = x_0 \cos t \oplus x_1 \sin t \oplus \int_0^t f(\tau) \sin(t-\tau) d\tau$$

and the fuzzy ii-differentiable solution is:

$$x(t) = x_0 \odot \cos t \oplus x_1 \odot \sin t \ominus_H (-1) \int_0^t f(\tau) \odot \sin(t-\tau) d\tau$$

As a case, consider that:

$$x''_{gH}(t) \oplus x(t) = (1, 5, 15) e^{2t} \oplus (2, 10, 30) e^{3t}, \ x(0) = (0.4, 2, 6), x'_{gH}(0) = (1, 5, 15)$$

the i-solution:

$$x(t) = (0.4, 2, 6) \odot \cos t \oplus (1, 5, 15) \odot \sin t \oplus \int_0^t \left((1, 5, 15) e^{2\tau} \oplus (2, 10, 30) e^{3\tau} \right) \odot \sin(t-\tau) d\tau$$

The final solution is obtained by fuzzy calculus:

$$x(t) = (0.2, 1, 3)e^{2t} \oplus (0.2, 1, 3)e^{3t}$$

4.4 *Z*-differential equations

In Chapter 2, we discussed the Z-numbers and calculations on these uncertain numbers. In the real world, most phenomena are based on doubt, and the information that we have from various subjects such as economics, politics, and physics is evaluated according to verbal values. Here, we try to formulate and investigate the mentioned information to the initial value problem while our initial data are Z-numbers. Now, in this section, first the differential operator will be introduced on the Z-number valued functions under *gH*-differentiability, then the differential equation with Z-number initial value will be introduced and discussed. To this purpose, we should first define a Z-process or a Z-valued function.

Definition—Z-process

A function x is called a Z-valued function if for any $t \in D_x$ the value $x(t)$ is a Z-number.

Definition—Continuity

A Z-valued function is continuous if and only if its first part is continuous. Indeed, if $x = (x_A, x_N)$ is a Z-process or Z-valued then the continuity of x is equivalent to continuity of x_A at the point t_0 and it is:

$$\forall \epsilon > 0 \exists \delta > 0 \forall t \, (|t - t_0| < \delta \Rightarrow D_H(x(t), x(t_0)) < \epsilon)$$

Note. In this definition, we assume that the probability part is always continuous.

We shall now define the derivative of a Z-process under *gH*-differentiability and then its corresponding differential equations.

Note. As we mentioned in Chapter 2, the special case of a Z-number occurs when the probability part is also a fuzzy number. In other words, it can be approximated by a trapezoidal or triangular fuzzy number. In this case, two parts of the Z-process are fuzzy numbers.

Example

Assume that $X = R$ is the set of real numbers, A is close to 10, and N is quite sure. Then the Z-number can be defined as:

$$Z = (\text{close to } 10, \text{quite sure})$$

The Z-valued function or process can be defined as $x(t) = Zt$. The membership function of A also can be defined as:

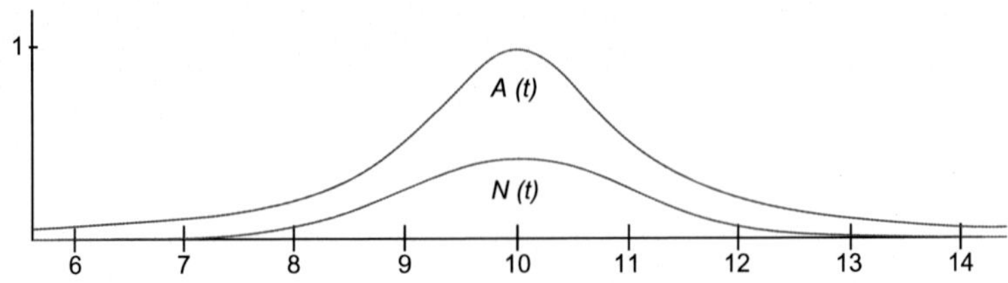

Fig. 4.22 Z-number Z=(close to 10, quite sure).

$$A(t)=\left(1+(t-10)^2\right)^{-1}$$

and the membership function for N:

$$N(t)=\frac{1}{\sigma\sqrt{2\pi}}\exp\left(-\frac{(t-\mu)^2}{2\sigma^2}\right),\ \mu=10,\ \sigma=1$$

See Fig. 4.22.

The level-wise form of this Z-number is:

$$Z[r]=(A,N)[r]=[A[r],N[r]],\ 0\le r\le 1,$$

where:

$$A[r]=[A_l(r),A_u(r)]=[5+5r,\ 15-5r],$$

$$N[r]=[N_l(r),N_u(r)]=[6+4r,\ 14-4r].$$

Moreover, it is clear both parts are continuous and immediately the continuity of the Z-process $x(t)=Zt$ can be concluded.

Definition—*gH*-differentiability of Z-process

A Z-process x is gH-differentiable on $[a,b]$ if for all $t\in[a,b]$:

$$x'_{gH}(t)=\left(x'_{A_{gH}}(t),x'_{N_{gH}}(t)\right)$$

$$=\left(\lim_{h\to 0}\frac{x_A(t+h)\ominus_{gH}x_A(t)}{h},\ \lim_{h\to 0}\frac{x_N(t+h)\ominus_{gH}x_N(t)}{h}\right)$$

Note. The necessary and sufficient conditions for the gH-differentiability of a Z-process are both parts gH-differentiable.

Note. The Z-process x is $i-gH$ differentiable if x_A and x_N both are $i-gH$ differentiable:

$$x'_{i-gH}(t)=\left(x'_{A_{i-gH}}(t),x'_{N_{i-gH}}(t)\right)$$

The level-wise form:

$$x'_{i-gH}(t)[r] = \left(\left[x'_{l,A}(t,r), x'_{u,A}(t,r)\right], \left[x'_{l,N}(t,r), x'_{u,N}(t,r)\right]\right)$$

Note. The Z-process x is $ii-gH$ differentiable if x_A and x_N both are $ii-gH$ differentiable:

$$x'_{ii-gH}(t) = \left(x'_{A_{ii-gH}}(t), x'_{N_{ii-gH}}(t)\right)$$

The level-wise form:

$$x'_{ii-gH}(t)[r] = \left(\left[x'_{u,A}(t,r), x'_{l,A}(t,r)\right], \left[x'_{u,N}(t,r), x'_{l,N}(t,r)\right]\right)$$

***Z*-number initial value problem**

Consider the following differential equation with Z-number initial value:

$$x'_{gH}(t) = f(t, x(t)), \ x(t_0) = x_0, \ t \in [t_0, T], \ T > 0$$

where x_0 is a Z-number and $x_0 = (x_{0,A}, x_{0,N})$ then the solution is also a Z-process, and it can be considered in the following form:

$$x(t) = (x_A(t), x_N(t))$$

Here, we also have two cases without considering the switching points.

Case 1. The Z-process x is $i-gH$ differentiable, then:

$$x'_{i-gH}(t)[r] = \left(\left[x'_{l,A}(t,r), x'_{u,A}(t,r)\right], \left[x'_{l,N}(t,r), x'_{u,N}(t,r)\right]\right) = f(t, x(t))[r]$$

where:

$$f(t,x(t))[r] = ((f_A(t, x_A(t), x_N(t)))[r], (f_N(t, x_A(t), x_N(t)))[r])[r],$$

$$(f_A(t, x_A(t), x_N(t)))[r] = [f_{l,A}(t, x_A(t), x_N(t), r), f_{u,A}(t, x_A(t), x_N(t), r)],$$

$$(f_N(t, x_A(t), x_N(t)))[r] = [f_{l,N}(t, x_A(t), x_N(t), r), f_{u,N}(t, x_A(t), x_N(t), r)].$$

It is concluded that:

$$\left[x'_{l,A}(t,r), x'_{u,A}(t,r)\right] = [f_{l,A}(t, x_A(t), x_N(t), r), f_{u,A}(t, x_A(t), x_N(t), r)],$$

$$\left[x'_{l,N}(t,r), x'_{u,N}(t,r)\right] = [f_{l,N}(t, x_A(t), x_N(t), r), f_{u,N}(t, x_A(t), x_N(t), r)].$$

Finally:

$$\begin{cases} \begin{cases} x'_{l,A}(t,r) = f_{l,A}(t, x_A(t), x_N(t), r) \\ x'_{u,A}(t,r) = f_{u,A}(t, x_A(t), x_N(t), r) \end{cases} \\ \begin{cases} x'_{l,N}(t,r) = f_{l,N}(t, x_A(t), x_N(t), r) \\ x'_{u,N}(t,r) = f_{u,N}(t, x_A(t), x_N(t), r) \end{cases} \\ \begin{cases} x_{l,A}(t_0,r) = x_{l,0,A}(r), x_{l,N}(t_0,r) = x_{l,0,N}(r) \\ x_{u,A}(t_0,r) = x_{u,0,A}(r), x_{u,N}(t_0,r) = x_{u,0,N}(r) \end{cases} \end{cases}$$

Case 2. The Z-process x is $ii-gH$ differentiable, then:

$$\begin{cases} \begin{cases} x'_{u,A}(t,r)=f_{l,A}(t,x_A(t),x_N(t),r) \\ x'_{l,A}(t,r)=f_{u,A}(t,x_A(t),x_N(t),r) \end{cases} \\ \begin{cases} x'_{u,N}(t,r)=f_{l,N}(t,x_A(t),x_N(t),r) \\ x'_{l,N}(t,r)=f_{u,N}(t,x_A(t),x_N(t),r) \end{cases} \\ \begin{cases} x_{l,A}(t_0,r)=x_{l,0,A}(r), x_{l,N}(t_0,r)=x_{l,0,N}(r) \\ x_{u,A}(t_0,r)=x_{u,0,A}(r), x_{u,N}(t_0,r)=x_{u,0,N}(r) \end{cases} \end{cases}$$

where:

$$f_{l,A}(t,x_A(t),x_N(t),r)=\min\{f_A(t,u,v)|\, u\in x_A(t)[r], v\in x_N(t)[r]\}$$

$$f_{u,A}(t,x_A(t),x_N(t),r)=\max\{f_A(t,u,v)|\, u\in x_A(t)[r], v\in x_N(t)[r]\}$$

$$f_{l,N}(t,x_A(t),x_N(t),r)=\min\{f_N(t,u,v)|\, u\in x_A(t)[r], v\in x_N(t)[r]\}$$

$$f_{u,N}(t,x_A(t),x_N(t),r)=\max\{f_N(t,u,v)|\, u\in x_A(t)[r], v\in x_N(t)[r]\}$$

Therefore, in those cases the Z-number initial value problem is transformed to the system of real differential equations and the characteristic theorem is necessary to find the solution of the original Z-valued differential equations.

Characteristic theorem

If the Z-process f is a continuous and gH-differentiable that satisfies the following fuzzy differential equation:

$$x'_{gH}(t)=f(t,x(t)),\ \ x(t_0)=x_0,\ \ t\in[t_0,T],\ \ T>0$$

and also suppose the following conditions:

- $f_A(t,x(t),r)=[f_{l,\ A}(t,x_A(t),x_N(t),r),f_{u,\ A}(t,x_A(t),x_N(t),r)]$
- $f_N(t,x(t),r)=[f_{l,\ N}(t,x_A(t),x_N(t),r),f_{u,\ N}(t,x_A(t),x_N(t),r)]$
- $f_{l,\ A}(t,x_l(t,r),x_u(t,r))$, $f_{u,\ A}(t,x_l(t,r),x_u(t,r))$, $f_{l,\ N}(t,x_A(t),x_N(t),r)$ and $f_{u,\ N}(t,x_A(t),x_N(t),r)$ are equicontinuous. It means, for any $\epsilon>0$ and any $(t,u,v)\in[t_0,T]\times R^2$ if $\|(t,u,v)-(t,u_1,v_1)\|<\delta$ we have the following inequalities for $\forall r\in[0,1]$:

$$|f_{l,A}(t,x_l(t,r),x_u(t,r))-f_{l,A}(t,x_l(t,r),x_u(t,r))|<\epsilon$$

$$|f_{l,A}(t,x_l(t,r),x_u(t,r))-f_{u,A}(t,x_l(t,r),x_u(t,r))|<\epsilon$$

$$|f_{u,A}(t,x_l(t,r),x_u(t,r))-f_{l,A}(t,x_l(t,r),x_u(t,r))|<\epsilon$$

$$|f_{u,A}(t,x_l(t,r),x_u(t,r))-f_{u,A}(t,x_l(t,r),x_u(t,r))|<\epsilon$$

$$|f_{l,N}(t,x_l(t,r),x_u(t,r))-f_{l,N}(t,x_l(t,r),x_u(t,r))|<\epsilon$$

$$|f_{l,N}(t,x_l(t,r),x_u(t,r))-f_{u,N}(t,x_l(t,r),x_u(t,r))|<\epsilon$$

$$|f_{u,N}(t,x_l(t,r),x_u(t,r))-f_{l,N}(t,x_l(t,r),x_u(t,r))|<\epsilon$$
$$|f_{u,N}(t,x_l(t,r),x_u(t,r))-f_{u,N}(t,x_l(t,r),x_u(t,r))|<\epsilon$$

- $f_{l,\ A}(t,x_l(t,r),x_u(t,r))$, $f_{u,\ A}(t,x_l(t,r),x_u(t,r))$, $f_{l,\ N}(t,x_A(t),x_N(t),r)$ and $f_{u,\ N}(t,x_A(t),x_N(t),r)$ are uniformly bounded on any bounded set.
- Lipschitz property. There exists $L>0$ such that:

$$|f_{l,A}(t,u_1,v_1,r)-f_{l,A}(t,u_2,v_2,r)|<L\max\{|u_1-u_2|,|v_1-v_2|\}$$
$$|f_{l,A}(t,u_1,v_1,r)-f_{u,A}(t,u_2,v_2,r)|<L\max\{|u_1-u_2|,|v_1-v_2|\}$$
$$|f_{u,A}(t,u_1,v_1,r)-f_{l,A}(t,u_2,v_2,r)|<L\max\{|u_1-u_2|,|v_1-v_2|\}$$
$$|f_{u,A}(t,u_1,v_1,r)-f_{u,A}(t,u_2,v_2,r)|<L\max\{|u_1-u_2|,|v_1-v_2|\}$$
$$|f_{l,N}(t,u_1,v_1,r)-f_{l,N}(t,u_2,v_2,r)|<L\max\{|u_1-u_2|,|v_1-v_2|\}$$
$$|f_{l,N}(t,u_1,v_1,r)-f_{u,N}(t,u_2,v_2,r)|<L\max\{|u_1-u_2|,|v_1-v_2|\}$$
$$|f_{u,N}(t,u_1,v_1,r)-f_{l,N}(t,u_2,v_2,r)|<L\max\{|u_1-u_2|,|v_1-v_2|\}$$
$$|f_{u,N}(t,u_1,v_1,r)-f_{u,N}(t,u_2,v_2,r)|<L\max\{|u_1-u_2|,|v_1-v_2|\}$$

for any $r\in[0,1]$.
Then the Z-differential equation is equivalent to the each of following real differential equations in the cone:

$$\begin{cases}\begin{cases}x'_{l,A}(t,r)=f_{l,A}(t,x_A(t),x_N(t),r)\\ x'_{u,A}(t,r)=f_{u,A}(t,x_A(t),x_N(t),r)\end{cases}\\ \begin{cases}x'_{l,N}(t,r)=f_{l,N}(t,x_A(t),x_N(t),r)\\ x'_{u,N}(t,r)=f_{u,N}(t,x_A(t),x_N(t),r)\end{cases}\\ \begin{cases}x_{l,A}(t_0,r)=x_{l,0,A}(r),x_{l,N}(t_0,r)=x_{l,0,N}(r)\\ x_{u,A}(t_0,r)=x_{u,0,A}(r),x_{u,N}(t_0,r)=x_{u,0,N}(r)\end{cases}\end{cases}$$

or

$$\begin{cases}\begin{cases}x'_{u,A}(t,r)=f_{l,A}(t,x_A(t),x_N(t),r)\\ x'_{l,A}(t,r)=f_{u,A}(t,x_A(t),x_N(t),r)\end{cases}\\ \begin{cases}x'_{u,N}(t,r)=f_{l,N}(t,x_A(t),x_N(t),r)\\ x'_{l,N}(t,r)=f_{u,N}(t,x_A(t),x_N(t),r)\end{cases}\\ \begin{cases}x_{l,A}(t_0,r)=x_{l,0,A}(r),x_{l,N}(t_0,r)=x_{l,0,N}(r)\\ x_{u,A}(t_0,r)=x_{u,0,A}(r),x_{u,N}(t_0,r)=x_{u,0,N}(r)\end{cases}\end{cases}$$

The proof is very similar to the same theorem that has been proved in this chapter previously.

Remark. An immediate conclusion of the theorem is, the solution of the Z-differential equation is unique (Pirmuhammadi et al., 2017).

Example—Population biology

Differential equations whose solutions involve exponential growth or decay were discussed earlier. Consider the differential equation:

$$x'_{gH}(t)=\lambda\odot x(t),\ \ x(t_0)=x_0$$

Clearly, the population does have the following statuses:

$$\text{population}:=\begin{cases}\text{stationary or } x(t)=x(t_0)\ \text{when } \lambda=0\\ \text{growth or } x(t)\to\infty\ \text{when } \lambda>0\\ \text{decay or } x(t)\to 0\ \text{when } \lambda<0\end{cases}$$

First, suppose that $\lambda=1$ and we have the growth model. The initial value is defined as a Z-number on the set of "the births in some country last month" and it is:

$$x_0=(\text{considerably close to } 20{,}000,\text{ not sure})$$

such that:

$$x_{0,A}=\text{considerably close to } 20{,}000,\ \ x_{0,B}=\text{not sure}$$

with the membership functions (19,20,21):

$$x_{0,A}(t)=\begin{cases}0,\ t<19\\ t-1,\ 19\le t<20\\ 1,\ t=20\\ 1-t,\ 20<t<21\\ 0,\ t>21\end{cases}$$

and $x_{0,\ N}(t)$ presents the normal probability density function:

$$N(t)=\frac{1}{\sigma\sqrt{2\pi}}\exp\left(-\frac{(t-\mu)^2}{2\sigma^2}\right),\ \ \mu=20,\ \ \sigma=2$$

It is very easy to show that:

$$x(t)=(x_A(t),x_N(t))=\left(x_{0,A}\odot e^{(t-t_0)},x_{0,N}\odot e^{(t-t_0)}\right)$$

$$x_{0,A}(t,r)=[19+r,21-r],\ \ x_{0,N}(t,r)=[4+16r,36-16r]$$

Now decay the model; assume $\lambda=-1$. The initial value is defined as a Z-number on the set of "the deaths in some country last month" and it is:

$$x_0=(\text{considerably close to 2 million, not sure})$$

such that:

$$x_{0,A} = \text{considerably close to 2 million}, x_{0,B} = \text{not sure}$$

With the same membership function (19,20,21), and $x_{0,\ N}(t)$ presents the same normal probability density function. It is also very easy to show that:

$$x_{l,A}(t,r) = \frac{x_{l,0,A}(r) - x_{u,0,A}(r)}{2} e^{(t-t_0)} + \frac{x_{l,0,A}(r) + x_{u,0,A}(r)}{2} e^{-(t-t_0)}$$

$$x_{u,A}(t,r) = \frac{x_{u,0,A}(r) - x_{l,0,A}(r)}{2} e^{(t-t_0)} + \frac{x_{l,0,A}(r) + x_{u,0,A}(r)}{2} e^{-(t-t_0)}$$

$$x_{l,N}(t,r) = \frac{x_{l,0,N}(r) - x_{u,0,N}(r)}{2} e^{(t-t_0)} + \frac{x_{l,0,N}(r) + x_{u,0,N}(r)}{2} e^{-(t-t_0)}$$

$$x_{u,N}(t,r) = \frac{x_{u,0,N}(r) - x_{l,0,N}(r)}{2} e^{(t-t_0)} + \frac{x_{l,0,N}(r) + x_{u,0,N}(r)}{2} e^{-(t-t_0)}$$

where:

$$x_{0,A}(t,r) = [19 + r, 21 - r],\ x_{0,N}(t,r) = [4 + 16r, 36 - 16r],\ 0 \le r \le 1.$$

Note. According to the solution of the growth model, we find that by increasing time, the fuzziness and distribution are increased as well. In other words, uncertainty tends to infinity and probability tends to zero. The same is true for the decay model. So, if at the initial point:

$$x_0 = (\text{the births in some country last month, considerably close to } 20{,}000, \text{ not sure})$$

it will be at other time points like:

$$x(t) = (\text{the births in some country last month, considerably close to } 20{,}000, \text{ not at all})$$

Example—Medicine

The rate of a certain drug that is eliminated from the bloodstream is proportional to the amount of the drug in the bloodstream. A patient now has about 10 mg deficiency of the drug in his or her bloodstream, quite sure. The drug is being administered to the patient intravenously at a constant rate of 5 mg/h. A differential equation reflecting the situation is:

$$x'_{gH}(t) = 5 \ominus_{gH} k \odot x(t)$$

where $x(t)$ is the amount of the drug in the patient's bloodstream at time t, and:

$$x(t_0) := (\text{deficiency of the drug, about 10 mg, quite sure})$$

such that $x_{0,\ A} :=$ (about 10 mg) is a triangular fuzzy number $(8, 10, 12)$ and:

$x_{0,\ N}$:= (quite sure) presents the normal probability density function:

$$N(t) = \frac{1}{\sigma\sqrt{2\pi}} \exp\left(-\frac{(t-\mu)^2}{2\sigma^2}\right), \quad \mu = 10, \quad \sigma = 0$$

and k is the proportionality constant determined by the drug. The solutions are:

$$[x_{l,A}(t,r), x_{u,A}(t,r)] = [e^{-t}(3 + 5e^t + 2r), e^{-t}(7 + 5e^t - 2r)]$$

$$[x_{l,N}(t,r), x_{u,N}(t,r)] = [5e^{-t}(1 + 5e^t), 5e^{-t}(1 + 5e^t)]$$

Note. According to the solutions of this example, we find that by increasing t the fuzziness (or uncertainty) tends to infinity and distribution (or probability) is fixed:

$$x(t_0) := (\text{deficiency of the drug, about } 10\,\text{mg, quite sure}) \rightarrow$$

$$x(t_n) := (\text{deficiency of the drug, not close to } 10\,\text{mg, quite sure}).$$

Example—Economics

Let us suppose the highest saved money by an employee in a country is significantly over 1000 dollars per month, very likely, which is deposited in a bank account, and assume $x(t)$ is the amount of money in a bank account at time t, given in years, and we have:

$$x'_{gH}(t) = 1300 \oplus 0.04 \odot x(t) - 50t$$

where:

$$x(t_0) := (\text{high saved money, significantly over } 1000 \text{ dollars, very likely})$$

such that $x_{0,\ A}$:= (significantly over 1000 dollars) is a triangular fuzzy number (999, 1000, 1001) and $x_{0,\ N}$:= (very likely) presents the normal probability density function:

$$N(t) = \frac{1}{\sigma\sqrt{2\pi}} \exp\left(-\frac{(t-\mu)^2}{2\sigma^2}\right), \quad \mu = 100, \quad \sigma = 1$$

The term $0.04 \odot x(t)$ must reflect the rate of growth due to interest. It is possible that the interest is nominally 4% per year, compounded continuously. The term 1300 reflects deposits into the account at a constant rate of 1300 dollars per year. The term $50t$ accounts for the contribution to the decrease in money, which represents the rate of withdrawal. The rate at which money is being withdrawn is increasing with time. The solutions are:

$$x_{l,A}(t,r) = -1250 + 2249e^{0.04t} + e^{0.04t}r + 1250t$$

$$x_{u,A}(t,r) = -1250 + 2251e^{0.04t} - e^{0.04t}r + 1250t$$

$$x_{l,N}(t,r) = -1250 + 2247e^{0.04t} + e^{0.04t}r + 1250t$$

$$x_{u,N}(t,r) = -1250 + 2253e^{0.04t} - e^{0.04t}r + 1250t$$

for any $0 \le r \le 1$.

Note. According to the solutions of this model, we can find out by increasing t that the fuzziness and distribution are fixed.

References

Allahviranloo, T., 2020. Uncertain information and linear systems. In: Studies in Systems, Decision and Control. 254 Springer.

Allahviranloo, T., Chehlabi, M., 2015. Solving fuzzy differential equations based on the length function properties. Soft Comput. 19, 307–320. https://doi.org/10.1007/s00500-014-1254-4.

Allahviranloo, S., Abbasbandy, S., Behzadi, S., 2014. Solving nonlinear fuzzy differential equations by using fuzzy variational iteration method. Soft Comput. 18, 2191–2200. https://10.1007/s00500-013-1193-5.

Allahviranloo, T., Gouyandeh, Z., Armand, A., Hasanoglu, A., 2015. On fuzzy solutions for heat equation based on generalized Hukuhara differentiability. Fuzzy Set. Syst. 265, 1–23.

Bede, B., Gal, S.G., 2005. Generalizations of the differentiability of fuzzy-number-valued functions with applications to fuzzy differential equations. Fuzzy Set Syst. 151, 581–599.

Bede, B., Rudas, I.J., Bencsik, A.L., 2007. First order linear fuzzy differential equations under generalized differentiability. Inform. Sci. 177, 1648–1662.

Chehlabi, M., Allahviranloo, T., 2018. Positive or negative solutions to first-order fully fuzzy linear differential equations under generalized differentiability. Appl. Soft Comput. 70, 359–370.

Gouyandeha, Z., Allahviranloob, T., Abbasbandyb, S., Armand, A., 2017. A fuzzy solution of heat equation under generalized Hukuhara differentiability by fuzzy Fourier transform. Fuzzy Set. Syst. 309, 81–97.

Liu, B., 2015. Uncertain Theory. Springer-Verlag, Berlin.

Pirmuhammadi, S., Allahviranloo, T., Keshavarz, M., 2017. The parametric form of Z-number and its application in Z-number initial value problem. Int. J. Intell. Syst. 00, 1–32.

Salahshour, S., Allahviranloo, T., 2013. Applications of fuzzy Laplace transforms. Soft Comput. 17, 145–158. https://doi.org/10.1007/s00500-012-0907-4.

Stefanini, L., Bede, B., 2009. Generalized Hukuhara differentiability of interval-valued functions and interval differential equations. Nonlinear Anal. 71, 1311–1328.

Tofigh Allahviranloo, M., Ahmadi, B., 2010. Fuzzy Laplace transforms. Soft Comput. 14, 235–243. https://doi.org/10.1007/s00500-008-0397-6.

Yao, K., 2016. Uncertain Differential Equations. Springer Uncertainty Research https://doi.org/10.1007/978-3-662-52729-0_6.

Chapter 5

Discrete numerical solutions of uncertain differential equations

5.1 Introduction

In the previous chapters, we talked about the fuzzy differential equations and their solutions. Despite the uniqueness of the fuzzy solutions of the equations, usually finding the exact solution of the equations is not an easy problem and perhaps the solution cannot even be found. In this situation, we must approximate the solutions. In this chapter, we introduce some numerical methods to approximate the exact solutions of fuzzy differential equations.

The fuzzy Taylor method is one of the numerical methods to find the fuzzy approximate and unique solution of fuzzy differential equations. This expansion was expressed in Chapter 3 up to the order three of differentiability, as follows, because of computing the complicity of the expansion involved with the type of differentiability.

Soft Numerical Computing in Uncertain Dynamic Systems. https://doi.org/10.1016/B978-0-12-822855-5.00005-7

To introduce the fuzzy Taylor method (Gouyandeha et al., 2017), we should discuss several cases. In each case, we have options in choosing the first two terms or the first three terms of the expansion to find and investigate the several numerical methods, such as the fuzzy Euler method, the fuzzy Tylor method of order two and three, etc. Since we are not able to compute and, as a matter of fact, we cannot evaluate the expansion with more terms or differentials, we thus claim that the fuzzy Taylor method with the first order of differentiability is known as a fuzzy Euler method, and the fuzzy modified Euler method is obtained with considering the first and the second derivative of the fuzzy function. The cases are as follows.

Case 1. Let us assume that $x(t)$ is a continuous fuzzy number valued function and all the derivatives are $(i-gH)$-differentiable for $n=1,2,\ldots,m$ without changing the type of differentiability. Then, based on the previous case, we have the following relation:

$$x(s)=x(a)\oplus x_{i-gH}^{(1)}(a)\odot(s-a)$$

$$\oplus x_{i-gH}^{(2)}(a)\odot\frac{(s-a)^2}{2!}\oplus\cdots\oplus x_{i-gH}^{(m-1)}(a)\odot\frac{(s-a)^{m-1}}{(m-1)!}\oplus R_n(a,s)$$

where $R_n(a,s)$ is noted as a reminder term of the expansion and it is:

$$R_n(a,s)=FR\int_a^s\left(\int_a^{s_1}\cdots\left(\int_a^{s_{n-1}}x_{i-gH}^{(n)}(s_n)\mathrm{d}s_n\right)\mathrm{d}s_{n-1}\cdots\right)\mathrm{d}s_1$$

Case 2. Let us now assume all the derivatives are $(ii-gH)$-differentiable for $n=1,2,\ldots,m$ without changing the type of differentiability. Then, based on the previous case, we have the following relation:

$$x(s)=x(a)\ominus_H(-1)x_{ii-gH}^{(1)}(a)\odot(s-a)\ominus_H(-1)x_{ii-gH}^{(2)}(a)\odot\frac{(s-a)^2}{2!}$$

$$\ominus_H(-1)\cdots\ominus_H(-1)x_{ii-gH}^{(m-1)}(a)\odot\frac{(s-a)^{m-1}}{(m-1)!}\ominus_H(-1)R_n(a,s)$$

where again $R_n(a,s)$ is noted as a reminder term of the expansion and it is:

$$R_n(a,s)=FR\int_a^s\left(\int_a^{s_1}\cdots\left(\int_a^{s_{n-1}}x_{ii-gH}^{(n)}(s_n)\mathrm{d}s_n\right)\mathrm{d}s_{n-1}\cdots\right)\mathrm{d}s_1$$

Case 3. Suppose that the same function is $i-gH$ differentiable for $n=2k-1$, $k\in\mathbb{N}$ and it is $ii-gH$ differentiable for $n=2k$, $k\in\mathbb{N}\cup\{0\}$:

$$x(s)=x(a)\ominus_H(-1)x_{ii-gH}^{(1)}(a)\odot(s-a)$$

$$\oplus x_{i-gH}^{(2)}(a)\odot\frac{(s-a)^2}{2!}\ominus_H(-1)\cdots\ominus_H(-1)x_{ii-gH}^{\left(\frac{m-1}{2}\right)}(a)\odot\frac{(s-a)^{\frac{m-1}{2}}}{\left(\frac{m-1}{2}\right)!}\oplus$$

$$\oplus x_{i-gH}^{\left(\frac{m}{2}\right)}(a)\odot\frac{(s-a)^{\frac{m}{2}}}{\left(\frac{m}{2}\right)!}\ominus_H(-1)\cdots\ominus_H(-1)R_n(a,s)$$

where again $R_n(a,s)$ is noted as:

$$R_n(a,s)=FR\int_a^s\left(\int_a^{s_1}\cdots\left(\int_a^{s_{n-1}}x_{i-gH}^{(n)}(s_n)\mathrm{d}s_n\right)\mathrm{d}s_{n-1}\cdots\right)\mathrm{d}s_1$$

Case 4. Suppose that the same function is $i-gH$ differentiable in interval $[a,\xi]$ and ξ is the switching point. So:

$$x(s)=x(a)\oplus x_{i-gH}^{(1)}(a)\odot(\xi-a)\ominus_H x_{ii-gH}^{(2)}(a)\odot(a-\zeta_1)\odot(\xi-a)$$

$$\oplus x_{i-gH}^{(2)}(\zeta_1)\odot\left(\frac{(\xi-\zeta_1)^2}{2}\right.$$

$$\left.-\frac{(a-\zeta_1)^2}{2}\right)\ominus_H(-1)FR\int_a^{\xi}\left(\int_a^{\zeta_1}\left(\int_a^{s_2}x_{ii-gH}^{(3)}(s_4)\mathrm{d}s_4\right)\mathrm{d}s_2\right)\mathrm{d}s_1$$

$$\oplus FR\int_a^{\xi}\left(\int_{\zeta_1}^{s_1}\left(\int_{\zeta_1}^{s_3}x_{i-gH}^{(3)}(s_5)\mathrm{d}s_5\right)\mathrm{d}s_3\right)ds_1\ominus_H(-1)\left(x_{ii-gH}^{(1)}(\xi)\right.$$

$$\odot(s-\xi)\oplus x_{ii-gH}^{(2)}(\xi)\odot\frac{(s-\xi)^2}{2!}$$

$$\left.\oplus FR\int_{\xi}^{s}\left(\int_{\xi}^{t}\left(\int_a^{t_2}x_{ii-gH}^{(3)}(t_3)\mathrm{d}t_3\right)\mathrm{d}t_2\right)\mathrm{d}t_1\right)$$

As we discussed before, we should rest assured that the solution exists and is unique. In Chapter 4 we proved the following theorem, in which, under the following conditions, the fuzzy solution exists, and it is unique.

1. The function $f:I_1\times I_2\rightarrow\mathbb{F}_R$ is continuous where I_1 is a closed interval containing the initial value x_0 and I_2 is any other area such that f is bounded on it.
2. The function f is bounded. It means $\exists M<0,\ D_H(f(t,x),0)\leq M,\forall(t,x)\in I_1\times I_2$.
3. The real function $g:I_1\times I_3\rightarrow R$ such that $g(t,u)\equiv 0$ is bounded on $I_1\times I_3$, $\exists M_1>0,\ 0\leq g(t,u)\leq M_1,\forall(t,u)\in I_1\times I_3$ where I_3 is another closed interval containing u. Moreover $g(t,u)$ is nondecreasing in u and its corresponding initial value problem:

$$u'(t)=g(t,u(t)),\ \ u(t_0)=0$$

has only the solution $u(t)\equiv 0$ on I_1.

4. Also:

$$D_H(f(t,x),f(t,y)) \leq g(t,|x-y|),\ \forall(t,x)\forall(t,y)\in I_1\times I_2, x,y\in I_3$$

Then the fuzzy initial value problem has both $(i-gH)$-solution $x_{i-gH}(t)$ and $(ii-gH)$-solution $x_{ii-gH}(t)$ and the following successive iterations converge to these two solutions:

$$x_{i,n+1}(t)=x_{i,0}\oplus\int_{t_0}^{t} f(t,x_{i,n}(z))\mathrm{d}z,\ x_{i,0}(t)=x_0$$

and:

$$x_{ii,n+1}(t)=x_{ii,0}\ominus(-1)\odot\int_{t_0}^{t} f(t,x_{ii,n}(z))\mathrm{d}z,\ x_{ii,0}(t)=x_0$$

5.2 Fuzzy Euler method

Consider the following fuzzy initial value problem:

$$x'_{gH}(t)=f(t,x),\ x(t_0)=x_0\in\mathbb{F}_R,\ t_0\leq t\leq T$$

As we know, the solution $x(t)$ is an unknown fuzzy number valued function and $f:[0,T]\times\mathbb{F}_R\to\mathbb{F}_R$ is a fuzzy continuous function.

To derive the fuzzy Euler method, let a partition $I_N=\{0=t_0<t_1<\cdots<t_N=T\}$ of the interval $[0,T]$, where $t_k=kh$, $k=0, 1, \ldots, N$. The step size is $h=\frac{T}{N}$ and the points are equidistant points. As a first case, suppose that the unique solution $x(t)$ is $(i-gH)$-differentiable and $x(t)\in C^2_{gH}([0,T],\mathbb{F}_R)$ (Allahviranloo et al., 2015, 2007; Allahviranloo & Salahshour, 2011; Armand et al., 2019; Gouyandeha et al., 2017).

Case 1. The fuzzy number valued solution function $x(t)$ is $(i-gH)$-differentiable and the type of differentiability does not change on $[0,T]$. So the fuzzy Taylor expansion is:

$$x(t_{k+1})=x(t_k)\oplus x'_{i-gH}(t_k)\odot(t_{k+1}-t_k)\oplus x''_{i-gH}(\eta_k)\odot\frac{(t_{k+1}-t_k)^2}{2!}$$

for some point $\eta_k\in[t_k,t_{k+1}]$. Since $h=t_{k+1}-t_k$ then it gives:

$$x(t_{k+1})=x(t_k)\oplus h\odot x'_{i-gH}(t_k)\oplus\frac{h^2}{2!}\odot x''_{i-gH}(\eta_k)$$

From the equation, we have:

$$x'_{i-gH}(t)=f(t,x(t))$$

then:

$$x(t_{k+1})=x(t_k)\oplus h\odot f(t_k,x(t_k))\oplus\frac{h^2}{2!}\odot x''_{i-gH}(\eta_k)$$

Using the Hausdorff distance and approaching it to zero, we will find the fuzzy Euler method with its error function. So we have:

$$D_H\left(x(t_{k+1}),x(t_k)\oplus h\odot f(t_k,x(t_k))\oplus\frac{h^2}{2!}\odot x''_{i-gH}(\eta_k)\right)\leq$$

$$D_H(x(t_{k+1}),x(t_k)\oplus h\odot f(t_k,x(t_k)))+D_H\left(0,\frac{h^2}{2!}\odot x''_{i-gH}(\eta_k)\right)\rightarrow 0$$

Hence we find:

$$D_H(x(t_{k+1}),x(t_k)\oplus h\odot f(t_k,x(t_k)))\rightarrow 0,\ D_H\left(0,\frac{h^2}{2!}\odot x''_{i-gH}(\eta_k)\right)\rightarrow 0$$

We know that the step size h is small enough and goes to zero. Then:

$$x(t_{k+1})\approx x(t_k)\oplus h\odot f(t_k,x(t_k))$$

It is clear that the right-hand side approximates the left-hand side. Based on this approximate method, we can introduce a similar iterative method to find or define the sequence of $\{x_k\}_{k=0}^{N-1}$ such that $x_k\approx x(t_k)$:

$$\begin{cases} x_{k+1}=x_k\oplus h\odot f(t_k,x_k), & k=0,1,\ldots,N-1 \\ x_0\in\mathbb{F}_R \end{cases}$$

Case 2. The solution $x(t)$ is $(ii-gH)$-differentiable and the type of differentiability does not change on $[0,T]$. So the fuzzy Taylor expansion is:

$$x(t_{k+1})=x(t_k)\ominus_H(-1)h\odot x'_{ii-gH}(t_k)\ominus_H(-1)\frac{h^2}{2!}\odot x''_{ii-gH}(\eta_k)$$

Since $x_{ii-gH}{}'(t)=f(t,x(t))$ then:

$$x(t_{k+1})=x(t_k)\ominus_H(-1)h\odot f(t_k,x(t_k))\ominus_H(-1)\frac{h^2}{2!}\odot x''_{ii-gH}(\eta_k)$$

Thus by a process similar to the previous one, the fuzzy Euler method takes the form:

$$\begin{cases} x_{k+1}=x_k\ominus_H(-1)h\odot f(t_k,x_k), & k=0,1,\ldots,N-1 \\ x_0\in\mathbb{F}_R \end{cases}$$

Case 3. Let us suppose that $x(t)$ has a switching point type (1) on the interval $[0, T]$ as like as ξ, and also assume that t_0, t_1, …, t_j, ξ, t_{j+1}, …, t_N. Thus the fuzzy Euler method is obtained as follows:

$$\begin{cases} x_{k+1} = x_k \oplus h \odot f(t_k, x_k), & k = 0, 1, \ldots, j \\ x_{k+1} = x_k \ominus_H (-1) h \odot f(t_k, x_k), & k = j+1, j+2, \ldots, N-1 \\ x_0 \in \mathbb{F}_R \end{cases}$$

Case 4. If ξ is a type (2) switching point, the fuzzy Euler method takes the form as follows:

$$\begin{cases} x_{k+1} = x_k \ominus_H (-1) h \odot f(t_k, x_k), & k = 0, 1, \ldots, j \\ x_{k+1} = x_k \oplus h \odot f(t_k, x_k), & k = j+1, j+2, \ldots, N-1 \\ x_0 \in \mathbb{F}_R \end{cases}$$

5.2.1 Analysis of the fuzzy Euler method

Since error in the numerical method is inevitable, so we are going to define local truncation and global truncation errors. Using this concept, the consistency of the Euler method and its convergence and stability are studied and proved (Armand et al., 2019).

5.2.1.1 Local truncation error and consistency

For all abovementioned cases of the fuzzy Euler method, we can define the local truncation error by using a residual value as follows:

$$R_k = x(t_{k+1}) \ominus_{gH} (x(t_k) \oplus f(t_k, x(t_k))) = \frac{h^2}{2} \odot x''_{i-gH}(\eta_k)$$

or:

$$R_k = x(t_{k+1}) \ominus_{gH} (x(t_k) \ominus_H (-1) f(t_k, x(t_k))) = \ominus_H (-1) \frac{h^2}{2} \odot x''_{ii-gH}(\eta_k)$$

and the mentioned error is defined as:

$$\tau_k = \frac{1}{h} R_k = \frac{h}{2} \odot x''_{i-gH}(\eta_k)$$

or:

$$\tau_k = \frac{1}{h} R_k = \ominus_H (-1) \frac{h}{2} \odot x''_{ii-gH}(\eta_k)$$

Note. In four cases, the residual values are in two mentioned forms.

Now we claim that the methods are said to be consistent if:

$$\lim_{h\to 0}\max_{0\le t_k\le T} D_H(\tau_k,0)=0$$

To this end, we suppose that the functions $x_{i-gH}''(\eta_k)$ and $x_{ii-gH}''(\eta_k)$ are bounded and this means:

$$\exists M_1>0;\ D_H\left(x''_{i-gH}(\eta_k),0\right)\le M_1,\ \ \exists M_2>0;\ D_H\left(x''_{ii-gH}(\eta_k),0\right)\le M_2$$

Thus the methods will be consistent, because:

$$\lim_{h\to 0}\max_{0\le t_k\le T} D_H(\tau_k,0)=\lim_{h\to 0}\max_{0\le t_k\le T} D_H\left(\frac{h}{2}\odot x''_{i-gH}(\eta_k),0\right)$$

$$=\lim_{h\to 0}\frac{h}{2}\max_{0\le t_k\le T} D_H\left(x''_{i-gH}(\eta_k),0\right)\le \lim_{h\to 0}\frac{h}{2}M_1=0$$

The same process is true for the $ii-gH$ differentiability:

$$\lim_{h\to 0}\max_{0\le t_k\le T} D_H(\tau_k,0)=\lim_{h\to 0}\max_{0\le t_k\le T} D_H\left(\ominus_H(-1)\frac{h}{2}\odot x''_{ii-gH}(\eta_k),0\right)$$

$$=\lim_{h\to 0}\left|(-1)\frac{h}{2}\right|\max_{0\le t_k\le T} D_H\left(\ominus_H x''_{ii-gH}(\eta_k),0\right)=\lim_{h\to 0}\frac{h}{2}\max_{0\le t_k\le T} D_H\left(x''_{ii-gH}(\eta_k),0\right)$$

$$\le \lim_{h\to 0}\frac{h}{2}M_2=0$$

So the fuzzy Euler method in each case is consistent so long as the fuzzy number valued solution is in $C^2_{gH}([0,T],\mathbb{F}_R)$.

5.2.1.2 Global truncation error and convergence

The global truncation error is the agglomeration of the local truncation error over all the iterations, assuming perfect knowledge of the true solution at the initial time step. Formally, for both case (1) and (2) the global truncation error is noted by e_{k+1} at the point t_{k+1} and defined as:

$$e_{k+1}=x(t_{k+1})\ominus_{gH}x_{k+1}=$$

$$=x(t_{k+1})\ominus_{gH}(x_0\oplus h\odot f(t_0,x_0)\oplus h\odot f(t_1,x_1)\oplus\cdots\oplus h\odot f(t_k,x_k))$$

and in the case (2):

$$e_{k+1}=x(t_{k+1})\ominus_{gH}x_{k+1}=$$

$$=x(t_{k+1})\ominus_{gH}(x_0\ominus_H(-1)h\odot f(t_0,x_0)\ominus_H(-1)h\odot$$

$$f(t_1,x_1)\ominus_H(-1)\cdots\ominus_H(-1)h\odot f(t_k,x_k))$$

for any $k=0,\ 1,\ \ldots,\ N-1$.

We claim that the fuzzy Euler method is convergent if the global truncation error goes to zero as the step size goes to zero; in other words, the numerical solution converges to the exact solution if:

$$\lim_{h\to 0}\max_k D_H(e_{k+1},0)=0\Rightarrow \lim_{h\to 0}\max_k D_H\left(x(t_{k+1})\ominus_{gH}x_{k+1},0\right)$$

$$=\lim_{h\to 0}\max_k D_H(x(t_{k+1}),x_{k+1})=0$$

5.2.1.3 Theorem—Convergence

Suppose that $x_{gH}{}''(t)$ exists and also $f(t,x(t))$ satisfies the Lipschitz condition that was defined in Chapter 4. Then the fuzzy Euler method converges to the fuzzy solution of the fuzzy initial value problem:

$$x'_{gH}(t)=f(t,x),\ \ x(t_0)=x_0\in\mathbb{F}_R,\ \ t_0\le t\le T$$

To prove the theorem, consider that $x(t)$ is $i-gH$ differentiable and also suppose that:

$$d_k:=\frac{h^2}{2}\odot x''_{i-gH}(t_k)$$

By this assumption, the exact solution satisfies the following relation:

$$x(t_{k+1})=x(t_k)\oplus h\odot f(t_k,x(t_k))\oplus d_k$$

On the other hand, we have:

$$x_{k+1}=x_k\oplus h\odot f(t_k,x_k)$$

Now let us consider the distances of both sides of the abovementioned relations, so:

$$D_H(x(t_{k+1}),x_{k+1})=D_H(x(t_k),x_k)+h[D_H(f(t_k,x(t_k),f(t_k,x_k))]+D_H(d_k,0)$$

Since the function $f(t,x(t))$ satisfies the Lipschitz condition, then:

$$D_H(f(t_k,x(t_k),f(t_k,x_k))\le L_k D_H(x(t_k),x_k)$$

Using the triangular inequality and Lipschitz condition, we arrive at:

$$D_H(x(t_{k+1}), x_{k+1}) \le (1+hL_k)D_H(x(t_k), x_k) + D_H(d_k, 0), \ \ k=0,1,\ldots,N-1$$

Also consider that:

$$L = \max_{0\le k\le N-1} L_k, \ \ d = \max_{0\le k\le N-1} D_H(d_k, 0)$$

then we have:

$$D_H(x(t_{k+1}), x_{k+1}) \le (1+hL)D_H(x(t_k), x_k) + d, \ \ k=0,1,\ldots,N-1$$

By backward substituting:

$$\begin{aligned} D_H(x(t_{k+1}), x_{k+1}) &\le (1+hL)[(1+hL)D_H(x(t_{k-1}), x_{k-1}) + d] + d \\ &= (1+hL)^2 D_H(x(t_{k-1}), x_{k-1}) + d[1+(1+hL)] \end{aligned}$$

Continuing this process:

$$D_H(x(t_{k+1}), x_{k+1}) \le (1+hL)^{k+1} D_H(x(t_0), x_0) + d\left[1+(1+hL)+\cdots+(1+hL)^k\right]$$

The last term does have the general formula and actually it is a geometric series:

$$(1+hL)+\cdots+(1+hL)^k = \frac{(1+hL)^{k+1}-1}{hL}$$

By substituting:

$$\begin{aligned} D_H(x(t_{k+1}), x_{k+1}) &\le (1+hL)^{k+1} D_H(x(t_0), x_0) + d\left[\frac{(1+hL)^{k+1}-1}{hL}\right] \\ &\le (1+hL)^{k+1} D_H(x(t_0), x_0) + \frac{d}{hL}\left[(1+hL)^{k+1}-1\right] \end{aligned}$$

On the other hand:

$$1+hL \le e^{hL} \Rightarrow (1+hL)^{k+1} \le \left(e^{hL}\right)^{k+1} \le e^{LT}, \ \ h(k+1) \le T$$

thus:

$$D_H(x(t_{k+1}), x_{k+1}) \le e^{LT} D_H(x(t_0), x_0) + \frac{d}{hL}\left[e^{LT}-1\right]$$

By substituting:

$$d = \max_{0\le k\le N-1} D_H(d_k, 0) = \frac{h}{2}\max_{0\le t\le T} D_H\left(x''_{i-gH}(t), 0\right), \ \ D_H(x(t_0), x_0) = 0$$

Finally:

$$D_H(x(t_{k+1}), x_{k+1}) \leq \frac{h}{2L}\left[e^{LT} - 1\right] \max_{0 \leq t \leq T} D_H\left(x''_{i-gH}(t), 0\right)$$

Taking the limit of two sides:

$$\lim_{h \to 0} D_H(x(t_{k+1}), x_{k+1}) = 0$$

Now consider that $x(t)$ is $ii - gH$ differentiable without any switching point and:

$$d_k := \ominus_H(-1)\frac{h^2}{2} \odot x''_{ii-gH}(t_k)$$

By this assumption, the exact solution satisfies the following relation:

$$x(t_{k+1}) = x(t_k) \ominus_H (-1) h \odot f(t_k, x(t_k)) \oplus d_k$$

On the other hand, we have:

$$x_{k+1} = x_k \ominus_H (-1) h \odot f(t_k, x_k)$$

Now let us consider the distances of both sides of the abovementioned relations, so:

$$D_H(x(t_{k+1}), x_{k+1}) = D_H(x(t_k), x_k) - h[D_H(f(t_k, x(t_k)), f(t_k, x_k))] + D_H(d_k, 0)$$

Since the function $f(t, x(t))$ satisfies the Lipschitz condition, then:

$$D_H(f(t_k, x(t_k)), f(t_k, x_k)) \leq L_k D_H(x(t_k), x_k)$$

Using the triangular inequality and Lipschitz condition, we arrive at:

$$D_H(x(t_{k+1}), x_{k+1}) \leq (1 - hL_k) D_H(x(t_k), x_k) + D_H(d_k, 0), \quad k = 0, 1, \ldots, N-1$$

Also consider that:

$$L = \max_{0 \leq k \leq N-1} L_k, \quad d = \max_{0 \leq k \leq N-1} D_H(d_k, 0)$$

then we have:

$$D_H(x(t_{k+1}), x_{k+1}) \leq (1 - hL) D_H(x(t_k), x_k) + d, \quad k = 0, 1, \ldots, N-1$$

By backward substituting:

$$\begin{aligned} D_H(x(t_{k+1}), x_{k+1}) &\leq (1 - hL)[(1 - hL) D_H(x(t_{k-1}), x_{k-1}) + d] + d \\ &= (1 - hL)^2 D_H(x(t_{k-1}), x_{k-1}) + d[1 + (1 - hL)] \end{aligned}$$

Continuing this process:

$$D_H(x(t_{k+1}), x_{k+1}) \leq (1 - hL)^{k+1} D_H(x(t_0), x_0) + d\left[1 + (1 - hL) + \cdots + (1 - hL)^k\right]$$

The last term does have the general formula and actually it is a geometric series:

$$(1-hL)+\cdots+(1-hL)^k=\frac{1-(1-hL)^{k+1}}{hL}$$

By substituting:

$$D_H(x(t_{k+1}),x_{k+1})\leq(1-hL)^{k+1}D_H(x(t_0),x_0)+d\left[\frac{1-(1-hL)^{k+1}}{hL}\right]$$

$$\leq(1-hL)^{k+1}D_H(x(t_0),x_0)+\frac{d}{hL}\left[1-(1-hL)^{k+1}\right]$$

On the other hand:

$$1+hL\leq e^{hL}\Rightarrow(1-hL)^{k+1}\leq\left(e^{-hL}\right)^{k+1}\leq e^{-LT},\ h(k+1)\leq T$$

thus:

$$D_H(x(t_{k+1}),x_{k+1})\leq e^{-LT}D_H(x(t_0),x_0)+\frac{d}{hL}\left[1-e^{-LT}\right]$$

By substituting:

$$d=\max_{0\leq k\leq N-1}D_H(d_k,0)=-\frac{h}{2}\max_{0\leq t\leq T}D_H\left(x''_{ii-gH}(t),0\right),\ D_H(x(t_0),x_0)=0$$

Finally:

$$D_H(x(t_{k+1}),x_{k+1})\leq\frac{-h}{2L}\left[1-e^{-LT}\right]\max_{0\leq t\leq T}D_H\left(x''_{ii-gH}(t),0\right)$$

Taking the limit of two sides:

$$\lim_{h\to 0}D_H(x(t_{k+1}),x_{k+1})=0$$

5.2.1.4 Stability

In addition, to ensure that the problem has a solution, we must be sure that the method is stable. This means that small perturbations in the initial data will only lead to small changes in the solutions (Armand et al., 2019). The stability can be defined as follows.

Let x_{k+1}, $k+1\geq 0$ be the fuzzy solution of the fuzzy Euler method with fuzzy initial value $x_0\in\mathbb{F}_R$ and let z_{k+1} be the solution of the same numerical method with a perturbed fuzzy initial condition $z_0=x_0\oplus\delta_0\in\mathbb{F}_R$. The fuzzy Euler method is stable if there exist positive constants $\tilde{h}$ and κ such that:

$$D_H(z_{k+1},y_{k+1})\leq\kappa\delta,\ \forall(k+1)h\leq T,\ k\leq N-1$$

whenever $D_H(\delta_0, 0) \le \delta$.

Now suppose that the solution *x*(*t*) is $i - gH$ differentiable and consider the perturbed problem as follows:

$$z_{k+1} = z_k \oplus h \odot f(t_k, z_k), \quad z_0 = x_0 \oplus \delta_0$$

and also consider the mentioned iterative method in the case (1):

$$x_{k+1} = x_k \oplus h \odot f(t_k, x_k)$$

Using the distance, we will get:

$$D_H(z_{k+1}, x_{k+1}) \le D_H(z_k, x_k) + hD_H(f(t_k, z_k), f(t_k, x_k))$$

Using the properties of the distance and also the Lipschitz condition:

$$D_H(z_{k+1}, x_{k+1}) \le (1 + hL) D_H(z_k, x_k)$$

and also:

$$D_H(z_{k+1}, x_{k+1}) \le (1 + hL)[(1 + hL) D_H(z_{k-1}, x_{k-1})] = (1 + hL)^2 D_H(z_{k-1}, x_{k-1})$$

Iterating this inequality and the previous similar process, we will find:

$$D_H(z_{k+1}, x_{k+1}) \le (1 + hL)^k D_H(z_0, x_0) \le e^{hL(k+1)} D_H(z_0 \ominus_H x_0, 0)$$
$$\le e^{LT} D_H(\delta_0, 0) \le \kappa \delta$$

where $\kappa = e^{LT}$. So based on the previous illustrations, the method is stable.

In the case that the solution *x*(*t*) is $ii - gH$ differentiable, we consider the perturbed problem as follows:

$$z_{k+1} = z_k \ominus_H (-1) h \odot f(t_k, z_k), \quad z_0 = x_0 \oplus \delta_0$$

and also consider the mentioned iterative method in case (2):

$$x_{k+1} = x_k \ominus_H (-1) h \odot f(t_k, x_k)$$

Using the distance, we will get:

$$D_H(z_{k+1}, x_{k+1}) \le D_H(z_k, x_k) - hD_H(f(t_k, z_k), f(t_k, x_k))$$

Using the properties of the distance and also the Lipschitz condition:

$$D_H(z_{k+1}, x_{k+1}) \le (1 - hL) D_H(z_k, x_k)$$

and also:

$$D_H(z_{k+1}, x_{k+1}) \le (1 - hL)[(1 - hL) D_H(z_{k-1}, x_{k-1})] = (1 - hL)^2 D_H(z_{k-1}, x_{k-1})$$

Iterating this inequality and the previous similar process, we will find:

$$D_H(z_{k+1}, x_{k+1}) \leq (1 - hL)^{k+1} D_H(z_0, x_0) \leq e^{-hL(k+1)} D_H(z_0 \ominus_H x_0, 0)$$

$$\leq e^{-LT} D_H(\delta_0, 0) \leq \kappa\delta$$

where $\kappa = e^{-LT}$. So based on the previous illustrations, the method is stable.

Note. The Euler method is not stable generally.

By this example, we show that the fuzzy Euler method is not stable generally. To this end, we explain the method by using the concept of the tangent line of a fuzzy number valued solution function. Consider the following example:

$$x'(t) = x(t), \ \ x(0) = (1, 2, 3), \ \ t \geq 0$$

The trivial solution of this fuzzy initial value problem is $x(t) = (0.9,1.2,1.4)e^t$ (see Fig. 5.1).

As can be seen in the figure:

$$D_H(x(t_1), x_1) < D_H(x(t_2), x_2) < \cdots$$

This is the main reason to claim that the fuzzy Euler method is unstable. In other words, the stability area is not so extended.

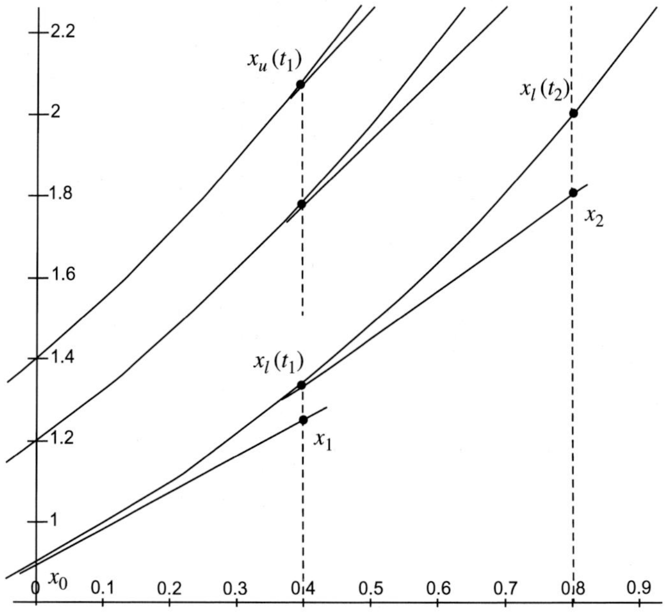

Fig. 5.1 Instability of the fuzzy Euler method.

Example. The following fuzzy initial value problem is assumed:

$$\begin{cases} x'_{i-gH}(t) = x(t) \oplus (1.3, 2, 2.1), \ \ 0 \leq t \leq 1 \\ x(0) = (0.82, 1, 1.2) \end{cases}$$

where (1.3,2,2.1) and (0.82,1,1.2) are triangular fuzzy numbers. The exact solution is obtained very easily, and it is:

$$x(t) = (x(0) \oplus (1.3, 2, 2.1))e^t \ominus_H (1.3, 2, 2.1)$$

The fuzzy Euler method in the sense of $i-gH$ differentiability does have the following form:

$$\begin{cases} x_{k+1} = x_k \oplus h \odot (x_k \oplus (1.3, 2, 2.1)), \\ x(0) = (0.82, 1, 1.2) \end{cases}$$

or:

$$\begin{cases} x_{k+1} = (1+h) \odot x_k \oplus h \odot (1.3, 2, 2.1), \\ x(0) = (0.82, 1, 1.2) \end{cases}$$

Since the fuzzy number valued solution function is $i-gH$ differentiable, the parametric form of the solution is:

$$x_l(t,r) = (0.82 + 0.18r + 1.3 + 0.7r)e^t - 1.3 - 0.7r = (2.12 + 0.88r)e^t - 1.3 - 0.7r$$

$$x_u(t,r) = (1.2 - 0.2r + 2.1 - 0.1r)e^t - 2.1 + 0.1r = (3.3 - 0.3r)e^t - 2.1 + 0.1r$$

These lower and upper functions are the solutions of the following parametric equations of fuzzy equations:

$$\begin{cases} x'_l(t,r) = x_l(t) + 1.3 + 0.7r, \ \ 0 \leq t \leq 1 \\ x_l(0) = 0.82 + 0.18r \end{cases}$$

$$\begin{cases} x'_u(t,r) = x_u(t) + 2.1 - 0.1r, \ \ 0 \leq t \leq 1 \\ x_l(0) = 1.2 - 0.2r \end{cases}$$

where:

$$(1.3, 2, 2.1)[r] = [1.3 + 0.7r, 2.1 - 0.1r], (0.82, 1, 1.2)[r] = [0.82 + 0.18r, 1.2 - 0.2r]$$

Fig. 5.2 shows the $i-gH$ differentiable solution of the fuzzy initial value problem. In addition, the global truncation errors have been reported for $h=0.025$ and $h=0.005$ in Table 5.1. It is seen that the results do have less error when the value of the step size is less. Moreover, for a fixed step size, the errors are going to increase when the time increases as well. This process is called error propagation.

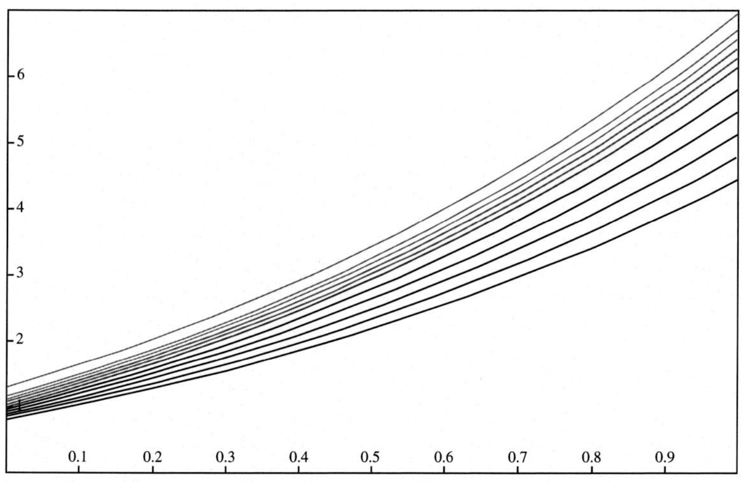

Fig. 5.2 The fuzzy $i-gH$ differentiable solution.

TABLE 5.1 Global error results.

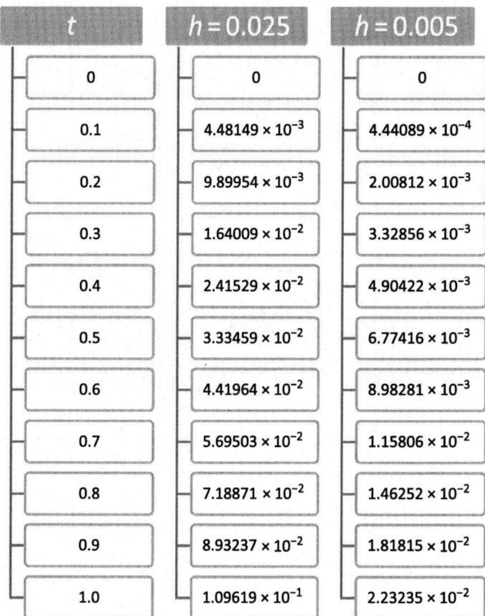

t	$h=0.025$	$h=0.005$
0	0	0
0.1	4.48149×10^{-3}	4.44089×10^{-4}
0.2	9.89954×10^{-3}	2.00812×10^{-3}
0.3	1.64009×10^{-2}	3.32856×10^{-3}
0.4	2.41529×10^{-2}	4.90422×10^{-3}
0.5	3.33459×10^{-2}	6.77416×10^{-3}
0.6	4.41964×10^{-2}	8.98281×10^{-3}
0.7	5.69503×10^{-2}	1.15806×10^{-2}
0.8	7.18871×10^{-2}	1.46252×10^{-2}
0.9	8.93237×10^{-2}	1.81815×10^{-2}
1.0	1.09619×10^{-1}	2.23235×10^{-2}

Example. Let us consider the following fuzzy initial value problem:

$$\begin{cases} x'_{ii-gH}(t) = -x(t) \oplus t \odot (0.7, 1, 1.8), \ 0 \le t \le 1 \\ x(0) = (0, 1, 2.2) \end{cases}$$

where (0.7,1, 1.8) and (0, 1,2.2) are triangular fuzzy numbers and their parametric forms are, respectively:

$$(0.7, 1, 1.8)[r] = [0.7 + 0.3r, 1.8 - 0.8r], \ (0, 1, 2.2)[r] = [r, 2.2 - 1.2r]$$

The exact solution of the fuzzy initial value problem can be obtained easily by using the parametric form of the problem and considering the $ii - gH$ differentiability of the solution. The parametric form is as follows:

$$\begin{cases} x'_l(t, r) = -x_l(t, r) + t(1.8 - 0.8r), \ 0 \le t \le 1 \\ x_l(0) = r \end{cases}$$

$$\begin{cases} x'_u(t, r) = -x_u(t, r) + t(0.7 + 0.3r), \ 0 \le t \le 1 \\ x_u(0) = 2.2 - 1.2r \end{cases}$$

The solutions of these parametric initial value problems are:

$$x_l(t, r) = (1.8 + 0.2r)e^{-t} + (1.8 - 0.8r)(t - 1)$$

$$x_u(t, r) = (2.9 - 0.9r)e^{-t} + (0.7 + 0.3r)(t - 1)$$

The fuzzy number valued solution function is in the form of:

$$x(t) = C \odot e^{-t} \oplus (0.7, 1, 1.8) \odot (t - 1), \ C = (0, 1, 2.2) \ominus_H (-1)(0.7, 1, 1.8)$$

In Fig. 5.3, the $ii - gH$ differentiable solution function is plotted and as we know, the length of the function is decreasing.

With the same explanation about the global error and its propagation of the previous example, Table 5.2 shows us the global error propagation with the same step sizes.

Example. In this example, there is a switching point and we will see that the type of differentiability is changed before and after the switching point. Consider the following fuzzy initial value problem:

$$\begin{cases} x'_{gH}(t) = (1 - t) \odot x(t), \quad 0 \le t \le 2 \\ x(0) = (0, 1, 2) \end{cases}$$

where $(0, 1,2)$ is again a triangular fuzzy number with the parametric form of:

$$(0, 1, 2)[r] = [r, 2 - r]$$

It is clear that in the interval $0 \le t < 1$ the solution is $i - gH$ differentiable and on another subinterval $1 < t \le 2$ it is $ii - gH$ differentiable. So considering these

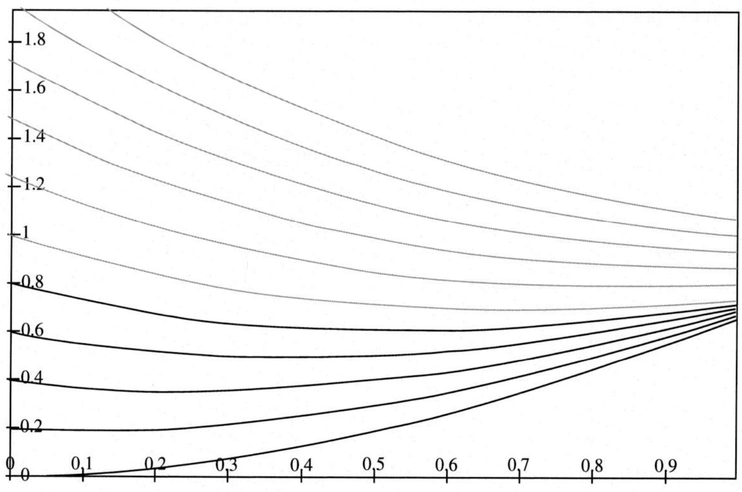

Fig. 5.3 The fuzzy $ii-gH$ differentiable solution.

TABLE 5.2 Global error results.

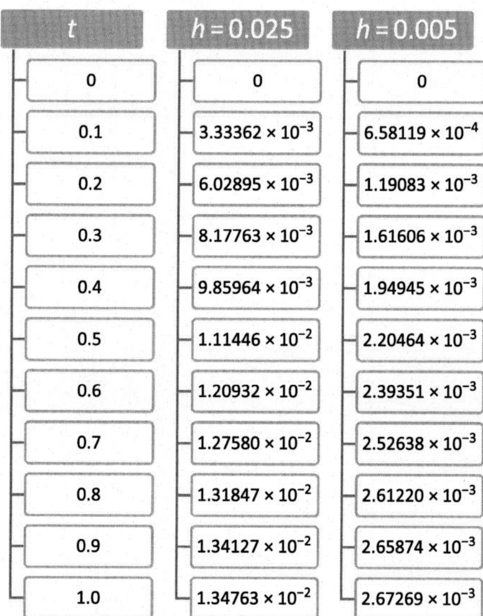

t	$h=0.025$	$h=0.005$
0	0	0
0.1	3.33362×10^{-3}	6.58119×10^{-4}
0.2	6.02895×10^{-3}	1.19083×10^{-3}
0.3	8.17763×10^{-3}	1.61606×10^{-3}
0.4	9.85964×10^{-3}	1.94945×10^{-3}
0.5	1.11446×10^{-2}	2.20464×10^{-3}
0.6	1.20932×10^{-2}	2.39351×10^{-3}
0.7	1.27580×10^{-2}	2.52638×10^{-3}
0.8	1.31847×10^{-2}	2.61220×10^{-3}
0.9	1.34127×10^{-2}	2.65874×10^{-3}
1.0	1.34763×10^{-2}	2.67269×10^{-3}

explanations, the switching point is $t=1$ and the parametric form of the fuzzy initial value problem can be explained as the following forms:

- In the case of $i-gH$ differentiability:

$$\begin{cases} x_l'(t,r)=\begin{cases}(1-t)x_l(t,r), & 0\le t\le 1\\ (1-t)x_u(t,r), & 1\le t\le 2\end{cases}\\ x_u'(t,r)=\begin{cases}(1-t)x_u(t,r), & 0\le t\le 1\\ (1-t)x_l(t,r), & 1\le t\le 2\end{cases}\\ x(0,r)=[r,2-r]\end{cases}$$

The $i-gH$ solution is obtained as follows (Figs. 5.4 and 5.5):

$$x_l(t,r)=r\cdot e^{t-\frac{t^2}{2}},\ x_u(t,r)=(2-r)\cdot e^{t-\frac{t^2}{2}},\ 0\le t\le 1$$

$$x_l(t,r)=e^{t-\frac{t^2}{2}}+(r-1)e^{\frac{1}{2}t(t-2)},\ x_u(t,r)=e^{t-\frac{t^2}{2}}-(r-1)e^{\frac{1}{2}t(t-2)},\ 1\le t\le 2$$

- In the case of $ii-gH$ differentiability:

$$\begin{cases} x_l'(t,r)=\begin{cases}(1-t)x_u(t,r), & 0\le t\le 1\\ (1-t)x_l(t,r), & 1\le t\le 2\end{cases}\\ x_u'(t,r)=\begin{cases}(1-t)x_l(t,r), & 0\le t\le 1\\ (1-t)x_u(t,r), & 1\le t\le 2\end{cases}\\ x(0,r)=[r,2-r]\end{cases}$$

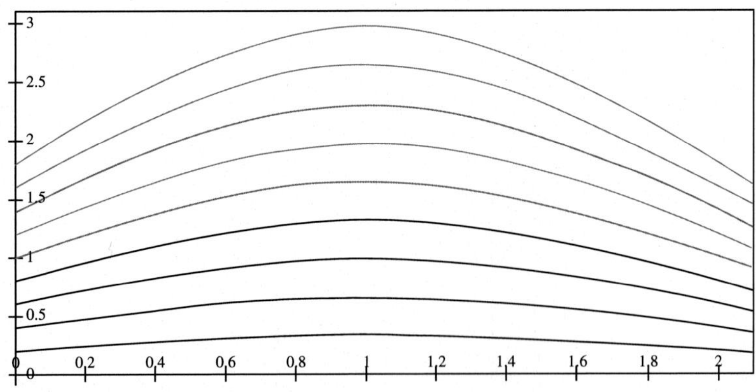

Fig. 5.4 The fuzzy $i-gH$ differentiable solution in $0\le t\le 1$.

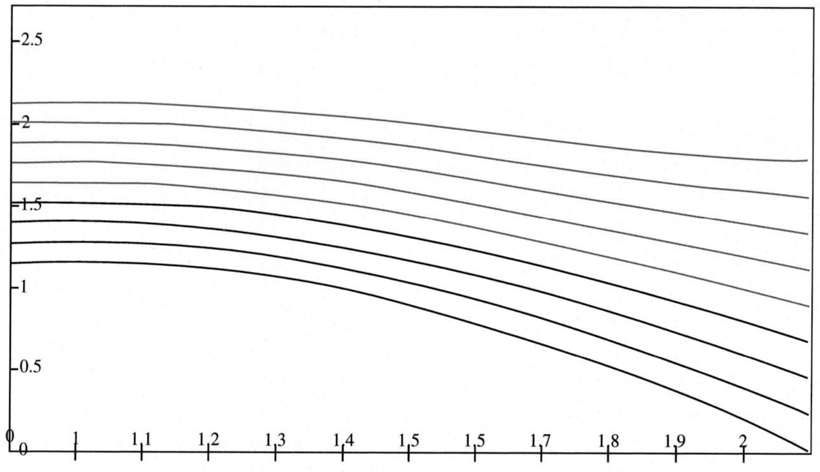

Fig. 5.5 The fuzzy $i-gH$ differentiable solution in $1\leq t\leq 2$.

It is clear that the parametric initial value problems in two subintervals $0\leq t\leq 1$ and $1\leq t\leq 2$ have symmetric displacements. The solutions and figures show the same behavior as well (Fig. 5.6).

The fuzzy Euler method for this problem is:

$$\begin{cases} x_{k+1}=x_k\oplus h\odot(1-t_k)\odot x_k, \quad 0\leq t_k\leq 1, \quad k=0,1,\ldots,\dfrac{N}{2}-1 \\ x_{k+1}=x_k\ominus_H(-1)h\odot(1-t_k)\odot x_k, \quad 1<t_k\leq 2, \quad k=\dfrac{N}{2},\ldots,N \\ x_0=(0,1,2) \end{cases}$$

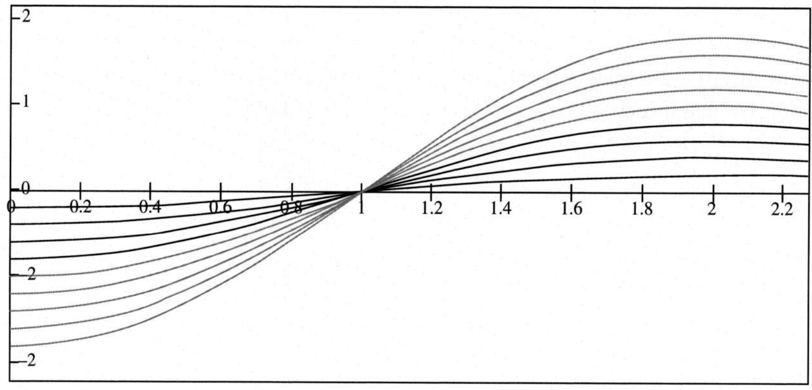

Fig. 5.6 The gH-differential of the solution with switching point in t=1

TABLE 5.3 Global error results.

t	$h = 0.025$	$h = 0.005$
0	0	0
0.2	1.05772×10^{-3}	2.21057×10^{-4}
0.4	4.62954×10^{-3}	9.48966×10^{-4}
0.6	1.07346×10^{-2}	2.18262×10^{-3}
0.8	1.87015×10^{-2}	3.78194×10^{-3}
1.0	2.72488×10^{-2}	5.48657×10^{-3}
1.2	1.84424×10^{-2}	3.73717×10^{-3}
1.4	8.95003×10^{-3}	1.85160×10^{-3}
1.6	6.46455×10^{-4}	5.51592×10^{-5}
1.8	9.62457×10^{-3}	1.84070×10^{-3}
2.0	1.72255×10^{-2}	3.35558×10^{-3}

The numerical results for this example with the same step sizes are presented in Table 5.3 and it can be seen that if the step size is going to be decreased then the errors are going to be decreased as well.

5.3 Fuzzy modified Euler method

In this section, we intend to introduce a modified approach for solving fuzzy differential equations. The modified Euler method is obtained by improving the Euler method discussed in the previous section. The proposed method can estimate the solution by using a two-stage predictor–corrector algorithm with local truncation error of order two. The consistency, convergence, and stability of the proposed method are also investigated in detail (Allahviranloo et al., 2007; Armand et al., 2019). To start, again consider the following fuzzy initial value problem:

$$x'_{gH}(t) = f(t, x),\ \ x(t_0) = x_0 \in \mathbb{F}_R,\ \ t_0 \le t \le T$$

where the fuzzy solution $x(t)$ is an unknown fuzzy number valued function and $f : [0, T] \times \mathbb{F}_R \to \mathbb{F}_R$ is a fuzzy continuous function.

Let us have the same partition on the interval $[t_0, T]$. As was the case previously, two cases are considered for $x(t) \in C^3_{gH}([0, T], \mathbb{F}_R)$.

Case 1. The fuzzy number valued solution function $x(t)$ is $(i-gH)$-differentiable and the type of differentiability does not change on $[0,T]$. So the fuzzy Taylor expansion is:

$$x(t_{k+1})=x(t_k)\oplus x'_{i-gH}(t_k)\odot(t_{k+1}-t_k)\oplus x''_{i-gH}(t_k)\odot\frac{(t_{k+1}-t_k)^2}{2!}$$

$$\oplus x'''_{i-gH}(\eta_k)\odot\frac{(t_{k+1}-t_k)^3}{3!}$$

for some point $\eta_k\in[t_k,t_{k+1}]$. Since $h=t_{k+1}-t_k$ then it gives:

$$x(t_{k+1})=x(t_k)\oplus h\odot x'_{i-gH}(t_k)\oplus\frac{h^2}{2!}\odot x''_{i-gH}(t_k)\oplus\frac{h^3}{3!}\odot x'''_{i-gH}(\eta_k)$$

We know that:

$$x''_{i-gH}(t_k)=\frac{x'_{i-gH}(t_{k+1})\ominus_H x'_{i-gH}(t_k)}{h}$$

since we have:

$$x'_{i-gH}(t_k)=f(t_k,x(t_k))$$

so:

$$x''_{i-gH}(t_k)=\frac{f(t_{k+1},x(t_{k+1}))\ominus_H f(t_k,x(t_k))}{h}$$

Then by using this second derivative in the abovementioned iterative equation, we have:

$$x(t_{k+1})=x(t_k)\oplus h\odot f(t_k,x(t_k))\oplus\frac{h^2}{2!}\odot\left(\frac{f(t_{k+1},x(t_{k+1}))\ominus_H f(t_k,x(t_k))}{h}\right)$$

$$\oplus\frac{h^3}{3!}\odot x'''_{i-gH}(\eta_k)$$

After simplification, we have:

$$x(t_{k+1})=x(t_k)\oplus h\odot\left(\frac{f(t_{k+1},x(t_{k+1}))\oplus f(t_k,x(t_k))}{2}\right)\oplus\frac{h^3}{3!}\odot x'''_{i-gH}(\eta_k)$$

Using the Hausdorff distance and approaching it to zero, we will find the fuzzy Euler method with its error function. So we have:

$$D_H\left(x(t_{k+1}),x(t_k)\oplus h\odot\left(\frac{f(t_{k+1},x(t_{k+1}))\oplus f(t_k,x(t_k))}{2}\right)\oplus\frac{h^3}{3!}\odot x''_{i-gH}(\eta_k)\right)\le$$

$$D_H\left(x(t_{k+1}), x(t_k)\oplus h\odot\left(\frac{f(t_{k+1}, x(t_{k+1}))\oplus f(t_k, x(t_k))}{2}\right)\right) + D_H\left(0, \frac{h^3}{3!}\odot x'''_{i-gH}(\eta_k)\right)$$
$$\to 0$$

Hence we find:

$$D_H\left(x(t_{k+1}), x(t_k)\oplus h\odot\left(\frac{f(t_{k+1}, x(t_{k+1}))\oplus f(t_k, x(t_k))}{2}\right)\right) \to 0,$$

and:

$$D_H\left(0, \frac{h^3}{3!}\odot x'''_{i-gH}(\eta_k)\right) \to 0$$

We know that the step size h is small enough and goes to zero. Then:

$$x(t_{k+1}) \approx x(t_k)\oplus h\odot\left(\frac{f(t_{k+1}, x(t_{k+1}))\oplus f(t_k, x(t_k))}{2}\right)$$

It is clear that the right-hand side approximates the left-hand side. Based on this approximate method, we can introduce a similar iterative method to find or define the sequence of $\{x_k\}_{k=0}^{N-1}$ such that $x_k \approx x(t_k)$:

$$\begin{cases} x_{k+1} = x_k\oplus h\odot\left(\dfrac{f(t_{k+1}, x_{k+1})\oplus f(t_k, x_k)}{2}\right), & k = 0, 1, \ldots, N-1 \\ x_0 \in \mathbb{F}_R \end{cases}$$

It is observed that the value $x(t_{k+1})$ appears in both sides of the iterative equation and this concludes the implicit iterative equation. To have an implicit iterative equation, $x(t_{k+1})$ can be provided with the fuzzy Euler method in case (1) as $x^{*(t_{k+1})}$:

$$\begin{cases} x^*_{k+1} = x_k\oplus h\odot f(t_k, x_k), & k = 0, 1, \ldots, N-1 \\ x_0 \in \mathbb{F}_R \end{cases}$$

So the final fuzzy modified Euler method is obtained as follows:

$$\begin{cases} x_{k+1} = x_k\oplus \dfrac{h}{2}\odot\left(f\left(t_{k+1}, x^*_{k+1}\right)\oplus f(t_k, x_k)\right), & k = 0, 1, \ldots, N-1 \\ x^*_{k+1} = x_k\oplus h\odot f(t_k, x_k), \\ x_0 \in \mathbb{F}_R \end{cases}$$

Case 2. The solution $x(t)$ is $(ii-gH)$-differentiable and the type of differentiability does not change on $[0, T]$. So the fuzzy Taylor expansion is:

$$x(t_{k+1}) = x(t_k)\ominus_H(-1)x'_{ii-gH}(t_k)\odot(t_{k+1}-t_k)\ominus_H(-1)x''_{ii-gH}(t_k)$$

$$\odot\frac{(t_{k+1}-t_k)^2}{2!}\ominus_H(-1)x'''_{ii-gH}(\eta_k)\odot\frac{(t_{k+1}-t_k)^3}{3!}$$

Thus, by a similar process, the fuzzy modified Euler method takes the form:

$$\begin{cases} x_{k+1}=x_k\ominus_H(-1)\dfrac{h}{2}\odot\left(f\left(t_{k+1},x^*_{k+1}\right)\oplus f(t_k,x_k)\right), & k=0,1,\ldots,N-1 \\ x^*_{k+1}=x_k\ominus_H(-1)h\odot f(t_k,x_k), & \\ x_0\in\mathbb{F}_R & \end{cases}$$

Case 3. Let us suppose that $x(t)$ has a switching point type (1) on the interval $[0,T]$ as like as ξ, and also assume that $t_0, t_1, \ldots, t_j, \xi, t_{j+1}, \ldots, t_N$. So the fuzzy Euler method is obtained as follows:

$$\begin{cases} x_{k+1}=x_k\oplus\dfrac{h}{2}\odot\left(f\left(t_{k+1},x^*_{k+1}\right)\oplus f(t_k,x_k)\right), & \\ x^*_{k+1}=x_k\oplus h\odot f(t_k,x_k), & k=0,1,\ldots,j \\ & \\ x_{k+1}=x_k\ominus_H(-1)\dfrac{h}{2}\odot\left(f\left(t_{k+1},x^*_{k+1}\right)\oplus f(t_k,x_k)\right), & \\ x^*_{k+1}=x_k\ominus_H(-1)h\odot f(t_k,x_k), & k=j+1,j+2,\ldots,N-1 \\ x_0\in\mathbb{F}_R & \end{cases}$$

Case 4. If ξ is a type (2) switching point, the fuzzy Euler method takes the form as follows:

$$\begin{cases} x_{k+1}=x_k\oplus\dfrac{h}{2}\odot\left(f\left(t_{k+1},x^*_{k+1}\right)\oplus f(t_k,x_k)\right), & \\ x^*_{k+1}=x_k\oplus h\odot f(t_k,x_k), & k=j+1,j+2,\ldots,N-1 \\ & \\ x_{k+1}=x_k\ominus_H(-1)\dfrac{h}{2}\odot\left(f\left(t_{k+1},x^*_{k+1}\right)\oplus f(t_k,x_k)\right), & \\ x^*_{k+1}=x_k\ominus_H(-1)h\odot f(t_k,x_k), & k=0,1,\ldots,j \\ x_0\in\mathbb{F}_R & \end{cases}$$

5.3.1 Analysis of the fuzzy modified Euler method

As with the fuzzy Euler method, in this section, consistency, convergence, and stability of the modified Euler method are discussed in detail.

5.3.1.1 Local truncation error and consistency

For all abovementioned cases of the fuzzy Euler method, we can define the local truncation error by using a residual value as follows:

$$R_k=x(t_{k+1})\ominus_{gH}\left(x(t_k)\oplus h\odot\left(\frac{f(t_{k+1},x^*(t_{k+1}))\oplus f(t_k,x(t_k))}{2}\right)\right)$$

$$=\frac{h^3}{3!}\odot x'''_{i-gH}(\eta_k)$$

or:

$$R_k = x(t_{k+1})\ominus_{gH}\left(x(t_k)\ominus_H(-1)\left(\frac{f(t_{k+1}, x^*(t_{k+1}))\oplus f(t_k, x(t_k))}{2}\right)\right)$$

$$=\ominus_H(-1)\frac{h^3}{3!}\odot x'''_{ii-gH}(\eta_k)$$

and the mentioned error is defined as:

$$\tau_k = \frac{1}{h}R_k = \frac{h^2}{3!}\odot x'''_{i-gH}(\eta_k)$$

or:

$$\tau_k = \frac{1}{h}R_k = \ominus_H(-1)\frac{h^2}{3!}\odot x'''_{ii-gH}(\eta_k)$$

Note. In four cases, the residual values are in two mentioned forms.

Now we claim that the methods are said to be consistent if:

$$\lim_{h\to 0}\max_{0\le t_k\le T} D_H(\tau_k, 0) = 0$$

To this end, we suppose that the functions $x''_{i-gH}(\eta_k)$ and $x''_{ii-gH}(\eta_k)$ are bounded and this means:

$$\exists M_1 > 0;\ D_H\left(x'''_{i-gH}(\eta_k), 0\right) \le M_1,\ \ \exists M_2 > 0;\ D_H\left(x'''_{ii-gH}(\eta_k), 0\right) \le M_2$$

Thus the methods will be consistent, because:

$$\lim_{h\to 0}\max_{0\le t_k\le T} D_H(\tau_k, 0) = \lim_{h\to 0}\max_{0\le t_k\le T} D_H\left(\frac{h^2}{3!}\odot x'''_{i-gH}(\eta_k), 0\right)$$

$$= \lim_{h\to 0}\frac{h}{2}\max_{0\le t_k\le T} D_H\left(x'''_{i-gH}(\eta_k), 0\right) \le \lim_{h\to 0}\frac{h}{2}M_1 = 0$$

The same process is true for the $ii-gH$ differentiability:

$$\lim_{h\to 0}\max_{0\le t_k\le T} D_H(\tau_k, 0) = \lim_{h\to 0}\max_{0\le t_k\le T} D_H\left(\ominus_H(-1)\frac{h^2}{3!}\odot x'''_{ii-gH}(\eta_k), 0\right)$$

$$= \lim_{h\to 0}\left|(-1)\frac{h^2}{3!}\right|\max_{0\le t_k\le T} D_H\left(\ominus_H x'''_{ii-gH}(\eta_k), 0\right) = \lim_{h\to 0}\frac{h^2}{3!}\max_{0\le t_k\le T} D_H\left(x'''_{ii-gH}(\eta_k), 0\right)$$

$$\le \lim_{h\to 0}\frac{h^2}{3!}M_2 = 0$$

So the fuzzy modified Euler method in each case is consistent so long as the fuzzy number valued solution is in $C^3_{gH}([0,T],\mathbb{F}_R)$.

5.3.1.2 Global truncation error and convergence

The global truncation error is the agglomeration of the local truncation error over all the iterations, assuming perfect knowledge of the true solution at the initial time step. Formally, for each case (1) and (2) the global truncation error is noted by e_{k+1} at the point t_{k+1} and defined as:

$$e_{k+1}=x(t_{k+1})\ominus_{gH}x_{k+1}=$$

$$=x(t_{k+1})\ominus_{gH}\left(x_0\oplus h\odot\left(\frac{f\left(t_0,x_0^*\right)\oplus f(t_0,x_0)}{2}\right)\oplus h\odot\left(\frac{f\left(t_1,x_1^*\right)\oplus f(t_1,x_1)}{2}\right)\right.$$

$$\left.\oplus\cdots\oplus h\odot\left(\frac{f\left(t_k,x_k^*\right)\oplus f(t_k,x_k)}{2}\right)\right)$$

and in case (2):

$$e_{k+1}=x(t_{k+1})\ominus_{gH}x_{k+1}=$$

$$=x(t_{k+1})\ominus_{gH}\left(x_0\ominus_H(-1)h\odot\left(\frac{f\left(t_0,x_0^*\right)\oplus f(t_0,x_0)}{2}\right)\ominus_H(-1)h\odot\right)$$

$$\left(\frac{f\left(t_1,x_1^*\right)\oplus f(t_1,x_1)}{2}\right)\ominus_H(-1)\cdots\ominus_H(-1)h\odot\left(\frac{f\left(t_k,x_k^*\right)\oplus f(t_k,x_k)}{2}\right)\Bigg)$$

for any $k=0,\ 1,\ \ldots,\ N-1$.

We claim that the fuzzy Euler method is convergent if the global truncation error goes to zero as the step size goes to zero; in other words, the numerical solution converges to the exact solution if:

$$\lim_{h\to 0}\max_k D_H(e_{k+1},0)=0\Rightarrow\lim_{h\to 0}\max_k D_H\left(x(t_{k+1})\ominus_{gH}x_{k+1},0\right)$$

$$=\lim_{h\to 0}\max_k D_H(x(t_{k+1}),x_{k+1})=0$$

5.3.1.3 Theorem—Convergence

Suppose that $x''_{gH}(t)$ exists and also $f(t,x(t))$ satisfies the Lipschitz condition. Then the fuzzy modified Euler method converges to the fuzzy solution of fuzzy initial value problem:

$$x'_{gH}(t)=f(t,x),\ \ x(t_0)=x_0\in\mathbb{F}_R,\ \ t_0\le t\le T$$

To prove the theorem, consider that $x(t)$ is $i-gH$ differentiable and also suppose that:

$$d_k := \frac{h^3}{3!} \odot x'''_{i-gH}(t_k)$$

By this assumption, the exact solution satisfies the following relation:

$$x(t_{k+1}) = x(t_k) \oplus h \odot \left(\frac{f(t_{k+1}, x^*(t_{k+1})) \oplus f(t_k, x(t_k))}{2} \right) \oplus d_k$$

On the other hand, we have:

$$x_{k+1} = x_k \oplus h \odot \left(\frac{f\left(t_{k+1}, x^*_{k+1}\right) \oplus f(t_k, x_k)}{2} \right), \quad k = 0, 1, \ldots, N-1$$
$$x^*_{k+1} = x_k \oplus h \odot f(t_k, x_k),$$

Now let us consider the distances of both sides of the abovementioned relations, so:

$$D_H(x(t_{k+1}), x_{k+1}) = D_H(x(t_k), x_k)$$
$$+ \frac{h}{2}\left[D_H\left(\left(f(t_{k+1}, x^*(t_{k+1})) \oplus f(t_k, x(t_k))\right), \left(f\left(t_{k+1}, x^*_{k+1}\right) \oplus f(t_k, x_k)\right)\right)\right]$$
$$+ D_H(d_k, 0)$$

Since the function $f(t, x(t))$ satisfies the Lipschitz condition, then:

$$D_H(f(t_k, x(t_k)), f(t_k, x_k)) \leq L_k D_H(x(t_k), x_k)$$
$$D_H\left(f(t_{k+1}, x^*(t_{k+1})), f\left(t_{k+1}, x^*_{k+1}\right)\right) \leq L_{k+1} D_H\left(x^*(t_{k+1}), x^*_{k+1}\right)$$

Using the triangular inequality and Lipschitz condition, we arrive at:

$$D_H\left(\left(f(t_{k+1}, x^*(t_{k+1})) \oplus f(t_k, x(t_k))\right), \left(f\left(t_{k+1}, x^*_{k+1}\right) \oplus f(t_k, x_k)\right)\right)$$
$$\leq D_H\left(f(t_{k+1}, x^*(t_{k+1})), f\left(t_{k+1}, x^*_{k+1}\right)\right) + D_H(f(t_k, x(t_k)), f(t_k, x_k))$$
$$\leq L_{k+1} D_H\left(x^*(t_{k+1}), x^*_{k+1}\right) + L_k D_H(x(t_k), x_k)$$

then:

$$D_H(x(t_{k+1}), x_{k+1}) \leq D_H(x(t_k), x_k) + \frac{h}{2}\left[L_{k+1} D_H\left(x^*(t_{k+1}), x^*_{k+1}\right) + L_k D_H(x(t_k), x_k)\right]$$
$$+ D_H(d_k, 0)$$

Suppose that:

$$L = \max_{0 \le k \le N-1} \{L_k, L_{k+1}\}$$

then:

$$D_H(x(t_{k+1}), x_{k+1}) \le D_H(x(t_k), x_k) + \frac{Lh}{2}\left[D_H\left(x^*(t_{k+1}), x^*_{k+1}\right) + D_H(x(t_k), x_k)\right]$$

On the other hand, we have the Lipschitz condition for the fuzzy Euler method:

$$D_H\left(x^*(t_{k+1}), x^*_{k+1}\right) \le D_H(x(t_k) + h \odot f(t_k, x(t_k)), x_k + h \odot f(t_k, x_k))$$
$$\le (1 + hL_k) D_H(x(t_k), x_k) \le (1 + hL) D_H(x(t_k), x_k)$$

Then it is obtained that:

$$D_H(x(t_{k+1}), x_{k+1}) \le D_H(x(t_k), x_k) + \frac{Lh}{2}[(1 + hL) D_H(x(t_k), x_k) + D_H(x(t_k), x_k)]$$

and:

$$D_H(x(t_{k+1}), x_{k+1}) \le D_H(x(t_k), x_k) + \frac{Lh}{2}[(2 + hL) D_H(x(t_k), x_k)]$$

Finally:

$$D_H(x(t_{k+1}), x_{k+1}) \le \left(1 + Lh + \frac{(Lh)^2}{2}\right) D_H(x(t_k), x_k) + D_H(d_k, 0), k = 0, 1, \ldots, N-1$$

Also consider that:

$$d = \max_{0 \le k \le N-1} D_H(d_k, 0)$$

then we have:

$$D_H(x(t_{k+1}), x_{k+1}) \le \left(1 + Lh + \frac{(Lh)^2}{2}\right) D_H(x(t_k), x_k) + d, \ \ k = 0, 1, \ldots, N-1$$

By backward substituting:

$$D_H(x(t_{k+1}), x_{k+1}) \le \left(1 + Lh + \frac{(Lh)^2}{2}\right)\left[\left(1 + Lh + \frac{(Lh)^2}{2}\right) D_H(x(t_{k-1}), x_{k-1}) + d\right] + d$$

$$= \left(1 + Lh + \frac{(Lh)^2}{2}\right)^2 D_H(x(t_{k-1}), x_{k-1}) + d\left[1 + \left(1 + Lh + \frac{(Lh)^2}{2}\right)\right]$$

Continuing this process:

$$D_H(x(t_{k+1}),x_{k+1}) \le \left(1+Lh+\frac{(Lh)^2}{2}\right)^{k+1} D_H(x(t_0),x_0)$$

$$+d\left[1+\left(1+Lh+\frac{(Lh)^2}{2}\right)+\cdots+\left(1+Lh+\frac{(Lh)^2}{2}\right)^{k}\right]$$

The last term does have the general formula and actually it is a geometric series:

$$1+\left(1+Lh+\frac{(Lh)^2}{2}\right)+\cdots+\left(1+Lh+\frac{(Lh)^2}{2}\right)^{k} \le 1+e^{Lh}+\cdots+e^{kLh}$$

$$=\frac{e^{(k+1)Lh}-1}{e^{Lh}}$$

since:

$$1+Lh+\frac{(Lh)^2}{2} \le e^{Lh}$$

By substituting:

$$D_H(x(t_{k+1}),x_{k+1}) \le \left(1+Lh+\frac{(Lh)^2}{2}\right)^{k+1} D_H(x(t_0),x_0)$$

$$+d\left[\frac{e^{(k+1)Lh}-1}{e^{Lh}}\right]$$

thus:

$$D_H(x(t_{k+1}),x_{k+1}) \le e^{Lh} D_H(x(t_0),x_0)+d\left[\frac{e^{(k+1)Lh}-1}{e^{Lh}}\right]$$

On the other hand:

$$(k+1)h \le T \Rightarrow e^{(k+1)Lh} \le e^{LT}$$

By substituting:

$$d=\max_{0\le k\le N-1} D_H(d_k,0)=\frac{h^3}{3!}\max_{0\le t\le T} D_H\left(x'''_{i-gH}(t_k),0\right),\ D_H(x(t_0),x_0)=0$$

Finally:

$$D_H(x(t_{k+1}),x_{k+1})\le\frac{h^3}{3!}\left[\frac{e^{LT}-1}{e^{Lh}}\right]\max_{0\le t\le T}D_H\left(x''_{i-gH}(t),0\right)$$

$$\le\frac{M_1h^3}{3!}\left[\frac{e^{LT}-1}{e^{Lh}}\right]=O\left(h^2\right)$$

Taking the limit of the two sides:

$$\lim_{h\to 0}D_H(x(t_{k+1}),x_{k+1})=0$$

Now consider that $x(t)$ is $ii-gH$ differentiable without any switching point and:

$$d_k:=\ominus_H(-1)\frac{h^3}{3!}\odot x'''_{ii-gH}(t_k)$$

Here we would like to change the strategy to prove the case. By this assumption, the iterative method is as follows:

$$x_{k+1}=x_k\ominus_H(-1)h\odot\phi(t_k,x_k,h)$$

where:

$$\phi(t_k,x_k,h)=\frac{1}{2}[f(t_k,x_k)\oplus f(t_k+h,x_k\ominus_H(-1)h\odot f(t_k,x_k))]$$

where $\phi(t_k,x_k,h)$ is a continuous fuzzy function. Now using the Lipschitz condition on $\phi(t_k,x_k,h)$ in terms of the second terms:

$$D_H(\phi(t_k,x(t_k),h),\phi(t_k,x_k,h))\le\frac{1}{2}D_H(f(t_k,x(t_k)),f(t_k,x_k))$$

$$+\frac{1}{2}D_H(f(t_k+h,x(t_k)\ominus_H(-1)h\odot f(t_k,x(t_k))),f(t_k+h,x_k\ominus_H(-1)h\odot f(t_k,x_k)))$$

$$\le\frac{L}{2}D_H(x(t_k),x_k)+$$

$$\frac{L}{2}D_H(x(t_k)\ominus_H(-1)h\odot f(t_k,x(t_k)),x_k\ominus_H(-1)h\odot f(t_k,x_k))$$

using the properties of the distance:

$$\le\frac{L}{2}D_H(x(t_k),x_k)+\frac{L}{2}D_H(x(t_k),x_k)-\frac{hL}{2}D_H(f(t_k,x(t_k)),f(t_k,x_k))$$

$$\le LD_H(x(t_k),x_k)+\frac{hL}{2}LD_H(x(t_k),x_k)=L\left(1-\frac{Lh}{2}\right)D_H(x(t_k),x_k)$$

It should be noted that the L is the maximum value of all Lipschitz constants. Finally:

$$D_H(x(t_{k+1}), x_{k+1}) \le \frac{h^2}{3!L_1}\left[1 - e^{-L_1 T}\right] \max_{0\le t\le T} D_H\left(x'''_{ii-gH}(t), 0\right)$$

where:

$$L_1 = L\left(1 + \frac{Lh}{2}\right)$$

Taking the limit of the two sides:

$$\lim_{h\to 0} D_H(x(t_{k+1}), x_{k+1}) = 0$$

5.3.1.4 Stability of the modified fuzzy Euler method

With the same illustrations about the fuzzy Euler method, we shall now discuss the stability of the modified method. To do this, again we assume that there is the same perturbation δ_0 in the fuzzy initial value and we try to show:

$$D_H(z_{k+1}, y_{k+1}) \le \kappa\delta, \ \forall (k+1)h \le T, \ k \le N-1$$

whenever $D_H(\delta_0, 0) \le \delta$.

Now suppose that the solution $x(t)$ is $i-gH$ differentiable and consider the perturbed problem as follows:

$$z_{k+1} = z_k \oplus \frac{h}{2} \odot (f(t_k, z_k \oplus h \odot f(t_k, z_k)) \oplus f(t_k, z_k)), \ z_0 = x_0 \oplus \delta_0$$

and also consider the mentioned iterative method in case (1):

$$x_{k+1} = x_k \oplus \frac{h}{2} \odot (f(t_k, x_k \oplus h \odot f(t_k, x_k)) \oplus f(t_k, x_k))$$

Using the distance, we will get:

$$D_H(z_{k+1}, x_{k+1})$$

$$\le D_H(z_k, x_k) + \frac{Lh}{2} D_H(z_k \oplus h \odot f(t_k, z_k), x_k \oplus h \odot f(t_k, x_k)) + \frac{Lh}{2} D_H(z_k, x_k)$$

$$\le D_H(z_k, x_k) + \frac{Lh}{2}(D_H(z_k, x_k) + hLD_H(z_k, x_k)) + \frac{Lh}{2} D_H(z_k, x_k)$$

$$= \left(1 + Lh + \frac{L^2h^2}{2}\right) D_H(z_k, x_k)$$

Finally:

$$D_H(z_{k+1}, x_{k+1}) \le \left(1 + Lh + \frac{L^2h^2}{2}\right) D_H(z_k, x_k)$$

and:

$$D_H(z_{k+1}, x_{k+1}) \le \left(1 + Lh + \frac{L^2h^2}{2}\right)^{k+1} D_H(z_0, x_0) \le e^{hL(k+1)} D_H(z_0 \ominus_H x_0, 0)$$
$$\le e^{LT} D_H(\delta_0, 0) \le \kappa\delta$$

where $\kappa = e^{LT}$. So based on the previous illustrations the method is stable.

In the case that the solution *x*(*t*) is $ii-gH$ differentiable, we consider the perturbed problem as follows:

$$z_{k+1} = z_k \ominus_H (-1)\frac{h}{2} \odot (f(t_k, z_k \oplus h \odot f(t_k, z_k)) \oplus f(t_k, z_k)),\ z_0 = x_0 \oplus \delta_0$$

and also consider the mentioned iterative method in case (2):

$$x_{k+1} = x_k \ominus_H (-1)\frac{h}{2} \odot (f(t_k, x_k \oplus h \odot f(t_k, x_k)) \oplus f(t_k, x_k))$$

Using the distance, we will get:

$$D_H(z_{k+1}, x_{k+1})$$
$$\le D_H(z_k, x_k) - \frac{Lh}{2} D_H(z_k \oplus h \odot f(t_k, z_k), x_k \oplus h \odot f(t_k, x_k)) - \frac{Lh}{2} D_H(z_k, x_k)$$
$$\le D_H(z_k, x_k) - \frac{Lh}{2}(D_H(z_k, x_k) + hLD_H(z_k, x_k)) - \frac{Lh}{2} D_H(z_k, x_k)$$
$$= \left(1 - Lh + \frac{L^2h^2}{2}\right) D_H(z_k, x_k)$$

Finally:

$$D_H(z_{k+1}, x_{k+1}) \le \left(1 - Lh + \frac{L^2h^2}{2}\right) D_H(z_k, x_k)$$

and:

$$D_H(z_{k+1}, x_{k+1}) \le \left(1 - Lh + \frac{L^2h^2}{2}\right)^{k+1} D_H(z_0, x_0) \le e^{-hL(k+1)} D_H(z_0 \ominus_H x_0, 0)$$
$$\le e^{-LT} D_H(\delta_0, 0) \le \kappa\delta$$

where $\kappa = e^{-LT}$. So based on the previous illustrations the method is stable.

To compare the fuzzy Euler method and fuzzy modified Euler method, we reconsider the previous examples (Allahviranloo et al., 2007).

Example. The following fuzzy initial value problem is assumed:

$$\begin{cases} x'_{i-gH}(t) = x(t) \oplus (1.3, 2, 2.1), \ 0 \le t \le 1 \\ x(0) = (0.82, 1, 1.2) \end{cases}$$

where (1.3,2,2.1) and (0.82,1,1.2) are triangular fuzzy numbers. The exact solution is obtained very easily, and it is:

$$x(t) = (x(0) \oplus (1.3, 2, 2.1))e^t \ominus_H (1.3, 2, 2.1)$$

The fuzzy Euler method in the sense of $i-gH$ differentiability has the following form:

$$\begin{aligned} x_{k+1} &= x_k \oplus \frac{h}{2} \odot \left(x^*_{k+1} \oplus (1.3, 2, 2.1) \oplus x_k \oplus (1.3, 2, 2.1)\right), \ k = 0, 1, \ldots, N-1 \\ x^*_{k+1} &= x_k \oplus h \odot (x_k \oplus (1.3, 2, 2.1)), \\ x_0 &= (0.82, 1, 1.2) \end{aligned}$$

After substituting and simplifying:

$$x_{k+1} = \left(1 + h + \frac{h^2}{2}\right) x_k \oplus \frac{h^3}{2} \odot (1.3, 2, 2.1) \oplus \frac{h}{2} (2.6, 4, 4.2)$$

$$x_0 = (0.82, 1, 1.2), \qquad k = 0, 1, \ldots, N-1$$

The global truncation errors have been reported for $h = 0.025$ and $h = 0.005$ in Table 5.4 to compare the results of the fuzzy Euler method and modified method. It is seen that the results of the modified method are much better than the Euler method. This is because the order of convergence of the modified method is higher than that of the fuzzy Euler method.

Example. Let us consider the following fuzzy initial value problem:

$$\begin{cases} x'_{ii-gH}(t) = -x(t) \oplus t \odot (0.7, 1, 1.8), \ 0 \le t \le 1 \\ x(0) = (0, 1, 2.2) \end{cases}$$

where (0.7,1,1.8) and (0,1,2.2) are triangular fuzzy numbers and their parametric forms are, respectively, as:

$$(0.7, 1, 1.8)[r] = [0.7 + 0.3r, 1.8 - 0.8r], \ (0, 1, 2.2)[r] = [r, 2.2 - 1.2r]$$

The exact solution of the fuzzy initial value problem can be obtained easily by using the parametric form of the problem and considering the $ii-gH$ differentiability of the solution. Here is the exact fuzzy number valued solution function:

$$x(t) = C \odot e^{-t} \oplus (0.7, 1, 1.8) \odot (t-1), \ C = (0, 1, 2.2) \ominus_H (-1)(0.7, 1, 1.8)$$

TABLE 5.4 Comparison of global errors.

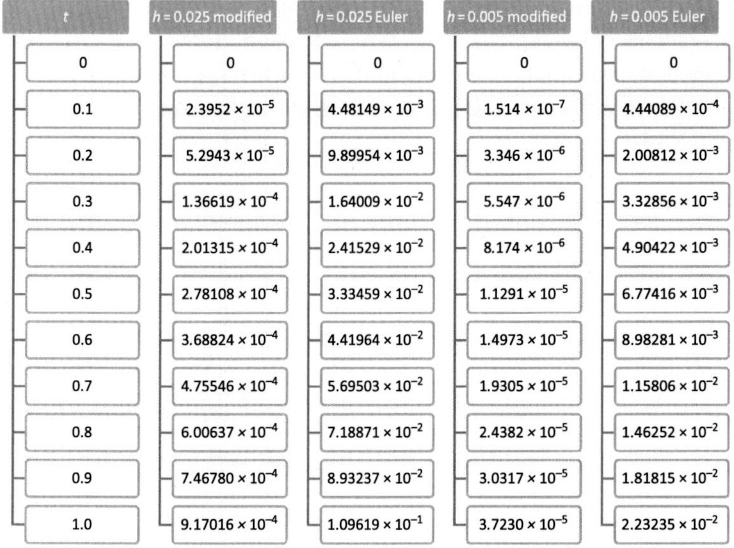

t	$h=0.025$ modified	$h=0.025$ Euler	$h=0.005$ modified	$h=0.005$ Euler
0	0	0	0	0
0.1	2.3952×10^{-5}	4.48149×10^{-3}	1.514×10^{-7}	4.44089×10^{-4}
0.2	5.2943×10^{-5}	9.89954×10^{-3}	3.346×10^{-6}	2.00812×10^{-3}
0.3	1.36619×10^{-4}	1.64009×10^{-2}	5.547×10^{-6}	3.32856×10^{-3}
0.4	2.01315×10^{-4}	2.41529×10^{-2}	8.174×10^{-6}	4.90422×10^{-3}
0.5	2.78108×10^{-4}	3.33459×10^{-2}	1.1291×10^{-5}	6.77416×10^{-3}
0.6	3.68824×10^{-4}	4.41964×10^{-2}	1.4973×10^{-5}	8.98281×10^{-3}
0.7	4.75546×10^{-4}	5.69503×10^{-2}	1.9305×10^{-5}	1.15806×10^{-2}
0.8	6.00637×10^{-4}	7.18871×10^{-2}	2.4382×10^{-5}	1.46252×10^{-2}
0.9	7.46780×10^{-4}	8.93237×10^{-2}	3.0317×10^{-5}	1.81815×10^{-2}
1.0	9.17016×10^{-4}	1.09619×10^{-1}	3.7230×10^{-5}	2.23235×10^{-2}

In the previous section, the figure of the exact solution and the process to find it were explained. Now the $ii-gH$ solution can be approximated by using case (2) in the fuzzy modified Euler method:

$$\begin{cases} x_{k+1}=x_k\ominus_H(-1)\frac{h}{2}\odot\left(f\left(t_{k+1},x_{k+1}^*\right)\oplus f(t_k,x_k)\right), & k=0,1,\ldots,N-1 \\ x_{k+1}^*=x_k\ominus_H(-1)h\odot f(t_k,x_k), \\ x_0=(0,1,2.2) \end{cases}$$

For this example, it is renewed as:

$$x_{k+1}=x_k\ominus_H(-1)\frac{h}{2}\odot\left((-1)x_{k+1}^*\oplus t_{k+1}\odot(0.7,1,1.8)\oplus(-1)x_k\oplus t_k\odot(0.7,1,1.8)\right),$$

$$x_{k+1}^*=x_k\ominus_H(-1)h\odot((-1)x_k\oplus t_k\odot(0.7,1,1.8)),$$

$$x_0=(0,1,2.2),\ k=0,1,\ldots,N-1$$

This can be simplified in the following format:

$$x_{k+1}=x_k\ominus_H\frac{h}{2}\odot([x_k\ominus_H h\odot(x_k\oplus t_k\odot(-1.8,-1,-0.7))]\oplus t_{k+1}$$
$$\odot(-1.8,-1,-0.7)\oplus x_k\oplus t_k\odot(-1.8,-1,-0.7))$$

With the same explanation about the global error and its propagation, Table 5.5 shows us the comparison of the global errors' propagations with the same step sizes for the classic fuzzy Euler method and its modification. Here also, the results of modified method are more accurate than the classic one.

Example. Consider the following fuzzy initial value problem, which is the same as the previous one:

$$\begin{cases} x'_{gH}(t) = (1-t)\odot x(t), & 0 \le t \le 2 \\ x(0) = (0, 1, 2) \end{cases}$$

with a switching point at $t = 1$.

- In the case of $i-gH$ differentiability, the fuzzy modified Euler method is reformed in the following form, which is defined in the interval $0 \le t_k < 1$:

$$x_{k+1} = x_k \oplus \frac{h}{2} \odot \left((1-t_{k+1})\odot x^*_{k+1} \oplus (1-t_k)\odot x_k\right),$$

$$x^*_{k+1} = x_k \oplus h \odot (1-t_k)\odot x_k,$$

TABLE 5.5 Comparison of global errors.

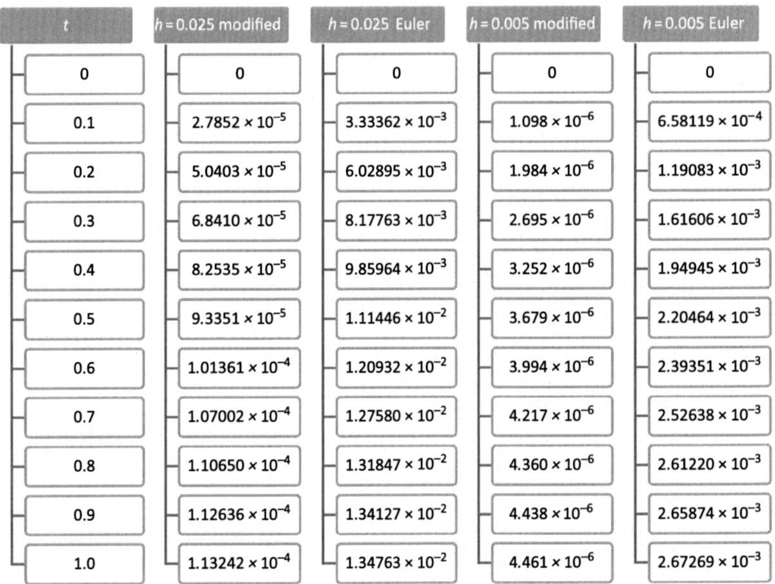

t	$h=0.025$ modified	$h=0.025$ Euler	$h=0.005$ modified	$h=0.005$ Euler
0	0	0	0	0
0.1	2.7852×10^{-5}	3.33362×10^{-3}	1.098×10^{-6}	6.58119×10^{-4}
0.2	5.0403×10^{-5}	6.02895×10^{-3}	1.984×10^{-6}	1.19083×10^{-3}
0.3	6.8410×10^{-5}	8.17763×10^{-3}	2.695×10^{-6}	1.61606×10^{-3}
0.4	8.2535×10^{-5}	9.85964×10^{-3}	3.252×10^{-6}	1.94945×10^{-3}
0.5	9.3351×10^{-5}	1.11446×10^{-2}	3.679×10^{-6}	2.20464×10^{-3}
0.6	1.01361×10^{-4}	1.20932×10^{-2}	3.994×10^{-6}	2.39351×10^{-3}
0.7	1.07002×10^{-4}	1.27580×10^{-2}	4.217×10^{-6}	2.52638×10^{-3}
0.8	1.10650×10^{-4}	1.31847×10^{-2}	4.360×10^{-6}	2.61220×10^{-3}
0.9	1.12636×10^{-4}	1.34127×10^{-2}	4.438×10^{-6}	2.65874×10^{-3}
1.0	1.13242×10^{-4}	1.34763×10^{-2}	4.461×10^{-6}	2.67269×10^{-3}

By substituting:

$$x_{k+1} = x_k \oplus \frac{h}{2} \odot ((1 - t_{k+1}) \odot x_k \oplus h(1 - t_{k+1})(1 - t_k) \odot x_k \oplus (1 - t_k) \odot x_k),$$

$$x_{k+1} = \left[1 + \left(h + \frac{h^2}{2}(1 - t_{k+1})\right)(1 - t_k)\right] \odot x_k,$$

- In the case of $ii - gH$ differentiability in the interval $1 < t_k \le 2$:

$$x_{k+1} = x_k \ominus_H (-1) \frac{h}{2} \odot ((1 - t_{k+1}) \odot x^*_{k+1} \oplus (1 - t_k) \odot x_k),$$

$$x^*_{k+1} = x_k \ominus_H (-1) h \odot (1 - t_k) \odot x_k$$

By substituting the x^*_{k+1} in x^*_{k+1} we will find:

$$x_{k+1} = x_k \ominus_H (-1) \frac{h}{2} \odot ((1 - t_{k+1}) \odot [x_k \ominus_H (-1) h \odot (1 - t_k) \odot x_k] \oplus (1 - t_k) \odot x_k),$$

Clearly, it can be simplified more but we skip it to the author. The comparison of the results between the fuzzy Euler and the modified one are shown in Table 5.6. The accuracy of the modified method can be observed in the results.

TABLE 5.6 Global error results.

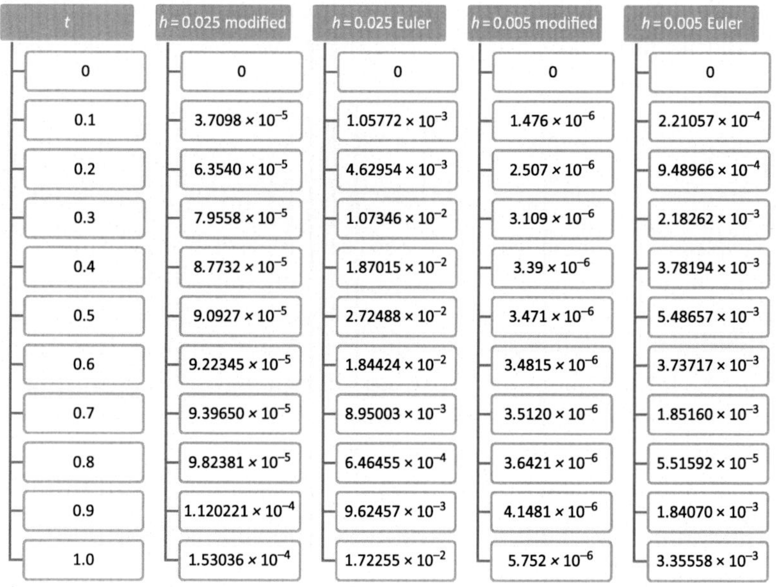

t	$h = 0.025$ modified	$h = 0.025$ Euler	$h = 0.005$ modified	$h = 0.005$ Euler
0	0	0	0	0
0.1	3.7098×10^{-5}	1.05772×10^{-3}	1.476×10^{-6}	2.21057×10^{-4}
0.2	6.3540×10^{-5}	4.62954×10^{-3}	2.507×10^{-6}	9.48966×10^{-4}
0.3	7.9558×10^{-5}	1.07346×10^{-2}	3.109×10^{-6}	2.18262×10^{-3}
0.4	8.7732×10^{-5}	1.87015×10^{-2}	3.39×10^{-6}	3.78194×10^{-3}
0.5	9.0927×10^{-5}	2.72488×10^{-2}	3.471×10^{-6}	5.48657×10^{-3}
0.6	9.22345×10^{-5}	1.84424×10^{-2}	3.4815×10^{-6}	3.73717×10^{-3}
0.7	9.39650×10^{-5}	8.95003×10^{-3}	3.5120×10^{-6}	1.85160×10^{-3}
0.8	9.82381×10^{-5}	6.46455×10^{-4}	3.6421×10^{-6}	5.51592×10^{-5}
0.9	1.120221×10^{-4}	9.62457×10^{-3}	4.1481×10^{-6}	1.84070×10^{-3}
1.0	1.53036×10^{-4}	1.72255×10^{-2}	5.752×10^{-6}	3.35558×10^{-3}

5.4 Fuzzy Euler method for fuzzy hybrid differential equations

The quadratic perturbations of nonlinear differential equations have attracted much attention recently. Such differential equations hybrid differential equations can be called hybrid differential equations. Here we are going to discuss the fuzzy version. In this section, the fuzzy Euler method is presented to solve hybrid fuzzy differential equations with fuzzy initial value. To start the discussion, we define the fuzzy hybrid differential equations in the following:

$$x'_{gH}(t) = f(t, x(t), \lambda_k(x_k)),\ \ x(t_k) = x_k,\ \ t \in [t_k, t_{k+1}]$$

where $0 \le t_0 < t_1 < t_2 < \cdots < t_k, t_k \to 0$, $f \in C[R^+ \times \mathbb{F}_R \times \mathbb{F}_R, \mathbb{F}_R], \lambda_k \in C[\mathbb{F}_R \times \mathbb{F}_R]$. These mean that the function f is a fuzzy continuous function and also λ_k is the fuzzy parameter of the fuzzy initial value. In this problem, the differential equation is defined on each subinterval $[t_k, t_{k+1}]$ and indeed we have piecewise differential equations or piecewise fuzzy initial value problems. In each subinterval, the fuzzy differential equation has a unique fuzzy solution. It is shown as the following piecewise equations:

$$x'_{gH}(t) = \begin{cases} f(t, x(t), \lambda_0(x_0)),\ x(t_0) = x_0,\ t \in [t_0, t_1] \\ f(t, x(t), \lambda_1(x_1)),\ x(t_1) = x_1,\ t \in [t_1, t_2] \\ \vdots \\ f(t, x(t), \lambda_k(x_k)),\ x(t_k) = x_k,\ t \in [t_k, t_{k+1}] \\ \vdots \end{cases}$$

But in general, we denote the fuzzy solution function as $x(t) := x_k(t)$ that is a function of t and the initial value, which is defined at the subinterval $[t_k, t_{k+1}]$, and show it as:

$$x(t) = x(t, t_0, x_0) = \begin{cases} x_0(t),\ t \in [t_0, t_1] \\ x_1(t),\ t \in [t_1, t_2] \\ \vdots \\ x_k(t),\ t \in [t_k, t_{k+1}] \end{cases}$$

As was explained earlier, for the existence and uniqueness of the solution we need the Lipschitz condition; and here, for the fuzzy hybrid differential equation, there is a unique fuzzy solution if and only if each piece does have a unique solution and if and only if each piece satisfies the Lipschitz condition. Now the fuzzy Euler method is used for the hybrid problem and this means that the fuzzy Euler method can be used for each piece even with different step size. Again, it is discussed in four cases as before.

Case 1. The fuzzy number valued solution function $x(t)$ is $(i-gH)$-differentiable and the type of differentiability does not change on $[0, T]$:

$$\begin{cases} x_{k,n+1} = x_{k,n} \oplus h_k \odot f(t, x_{k,n}, \lambda_k(x_{k,n})),\ \ n = 0, 1, \ldots, N-1 \\ x_0 \in \mathbb{F}_R \end{cases}$$

Case 2. The solution $x(t)$ is $(ii-gH)$-differentiable and the type of differentiability does not change on $[0,T]$:

$$\begin{cases} x_{k,n+1}=x_{k,n}\ominus_H(-1)h\odot f(t,x_{k,n},\lambda_k(x_{k,n})), & n=0,1,\ldots,N-1 \\ x_0\in\mathbb{F}_R \end{cases}$$

Case 3. Let us suppose that $x(t)$ has a switching point type (1) on the interval $[0,T]$ as like as ξ, and also assume that $t_0, t_1, \ldots, t_j, \xi, t_{j+1}, \ldots, t_N$. So the fuzzy Euler method is obtained as follows:

$$\begin{cases} x_{k,n+1}=x_{k,n}\oplus h\odot f(t,x_{k,n},\lambda_k(x_{k,n})), & n=0,1,\ldots,j \\ x_{k,n+1}=x_{k,n}\ominus_H(-1)h\odot f(t,x_{k,n},\lambda_k(x_{k,n})), & n=j+1,j+2,\ldots,N-1 \\ x_0\in\mathbb{F}_R \end{cases}$$

Case 4. If ξ is a type (2) switching point, the fuzzy Euler method takes the form as follows:

$$\begin{cases} x_{k,n+1}=x_{k,n}\ominus_H(-1)h\odot f(t,x_{k,n},\lambda_k(x_{k,n})), & n=0,1,\ldots,j \\ x_{k,n+1}=x_{k,n}\oplus h\odot f(t,x_{k,n},\lambda_k(x_{k,n})), & n=j+1,j+2,\ldots,N-1 \\ x_0\in\mathbb{F}_R \end{cases}$$

We have the same properties of the fuzzy Euler method for these fuzzy hybrid problems. We shall now solve some numerical examples.

Example. Consider the following fuzzy hybrid differential equations:

$$x'_{gH}(t)=(-1)\odot x(t)\oplus m(t)\odot\lambda_k(x(t_k)),\ t_k=k,\ k=0,1,2,\ldots$$

$$x(0)=(0.75, 1, 1.25)$$

where:

$$m(t)=\begin{cases} 2(t(\bmod 1)), & t(\bmod 1)<0.5 \\ 2(1-t(\bmod 1)), & t(\bmod 1)>0.5 \end{cases},\ \lambda_k(\mu)=\begin{cases} 0, & k=0 \\ \mu, & k\in\{1,2,\ldots\} \end{cases}$$

The level-wise form of the triangular fuzzy initial value is as:

$$x(0,r)=[0.75+0.25r,\ 1.125-0.125r].$$

The abovementioned fuzzy hybrid differential equation is equivalent to the following problem:

$$\begin{cases} x'_{0,gH}(t)=(-1)\odot x_0(t),\ 0\le t\le 1 \\ x(0,r)=[0.75+0.25r,\ 1.125-0.125r] \end{cases}$$

$$\begin{cases} x'_{k,gH}(t)=(-1)\odot x_k(t)\oplus m(t)\odot x_k(t_k),\ t_k\le t\le t_{k+1} \\ x_k(t_k)=x_{k-1}(t_k),\ k=1,2,\ldots \end{cases}$$

To this purpose, first of all the first fuzzy differential equation should be solved to find the fuzzy solution $x_0(t)$. It is obtained by the fuzzy Euler method, but for comparing the approximate solution and the exact solution, we need to investigate the exact solution and it is in the level-wise $[x_{0,l}(r), x_{0,u}(r)]$ form and does have the following relations, which were discussed in Chapter 4

It should be observed that we have these notations here:

$$x_0(t,r) = [x_{0,l}(r), x_{0,u}(r)], \quad x_0(r) = [x_{l,0}(r), x_{u,0}(r)]$$

To find the exact solution in level-wise form, we use the parametric form or level-wise form of the derivative. If type (1) of the differentiability is used, we will see that the fuzzy solution will not satisfy our differential equations, which means the type of differentiability is changed to type (2). So in the following, we use the routine level-wise form and we find a system of two lower and upper form differential equations and the solutions in lower and upper case are as follows:

$$x_{0,l}(t,r) = \frac{A-B}{2} x_{u,0}(r) + \frac{A+B}{2} x_{l,0}(r)$$

$$x_{0,u}(t,r) = \frac{A+B}{2} x_{u,0}(r) + \frac{A-B}{2} x_{l,0}(r)$$

where $A = \frac{1}{2}\exp\left(\frac{t^2-t_0^2}{2}\right), B = \frac{1}{A}$.

At the point $t=1$, $t_0=0$ we have:

$$x_{0,l}(1,r) = \frac{1}{2}\left(\exp\left(\frac{1}{2}\right) + \frac{2}{\exp\left(\frac{1}{2}\right)}\right) x_{u,0}(r) + \frac{1}{2}\left(\exp\left(\frac{1}{2}\right) - \frac{2}{\exp\left(\frac{1}{2}\right)}\right) x_{l,0}(r)$$

$$x_{0,u}(1,r) = \frac{1}{2}\left(\exp\left(\frac{1}{2}\right) - \frac{2}{\exp\left(\frac{1}{2}\right)}\right) x_{u,0}(r) + \frac{1}{2}\left(\exp\left(\frac{1}{2}\right) + \frac{2}{\exp\left(\frac{1}{2}\right)}\right) x_{l,0}(r)$$

$$x_{l,0}(r) = 0.75 + 0.25r, \quad x_{u,0}(r) = 1.125 - 0.125r$$

Now in the sense of *ii*-differentiability we will have the right solution and it is:

$$x_0(t) = x_0(0)\exp(t),$$

$$x_0(t,r) = [(0.75+0.25r)\exp(-t), (1.125-0.125r)\exp(-t)]$$

and at the point $t=1$ it is:

$$x_0(1,r) = [(0.75+0.25r)\exp(-1), (1.125-0.125r)\exp(-1)]$$

To find the approximate solution, we use the fuzzy Euler method in the sense of ii-differentiability and we have:

$$x_{0,n+1} = x_{0,n} \ominus_H (-1) h \odot f(t_n, x_{0,n}) = x_{0,n} \ominus_H (-1) h \odot (-1) \odot x_{0,n}$$

$$= x_{0,n} \ominus_H h \odot x_{0,n} = (1-h) \odot x_{0,n} = (1-h)^2 \odot x_{0,n-1} = \cdots$$

$$= (1-h)^{n+1} \odot x_{0,0} = \left(1 - \frac{1}{n+1}\right)^{n+1} \odot x_{0,0}$$

In the level-wise form it is:

$$x_{0,n+1,l}(r) = (1-h)^{n+1} x_{0,0,l}(r) = \left(1 - \frac{1}{n+1}\right)^{n+1} (0.75 + 0.25r)$$

$$x_{0,n+1,u}(r) = (1-h)^{n+1} x_{0,0,u}(r) = \left(1 - \frac{1}{n+1}\right)^{n+1} ((1.125 - 0.125r))$$

For instance, for nine iterations we have:

$$x_0(1,r) \approx x_{0,n}(r) = \left[(0.75 + 0.25r)\left(1 - \frac{1}{10}\right)^{10}, (1.125 - 0.125r)\left(1 - \frac{1}{10}\right)^{10} \right]$$

for any $0 \le r \le 1$.

Now we use the fuzzy Euler method to solve the second part of the hybrid differential equation:

$$\begin{cases} x'_{k,gH}(t) = (-1) \odot x_k(t) \oplus m(t) \odot x_k(t_k), \; t_k \le t \le t_{k+1} \\ x_k(t_k) = x_{k-1}(t_k), \; k = 1, 2, \ldots \end{cases}$$

If we choose $k=1$ then $x_1(t_1) = x_0(t_1)$ and from the first part we found the approximate values of $x_0(t)$ at any points including t_1, so we already have computed the $x_0(t_1)$ and also the same for $x_1(t_1)$. Since $t(\text{mod } 1) < 0.5$ for any $t_k \in [0,1]$ with the step size 0.1 then $m(t_k) = 2(t_k(\text{mod } 1))$ is computed easily. Then using the fuzzy Euler method is easier because all information is provided. Indeed, in each piece we use the fuzzy Euler method at 11 points. Now the fuzzy Euler method is used in the sense of ii-differentiability and we have:

For $k=1$:

$$\begin{cases} x_{1,n+1} = x_{1,n} \ominus_H (-1) h \odot (-1) \odot x_{1,n} \oplus m(t_n) \odot x_1(t_1), \; n = 0, 1, \ldots, 9 \\ x_0(0,r) = [(0.75 + 0.25r), (1.125 - 0.125r)] \end{cases}$$

or:

$$\begin{cases} x_{1,n+1} = x_{1,n} \ominus_H h \odot x_{1,n} \oplus m(t_n) \odot x_1(t_1), \; n = 0, 1, \ldots, 9 \\ x_0(0,r) = [(0.75 + 0.25r), (1.125 - 0.125r)] \end{cases}$$

since:

$$x_1(t_1)=x_0(t_1)=x_0(0.1)=x_{0,1}(r)$$

$$=\left[(0.75+0.25r)\left(1-\frac{1}{2}\right)^2,(1.125-0.125r)\left(1-\frac{1}{2}\right)^2\right]$$

Then in the subinterval $[t_1,t_2]$, the fuzzy Euler method has been shown as the following form:

$$\begin{cases} x_{1,n+1}=x_{1,n}\ominus_H h\odot x_{1,n}\oplus m(t_n)\odot x_1(t_1), \quad n=0,1,\ldots,9 \\ x_{0,1}(r)=\left[(0.75+0.25r)\left(1-\frac{1}{2}\right)^2,(1.125-0.125r)\left(1-\frac{1}{2}\right)^2\right] \end{cases}$$

After finding the $x_{1,10}$ then we choose $k=2$, repeat the same procedure, and find the $x_{2,10}\approx x(t_2)$. By repeating this process on each subinterval and using the Euler method in each subinterval with $n=0$, 1, ..., 9, the solution in each subinterval is found (Allahviranloo & Salahshour, 2011).

5.5 Fuzzy Euler method for fuzzy impulsive differential equations

In this section we shall find the numerical solution of fuzzy impulsive differential equations by using both the fuzzy Euler and fuzzy modified Euler methods.

Generally, the analytical solution of these fuzzy impulsive equations is a complex solution and usually it is impossible to obtain, and therefore the numerical solution is suggested. The fuzzy impulsive differential equation is introduced in the following form:

$$\begin{cases} x'_{gH}(t)=f(t,x(t)), \quad t\in J=[0,T], \quad t\neq t_k, k=1,2,\ldots,N \\ \Delta x|_{t=t_k}=I_k(x(t_k)), \ t=t_k, \quad k=1,2,\ldots,N \\ x(t_0)=x_0 \end{cases}$$

where:

$$x_0\in\mathbb{F}_R, \quad f:J\times\mathbb{F}_R\rightarrow\mathbb{F}_R, \quad I_k:\mathbb{F}_R\rightarrow\mathbb{F}_R, \quad k=1,2,\ldots,N$$

and:

$$\Delta x|_{t=t_k}=x\left(t_k^+\right)\ominus_{gH}x\left(t_k^-\right), \ k=1,2,\ldots,N$$

where:

$$\lim_{t\to t_k^-}x(t)=x\left(t_k^-\right), \quad \lim_{t\to t_k^+}x(t)=x\left(t_k^+\right)$$

Indeed, it seems that we have some points like t_k, $k=1, 2, \ldots, N$, and at these points the fuzzy derivative cannot be defined and there is only a fuzzy difference, but between these points or in the subinterval a fuzzy differential equation is defined. So in the arbitrary subinterval $(t_k, t_{k+1}]$, the fuzzy differential equations is solved numerically or analytically, then the obtained solution is determined at the point t_{k+1}, again at this point we have only difference (one can call it by a jump from the left limit to the right limit), the difference is a fuzzy difference and it can be defined in two cases. For more clarity, the procedure of finding the numerical solution of the impulsive equation is explained by the following steps:

Step 1. We use the fuzzy Euler method for the impulsive equation in the interval $(t_k, t_{k+1}]$. It should be noted that in each half segment or subinterval the initial value for the fuzzy Euler method is as $x_0=x(t_k^+)$. It is clear that the Euler method can be used in two cases of differentiability.

Step 2. The numerical solution obtained from step 1, is used in the difference function, at the point $t=t_{k+1}$:

$$\Delta x|_{t=t_{k+1}} = I_k\left(x\left(t_{k+1}^-\right)\right) = I_k(x(t_k) \oplus h \odot f(t_k, x(t_k)))$$

On the other hand:

$$x\left(t_{k+1}^+\right) \ominus_{gH} x\left(t_{k+1}^-\right) = I_k(x(t_k) \oplus h \odot f(t_k, x(t_k))) = I\left(x\left(t_{k+1}^-\right)\right)$$

The $x(t_k)$ is a scalar and we know:

$$\lim_{t \to t_{k+1}^-} x(t) = x\left(t_{k+1}^-\right), \quad \lim_{t \to t_{k+1}^+} x(t) = x\left(t_{k+1}^+\right)$$

Now if $I(x(t_{k+1}^-))$ is a fuzzy number then the gH-difference is defined and:

$$x\left(t_{k+1}^+\right) \ominus_{gH} x\left(t_{k+1}^-\right) = I\left(x\left(t_{k+1}^-\right)\right)$$

$$x\left(t_{k+1}^+\right) \ominus_{gH} x\left(t_{k+1}^-\right) = I\left(x\left(t_{k+1}^-\right)\right) = \begin{cases} x\left(t_{k+1}^+\right) = I\left(x\left(t_{k+1}^-\right)\right) \oplus x\left(t_{k+1}^-\right) \\ x\left(t_{k+1}^-\right) = x\left(t_{k+1}^+\right) \oplus (-1) I\left(x\left(t_{k+1}^-\right)\right) \end{cases}$$

Now in each subinterval, $(t_k, t_{k+1}]$, $x(t_k^+)$ is the initial point for the Euler method and by applying the fuzzy Euler method and even the modified version, we will find the $x(t_{k+1}^-)$, and this satisfies the jump, so we have obtained the $x(t_{k+1}^+)$. At each stage, we determine the left limit point and right limit point, and the jumps are skipped, so to find the final solution, all the jumps must be added to the approximate solution. This process is continued in every subinterval.

Step 3. The steps 1 and 2 are repeated while $t_{k+1} \leq t_z$ where t_z is known and fixed time.

Step 4. All the jumps are added to the solution to introduce the general solution of the fuzzy impulsive differential equations. See the abovementioned explanations.

5.5.1 Error analysis

In the numerical investigation of the problem, we know that we need the convergence solution, consistency of the problem, and the stability of the method. The presented numerical methods have been analyzed before in accordance with convergency and consistency, and now we only discuss the stability of the fuzzy impulsive problem.

5.5.1.1 *Stability*

To investigate the stability of the problem, we add a small perturbation δ_3 in the fuzzy initial value. Clearly, it causes some small perturbations like δ_2, δ_1 in the other equations. It is expected that the created or forced perturbation δ in the solution of the problem should be small as well. To this end, consider the perturbed fuzzy impulsive differential equation in the following form:

$$\begin{cases} z'_{gH}(t) = f(t,z(t)) \oplus (\delta_1 \odot f(t,z(t))), \ t \in J = [0,T], \ t \neq t_k, k = 1,2,\ldots,N \\ \Delta z|_{t=t_k} = I_k(z(t_k)) \oplus (\delta_2 \odot I_k(z(t_k))), \ t = t_k, \ k = 1,2,\ldots,N \\ z(t_0) = \delta_3 \odot x_0 \end{cases}$$

The solution of this perturbed problem is $z(t)$ and we expect that the perturbation in the solution will be δ and:

$$z(t) = x(t) \oplus (x(t) \odot \delta)$$

where:

$$\forall t \exists \epsilon > 0; \delta \in N(x(t), \epsilon), \quad \exists \epsilon_3 > 0; \delta \in N(z_0, \epsilon_3),$$

$$\exists \epsilon_2 > 0; \delta \in N(I_k(z(t_k)), \epsilon_2), \quad \forall t \exists \epsilon_1 > 0; \delta \in N(f(t,z(t)), \epsilon_1)$$

$$\epsilon = \min\{\epsilon_1, \epsilon_2, \epsilon_3\}$$

Now consider the following relation, which means the perturbation in the $I_k(x(t_k))$ concludes the $I_k(z(t_k))$:

$$z(t_k^+) \ominus_{gH} z(t_k^-) = x(t_k^+) \ominus_{gH} x(t_k^-) \oplus (\delta_2 \odot I_k(x(t_k)))$$

Based on the definition of the gH-difference, we have:

$$(z(t_k^+) \ominus_{gH} z(t_k^-)) \ominus_{gH} (x(t_k^+) \ominus_{gH} x(t_k^-)) = \delta_2 \odot I_k(x(t_k))$$

since:

$$z(t_k^+) = x(t_k^+) \oplus \delta \odot x(t_k^+), \quad z(t_k^-) = x(t_k^-) \oplus \delta \odot x(t_k^-)$$

By substituting:

$$(x(t_k^+) \oplus \delta \odot x(t_k^+)) \ominus_{gH} (x(t_k^-) \oplus \delta \odot x(t_k^-)) \ominus_{gH} (x(t_k^+) \ominus_{gH} x(t_k^-))$$
$$= \delta_2 \odot I_k(x(t_k))$$

Assuming all gH-differences exist, for instance, suppose that the:

$$\left(x\left(t_k^+\right)\oplus\delta\odot x\left(t_k^+\right)\right)\ominus_{gH}\left(x\left(t_k^-\right)\oplus\delta\odot x\left(t_k^-\right)\right)$$

exists in case (1):

$$\left(x\left(t_k^+\right)\oplus\delta\odot x\left(t_k^+\right)\right)\ominus_{i-gH}\left(x\left(t_k^-\right)\oplus\delta\odot x\left(t_k^-\right)\right)$$

then:

$$\begin{aligned}&\left(x_l\left(t_k^+\right)\oplus\delta\odot x_l\left(t_k^+\right)\right)-\left(x_l\left(t_k^-\right)\oplus\delta\odot x_l\left(t_k^-\right)\right)\\&=x_l\left(t_k^+\right)-\delta\odot x_l\left(t_k^+\right)-x_l\left(t_k^-\right)-\delta\odot x_l\left(t_k^-\right)\end{aligned}$$

and:

$$\begin{aligned}&\left(x_u\left(t_k^+\right)\oplus\delta\odot x_u\left(t_k^+\right)\right)-\left(x_u\left(t_k^-\right)\oplus\delta\odot x_u\left(t_k^-\right)\right)\\&=x_u\left(t_k^+\right)-\delta\odot u\left(t_k^+\right)-x_u\left(t_k^-\right)-\delta\odot x_u\left(t_k^-\right)\end{aligned}$$

then the gH-difference in the interval form is as:

$$\left(x\left(t_k^+\right)\oplus\delta\odot x\left(t_k^+\right)\right)\ominus_{i-gH}\left(x\left(t_k^-\right)\oplus\delta\odot x\left(t_k^-\right)\right)$$

$$\left[x_l\left(t_k^+\right)-\delta\odot x_l\left(t_k^+\right)-x_l\left(t_k^-\right)-\delta\odot x_l\left(t_k^-\right),x_u\left(t_k^+\right)-\delta\odot u\left(t_k^+\right)-x_u\left(t_k^-\right)-\delta\odot x_u\left(t_k^-\right)\right]$$

and also, in case (2) of gH-difference, the interval form is as:

$$\left(x\left(t_k^+\right)\oplus\delta\odot x\left(t_k^+\right)\right)\ominus_{ii-gH}\left(x\left(t_k^-\right)\oplus\delta\odot x\left(t_k^-\right)\right)$$

$$\left[x_u\left(t_k^+\right)-\delta\odot u\left(t_k^+\right)-x_u\left(t_k^-\right)-\delta\odot x_u\left(t_k^-\right),x_l\left(t_k^+\right)-\delta\odot x_l\left(t_k^+\right)-x_l\left(t_k^-\right)-\delta\odot x_l\left(t_k^-\right)\right]$$

All these mean that in each case of the difference we have the following relations immediately:

$$\begin{aligned}&\left(x\left(t_k^+\right)\oplus\delta\odot x\left(t_k^+\right)\right)\ominus_{gH}\left(x\left(t_k^-\right)\oplus\delta\odot x\left(t_k^-\right)\right)\ominus_{gH}\left(x\left(t_k^+\right)\ominus_{gH}x\left(t_k^-\right)\right)=\\&\left(x\left(t_k^+\right)\ominus_{gH}x\left(t_k^-\right)\right)\oplus\left(\delta\odot x\left(t_k^+\right)\ominus_{gH}\delta\odot x\left(t_k^-\right)\right)\ominus_{gH}\left(x\left(t_k^+\right)\ominus_{gH}x\left(t_k^-\right)\right)\\&=\delta\odot x\left(t_k^+\right)\ominus_{gH}\delta\odot x\left(t_k^-\right)\end{aligned}$$

then:

$$\delta\odot x\left(t_k^+\right)\ominus_{gH}\delta\odot x\left(t_k^-\right)=\delta_2\odot I_k(x(t_k))$$

since δ is positive:

$$\delta\odot\left(x\left(t_k^+\right)\ominus_{gH}x\left(t_k^-\right)\right)=\delta_2\odot I_k(x(t_k))$$

or:

$$\delta \odot \left(x\left(t_k^+\right) \ominus_{gH} x\left(t_k^-\right)\right) = \delta_2 \odot \left(x\left(t_k^+\right) \ominus_{gH} x\left(t_k^-\right)\right)$$

This means the perturbations in the difference equation corresponding to the jump are the same: $\delta = \delta_2$.

What about other perturbations?

In the case that we use the fuzzy Euler method and it does not matter which case of Euler we use, then:

$$z_{k+1} = z_k \oplus h \odot (f(t_k, z_k) \oplus (\delta_1 \odot f(t_k, z_k))), \quad z_0 = \delta_3 \odot x_0$$

By backward substituting:

$$z_k = z_{k-1} \oplus h \odot (f(t_{k-1}, z_{k-1}) \oplus (\delta_1 \odot f(t_{k-1}, z_{k-1})))$$

Since δ_1 is positive we have:

$$z_{k+1} = z_{k-1} \oplus h \odot [f(t_{k-1}, z_{k-1}) \oplus f(t_k, z_k)] \oplus \delta_1 \odot [f(t_{k-1}, z_{k-1}) \oplus f(t_k, z_k)]$$

Finally, by continuing this process we get:

$$z_{k+1} = z_0 \oplus h \odot \sum_{i=0}^{k} f(t_i, z_i) \oplus \delta_1 \odot \sum_{i=0}^{k} f(t_i, z_i)$$

Since $z_0 = \delta_3 \odot x_0$ and $z_i = z_i \oplus \delta \odot z_i$ then:

$$z_{k+1} \oplus \delta \odot z_{k+1} = \delta_3 \odot x_0 \oplus h \odot \sum_{i=0}^{k} f(t_i, z_i) \oplus \delta_1 \odot \sum_{i=0}^{k} f(t_i, z_i)$$

If you look at to both sides, the perturbation on the left-hand side is $\delta \odot z_{k+1}$ and the perturbations on the right-hand side are:

$$\delta_3 \odot x_0 \oplus \delta_1 \odot \sum_{i=0}^{k} f(t_i, z_i)$$

Now we should claim that:

$$\delta \odot z_{k+1} \leq \delta_3 \odot x_0 \oplus \delta_1 \odot \sum_{i=0}^{k} f(t_i, z_i)$$

This inequality or ordering of fuzzy numbers in the level-wise form is:

$$\delta \odot z_{l,k+1} \leq \delta_3 \odot x_{l,0} \oplus \delta_1 \odot \sum_{i=0}^{k} f_l(t_i, z_i)$$

$$\delta \odot z_{u,k+1} \leq \delta_3 \odot x_{u,0} \oplus \delta_1 \odot \sum_{i=0}^{k} f_u(t_i, z_i)$$

thus:

$$\delta \leq \frac{\delta_3 \odot x_{l,0} \oplus \delta_1 \odot \sum_{i=0}^{k} f_l(t_i, z_i)}{z_{l,k+1}}$$

$$\delta \leq \frac{\delta_3 \odot x_{u,0} \oplus \delta_1 \odot \sum_{i=0}^{k} f_u(t_i, z_i)}{z_{u,k+1}}$$

Considering $\delta = \delta_2$ the maximum error or perturbation is:

$$\delta \leq \max \left\{ \frac{\delta_3 \odot x_{u,0} \oplus \delta_1 \odot \sum_{i=0}^{k} f_u(t_i, z_i)}{z_{u,k+1}}, \delta_2 \right\}$$

We shall now solve some examples for further illustration.

Example. Consider the following impulsive differential equation with fuzzy initial value:

$$\begin{cases} x'_{gH}(t) = (-1) \odot x(t), \ t \in J = [0, 3], \ t \neq 1,2,3 \\ x\left(t_k^+\right) = 0.01 \odot x\left(t_k^+\right), \ t = t_k = 1,2,3 \\ x(0) = (0.75 + 0.25r, \ 1.25 - 0.75r), \ 0 \leq r \leq 1 \end{cases}$$

Let us consider $t_z = 3$ and the jump points are $t = 1$, $t = 2$, $t = 3$. So we have three intervals to approximations: $(0, 1^-]$, $(1, 2^-]$, $(2, 3^-]$.

The mentioned four steps are now done and the results of local truncation error for the Euler method with $h = 0.025$ and in the level $r = 0.9$ are displayed in Tables 5.7–5.9.

Example. Consider the following impulsive differential equation with fuzzy initial value:

$$\begin{cases} x'_{gH}(t) = (-1) \odot x^2(t), \ t \in J = [0, 5], \ t \neq 3,4,5 \\ x\left(t_k^+\right) = 0.01 \odot x\left(t_k^+\right), \ t = t_k = 3,4,5 \\ x(0) = (0.75 + 0.25r, \ 1.25 - 0.75r), \ 0 \leq r \leq 1 \end{cases}$$

Let us consider $t_z = 5.5$ and the jump points are $t = 3$, $t = 4$, $t = 5$. So we have three intervals to approximations: $(3, 4^-]$, $(4, 5^-]$, $(5, 5.5^-]$.

The mentioned four steps are now done and the results of local truncation error for the Euler method with $h = 0.025$ and in the level $r = 0.9$ are displayed in Tables 5.10–5.12.

TABLE 5.7 The truncation error in the first interval.

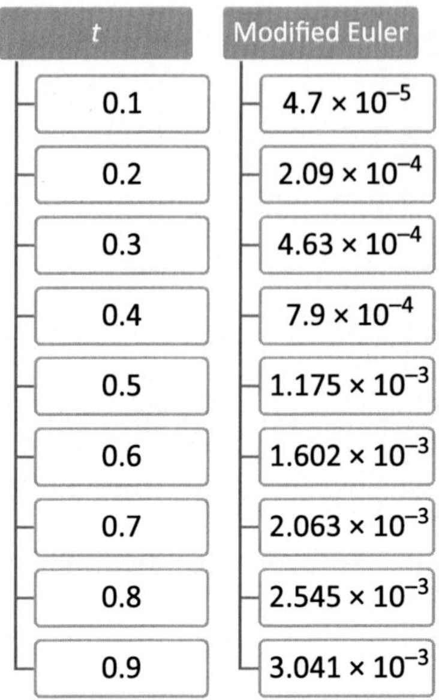

t	Modified Euler
0.1	4.7×10^{-5}
0.2	2.09×10^{-4}
0.3	4.63×10^{-4}
0.4	7.9×10^{-4}
0.5	1.175×10^{-3}
0.6	1.602×10^{-3}
0.7	2.063×10^{-3}
0.8	2.545×10^{-3}
0.9	3.041×10^{-3}

TABLE 5.8 The truncation error in the second interval.

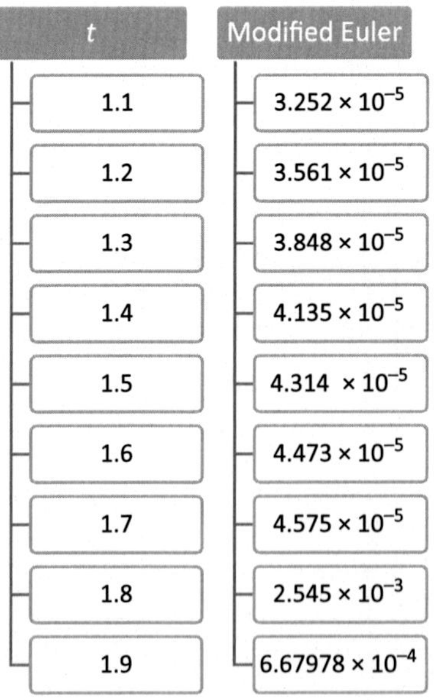

t	Modified Euler
1.1	3.252×10^{-5}
1.2	3.561×10^{-5}
1.3	3.848×10^{-5}
1.4	4.135×10^{-5}
1.5	4.314×10^{-5}
1.6	4.473×10^{-5}
1.7	4.575×10^{-5}
1.8	2.545×10^{-3}
1.9	6.67978×10^{-4}

TABLE 5.9 The truncation error in the third interval.

t	Modified Euler
2.1	1.3976×10^{-6}
2.2	1.5398×10^{-6}
2.3	1.689×10^{-6}
2.4	1.8449×10^{-6}
2.5	2.0074×10^{-6}
2.6	2.2958×10^{-6}
2.7	2.531×10^{-6}
2.8	2.714×10^{-6}
2.9	2.901×10^{-6}

TABLE 5.10 The truncation error in the first interval.

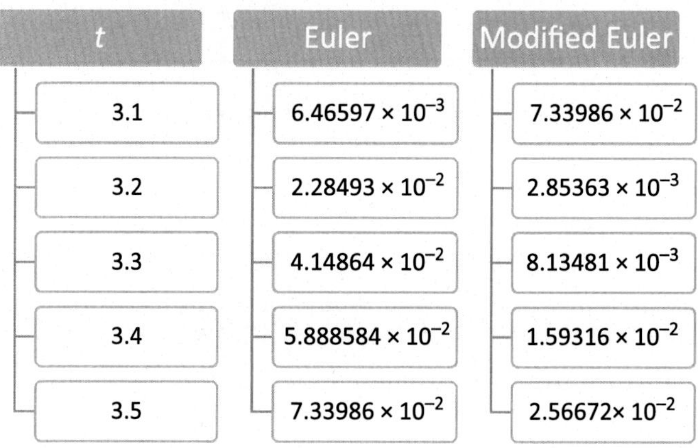

t	Euler	Modified Euler
3.1	6.46597×10^{-3}	7.33986×10^{-2}
3.2	2.28493×10^{-2}	2.85363×10^{-3}
3.3	4.14864×10^{-2}	8.13481×10^{-3}
3.4	5.888584×10^{-2}	1.59316×10^{-2}
3.5	7.33986×10^{-2}	2.56672×10^{-2}

TABLE 5.11 The truncation error in the second interval.

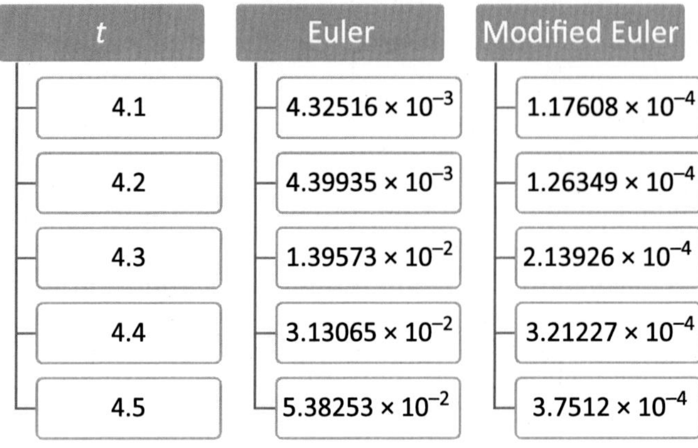

t	Euler	Modified Euler
4.1	4.32516×10^{-3}	1.17608×10^{-4}
4.2	4.39935×10^{-3}	1.26349×10^{-4}
4.3	1.39573×10^{-2}	2.13926×10^{-4}
4.4	3.13065×10^{-2}	3.21227×10^{-4}
4.5	5.38253×10^{-2}	3.7512×10^{-4}

TABLE 5.12 The truncation error in the third interval.

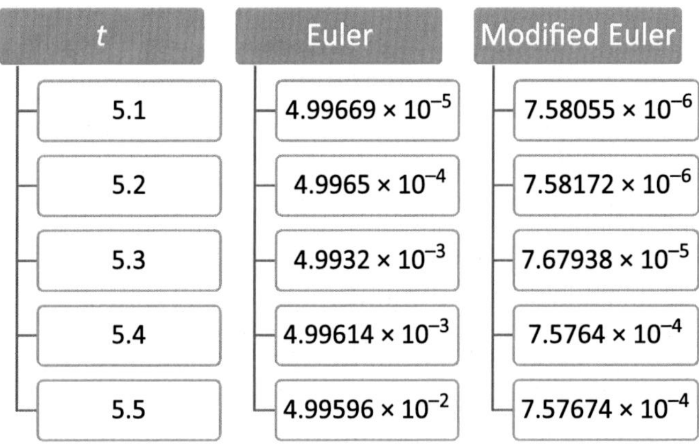

t	Euler	Modified Euler
5.1	4.99669×10^{-5}	7.58055×10^{-6}
5.2	4.9965×10^{-4}	7.58172×10^{-6}
5.3	4.9932×10^{-3}	7.67938×10^{-5}
5.4	4.99614×10^{-3}	7.5764×10^{-4}
5.5	4.99596×10^{-2}	7.57674×10^{-4}

5.6 Fuzzy predictor and corrector methods

In this section, we are going to cover a fuzzy numerical method with combinations of two other fuzzy numerical methods. To do this, first a fuzzy explicit numerical method is introduced to investigate the initial approximation and then it is improved by another implicit fuzzy method. To this purpose, we should first discuss the fuzzy explicit and implicit methods (Allahviranloo et al., 2007, 2009).

5.6.1 Definition—Fuzzy explicit method

Consider the following fuzzy recursive relation:

$$\begin{cases} x_{k+1} = x_k \oplus h \odot F(t, x_{k-1}, x_{k-2}, \ldots, x_1, h), \ 0 \le t \le T \\ x_0 \in \mathbb{F}_R \end{cases}$$

where $h = \frac{T}{N}$ for any $k = 0, 1, \ldots, N$. This recursive relation is called the fuzzy k-step explicit method, because it uses the previous $x_k, x_{k-1}, x_{k-2}, \ldots, x_1$ to investigate the x_{k+1}.

5.6.2 Definition—Fuzzy implicit method

Consider the following fuzzy recursive relation:

$$\begin{cases} x_{k+1} = x_k \oplus h \odot F(t, x_{k+1}, x_{k-1}, x_{k-2}, \ldots, x_1, h), \ 0 \le t \le T \\ x_0 \in \mathbb{F}_R \end{cases}$$

with the same characteristics as the previous example. The value x_{k+1} appears in two sides of the relation and this is why we call it the implicit method.

To introduce the methods, we need to define an interpolation problem to interpolate or approximate the behavior of the points (t_i, x_i) in which the t_i is real and x_i is a fuzzy number for $i = 0, 1, \ldots, n$.

As we know, there are several interpolation methods to approximate the data. Here we are going to discuss the fuzzy spline interpolation method. The fuzzy spline method is defined based on piecewise fuzzy polynomials functions to approximate a fuzzy continuous function. So, to approximate a fuzzy continuous function $x(t)$ at the nodes (t_i, x_i), we need to define the piecewise fuzzy polynomial $s(t)$ with degree at most k such that $s(t) \in C^{k-1}[t_0, t_n]$ at the points $t_0 < t_1 < \ldots < t_n$:

$$s(t) = \begin{cases} s_0(t), & t \in [t_0, t_1] \\ s_1(t), & t \in [t_1, t_2] \\ & \vdots \\ s_{n-1}(t), & t \in [t_{n-1}, t_n] \end{cases}$$

where $s_i(t) \in C^{k-1}[t_i, t_{i+1}]$, $i=0, 1..., n-1$ are the fuzzy polynomials of the degree k with fuzzy number coefficients, such that:

$$s_{i-1}^{(k-1)}(t_i) = s_i^{(k-1)}(t_i), \quad i=1,\ldots,n-1$$

$$s_{i-1}(t_i) = x_i, i=1,\ldots,n, \quad s_i(t_i) = x_i, i=0,1,\ldots,n-1$$

Now let us consider the triple form of a triangular fuzzy number as $x_i = (x_i^l, x_i^c, x_i^r)$ and suppose that $f(t) = (f^l(t), f^c(t), f^r(t))$ is a fuzzy function that we want to approximate in the $[t_0, t_n]$. The mentioned spline should be defined for each element of the fuzzy number separately, and we have:

$$\begin{cases} f^l(t) = \sum\limits_{s_i(t)\geq 0} s_i(t)x_i^l + \sum\limits_{s_i(t)<0} s_i(t)x_i^r \\ f^c(t) = \sum\limits_{i=0}^{n} s_i(t)x_i^c \\ f^r(t) = \sum\limits_{s_i(t)\geq 0} s_i(t)x_i^r + \sum\limits_{s_i(t)<0} s_i(t)x_i^l \end{cases}$$

Note. In this section, we suppose that the Hukuhara difference always exists and it is only considered in type one difference or i-difference. So we consider the fuzzy initial value with H-differentiability as the following form:

$$x_H'(t) = f(t, x(t)), \quad x(t_0) = x_0 \in \mathbb{F}_R$$

5.6.3 Fuzzy explicit three steps method

To introduce the method, we need the points $x(t_{i-1})$, $x(t_i)$, $x(t_{i+1})$ and $f(t_{i-1}, x(t_{i-1}))$, $f(t_i, x(t_i))$, $f(t_{i+1}, x(t_{i+1}))$, which are triangular fuzzy numbers, and:

$$\left(f^l(t_{i-1}, x(t_{i-1})), f^c(t_{i-1}, x(t_{i-1})), f^r(t_{i-1}, x(t_{i-1}))\right)$$

$$\left(f^l(t_i, x(t_i)), f^c(t_i, x(t_i)), f^r(t_i, x(t_i))\right)$$

$$\left(f^l(t_{i+1}, x(t_{i+1})), f^c(t_{i+1}, x(t_{i+1})), f^r(t_{i+1}, x(t_{i+1}))\right)$$

The fuzzy linear spline of in the intervals $[t_{i-1}, t_i]$ and $[t_i, t_{i+1}]$ are defined as:

$$s_{i-1}(t) = \frac{t_i - t}{t_i - t_{i-1}} f(t_{i-1}, x(t_{i-1})) + \frac{t - t_{i-1}}{t_i - t_{i-1}} f(t_i, x(t_i)), \quad t \in [t_{i-1}, t_i]$$

$$s_i(t) = \frac{t_{i+1} - t}{t_{i+1} - t_i} f(t_i, x(t_i)) + \frac{t - t_i}{t_{i+1} - t_i} f(t_{i+1}, x(t_{i+1})), \quad t \in [t_i, t_{i+1}]$$

The left-center-right of $s_{i-1}(t)$ is defined as:

$$s_{i-1}^{l}(t)=\frac{t_i-t}{t_i-t_{i-1}}f^{l}(t_{i-1},x(t_{i-1}))+\frac{t-t_{i-1}}{t_i-t_{i-1}}f^{l}(t_i,x(t_i)),\ t\in[t_{i-1},t_i]$$

$$s_{i-1}^{c}(t)=\frac{t_i-t}{t_i-t_{i-1}}f^{c}(t_{i-1},x(t_{i-1}))+\frac{t-t_{i-1}}{t_i-t_{i-1}}f^{c}(t_i,x(t_i)),\ t\in[t_{i-1},t_i]$$

$$s_{i-1}^{r}(t)=\frac{t_i-t}{t_i-t_{i-1}}f^{r}(t_{i-1},x(t_{i-1}))+\frac{t-t_{i-1}}{t_i-t_{i-1}}f^{r}(t_i,x(t_i)),\ t\in[t_{i-1},t_i]$$

because:

$$\frac{t_i-t}{t_i-t_{i-1}}\geq 0,\ \frac{t-t_{i-1}}{t_i-t_{i-1}}\geq 0,\ t\in[t_{i-1},t_i]$$

The same is defined for the right point of fuzzy function $s(t)$:

$$s_{i}^{l}(t)=\frac{t_{i+1}-t}{t_{i+1}-t_i}f^{l}(t_i,x(t_i))+\frac{t-t_i}{t_{i+1}-t_i}f^{l}(t_{i+1},x(t_{i+1})),\ t\in[t_i,t_{i+1}]$$

$$s_{i}^{c}(t)=\frac{t_{i+1}-t}{t_{i+1}-t_i}f^{c}(t_i,x(t_i))+\frac{t-t_i}{t_{i+1}-t_i}f^{c}(t_{i+1},x(t_{i+1})),\ t\in[t_i,t_{i+1}]$$

$$s_{i}^{r}(t)=\frac{t_{i+1}-t}{t_{i+1}-t_i}f^{r}(t_i,x(t_i))+\frac{t-t_i}{t_{i+1}-t_i}f^{r}(t_{i+1},x(t_{i+1})),\ t\in[t_i,t_{i+1}]$$

because:

$$\frac{t_{i+1}-t}{t_{i+1}-t_i}\geq 0,\ \frac{t-t_i}{t_{i+1}-t_i}\geq 0,\ t\in[t_i,t_{i+1}]$$

In addition, we have:

$$x(t_{i+2})=x(t_{i-1})\oplus\int_{t_{i-1}}^{t_{i+2}}f(t,x(t))\mathrm{d}t$$

The level-wise form of this integral equation is as:

$$x_l(t_{i+2},r)=x_l(t_{i-1},r)+\int_{t_{i-1}}^{t_i}\left(rs_{i-1}^{c}(t)+(1-r)s_{i-1}^{l}(t)\right)\mathrm{d}t$$

$$+\int_{t_i}^{t_i+2}\left(rs_{i}^{c}(t)+(1-r)s_{i}^{l}(t)\right)\mathrm{d}t$$

$$x_u(t_{i+2},r)=x_u(t_{i-1},r)+\int_{t_{i-1}}^{t_i}\left(rs_{i-1}^{c}(t)+(1-r)s_{i-1}^{r}(t)\right)\mathrm{d}t$$

$$+\int_{t_i}^{t_i+2}\left(rs_{i}^{c}(t)+(1-r)s_{i}^{r}(t)\right)\mathrm{d}t$$

Now by substituting, we find:

$$x_l(t_{i+2},r)=x_l(t_{i-1},r)+\int_{t_{i-1}}^{t_i}\left(r\left\{\frac{t_i-t}{t_i-t_{i-1}}f^c(t_{i-1},x(t_{i-1}))+\frac{t-t_{i-1}}{t_i-t_{i-1}}f^c(t_i,x(t_i))\right\}\right.$$

$$\left.+(1-r)\left\{\frac{t_i-t}{t_i-t_{i-1}}f^l(t_{i-1},x(t_{i-1}))+\frac{t-t_{i-1}}{t_i-t_{i-1}}f^l(t_i,x(t_i))\right\}\right)\mathrm{d}t$$

$$+\int_{t_i}^{t_i+2}\left(r\left\{\frac{t_{i+1}-t}{t_{i+1}-t_i}f^c(t_i,x(t_i))+\frac{t-t_i}{t_{i+1}-t_i}f^c(t_{i+1},x(t_{i+1}))\right\}\right)$$

$$+(1-r)\left\{\frac{t_{i+1}-t}{t_{i+1}-t_i}f^l(t_i,x(t_i))+\frac{t-t_i}{t_{i+1}-t_i}f^l(t_{i+1},x(t_{i+1}))\right\}\Bigg)\mathrm{d}t$$

$$x_u(t_{i+2},r)=x_u(t_{i-1},r)+\int_{t_{i-1}}^{t_i}\left(r\left\{\frac{t_i-t}{t_i-t_{i-1}}f^c(t_{i-1},x(t_{i-1}))+\frac{t-t_{i-1}}{t_i-t_{i-1}}f^c(t_i,x(t_i))\right\}\right)$$

$$+(1-r)\left\{\frac{t_i-t}{t_i-t_{i-1}}f^r(t_{i-1},x(t_{i-1}))+\frac{t-t_{i-1}}{t_i-t_{i-1}}f^r(t_i,x(t_i))\right\}\Bigg)\mathrm{d}t$$

$$+\int_{t_i}^{t_i+2}\left(r\left\{\frac{t_{i+1}-t}{t_{i+1}-t_i}f^c(t_i,x(t_i))+\frac{t-t_i}{t_{i+1}-t_i}f^c(t_{i+1},x(t_{i+1}))\right\}\right)$$

$$+(1-r)\left\{\frac{t_{i+1}-t}{t_{i+1}-t_i}f^r(t_i,x(t_i))+\frac{t-t_i}{t_{i+1}-t_i}f^r(t_{i+1},x(t_{i+1}))\right\}\Bigg)\mathrm{d}t$$

By integrating, the following results are obtained:

$$x_l(t_{i+2},r)=x_l(t_{i-1},r)+\frac{h}{2}\left[rf^c(t_{i-1},x(t_{i-1}))+(1-r)f^l(t_{i-1},x(t_{i-1}))\right]$$

$$+\frac{h}{2}\left[rf^c(t_i,x(t_i))+(1-r)f^l(t_i,x(t_i))\right]$$

$$+2h\left[rf^c(t_{i+1},x(t_{i+1}))+(1-r)f^l(t_{i+1},x(t_{i+1}))\right]$$

$$x_u(t_{i+2},r)=x_u(t_{i-1},r)+\frac{h}{2}[rf^c(t_{i-1},x(t_{i-1}))+(1-r)f^r(t_{i-1},x(t_{i-1}))]$$

$$+\frac{h}{2}[rf^c(t_i,x(t_i))+(1-r)f^r(t_i,x(t_i))]$$

$$+2h[rf^c(t_{i+1},x(t_{i+1}))+(1-r)f^r(t_{i+1},x(t_{i+1}))]$$

Finally:

$$x_l(t_{i+2},r)=x_l(t_{i-1},r)+\frac{h}{2}[f_l(t_{i-1},x(t_{i-1}),r)+f_l(t_i,x(t_i),r)+4f_l(t_{i+1},x(t_{i+1}),r)]$$

$$x_u(t_{i+2},r)=x_u(t_{i-1},r)+\frac{h}{2}[f_u(t_{i-1},x(t_{i-1}),r)+f_u(t_i,x(t_i),r)+4f_u(t_{i+1},x(t_{i+1}),r)]$$

It is indeed:

$$x(t_{i+2})=x(t_{i-1})\oplus\frac{h}{2}[f(t_{i-1},x(t_{i-1}))+f(t_i,x(t_i))+4\odot f(t_{i+1},x(t_{i+1}))]$$

Therefore, the three steps fuzzy explicit method is defined as:

$$\begin{cases} x_l(t_{i+2},r)=x_l(t_{i-1},r)+\frac{h}{2}[f_l(t_{i-1},x(t_{i-1}),r)+f_l(t_i,x(t_i),r)+4f_l(t_{i+1},x(t_{i+1}),r)] \\ x_u(t_{i+2},r)=x_u(t_{i-1},r)+\frac{h}{2}[f_u(t_{i-1},x(t_{i-1}),r)+f_u(t_i,x(t_i),r)+4f_u(t_{i+1},x(t_{i+1}),r)] \\ x_l(t_{i+2},r)=x_{l,i+2}(r),\quad x_l(t_{i+1},r)=x_{l,i+1}(r),\quad x_l(t_i,r)=x_{l,i}(r) \\ x_u(t_{i+2},r)=x_{u,i+2}(r),\quad x_u(t_{i+1},r)=x_{u,i+1}(r),\quad x_u(t_i,r)=x_{u,i}(r) \end{cases}$$

Note. It should be observed that:

$$f_l(t_{i-1},x(t_{i-1}),r):=f_l(t_{i-1},x_l(t_{i-1},r),x_u(t_{i-1},r))$$

$$f_u(t_{i-1},x(t_{i-1}),r):=f_u(t_{i-1},x_l(t_{i-1},r),x_u(t_{i-1},r))$$

5.6.4 Fuzzy implicit two steps method

To introduce the method, we need the points $x(t_{i-1})$, $x(t_i)$ and $f(t_{i-1},x(t_{i-1}))$, $f(t_i,x(t_i))$, which are triangular fuzzy numbers, and:

$$\left(f^l(t_{i-1},x(t_{i-1})),f^c(t_{i-1},x(t_{i-1})),f^r(t_{i-1},x(t_{i-1}))\right)$$

$$\left(f^l(t_i,x(t_i)),f^c(t_i,x(t_i)),f^r(t_i,x(t_i))\right)$$

By using the same fuzzy linear splines for $f(t_{i-1},x(t_{i-1}))$, $f(t_i,x(t_i))$ and $f(t_{i+1},x(t_{i+1}))$ at the same intervals, and considering the following integral equation:

$$x(t_{i+1})=x(t_{i-1})\oplus\int_{t_{i-1}}^{t_{i+1}}f(t,x(t))\mathrm{d}t$$

the level-wise form of this integral equation is as follows:

$$x_l(t_{i+1},r)=x_l(t_{i-1},r)+\int_{t_{i-1}}^{t_i}\left(rs_{i-1}^c(t)+(1-r)s_{i-1}^l(t)\right)\mathrm{d}t$$

$$+\int_{t_i}^{t_i+1}\left(rs_i^c(t)+(1-r)s_i^l(t)\right)\mathrm{d}t$$

$$x_u(t_{i+1},r)=x_u(t_{i-1},r)+\int_{t_{i-1}}^{t_i}\left(rs_{i-1}^c(t)+(1-r)s_{i-1}^r(t)\right)\mathrm{d}t$$

$$+\int_{t_i}^{t_i+1}\left(rs_i^c(t)+(1-r)s_i^r(t)\right)\mathrm{d}t$$

The same process as that above is done here and finally we have:

$$x_l(t_{i+1},r)=x_l(t_{i-1},r)+\frac{h}{2}[f_l(t_{i-1},x(t_{i-1}),r)+2f_l(t_i,x(t_i),r)+f_l(t_{i+1},x(t_{i+1}),r)]$$

$$x_u(t_{i+1},r)=x_u(t_{i-1},r)+\frac{h}{2}[f_u(t_{i-1},x(t_{i-1}),r)+2f_u(t_i,x(t_i),r)+f_u(t_{i+1},x(t_{i+1}),r)]$$

It is indeed:

$$x(t_{i+1})=x(t_{i-1})\oplus\frac{h}{2}[f(t_{i-1},x(t_{i-1}))+2\odot f(t_i,x(t_i))+f(t_{i+1},x(t_{i+1}))]$$

Therefore, the two steps fuzzy implicit method is defined as:

$$\begin{cases} x_l(t_{i+1},r)=x_l(t_{i-1},r)+\frac{h}{2}[f_l(t_{i-1},x(t_{i-1}),r)+2f_l(t_i,x(t_i),r)+f_l(t_{i+1},x(t_{i+1}),r)] \\ x_u(t_{i+1},r)=x_u(t_{i-1},r)+\frac{h}{2}[f_u(t_{i-1},x(t_{i-1}),r)+2f_u(t_i,x(t_i),r)+f_u(t_{i+1},x(t_{i+1}),r)] \\ x_l(t_{i+1},r)=x_{l,i+1}(r),\ x_l(t_i,r)=x_{l,i}(r) \\ x_u(t_{i-1},r)=x_{u,i-1}(r),\ x_u(t_i,r)=x_{u,i}(r) \end{cases}$$

5.6.5 FUZZY PREDICTOR AND CORRECTOR THREE STEPS METHODS

We have introduced two methods: the fuzzy three steps explicit method and the fuzzy two steps implicit method. In the following method, we shall introduce a predictor and corrector method to obtain an accurate result. Consider the same fuzzy differential equations in the form of:

$$x'_{gH}(t)=f(tx(t)),\ x(t_0)=x_0\in\mathbb{F}_R$$

In this method, we need more initial values as initial steps. To do this, we can use the fuzzy Euler method to find the $x(t_1)\approx x_1$, $x(t_2)\approx x_2$. Then we have three initial values. Now the algorithm is introduced as follows:

1. $h=\frac{T-t_0}{N}$
2. The initial values x_1, x_2 are obtained by the fuzzy Euler method.
3. We have x_0, x_1, x_2.
4. $x_{i+2}^{(0)}=x_{i-1}\oplus\frac{h}{2}\odot[f(t_{i-1},x_{i-1})\oplus f(t_i,x_i)\oplus 4\odot f(t_{i+1},x_{i+1})]$
5. $x_{i+2}=x_i\oplus\frac{h}{2}\odot f(t_i,x_i)\oplus h\odot f(t_{i+1},x_{i+1})\oplus\frac{h}{2}\odot f\left(t_{i+2},x_{i+2}^{(0)}\right)$
6. Repeat until $i>N-2$.

Convergency

To discuss convergency, we must consider the uniform convergence and especially should show that at the end point of the interval $[t_0, T]$ we have convergence. Because the approximate values, at the end point, T, do have more error propagation:

$$\lim_{h\to 0} D_H(x(T), x_N) = 0$$

using the definition of the Hausdorff distance, we should discuss in the level-wise form:

$$\lim_{h\to 0} x_l(T,r) = x_{l,N}(r), \quad \lim_{h\to 0} x_u(T,r) = x_{u,N}(r)$$

where:

$$h = \frac{T - t_0}{N}, \quad t_0 < t_1 < \cdots < t_N, \quad t_i = t_0 + ih, \quad i = 1, 2, \ldots, N$$

To prove the convergence we need the following lemma, which is proved very easily by using mathematical induction.

Lemma

Let us consider that the sequence of numbers $\{w_i\}_{i=0}^{N}$ satisfy:

$$|w_{i+1}| \le A|w_i| + B|w_{i-1}| + C, \quad A.B, C > 0, \quad 0 \le i \le N$$

Then, if i is odd:

$$|w_i| \le \left(A^{i-1} + \beta_1 A^{i-3} B + \beta_2 A^{i-5} B^2 + \cdots + \beta_s B^{\left[\frac{i}{2}\right]} \right) |w_1|$$

$$+ \left(A^{i-2} + \gamma_1 A^{i-4} B^2 + \cdots + \beta_t AB^{\left[\frac{i}{2}\right]} \right) |w_0| + \left(A^{i-2} + A^{i-3} + \cdots 1 \right) C$$

$$+ \left(\delta_1 A^{i-4} + \delta_2 A^{i-5} + \cdots + \delta_m A + 1 \right) BC$$

$$+ \left(\zeta_1 A^{i-6} + \zeta_2 A^{i-7} + \cdots + \zeta_l A + 1 \right) B^2 C + \left(\lambda_1 A^{i-8} + \lambda_2 A^{i-9} + \lambda_p A + 1 \right) B^3 C + \cdots$$

Then, if i is even:

$$|w_i| \le \left(A^{i-1} + \beta_1 A^{i-3} B + \beta_2 A^{i-5} B^2 + \cdots + \beta_s B^{\left[\frac{i}{2}\right]-1} \right) |w_1|$$

$$+ \left(A^{i-2} + \gamma_1 A^{i-4} B^2 + \cdots + \beta_t AB^{\left[\frac{i}{2}\right]} \right) |w_0| + \left(A^{i-2} + A^{i-3} + \cdots 1 \right) C$$

$$+\left(\delta_1 A^{i-4}+\delta_2 A^{i-5}+\cdots+\delta_m A+1\right)BC$$
$$+\left(\zeta_1 A^{i-6}+\zeta_2 A^{i-7}+\cdots+\zeta_l A+1\right)B^2C+\left(\lambda_1 A^{i-8}+\lambda_2 A^{i-9}+\lambda_p A+1\right)B^3C+\cdots$$

where β_s, γ_t, δ_m, ζ_l, λ_p are constants for all s, t, m, j, p.

Convergence theorem

For any arbitrary but fixed $0\leq r\leq 1$ the implicit two steps approximations converge to $x_l(T,r)$, $x_u(T,r)$ for x_l, $x_u\in C^3[t_0,T]$.

To prove this, it is enough to show that:

$$\lim_{h\to 0} x_l(T,r)=x_{l,N}(r),\quad \lim_{h\to 0} x_u(T,r)=x_{u,N}(r)$$

The approximate solution satisfies the recursive method for the implicit two steps method exactly, while the exact solution satisfies it approximately. This means:

$$x_l(t_{i+1},r)\approx x_l(t_{i-1},r)+\frac{h}{2}[f_l(t_{i-1},x(t_{i-1}),r)+2f_l(t_i,x(t_i),r)+f_l(t_{i+1},x(t_{i+1}),r)]$$

and:

$$x_{l,i+1}(r)=x_{l,i-1}(r)+\frac{h}{2}[f_l(t_{i-1},x_{l,i-1}(r))+2f_l(t_i,x_{l,i}(r))+f_l(t_{i+1},x_{l,i+1}(r))]$$

To have equality for the exact solution, we must add the error term to the recursive relation, so we have:

$$x_l(t_{i+1},r)=x_l(t_{i-1},r)+\frac{h}{2}[f_l(t_{i-1},x(t_{i-1}),r)+2f_l(t_i,x(t_i),r)+f_l(t_{i+1},x(t_{i+1}),r)]$$
$$+\frac{h^3}{6}x_l'''(\eta_i)$$

It should be remembered that the lower and upper functions f in the recursive relations are in terms of lower and upper functions of x:

$$f_l(t_{i-1},x(t_{i-1}),r):=f_l(t_{i-1},x_l(t_{i-1},r),x_u(t_{i-1},r))$$
$$f_u(t_{i-1},x(t_{i-1}),r):=f_u(t_{i-1},x_l(t_{i-1},r),x_u(t_{i-1},r))$$

Now consider the following recursive relations for the lower and upper values:

$$x_l(t_{i+1},r)=x_l(t_{i-1},r)+\frac{h}{2}[f_l(t_{i-1},x(t_{i-1}),r)+2f_l(t_i,x(t_i),r)+f_l(t_{i+1},x(t_{i+1}),r)]$$
$$+\frac{h^3}{6}x_l'''(\eta_{l,i})$$

$$x_{l,i+1}(r)=x_{l,i-1}(r)+\frac{h}{2}[f_l(t_{i-1},x_{l,i-1}(r))+2f_l(t_i,x_{l,i}(r))+f_l(t_{i+1},x_{l,i+1}(r))]$$

and:

$$x_u(t_{i+1},r)=x_u(t_{i-1},r)+\frac{h}{2}[f_u(t_{i-1},x(t_{i-1}),r)+2f_u(t_i,x(t_i),r)+f_u(t_{i+1},x(t_{i+1}),r)]$$
$$+\frac{h^3}{6}x_u'''(\eta_{u,i})$$

$$x_{u,i+1}(r)=x_{u,i-1}(r)+\frac{h}{2}[f_u(t_{i-1},x_{l,i-1}(r))+2f_u(t_i,x_{l,i}(r))+f_u(t_{i+1},x_{l,i+1}(r))]$$

for $\eta_{l,i}, \eta_{u,i}\in[t_i,t_{i+1}]$. Consider the Hausdorff distance of two values $x_l(t_{i+1})$ and $x_{l,\,i+1}$ or the real absolute values in the level-wise form:

$$x_l(t_{i+1},r)-x_{l,i+1}(r)=x_l(t_{i-1},r)-x_{l,i-1}(r)+\frac{h}{2}[f_l(t_{i-1},x(t_{i-1}),r)-f_l(t_{i-1},x_{l,i-1}(r))]$$

$$h[f_l(t_i,x(t_i),r)-f_l(t_i,x_{l,i}(r))]+\frac{h}{2}[f_l(t_{i+1},x(t_{i+1}),r)-f_l(t_{i+1},x_{l,i+1}(r))]$$
$$+\frac{h^3}{6}x_l'''(\eta_{l,i})$$

and:

$$x_u(t_{i+1},r)-x_{u,i+1}(r)=x_u(t_{i-1},r)-x_{u,i-1}(r)$$
$$+\frac{h}{2}[f_u(t_{i-1},x(t_{i-1}),r)-f_u(t_{i-1},x_{l,i-1}(r))]$$

$$h[f_u(t_i,x(t_i),r)-f_u(t_i,x_{l,i}(r))]+\frac{h}{2}[f_u(t_{i+1},x(t_{i+1}),r)-f_u(t_{i+1},x_{l,i+1}(r))]$$
$$+\frac{h^3}{6}x_u'''(\eta_{u,i})$$

Let us assume that $w_i=x_l(t_i,r)-x_{l,i}(r)$ and $v_i=x_u(t_i,r)-x_{u,i}(r)$, then the following relations are concluded immediately:

$$|w_{i+1}|\le hL_1|w_i|+\left(1+\frac{hL_2}{2}\right)|w_{i-1}|+\left(\frac{hL_3}{2}\right)|w_{i+1}|+\frac{h^3}{6}M_l$$

$$|v_{i+1}|\le hL_4|v_i|+\left(1+\frac{hL_5}{2}\right)|v_{i-1}|+\left(\frac{hL_6}{2}\right)|v_{i+1}|+\frac{h^3}{6}M_u$$

where:

$$M_l=\max_{t_0\le t\le T}x_l'''(\eta_{l,i}),\quad M_u=\max_{t_0\le t\le T}x_u'''(\eta_{u,i})$$

where $L_1, L_2, L_3, L_4, L_5, L_6$ are Lipschitz constants and:

$$L = \max\{L_1, L_2, L_3, L_4, L_5, L_6\} < \frac{2}{h}$$

then:

$$|w_{i+1}| \le \left(\frac{2hL}{2-hL}\right)|w_i| + \left(\frac{2+hL}{2-hL}\right)|w_{i-1}| + \left(\frac{1}{6-3hL}\right)h^3 M_l$$

$$|v_{i+1}| \le \left(\frac{2hL}{2-hL}\right)|v_i| + \left(\frac{2+hL}{2-hL}\right)|v_{i-1}| + \left(\frac{1}{6-3hL}\right)h^3 M_u$$

where $v_0 = w_0 = v_1 = w_1 = 0$. Now let us suppose that $|u_i| = |w_i| + |v_i|$. By adding the two abovementioned inequalities:

$$|u_{i+1}| \le \left(\frac{2hL}{2-hL}\right)|u_i| + \left(\frac{2+hL}{2-hL}\right)|u_{i-1}| + \left(\frac{1}{6-3hL}\right)h^3 (M_l + M_u)$$

Using the lemma and assuming:

$$A = \frac{2hL}{2-hL}, \quad B = \frac{2+hL}{2-hL}, \quad C = \left(\frac{1}{6-3hL}\right)h^3 (M_l + M_u)$$

it can be concluded that:

$$|u_i| \le \frac{\left(\frac{2hL}{2-hL}\right)^{i-1} - 1}{\frac{3hL-2}{2-hL}} \times \left(\frac{1}{6-3hL}\right)h^3 (M_l + M_u)$$

$$+\left\{\delta_1\left(\frac{2hL}{2-hL}\right)^{i-4} + \delta_2\left(\frac{2hL}{2-hL}\right)^{i-5} + \cdots + \delta_m\left(\frac{2hL}{2-hL}\right) + 1\right\}$$

$$\times\left(\frac{1+hL}{1-hL}\right)\left(\frac{1}{6-3hL}\right)h^3 (M_l + M_u)$$

$$+\left\{\zeta_1\left(\frac{2hL}{2-hL}\right)^{i-6} + \zeta_2\left(\frac{2hL}{2-hL}\right)^{i-7} + \cdots + \zeta_n\left(\frac{2hL}{2-hL}\right) + 1\right\}$$

$$\times\left(\frac{1+hL}{1-hL}\right)^2\left(\frac{1}{6-3hL}\right)h^3 (M_l + M_u)$$

$$+\left\{\lambda_1\left(\frac{2hL}{2-hL}\right)^{i-8} + \lambda_2\left(\frac{2hL}{2-hL}\right)^{i-9} + \cdots + \delta_p\left(\frac{2hL}{2-hL}\right) + 1\right\}$$

$$\times\left(\frac{1+hL}{1-hL}\right)^3\left(\frac{1}{6-3hL}\right)h^3 (M_l + M_u)$$

when $h \to 0$ then $|u_i| \to 0$ then $|w_i| \to 0$, $|v_i| \to 0$ and the order of the convergence is $O(h^2)$.

The same process as a proof can be used for the three steps explicit method.

Example. Consider the following fuzzy initial value problem:

$$x'(t) = (-1) \odot x(t), \quad 0 \le t \le 1, \; x(0,r) = (0.96 + 0.04r, 1.01 - 0.01r)$$

This example has an exact solution and it has been discussed before in two cases of differentiability. Here we use the H-difference and the solution can be obtained as a linear combination of e^{-t} and e^t:

$$x_{0,l}(t,r) = \frac{A-B}{2} x_{u,0}(r) + \frac{A+B}{2} x_{l,0}(r)$$

$$x_{0,u}(t,r) = \frac{A+B}{2} x_{u,0}(r) + \frac{A-B}{2} x_{l,0}(r)$$

where $A = \frac{1}{2}\exp\left(\frac{t^2 - t_0^2}{2}\right), B = \frac{1}{A}$.

So, the exact solution can be determined as:

$$x_l(t,r) = (0.985 + 0.015r)e^{-t} - (1-r)(0.025)e^t$$

$$x_u(t,r) = (0.985 + 0.015r)e^{-t} + (1-r)(0.025)e^t$$

Clearly, the three initial values can be obtained because we already have the exact solution in this example. Now, based on the algorithm, we can calculate the steps:

- $h = \frac{1}{100}, N = 100$
- The initial values x_1, x_2 are available and:

$$x_{l,0}(r) = 0.96 + 0.04r, \; x_{u,0}(r) = 1.01 - 0.01r$$

$$x_{l,1}(r) = (0.985 + 0.015r)e^{-0.01} - (1-r)(0.025)e^{0.01}$$

$$x_{u,1}(r) = (0.985 + 0.015r)e^{-0.01} + (1-r)(0.025)e^{0.01}$$

$$x_{l,2}(r) = (0.985 + 0.015r)e^{-0.02} - (1-r)(0.025)e^{0.02}$$

$$x_{u,2}(r) = (0.985 + 0.015r)e^{-0.02} + (1-r)(0.025)e^{0.02}$$

$$x_{l,i+2}^{(0)}(r) = x_{l,i-1}(r) + \frac{h}{2}[-x_{u,i-1} - x_{u,i} - 4x_{u,i+1}]$$

$$x_{u,i+2}^{(0)}(r) = x_{u,i-1}(r) + \frac{h}{2}[-x_{l,i-1} - x_{l,i} - 4x_{l,i+1}]$$

$$i = 1,$$

$$x_{l,3}^{(0)}(r) = x_{l,0}(r) + \frac{h}{2}[-x_{u,0} - x_{u,1} - 4x_{u,2}]$$

$$x_{u,i+3}^{(0)}(r) = x_{u,0}(r) + \frac{h}{2}[-x_{l,0} - x_{l,1} - 4x_{l,2}]$$

$$x_{l,i+2}(r) = x_{l,i}(r) - \frac{h}{2}x_{u,i}(r) - hx_{u,i+1}(r) - \frac{h}{2}x_{u,i+2}^{(0)}(r)$$

$$x_{u,i+2}(r) = x_{u,i}(r) - \frac{h}{2}x_{l,i}(r) - hx_{l,i+1}(r) - \frac{h}{2}x_{l,i+2}^{(0)}(r)$$

$$i = 1,$$

$$x_{l,3}(r) = x_{l,1}(r) - \frac{h}{2}x_{u,1}(r) - hx_{u,2}(r) - \frac{h}{2}x_{u,3}^{(0)}(r)$$

$$x_{u,3}(r) = x_{u,1}(r) - \frac{h}{2}x_{l,1}(r) - hx_{l,2}(r) - \frac{h}{2}x_{l,3}^{(0)}(r)$$

All the values can be computed very easily. The iterative process is continued to reach the target (Fig. 5.7).

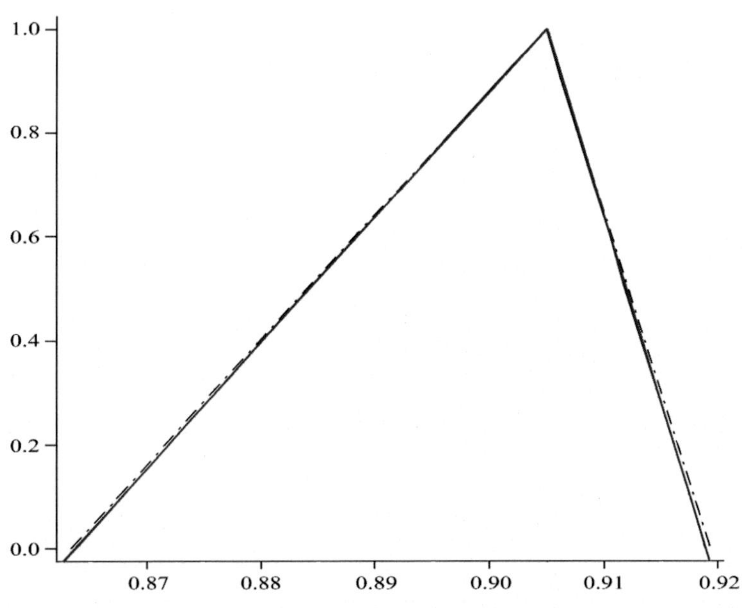

Fig. 5.7 *Solid* is the exact solution, and *dash dotted* is the approximate solution at $t=0.1$.

5.7 Numerical solution of fuzzy *n*th-order differential equations

In this section, a numerical method for solving *n*th-order linear differential equations with fuzzy initial conditions is considered. The idea is based on the collocation method. This means the coefficients and also the solution can be produced by the basis functions. To this purpose, the fuzzy solutions are formed as a linear combination of the basis functions with fuzzy number coefficients. Then this combination is used in the differential equations instead of the fuzzy solution. Finally, in the obtained equations, collocated points are used to have a linear system of equations. Ultimately, the components of the fuzzy vector solution of the fuzzy linear system of equations are exactly the values of the coefficients in the linear combination. Indeed, the fuzzy solution is now computed (Allahviranloo et al., 2008).

Note. In this method, we assume that the H-differences in any order of differentiability exist.

Let us assume the following *n*th-order fuzzy differential equations with fuzzy initial values:

$$x^{(n)}(t)\oplus a_{n-1}(t)\odot x^{(n-1)}(t)\oplus\cdots\oplus a_1(t)\odot x'(t)\oplus a_0(t)=g(t)$$

where $a_i(t)$ are continuous functions for $i=0,\ 1,\ \ldots,\ n-1$ and $0\le t\le T$. The fuzzy initial values are:

$$x(0)=b_0,\ \ x'(0)=b_1,\ \ \ldots,\ \ x^{(n-1)}(0)=b_{n-1}$$

Suppose that the sequence $\{\phi_k(t)\}_{k=0}^{N}$ is the sequence of positive basis functions whose differentiations are all positive as well. The fuzzy solution of the *n*th-order differential equations is as a linear combination of these functions. So:

$$x(t)=x_N(t)\oplus R_N(t),\ \ x_N(t)=\sum_{k=0}^{N}\alpha_k\odot\phi_k(t),\ \ \alpha_k\in\mathbb{F}_R$$

Our aim is to compute the fuzzy coefficients by setting the following error to zero:

$$\text{Error}=D_H\left(x^{(n)}(t)\oplus a_{n-1}(t)\odot x^{(n-1)}(t)\oplus\cdots\oplus a_1(t)\odot x'(t)\oplus a_0(t),g(t)\right)$$
$$+D_H(x(0),b_0)+D_H(x'(0),b_1)+\cdots+D_H\left(x^{(n-1)}(0),b_{n-1}\right)$$

For more illustration, if the error term $R_N(t)$ is zero then the function $x_N(t)$ satisfies our nth-order equations as a fuzzy solution. Based on the definition of H-difference, we have:

$$x_{l,N}^{(i)}(t,r)=\sum_{k=0}^{N}\alpha_{l,k}(r)\phi_k^{(i)}(t),\ \ x_{u,N}^{(i)}(t,r)=\sum_{k=0}^{N}\alpha_{u,k}(r)\phi_k^{(i)}(t),\ \ i=0,1,\ldots,n$$

This means the derivatives of lower and upper functions are the same as the lower and upper of the derivatives. Now using the definition of the distance:

$$\begin{cases} \left(x^{(n)}(t)+a_{n-1}(t)x^{(n-1)}(t)+\cdots+a_1(t)x'(t)+a_0(t)\right)_l(r)=g_l(t,r) \\ x_l(0,r)=b_{l,0}(r) \\ x_l'(0,r)=b_{l,1}(r) \\ \vdots \\ x_l^{(n-1)}(0,r)=b_{l,n-1}(r) \end{cases}$$

$$\begin{cases} \left(x^{(n)}(t)+a_{n-1}(t)x^{(n-1)}(t)+\cdots+a_1(t)x'(t)+a_0(t)\right)_u(r)=g_u(t,r) \\ x_u(0,r)=b_{u,0}(r) \\ x_u'(0,r)=b_{u,1}(r) \\ \vdots \\ x_u^{(n-1)}(0,r)=b_{u,n-1}(r) \end{cases}$$

To investigate the lower and upper functions in the first equation of the above-mentioned nth-order differential equations, we need to discuss the signs of the coefficients.

Case 1. All the coefficients $a_i(t)$, $i=0, 1, \ldots, n-1$ are nonnegative. Then we have:

$$\begin{cases} x_l^{(n)}(t,r)+a_{n-1}(t)x_l^{(n-1)}(t,r)+\cdots+a_1(t)x_l'(t,r)+a_0(t)=g_l(t,r) \\ x_l(0,r)=b_{l,0}(r) \\ x_l'(0,r)=b_{l,1}(r) \\ \vdots \\ x_l^{(n-1)}(0,r)=b_{l,n-1}(r) \end{cases}$$

$$\begin{cases} x_u^{(n)}(t,r)+a_{n-1}(t)x_u^{(n-1)}(t,r)+\cdots+a_1(t)x_u'(t,r)+a_0(t)=g_u(t,r) \\ x_u(0,r)=b_{u,0}(r) \\ x_u'(0,r)=b_{u,1}(r) \\ \vdots \\ x_u^{(n-1)}(0,r)=b_{u,n-1}(r) \end{cases}$$

Now, by using these equations:

$$x_{l,N}^{(i)}(t,r)=\sum_{k=0}^{N}\alpha_{l,k}(r)\phi_k^{(i)}(t),\quad x_{u,N}^{(i)}(t,r)=\sum_{k=0}^{N}\alpha_{u,k}(r)\phi_k^{(i)}(t),\quad i=0,1,\ldots,n$$

we will have the following system of equations:

$$\sum_{k=0}^{N}\alpha_{l,k}(r)\phi_k^{(n)}(t)+a_{n-1}(t)\sum_{k=0}^{N}\alpha_{l,k}(r)\phi_k^{(n-1)}(t)+\cdots+a_1(t)\sum_{k=0}^{N}\alpha_{l,k}(r)\phi_k'(t)$$

$$+a_0(t)\sum_{k=0}^{N}\alpha_{l,k}(r)\phi_k(t)=g_l(t,r)$$

$$\sum_{k=0}^{N} \alpha_{l,k}(r)\phi_k(0) = b_{l,0}, \sum_{k=0}^{N} \alpha_{l,k}(r)\phi'_k(0) = b_{l,1}(r), \ldots, \sum_{k=0}^{N} \alpha_{l,k}(r)\phi_k^{(n-1)}(0) = b_{l,n-1}(r)$$

$$\sum_{k=0}^{N} \alpha_{u,k}(r)\phi_k^{(n)}(t) + a_{n-1}(t)\sum_{k=0}^{N} \alpha_{u,k}(r)\phi_k^{(n-1)}(t) + \cdots + a_1(t)\sum_{k=0}^{N} \alpha_{u,k}(r)\phi'_k(t) + a_0(t)\sum_{k=0}^{N} \alpha_{u,k}(r)\phi_k(t) = g_u(t,r)$$

$$\sum_{k=0}^{N} \alpha_{u,k}(r)\phi_k(0) = b_{u,0}, \sum_{k=0}^{N} \alpha_{u,k}(r)\phi'_k(0) = b_{u,1}(r), \ldots, \sum_{k=0}^{N} \alpha_{u,k}(r)\phi_k^{(n-1)}(0) = b_{u,n-1}(r)$$

By setting:

$$\phi_k^{(n)}(t) + a_{n-1}(t)\phi_k^{(n-1)}(t) + a_{n-2}(t) + \phi_k^{(n-2)}(t) + \cdots + a_0(t)\phi_k(t) = \beta_k$$

$$\phi_k^{(j)}(0) = \sigma_{jk}, \ \ j = 0, 1, \ldots, n-1, \ \ k = 0, 1, \ldots, N$$

and substituting, we get:

$$\begin{cases} \sum_{k=0}^{N} \alpha_{l,k}(r)\beta_k = g_l(t,r) \\ \sum_{k=0}^{N} \alpha_{l,k}(r)\sigma_{0k} = b_{l,0}(r) \\ \vdots \\ \sum_{k=0}^{N} \alpha_{l,k}(r)\sigma_{n-1,k} = b_{l,n-1}(r) \end{cases}$$

$$\begin{cases} \sum_{k=0}^{N} \alpha_{u,k}(r)\beta_k = g_u(t,r) \\ \sum_{k=0}^{N} \alpha_{u,k}(r)\sigma_{0k} = b_{u,0}(r) \\ \vdots \\ \sum_{k=0}^{N} \alpha_{u,k}(r)\sigma_{n-1,k} = b_{u,n-1}(r) \end{cases}$$

The matrix form of these system of linear equations can be formed as the following block-wise linear system $SX = Y$, where:

$$S = \begin{bmatrix} S_1 & S_2 \\ S_2 & S_1 \end{bmatrix}_{2(N+1)(N+1)}, \quad S_1 = \begin{bmatrix} \beta_0 & \beta_1 & \cdots & \beta_N \\ \sigma_{0,0} & \sigma_{0,1} & \cdots & \sigma_{0,N-1} \\ \vdots & \vdots & \cdots & \vdots \\ \sigma_{n-1,0} & \sigma_{n-1,1} & \cdots & \sigma_{n-1,N-1} \end{bmatrix}_{(N+1)(N+1)}$$

$$S_1 = \begin{bmatrix} 0 & 0 & \cdots & 0 \\ 0 & 0 & \cdots & 0 \\ \vdots & \vdots & \cdots & \vdots \\ 0 & 0 & \cdots & 0 \end{bmatrix}_{(N+1)(N+1)}$$

$$X = [\alpha_{l,0}(r), \alpha_{l,1}(r), \alpha_{l,2}(r), \ldots, \alpha_{l,N}(r), \alpha_{u,0}(r), \alpha_{u,1}(r), \alpha_{u,2}(r), \ldots, \alpha_{u,N}(r)]^T$$

$$Y = [g_l(t,r), b_{l,0}(r), \ldots, b_{l,n-1}(r), g_u(t,r), b_{u,0}(r), \ldots, b_{u,n-1}(r)]$$

For more explanation on this topic, see Allahviranloo (2020).

Now we can use the collocation points like $t = a \in [0, T]$:

$$\phi_k^{(n)}(a) + a_{n-1}(a)\phi_k^{(n-1)}(a) + a_{n-2}(a)\phi_k^{(n-2)}(a) + \cdots + a_0(a)\phi_k(a) = \beta_k$$

$$\phi_k^{(j)}(0) = \sigma_{jk},\ j = 0, 1, \ldots, n-1,\ k = 0, 1, \ldots, N$$

$$\begin{cases} \sum_{k=0}^{N} \alpha_{l,k}(r)\beta_k = g_l(a,r) \\ \sum_{k=0}^{N} \alpha_{l,k}(r)\sigma_{0k} = b_{l,0}(r) \\ \vdots \\ \sum_{k=0}^{N} \alpha_{l,k}(r)\sigma_{n-1,k} = b_{l,n-1}(r) \end{cases}, \quad \begin{cases} \sum_{k=0}^{N} \alpha_{u,k}(r)\beta_k = g_u(a,r) \\ \sum_{k=0}^{N} \alpha_{u,k}(r)\sigma_{0k} = b_{u,0}(r) \\ \vdots \\ \sum_{k=0}^{N} \alpha_{u,k}(r)\sigma_{n-1,k} = b_{u,n-1}(r) \end{cases}$$

Then all:

$$\alpha_{l,0}(r), \alpha_{l,1}(r), \alpha_{l,2}(r), \ldots, \alpha_{l,N}(r), \alpha_{u,0}(r), \alpha_{u,1}(r), \alpha_{u,2}(r), \ldots, \alpha_{u,N}(r)$$

are determined very easily for arbitrary but fixed $r \in [0, 1]$. Therefore, the solutions $x_l(t,r)$ and $x_u(t,r)$ are approximated.

Example

Consider the following second-order fuzzy linear differential equation:

$$\begin{cases} x''_{gH}(t) \oplus x(t) = -t,\ 0 \le t \le 1 \\ x(0) = (0.1r - 0.1, 0.1 - 0.1r) \\ x'_{gH}(0) = (0.088 + 0.1r, 0.288 - 0.1r) \end{cases}$$

The fuzzy exact solution of the problem is:

$$x_l(t,r) = (0.1r - 0.1)\cos t + (1.088 + 0.1r)\sin t - t$$

$$x_u(t,r) = (0.1 - 0.1r)\cos t + (1.288 - 0.1r)\sin t - t$$

If the basis functions is $\phi_k(t) = t^k$, $k = 0$, 1, 2 and we have:

$$x_{l,2}(t,r) = \alpha_{l,0}(r) + \alpha_{l,1}(r)t + \alpha_{l,2}(r)t^2$$

$$x_{u,2}(t,r) = \alpha_{u,0}(r) + \alpha_{u,1}(r)t + \alpha_{u,2}(r)t^2$$

the linear system to determine the coefficients is:

$$\begin{cases} 2\alpha_{l,2}(r)+\alpha_{l,0}(r)+\alpha_{l,1}(r)t+\alpha_{l,2}(r)t^2=-t \\ \alpha_{l,0}(r)=0.1-0.1r \\ \alpha_{l,1}(r)=0.088+0.1r \end{cases}$$

$$\begin{cases} 2\alpha_{u,2}(r)+\alpha_{u,0}(r)+\alpha_{u,1}(r)t+\alpha_{u,2}(r)t^2=-t \\ \alpha_{u,0}(r)=0.1-0.1r \\ \alpha_{l,1}(r)=0.288-0.1r \end{cases}$$

$$SX=Y$$

$$S=\begin{bmatrix} S_1 & S_2 \\ S_2 & S_1 \end{bmatrix},\quad S_1=\begin{bmatrix} 1 & t & 2+t^2 \\ 1 & 0 & 0 \\ 0 & 1 & 1 \end{bmatrix},\quad S_2=\begin{bmatrix} 0 & 0 & 0 \\ 0 & 0 & 0 \\ 0 & 0 & 0 \end{bmatrix},\quad X=\begin{bmatrix} \alpha_{l,0}(r) \\ \alpha_{l,1}(r) \\ \alpha_{l,1}(r) \\ \alpha_{u,0}(r) \\ \alpha_{u,1}(r) \\ \alpha_{u,2}(r) \end{bmatrix},$$

$$Y=\begin{bmatrix} -t \\ 0.1-0.1r \\ 0.088+0.1r \\ -t \\ 0.1-0.1r \\ 0.288-0.1r \end{bmatrix}$$

Choosing the collocation point as $=\frac{1}{2}$:

$$S_1=\begin{bmatrix} 1 & \frac{1}{2} & \frac{9}{4} \\ 1 & 0 & 0 \\ 0 & 1 & 1 \end{bmatrix},\quad Y=\begin{bmatrix} -\frac{1}{2} \\ 0.1-0.1r \\ 0.088+0.1r \\ -\frac{1}{2} \\ 0.1-0.1r \\ 0.288-0.1r \end{bmatrix}$$

$$S=\begin{bmatrix} 1 & 1/2 & 9/4 & 0 & 0 & 0 \\ 1 & 0 & 0 & 0 & 0 & 0 \\ 0 & 1 & 1 & 0 & 0 & 0 \\ 0 & 0 & 0 & 1 & 1/2 & 9/4 \\ 0 & 0 & 0 & 1 & 0 & 0 \\ 0 & 0 & 0 & 0 & 1 & 1 \end{bmatrix}$$

the matrix S is nonsingular, and by solving the $SX=Y$ the vector solution X can be determined easily and the solution in level-wise form is:

$$x_l(t,r)=0.1r-0.1+(0.88e-1+0.1r)t$$

$$+(-0.1973333334-0.6666666666e-1r)t^2$$

$$x_u(t,r) = 0.1 - 0.1r + (0.288 - 0.1r)t + (-0.3306666666 + 0.6666666666e - 1r)t^2$$

For more illustration, Tables 5.13–5.15 show the comparison of the exact and approximate solutions at $t=0$, 0.001, 0.01 for $r \in [0,1]$ with step size 0.1.

Case 2. All the coefficients $a_i(t)$, $i=0, 1, \ldots, n-1$ are negative. Then we have:

$$\begin{cases} x_l^{(n)}(t,r) + a_{n-1}(t)x_u^{(n-1)}(t,r) + \cdots + a_1(t)x_u'(t,r) + a_0(t) = g_l(t,r) \\ x_l(0,r) = b_{l,0}(r) \\ x_l'(0,r) = b_{l,1}(r) \\ \vdots \\ x_l^{(n-1)}(0,r) = b_{l,n-1}(r) \end{cases}$$

$$\begin{cases} x_u^{(n)}(t,r) + a_{n-1}(t)x_l^{(n-1)}(t,r) + \cdots + a_1(t)x_l'(t,r) + a_0(t) = g_u(t,r) \\ x_u(0,r) = b_{u,0}(r) \\ x_u'(0,r) = b_{u,1}(r) \\ \vdots \\ x_u^{(n-1)}(0,r) = b_{u,n-1}(r) \end{cases}$$

Now by using the same previously mentioned linear combinations, we will have the following system of equations:

TABLE 5.13 Comparison of the exact and approximate solutions at $t=0$.

r	$x_{l,N}$	x_l	Error	$x_{u,N}$	x_u	Error
0	−0.1	−0.1	0	0.1	0.1	0
0.1	−0.09	−0.09	0	0.09	0.09	0
0.2	−0.08	−0.08	0	0.08	0.08	0
0.3	−0.07	−0.07	0	0.07	0.07	0
0.4	−0.06	−0.06	0	0.06	0.06	0
0.5	−0.05	−0.05	0	0.05	0.05	0
0.6	−0.04	−0.04	0	0.04	0.04	0
0.7	−0.03	−0.03	0	0.03	0.03	0
0.8	−0.02	−0.02	0	0.02	0.02	0
0.9	−0.01	−0.01	0	0.01	0.01	0
1	0	0	0	0	0	0

TABLE 5.14 Comparison of the exact and approximate solutions at $t=0.001$.

r	$x_{l, N}$	x_l	Error	$x_{u, N}$	x_u	Error
0	0.9991219733e−1	0.9991195018e−1	0.24715e−6	0.1002876693	0.1002879498	0.2805e−6
0.1	0.8990220400e−1	0.8990195518e−1	0.24882e−6	0.9027767600e−1	0.9027795479e−1	0.27879e−6
0.2	0.7989221067e−1	0.7989196018e−1	0.25049e−6	0.8026768267e−1	0.8026795979e−1	0.27712e−6
0.3	0.6988221733e−1	0.6988196519e−1	0.25214e−6	0.7025768933e−1	0.7025796479e−1	0.27546e−6
0.4	0.5987222400e−1	0.5987197019e−1	0.25381e−6	0.6024769600e−1	0.6024796979e−1	0.27379e−6
0.5	0.4986223067e−1	0.4986197519e−1	0.25548e−6	0.5023770267e−1	0.5023797479e−1	0.27212e−6
0.6	0.3985223733e−1	0.3985198019e−1	0.25714e−6	0.4022770933e−1	0.4022797980e−1	0.27047e−6
0.7	0.2984224400e−1	0.2984198519e−1	0.25881e−6	0.3021771600e−1	0.3021798480e−1	0.26880e−6
0.8	0.1983225067e−1	0.1983199020e−1	0.26047e−6	0.2020772267e−1	0.2020798980e−1	0.26713e−6
0.9	0.9822257333e−2	0.9821995196e−2	0.262137e−6	0.1019772933e−1	0.1019799480e−1	0.26713e−6
1	0.1877360000e−3	0.187999802e−3	0.2638020e−6	0.1877360000e−3	0.187999802e−3	0.2638020e−6

TABLE 5.15 Comparison of the exact and approximate solutions at $t=0.01$.

r	$x_{l,N}$	x_l	Error	$x_{u,N}$	x_u	Error
0	−0.9913973333e−1	−0.9911518137e−1	0.2455196e−4	0.1028469333	0.1028747854	0.278521e−4
0.1	−0.8904040000e−1	−0.8901568304e−1	0.2471696e−4	0.9274760000e−1	0.927752870e−1	0.2768700e−4
0.2	−0.7894106667e−1	−0.7891618470e−1	0.2488197e−4	0.8264826667e−1	0.8267578870e−1	0.2752203e−4
0.3	−0.6884173333e−1	−0.6881668636e−1	0.2504697e−4	0.7254893333e−1	0.7257629036e−1	0.2735703e−4
0.4	−0.5874240000e−1	−0.5871718802e−1	0.2521198e−4	0.6244960000e−1	0.6247679202e−1	0.2719202e−4
0.5	−0.4864306667e−1	−0.4861768969e−1	0.2537698e−4	0.5235026667e−1	0.5237729369e−1	0.2702702e−4
0.6	−0.3854373333e−1	−0.3851819135e−1	0.2554198e−4	0.4225093333e−1	0.4227779535e−1	0.2686202e−4
0.7	−0.2844440000e−1	−0.2841869301e−1	0.2570699e−4	0.3215160000e−1	0.3217829701e−1	0.2669701e−4
0.8	−0.1834506667e−1	−0.1831919468e−1	0.2587199e−4	0.2205226667e−1	0.2207879868e−1	0.2653201e−4
0.9	−0.8245733333e−2	−0.8219696334e−2	0.26036999e−4	0.1195293333e−1	0.1197930033e−1	0.2636700e−4
1	0.1853600000e−2	0.187980200e−2	0.26202000e−4	0.1853600000e−2	0.187980200e−2	0.26202000e−4

$$\sum_{k=0}^{N} \alpha_{l,k}(r)\phi_k^{(n)}(t) + a_{n-1}(t)\sum_{k=0}^{N} \alpha_{u,k}(r)\phi_k^{(n-1)}(t) + \cdots + a_1(t)\sum_{k=0}^{N} \alpha_{u,k}(r)\phi_k'(t)$$

$$+ a_0(t)\sum_{k=0}^{N} \alpha_{u,k}(r)\phi_k(t) = g_l(t,r)$$

$$\sum_{k=0}^{N} \alpha_{l,k}(r)\phi_k(0) = b_{l,0}, \sum_{k=0}^{N} \alpha_{l,k}(r)\phi_k'(0) = b_{l,1}(r), \ldots, \sum_{k=0}^{N} \alpha_{l,k}(r)\phi_k^{(n-1)}(0)$$
$$= b_{l,n-1}(r)$$

$$\sum_{k=0}^{N} \alpha_{u,k}(r)\phi_k^{(n)}(t) + a_{n-1}(t)\sum_{k=0}^{N} \alpha_{u,k}(r)\phi_k^{(n-1)}(t) + \cdots + a_1(t)\sum_{k=0}^{N} \alpha_{u,k}(r)\phi_k'(t)$$

$$+ a_0(t)\sum_{k=0}^{N} \alpha_{u,k}(r)\phi_k(t) = g_l(t,r)$$

$$\sum_{k=0}^{N} \alpha_{u,k}(r)\phi_k(0) = b_{u,0}, \sum_{k=0}^{N} \alpha_{u,k}(r)\phi_k'(0) = b_{u,1}(r), \ldots, \sum_{k=0}^{N} \alpha_{u,k}(r)\phi_k^{(n-1)}(0)$$
$$= b_{u,n-1}(r)$$

By setting:

$$\phi_k^{(n)}(t) + a_{n-1}(t)\phi_k^{(n-1)}(t) + a_{n-2}(t) + \phi_k^{(n-2)}(t) + \cdots + a_0(t)\phi_k(t) = \delta_k$$

$$\phi_k^{(n)}(t) = \gamma_{nk},\ \ \phi_k^{(j)}(0) = \sigma_{jk},\ \ j = 0,1,\ldots,n-1,\ \ k = 0,1,\ldots,N$$

and substituting, we get:

$$\begin{cases} \sum_{k=0}^{N} (\alpha_{l,k}(r)\gamma_{nk} + \alpha_{u,k}(r)\delta_k) = g_l(t,r) \\ \sum_{k=0}^{N} \alpha_{l,k}(r)\sigma_{0k} = b_{l,0}(r) \\ \vdots \\ \sum_{k=0}^{N} \alpha_{l,k}(r)\sigma_{n-1,k} = b_{l,n-1}(r) \end{cases} \qquad \begin{cases} \sum_{k=0}^{N} (\alpha_{u,k}(r)\gamma_{nk} + \alpha_{l,k}(r)\delta_k) = g_u(t,r) \\ \sum_{k=0}^{N} \alpha_{u,k}(r)\sigma_{0k} = b_{u,0}(r) \\ \vdots \\ \sum_{k=0}^{N} \alpha_{u,k}(r)\sigma_{n-1,k} = b_{u,n-1}(r) \end{cases}$$

The matrix form of these system of linear equations can be formed as the following block-wise linear system $SX = Y$, where:

$$S = \begin{bmatrix} S_1 & S_2 \\ S_2 & S_1 \end{bmatrix}_{2(N+1)(N+1)},\quad S_1 = \begin{bmatrix} \gamma_{n0} & \gamma_{n1} & \cdots & \gamma_{nN} \\ \sigma_{0,0} & \sigma_{0,1} & \cdots & \sigma_{0,N-1} \\ \vdots & \vdots & \cdots & \vdots \\ \sigma_{n-1,0} & \sigma_{n-1,1} & \cdots & \sigma_{n-1,N-1} \end{bmatrix}_{(N+1)(N+1)}$$

$$S_1 = \begin{bmatrix} \delta_0 & \delta_1 & \cdots & \delta_N \\ 0 & 0 & \cdots & 0 \\ \vdots & \vdots & \cdots & \vdots \\ 0 & 0 & \cdots & 0 \end{bmatrix}_{(N+1)(N+1)}$$

$$X = [\alpha_{l,0}(r), \alpha_{l,1}(r), \alpha_{l,2}(r), \ldots, \alpha_{l,N}(r), \alpha_{u,0}(r), \alpha_{u,1}(r), \alpha_{u,2}(r), \ldots, \alpha_{u,N}(r)]^T$$

$$Y = [g_l(t,r), b_{l,0}(r), \ldots, b_{l,n-1}(r), g_u(t,r), b_{u,0}(r), \ldots, b_{u,n-1}(r)]$$

By the same process that we have discussed in Case 1, we can use the collocation points like $t=a\in[0,T]$ to realize the system of linear equations to find the coefficients:

$$\begin{cases} \sum_{k=0}^{N} (\alpha_{l,k}(r)\gamma_{nk} + \alpha_{u,k}(r)\delta_k) = g_l(a,r) \\ \sum_{k=0}^{N} \alpha_{l,k}(r)\sigma_{0k} = b_{l,0}(r) \\ \vdots \\ \sum_{k=0}^{N} \alpha_{l,k}(r)\sigma_{n-1,k} = b_{l,n-1}(r) \end{cases} \quad \begin{cases} \sum_{k=0}^{N} (\alpha_{u,k}(r)\gamma_{nk} + \alpha_{l,k}(r)\delta_k) = g_u(a,r) \\ \sum_{k=0}^{N} \alpha_{u,k}(r)\sigma_{0k} = b_{u,0}(r) \\ \vdots \\ \sum_{k=0}^{N} \alpha_{u,k}(r)\sigma_{n-1,k} = b_{u,n-1}(r) \end{cases}$$

Then all:

$$\alpha_{l,0}(r), \alpha_{l,1}(r), \alpha_{l,2}(r), \ldots, \alpha_{l,N}(r), \alpha_{u,0}(r), \alpha_{u,1}(r), \alpha_{u,2}(r), \ldots, \alpha_{u,N}(r)$$

are determined very easily for arbitrary but fixed $r\in[0,1]$. Therefore, the solutions $x_l(t,r)$ and $x_u(t,r)$ are approximated.

Example

Consider the following second-order fuzzy linear differential equation:

$$\begin{cases} x''_{gH}(t) \ominus_H \frac{2}{t^2} \odot x(t) = \frac{2}{t}, \ t \geq 1 \\ x(1) = (0.1r - 0.1, 0.1 - 0.1r) \\ x'_{gH}(1) = (-0.25 + 0.25r, 0.25 - 0.25r) \end{cases}$$

The fuzzy exact solution of the problem is:

$$x_l(t,r) = \left(\frac{1}{t}\right)(-0.500000001e - r + 0.3833333334) + (0.15r + 0.5166666666)t^2 - t$$

$$x_u(t,r) = \left(\frac{1}{t}\right)(0.500000003e - r + 0.2833333337) + (-0.15r + 0.8166666666)t^2 - t$$

If the basis functions is $\phi_k(t) = t^k$, $k=0$, 1, 2 and we have:

$$x_{l,2}(t,r)=\alpha_{l,0}(r)+\alpha_{l,1}(r)t+\alpha_{l,2}(r)t^2$$

$$x_{u,2}(t,r)=\alpha_{u,0}(r)+\alpha_{u,1}(r)t+\alpha_{u,2}(r)t^2$$

the linear system to determine the coefficients is $SX=Y$ where:

$$S=\begin{bmatrix} S_1 & S_2 \\ S_2 & S_1 \end{bmatrix},\quad S_2=\begin{bmatrix} -\frac{2}{t^2} & -\frac{2}{t} & -2 \\ 0 & 0 & 0 \\ 0 & 0 & 0 \end{bmatrix},\quad S_1=\begin{bmatrix} 0 & 0 & 2 \\ 1 & 1 & 1 \\ 0 & 1 & 2 \end{bmatrix},$$

$$X=\begin{bmatrix} \alpha_{l,0}(r) \\ \alpha_{l,1}(r) \\ \alpha_{l,1}(r) \\ \alpha_{u,0}(r) \\ \alpha_{u,1}(r) \\ \alpha_{u,2}(r) \end{bmatrix},\quad Y=\begin{bmatrix} 2/t \\ 0.1-0.1r \\ -0.25+0.25r \\ 2/t \\ 0.1-0.1r \\ 0.25-0.25r \end{bmatrix}$$

Choosing the collocation point as $=\frac{3}{2}$:

$$S_1=\begin{bmatrix} 1 & \frac{1}{2} & \frac{9}{4} \\ 1 & 0 & 0 \\ 0 & 1 & 1 \end{bmatrix},\quad Y=\begin{bmatrix} \frac{4}{3} \\ 0.1-0.1r \\ -0.25+0.25r \\ \frac{4}{3} \\ 0.1-0.1r \\ 0.25-0.25r \end{bmatrix},$$

$$S=\begin{bmatrix} 0 & 0 & 2 & -8/9 & -4/3 & -2 \\ 1 & 1 & 1 & 0 & 0 & 0 \\ 0 & 1 & 2 & 0 & 0 & 0 \\ -8/9 & -4/3 & -2 & 0 & 0 & 2 \\ 0 & 0 & 0 & 1 & 1 & 1 \\ 0 & 0 & 0 & 0 & 1 & 2 \end{bmatrix}$$

the matrix S is nonsingular and by solving the $SX=Y$ the vector solution X can be determined easily and the solution in level-wise form is:

$$x_l(t,r)=0.99-0.24r+(-1.93+0.43r)t$$
$$+(0.84-0.8999999996e-1r)t^2$$
$$x_l(t,r)=0.51-0.24r+(-1.07+0.43r)t$$
$$+(0.66-0.8999999996e-1r)t^2$$

For more illustration, Tables 5.16–5.18 show the comparison of the exact and approximate solutions at $t=1$, 1.001, 1.01 for $r\in[0,1]$ with step size 0.1.

TABLE 5.16 Comparison of the exact and approximate solutions at $t=1$.

r	$x_{l,N}$	x_l	Error	$x_{u,N}$	x_u	Error
0	−0.1	−0.1	0	0.1	0.1	0
0.1	−0.09	−0.09	0	0.09	0.09	0
0.2	−0.08	−0.08	0	0.08	0.08	0
0.3	−0.07	−0.07	0	0.07	0.07	0
0.4	−0.06	−0.06	0	0.06	0.06	0
0.5	−0.05	−0.05	0	0.05	0.05	0
0.6	−0.04	−0.40000000e−1	0.1e−9	0.04	0.04	0
0.7	−0.03	−0.30000000e−1	0.1e−9	0.03	0.03	0
0.8	−0.02	−0.02	0	0.02	0.02	0
0.9	−0.01	−0.10000000e−1	0.1e−9	0.01	0.01	0
1	−0.1e−9	−0.1e−9	0	0	0	0

Case 3. Suppose that some coefficients as the following are negative and the rest are nonnegative:

$$a_{n-m-1}(t), a_{n-m-2}(t), \ldots, a_1(t), a_0(t)$$

Then we have:

$$\begin{cases} x_l^{(n)}(t,r) + a_{n-1}(t)x_l^{(n-1)}(t,r) + \cdots + a_{n-m}(t)x_l^{(n-m)}(t,r) \\ \qquad + a_{n-m-1}(t)x_u^{(n-m-1)}(t,r) + \cdots + a_0(t)x_u(t,r) = g_l(t,r) \\ x_l(0,r) = b_{l,0}(r) \\ x_l'(0,r) = b_{l,1}(r) \\ \quad \vdots \\ x_l^{(n-1)}(0,r) = b_{l,n-1}(r) \end{cases}$$

$$\begin{cases} x_u^{(n)}(t,r) + a_{n-1}(t)x_u^{(n-1)}(t,r) + \cdots + a_{n-m}(t)x_u^{(n-m)}(t,r) \\ \qquad + a_{n-m-1}(t)x_l^{(n-m-1)}(t,r) + \cdots + a_0(t)x_l(t,r) = g_u(t,r) \\ x_u(0,r) = b_{u,0}(r) \\ x_u'(0,r) = b_{u,1}(r) \\ \quad \vdots \\ x_u^{(n-1)}(0,r) = b_{u,n-1}(r) \end{cases}$$

Now by using the same previously mentioned linear combinations, we will have the following system of equations:

TABLE 5.17 Comparison of the exact and approximate solutions at $t = 1.001$.

r	$x_{l,N}$	x_l	Error	$x_{u,N}$	x_u	Error
0	0.1002491600	0.1003491004	0.999404e−4	0.1002506600	0.100351100	0.1004400e−3
0.1	0.902241690e−1	0.903140904e−1	0.899214e−4	0.902256690e−1	0.90316090e−1	0.904210e−4
0.2	0.801991780e−1	0.802790804e−1	0.799024e−4	0.802006780e−1	0.80281080e−1	0.804020e−4
0.3	0.701741870e−1	0.702440704e−1	0.698834e−4	0.701756870e−1	0.70246070e−1	0.703830e−4
0.4	0.601491960e−1	0.602090604e−1	0.598644e−4	0.601506960e−1	0.60211060e−1	0.603640e−4
0.5	0.501242050e−1	0.501740504e−1	0.498454e−4	0.501257050e−1	0.50176050e−1	0.503450e−4
0.6	0.400992140e−1	0.401390405e−1	0.398265e−4	0.401007140e−1	0.40141040e−1	0.403260e−4
0.7	0.300742230e−1	0.301040304e−1	0.298074e−4	0.300757230e−1	0.30106030e−1	0.303070e−4
0.8	0.200492320e−1	0.200690204e−1	0.197884e−4	0.200507320e−1	0.20071020e−1	0.202880e−4
0.9	0.100242410e−1	0.100340104e−1	0.97694e−5	0.100257410e−1	0.10036010e−1	0.102690e−4
1	0.7500e−6	0.1000e−5	0.2500e−6	0.7500e−6	0.1000e−5	0.2500e−6

TABLE 5.18 Comparison of the exact and approximate solutions at $t=1.01$.

r	$x_{l,N}$	x_l	Error	$x_{u,N}$	x_u	Error
0	0.1024160000	0.1034103795	0.99670e−4	0.1025660000	0.103609720	0.10437200e−2
0.1	0.921669000e−1	0.930593746e−1	0.8924746e−3	0.923169000e−1	0.93258715e−1	0.9418150e−3
0.2	0.819178000e−1	0.827083696e−1	0.7905696e−3	0.820678000e−1	0.82907710e−1	0.8399100e−3
0.3	0.614196000e−1	0.723573647e−1	0.6886647e−3	0.718187000e−1	0.72556705e−1	0.7380050e−3
0.4	0.511705000e−1	0.620063597e−1	0.5867597e−3	0.615696000e−1	0.62205700e−1	0.6361000e−3
0.5	0.409214000e−1	0.516553548e−1	0.4848548e−3	0.513205000e−1	0.51854695e−1	0.5341950e−3
0.6	0.306723000e−1	0.413043499e−1	0.3829499e−3	0.410714000e−1	0.41503690e−1	0.4322900e−3
0.7	0.306723000e−1	0.309533450e−1	0.2810450e−3	0.308223000e−1	0.31152685e−1	0.3303850e−3
0.8	0.204232000e−1	0.206023400e−1	0.1791400e−3	0.205732000e−1	0.20801680e−1	0.2284800e−3
0.9	0.101741000e−1	0.102513351e−1	0.772351e−4	0.103241000e−1	0.10450675e−1	0.1265750e−3
1	0.750000e−4	0.99670e−4	0.246700e−4	0.750000e−4	0.99670e−4	0.246700e−4

$$\sum_{k=0}^{N}\alpha_{l,k}(r)\phi_k^{(n)}(t)+a_{n-1}(t)\sum_{k=0}^{N}\alpha_{l,k}(r)\phi_k^{(n-1)}(t)+\cdots+a_{n-m}(t)\sum_{k=0}^{N}\alpha_{l,k}(r)\phi_k^{(n-m)}(t)$$

$$+a_{n-m-1}(t)\sum_{k=0}^{N}\alpha_{u,k}(r)\phi_k^{(n-m-1)}(t)+\cdots+a_0(t)\sum_{k=0}^{N}\alpha_{u,k}(r)\phi_k(t)=g_l(t,r)$$

$$\sum_{k=0}^{N}\alpha_{l,k}(r)\phi_k(0)=b_{l,0},\ \sum_{k=0}^{N}\alpha_{l,k}(r)\phi_k'(0)=b_{l,1}(r),\ldots,\ \sum_{k=0}^{N}\alpha_{l,k}(r)\phi_k^{(n-1)}(0)=b_{l,n-1}(r)$$

$$\sum_{k=0}^{N}\alpha_{u,k}(r)\phi_k^{(n)}(t)+a_{n-1}(t)\sum_{k=0}^{N}\alpha_{u,k}(r)\phi_k^{(n-1)}(t)+\cdots+a_{n-m}(t)\sum_{k=0}^{N}\alpha_{u,k}(r)\phi_k^{(n-m)}(t)$$

$$+a_{n-m-1}(t)\sum_{k=0}^{N}\alpha_{l,k}(r)\phi_k^{(n-m-1)}(t)+\cdots+a_0(t)\sum_{k=0}^{N}\alpha_{l,k}(r)\phi_k(t)=g_l(t,r)$$

$$\sum_{k=0}^{N}\alpha_{u,k}(r)\phi_k(0)=b_{u,0},\ \sum_{k=0}^{N}\alpha_{u,k}(r)\phi_k'(0)=b_{u,1}(r),\ldots,\ \sum_{k=0}^{N}\alpha_{u,k}(r)\phi_k^{(n-1)}(0)=b_{u,n-1}(r)$$

By setting:

$$\phi_k^{(n)}(t)+a_{n-1}(t)\phi_k^{(n-1)}(t)+\cdots+a_{n-m}(t)\phi_k^{(n-m)}(t)=\eta_k$$

$$a_{n-m-1}(t)\phi_k^{(n-m-1)}(t)+a_{n-m-2}(t)+\phi_k^{(n-m-2)}(t)+\cdots+a_0(t)\phi_k(t)=\xi_k$$

$$\phi_k^{(j)}(0)=\sigma_{jk},\quad j=0,1,\ldots,n-1,\quad k=0,1,\ldots,N$$

and substituting, we get:

$$\begin{cases}\sum_{k=0}^{N}(\alpha_{l,k}(r)\eta_k+\alpha_{u,k}(r)\xi_k)=g_l(t,r)\\ \sum_{k=0}^{N}\alpha_{l,k}(r)\sigma_{0k}=b_{l,0}(r)\\ \vdots\\ \sum_{k=0}^{N}\alpha_{l,k}(r)\sigma_{n-1,k}=b_{l,n-1}(r)\end{cases}\qquad \begin{cases}\sum_{k=0}^{N}(\alpha_{u,k}(r)\eta_k+\alpha_{l,k}(r)\xi_k)=g_u(t,r)\\ \sum_{k=0}^{N}\alpha_{u,k}(r)\sigma_{0k}=b_{u,0}(r)\\ \vdots\\ \sum_{k=0}^{N}\alpha_{u,k}(r)\sigma_{n-1,k}=b_{u,n-1}(r)\end{cases}$$

The matrix form of these systems of linear equations can be formed as the following block-wise linear system $SX=Y$, where:

$$S=\begin{bmatrix} S_1 & S_2 \\ S_2 & S_1 \end{bmatrix}_{2(N+1)(N+1)}, \quad S_1=\begin{bmatrix} \eta_0 & \eta_1 & \cdots & \eta_N \\ \sigma_{0,0} & \sigma_{0,1} & \cdots & \sigma_{0,N-1} \\ \vdots & \vdots & \cdots & \vdots \\ \sigma_{n-1,0} & \sigma_{n-1,1} & \cdots & \sigma_{n-1,N-1} \end{bmatrix}_{(N+1)(N+1)}$$

$$S_2=\begin{bmatrix} \xi_0 & \xi_1 & \cdots & \xi_N \\ 0 & 0 & \cdots & 0 \\ \vdots & \vdots & \cdots & \vdots \\ 0 & 0 & \cdots & 0 \end{bmatrix}_{(N+1)(N+1)}$$

$$X=\left[\alpha_{l,0}(r),\alpha_{l,1}(r),\alpha_{l,2}(r),\ldots,\alpha_{l,N}(r),\alpha_{u,0}(r),\alpha_{u,1}(r),\alpha_{u,2}(r),\ldots,\alpha_{u,N}(r)\right]^T$$

$$Y=\left[g_l(t,r),b_{l,0}(r),\ldots,b_{l,n-1}(r),g_u(t,r),b_{u,0}(r),\ldots,b_{u,n-1}(r)\right]$$

By the same process that we have discussed in Case 1, we can use the collocation points like $t=a\in[0,T]$ to realize the system of linear equations to find the coefficients:

$$\begin{cases} \sum_{k=0}^{N}\left(\alpha_{l,k}(r)\eta_k+\alpha_{u,k}(r)\xi_k\right)=g_l(a,r) \\ \sum_{k=0}^{N}\alpha_{l,k}(r)\sigma_{0k}=b_{l,0}(r) \\ \vdots \\ \sum_{k=0}^{N}\alpha_{l,k}(r)\sigma_{n-1,k}=b_{l,n-1}(r) \end{cases} \qquad \begin{cases} \sum_{k=0}^{N}\left(\alpha_{u,k}(r)\eta_k+\alpha_{l,k}(r)\xi_k\right)=g_u(a,r) \\ \sum_{k=0}^{N}\alpha_{u,k}(r)\sigma_{0k}=b_{u,0}(r) \\ \vdots \\ \sum_{k=0}^{N}\alpha_{u,k}(r)\sigma_{n-1,k}=b_{u,n-1}(r) \end{cases}$$

Then all:

$$\alpha_{l,0}(r),\alpha_{l,1}(r),\alpha_{l,2}(r),\ldots,\alpha_{l,N}(r),\alpha_{u,0}(r),\alpha_{u,1}(r),\alpha_{u,2}(r),\ldots,\alpha_{u,N}(r)$$

are determined very easily for arbitrary but fixed $r\in[0,1]$. Therefore, the solutions $x_l(t,r)$ and $x_u(t,r)$ are approximated.

Example

Consider the following second-order fuzzy linear differential equation:

$$\begin{cases} x''_{gH}(t)\ominus_H 4x'_{gH}(t)\oplus 4\odot x(t)=0, \ t\geq 0 \\ x(0)=(2+r,4-r) \\ x'_{gH}(0)=(5+r,7-r) \end{cases}$$

The fuzzy exact solution of the problem is:

$$x_l(t,r)=(2+r)e^{2t}+(1-r)te^{2t}$$

$$x_u(t,r)=(4-r)e^{2t}+(r-1)te^{2t}$$

If the basis functions is $\phi_k(t)=t^k$, $k=0$, 1, 2 and we have:

$$x_{l,2}(t,r)=\alpha_{l,0}(r)+\alpha_{l,1}(r)t+\alpha_{l,2}(r)t^2$$

$$x_{u,2}(t,r)=\alpha_{u,0}(r)+\alpha_{u,1}(r)t+\alpha_{u,2}(r)t^2$$

the linear system to determine the coefficients is $SX=Y$ where:

$$S=\begin{bmatrix} S_1 & S_2 \\ S_2 & S_1 \end{bmatrix},\quad S_2=\begin{bmatrix} 4 & 4t & 2+4t^2 \\ 1 & 0 & 0 \\ 0 & 1 & 0 \end{bmatrix},\quad S_1=\begin{bmatrix} 0 & -4 & -8t \\ 0 & 0 & 0 \\ 0 & 0 & 0 \end{bmatrix},$$

$$X=\begin{bmatrix} \alpha_{l,0}(r) \\ \alpha_{l,1}(r) \\ \alpha_{l,1}(r) \\ \alpha_{u,0}(r) \\ \alpha_{u,1}(r) \\ \alpha_{u,2}(r) \end{bmatrix},\quad Y=\begin{bmatrix} -0.25+0.25r \\ 2+r \\ 5+r \\ 0.25-0.25r \\ 4-r \\ 7-r \end{bmatrix}$$

Choosing the collocation point as $t=\frac{1}{2}$, we will have a system of linear equations. The solution in level-wise form is:

$$x_l(t,r)=(2+r)+(5+r)t+(1.42851427-1.428571430r)t^2$$

$$x_l(t,r)=(4-r)+(7-r)t+(-1.42851429+1.428571430r)t^2$$

For more illustration, Table 5.19 shows the comparison of the exact and approximate solutions at $t=0.01$ for $r\in[0,1]$ with step size 0.1.

Example. Electrical circuit

Consider the electrical circuit in Fig. 5.8, where $L=1h$, $R=2\Omega$, $C=0.25f$ and $E(t)=20\cos t$. If $x(t)$ is the charge on the capacitor at time $t>0$, then we have:

$$x''_{gH}(t)\oplus 2\odot x'_{gH}(t)\oplus 4\odot x(t)=50\cos t$$

subject to:

$$x(0)=(4+r,6-r),\quad x'_{gH}(0)=(r,2-r)$$

The exact solution in level-wise form is as the following form:

$$x_l(t,r)=e^{-t}\left(4+r-\frac{150}{13}\right)\cos\sqrt{3}t+6-\frac{\left(\frac{250}{13}\right)}{\sqrt{3}}\cdot\sin\sqrt{3}t+\left(\frac{150}{13}\right)\cos t$$
$$+\left(\frac{100}{13}\right)\sin t$$

$$x_l(t,r)=e^{-t}\left(6-r-\frac{150}{13}\right)\cos\sqrt{3}t+6-\frac{\left(\frac{250}{13}\right)}{\sqrt{3}}\cdot\sin\sqrt{3}t+\left(\frac{150}{13}\right)\cos t$$
$$+\left(\frac{100}{13}\right)\sin t$$

TABLE 5.19 Comparison of the exact and approximate solutions at $t = 1.01$.

r	$x_{l,N}$	x_l	Error	$x_{u,N}$	x_u	Error
0	2.050142857	2.050604693	0.461836e−3	4.069857143	4.070603347	0.746204e−3
0.1	2.151128571	2.151604626	0.476055e−3	3.968871429	3.969603414	0.731985e−3
0.2	2.252114286	2.252604559	0.490273e−3	3.867885714	3.868603481	0.717767e−3
0.3	2.353100000	2.353604491	0.504491e−3	3.766900000	3.767603549	0.703549e−3
0.4	2.454085714	2.454604424	0.518710e−3	3.665914286	3.666603616	0.689330e−3
0.5	2.555071429	2.555604357	0.532928e−3	3.564928571	3.565603683	0.675112e−3
0.6	2.656057143	2.656604289	0.547146e−3	3.463942857	3.464603751	0.660894e−3
0.7	2.757042857	2.757604222	0.561365e−3	3.362957143	3.363603818	0.646675e−3
0.8	2.858028571	2.858604155	0.575584e−3	3.261971429	3.262603885	0.632456e−3
0.9	2.959014286	2.959604087	0.589801e−3	3.160985714	3.161603953	0.618239e−3
1	3.060	3.060604020	0.604020e−3	3.060	3.060604020	0.604020e−3

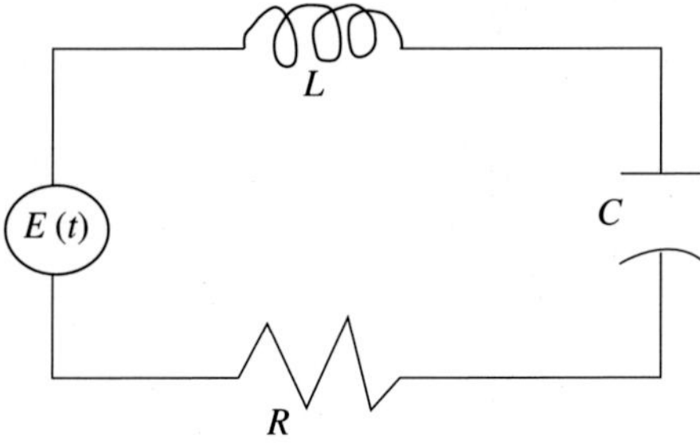

Fig. 5.8 Electrical circuit.

If $\phi_k(t)=e^k$, $k=0, 1, 2, 3, 4$ and using the same process we have the approximate values for $x_{l,\ 4}$, $x_{u,\ 4}$ in the form of:

$$x_l(t,r)=\alpha_{l,0}(r)+\alpha_{l,1}(r)e^t+\alpha_{l,2}(r)e^{2t}+\alpha_{l,3}(r)e^{3t}++\alpha_{l,4}(r)e^{4t}$$

$$x_u(t,r)=\alpha_{u,0}(r)+\alpha_{u,1}(r)e^t+\alpha_{u,2}(r)e^{2t}+\alpha_{u,3}(r)e^{3t}++\alpha_{u,4}(r)e^{4t}$$

It is clear this case is exactly Case 1 of our discussion in this section and we should solve an 8×8 linear system of equations. To this end, we need three collocation points like $=1, 1.1, 1.2$; so finally, the following system is realized:

$$S=\begin{bmatrix} S_1 & S_2 \\ S_3 & S_4 \end{bmatrix},\quad S_1=\begin{bmatrix} 4 & 7e^1 & 12e^2 & 19e^3 & 28e^4 \\ 4 & 7e^{1.1} & 12e^{2.2} & 19e^{3.3} & 28e^{4.4} \\ 4 & 7e^{1.2} & 12e^{2.4} & 19e^{3.6} & 28e^{4.8} \\ 1 & 1 & 1 & 1 & 1 \\ 0 & 1 & 1 & 1 & 1 \end{bmatrix},\quad S_2=[0]$$

In conclusion, the approximate solutions are:

$$\begin{aligned} x_{l,4}(t,r)=4&+(-2.255809230+1.889692363r)e^t \\ &+(3.042557688-1.104464241r)e^{2t} \\ &+(0.8603224932+0.2321963367r)e^{3t} \\ &+(0.7357403924e-1-0.1742445864e-1r)e^{4t} \end{aligned}$$

$$\begin{aligned} x_{u,4}(t,r)=4&+(1.523575496-1.889692363r)e^t \\ &+(0.833629204+1.104464241r)e^{2t} \\ &+(-0.3959298198-0.2321963367r)e^{3t} \\ &+(0.3872512196e-1+0.1742445864e-1r)e^{4t} \end{aligned}$$

Table 5.20 compares the exact solution and the results of approximate solution at the point $t=0.001$.

TABLE 5.20 Comparison of the exact and approximate solutions at $t=0.001$.

r	$x_{l,N}$	x_l	Error	$x_{u,N}$	x_u	Error
0	4.001544314	4.002014989	0.470675e−3	6.002158904	6.000012991	0.2145913e−2
0.1	4.101575043	4.101914890	0.339847e−3	5.902128174	5.900113092	0.2015082e−2
0.2	4.201605773	4.201814790	0.209017e−3	5.802097444	5.800213192	0.1884252e−2
0.3	4.301636502	4.301714690	0.78188e−4	5.702066714	5.700313292	0.1753422e−2
0.4	4.401667231	4.401614590	0.52641e−4	5.602035984	5.600413392	0.1622592e−2
0.5	4.501697961	4.501514490	0.183471e−3	5.502005255	5.500513492	0.1491763e−2
0.6	4.601728690	4.601414390	0.314300e−3	5.401974526	5.400613591	0.1360935e−2
0.7	4.701759421	4.701314291	0.445130e−3	5.301943796	5.300713691	0.1230105e−2
0.8	4.801790150	4.801214191	0.575959e−3	5.201913068	5.200813791	0.1099277e−2
0.9	4.901820879	4.901114091	0.706788e−3	5.101882337	5.100913891	0.968446e−3
1	5.001851609	5.001013991	0.837618e−3	5.001851607	5.001013991	0.837616e−3

References

Allahviranloo, T., 2020. Uncertain information and linear systems. In: Studies in Systems, Decision and Control. vol. 254. Springer.

Allahviranloo, T., Salahshour, S., 2011. Euler method for solving hybrid fuzzy differential equation. Soft Comput. 15, 1247–1253.

Allahviranloo, T., Ahmady, N., Ahmady, E., 2007. Numerical solution of fuzzy differential equations by predictor–corrector method. Inform. Sci. 177, 1633–1647.

Allahviranloo, T., Ahmady, E., Ahmady, N., 2008. Nth-order fuzzy linear differential equations. Inform. Sci. 178, 1309–1324.

Allahviranloo, T., Abbasbandy, S., Ahmady, N., Ahmady, E., 2009. Improved redictor–corrector method for solving fuzzy initial value problems. Inform. Sci. 179, 945–955.

Allahviranloo, T., Gouyandeh, Z., Armand, A., Hasanoglu, A., 2015. On fuzzy solutions for heat equation based on generalized Hukuhara differentiability. Fuzzy Set. Syst. 265, 1–23.

Armand, A., Allahviranloo, T., Abbasbandy, S., Gouyandeh, Z., 2019. The fuzzy generalized Taylor's expansion with application in fractional differential equations. Iran J. Fuzzy Syst. 16 (2), 57–72.

Gouyandeha, Z., Allahviranloob, T., Abbasbandyb, S., Armand, A., 2017. A fuzzy solution of heat equation under generalized Hukuhara differentiability by fuzzy Fourier transform. Fuzzy Set. Syst. 309, 81–97.

Further reading

Ahmady, N., Allahviranloo, T., Ahmady, E., 2020. A modified Euler method for solving fuzzy differential equations under generalized differentiability. Comput. Appl. Math. 39, 104.

Chapter 6

Numerical solutions of uncertain fractional differential equations

6.1 Introduction

The objectives for this chapter are introducing the Caputo fractional derivative on the fuzzy number valued functions and fuzzy fractional differential equations under this Caputo operator. After showing the existence and uniqueness of the fuzzy solution, the fuzzy Taylor method will be illustrated, and its consequence as the fuzzy fractional Euler method will be applied as numerical methods to solve the fuzzy fractional differential equations. To define the Caputo fractional operator, the Riemann-Liouville fractional operator should be defined first.

6.2 Fuzzy Riemann-Liouville Derivative—Fuzzy RL Derivative

The fuzzy Riemann-Liouville derivative is defined as:

$$\boldsymbol{I}_{\boldsymbol{RL}}^{\alpha} x(s) := \boldsymbol{D}_{\boldsymbol{RL}}^{-\alpha} x(s) = \frac{1}{\Gamma(\alpha)} \odot \int_{t_0}^{s} (s-t)^{\alpha-1} \odot x(t) \mathrm{d}t, \;\; s \in [t_0, T],$$

Soft Numerical Computing in Uncertain Dynamic Systems. https://doi.org/10.1016/B978-0-12-822855-5.00006-9

for any $0<\alpha<1$.

Indeed, it is the antioperator of the RL fractional integral:

$$\boldsymbol{I}_{\boldsymbol{RL}}^{\alpha}x(s,r)=\frac{1}{\Gamma(\alpha)}\odot\int_{t_0}^{s}(s-t)^{\alpha-1}\odot x(t,r)\mathrm{d}t$$

One of the properties of this derivative entitled combination property can be explained as follows (Mathai & Haubold, 2017; Van Hoa et al., 2019).

6.2.1.1 Note—Combination Property

$$\boldsymbol{D}_{\boldsymbol{RL}}^{-\alpha}\boldsymbol{D}_{\boldsymbol{RL}}^{-\beta}x(t)=\boldsymbol{D}_{\boldsymbol{RL}}^{-\beta}\boldsymbol{D}_{\boldsymbol{RL}}^{-\alpha}x(t)=\boldsymbol{D}_{\boldsymbol{RL}}^{-(\alpha+\beta)}x(t),\;\; 0<\alpha<1,\;\; 0<\beta<1$$

$$\boldsymbol{D}_{\boldsymbol{RL}}^{-\alpha}x(s)=\frac{1}{\Gamma(\alpha)}\odot\int_{t_0}^{s}(s-t)^{\alpha-1}\odot x(t)\mathrm{d}t,\;\; 0<\alpha<1.$$

$$\boldsymbol{D}_{\boldsymbol{RL}}^{-\beta}x(s)=\frac{1}{\Gamma(\beta)}\odot\int_{t_0}^{s}(s-t)^{\beta-1}\odot x(t)\mathrm{d}t,\;\; 0<\beta<1$$

Now:

$$\boldsymbol{D}_{\boldsymbol{RL}}^{-\alpha}\boldsymbol{D}_{\boldsymbol{RL}}^{-\beta}x(s)=\frac{1}{\Gamma(\alpha)}\odot\int_{t_0}^{s}(s-t)^{\alpha-1}\odot\left[\frac{1}{\Gamma(\beta)}\odot\int_{u}^{s}(t-u)^{\beta-1}\odot x(u)\mathrm{d}u\right]\mathrm{d}t$$

Since the functions $s-t, t-u, \Gamma(\alpha), \Gamma(\beta)$ are positive, the same procedure for the real cases occurs here.

$$\boldsymbol{D}_{\boldsymbol{RL}}^{-\alpha}\boldsymbol{D}_{\boldsymbol{RL}}^{-\beta}x(s)=\frac{1}{\Gamma(\alpha+\beta)}\odot\int_{t_0}^{s}x(u)\mathrm{d}u\odot\left[\int_{u}^{s}(s-t)^{\alpha-1}(t-u)^{\beta-1}\mathrm{d}t\right]$$

By changing some variables such as $\frac{t-u}{s-u}=v$, where s, u are fixed, then:

$$\frac{1}{s-u}\mathrm{d}t=\mathrm{d}v,\;\; (t-u)^{\beta-1}=v^{\beta-1}(s-u)^{\beta-1},$$

$$1-v=\frac{s-t}{s-u}\Longrightarrow(s-t)^{\alpha-1}=(1-v)^{\alpha-1}(s-u)^{\alpha-1}$$

then:

$$\begin{aligned}(s-t)^{\alpha-1}(t-u)^{\beta-1}&=(1-v)^{\alpha-1}(s-u)^{\alpha-1}v^{\beta-1}(s-u)^{\beta-1}\\&=(s-u)^{\alpha+\beta-2}(1-v)^{\alpha-1}v^{\beta-1}\end{aligned}$$

By substituting:

$$\boldsymbol{D}_{\boldsymbol{RL}}^{-\alpha}\boldsymbol{D}_{\boldsymbol{RL}}^{-\beta}x(s)=\frac{1}{\Gamma(\alpha+\beta)}\odot\int_{t_0}^{s}x(u)\mathrm{d}u\odot\left[\int_{0}^{1}(s-u)^{\alpha+\beta-1}(1-v)^{\alpha-1}v^{\beta-1}\mathrm{d}v\right]$$

$$=\frac{1}{\Gamma(\alpha+\beta)}\odot\int_{t_0}^{s}(s-u)^{\alpha+\beta-1}\odot x(u)\mathrm{d}u\left[\int_{0}^{1}(1-v)^{\alpha-1}v^{\beta-1}\mathrm{d}v\right]$$

Since:

$$\int_{0}^{1}(1-v)^{\alpha-1}v^{\beta-1}\mathrm{d}v=1$$

then:

$$\boldsymbol{D}_{\boldsymbol{RL}}^{-\alpha}\boldsymbol{D}_{\boldsymbol{RL}}^{-\beta}x(s)=\frac{1}{\Gamma(\alpha+\beta)}\odot\int_{t_0}^{s}(s-u)^{\alpha+\beta-1}\odot x(u)\mathrm{d}u=\boldsymbol{D}_{\boldsymbol{RL}}^{-(\alpha+\beta)}x(s)$$

The same procedure can be used to prove $\boldsymbol{D}_{\boldsymbol{RL}}^{-\beta}\boldsymbol{D}_{\boldsymbol{RL}}^{-\alpha}x(t)$.

6.2.1.2 Level-Wise form of Fuzzy Riemann-Liouville Integral Operators

Based on the definition of the integral and its level-wise form, we know that the level-wise form of integral is the integrals of end points of the interval in the level-wise form of integrand function.

6.2.1.3 The RL Fractional Integral Operator

$$\boldsymbol{I}_{\boldsymbol{RL}}^{\alpha}x(s,r)=\left[\boldsymbol{I}_{\boldsymbol{RL}}^{\alpha}x_l(s,r),\boldsymbol{I}_{\boldsymbol{RL}}^{\alpha}x_u(s,r)\right],\ \ s\in[t_0,T]$$

where:

$$\boldsymbol{I}_{\boldsymbol{RL}}^{\alpha}x_l(s,r)=\frac{1}{\Gamma(\alpha)}\int_{t_0}^{s}(s-t)^{\alpha-1}x_l(t,r)\mathrm{d}t$$

$$\boldsymbol{I}_{\boldsymbol{RL}}^{\alpha}x_u(s,r)=\frac{1}{\Gamma(\alpha)}\int_{t_0}^{s}(s-t)^{\alpha-1}x_u(t,r)\mathrm{d}t$$

because, $\Gamma(\alpha)>0$ and $(s-t)^{\alpha-1}>0$.

6.2.1.4 The Fuzzy Riemann-Liouville Derivative Operators

In the definition of RL fractional integral:

$$D_{RL}^{-\alpha}x(s)=\frac{1}{\Gamma(\alpha)}\odot\int_{t_0}^{s}(s-t)^{\alpha-1}\odot x(t)\mathrm{d}t,\ 0<\alpha<1$$

or:

$$D_{RL}^{\alpha}x(s):=\frac{1}{\Gamma(1-\alpha)}\odot\int_{t_0}^{s}(s-t)^{-\alpha}\odot x(t)\mathrm{d}t,\ 0<\alpha<1$$

assume:

$$\int_{t_0}^{s}\frac{x(t)}{(s-t)^{\alpha}}\mathrm{d}t=f(s)\in\mathbb{F}_R,\ x(t)\in\mathbb{F}_R$$

so:

$$\frac{\mathrm{d}}{\mathrm{d}s}\int_{t_0}^{s}\frac{x(t)}{(s-t)^{\alpha}}\mathrm{d}t=f'_{gH}(s),\ s\in[t_0,T]$$

Remark. The function $f(t)$ is gH-differentiable if and only if $f_l'(t,r)$ and $f_u'(t,r)$ are differentiable with respect to t for all $0\le r\le 1$ and:

$$f'_{gH}(t)=\left[\min\left\{f_l'(t,r),f_u'(t,r)\right\},\ \max\left\{f_l'(t,r),f_u'(t,r)\right\}\right]$$

Theorem. The necessary and sufficient condition for RL gH-differentiability of $x(t)$ is gH-differentiability of $f(s)$. This means:

$$D_{RL_{gH}}^{\alpha}x(t,r)=\left[\min\left\{D_{RL}^{\alpha}x_l(t,r),D_{RL}^{\alpha}x_u(t,r)\right\},\ \max\left\{D_{RL}^{\alpha}x_l(t,r),D_{RL}^{\alpha}x_u(t,r)\right\}\right]$$

The proof is very easy, since $s-t>0$:

$$f_l(s,r)=\int_{t_0}^{s}\frac{x_l(t,r)}{(s-t)^{\alpha}}\mathrm{d}t,\ f_u(s,r)=\int_{t_0}^{s}\frac{x_u(t,r)}{(s-t)^{\alpha}}\mathrm{d}t$$

$$\min\left\{\frac{1}{\Gamma(1-\alpha)}f_l'(t,r),\ \frac{1}{\Gamma(1-\alpha)}f_u'(t,r)\right\}$$

$$\le\max\left\{\frac{1}{\Gamma(1-\alpha)}f_l'(t,r),\ \frac{1}{\Gamma(1-\alpha)}f_u'(t,r)\right\}$$

then:

$$\min\left\{D_{RL}^{\alpha}x_l(t,r),D_{RL}^{\alpha}x_u(t,r)\right\}\le\max\left\{D_{RL}^{\alpha}x_l(t,r),D_{RL}^{\alpha}x_u(t,r)\right\}$$

This means that the following interval defines an interval for all $r\in[0,1]$:

$$D_{RL_{gH}}^{\alpha}x(t,r)=\left[D_{RL}^{\alpha}x_l(t,r),D_{RL}^{\alpha}x_u(t,r)\right]$$

6.3 Fuzzy Caputo Fractional Derivative

In this section, another form of the fractional derivative entitled the fuzzy Caputo fractional derivative is expressed (Chehlabi & Allahviranloo, 2016; Garrappa et al., 2019; Mathai & Haubold, 2017; Van Hoa et al., 2019).

6.3.1.1 *Caputo* gH*-Differentiability*

The fuzzy number valued function $x(t)$ is Caputo gH-differentiable if and only if $x_l'(t,r)$ and $x_u'(t,r)$ are differentiable with respect to t for all $0 \leq r \leq 1$ and:

$$\boldsymbol{D}^{\alpha}_{C_{gH}}x(t,r) = \left[\min\left\{\boldsymbol{D}^{\alpha}_{C}x_l(t,r), \boldsymbol{D}^{\alpha}_{C}x_u(t,r)\right\},\ \max\left\{\boldsymbol{D}^{\alpha}_{C}x_l(t,r), \boldsymbol{D}^{\alpha}_{C}x_u(t,r)\right\}\right]$$

where:

$$\boldsymbol{D}^{\alpha}_{C}x_l(s,r) = \frac{1}{\Gamma(1-\alpha)}\int_{t_0}^{s}\frac{x_l'(t,r)}{(s-t)^{\alpha}}\mathrm{d}t,\ D^{\alpha}_{C}x_u(t,r) = \frac{1}{\Gamma(1-\alpha)}\int_{t_0}^{s}\frac{x_u'(t,r)}{(s-t)^{\alpha}}\mathrm{d}t$$

The proof is straight:

$$\boldsymbol{D}^{\alpha}_{C_{gH}}x(s,r) = \frac{1}{\Gamma(1-\alpha)} \odot \int_{t_0}^{s}\frac{x_{gH}'(t,r)}{(s-t)^{\alpha}}\mathrm{d}t$$

We have:

$$x_{gH}'(s,r) = \left[\min\left\{x_l'(s,r), x_u'(s,r)\right\},\ \max\left\{x_l'(s,r), x_u'(s,r)\right\}\right]$$

then:

$$x_{gH}'(s,r) = \left[\min\left\{\frac{1}{\Gamma(1-\alpha)}\int_{t_0}^{s}\frac{x_l'(t,r)}{(s-t)^{\alpha}}\mathrm{d}t, \frac{1}{\Gamma(1-\alpha)}\int_{t_0}^{s}\frac{x_u'(t,r)}{(s-t)^{\alpha}}\mathrm{d}t\right\},\right.$$
$$\left.\max\left\{\frac{1}{\Gamma(1-\alpha)}\int_{t_0}^{s}\frac{x_l'(t,r)}{(s-t)^{\alpha}}\mathrm{d}t, \frac{1}{\Gamma(1-\alpha)}\int_{t_0}^{s}\frac{x_u'(t,r)}{(s-t)^{\alpha}}\mathrm{d}t\right\}\right]$$

This is exactly:

$$\boldsymbol{D}^{\alpha}_{C_{gH}}x(t,r) = \left[\min\left\{\boldsymbol{D}^{\alpha}_{C}x_l(t,r), \boldsymbol{D}^{\alpha}_{C}x_u(t,r)\right\},\ \max\left\{\boldsymbol{D}^{\alpha}_{C}x_l(t,r), \boldsymbol{D}^{\alpha}_{C}x_u(t,r)\right\}\right]$$

Also, in the case where $0 < \alpha < 1$, we have two cases of differentiability:

- $i-gH$ (differentiable)

$$x_{i-gH}'(t) = \lim_{h\to 0}\frac{x(t+h)\ominus_H x(t)}{h}$$

Its level-wise form:

$$\boldsymbol{D}^{\alpha}_{C_{i-gH}}x(s,r) = \left[\boldsymbol{D}^{\alpha}_{C}x_l(s,r), \boldsymbol{D}^{\alpha}_{C}x_u(s,r)\right]$$

- $ii-gH$ (differentiable)

$$x'_{ii-gH}(t)=\lim_{h\to 0}\frac{x(t)\ominus_H x(t+h)}{h}$$

Its level-wise form:

$$\boldsymbol{D}^{\alpha}_{C_{ii-gH}}x(s,r)=\left[\boldsymbol{D}^{\alpha}_{C}x_u(s,r),\boldsymbol{D}^{\alpha}_{C}x_l(s,r)\right]$$

Example. Consider the same fuzzy exponential function $x(t)=e^{c\odot t}$, $t\in(t_0,T]$, $c\in\mathbb{F}_R$, $c(r)=(c_l(r),c_u(r))$:

$$\boldsymbol{D}^{\alpha}_{C_{gH}}e^{c\odot s}=\frac{1}{\Gamma(1-\alpha)}\odot\int_{t_0}^{s}\frac{c\odot e^{c\odot t}}{(s-t)^{\alpha}}dt$$

We know that:

$$x_l(t,r)=e^{c_l(r)t},\ x_u(t,r)=e^{c_u(r)t}$$

$$x'_l(t,r)=c_l(r)e^{c_l(r)t},\ x'_u(t,r)=c_u(r)e^{c_u(r)t}$$

because $t>0$ and the exponential function is increasing. Thus:

$$x'_{gH}(t,r)=\left[c_l(r)e^{c_l(r)t},c_u(r)e^{c_u(r)t}\right]$$

Finally, the i-differential is found as follows:

$$\boldsymbol{D}^{\alpha}_{C_{i-gH}}x(s,r)=\left[\boldsymbol{D}^{\alpha}_{C}x_l(s,r),\boldsymbol{D}^{\alpha}_{C}x_u(s,r)\right]$$

where:

$$\boldsymbol{D}^{\alpha}_{C}x_l(s,r)=\frac{1}{\Gamma(1-\alpha)}\int_{t_0}^{s}\frac{c_l(r)e^{c_l(r)t}}{(s-t)^{\alpha}}dt=\frac{c_l(r)}{\Gamma(1-\alpha)}\int_{t_0}^{s}\frac{e^{c_l(r)t}}{(s-t)^{\alpha}}dt$$

Let $v=s-t$, and then $dt=-dv$, and $e^{c\odot t}=e^{c\odot(s-v)}$, $s-v\geq 0$. By these conditions, the integral equation $\int_{t_0}^{s}(s-t)^{-\alpha}\odot e^{c\odot t}dt$ is always $i-gH$ differentiable, and:

$$\boldsymbol{D}^{\alpha}_{C}x_l(s,r)=\frac{c_l(r)}{\Gamma(1-\alpha)}\int_{0}^{s-t_0}\frac{e^{c_l(r)(s-v)}}{v^{\alpha}}dv=\frac{c_l(r)e^{c_l(r)s}}{\Gamma(1-\alpha)}\int_{0}^{s-t_0}\frac{e^{-c_l(r)v}}{v^{\alpha}}dv$$

The integral equation:

$$\frac{1}{\Gamma(1-\alpha)}\int_{0}^{s-t_0}\frac{e^{-c_l(r)v}}{v^{\alpha}}dv=\frac{1}{\Gamma(1-\alpha)}\int_{0}^{s-t_0}v^{-\alpha}e^{-c_l(r)v}dv$$

where $\int_0^{s-t_0}v^{-\alpha}e^{-c_l(r)v}dv$ is an incomplete $\gamma(v,t)$ function, thus:

$$\boldsymbol{D}^{\alpha}_{C}x_l(s,r)=\frac{c_l(r)e^{c_l(r)s}}{\Gamma(1-\alpha)}\gamma(v,t)$$

Using the same process:

$$\boldsymbol{D}_{C}^{\alpha} x_u(s,r) = \frac{c_l(r)e^{c_l(r)s}}{\Gamma(1-\alpha)}\gamma(v,t),\quad 0<\alpha<1$$

Now if for any $r\in[0,1]$, the conditions of the interval are satisfied then the Caputo derivative for this exponential function exists. This is exactly depending on the sign of $\gamma(v,t)$ and it can be variational. Then it is not easy to claim that:

$$\boldsymbol{D}_{C}^{\alpha} x_l(s,r) \le \boldsymbol{D}_{C}^{\alpha} x_u(s,r),\quad 0\le r\le 1$$

Remark. For $x(t)\in\mathbb{F}_R$ and $0<\alpha<\beta<1$ we have:

- $(\boldsymbol{D}_{RL_{gH}}{}^{\alpha}\boldsymbol{I}_{RL}^{\alpha}x)(t) = x(t)$
- $(\boldsymbol{D}_{RL_{gH}}{}^{\alpha}\boldsymbol{I}_{RL}^{\beta}x)(t) = \boldsymbol{I}_{RL}^{(\beta-\alpha)}x(t)$

To show the first item:

$$\boldsymbol{D}_{RL_{gH}}^{\alpha}\boldsymbol{I}_{RL}^{\alpha}x(t) = \left(\boldsymbol{I}_{RL}^{(1-\alpha)}\boldsymbol{I}_{RL}^{\alpha}x\right)'_{gH}(t)$$

$$= \frac{1}{\Gamma(1-\alpha)} \odot \left(\int_{t_0}^{t} (t-s)^{-\alpha} \odot \boldsymbol{I}_{RL}^{\alpha}x(s)\mathrm{d}s\right)'_{gH}$$

where:

$$\boldsymbol{I}_{RL}^{\alpha}x(s) = \frac{1}{\Gamma(\alpha)} \odot \int_{t_0}^{s} (t-u)^{\alpha-1} \odot x(u)\mathrm{d}u$$

By substituting and by using the Dirichlet formula, the known formula for the Beta function, and setting $= \dfrac{u-s}{t-s}$:

$$\boldsymbol{D}_{RL_{gH}}^{\alpha}\boldsymbol{I}_{RL}^{\alpha}x(t) =$$

$$= \frac{1}{\Gamma(1-\alpha)} \odot \left(\int_{t_0}^{t} \frac{1}{(t-s)^{\alpha}} \odot \left(\frac{1}{\Gamma(\alpha)}\int_{t_0}^{s} \frac{1}{(s-u)^{1-\alpha}}x(u)\mathrm{d}u\right)\mathrm{d}s\right)'_{gH}$$

$$= \frac{1}{\Gamma(\alpha)\Gamma(1-\alpha)} \odot \left(\int_{t_0}^{t} x(s) \odot \int_{s}^{t} \frac{u-s)^{\alpha-1}}{(t-u)^{\alpha}}\mathrm{d}u\mathrm{d}s\right)'_{gH}$$

$$= \frac{1}{\Gamma(\alpha)\Gamma(1-\alpha)} \odot \left(\int_{t_0}^{t} x(s)\mathrm{d}s \odot \underbrace{\int_{0}^{1} (1-v)^{-\alpha}v^{\alpha-1}\mathrm{d}u}_{1}\right)'_{gH}$$

$$= \frac{B(1-\alpha,\alpha)}{\Gamma(\alpha)\Gamma(1-\alpha)} \odot \left(\int_{t_0}^{t} x(s)s^{p-1}\mathrm{d}s\right)'_{gH} = x(t)$$

The second property:

$$\boldsymbol{D}^{\alpha}_{RL_{gH}}\boldsymbol{I}^{\beta}_{RL}x(t)=$$

$$=\frac{1}{\Gamma(\beta)\Gamma(1-\alpha)}\odot\left(\int_{t_0}^{t}\frac{1}{(t-s)^{\alpha-\beta}}\odot x(s)ds\odot\int_0^1(1-v)^{-\alpha}v^{\alpha-1}du\right)'_{gH}$$

$$=\frac{1}{\Gamma(\beta-\alpha+1)}\odot\int_{t_0}^{t}\frac{1}{(t-s)^{\alpha-\beta}}\odot x(s)ds=I_{RL}^{(\beta-\alpha)}x(t)$$

Remark. If in the interval $(t_0,T]$ the type of differentiability does not change, it means it is either $i-gH$ differentiable or $ii-gH$ differentiable. Then the following relation as a relation of fractional integral and derivative operators is established:

$$\boldsymbol{I}^{\alpha}_{RL}\boldsymbol{D}^{\alpha}_{RL_{gH}}x(t)=x(t)\ominus_{gH}\frac{(t-t_0)^{\alpha-1}}{\Gamma(\alpha)}\odot I_{RL}^{(1-\alpha)}x(t_0),\ \ t\in(t_0,T]$$

where $\boldsymbol{I}_{RL}^{(1-\alpha)}x(t_0)$ exists and:

$$\lim_{t\to t_0+}\boldsymbol{I}_{RL}^{(1-\alpha)}x(t)=\boldsymbol{I}_{RL}^{(1-\alpha)}x(t_0)$$

To show the assertion, we consider two cases:

- $i-gH$ (differentiability)

$$\boldsymbol{I}^{\alpha}_{RL}\boldsymbol{D}^{\alpha}_{RL_{i-gH}}x(t,r)=\left[\boldsymbol{I}^{\alpha}_{RL}\boldsymbol{D}^{\alpha}_{RL_{gH}}x_l(t,r),\boldsymbol{I}^{\alpha}_{RL}\boldsymbol{D}^{\alpha}_{RL_{gH}}x_u(t,r)\right]$$

where:

$$\boldsymbol{I}^{\alpha}_{RL}\boldsymbol{D}^{\alpha}_{RL_{gH}}x_l(t,r)=x_l(t,r)-\frac{(t-t_0)^{\alpha-1}}{\Gamma(\alpha)}I_{RL}^{(1-\alpha)}x_l(t_0,r)$$

$$\boldsymbol{I}^{\alpha}_{RL}\boldsymbol{D}^{\alpha}_{RL_{gH}}x_u(t,r)=x_u(t,r)-\frac{(t-t_0)^{\alpha-1}}{\Gamma(\alpha)}I_{RL}^{(1-\alpha)}x_u(t_0,r)$$

Now, since $x_l(t,r)$ is increasing, then $\boldsymbol{I}^{\alpha}_{RL}\boldsymbol{D}_{RL_{gH}}{}^{\alpha}x_l(t,r)$ is also increasing and $\boldsymbol{I}^{\alpha}_{RL}\boldsymbol{D}_{RL_{gH}}{}^{\alpha}x_u(t,r)$ is decreasing because $x_u(t,r)$ is decreasing.

6.3.1.2 *Caputo-Katugampola* gH*-Fractional Derivative*

If the RL derivative $\boldsymbol{D}_{RL_{gH}}{}^{\alpha}x(t)$ exists in $[t_o,T]$ and $0<\alpha<1$:

$$\boldsymbol{D}^{\alpha}_{CK_{gH}}x(t)=\boldsymbol{D}^{\alpha}_{RL_{gH}}\left(x(t)\ominus_{gH}x(t_0)\right)$$

In the sequel, some relations between fuzzy type Riemann-Liouville-Katugampola generalized fractional derivative and fuzzy type Caputo-Katugampola fractional derivative are shown (Mathai & Haubold, 2017; Van Hoa et al., 2019).

Remark. Assume $x(t)$ is an absolutely continuous fuzzy number valued function that does have increasing or decreasing length, i.e., it is $i-gH$ differentiable or $ii--$ gH differentiable, then:

$$\boldsymbol{D}^{\alpha}_{\boldsymbol{CK_{gH}}}x(t)=\frac{1}{\Gamma(1-\alpha)}\int_{t_0}^{t}(t-s)^{-\alpha}\odot x'(s)\mathrm{d}s,\ \ t\in[t_0,T],\ \ 0<\alpha<1$$

To show the relation, we know the fuzzy function $\boldsymbol{I}_{\boldsymbol{RL}}^{(1-\alpha)}x(t)$ is absolutely continuous because in its relation:

$$\boldsymbol{I}_{\boldsymbol{RL}}^{(1-\alpha)}x(t)=\frac{1}{\Gamma(1-\alpha)}\odot\int_{t_0}^{t}(t-s)^{-\alpha}\odot x(s)\mathrm{d}s$$

the coefficients $(t-s)^{-\alpha}>0$, $\frac{1}{\Gamma(1-\alpha)}>0$ and the fuzzy function $x(s)$ is absolutely continuous; thus $(\boldsymbol{I}_{\boldsymbol{RL}}^{(1-\alpha)}x)'_{gH}(t)$ exists and finally, $\boldsymbol{D}_{\boldsymbol{RL_{gH}}}{}^{\alpha}x(t)$ exists for $t\in(t_0,T]$:

$$\boldsymbol{D}^{\alpha}_{\boldsymbol{RL_{gH}}}x(t)=\left(\boldsymbol{I}_{\boldsymbol{RL}}^{(1-\alpha)}x\right)'_{gH}(t).$$

Now, let us consider a constant fuzzy function like $y\in\mathbb{F}_R$, which is $y(t):=x(t_0)$. Then:

$$\boldsymbol{I}_{\boldsymbol{RL}}^{(1-\alpha)}y(t)=\boldsymbol{I}_{\boldsymbol{RL}}^{(1-\alpha)}x(t_0)=\frac{(t-t_0)^{1-\alpha}}{\Gamma(2-\alpha)}\odot x(t_0)$$

and if $\alpha:\rightarrow 1+\alpha$:

$$\boldsymbol{D}^{\alpha}_{\boldsymbol{RL_{gH}}}y(t)=\boldsymbol{I}_{\boldsymbol{RL}}^{-\alpha}y(t)=\frac{(t-t_0)^{-\alpha}}{\Gamma(1-\alpha)}\odot x(t_0)$$

This is the reason for gH-differentiability of $\boldsymbol{I}_{\boldsymbol{RL}}^{(1-\alpha)}x$ (in two cases) on $(t_0,T]$ and it follows that:

$$\boldsymbol{D}^{\alpha}_{\boldsymbol{CK_{gH}}}x(t)=\boldsymbol{D}^{\alpha}_{\boldsymbol{RL_{gH}}}\left(x(t)\ominus_{gH}x(t_0)\right)=\boldsymbol{D}^{\alpha}_{\boldsymbol{RL_{gH}}}\left(x(t)\ominus_{gH}y(t)\right)$$

$$=\boldsymbol{D}^{\alpha}_{\boldsymbol{RL_{gH}}}x(t)\ominus_{gH}\boldsymbol{D}^{\alpha}_{\boldsymbol{RL_{gH}}}y(t)=\boldsymbol{D}^{\alpha}_{\boldsymbol{RL_{gH}}}x(t)\ominus_{gH}\frac{(t-t_0)^{-\alpha}}{\Gamma(1-\alpha)}\odot x(t_0)$$

so:

$$\boldsymbol{D}^{\alpha}_{\boldsymbol{CK_{gH}}}x(t)=\boldsymbol{D}^{\alpha}_{\boldsymbol{RL_{gH}}}x(t)\ominus_{gH}\frac{(t-t_0)^{-\alpha}}{\Gamma(1-\alpha)}\odot x(t_0)$$

Two sides in the level-form and based on the first case of gH-difference, we have:

Case $i-gH$ difference:

$$\boldsymbol{D}^{\alpha}_{\boldsymbol{RL}_{gH}}x(t,r)=\boldsymbol{D}^{\alpha}_{\boldsymbol{CK}_{gH}}x(t,r)\oplus\frac{(t-t_0)^{-\alpha}}{\Gamma(1-\alpha)}x(t_0,r)$$

In the interval form:

$$\left[\boldsymbol{D}^{\alpha}_{\boldsymbol{RL}_{gH}}x_l(t,r),\boldsymbol{D}^{\alpha}_{\boldsymbol{RL}_{gH}}x_u(t,r)\right]=$$

$$=\left[\boldsymbol{D}^{\alpha}_{\boldsymbol{CK}_{gH}}x_l(t,r),\boldsymbol{D}^{\alpha}_{\boldsymbol{CK}_{gH}}x_u(t,r)\right]+\frac{(t-t_0)^{-\alpha}}{\Gamma(1-\alpha)}[x_l(t_0,r),x_u(t_0,r)]$$

Therefore, for any $r\in[0,1]$ and $t\in(t_0,T]$:

$$\boldsymbol{D}^{\alpha}_{\boldsymbol{RL}_{gH}}x(t)=\boldsymbol{D}^{\alpha}_{\boldsymbol{CK}_{gH}}x(t)\oplus\frac{(t-t_0)^{-\alpha}}{\Gamma(1-\alpha)}\odot x(t_0)$$

$$=\left(\boldsymbol{I}^{(1-\alpha)}_{\boldsymbol{RL}}\frac{\mathrm{d}}{\mathrm{d}s}x\right)(t)\oplus\frac{(t-t_0)^{-\alpha}}{\Gamma(1-\alpha)}\odot x(t_0)$$

Substituting in the following:

$$\boldsymbol{D}^{\alpha}_{\boldsymbol{CK}_{gH}}x(t)=\boldsymbol{D}^{\alpha}_{\boldsymbol{RL}_{gH}}x(t)\ominus_{gH}\frac{(t-t_0)^{-\alpha}}{\Gamma(1-\alpha)}\odot x(t_0)$$

we get:

$$\boldsymbol{D}^{\alpha}_{\boldsymbol{CK}_{gH}}x(t)=\left(\boldsymbol{I}^{(1-\alpha)}_{\boldsymbol{RL}}\frac{\mathrm{d}}{\mathrm{d}s}x\right)(t)$$

Based on the definition of:

$$\boldsymbol{I}^{(1-\alpha)}_{\boldsymbol{RL}}x(t)=\frac{1}{\Gamma(1-\alpha)}\odot\int_{t_0}^{t}s^{p-1}(t-s)^{-\alpha}\odot x(s)\mathrm{d}s$$

it is concluded:

$$\left(\boldsymbol{I}^{(1-\alpha)}_{\boldsymbol{RL}}\frac{\mathrm{d}}{\mathrm{d}s}x\right)(t)=\frac{1}{\Gamma(1-\alpha)}\odot\int_{t_0}^{t}(t-s)^{-\alpha}\odot x'(s)\mathrm{d}s$$

Thus, the proof is completed in the case of $i-gH$ difference.
Case $ii-gH$ difference:

$$\boldsymbol{D}^{\alpha}_{\boldsymbol{CK}_{gH}}x(t,r)=\boldsymbol{D}^{\alpha}_{\boldsymbol{RL}_{gH}}x(t,r)\oplus(-1)\frac{(t-t_0)^{-\alpha}}{\Gamma(1-\alpha)}\odot x(t_0,r)$$

Because in level-wise form, since the function $x(t)$ is $ii-gH$ differentiable, so:

$$\boldsymbol{D}^{\alpha}_{\boldsymbol{RL}_{gH}}x(t,r)=\left[\boldsymbol{D}^{\alpha}_{\boldsymbol{RL}_{gH}}x_u(t,r),\boldsymbol{D}^{\alpha}_{\boldsymbol{RL}_{gH}}x_l(t,r)\right],$$

$$\boldsymbol{D}^{\alpha,p}_{CK_{gH}}x(t,r) = \left[\boldsymbol{D}^{\alpha,p}_{CK_{gH}}x_u(t,r), \boldsymbol{D}^{\alpha,p}_{CK_{gH}}x_l(t,r)\right]$$

$$\left[\boldsymbol{D}^{\alpha}_{CK_{gH}}x_u(t,r), \boldsymbol{D}^{\alpha}_{CK_{gH}}x_l(t,r)\right] =$$

$$= \left[\boldsymbol{D}^{\alpha}_{RL_{gH}}x_u(t,r), \boldsymbol{D}^{\alpha}_{RL_{gH}}x_l(t,r)\right] + (-1)\frac{(t-t_0)^{-\alpha}}{\Gamma(1-\alpha)}[x_l(t_0,r), x_u(t_0,r)]$$

Therefore, for any $r \in [0,1]$ and $t \in (t_0, T]$:

$$\left[\left(\boldsymbol{I}^{(1-\alpha)}_{RL}\frac{\mathrm{d}}{\mathrm{d}s}x_l\right)(t,r), \left(\boldsymbol{I}^{(1-\alpha)}_{RL}\frac{\mathrm{d}}{\mathrm{d}s}x_u\right)(t,r)\right] =$$

$$= \left[\boldsymbol{D}^{\alpha}_{RL_{gH}}x_u(t,r), \boldsymbol{D}^{\alpha}_{RL_{gH}}x_l(t,r)\right] + (-1)\frac{(t-t_0)^{-\alpha}}{\Gamma(1-\alpha)}[x_l(t_0,r), x_u(t_0,r)]$$

so we have:

$$\left(\boldsymbol{I}^{(1-\alpha)}_{RL}\frac{\mathrm{d}}{\mathrm{d}s}x\right)(t) = \boldsymbol{D}^{\alpha}_{RL_{gH}}x(t) \oplus \frac{(t-t_0)^{-\alpha}}{\Gamma(1-\alpha)}(-1) \odot x(t_0)$$

Substituting in the following:

$$\boldsymbol{D}^{\alpha}_{CK_{gH}}x(t) = \boldsymbol{D}^{\alpha}_{RL_{gH}}x(t) \ominus_{gH} \frac{(t-t_0)^{-\alpha}}{\Gamma(1-\alpha)} \odot x(t_0)$$

we get:

$$\boldsymbol{D}^{\alpha}_{CK_{gH}}x(t) = \left(\boldsymbol{I}^{(1-\alpha)}_{RL}\frac{\mathrm{d}}{\mathrm{d}s}x\right)(t)$$

Based on the definition of:

$$\boldsymbol{I}^{(1-\alpha)}_{RL}x(t) = \frac{1}{\Gamma(1-\alpha)} \odot \int_{t_0}^{t} (t-s)^{-\alpha} \odot x(s)\mathrm{d}s$$

it is concluded:

$$\left(\boldsymbol{I}^{(1-\alpha)}_{RL}\frac{\mathrm{d}}{\mathrm{d}s}x\right)(t) = \frac{1}{\Gamma(1-\alpha)} \odot \int_{t_0}^{t} (t-s)^{-\alpha} \odot x'(s)\mathrm{d}s$$

Thus, the proof is also completed in the case of $ii - gH$ difference.

Remark. The RL integral operator is bounded:

$$\boldsymbol{I}^{\alpha}_{RL}x(t) = \frac{1}{\Gamma(\alpha)} \odot \int_{t_0}^{t} (t-s)^{\alpha-1} \odot x(s)\mathrm{d}s$$

It can be shown by Hausdorff distance:

$$\sup_{t\in[t_0,T]} D_H\left(\boldsymbol{I}_{\boldsymbol{RL}}^{\alpha}x(t),0\right)\leq D_H(x(s),0)\frac{1}{\Gamma(\alpha)}\int_{t_0}^{t}(t-s)^{\alpha-1}\mathrm{d}s=$$

$$=\frac{1}{\Gamma(\alpha+1)}D_H(x(s),0)(T-t_0)^{\alpha}$$

As mentioned before, the existence of the Caputo-Katugampola depends on the continuity of $x(t)$ and it has been supposed that it is absolutely continuous. Then we claim the following remark.

Remark. $\boldsymbol{D}_{\boldsymbol{CK}_{gH}}{}^{\alpha}x(t)=0$ at $t=0$.

Since $\boldsymbol{I}_{\boldsymbol{RL}}^{(1-\alpha)}$ is bounded, the Caputo-Katugampola derivative is continuous:

$$\boldsymbol{D}_{\boldsymbol{CK}_{gH}}^{\alpha}x(t)=\left(\boldsymbol{I}_{\boldsymbol{RL}}^{(1-\alpha)}\frac{\mathrm{d}}{\mathrm{d}s}x\right)(t)$$

To show the assertion, it is enough to show that the upper bound of the derivative goes to zero at the point $t=0$. Then:

$$D_H\left(\boldsymbol{D}_{\boldsymbol{CK}_{gH}}^{\alpha}x(t),0\right)=D_H\left(\left(\boldsymbol{I}_{\boldsymbol{RL}}^{(1-\alpha)}x'\right)(t),0\right)$$

$$\leq\frac{1}{\Gamma(2-\alpha)}D_H(x',0)(t-t_0)^{1-\alpha}$$

$$\leq\frac{1}{\Gamma(2-\alpha)}\sup_{s\in[t_0,T]}D_H(x',0)(t-t_0)^{1-\alpha}$$

The supremum $\sup_{s\in[t_0,T]}D_H(x',0)$ is a real number like k, then:

$$D_H\left(\boldsymbol{D}_{\boldsymbol{CK}_{gH}}^{\alpha}x(t),0\right)\leq\frac{1}{\Gamma(2-\alpha)}k(t-t_0)^{1-\alpha}$$

It is clear that, at the point $t=0$, the distance goes to zero, and this completes the proof.

Remark. If the function $x(t)$ is $i-gH$ or $ii-gH$ differentiable on $(t_0,T]$, for $0<\alpha<1$, we have:

- $\boldsymbol{I}_{\boldsymbol{RL}}^{\alpha}\boldsymbol{D}_{\boldsymbol{CK}_{gH}}{}^{\alpha}x(t)=x(t)\ominus_{gH}x(t_0)$
- $\boldsymbol{D}_{\boldsymbol{CK}_{gH}}{}^{\alpha}\boldsymbol{I}_{\boldsymbol{RL}}^{\alpha}x(t)=x(t)$

The first item:

$$\boldsymbol{I}_{\boldsymbol{RL}}^{\alpha}\boldsymbol{D}_{\boldsymbol{CK}_{gH}}^{\alpha}x(t)=\boldsymbol{I}_{\boldsymbol{RL}}^{\alpha}\left(\boldsymbol{I}_{\boldsymbol{RL}}^{(1-\alpha)}\frac{\mathrm{d}}{\mathrm{d}s}x\right)(t)$$

$$=\left(\boldsymbol{I}_{\boldsymbol{RL}}^{1}\frac{\mathrm{d}}{\mathrm{d}s}x\right)(t)=\int_{t_0}^{t}x'(s)\mathrm{d}s=x(t)\ominus_{gH}x(t_0)$$

because in the definition:

$$\boldsymbol{I}_{\boldsymbol{RL}}^{\alpha}x(t)=\frac{1}{\Gamma(\alpha)}\odot\int_{t_0}^{t}(t-s)^{\alpha-1}\odot x(s)\mathrm{d}s$$

If $\alpha=1$ then:

$$\boldsymbol{I}_{\boldsymbol{RL}}^{1}x(t)=\int_{t_0}^{t}x(s)\mathrm{d}s$$

To prove the second item, we have the following relations.

For $x(t_0)$ as a constant fuzzy, we have:

$$\boldsymbol{I}_{\boldsymbol{RL}}^{(1-\alpha)}x(t_0)=\frac{1}{\Gamma(1-\alpha)}\odot\int_{t_0}^{t}(t-s)^{-\alpha}\odot x(t_0)\mathrm{d}s=\frac{(t-t_0)^{1-\alpha}}{\Gamma(2-\alpha)}\odot x(t_0)$$

and if $\alpha:\to 1+\alpha$:

$$\boldsymbol{D}_{\boldsymbol{RL}_{gH}}^{\alpha}x(t_0)=\boldsymbol{I}_{\boldsymbol{RL}}^{-\alpha}y(t)=\frac{(t-t_0)^{-\alpha}}{\Gamma(1-\alpha)}\odot x(t_0)$$

$$\boldsymbol{D}_{\boldsymbol{CK}_{gH}}^{\alpha}x(t)=\boldsymbol{D}_{\boldsymbol{RL}_{gH}}^{\alpha}\left(x(t)\ominus_{gH}x(t_0)\right)=\boldsymbol{D}_{\boldsymbol{RL}_{gH}}^{\alpha}x(t)\ominus_{gH}\frac{(t-t_0)^{-\alpha}}{\Gamma(1-\alpha)}\odot x(t_0)$$

Now by substituting $\boldsymbol{I}_{\boldsymbol{RL}}^{\alpha}x(t)\to x(t)$, we get:

$$\boldsymbol{D}_{\boldsymbol{CK}_{gH}}^{\alpha}\boldsymbol{I}_{\boldsymbol{RL}}^{\alpha}x(t)=\boldsymbol{D}_{\boldsymbol{RL}_{gH}}^{\alpha}\boldsymbol{I}_{\boldsymbol{RL}}^{\alpha}x(t)\ominus_{gH}\frac{(t=t_0)^{-\alpha}}{\Gamma(1-\alpha)}\odot\left(\boldsymbol{I}_{\boldsymbol{RL}}^{\alpha}x\right)(t_0)$$

If we show $(\boldsymbol{I}_{\boldsymbol{RL}}^{\alpha}x)(t_0)=0$, the proof is completed. To do this, we use the distance:

$$D_H\left(\left(\boldsymbol{I}_{\boldsymbol{RL}}^{\alpha}x\right)(t_0),0\right)\leq k\frac{1}{\Gamma(\alpha)}\int_{t_0}^{t}(t-s)^{\alpha-1}\mathrm{d}s=k\frac{(t-t_0)^{\alpha}}{\Gamma(1+\alpha)}$$

where $\sup_{t\in[t_0,T]}D_H(x(t),0)=k$. Then:

$$D_H\left(\left(\boldsymbol{I}_{\boldsymbol{RL}}^{\alpha}x\right)(t_0),0\right)\leq k\frac{(t-t_0)^{\alpha}}{\Gamma(1+\alpha)}\to 0$$

6.4 Fuzzy Fractional Differential Equations—Caputo-Katugampola Derivative

In this section, we are going to cover the fuzzy fractional differential equations that can be defined by each operator, which were defined earlier (Chehlabi & Allahviranloo, 2016; Van Hoa et al., 2019).

6.4.1.1 Definition—Fuzzy Fractional Differential Equations

Consider the following fuzzy fractional differential equation with fuzzy initial value:

$$D^{\alpha}_{CK_{gH}}x(t)=f(t,x(t)),\ x(t_0)=x_0,\ t\in[t_0,T],\ 0<\alpha<1.$$

where $f:[t_0,T]\times\mathbb{F}_R\to\mathbb{F}_R$ is a fuzzy number valued function, $x(t)$ is a continuous fuzzy set valued solution, and ${D_{CK_{gH}}}^{\alpha}$ is the fractional Caputo-Katugampola fractional operator. The first discussion is about the relation between the solution of fractional differential equations and solution of its corresponding fuzzy fractional differential equation. This means the fuzzy solution is the common solution of two fractional operators, differential and integral. In the following remark, we suppose that the fuzzy solution is $i-gH$ differentiable or $ii-gH$ differentiable on $(t_0,T]$.

Remark. Considering the abovementioned assumptions, the continuous fuzzy function $x(t)$ is the solution of:

$$D^{\alpha}_{CK_{gH}}x(t)=f(t,x(t)),\ x(t_0)=x_0,\ t\in[t_0,T],\ 0<\alpha<1$$

if, and only if, $x(t)$ satisfies the following integral equation:

$$x(t)\ominus_{gH}x(t_0)=\frac{1}{\Gamma(\alpha)}\int_{t_0}^{t}(t-s)^{\alpha-1}f(s,x(s))\mathrm{d}s,\ t\in[t_0,T]$$

Before we show the assertion, it should be noted that the function $x(t)$ can be $i-gH$ differentiable (increasing length) or $ii-gH$ differentiable (decreasing length) on $(t_0,T]$ but the fractional integral operator $I^{\alpha,p}_{RL}$ always has increasing length. To prove the remark, first suppose that $x(t)$ is the solution of the differential equation, and moreover, suppose $x(t)\ominus_{gH}x(t_0):=y(t)$. The length of $y(t)$ is increasing and it is $i-gH$ differentiable because if $x(t)$ is $i-gH$ differentiable, then:

$$t_0<t\Longrightarrow x_u(t_0,r)-x_l(t_0,r)<x_u(t,r)-x_l(t,r)$$

then:

$$y_l(t,r)=x_l(t,r)-x_l(t_0,r)<x_u(t,r)-x_u(t_0,r)=y_u(t,r)$$

This means $y(t,r)$ is an interval for any $r\in[0,1]$ and we conclude that it satisfies the type (1) of gH-difference. As shown before:

$$I^{\alpha}_{RL}D^{\alpha,}_{CK_{gH}}x(t)=x(t)\ominus_{gH}x(t_0)$$

and ${D_{CK_{gH}}}^{\alpha}x(t)=f(t,x(t))$, then the following relation is concluded:

$$I^{\alpha}_{RL}f(t,x(t))=x(t)\ominus_{gH}x(t_0)$$

On the other hand, based on the definition of the fractional integral:

$$I^{\alpha}_{RL}x(t)=\frac{1}{\Gamma(\alpha)}\odot\int_{t_0}^{t}(t-s)^{\alpha-1}\odot x(s)\mathrm{d}s$$

then:

$$\boldsymbol{I}_{RL}^{\alpha} f(t, x(t)) = \frac{1}{\Gamma(\alpha)} \odot \int_{t_0}^{t} (t-s)^{\alpha-1} \odot f(s, x(s)) \mathrm{d}s$$

The necessary condition is thus proved. Next, the sufficient condition will be proved. Suppose we have:

$$x(t) \ominus_{gH} x(t_0) = \frac{1}{\Gamma(\alpha)} \int_{t_0}^{t} (t-s)^{\alpha-1} f(s, x(s)) \mathrm{d}s$$

Effecting the fractional derivative $\boldsymbol{D}_{\boldsymbol{RL}_{gH}}{}^{\alpha}$ to both sides:

$$\boldsymbol{D}_{\boldsymbol{RL}_{gH}}^{\alpha} \left(x(t) \ominus_{gH} x(t_0) \right) = \boldsymbol{D}_{\boldsymbol{RL}_{gH}}^{\alpha} \frac{1}{\Gamma(\alpha)} \int_{t_0}^{t} (t-s)^{\alpha-1} f(s, x(s)) \mathrm{d}s$$

thus:

$$\boldsymbol{D}_{\boldsymbol{RL}_{gH}}^{\alpha} \left(x(t) \ominus_{gH} x(t_0) \right) = \boldsymbol{D}_{\boldsymbol{RL}_{gH}}^{\alpha} \boldsymbol{I}_{RL}^{\alpha} f(t, x(t)) = f(t, x(t))$$

therefore:

$$\boldsymbol{D}_{\boldsymbol{RL}_{gH}}^{\alpha} \left(x(t) \ominus_{gH} x(t_0) \right) = f(t, x(t))$$

Since we had:

$$\boldsymbol{D}_{\boldsymbol{CK}_{gH}}^{\alpha} x(t) = \boldsymbol{D}_{\boldsymbol{RL}_{gH}}^{\alpha} \left(x(t) \ominus_{gH} x(t_0) \right)$$

thus:

$$\boldsymbol{D}_{\boldsymbol{CK}_{gH}}^{\alpha} x(t) = f(t, x(t))$$

and the proof is completed.

Note. Based on the definition of the *gH*-difference in the integral equation:

$$x(t) \ominus_{gH} x(t_0) = \frac{1}{\Gamma(\alpha)} \int_{t_0}^{t} (t-s)^{\alpha-1} f(s, x(s)) \mathrm{d}s, \quad t \in [t_0, T]$$

- In the case where the *gH*-difference is $i-gH$ difference:

$$x(t) = x(t_0) \oplus \frac{1}{\Gamma(\alpha)} \int_{t_0}^{t} (t-s)^{\alpha-1} f(s, x(s)) \mathrm{d}s, \quad t \in [t_0, T]$$

- In the case where the *gH*-difference is $ii-gH$ difference:

$$x(t) = x(t_0) \ominus_H (-1) \frac{1}{\Gamma(\alpha)} \int_{t_0}^{t} (t-s)^{\alpha-1} f(s, x(s)) \mathrm{d}s, \quad t \in [t_0, T]$$

Example. Consider the following fuzzy initial value problem:

$$D^{\frac{1}{2}}_{CK_{gH}}x(t)=\left(\sqrt{t},\frac{1}{\sqrt{t}},\frac{2}{\sqrt{t}}\right)=f(t),\ x(0)=(-2,0,1),\ t\in(0,1]$$

Now using the fractional derivative operator on both sides:

$$I^{\frac{1}{2}}_{RL}D^{\frac{1}{2}}_{CK_{gH}}x(t)=x(t)\ominus_{gH}x(t_0)$$

with:

$$x(t)\ominus_{gH}x(t_0)=I^{\frac{1}{2}}_{RL}f(t)=\frac{1}{\Gamma(\alpha)}\int_{t_0}^{t}(t-s)^{\alpha-1}f(s,x(s))\mathrm{d}s,\ t\in(0,1]$$

and we have:

$$I^{\frac{1}{2}}_{RL}f(t)=\frac{1}{\Gamma\left(\frac{1}{2}\right)}\odot\int_0^t(t-s)^{-\frac{1}{2}}\odot\left(\sqrt{s},\frac{1}{\sqrt{s}},\frac{2}{\sqrt{s}}\right)\mathrm{d}s=\left(\frac{\sqrt{\pi}}{2}t,\sqrt{\pi},2\sqrt{\pi}\right)$$

then:

$$x(t)\ominus_{gH}x(t_0)=\left(\frac{\sqrt{\pi}}{2}t,\sqrt{\pi},2\sqrt{\pi}\right)$$

By substituting the initial value:

$$x(t)\ominus_{gH}(-2,0,1)=\left(\frac{\sqrt{\pi}}{2}t,\sqrt{\pi},2\sqrt{\pi}\right)$$

The length of $\left(\frac{\sqrt{\pi}}{2}t,\sqrt{\pi},2\sqrt{\pi}\right)$ is $(1-r)\sqrt{\pi}(2-\frac{t}{2}),t\in(0,1],r\in[0,1]$. The length function is decreasing because:

$$\frac{\mathrm{d}}{\mathrm{d}t}\left[(1-r)\sqrt{\pi}\left(2-\frac{t}{2}\right)\right]<0,\ r\in[0,1]$$

In the case of $i-gH$ difference:

$$x(t)=(-2,0,1)\oplus\left(\frac{\sqrt{\pi}}{2}t,\sqrt{\pi},2\sqrt{\pi}\right)=\left(-2+\frac{\sqrt{\pi}}{2}t,\sqrt{\pi},1+2\sqrt{\pi}\right)$$

The level-wise form of the solution is:

$$x_l(t,r)=\sqrt{\pi}+\left(\sqrt{\pi}+2-\frac{\sqrt{\pi}}{2}t\right)(r-1),\ x_u(t,r)=\sqrt{\pi}+\left(1+\sqrt{\pi}\right)(1-r)$$

and:

$$\mathrm{length}(x(t))=\left(3+2\sqrt{\pi}-\frac{\sqrt{\pi}}{2}t\right)(1-r),\ \frac{\mathrm{d}}{\mathrm{d}t}\left[3+2\sqrt{\pi}-\frac{\sqrt{\pi}}{2}t\right]<0,\ r\in[0,1]$$

It can be seen from Figs. 6.1 and 6.2 that both $x(t)$ and $x(t)\ominus_{gH}x_0$ have decreasing length and the solution is as follows:

$$x(t) = x_0 \oplus \boldsymbol{I}_{RL}^{\frac{1}{2}} f(t) = \left(-2 + \frac{\sqrt{\pi}}{2}t, \sqrt{\pi}, 1 + 2\sqrt{\pi}\right)$$

The figures show that the solution is a fuzzy number at each point, like $t=1$. Checking the function will provide the solution to the problem:

$$\boldsymbol{D}_{CK_{gH}}^{\alpha} x(t) = \frac{1}{\Gamma\left(\frac{1}{2}\right)} \int_0^t (t-s)^{-\frac{1}{2}} \odot \left(-2 + \frac{\sqrt{\pi}}{2}s, \sqrt{\pi}, 1 + 2\sqrt{\pi}\right)' \mathrm{d}s$$

$$= \left(\frac{\frac{2}{3}\sqrt{\pi}t^{\frac{3}{2}} - 4\sqrt{t}}{\sqrt{\pi}}, 2\sqrt{t}, \frac{2(1+2\sqrt{\pi})\sqrt{t}}{\sqrt{\pi}}\right) \neq \left(\sqrt{t}, \frac{1}{\sqrt{t}}, \frac{2}{\sqrt{t}}\right)$$

Despite the fuzzy function $x(t)$ is a fuzzy number valued function but it is not the solution of the fuzzy fractional differential equation. This is because the length of $x(t)\ominus_{gH}x(t_0)$ is not increasing.

Example. Consider the following fuzzy initial value problem:

$$\boldsymbol{D}_{CK_{gH}}^{\frac{1}{2}} x(t) = \sqrt{\pi}\left(-t^2, 0, 2t - t^2\right) = f(t), \ \ x(0) = (-2, 0, 2), \ \ t \in (0, 1],$$

Now, using the fractional derivative operator on both sides:

$$\boldsymbol{I}_{RL}^{\frac{1}{2}} \boldsymbol{D}_{CK_{gH}}^{\frac{1}{2}} x(t) = x(t) \ominus_{gH} x(t_0)$$

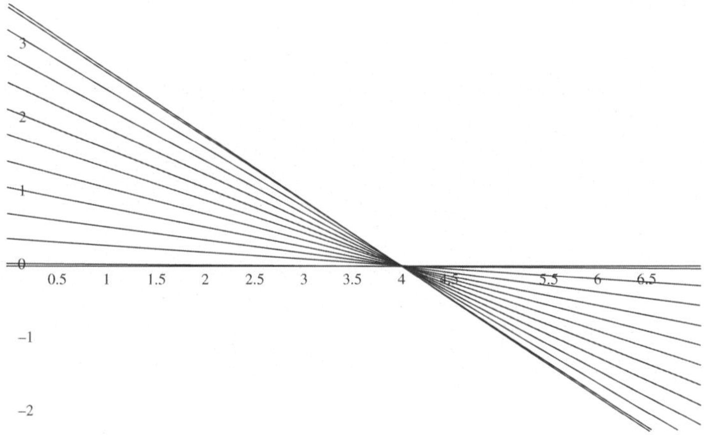

Fig. 6.1 The length of $x(t)\ominus_{gH}x(t_0)$ is decreasing.

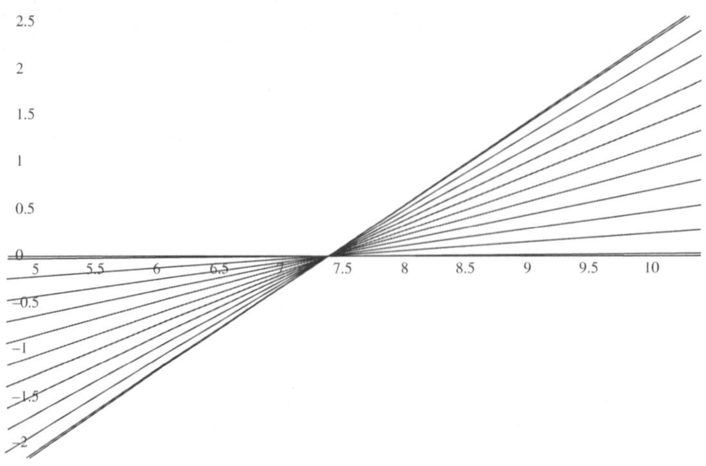

Fig. 6.2 Length of $x(t)$ is decreasing.

with:

$$x(t) \ominus_{gH} x(t_0) = I_{RL}^{\frac{1}{2}} f(t) = \frac{1}{\Gamma(\alpha)} \int_{t_0}^{t} (t-s)^{\alpha-1} f(s, x(s)) \mathrm{d}s, \quad t \in (0, 1]$$

$$I_{RL}^{\frac{1}{2}} f(t) = \frac{1}{\Gamma\left(\frac{1}{2}\right)} \odot \int_0^t (t-s)^{-\frac{1}{2}} \odot \sqrt{\pi}\left(-s^2, 0, 2s - s^2\right) \mathrm{d}s$$

$$= \left(-\frac{16}{15} t^{\frac{5}{2}}, 0, \frac{8}{3} t^{\frac{3}{2}} - \frac{16}{15} t^{\frac{5}{2}}\right)$$

then (Fig. 6.3):

$$x(t) \ominus_{gH} x(t_0) = \left(-\frac{16}{15} t^{\frac{5}{2}}, 0, \frac{8}{3} t^{\frac{3}{2}} - \frac{16}{15} t^{\frac{5}{2}}\right)$$

Now, the two types of the solution we should have are:

- $i-gH$ (solution) (Fig. 6.4)

$$x_{i-gH}(t) = (-2, 0, 2) \oplus \left(-\frac{16}{15} t^{\frac{5}{2}}, 0, \frac{8}{3} t^{\frac{3}{2}} - \frac{16}{15} t^{\frac{5}{2}}\right)$$

$$= \left(-2 - \frac{16}{15} t^{\frac{5}{2}}, 0, \frac{8}{3} t^{\frac{3}{2}} - \frac{16}{15} t^{\frac{5}{2}} + 2\right)$$

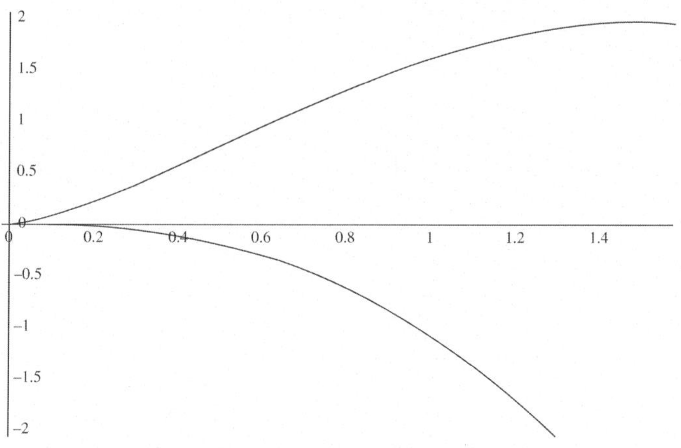

Fig. 6.3 Length of $x(t)\ominus_{gH}x(t_0)$ is increasing.

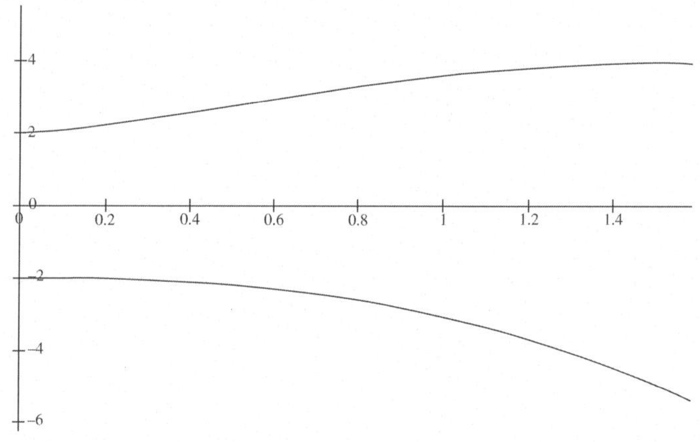

Fig. 6.4 Length of $x_{i-gH}(t)$ is increasing.

- $ii-gH$ (solution) (Fig. 6.5)

$$x_{ii-gH}(t) = (-2,0,2)\ominus_H(-1)\left(-\frac{16}{15}t^{\frac{5}{2}}, 0, \frac{8}{3}t^{\frac{3}{2}}-\frac{16}{15}t^{\frac{5}{2}}\right)$$

$$= \left(\frac{8}{3}t^{\frac{3}{2}}-\frac{16}{15}t^{\frac{5}{2}}-2, 0, 2-\frac{16}{15}t^{\frac{5}{2}}\right)$$

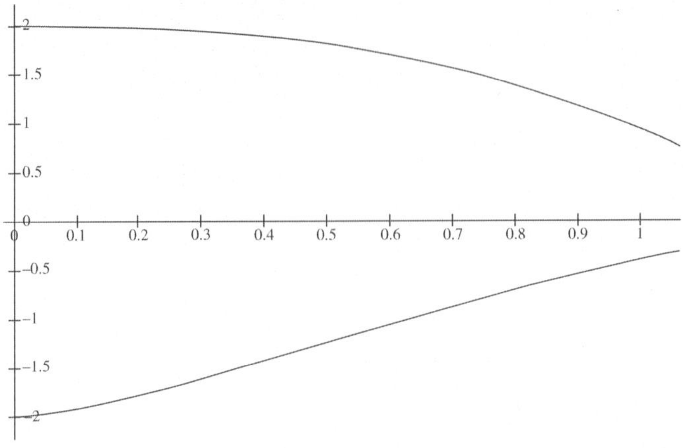

Fig. 6.5 Length of $x_{ii-gH}(t)$ is decreasing.

To check the solutions:

$$D^{\frac{1}{2}}_{CK_{gH}} x_{i-gH}(t) = D^{\frac{1}{2}}_{CK_{gH}}\left(-2-\frac{16}{15}t^{\frac{5}{2}}, 0, \frac{8}{3}t^{\frac{3}{2}}-\frac{16}{15}t^{\frac{5}{2}}+2\right) =$$

$$= \left(D^{\frac{1}{2}}_{CK}\left(-2-\frac{16}{15}t^{\frac{5}{2}}\right), 0, D^{\frac{1}{2}}_{CK}\left(\frac{8}{3}t^{\frac{3}{2}}-\frac{16}{15}t^{\frac{5}{2}}+2\right)\right)$$

$$= \left(\frac{-1}{\Gamma\left(\frac{1}{2}\right)}\int_0^t \frac{8s^{\frac{3}{2}}}{3\sqrt{t-s}}ds, 0, \frac{1}{\Gamma\left(\frac{1}{2}\right)}\int_0^t \frac{4s^{\frac{1}{2}}-\frac{8}{3}s^{\frac{3}{2}}}{\sqrt{t-s}}ds\right)$$

$$= \sqrt{\pi}\left(-t^2, 0, 2t-t^2\right)$$

Then the $i-gH$ solution satisfies the fractional problem. The same process can be carried out for checking the $ii-gH$ solution:

$$D^{\frac{1}{2}}_{CK_{gH}} x_{ii-gH}(t) = D^{\frac{1}{2}}_{CK_{gH}}\left(\frac{8}{3}t^{\frac{3}{2}}-\frac{16}{15}t^{\frac{5}{2}}-2, 0, 2-\frac{16}{15}t^{\frac{5}{2}}\right) =$$

$$= \left(D^{\frac{1}{2}}_{CK}\left(-2-\frac{16}{15}t^{\frac{5}{2}}\right), 0, D^{\frac{1}{2}}_{CK}\left(\frac{8}{3}t^{\frac{3}{2}}-\frac{16}{15}t^{\frac{5}{2}}+2\right)\right)$$

$$= \sqrt{\pi}\left(-t^2, 0, 2t-t^2\right)$$

Both are $i-gH$ and $ii-gH$ solutions of the problem because the length of $x(t)\ominus_{gH}x(t_0)$ is increasing.

6.4.1.2 Existence and Uniqueness of the Solution

In this section, the existence and uniqueness of the results of the solutions to fuzzy fractional differential equations by using an idea of successive approximations under generalized Lipschitz condition of the right-hand side are investigated. Furthermore, the formula of solution to the linear fuzzy Caputo-Katugampola fractional differential equation is given. Since the real intervals in the level-wise form are used for any arbitrary level, so to reach the aims, we should consider the following theorem in the real case of Caputo fractional derivative (Van Hoa et al., 2019).

6.4.1.3 Theorem—Existence and Uniqueness in Real Fractional Differential Equation

Consider the initial value problem as follows:

$$\boldsymbol{D}_{CK}^{\alpha}u(t)=g(t,u(t)),\ \ u(t_0)=u_0=0,\ \ t\in[t_0,T]$$

Let $\eta>0$ be a given constant and $B(u_0,\eta)=\{u\in R;\ |u-u_0|\le\eta\}$ is a ball around u_0 with radius η. Also assume a real valued function $g:[t_0,T]\times[0,\eta]\to R^{+}$ satisfies the following conditions:

1. $g\in C([t_0,T]\times[0,\eta],R^{+}),\ g(t,0)\equiv 0,\ \exists M_g\ge 0,\ 0\le g(t,u)\le M_g,$ for all $(t,u)\in[t_0,T]\times[0,\eta]$.
2. $g(t,u)$ is a nondecreasing function with respect to x for any $t\in[t_0,T]$.

Then the mentioned fractional problem has at least one solution on $[t_0,T]$ and $u(t)\in B(u_0,\eta)$.

Proof. The solution of the mentioned above fractional differential equation is the solution of following fractional integral equation:

$$u(t)=\frac{1}{\Gamma(\alpha)}\int_{t_0}^{t}(t-s)^{\alpha-1}g(s,u(s))\mathrm{d}s$$

The following successive method for approximation of the solution of fractional differential equation is defined:

$$u_{n+1}(t)=\frac{1}{\Gamma(\alpha)}\int_{t_0}^{t}(t-s)^{\alpha-1}g(s,u_n(s))\mathrm{d}s,\ \ t\in[t^*,T^*]$$

such that:

$$u_0(t)=\frac{M_g(t-a)^{\alpha}}{\Gamma(\alpha+1)},\ \ t_0<t\le\left(\frac{\eta\Gamma(\alpha+1)}{M_g}\right)^{\frac{1}{\alpha}}+a,\ \ T^*=\min\{t^*,T\}$$

For $n=0$ and $t\in[t_0,T^{*]}$ we have:

$$u_1(t) = \frac{1}{\Gamma(\alpha)} \int_{t_0}^{t} (t-s)^{\alpha-1} g(s, u_0(s)) ds \leq \frac{M_g (t-a)^{\alpha}}{\Gamma(\alpha+1)} = u_0(t) \leq \eta,$$

so we found:

$$u_1(t) \leq u_0(t)$$

for $n = 1$ and $t \in [t_0, T^*]$:

$$u_2(t) = \frac{1}{\Gamma(\alpha)} \int_{t_0}^{t} (t-s)^{\alpha-1} g(s, u_1(s)) ds \leq \frac{M_g (t-a)^{\alpha}}{\Gamma(\alpha+1)} = u_0(t) \leq \eta,$$

Since g is a nondecreasing function in u and $u_1(t) \leq u_0(t)$, then $g(s, u_1(s)) \leq g(s, u_0(s))$; thus, $u_2(t) \leq u_1(t)$. Now we have:

$$u_2(t) \leq u_1(t) \leq u_0(t)$$

Proceeding recursively, we will have:

$$u_{n+1}(t) \leq u_n(t) \leq \cdots \leq u_1(t) \leq u_0(t) \leq \eta, \ t \in [t_0, T^*]$$

It follows that the sequence $\{u_n(t)\}_n$ is uniformly bounded for $n \geq 0$. On the other hand:

$$\left| D_{CK}^{\alpha} u_n(t) \right| = |g(t, u_n(t))| = g(t, u_n(t)) \leq M_g$$

Then, in the interval $[t_0, T^*]$, we can use the mean value theorem for t', $t_2 \in [t_0, T^*]$, $n \geq 0$:

$$|u_n(t_2) - u_n(t_1)| = \frac{2M_g (t-a)^{\alpha}}{\Gamma(\alpha+1)} \leq \frac{2M_g (t_2 - t_1)^{\alpha}}{\Gamma(\alpha+1)} \tau^{\alpha}, \ \tau \in [t_1, t_2] \subseteq [t_0, T^*]$$

Therefore, the sequence $\{u_n(t)\}_n$ is equicontinuous, and then:

$$\forall \epsilon > 0, \ \exists \delta = \left(\frac{\epsilon \Gamma(\alpha+1) \tau^{\alpha}}{2M_g} \right)^{\frac{1}{\alpha}} > 0, \ (|t_2 - t_1| < \delta \Longrightarrow |u_n(t_2) - u_n(t_1)| < \epsilon)$$

Hence, by the Arzela-Ascoli Theorem and the monotonicity of the sequence $\{u_n(t)\}_{n}$, we conclude the convergency of the sequence and $\lim_{n \to \infty} u_n(t) = u(t), t \in [t_0, T^*]$.

6.4.1.4 Theorem—Existence and Uniqueness in Fuzzy Fractional Differential Equation

Consider the fuzzy initial value problem as follows:

$$D_{CK_{gH}}^{\alpha} x(t) = f(t, x(t)), \ x(t_0) = x_0, \ t \in [t_0, T], \ 0 < \alpha < 1$$

Let $\eta > 0$ be a given constant and $B(x_0, \eta) = \{x \in R; |x - x_0| \leq \eta\}$ is a ball around x_0 with radius η. Also assume a fuzzy number valued function $f : [t_0, T] \times [0, \eta] \to \mathbb{F}_R$ satisfies the following conditions:

i. $f \in C([t_0, T] \times [0, \eta], \mathbb{F}_R)$, $\exists M_g \geq 0$, $D_H(g(t,x), 0) \leq M_g$, for all $(t,x) \in [t_0, T] \times B(x_0, \eta)$.

ii. For any $z, w \in B(x_0, \eta)$, $D_H(f(t,z), f(t,w)) \leq g(t, D_H(z,w))$ where $g \in C([t_0, T] \times [0, \eta], R^+)$ in the problem:

$$\boldsymbol{D}^{\alpha}_{\boldsymbol{CK}} x(t) = g(t, x(t)), \ \ x(t_0) = x_0 = 0, \ \ t \in [t_0, T]$$

has only the solution $x(t) \equiv 0$ on $[t_0, T]$ (the previous theorem of existence and uniqueness in real case).

Then the following successive approximations given by $x_0(t) = x_0$:

$$x_n(t) \ominus_{gH} x_0 = \frac{1}{\Gamma(\alpha)} \int_{t_0}^{t} (t-s)^{\alpha-1} \odot f(s, x_{n-1}(s)) \mathrm{d}s, \ \ n = 1, 2, \ldots,$$

converge to a unique solution of:

$$\boldsymbol{D}^{\alpha}_{\boldsymbol{CK_{gH}}} x(t) = f(t, x(t)), \ \ x(t_0) = x_0, \ \ 0 < \alpha < 1$$

on $t \in [t_0, T^*]$, $T^* \in (t0, T]$, provided that $x_n(t) \ominus_{gH} x_0$ does have increasing length.

Proof. Let us consider the point t^*:

$$t_0 < t^* \leq \left(\frac{\eta \Gamma(\alpha+1)}{M}\right)^{\frac{1}{\alpha}} + a, \ \ M = \max\{M_f, M_g\}, \ \ T^* = \min\{t^*, T\}$$

Now consider the sequence of fuzzy continuous functions $\{x_n(t)\}_n$, $x_0(t) = x_0$, $t \in [t_0, T^*]$:

$$x_n(t) \ominus_{gH} x_0 = \frac{1}{\Gamma(\alpha)} \int_{t_0}^{t} (t-s)^{\alpha-1} \odot f(s, x_{n-1}(s)) \mathrm{d}s, \ \ n = 1, 2, \ldots,$$

First, we prove the $x_n(t) \in C([t_0, T^*], B(x^{\circ}, \eta))$. To this end, assume t_1, $t_2 \in [t_0, T^*]$ and $t^{1} < t_2$:

$$D_H\left(x_n(t_1) \ominus_{gH} x_0, x_n(t_2) \ominus_{gH} x_0\right)$$

$$\leq \frac{1}{\Gamma(\alpha)} \int_{t_0}^{t_1} \left[(t_1 - s)^{\alpha-1} - (t_2 - s)^{\alpha-1}\right] D_H(f(s, x_n(s)), 0) \mathrm{d}s$$

$$+ \frac{1}{\Gamma(\alpha)} \int_{t_1}^{t_2} \left[(t_2 - s)^{\alpha-1}\right] D_H(f(s, x_n(s)), 0) \mathrm{d}s$$

and:

$$\frac{1}{\Gamma(\alpha)}\int_{t_1}^{t_2}\left[(t_2-s)^{\alpha-1}\right]\mathrm{d}s=\frac{1}{\Gamma(\alpha+1)}(t_2-t_1)^{\alpha}$$

$$\frac{1}{\Gamma(\alpha)}\int_{t_0}^{t_1}\left[(t_1-s)^{\alpha-1}-(t_2-s)^{\alpha-1}\right]\mathrm{d}s=$$

$$=\frac{1}{\Gamma(\alpha+1)}[(t_1-t_0)^{\alpha}-(t_2-t_1)^{\alpha}]$$

and:

$$D_H(f(s,x_n(s)),0)\le M_f, D_H\left(x_n(t_1)\ominus_{gH}x_0, x_n(t_2)\ominus_{gH}x_0\right)=D_H(x_n(t_1),x_n(t_2))$$

hence:

$$D_H(x_n(t_1),x_n(t_2))\le\frac{M_f}{\Gamma(\alpha+1)}[(t_2-t_1)^{\alpha}+(t_1-t_0)^{\alpha}+(t_2-t_1)^{\alpha}]$$

Finally:

$$D_H(x_n(t_1),x_n(t_2))\le\frac{2M_f}{\Gamma(\alpha+1)}(t_2-t_1)^{\alpha}\le\eta$$

This means, if $t_2\to t_1$ then $D_H(x_n(t_1),x_n(t_2))\to 0$ and follows the function $x_n(t)$ is continuous on $[t_0,T^*]$. In addition, it follows for $n\ge 1$, $t\in[t^o,T^*]$:

$$x_n(t)\in B(x_0,\eta)\Leftrightarrow x_n(t)\ominus_{gH}x_0\in B(x_0,\eta)$$

Now, if $x_{n-1}(t)\in B(x_0,\eta)$:

$$D_H\left(x_n(t)\ominus_{gH}x_0,0\right)\le\frac{1}{\Gamma(\alpha)}\int_{t_0}^{t}(t-s)^{\alpha-1}D_H(f(s,x_{n-1}(s)),0)\mathrm{d}s$$

$$\le\frac{M_f}{\Gamma(\alpha+1)}(t-t_0)^{\alpha}\le\eta$$

In conclusion, the fuzzy function $x_n(t)\in B(x_0,\eta)$ for all $n\ge 1$ and all $t\in[t_0,T^*]$. Now our next step is proving the convergence, for $x_n(t)$, $x(t)\in C([t_0,T^*],B(x^o,\eta))$:

$$\lim_{n\to 0}x_n(t)=x(t)$$

To this purpose, we need some relations:

$$D_H\left(x_{n+1}(t)\ominus_{gH}x_0, x_n(t)\ominus_{gH}x_0\right)$$

$$\le\frac{1}{\Gamma(\alpha)}\int_{t_0}^{t}(t-s)^{\alpha-1}D_H(f(s,x_n(s)),f(s,x_{n-1}(s))\mathrm{d}s$$

$$\leq \frac{1}{\Gamma(\alpha)} \int_{t_0}^{t} (t-s)^{\alpha-1} D_H \left(g(x_n(s), x_{n-1}(s)) \mathrm{d}s \leq u_n(t) \leq \frac{M_g (t-a)^{\alpha}}{\Gamma(\alpha+1)} \leq \eta \right.$$

since:

$$\boldsymbol{D}^{\alpha}_{\boldsymbol{CK_{gH}}} x(t) = x(t) \ominus_{gH} x_0$$

Thus, based on the properties of the distance:

$$D_H \left(D^{\alpha}_{CK_{gH}} x_{n+1}(t), D^{\alpha}_{CK_{gH}} x_n(t) \right) \leq D_H (f(t, x_n(t)), f(t, x_{n-1}(t)))$$

$$\leq g(D_H(x_n(t), x_{n-1}(t))) \leq g(t, u_{n-1}(t))$$

Finally:

$$D_H \left(D^{\alpha}_{CK_{gH}} x_{n+1}(t), D^{\alpha}_{CK_{gH}} x_n(t) \right) \leq g(t, u_{n-1}(t))$$

Continuing:

$$D_H \left(\boldsymbol{D}^{\alpha}_{\boldsymbol{CK_{gH}}} x_n(t), \boldsymbol{D}^{\alpha}_{\boldsymbol{CK_{gH}}} x_{n-1}(t) \right) \leq g(t, u_{n-2}(t))$$

then:

$$D_H \left(\boldsymbol{D}^{\alpha}_{\boldsymbol{CK_{gH}}} x_{n+1}(t), \boldsymbol{D}^{\alpha}_{\boldsymbol{CK_{gH}}} x_{n-1}(t) \right)$$

$$\leq D_H \left(\boldsymbol{D}^{\alpha}_{\boldsymbol{CK_{gH}}} x_{n+1}(t), \boldsymbol{D}^{\alpha}_{\boldsymbol{CK_{gH}}} x_n(t) \right) + D_H \left(\boldsymbol{D}^{\alpha}_{\boldsymbol{CK_{gH}}} x_n(t), \boldsymbol{D}^{\alpha}_{\boldsymbol{CK_{gH}}} x_{n-1}(t) \right)$$

$$\leq g(t, u_{n-1}(t)) + g(t, u_{n-2}(t))$$

$$\vdots$$

$$D_H \left(\boldsymbol{D}^{\alpha}_{\boldsymbol{CK_{gH}}} x_n(t), \boldsymbol{D}^{\alpha}_{\boldsymbol{CK_{gH}}} x_1(t) \right) \leq \sum_{i=0}^{n-1} g(t, u_i(t)) \to 0$$

hence:

$$D_H \left(x_n(t) \ominus_{gH} x_0, x_1(t) \ominus_{gH} x_0 \right) \leq \sum_{i=0}^{n-1} g(t, u_i(t)) \to 0$$

and:

$$D_H(x_n(t), x_1(t)) \leq \sum_{i=0}^{n-1} g(t, u_i(t)) \to 0$$

In general, assume for $m \geq n$:

$$D_H(x_m(t), x_n(t)) \to 0$$

then using the definition of the Cauchy sequence the sequence $\{x_n(t)\}_n \to x(t)$.

Uniqueness. To show this, let us suppose that $y(t)$ is another solution of the fuzzy fractional differential equation, and assume:

$$D_H(x(t), y(t)) = k(t), D_{CK}^{\alpha} D_H(x(t), y(t)) = D_{CK}^{\alpha} k(t) \leq D_H\left(D_{CK}^{\alpha} x(t), D_{CK}^{\alpha} y(t)\right)$$
$$\leq D_H(f(t, x(t)), f(t, y(t))) \leq g(t, k(t))$$

Finally, we have:

$$D_{CK}^{\alpha} k(t) \leq g(t, k(t))$$

The only solution (because of $\leq$, the maximal solution) is $k(t) \equiv 0$.

Remark. In conclusion, if the fuzzy function $f : [t_0, T] \times \mathbb{F}_R \to \mathbb{F}_R$ in the following fuzzy fractional initial value problem:

$$D_{CK_{gH}}^{\alpha} x(t) = f(t, x(t)), \quad x(t_0) = x_0, \quad t \in [t_0, T] \; 0 < \alpha < 1$$

satisfies in the Lipchitz condition:

$$D_H(f(t, x(t)), f(t, y(t))) \leq L D_H(x(t), y(t)), \quad D_H(f(t, x(t)), 0) \leq M_f$$

then the following successive approximations converge uniformly to the unique solution of the problem on $[t_0, T]$, subject to $x_n(t) \ominus_{gH} x_0$ does have increasing length:

$$x_n(t) \ominus_{gH} x_0 = \frac{1}{\Gamma(\alpha)} \int_{t_0}^{t} (t-s)^{\alpha-1} \odot f(s, x_{n-1}(s)) ds, \quad n = 1, 2, \ldots,$$

Example. Consider:

$$D_{CK_{gH}}^{\alpha} x(t) = \lambda \odot x(t) \oplus h(t), \quad x(t_0) = x_0, \quad \lambda \in R, \quad t \in (t_0, T]$$

such that $x(t), h(t) \in C((t_0, T], \mathbb{F}_R)$. Since $I_{RL}^{\alpha} D_{CK_{gH}}{}^{\alpha} x(t) = x(t) \ominus_{gH} x(t_0)$ then:

$$x(t) \ominus_{gH} x(t_0) = \lambda I_{RL}^{\alpha} x(t) \oplus I_{RL}^{\alpha} h(t)$$

If we consider the $\lambda \geq 0$ then $\lambda I_{RL}^{\alpha} x(t) \oplus I_{RL}^{\alpha} h(t)$ has increasing length because $x(t)$ and $h(t)$ are two fuzzy number valued functions. Now we can use the successive approximation method:

$$x_n(t) \ominus_{gH} x(t_0) = \lambda I_{RL}^{\alpha} x_{n-1}(t) \oplus I_{RL}^{\alpha} h(t), \quad n = 1, 2, \ldots,$$

if $n = 1$.

Let us consider $\lambda \geq 0$ and x is $i - gH$ differentiable (increasing length):

$$x_1(t) \ominus_{gH} x(t_0) = x_0 \odot \frac{\lambda (t - t_0)^{\alpha}}{\Gamma(\alpha + 1)} \oplus I_{RL}^{\alpha} h(t),$$

Let us consider $\lambda < 0$ and x is $ii - gH$ differentiable (decreasing length):

$$(-1)\left(x(t_0)\ominus_{gH}x_1(t)\right)=x_0\odot\frac{\lambda(t-t_0)^{\alpha}}{\Gamma(\alpha+1)}\oplus \boldsymbol{I}_{RL}^{\alpha}h(t),$$

if $n=2$.

Let us consider $\lambda\geq 0$ and x is $i-gH$ differentiable (increasing length):

$$x_2(t)\ominus_{gH}x(t_0)=$$

$$=x_0\odot\left[\frac{\lambda(t-t_0)^{\alpha}}{\Gamma(\alpha+1)}+\frac{\lambda(t-t_0)^{2\alpha}}{\Gamma(2\alpha+1)}\right]\oplus \boldsymbol{I}_{RL}^{\alpha}h(t)\oplus \boldsymbol{I}_{RL}^{2\alpha}h(t),$$

Let us consider $\lambda<0$ and x is $ii-gH$ differentiable (decreasing length):

$$(-1)\left(x(t_0)\ominus_{gH}x_2(t)\right)=$$

$$=x_0\odot\left[\frac{\lambda(t-t_0)^{\alpha}}{\Gamma(\alpha+1)}+\frac{\lambda(t-t_0)^{2\alpha}}{\Gamma(2\alpha+1)}\right]\oplus \boldsymbol{I}_{RL}^{\alpha}h(t)\oplus \boldsymbol{I}_{RL}^{2\alpha}h(t),$$

If it is proceeding to more $n\rightarrow\infty$:

$$x_n(t)\ominus_{gH}x(t)=$$

$$=x_0\odot\sum_{i=1}^{\infty}\frac{\lambda^i(t-t_0)^{i\alpha}}{\Gamma(i\alpha+1)}\oplus\int_{t_0}^{t}\sum_{i=1}^{\infty}\frac{\lambda^{i-1}(t-s)^{i\alpha-1}}{\Gamma(i\alpha)}\odot h(s)\mathrm{d}s$$

$$=x_0\odot\sum_{i=1}^{\infty}\frac{\lambda^i(t-t_0)^{i\alpha}}{\Gamma(i\alpha+1)}\oplus\int_{t_0}^{t}\sum_{i=0}^{\infty}\frac{\lambda^{i}(t-s)^{i\alpha+(\alpha-1)}}{\Gamma(i\alpha+\alpha)}\odot h(s)\mathrm{d}s$$

$$=x_0\odot\sum_{i=1}^{\infty}\frac{\lambda^i(t-t_0)^{i\alpha}}{\Gamma(i\alpha+1)}\oplus\int_{t_0}^{t}(t-s)^{\alpha-1}\sum_{i=0}^{\infty}\frac{\lambda^{i}(t-s)^{i\alpha}}{\Gamma(i\alpha+\alpha)}\odot h(s)\mathrm{d}s$$

Let us consider $\lambda\geq 0$ and x is $i-gH$ differentiable (increasing length):

$$x(t)=x_0E_{\alpha,1}(\lambda(t-t_0)^{\alpha})\oplus\int_{t_0}^{t}(t-s)^{\alpha-1}E_{\alpha,\alpha}(\lambda(t-s)^{\alpha})\odot h(s)\mathrm{d}s$$

Let us consider $\lambda<0$ and x is $ii-gH$ differentiable (decreasing length):

$$x(t)=x_0E_{\alpha,1}(\lambda(t-t_0)^{\alpha})\ominus_H(-1)\int_{t_0}^{t}(t-s)^{\alpha-1}E_{\alpha,\alpha}(\lambda(t-s)^{\alpha})\odot h(s)\mathrm{d}s$$

such that the following function is called the Mittag-Leffler function:

$$E_{\alpha,\beta}(t)=\sum_{i=0}^{\infty}\frac{t^i}{\Gamma(i\alpha+\beta)},\quad \alpha>0,\ \beta>0$$

6.4.1.5 *Some Properties of the Mittag-Leffler Function*

The basic Mittag-Leffler function is defined as follows:

$$E_\alpha(t) = \sum_{i=0}^{\infty} \frac{t^i}{\Gamma(i\alpha+1)}, \quad \alpha>0$$

If $\alpha=1$:

$$E_1(t) = \sum_{i=0}^{\infty} \frac{t^i}{\Gamma(i+1)} = \sum_{i=1}^{\infty} \frac{t^i}{i!} = e^t$$

Hence $E_\alpha(t)$ is a generalization of exponential series. One generalization of $E_\alpha(t)$ as a two-parameter generalization of is $E_\alpha(t)$ is:

$$E_{\alpha,\beta}(t) = \sum_{i=0}^{\infty} \frac{t^i}{\Gamma(i\alpha+\beta)}, \quad \alpha>0, \ \beta>0$$

A three-parameter generalization of $E_\alpha(t)$ is denoted by $E^{\gamma}_{\alpha,\beta}(t)$ and is defined as:

$$E^{\gamma}_{\alpha,\beta}(t) = \sum_{i=0}^{\infty} \frac{(\gamma)_i}{i!\Gamma(i\alpha+\beta)}, \quad \alpha>0, \ \beta>0$$

where $(\gamma)_i$ is the Pochhammer symbol standing for:

$$(\gamma)_i = \gamma(\gamma+1)(\gamma+2)\ldots(\gamma+i-1), \ (\gamma)_0=1, \ \gamma\neq0$$

Here, there is no other condition on $(\gamma)_i$, and γ could be a negative integer also. In that case, the series is going to terminate into a polynomial. However, if $(\gamma)_i$ is to be written in terms of a gamma function as:

$$(\gamma)_i = \frac{\Gamma(\gamma+i)}{\Gamma(\gamma)}, \quad \gamma>0$$

if more parameters are to be incorporated, then we can consider:

$$E^{\gamma_1,\gamma_2,\ldots,\gamma_p}_{\alpha,\beta,\delta_1,\ldots,\delta_q}(x) = \sum_{i=0}^{\infty} \frac{(\gamma_1)_i \cdots (\gamma_p)_i}{i!(\delta_1)_i \cdots (\delta_q)_i} \frac{x^i}{\Gamma(i\alpha+\beta)}, \quad \alpha>0, \ \beta>0$$

where:

$$\delta_j \neq 0, -1, -2, \ldots, \ j=1,2,\ldots,q.$$

No other restrictions on $\gamma_1, \ldots, \gamma_p$ and $\delta_1, \ldots, \delta_q$ are there other than the conditions for the convergence of the series. A δ_j can be a negative integer provided there is a γ_r, a negative integer such that $(\gamma_r)_k=0$ first before $(\delta_r)_k=0$, such as $\gamma_2=-3$ and $\delta_1=-5$ so that $(\gamma_2)_4=0$ and $(\delta_1)_4\neq0$ (Mathai & Haubold, 2017).

Example. Consider the following fuzzy fractional initial value problem with:

$$\lambda = 1, \ \alpha = \frac{1}{2}, \ h(t) = 0, \ t \in (0, 1]$$

$$\boldsymbol{D}^{\frac{1}{2}}_{\boldsymbol{CK_{gH}}} x(t) = x(t), \ x(t_0, r) = x_0(r) = (2, 2 - r)$$

such that $x(t) \in C((t_0, T], \mathbb{F}_R)$. Since $\boldsymbol{I}^{\frac{1}{2}}_{\boldsymbol{RL}} \boldsymbol{D}^{\frac{1}{2}}_{\boldsymbol{CK_{gH}}} x(t) = x(t) \ominus_{gH} x_0 = \boldsymbol{I}^{\frac{1}{2}}_{\boldsymbol{RL}} x(t)$ and it has increasing length then we can use the successive approximation method:

$$x_n(t) \ominus_{gH} x_0 = \boldsymbol{I}^{\alpha}_{\boldsymbol{RL}} x_{n-1}(t), \ n = 1, 2, \ldots,$$

The $i - gH$ differentiable solution (with increasing length) is:

$$x(t) = x_0 \odot E_{\frac{1}{2},1}\left(t^{\frac{1}{2}}\right) = x_0 \odot \left(1 + \frac{2}{\sqrt{\pi}} \int_0^t e^{-s^2} \mathrm{d}s\right) e^{t^2}$$

Example. Consider the following fuzzy fractional initial value problem with:

$$\lambda \in \{-1, 1\}, \ \alpha = \frac{1}{2}, \ h(t) = c \odot t^2, \ t \in (0, 1]$$

$$\boldsymbol{D}^{\frac{1}{2}}_{\boldsymbol{CK_{gH}}} x(t) = \lambda \odot x(t) \oplus h(t), \ c, x_0 \in \mathbb{F}_R$$

Let us consider that $\lambda = 1$ and x is $i - gH$ differentiable:

$$x_{i-gH}(t) = x_0 E_{\alpha,1}\left(t^{\frac{1}{2}}\right) \oplus \int_0^t (t-s)^{-\frac{1}{2}} E_{\frac{1}{2},\frac{1}{2}}\left((t-s)^{\frac{1}{2}}\right) \odot c \odot s^2 \mathrm{d}s$$

where:

$$E_{\frac{1}{2},1}\left(t^{\frac{1}{2}}\right) = \sum_{i=0}^{\infty} \frac{t^{\frac{i}{2}}}{\Gamma\left(\frac{i}{2} + 1\right)},$$

$$E_{\frac{1}{2},\frac{1}{2}}\left((t-s)^{\frac{1}{2}}\right) = \sum_{i=0}^{\infty} \frac{(t-s)^{\frac{i}{2}}}{\Gamma\left(\frac{i}{2} + \frac{1}{2}\right)} = \sqrt{t}\left(1 + \frac{2}{\sqrt{\pi}} \int_0^t e^{-s^2} \mathrm{d}s\right) + \frac{1}{\Gamma\left(\frac{1}{2}\right)}$$

The solution is obtained as follows:

$$x_{i-gH}(t) = x_0 \odot \left(1 + \frac{2}{\sqrt{\pi}} \int_0^t e^{-s^2} \mathrm{d}s\right) e^{t^2} \oplus \int_0^t (t-s)^{-\frac{1}{2}} E_{\frac{1}{2},\frac{1}{2}}\left((t-s)^{\frac{1}{2}}\right) \odot c \odot s^2 \mathrm{d}s$$

Now let us consider that $\lambda = -1$ and x is $ii-gH$ differentiable:

$$x_{ii-gH}(t) = x_0 \odot \left(1 + \frac{2}{\sqrt{\pi}}\int_0^t e^{-s^2}\mathrm{ds}\right)e^{t^2} \ominus_H (-1)\int_0^t (t-s)^{-\frac{1}{2}} E_{\frac{1}{2},\frac{1}{2}}\left((t-s)^{\frac{1}{2}}\right) \odot c \odot s^2 \mathrm{ds}$$

6.5 Fuzzy Generalized Taylor'S Expansion

Let us consider the fuzzy continuous function $\boldsymbol{D}_{C_{gH}}^{k\alpha} x(t) \in \mathbb{F}_R$ in (a,b) for $k=0, 1, \ldots, n$, such that $0<\alpha\leq 1$. Then we have the following items (Armand et al., 2019).

Case 1. If $x(t)$ is $i-C_{gH}$ differentiable of order $k\alpha$, then there exists $\xi \in (a,b)$ such that:

$$x(t) = x(a) \oplus \sum_{k=1}^{n} \frac{(t-a)^{k\alpha}}{\Gamma(k\alpha+1)} \odot \boldsymbol{D}_{C_{gH}}^{k\alpha} x(a) \oplus \frac{\boldsymbol{D}_{C_{gH}}^{(n+1)\alpha} x(\xi)}{\Gamma((n+1)\alpha+1)} \odot (t-a)^{(n+1)\alpha}$$

Case 2. If $x(t)$ is $ii-C_{gH}$ differentiable of order $k\alpha$, then there exists $\xi \in (a,b)$ such that:

$$x(t) = x(a) \ominus_H (-1)\sum_{k=1}^{n} \frac{(t-a)^{k\alpha}}{\Gamma(k\alpha+1)} \odot \boldsymbol{D}_{C_{gH}}^{k\alpha} x(a) \ominus_H (-1)\frac{\boldsymbol{D}_{C_{gH}}^{(n+1)\alpha} x(\xi)}{\Gamma((n+1)\alpha+1)} \odot (t-a)^{(n+1)\alpha}$$

Case 3. If $x(t)$ is $i-C_{gH}$ differentiable of order $2k\alpha, k=0,1,\ldots,\left[\frac{n}{2}\right]$ and also it is $ii-C_{gH}$ differentiable of order $(2k-1)\alpha, k=0,1,\ldots,\left[\frac{n}{2}\right]$, then there exists $\xi \in (a,b)$ such that:

$$x(t) = x(a) \ominus_H (-1) \sum_{k=1,\mathrm{odd}}^{n} \frac{(t-a)^{k\alpha}}{\Gamma(k\alpha+1)} \odot \boldsymbol{D}_{C_{gH}}^{k\alpha} x(a) \oplus \sum_{k=1,\mathrm{even}}^{n} \frac{(t-a)^{k\alpha}}{\Gamma(k\alpha+1)} \odot \boldsymbol{D}_{C_{gH}}^{k\alpha} x(a)$$
$$\ominus_H (-1)\frac{\boldsymbol{D}_{C_{gH}}^{(n+1)\alpha} x(\xi)}{\Gamma((n+1)\alpha+1)} \odot (t-a)^{(n+1)\alpha}$$

Case 4. If $\zeta \in [a,b]$, and $x(t)$ is $ii-C_{gH}$ differentiable before ζ and $i-C_{gH}$ after it, and types of differentiability for $\boldsymbol{D}_{C_{gH}}{}^{k\alpha} x(t)$, $k=1, 2, \ldots, n$ are $i-C_{gH}$ differentiable, then there exists $\xi \in (a,b)$ such that:

$$x(t) = \begin{cases} x(a) \ominus_H (-1)\dfrac{(t-a)^{\alpha}}{\Gamma(\alpha+1)} \odot \boldsymbol{D}_{C_{gH}}^{\alpha} x(a) \oplus \displaystyle\sum_{k=2}^{n} \frac{(t-a)^{k\alpha}}{\Gamma(k\alpha+1)} \odot \boldsymbol{D}_{C_{gH}}^{k\alpha} x(a) \\ \qquad \oplus \dfrac{\boldsymbol{D}_{C_{gH}}^{(n+1)\alpha} x(\xi)}{\Gamma((n+1)\alpha+1)} \odot (t-a)^{(n+1)\alpha}, & a \leq t \leq \zeta \\ x(a) \oplus \displaystyle\sum_{k=1}^{n} \frac{(t-a)^{k\alpha}}{\Gamma(k\alpha+1)} \odot \boldsymbol{D}_{C_{gH}}^{k\alpha} x(a) \oplus \dfrac{\boldsymbol{D}_{C_{gH}}^{(n+1)\alpha} x(\xi)}{\Gamma((n+1)\alpha+1)} \odot (t-a)^{(n+1)\alpha}, & \zeta \leq t \leq b \end{cases}$$

Case 5. If $\zeta \in [a,b]$, and $x(t)$ is $i-C_{gH}$ differentiable before ζ and $ii-C_{gH}$ after it, and types of differentiability for $\boldsymbol{D}_{C_{gH}}{}^{k\alpha}x(t)$, $k=1, 2, \ldots, n$ are $ii-C_{gH}$ differentiable, then there exists $\xi \in (a,b)$ such that:

$$
x(t)=\begin{cases} x(a)\oplus\dfrac{(t-a)^{\alpha}}{\Gamma(\alpha+1)}\odot \boldsymbol{D}_{C_{gH}}^{\alpha}x(a)\ominus_H(-1)\displaystyle\sum_{k=2}^{n}\frac{(t-a)^{k\alpha}}{\Gamma(k\alpha+1)}\odot \boldsymbol{D}_{C_{gH}}^{k\alpha}x(a) \\ \qquad\ominus_H(-1)\dfrac{\boldsymbol{D}_{C_{gH}}^{(n+1)\alpha}x(\xi)}{\Gamma((n+1)\alpha+1)}\odot(t-a)^{(n+1)\alpha}, \quad a\le t\le \zeta \\ x(a)\ominus_H(-1)\displaystyle\sum_{k=1}^{n}\frac{(t-a)^{k\alpha}}{\Gamma(k\alpha+1)}\odot \boldsymbol{D}_{C_{gH}}^{k\alpha}x(a)\ominus_H \\ \qquad(-1)\dfrac{\boldsymbol{D}_{C_{gH}}^{(n+1)\alpha}x(\xi)}{\Gamma((n+1)\alpha+1)}\odot(t-a)^{(n+1)\alpha}, \quad \zeta\le t\le b \end{cases}
$$

In general, in accordance with gH-difference, we have the following relations. Since:

$$
\boldsymbol{I}_{\boldsymbol{RL}}^{n\alpha}\boldsymbol{D}_{C_{gH}}^{n\alpha}x(t)\ominus_{gH}\boldsymbol{I}_{\boldsymbol{RL}}^{(n+1)\alpha}\boldsymbol{D}_{C_{gH}}^{(n+1)\alpha}x(t)=\frac{(t-a)^{n\alpha}}{\Gamma(n\alpha+1)}\odot \boldsymbol{D}_{C_{gH}}^{n\alpha}x(a)
$$

$$
\sum_{k=0}^{n}\left(\boldsymbol{I}_{\boldsymbol{RL}}^{k\alpha}\boldsymbol{D}_{C_{gH}}^{k\alpha}x(t)\ominus_{gH}\boldsymbol{I}_{\boldsymbol{RL}}^{(k+1)\alpha}\boldsymbol{D}_{C_{gH}}^{(k+1)\alpha}x(t)\right)=x(t)\ominus_{gH}\boldsymbol{I}_{\boldsymbol{RL}}^{(n+1)\alpha}\boldsymbol{D}_{C_{gH}}^{(n+1)\alpha}x(t)
$$

$$
\sum_{k=0}^{n}\left(\boldsymbol{I}_{\boldsymbol{RL}}^{k\alpha}\boldsymbol{D}_{C_{gH}}^{k\alpha}x(t)\ominus_{gH}\boldsymbol{I}_{\boldsymbol{RL}}^{(k+1)\alpha}\boldsymbol{D}_{C_{gH}}^{(k+1)\alpha}x(t)\right)=\sum_{k=0}^{n}\frac{(t-a)^{k\alpha}}{\Gamma(k\alpha+1)}\odot \boldsymbol{D}_{C_{gH}}^{k\alpha}x(a)
$$

$$
x(t)\ominus_{gH}\boldsymbol{I}_{\boldsymbol{RL}}^{(n+1)\alpha}\boldsymbol{D}_{C_{gH}}^{(n+1)\alpha}x(t)=\sum_{k=0}^{n}\frac{(t-a)^{k\alpha}}{\Gamma(k\alpha+1)}\odot \boldsymbol{D}_{C_{gH}}^{k\alpha}x(a)
$$

$$
x(t)=\sum_{k=0}^{n}\frac{(t-a)^{k\alpha}}{\Gamma(k\alpha+1)}\odot \boldsymbol{D}_{C_{gH}}^{k\alpha}x(a)\oplus\boldsymbol{I}_{\boldsymbol{RL}}^{(n+1)\alpha}\boldsymbol{D}_{C_{gH}}^{(n+1)\alpha}x(t)
$$

$$
x(t)=x(a)\oplus\sum_{k=1}^{n}\frac{(t-a)^{k\alpha}}{\Gamma(k\alpha+1)}\odot \boldsymbol{D}_{C_{gH}}^{k\alpha}x(a)\oplus\boldsymbol{I}_{\boldsymbol{RL}}^{(n+1)\alpha}\boldsymbol{D}_{C_{gH}}^{(n+1)\alpha}x(t)
$$

using the fractional mean value theorem:

$$
\begin{aligned}
\boldsymbol{I}_{\boldsymbol{RL}}^{(n+1)\alpha}\boldsymbol{D}_{C_{gH}}^{(n+1)\alpha}x(t)&=\frac{1}{\Gamma((n+1)\alpha)}\odot\int_a^t(t-\tau)^{(n+1)\alpha-1}\odot \boldsymbol{D}_{C_{gH}}^{(n+1)\alpha}x(\tau)\mathrm{d}\tau \\
&=\frac{\boldsymbol{D}_{C_{gH}}^{(n+1)\alpha}x(\xi)}{\Gamma((n+1)\alpha+1)}\odot(t-a)^{(n+1)\alpha}
\end{aligned}
$$

Proof of Case 1.

Since $x(t)$ is $i-C_{gH}$ differentiable of order $k\alpha$, then all gH-differences are defined in the sense of $i-gH$ difference and we have:

$$x(t)=x(a)\oplus\sum_{k=1}^{n}\frac{(t-a)^{k\alpha}}{\Gamma(k\alpha+1)}\odot \boldsymbol{D}_{C_{gH}}^{k\alpha}x(a)\oplus \boldsymbol{I}_{RL}^{(n+1)\alpha}\boldsymbol{D}_{C_{gH}}^{(n+1)\alpha}x(\zeta)$$

Proof of Case 2.

Since $x(t)$ is $ii-C_{gH}$ differentiable of order $k\alpha$, then all gH-differences are defined in the sense of $ii-gH$ difference and also fractional mean value theorem we have:

$$\boldsymbol{I}_{RL}^{n\alpha}\boldsymbol{D}_{C_{gH}}^{n\alpha}x(t)\oplus(-1)\boldsymbol{I}_{RL}^{(n+1)\alpha}\boldsymbol{D}_{C_{gH}}^{(n+1)\alpha}x(t)=\frac{(t-a)^{n\alpha}}{\Gamma(n\alpha+1)}\odot \boldsymbol{D}_{C_{gH}}^{n\alpha}x(a)$$

$$x(t)=x(a)\ominus_H(-1)\sum_{k=1}^{n}\frac{(t-a)^{k\alpha}}{\Gamma(k\alpha+1)}\odot \boldsymbol{D}_{C_{gH}}^{k\alpha}x(a)\ominus_H(-1)\frac{\boldsymbol{D}_{C_{gH}}^{(n+1)\alpha}x(\xi)}{\Gamma((n+1)\alpha+1)}\odot(t-a)^{(n+1)\alpha}$$

Proof of Case 3.

If $x(t)$ is $i-C_{gH}$ differentiable of order $2k\alpha, k=0,1,\ldots,\left[\frac{n}{2}\right]$ and also it is $ii-C_{gH}$ differentiable of order $(2k-1)\alpha, k=0,1,\ldots,\left[\frac{n}{2}\right]$, then there exists $\xi\in(a,b)$:

$$\sum_{k=0}^{n}\left(\boldsymbol{I}_{RL}^{k\alpha}\boldsymbol{D}_{C_{gH}}^{k\alpha}x(t)\ominus_{gH}\boldsymbol{I}_{RL}^{(k+1)\alpha}\boldsymbol{D}_{C_{gH}}^{(k+1)\alpha}x(t)\right)=x(t)\oplus(-1)\boldsymbol{I}_{RL}^{\alpha}\boldsymbol{D}_{C_{gH}}^{\alpha}x(t)$$

$$\ominus_H(-1)\boldsymbol{I}_{RL}^{\alpha}\boldsymbol{D}_{C_{gH}}^{\alpha}x(t)\ominus_H\boldsymbol{I}_{RL}^{2\alpha}\boldsymbol{D}_{C_{gH}}^{2\alpha}x(t)$$

$$\oplus\cdots\oplus\boldsymbol{I}_{RL}^{n\alpha}\boldsymbol{D}_{C_{gH}}^{n\alpha}x(t)\ominus_H(-1)\boldsymbol{I}_{RL}^{(n+1)\alpha}\boldsymbol{D}_{C_{gH}}^{(n+1)\alpha}x(t)$$

By similar reasoning in Case 1:

$$x(t)\oplus(-1)\boldsymbol{I}_{RL}^{(n+1)\alpha}\boldsymbol{D}_{C_{gH}}^{(n+1)\alpha}x(t)=x(a)\ominus_H\sum_{k=1,\text{odd}}^{n}\boldsymbol{I}_{RL}^{k\alpha}\boldsymbol{D}_{C_{gH}}^{k\alpha}x(a)\oplus\sum_{k=1,\text{even}}^{n}\boldsymbol{I}_{RL}^{k\alpha}\boldsymbol{D}_{C_{gH}}^{k\alpha}x(a)$$

$$=x(a)\ominus_H\sum_{k=1,\text{odd}}^{n}\frac{(t-a)^{k\alpha}}{\Gamma(k\alpha+1)}\odot\boldsymbol{D}_{C_{gH}}^{k\alpha}x(a)\oplus\sum_{k=1,\text{even}}^{n}\frac{(t-a)^{k\alpha}}{\Gamma(k\alpha+1)}\odot\boldsymbol{D}_{C_{gH}}^{k\alpha}x(a)$$

By using the definition of H-difference:

$$x(t)=x(a)\ominus_H(-1)\sum_{k=1,\text{odd}}^{n}\frac{(t-a)^{k\alpha}}{\Gamma(k\alpha+1)}\odot\boldsymbol{D}_{C_{gH}}^{k\alpha}x(a)\oplus\sum_{k=1,\text{even}}^{n}\frac{(t-a)^{k\alpha}}{\Gamma(k\alpha+1)}\odot\boldsymbol{D}_{C_{gH}}^{k\alpha}x(a)$$

$$\ominus_H(-1)\frac{D_{C_{gH}}^{(n+1)\alpha}x(\xi)}{\Gamma((n+1)\alpha+1)}\odot(t-a)^{(n+1)\alpha}$$

The proof of Cases 4 and 5 are very similar to Cases 1–3.

One of the applications of fuzzy fractional Taylor is the fuzzy Euler fractional method, which is the immediate consequence of the Taylor expansion. We shall now cover the Fuzzy fractional Euler method.

6.6 Fuzzy Fractional Euler Method

Consider the following fuzzy fractional differential equation:

$$D_{C_{gH}}^{\alpha}x(t)=f(t,x(t)),\ x(t_0)=x_0,\ t\in[t_0,T],\ 0<\alpha\le 1$$

where $f:[t_0,T]\times\mathbb{F}_R\to\mathbb{F}_R$ is a fuzzy number valued function, $x(t)$ is a continuous fuzzy set valued solution, and ${D_{C_{gH}}}^{\alpha}$ is the fractional Caputo fractional operator. In this method, a sequence of approximations to the solution $x(t)$ will be obtained at several points, called grid points. To derive Euler's method, the interval $[t_0,T]$ is divided to into N equal subintervals, each of length h, by the grid points $t_i=t_0+ih$, $i=0,\ 1,\ 2,\ \ldots,\ N$. The distance between points, $h=\frac{T-t_0}{N}$, is called the grid size. To explain the method, we should discuss the type of differentiability of the solution and to this end we will have several cases, as with fuzzy Taylor expansion (Armand et al., 2019).

Case 1. Suppose that the fuzzy solution $x(t)$ is $i-C_{gH}$ differentiable on $[t_0,T]$. The Taylor expansion about t_k on any subinterval $[t_k,t_{k+1}]$ for $k=0,\ 1,\ \ldots,\ N-1$ can be expressed as the following form, where $h=t_{k+1}-t_k, \exists\zeta_k\in[t_k,t_{k+1}]$:

$$x(t_{k+1})=x(t_k)\oplus\frac{(t_{k+1}-t_k)^{\alpha}}{\Gamma(\alpha+1)}\odot D_{C_{gH}}^{\alpha}x(t_k)\oplus\frac{(t_{k+1}-t_k)^{2\alpha}}{\Gamma(2\alpha+1)}\odot D_{C_{gH}}^{2\alpha}x(\zeta_k)$$

$$x(t_{k+1})=x(t_k)\oplus\frac{h^{\alpha}}{\Gamma(\alpha+1)}\odot D_{C_{gH}}^{k\alpha}x(t_k)\oplus\frac{h^{2\alpha}}{\Gamma(2\alpha+1)}\odot D_{C_{gH}}^{2\alpha}x(\zeta_k)$$

Since ${D_{C_{gH}}}^{\alpha}x(t_k)=f(t,x(t_k))$, then by substituting, we have:

$$x(t_{k+1})=x(t_k)\oplus\frac{h^{\alpha}}{\Gamma(\alpha+1)}\odot f(t_k,x(t_k))\oplus\frac{h^{2\alpha}}{\Gamma(2\alpha+1)}\odot D_{C_{gH}}^{2\alpha}x(\zeta_k)$$

where the term $\frac{h^{2\alpha}}{\Gamma(2\alpha+1)}\odot D_{C_{gH}}^{2\alpha}x(\zeta_k)$ can be denoted as the error for the numerical method. As a result, the Fuzzy fractional Euler method on $[t_k,t_{k+1}]$ can be introduced as:

$$x(t_{k+1})=x(t_k)\oplus\frac{h^{\alpha}}{\Gamma(\alpha+1)}\odot f(t_k,x(t_k)),\ h=t_{k+1}-t_k,\ k=0,1,\ldots,N-1$$

Case 2. Suppose that the fuzzy solution $x(t)$ is $ii-C_{gH}$ differentiable on $[t_0,T]$. The Taylor expansion about t_k on any subinterval $[t_k,t_{k+1}]$ for $k=0, 1, \ldots, N-1$ can be expressed as the following form, where $h=t_{k+1}-t_k, \exists\zeta_k\in[t_k,t_{k+1}]$:

$$x(t_{k+1})=x(t_k)\ominus_H(-1)\frac{h^\alpha}{\Gamma(\alpha+1)}\odot \boldsymbol{D}^{\alpha}_{C_{gH}}x(t_k)\ominus_H(-1)\frac{h^\alpha}{\Gamma(2\alpha+1)}\odot \boldsymbol{D}^{2\alpha}_{C_{gH}}x(\zeta_k)$$

Since $\boldsymbol{D}_{C_{gH}}{}^{\alpha}x(t_k)=f(t,x(t_k))$, then by substituting, we have:

$$x(t_{k+1})=x(t_k)\ominus_H(-1)\frac{h^\alpha}{\Gamma(\alpha+1)}\odot f(t_k,x(t_k))\ominus_H(-1)\frac{h^{2\alpha}}{\Gamma(2\alpha+1)}\odot \boldsymbol{D}^{2\alpha}_{C_{gH}}x(\zeta_k)$$

where the term $\frac{h^{2\alpha}}{\Gamma(2\alpha+1)}\odot \boldsymbol{D}^{2\alpha}_{C_{gH}}x(\zeta_k)$ can be denoted as the error for the numerical method. As a result, the Fuzzy fractional Euler method on $[t_k,t_{k+1}]$ can be introduced as follows:

$$x(t_{k+1})=x(t_k)\ominus_H(-1)\frac{h^\alpha}{\Gamma(\alpha+1)}\odot f(t_k,x(t_k)),\ h=t_{k+1}-t_k,\ k=0,1,\ldots,N-1$$

Case 3. Suppose that the fuzzy solution $x(t)$ has a switching point at $\xi\in[t_0,T]$ and it is $i-C_{gH}$ differentiable at the points $t_0, t_1, \ldots, t_j$ and $ii-C_{gH}$ differentiable at the points $t_{j+1}, t_{j+2}, \ldots, t_N$ on $[t_0,T]$. The Taylor expansion about t_k on any subinterval $[t_k,t_{k+1}]$ for $k=0, 1, \ldots, N-1$ can be expressed as the following form:

$$\begin{cases} x(t_{k+1})=x(t_k)\oplus\frac{h^\alpha}{\Gamma(\alpha+1)}\odot f(t_k,x(t_k)), & k=1,2,\ldots,j \\ x(t_{k+1})=x(t_k)\ominus_H(-1)\frac{h^\alpha}{\Gamma(\alpha+1)}\odot f(t_k,x(t_k)), & k=j+1,j+2,\ldots,N \end{cases}$$

Case 4. Suppose that the fuzzy solution $x(t)$ has a switching point at $\xi\in[t_0,T]$ and it is $ii-C_{gH}$ differentiable at the points $t_0, t_1, \ldots, t_j$ and $i-C_{gH}$ differentiable at the points $t_{j+1}, t_{j+2}, \ldots, t_N$ on $[t_0,T]$. The Taylor expansion about t_k on any subinterval $[t_k,t_{k+1}]$ for $k=0, 1, \ldots, N-1$ can be expressed as the following form:

$$\begin{cases} x(t_{k+1})=x(t_k)\ominus_H(-1)\frac{h^\alpha}{\Gamma(\alpha+1)}\odot f(t_k,x(t_k)), & k=1,2,\ldots,j \\ x(t_{k+1})=x(t_k)\oplus\frac{h^\alpha}{\Gamma(\alpha+1)}\odot f(t_k,x(t_k)), & k=j+1,j+2,\ldots,N \end{cases}$$

Example. Consider the following fuzzy fractional differential equation:

$$\boldsymbol{D}^{\alpha}_{C_{gH}}x(t)=(0,1,1.5)\odot\Gamma(\alpha+1),\ x(0)=0,\ t\in[0,1],\ 0<\alpha\leq 1$$

The exact solution is:

$$x(t)=(0,1,1.5)\odot t^\alpha:=c\odot t^\alpha$$

This function is $i-gH$ differentiable, because the length of $x(t)$ is increasing.
Note. The Caputo gH-derivative of $x(t)=(0,1,1.5)\odot t^{\alpha}$ is:

$$D^{\alpha}_{C_{gH}}((0,1,1.5)\odot t^{\alpha})=\frac{1}{\Gamma(1-\alpha)}\odot\int_0^t\frac{((0,1,1.5)\odot\tau^{\alpha})'}{(t-\tau)^{\alpha}}d\tau$$

$$=\frac{(0,1,1.5)\alpha}{\Gamma(1-\alpha)}\odot\int_0^t\frac{\tau^{\alpha-1}}{(t-\tau)^{\alpha}}d\tau$$

Since:

$$\int_0^t\frac{\tau^{\alpha-1}}{(t-\tau)^{\alpha}}d\tau=\frac{4^{-\alpha}\sqrt{\pi}\Gamma(\alpha)t^{2\alpha}}{\Gamma\left(\alpha+\frac{1}{2}\right)}$$

then:

$$D^{\alpha}_{C_{gH}}((0,1,1.5)\odot t^{\alpha})=(0,1,1.5)\odot\frac{\alpha 4^{-\alpha}\sqrt{\pi}\Gamma(\alpha)t^{2\alpha}}{\Gamma\left(\alpha+\frac{1}{2}\right)\Gamma(1-\alpha)}$$

In the level-wise form:

$$D^{\alpha}_{C}(rt^{\alpha})=r\cdot\frac{\alpha 4^{-\alpha}\sqrt{\pi}\Gamma(\alpha)t^{2\alpha}}{\Gamma\left(\alpha+\frac{1}{2}\right)\Gamma(1-\alpha)}$$

$$D^{\alpha}_{C}((1.5-1.5r)t^{\alpha})=(1.5-1.5r)\cdot\frac{\alpha 4^{-\alpha}\sqrt{\pi}\Gamma(\alpha)t^{2\alpha}}{\Gamma\left(\alpha+\frac{1}{2}\right)\Gamma(1-\alpha)}$$

so the Euler method is in the form of Case 1:

$$x(t_{k+1})=x(t_k)\oplus\frac{h^{\alpha}}{\Gamma(\alpha+1)}\odot(0,1,1.5)\odot\Gamma(\alpha+1),\ k=0,1,\ldots,N-1$$

For instance, consider the step size $h=0.1$ and $\alpha=0.5$. The level-wise form of the Euler method is:

$$x(t_{k+1},r)=x(t_k,r)\oplus(0.1)^{0.5}\odot(r,1.5-1.5r),\ k=0,1,\ldots,N-1$$

$$x(t_{k+1},r)=x(t_k,r)\oplus\left((0.1)^{0.5}r,(0.1)^{0.5}(1.5-1.5r)\right),\ k=0,1,\ldots,N-1$$

In the level-wise form:

$$x_l(t_{k+1},r)=x_l(t_k,r)+(0.1)^{0.5}r,\ k=0,1,\ldots,N-1,0\le r\le 1$$

$$x_u(t_{k+1}, r) = x_u(t_k, r) + (0.1)^{0.5}(1.5 - 1.5r), \quad k = 0, 1, \dots, N-1, 0 \le r \le 1$$

Using the recursive method and finding the values for $x(t_k)$, $k=0, 1, \dots, 9$, finally we get:

$$x_l(t_{10}, r) = 10(0.1)^{0.5} r, \quad x_u(t_{10}, r) = 10(0.1)^{0.5}(1.5 - 1.5r), \quad 0 \le r \le 1$$

In Table 6.1, the numerical solutions with order $\alpha = 0.5$ and $h = 0.1$ are expressed.

Example. Consider the following fuzzy fractional differential equation:

$$\boldsymbol{D}^{\alpha}_{C_{gH}} x(t) = (-1) \odot x(t), \quad x(0) = (0, 1, 2), \quad t \in [0, 1], \quad 0 < \alpha \le 1$$

The exact solution is:

$$x(t) = (0, 1, 2) \odot E_\alpha(-t^\alpha) := c \odot E_\alpha(-t^\alpha)$$

where:

$$E_\alpha(-t^\alpha) = \sum_{i=0}^{\infty} \frac{(-t^\alpha)^i}{\Gamma(i\alpha + 1)}$$

This function is $ii - gH$ differentiable, because the length of $x(t)$ is decreasing. Therefore, the Euler method is in the form of Case 2:

$$x(t_{k+1}) = x(t_k) \ominus_H (-1) \frac{h^\alpha}{\Gamma(\alpha + 1)} \odot (0, 1, 2) \odot E_\alpha(-t_k^\alpha), \quad k = 0, 1, \dots, N-1$$

TABLE 6.1 Numerical results for step size $h = 0.1$.

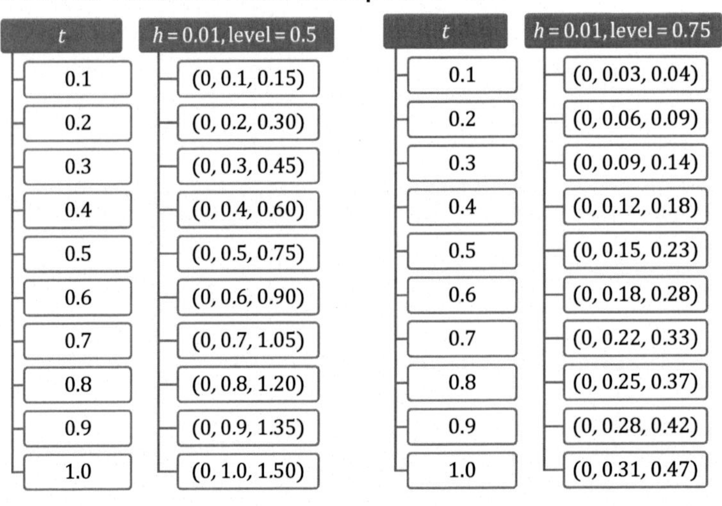

t	$h = 0.01$, level = 0.5	t	$h = 0.01$, level = 0.75
0.1	(0, 0.1, 0.15)	0.1	(0, 0.03, 0.04)
0.2	(0, 0.2, 0.30)	0.2	(0, 0.06, 0.09)
0.3	(0, 0.3, 0.45)	0.3	(0, 0.09, 0.14)
0.4	(0, 0.4, 0.60)	0.4	(0, 0.12, 0.18)
0.5	(0, 0.5, 0.75)	0.5	(0, 0.15, 0.23)
0.6	(0, 0.6, 0.90)	0.6	(0, 0.18, 0.28)
0.7	(0, 0.7, 1.05)	0.7	(0, 0.22, 0.33)
0.8	(0, 0.8, 1.20)	0.8	(0, 0.25, 0.37)
0.9	(0, 0.9, 1.35)	0.9	(0, 0.28, 0.42)
1.0	(0, 1.0, 1.50)	1.0	(0, 0.31, 0.47)

For instance, consider the step size $h=0.1$ and $\alpha=0.5$. The level-wise form of the Euler method is:

$$x(t_{k+1},r)=x(t_k,r)\ominus_H(-1)\frac{0.5^{\alpha}E_{0.5}\left(-t_k^{0.5}\right)}{\Gamma(0.5+1)}\odot(r-1,2-r),$$

for $k=0,\ 1,\ \ldots,\ N-1$:

$$\frac{0.687498}{(\sqrt{t_k}+1)\Gamma(0.5+1)}=\frac{0.775758}{(\sqrt{t_k}+1)}$$

Since the value $\frac{0.5^{\alpha}E_{0.5}\left(-t^{0.5}\right)}{\Gamma(0.5+1)}>0$, then, in the level-wise form:

$$x_l(t_{k+1},r)=x_l(t_k,r)+\frac{0.775758}{(\sqrt{t_k}+1)}(2-r),\ \ k=0,1,\ldots,N-1,\ \ 0\le r\le 1$$

$$x_u(t_{k+1},r)=x_u(t_k,r)+\frac{0.775758}{(\sqrt{t_k}+1)}(r-1),\ \ k=0,1,\ldots,N-1,\ \ 0\le r\le 1$$

In Table 6.2, the numerical solutions with order $\alpha=0.5$ and $h=0.1$ are expressed.

Example. Consider another fuzzy fractional differential equation:

$$\boldsymbol{D}^{\alpha}_{C_{gH}}x(t)=\frac{\pi t^{1-\alpha}\alpha}{\Gamma(2-\alpha)}\odot\left(0,\frac{1}{2},1\right)\odot{}_1F_1\left(1;\left[1-\frac{\alpha}{2},\frac{3}{2}-\frac{\alpha}{2}\right];-\frac{1}{4}\pi^2t^2\alpha^2\right),\ 1\le t\le 2$$

TABLE 6.2 Numerical results for step size $h=0.01$.

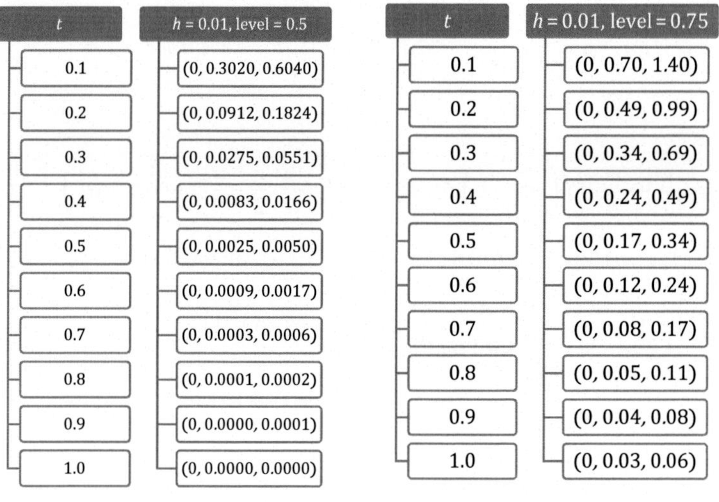

t	$h = 0.01$, level = 0.5	t	$h = 0.01$, level = 0.75
0.1	(0, 0.3020, 0.6040)	0.1	(0, 0.70, 1.40)
0.2	(0, 0.0912, 0.1824)	0.2	(0, 0.49, 0.99)
0.3	(0, 0.0275, 0.0551)	0.3	(0, 0.34, 0.69)
0.4	(0, 0.0083, 0.0166)	0.4	(0, 0.24, 0.49)
0.5	(0, 0.0025, 0.0050)	0.5	(0, 0.17, 0.34)
0.6	(0, 0.0009, 0.0017)	0.6	(0, 0.12, 0.24)
0.7	(0, 0.0003, 0.0006)	0.7	(0, 0.08, 0.17)
0.8	(0, 0.0001, 0.0002)	0.8	(0, 0.05, 0.11)
0.9	(0, 0.0000, 0.0001)	0.9	(0, 0.04, 0.08)
1.0	(0, 0.0000, 0.0000)	1.0	(0, 0.03, 0.06)

with fuzzy initial value $x(1)=(0,0.5,1)\odot\sin\alpha\pi$, where ${}_1F_1(a;b;z)$ is a generalized hypergeometric function and defined as the following form:

$$ {}_pF_q\left(a_1,a_2,\ldots,a_p;b_1,b_2,\ldots,b_q;z\right)=\sum_{n=0}^{\infty}\frac{\left(a_1\right)_n\cdots\left(a_p\right)_n}{\left(b_1\right)_n\cdots\left(b_q\right)_n}\cdot\frac{z^n}{n!} $$

Here:

$$ {}_1F_1(a;b;z)=\sum_{n=0}^{\infty}\frac{(a)_n}{(b)_n}\cdot\frac{z^n}{n!}=\sum_{n=0}^{\infty}\frac{\Gamma(a+n)}{\Gamma(a)}\cdot\frac{\Gamma(b)}{\Gamma(b+n)}\cdot\frac{z^n}{n!} $$

where:

$$ (\cdot)_n=\frac{\Gamma(\cdot+n)}{\Gamma(\cdot)} $$

Note that by the ratio test, the series is convergent. In this example, using $\alpha=0.5$, the exact solution is:

$$ x(t)=(0,0.5,1)\odot\sin(\alpha\pi t) $$

The solution has a switching point at the point $t=1.463$ and the switching point is type I; before the point it is $i-gH$ differentiable and after it is $ii-gH$ differentiable. In the subintervals $[t_k,t_{k+1}]$, $k=0,\ 1,\ \ldots,\ N-1$ with assumption that switching point is in the interval $[t_j,t_{j+1}]$, the fuzzy Euler's method is denoted as:

$$ \begin{cases} x(t_{k+1})=x(t_k)\oplus\dfrac{h^{\alpha}}{\Gamma(\alpha+1)}\odot f(t_k,x(t_k)), & k=1,2,\ldots,j \\ x(t_{k+1})=x(t_k)\ominus_H(-1)\dfrac{h^{\alpha}}{\Gamma(\alpha+1)}\odot f(t_k,x(t_k)), & k=j+1,j+2,\ldots,N \end{cases} $$

where:

$$ f(t_k,x(t_k))=\frac{\pi t_k^{1-\alpha}\alpha}{\Gamma(2-\alpha)}\odot\left(0,\frac{1}{2},1\right)\odot{}_1F_1\left(1;\left[1-\frac{\alpha}{2},\frac{3}{2}-\frac{\alpha}{2}\right];-\frac{1}{4}\pi^2t_k^2\alpha^2\right) $$

Suppose $h=0.1$, $k=0$, $\alpha=0.5$, $t_0=1$, $x(1)=(0,0.5,1)\odot\sin\alpha\pi$. Then:

$$ x(t_1)=(0,0.5,1)\oplus\frac{h^{0.5}}{\Gamma(0.5+1)}\odot f(1,(0,0.5,1)) $$

where:

$$ f(1,(0,0.5,1))=\frac{\pi 0.5}{\Gamma\left(\frac{3}{2}\right)}\odot\left(0,\frac{1}{2},1\right)\odot{}_1F_1\left(1;\left[\frac{3}{4},\frac{5}{4}\right];-\frac{1}{16}\pi^2\right) $$

$$ {}_1F_1\left(1;\left[\frac{3}{4},\frac{5}{4}\right];-\frac{1}{16}\pi^2\right)\sum_{n=0}^{\infty}\frac{\Gamma(1+n)}{\Gamma(1)}\cdot\frac{\Gamma\left(\left[\frac{3}{4},\frac{5}{4}\right]\right)}{\Gamma\left(\left[\frac{3}{4}+n,\frac{5}{4}+n\right]\right)}\cdot\frac{\left(-\frac{1}{16}\pi^2\right)^n}{n!}= $$

$$ =\left[\sum_{n=0}^{\infty}\frac{\Gamma(1+n)}{\Gamma(1)}\cdot\frac{\Gamma\left(\frac{3}{4}\right)}{\Gamma\left(\frac{3}{4}\right)}\cdot\frac{\left(-\frac{1}{16}\pi^2\right)^n}{n!},\sum_{n=0}^{\infty}\frac{\Gamma(1+n)}{\Gamma(1)}\cdot\frac{\Gamma\left(\frac{5}{4}\right)}{\Gamma\left(\frac{5}{4}\right)}\cdot\frac{\left(-\frac{1}{16}\pi^2\right)^n}{n!}\right]= $$

$$ =\left[\frac{16}{16+\pi^2},\frac{16}{16+\pi^2}\right]=\frac{16}{16+\pi^2} $$

thus:

$$ f(t_0,x(t_0))=f(1,(0,0.5,1))=\frac{\pi 0.5}{\Gamma\left(\frac{3}{2}\right)}\odot\left(0,\frac{1}{2},1\right)\odot\frac{16}{16+\pi^2} $$

Since $\frac{\pi 0.5}{\Gamma\left(\frac{3}{2}\right)}\frac{16}{16+\pi^2}\approx 1.1$ and positive, then $f(t_0,x(t_0))=1.1\odot(0{,}0.5{,}1)$ and in the level-wise form:

$$ f_l(t_0,x(t_0),r)=\frac{1.1}{2}r,\ f_u(t_0,x(t_0),r)=1.1-\frac{1.1}{2}r $$

and the method for approximate the solution at the second point $x(t_1)$ is:

$$ x_l(t_1,r)=\frac{1}{2}r+\frac{h^{0.5}}{\Gamma(0.5+1)}\cdot\frac{1.1}{2}r, x_u(t_1,r)=1-\frac{1}{2}r+\frac{h^{0.5}}{\Gamma(0.5+1)}\cdot\left(1.1-\frac{1.1}{2}r\right) $$

Putting $h=0.1$ and in the level, for instance, $r=0.5$, we have:

$$ x_l(t_1,0.5)=\frac{1}{4}+\frac{0.5^{0.5}}{\Gamma(1.5)}\cdot\frac{1.1}{4}\approx 0.47,\ x_u(t_1,r)=\frac{3}{4}+\frac{0.5^{0.5}}{\Gamma(1.5)}\cdot\frac{3}{4}\cdot 1.1\approx 1.41 $$

In general, for $\alpha=0.5$ we have:

$$ f(t_k,x(t_k))=\frac{\pi t_k^{0.5}0.5}{\Gamma(1.5)}\odot\left(0,\frac{1}{2},1\right)\odot {}_1F_1\left(1;[0.5,1];-\frac{1}{16}\pi^2 t_k^2\right) $$

and:

$$ \begin{cases} x(t_{k+1})=x(t_k)\oplus\dfrac{h^{0.5}}{\Gamma(1.5)}\odot f(t_k,x(t_k)), & k=1,2,\ldots,j \\ x(t_{k+1})=x(t_k)\ominus_H(-1)\dfrac{h^{0.5}}{\Gamma(1.5)}\odot f(t_k,x(t_k)), & k=j+1,j+2,\ldots,N \end{cases} $$

The results for $h=0.01$ are listed in Table 6.3.

TABLE 6.3 Numerical results with order $\alpha=0.5$ for step size $h=0.01$, 0.001.

t	$h=0.01$	$h=0.01$
1.1	(0, 0.4936, 0.9875)	(0, 0.4942, 0.9823)
1.2	(0, 0.4745, 0.9514)	(0, 0.4747, 0.9512)
1.3	(0, 0.4468, 0.8923)	(0, 0.4452, 0.8920)
1.4	(0, 0.4024, 0.8092)	(0, 0.4023, 0.8031)
1.5	(0, 0.3526, 0.7072)	(0, 0.3523, 0.7062)
1.6	(0, 0.2945, 0.5835)	(0, 0.2923, 0.5832)
1.7	(0, 0.2248, 0.4583)	(0, 0.2246, 0.4545)
1.8	(0, 0.1536, 0.3148)	(0, 0.1536, 0.3903)
1.9	(0, 0.0264, 0.1265)	(0, 0.0011, 0.0234)
1.0	(0, −0.018, −0.012)	(0, 0.0000, 0.0000)

References

Armand, A., Allahviranloo, T., Abbasbandy, S., Gouyandeh, Z., 2019. The fuzzy generalized Taylor's expansion with application in fractional differential equations. Iran. J. Fuzzy Syst. 16 (2), 57–72.

Chehlabi, M., Allahviranloo, T., 2016. Concreted solutions to fuzzy linear fractional differential equations. Appl. Soft Comput. 44, 108–116.

Garrappa, R., Kaslik, E., Popolizio, M., 2019. Evaluation of fractional integrals and derivatives of elementary functions: overview and tutorial. Mathematics 7, 407.

Mathai, A.M., Haubold, H.J., 2017. An Introduction to Fractional Calculus. Nova Science Publishers, Inc., Hauppauge, New York

Van Hoa, N., Ho, V., Duc, T.M., 2019. Fuzzy fractional differential equations under Caputo–Katugampola fractional derivative approach. Fuzzy Sets Syst. 375, 70–99.

Chapter 7

Numerical solutions of uncertain partial differential equations

7.1 Introduction

In this chapter, first fuzzy heat and Poisson equations with fuzzy initial values are considered. The concept of generalized Hukuhara differentiation is interpreted thoroughly in the univariate and multivariate cases. The first objective of this chapter is to prove the uniqueness of a solution for a fuzzy heat equation and show that a fuzzy heat equation can be modeled as two systems of fuzzy differential equations by considering the type of differentiability of solutions. Then the fuzzy Fourier transform is applied for solving the fuzzy heat equation.

As the second object, the fuzzy Poisson's equation and the fuzzy finite difference method are introduced. Then, the fuzzy Poisson's equation is discretized by the fuzzy finite difference method and it is solved as a linear system of equations. In addition, we discuss the fuzzy Laplace equation as a special case of the fuzzy Poisson's equation. In addition, the convergence of method is taken into account.

Soft Numerical Computing in Uncertain Dynamic Systems. https://doi.org/10.1016/B978-0-12-822855-5.00007-0

7.1.1 Partial ordering

For two fuzzy numbers $A, B \in \mathbb{F}_R$, we call $\preccurlyeq$ a partial order notation and:

$$A \preccurlyeq (\prec) B \text{ if any only if } A_l(r) \leq (<) B_l(r) \text{ and } A_u(r) \leq (<) B_u(r)$$

$$\text{If } A \preccurlyeq (\succcurlyeq) B \text{ then } A \ominus_{gH} B \ \preccurlyeq (\succcurlyeq) 0$$

for any $r \in [0, 1]$ (see Allahviranloo, 2020).

7.1.2 Continuity

Consider the fuzzy number valued function $x : [a, b] \to \mathbb{F}_R$ we say the function is continuous at a point like $t_0 \in [a, b]$ if for any $\epsilon > 0 \exists \delta > 0$ subject to $D_H(x(t), x(t_0)) < \epsilon$ whenever x is an arbitrary value from $|x - x_0| < \delta$.

7.1.3 Minimum and maximum

For any gH-differentiable fuzzy number function $x(t)$ at the inner point, such as $c \in (a, b)$, if the function has local minimum or maximum, then $x_{gH}{}'(c) = 0$ and:

$$\forall t \in [a, b] \ \exists t_{\text{Min}} \ \exists t_{\text{Max}} \in [a, b] \text{ s.t. } x(t_{\text{Min}}) \preccurlyeq x(t) \preccurlyeq x(t_{\text{Max}})$$

where $\max_{a \leq t \leq b} x(t) = x(t_{\text{Max}})$ and $\min_{a \leq t \leq b} x(t) = x(t_{\text{Min}})$.

For more information, see Allahviranloo et al. (2015) and Gouyandeha et al. (2017).

7.1.4 Production in partial gH-differentiability

Suppose that $u(x, t) : R \times R^{\geq 0} \to \mathbb{F}_R$ is a fuzzy number valued function and it is gH-partial differentiable at (x, t) on $\overline{D}$ (Bede & Gal, 2005a, b; Stefanini & Bede, 2009). Also let us suppose the function $v(x, t) : R \times R^{\geq 0} \to R$ is a differentiable real function in the same region. Then:

$$\partial_{tgH}(u \odot v)(x, t) = \partial_{tgH} u(x, t) \odot v(x, t) \oplus v'(x, t) \odot u(x, t)$$

7.1.5 Fuzzy integrating factor

Consider the following two-point fuzzy boundary value problem for $t \in [a, b]$:

$$y''_{gH}(t) \oplus p(t) \odot y'_{gH}(t) = 0, \ y(a) = c_0, \ y(b) = c_1$$

where $p(t) \in R, c_0, c_1 \in \mathbb{F}_R$. Multiplying both sides by the integrating factor $e^{\int p(t) dt}$, we get:

$$e^{\int p(t)\mathrm{d}t} \odot y''_{gH}(t) \oplus p(t)e^{\int p(t)\mathrm{d}t} \odot y'_{gH}(t) = 0$$

Using the production in gH-derivative, we have:

$$\left(e^{\int p(t)\mathrm{d}t} \odot y'_{gH}(t)\right)'_{gH} = 0$$

So, by taking the integral:

$$e^{\int p(t)\mathrm{d}t} \odot y'_{gH}(t) = \lambda_0 \in \mathbb{F}_R$$

Again, integrating both sides:

$$\int_a^t y'_{gH}(s)\mathrm{d}s = \lambda_0 \odot \int_a^t e^{-\int p(s)\mathrm{d}s} \mathrm{d}s$$

Hence:

$$y(t) \ominus_{gH} c_0 = \lambda_0 \odot \int_a^t e^{-\int p(s)\mathrm{d}s} \mathrm{d}s$$

Therefore, if $y(t)$ is $i-gH$ differentiable, we obtain $y(t) = c_0 \oplus \lambda_0 \odot \int_a^t e^{-\int p(s)\mathrm{d}s}\mathrm{d}s$ and if $y(t)$ is $ii-gH$ differentiable, we obtain $y(t) = c_0 \ominus_H (-1)\lambda_0 \odot \int_a^t e^{-\int p(s)\mathrm{d}s}\mathrm{d}s$:

$$\lambda_0 = \frac{c_1 \ominus_{gH} c_0}{\int_a^b e^{-\int p(s)\mathrm{d}s} \mathrm{d}s}$$

7.2 The fuzzy heat equation

Assume that we have a rod of some material of constant cross-section that is surrounded by insulation so that heat can only flow along the rod and not out of the cylindrical surface. We assume that the rod is infinitely long ($-\infty < x < \infty$) and that no boundary conditions are required. Moreover, the temperature is uniform across each cross-section. A fuzzy heat equation models the flow of heat in this rod that is insulated everywhere except at the two ends. We start with an initial temperature distribution $u(x,0) = f(x)$, such that $f(x) \in \mathbb{F}_\mathrm{R}$, then the fuzzy heat equation is as follows:

$$\partial_{tgH}u(x,t) \ominus_{gH}\kappa \odot \partial_{xxgH}u(x,t) = F(x,t), \ \ \kappa \in R^{\geq 0}$$

where κ is the constant heat conductivity coefficient and the fuzzy function $u(x,t): R \times R^{\geq 0} \to \mathbb{F}_R$ that models heat flow should satisfy the fuzzy heat equation.

First, we shall discuss the existence and uniqueness of the solution, and to this end we need the maximum principle. This principle has a simple interpretation: if we have an insulated rod of length L that can only be heated at the ends of the rod when $x=0$ or $x=L$, then the temperature cannot rise above the maximum of the initial temperatures and the temperatures at the ends of the rod.

7.2.1 Theorem—Fuzzy maximum principle

Let us consider that the fuzzy number valued function $u(x,t)$ is the solution of the fuzzy heat equation:

$$\partial_{tgH}u(x,t) \ominus_{gH}\kappa \odot \partial_{xxgH}u(x,t) \preccurlyeq 0$$

in $D=\{(x,t)|0<x<L, 0<t\leq T\}$ and is a fuzzy continuous in $\overline{D}=\{(x,t) \,|\, 0<x<L, 0<t\leq T\}$. Hence $u(x,t)$ attains its maximal values on the set:

$$\Gamma=\{(x,t)|\ x=0, 0\leq t\leq T; x=L, 0\leq t\leq T; 0<x<L, t=0\}$$

Proof. We first prove that if $v(x,t)$ is a fuzzy continuous function in $\overline{D}$ and satisfies the inequality in D:

$$\partial_{tgH}v(x,t) \ominus_{gH}\partial_{xxgH}v(x,t) \prec 0$$

and it assumes its maximum on Γ. Suppose that v has a local maximum at $P=(x_0,t_0)$ in D. According to the maximum and minimum theorem, we have:

$$\partial_{tgH}v(x_0,t_0)=0, \ \ \partial_{xxgH}v(x_0,t_0) \preccurlyeq 0$$

Since $\kappa>0$, and based on the properties of the partial ordering, we have:

$$\partial_{tgH}v(x,t) \ominus_{gH}\kappa \odot \partial_{xxgH}v(x,t) \succcurlyeq 0$$

and indeed, it contradicts the fact that $v(x,t)$ satisfies:

$$\partial_{tgH}v(x,t) \ominus_{gH}\partial_{xxgH}v(x,t) \prec 0$$

Moreover, since $v(x,t)$ is continuous in $\overline{D}$, we suppose that $M=\max_{\Gamma} v(x,t)$ and $M\in\mathbb{F}_R$. Now if we define:

$$v(x,t)=u(x,t)+\epsilon x^2, \ \ \epsilon>0$$

then:

$$\partial_{tgH}v(x,t) \ominus_{gH}\kappa \odot \partial_{xxgH}v(x,t) = \partial_{tgH}u(x,t) \ominus_{gH}\kappa \odot \partial_{xxgH}\left(u(x,t)+\epsilon x^2\right)$$

$$= \partial_{tgH} u(x,t) \ominus_{gH} \kappa \odot \partial_{xxgH}\left(u(x,t) + \epsilon x^2\right) - 2\kappa\epsilon = -2\kappa\epsilon \prec 0$$

then:

$$\partial_{tgH} v(x,t) \ominus_{gH} \kappa \odot \partial_{xxgH} v(x,t) \prec 0$$

and it assumes its maximum on Γ. Therefore:

$$\forall (x,t) \in \overline{R}, v(x,t) = u(x,t) + \epsilon x^2 \preccurlyeq M + \epsilon L^2$$

By removing the arbitrary small ϵ we have:

$$u(x,t) \preccurlyeq v(x,t) \preccurlyeq M$$

The proof is completed (Allahviranloo et al., 2015; Armand et al., 2019; Gouyandeha et al., 2017).

7.2.2 Theorem—Existence

There exists at most one solution of the fuzzy heat equation:

$$\begin{cases} \partial_{tgH} u(x,t) \ominus_{gH} \partial_{xxgH} u(x,t) = F(x,t), & -\infty < x < \infty, t > 0 \\ u(x,0) = f(x), & -\infty < x < \infty \end{cases}$$

which is continuous and bounded in the region $R = \{(x,t) | -\infty < x < \infty, t \geq 0\}$.

Proof. Suppose that w and v are two arbitrary solutions for the fuzzy heat equation and there is a $M \in \mathbb{F}_R, M \succcurlyeq 0$ such that $|w| \preccurlyeq M$ and $|v| \preccurlyeq M$. Let us consider $u = w \ominus_{gH} v$, then u satisfies the following relations:

$$\partial_{tgH} u(x,t) \ominus_{gH} \partial_{xxgH} u(x,t) = 0, \quad u(x,0) = 0, \quad |u| \preccurlyeq M$$

For two arbitrary positive L and T, consider a rectangle as a region:

$$S = \{(x,t) | -L \leq x \leq L, 0 \leq t \leq T\}$$

Define:

$$g(x,t) = \frac{4M}{L^2}\left(\frac{x^2}{2} + \kappa t\right)$$

We have:

$$\partial_{tgH} g(x,t) = \frac{4M\kappa}{L^2}, \quad \partial_{xxgH} g(x,t) = \frac{4M}{L^2}$$

Therefore, in S:

$$\partial_{tgH} g(x,t) \ominus_{gH} \partial_{xxgH} g(x,t) = 0$$

and:

$$g(x,0)=\frac{2Mx^2}{L^2}\succcurlyeq 0=u(x,0),\ \ g(\pm L,t)=2M+\frac{4M\kappa t}{L^2}\succcurlyeq 2M\succcurlyeq u(\pm L,t).$$

By using the maximum principle in $\overline{S}$, we have $g(x,t)\succcurlyeq u(x,t)$. Similarly, we obtain $u(x,t)\succcurlyeq -g(x,t)$, then:

$$-g(x,t)\preccurlyeq u(x,t)\preccurlyeq g(x,t)$$

and it means:

$$|u(x,t)|\preccurlyeq g(x,t)=\frac{4M}{L^2}\left(\frac{x^2}{2}+\kappa t\right).$$

Since $L>0$ and if $L\to\infty$ then $|u(x,t)|=0$ and it concludes:

$$u(x,t)=w(x,t)\ominus_{gH}v(x,t)=0$$

then in the areas $-\infty<x<\infty,\ 0\le t\le T,\ \ \forall(x,t),\ w(x,t)=v(x,t)$. So these two arbitrary solutions are the same and it means the fuzzy solution of the fuzzy heat equation is unique.

7.3 Analytical solution of the fuzzy heat equation

Consider the following fuzzy heat equation:

$$\partial_{tgH}u(x,t)\ominus_{gH}\kappa\odot\partial_{xxgH}u(x,t)=0,\ \ u(x,0)=\begin{cases}u_0\in\mathbb{F}_R, & x>0\\ 0, & x<0\end{cases}$$

Consider a fuzzy function $u(x,t):R\times R^{\geq 0}\to\mathbb{F}_R$ is the fuzzy analytical solution of the mentioned above equation. To find the analytical solution of the fuzzy heat equation, we introduce the dilatation transformation:

$$\xi(x)=\epsilon^a x,\ \ \tau(t)=\epsilon^b t,\ \ a,b>0$$

Then we define:

$$w(\xi,\tau)=\epsilon^c u\left(\epsilon^{-a}\xi,\epsilon^{-b}\tau\right),\ \ \epsilon\in R,\ \ c>0$$

Note that $\xi(x)$ and $\tau(t)$ are strictly increasing, so this changing variable gives:

$$\partial_{tgH}u(x,t)=\epsilon^{-c}\odot\partial_{\tau gH}w(\xi,\tau)\odot\partial_{tgH}\tau=\epsilon^{b-c}\odot\partial_{\tau gH}w(\xi,\tau)$$

$$\partial_{xgH}u(x,t)=\epsilon^{-c}\odot\partial_{\xi gH}w(\xi,\tau)\odot\partial_{xgH}\xi=\epsilon^{a-c}\odot\partial_{\xi gH}w(\xi,\tau)$$

$$\partial_{xxgH}u(x,t)=\epsilon^{a-c}\odot\partial_{\xi gH}\left(\partial_{\xi gH}w(\xi,\tau)\right)\odot\partial_{xgH}\xi=\epsilon^{2a-c}\odot\partial_{\xi\xi gH}w(\xi,\tau)$$

So, the fuzzy heat equation transforms into:

$$\epsilon^{b-c} \odot \partial_{\tau gH} w(\xi, \tau) \ominus_{gH} \kappa \epsilon^{2a-c} \odot \partial_{\xi\xi gH} w(\xi, \tau) = 0$$

and is invariant under the dilatation transformation if $b=2a$ for all ε. Thus, if u solves the equation at x, t then $w=\epsilon^{-c}u$ solves the equation at $x=\varepsilon^{-a}\xi$, $t=\varepsilon^{-b}\tau$. We can build some groupings of independent variables, such as:

$$\frac{\xi}{\tau^{\frac{a}{b}}} = \frac{x}{t^{\frac{a}{b}}} = \frac{\epsilon^a x}{(\epsilon^b t)^{\frac{a}{b}}}$$

which define the variable $\eta(x, t) = \frac{x}{\sqrt{2\kappa\tau}}$, since $b=2a$. This implies that:

$$\frac{w}{\tau^{\frac{c}{b}}} = \frac{u}{t^{\frac{c}{b}}} = \frac{\epsilon^c}{(\epsilon^b t)^{\frac{c}{b}}} = v(\eta)$$

We look for the solution of fuzzy heat equation of the form $u(x, t) = t^{\frac{c}{2a}} \odot v(\eta)$, where $v(\eta) \in \mathbb{F}_R$. Under the assumptions that all $gH-p-$derivatives of $u(x,t)$ exist, we examine the solution of the fuzzy heat equation:

- If $x>0$ then $\partial_{tgH}\eta(x, t) = \frac{-x}{2t\sqrt{2\kappa t}} = \frac{-1}{2t}\eta(x, t) := \frac{-\eta}{2t} < 0$, then:

$$\partial_{t,i-gH} u(x, t) = \frac{c}{2a} t^{\frac{c}{2a}-1} \odot v(\eta) \oplus t^{\frac{c}{2a}} \odot \partial_{t,ii-gH}\eta v'_{ii-gH}(\eta) =$$

$$= \frac{1}{2} t^{\frac{c}{2a}-1} \left(\frac{c}{a} \odot v(\eta) \ominus_{gH} \eta \odot v'_{ii-gH}(\eta) \right)$$

$$\partial_{t,ii-gH} u(x, t) = \frac{c}{2a} t^{\frac{c}{2a}-1} \odot v(\eta) \oplus t^{\frac{c}{2a}} \odot \partial_{t,i-gH}\eta v'_{ii-gH}(\eta) =$$

$$= \frac{1}{2} t^{\frac{c}{2a}-1} \left(\frac{c}{a} \odot v(\eta) \ominus_{gH} \eta \odot v'_{i-gH}(\eta) \right)$$

- If $x<0$ then $\partial_{tgH}\eta(x, t) = \frac{-x}{2t\sqrt{2\kappa t}} = \frac{\eta}{2t} > 0$, then:

$$\partial_{t,i-gH} u(x, t) = \frac{c}{2a} t^{\frac{c}{2a}-1} \odot v(\eta) \oplus t^{\frac{c}{2a}} \odot \partial_{t,i-gH}\eta v'_{i-gH}(\eta) =$$

$$= \frac{1}{2} t^{\frac{c}{2a}-1} \left(\frac{c}{a} \odot v(\eta) \ominus_{gH} \eta \odot v'_{i-gH}(\eta) \right)$$

$$\partial_{t,ii-gH} u(x, t) = \frac{c}{2a} t^{\frac{c}{2a}-1} \odot v(\eta) \oplus t^{\frac{c}{2a}} \odot \partial_{t,i-gH}\eta v'_{ii-gH}(\eta) =$$

$$=\frac{1}{2}t^{\frac{c}{2a}-1}\left(\frac{c}{a}\odot v(\eta)\ominus_{gH}\eta\odot v'_{ii-gH}(\eta)\right)$$

Also, considering that $\partial_x\eta=\frac{1}{\sqrt{2\kappa t}}>0$, we get:

$$\partial_{xgH}u(x,t)=t^{\frac{c}{2a}}\odot v'_{gH}(\eta)\odot\partial_x\eta=\frac{t^{\frac{c}{2a}-\frac{1}{2}}}{\sqrt{2\kappa}}\odot v'_{gH}(\eta)$$

Therefore, we observe that:

$$\partial_{xxgH}u(x,t)=\frac{t^{\frac{c}{2a}-\frac{1}{2}}}{\sqrt{2\kappa}}\odot v''_{gH}(\eta)$$

This means that $\partial_x\eta$ does not change the type of differentiability of $u(x,t)$ with respect to x. We then obtain the following expressions.

Case 1. Let assume that the type of $gH-p$-differentiability for $u(x,t)$ and $\partial_x u(x,t)$ do not change with respect to x, so we obtain the following:

1.1. If $u(x,t)$ is $i-gH-p$ differentiable with respect to t then using the mentioned partial differentiability in two cases $x>0$ and $x<0$, and:

$$\partial_{xxgH}u(x,t)=\frac{t^{\frac{c}{2a}-\frac{1}{2}}}{\sqrt{2\kappa}}\odot v''_{gH}(\eta)$$

The fuzzy heat equation reduces to the following fuzzy heat equations:

$$\begin{cases} t^{\frac{\gamma}{2}-1}\left(v''_{i,gH}(\eta)\oplus\eta\odot v'_{ii,gH}(\eta)\ominus_{gH}\gamma\odot v(\eta)\right)=0, & \text{if } x>0 \\ t^{\frac{\gamma}{2}-1}\left(v''_{i,gH}(\eta)\oplus\eta\odot v'_{i,gH}(\eta)\ominus_{gH}\gamma\odot v(\eta)\right)=0, & \text{if } x<0 \end{cases}$$

with $\gamma=\frac{c}{a}$ such that $u(x,t)=t^{\frac{\gamma}{2}}v(\eta)$ and $=\frac{x}{\sqrt{2\kappa t}}$. Since $u=t^{\frac{\gamma}{2}}v(\eta)\to u_0$ as $\eta\to+\infty$ where u_0 does not depend on t, γ must be zero. Hence, $v(\eta)$ is the solution of the fuzzy boundary value differential equations:

$$\begin{cases} \begin{cases} v''_{i,gH}(\eta)\oplus\eta\odot v'_{ii,gH}(\eta)=0 \\ v(+\infty)=u_0\in\mathbb{F}_R \end{cases} & \text{if } x>0 \\ \begin{cases} v''_{i,gH}(\eta)\oplus\eta\odot v'_{i,gH}(\eta)=0 \\ v(-\infty)=0\in\mathbb{F}_R \end{cases} & \text{if } x<0 \end{cases}$$

In the case where $x>0$, we use the fuzzy integrating factoring method to get the following relations:

$$e^{\frac{\eta^2}{2}}\odot v''_{i,gH}(\eta)\oplus\eta e^{\frac{\eta^2}{2}}\odot v'_{ii,gH}(\eta)=\left(e^{\frac{\eta^2}{2}}\odot v'_{ii,gH}(\eta)\right)'_{i,gH}=0$$

then:

$$e^{\frac{\eta^2}{2}} \odot v'_{ii,gH}(\eta) = \lambda_0 \Longrightarrow v'_{ii,gH}(\eta) = \lambda_0 \odot e^{\frac{-\eta^2}{2}}$$

hence:

$$\int_{\eta}^{+\infty} v'_{ii,gH}(y)dy = \lambda_0 \odot \int_{\eta}^{+\infty} e^{\frac{-y^2}{2}} dy$$

since:

$$\int_{\eta}^{+\infty} v'_{ii,gH}(y)\mathrm{d}y = v(+\infty) \ominus_{gH} v(\eta), \quad \int_{\eta}^{+\infty} e^{\frac{-y^2}{2}} \mathrm{d}y = \sqrt{2}\lambda_0 \odot \int_{\frac{\eta}{\sqrt{2}}}^{+\infty} e^{-s^2} \mathrm{d}s$$

so:

$$v(+\infty) \ominus_{gH} v(\eta) = \sqrt{2}\lambda_0 \odot \int_{\frac{\eta}{\sqrt{2}}}^{+\infty} e^{-s^2} \mathrm{d}s$$

$$v(\eta) = u_0 \oplus (-1)\sqrt{2}\lambda_0 \odot \int_{\frac{\eta}{\sqrt{2}}}^{+\infty} e^{-s^2} \mathrm{d}s$$

It is concluded that in this case, $v(\eta)$ is $ii-gH$ differentiable.

In the case where $x<0$, we use the fuzzy integrating factoring method to get the following relations:

$$e^{\frac{\eta^2}{2}} \odot v''_{i,gH}(\eta) \oplus \eta e^{\frac{\eta^2}{2}} \odot v'_{i,gH}(\eta) = \left(e^{\frac{\eta^2}{2}} \odot v'_{i,gH}(\eta)\right)'_{i,gH} = 0$$

then:

$$e^{\frac{\eta^2}{2}} \odot v'_{i,gH}(\eta) = \lambda_0 \Longrightarrow v'_{i,gH}(\eta) = \lambda_0 \odot e^{\frac{-\eta^2}{2}}$$

hence:

$$\int_{-\infty}^{\eta} v'_{i,gH}(y)dy = \lambda_0 \odot \int_{-\infty}^{\eta} e^{\frac{-y^2}{2}} \mathrm{d}y$$

since:

$$\int_{-\infty}^{\eta} v'_{i,gH}(y)\mathrm{d}y = v(\eta) \ominus_{gH} v(-\infty), \quad \int_{-\infty}^{\eta} e^{\frac{-y^2}{2}} \mathrm{d}y = \sqrt{2}\lambda_0 \odot \int_{-\infty}^{\frac{\eta}{\sqrt{2}}} e^{-s^2} \mathrm{d}s$$

so:

$$v(\eta) \ominus_{gH} v(-\infty) = \sqrt{2}\lambda_0 \odot \int_{-\infty}^{\frac{\eta}{\sqrt{2}}} e^{-s^2} \mathrm{d}s$$

$$v(\eta) = v(-\infty) \oplus \sqrt{2}\lambda_0 \odot \int_{-\infty}^{\frac{\eta}{\sqrt{2}}} e^{-s^2} ds$$

Finally, by adding both sides of the following relations, we get:

$$v(+\infty) \ominus_{gH} v(\eta) = \sqrt{2}\lambda_0 \odot \int_{\frac{\eta}{\sqrt{2}}}^{+\infty} e^{-s^2} ds, v(\eta) \ominus_{gH} v(-\infty) = \sqrt{2}\lambda_0 \odot \int_{-\infty}^{\frac{\eta}{\sqrt{2}}} e^{-s^2} ds$$

We have:

$$v(+\infty) \ominus_{gH} v(-\infty) = \sqrt{2}\lambda_0 \odot \int_{\frac{\eta}{\sqrt{2}}}^{+\infty} e^{-s^2} ds \oplus \sqrt{2}\lambda_0 \odot \int_{-\infty}^{\frac{\eta}{\sqrt{2}}} e^{-s^2} ds$$

$$= \sqrt{2}\lambda_0 \odot \left(\int_{-\infty}^{\frac{\eta}{\sqrt{2}}} e^{-s^2} ds + \int_{\frac{\eta}{\sqrt{2}}}^{+\infty} e^{-s^2} ds \right) = \sqrt{2}\lambda_0 \odot \int_{-\infty}^{\infty} e^{-s^2} ds$$

Indeed:

$$u_0 \ominus_{gH} 0 = \sqrt{2}\lambda_0 \odot \int_{-\infty}^{+\infty} e^{-s^2} ds$$

Since, $\int_{-\infty}^{+\infty} e^{-s^2} ds = \sqrt{\pi}$ then:

$$\lambda_0 = \frac{u_0}{\sqrt{2\pi}}$$

Case $x > 0$ and $v(\eta)$ is $ii - gH$ differentiable:

$$v(\eta) = u_0 \oplus (-1) \frac{u_0}{\sqrt{\pi}} \odot \int_{\frac{\eta}{\sqrt{2}}}^{+\infty} e^{-s^2} ds$$

Case $x < 0$ and $v(\eta)$ is $i - gH$ differentiable:

$$v(\eta) = \frac{u_0}{\sqrt{\pi}} \odot \int_{-\infty}^{\frac{\eta}{\sqrt{2}}} e^{-s^2} ds$$

since:

$$\gamma = \frac{c}{a}, \ u(x,t) = t^{\frac{\gamma}{2}} v(\eta), \ \eta = \frac{x}{\sqrt{2\kappa t}}$$

Hence the analytical solution of the fuzzy heat equations can be obtained as follows:

$$\begin{cases} u(x,t) = t^{\frac{\gamma}{2}}\left(u_0 \oplus (-1)\dfrac{u_0}{\sqrt{\pi}} \odot \displaystyle\int_{\frac{x}{2\sqrt{\kappa t}}}^{+\infty} e^{-s^2}\,ds\right), & x>0 \\ u(x,t) = t^{\frac{\gamma}{2}} \odot \left(\dfrac{u_0}{\sqrt{\pi}} \odot \displaystyle\int_{-\infty}^{\frac{x}{2\sqrt{\kappa t}}} e^{-s^2}\,ds\right), & x<0 \end{cases}$$

1.2. If $u(x,t)$ is $ii-gH-p$ differentiable with respect to t, then according to the process described above, we obtain the following equations:

$$\begin{cases} \begin{cases} v''_{i,gH}(\eta) \oplus \eta \odot v'_{i,gH}(\eta) = 0 \\ v(+\infty) = u_0 \in \mathbb{F}_R \end{cases} & \text{if } x>0 \\ \begin{cases} v''_{i,gH}(\eta) \oplus \eta \odot v'_{ii,gH}(\eta) = 0 \\ v(-\infty) = 0 \in \mathbb{F}_R \end{cases} & \text{if } x<0 \end{cases}$$

Using the same process, the analytical solution of the fuzzy heat equations can be obtained as follows:

$$\begin{cases} u(x,t) = t^{\frac{\gamma}{2}}\left(u_0 \ominus_{gH} \dfrac{u_0}{\sqrt{\pi}} \odot \displaystyle\int_{\frac{x}{2\sqrt{\kappa t}}}^{+\infty} e^{-s^2}\,ds\right), & x>0 \\ u(x,t) = t^{\frac{\gamma}{2}} \odot \left(\dfrac{u_0}{\sqrt{\pi}} \odot \displaystyle\int_{-\infty}^{\frac{x}{2\sqrt{\kappa t}}} e^{-s^2}\,ds\right), & x<0 \end{cases}$$

Case 2. Let assume that the type of $gH-p$-differentiability for $u(x,t)$ and $\partial_x u(x,t)$ changes with respect to x, so we obtain the following:

2.1. If $u(x,t)$ is $i-gH-p$ differentiable with respect to t then, according to the process described above, we obtain the following equations:

$$\begin{cases} \begin{cases} v''_{ii,gH}(\eta) \oplus \eta \odot v'_{ii,gH}(\eta) = 0 \\ v(+\infty) = u_0 \in \mathbb{F}_R \end{cases} & \text{if } x>0 \\ \begin{cases} v''_{ii,gH}(\eta) \oplus \eta \odot v'_{i,gH}(\eta) = 0 \\ v(-\infty) = 0 \in \mathbb{F}_R \end{cases} & \text{if } x<0 \end{cases}$$

Hence the analytical solution of the fuzzy heat equations can be obtained as follows:

$$\begin{cases} u(x,t) = t^{\frac{\gamma}{2}}\left(u_0 \oplus (-1)\dfrac{u_0}{\sqrt{\pi}} \odot \displaystyle\int_{\frac{x}{2\sqrt{\kappa t}}}^{+\infty} e^{-s^2}\mathrm{d}s\right), & x>0 \\ u(x,t) = t^{\frac{\gamma}{2}} \odot \left(\dfrac{u_0}{\sqrt{\pi}} \odot \displaystyle\int_{-\infty}^{\frac{x}{2\sqrt{\kappa t}}} e^{-s^2}\mathrm{d}s\right), & x<0 \end{cases}$$

2.2. If $u(x,t)$ is $ii-gH-p$ differentiable with respect to t then, according to the process described above, we obtain the following equations:

$$\begin{cases} \begin{cases} v''_{ii,gH}(\eta) \oplus \eta \odot v'_{i,gH}(\eta) = 0 \\ v(+\infty) = u_0 \in \mathbb{F}_R \end{cases} & \text{if } x>0 \\ \begin{cases} v''_{ii,gH}(\eta) \oplus \eta \odot v'_{ii,gH}(\eta) = 0 \\ v(-\infty) = 0 \in \mathbb{F}_R \end{cases} & \text{if } x<0 \end{cases}$$

$$\begin{cases} u(x,t) = t^{\frac{\gamma}{2}}\left(u_0 \ominus_{gH} \dfrac{u_0}{\sqrt{\pi}} \odot \displaystyle\int_{\frac{x}{2\sqrt{\kappa t}}}^{+\infty} e^{-s^2}\mathrm{d}s\right), & x>0 \\ u(x,t) = t^{\frac{\gamma}{2}} \odot \left(\dfrac{u_0}{\sqrt{\pi}} \odot \displaystyle\int_{-\infty}^{\frac{x}{2\sqrt{\kappa t}}} e^{-s^2}\mathrm{d}s\right), & x<0 \end{cases}$$

To summarize, in all cases we have:

- $u(x,t)$ is $i-p-gH$ differentiable:

$$\begin{cases} u(x,t) = t^{\frac{\gamma}{2}}\left(u_0 \oplus (-1)\dfrac{u_0}{\sqrt{\pi}} \odot \displaystyle\int_{\frac{x}{2\sqrt{\kappa t}}}^{+\infty} e^{-s^2}\mathrm{d}s\right), & x>0 \\ u(x,t) = t^{\frac{\gamma}{2}} \odot \left(\dfrac{u_0}{\sqrt{\pi}} \odot \displaystyle\int_{-\infty}^{\frac{x}{2\sqrt{\kappa t}}} e^{-s^2}\mathrm{d}s\right), & x<0 \end{cases}$$

- $u(x,t)$ is $ii-p-gH$ differentiable:

$$\begin{cases} u(x,t) = t^{\frac{\gamma}{2}}\left(u_0 \ominus_{gH} \frac{u_0}{\sqrt{\pi}} \odot \int_{\frac{x}{2\sqrt{\kappa t}}}^{+\infty} e^{-s^2} ds\right), & x>0 \\ u(x,t) = t^{\frac{\gamma}{2}} \odot \left(\frac{u_0}{\sqrt{\pi}} \odot \int_{-\infty}^{\frac{x}{2\sqrt{\kappa t}}} e^{-s^2} ds\right), & x<0 \end{cases}$$

Example. Consider the following heat equation:

$$\partial_{t,i-gH} u(x,t) \ominus_{gH} \partial_{xx,ii-gH} u(x,t) = 0,\ u(x,0) = \begin{cases} (1,3,5), & x>0 \\ 0, & x<0 \end{cases}$$

Since $u(x,t)$ is $i-p-gH$ differentiable with respect to t, then for $x>0$ we have:

$$u(x,t,r) = \left[(2r+1) + \frac{1}{2}(-2r+5)\left(\operatorname{erf}\left(\frac{x}{2\sqrt{\pi}}\right) - 1\right),\right.$$

$$\left.(-2r+5) + \frac{1}{2}(2r+1)\left(\operatorname{erf}\left(\frac{x}{2\sqrt{\pi}}\right) - 1\right)\right]$$

If $x<0$:

$$u(x,t,r) = \left[\frac{1}{2}(2r+1)\left(\operatorname{erf}\left(\frac{x}{2\sqrt{\pi}}\right) + 1\right), \frac{1}{2}(-2r+5)\left(\operatorname{erf}\left(\frac{x}{2\sqrt{\pi}}\right) + 1\right)\right]$$

For $r=\frac{1}{2}$ and $t \in [1,4]$, Fig. 7.1 shows the fuzzy solutions in two cases $x>0$ and $x<0$.

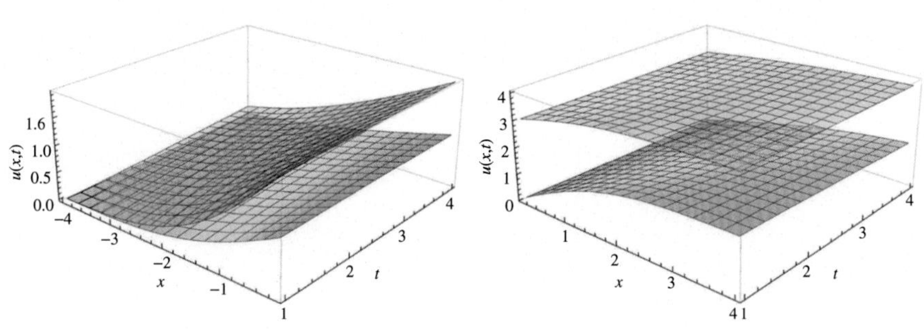

Fig. 7.1 The fuzzy solutions in two cases $x>0$ (*left*) and $x<0$ (*right*) for $r=\frac{1}{2}$.

Example. Consider the following heat equation:

$$\partial_{t,ii-gH}u(x,t)\ominus_{gH}2\odot\partial_{xx,i-gH}u(x,t)=0,\qquad u(x,0)=\begin{cases}(-3.5,\,-2,\,-1), & x<0\\ 0, & x>0\end{cases}$$

Since $u(x,t)$ is $ii-p-gH$ differentiable with respect to t, then for $x>0$ we have:

$$u(x,t,r)=\left[\left(\frac{3}{2}r-3.5\right)+\frac{1}{2}\left(\frac{3}{2}r-3.5\right)\left(\operatorname{erf}\left(\frac{\sqrt{2}x}{4\sqrt{\pi}}\right)-1\right),\right.$$
$$\left.(-r-1)+\frac{1}{2}(-r-1)\left(\operatorname{erf}\left(\frac{\sqrt{2}x}{4\sqrt{\pi}}\right)-1\right)\right]$$

If $x<0$:

$$u(x,t,r)=\left[\frac{1}{2}\left(\frac{3}{2}r-3.5\right)\left(\operatorname{erf}\left(\frac{\sqrt{2}x}{4\sqrt{\pi}}\right)+1\right),\frac{1}{2}(-r-1)\left(\operatorname{erf}\left(\frac{\sqrt{2}x}{4\sqrt{\pi}}\right)+1\right)\right]$$

For $r=\frac{1}{3}$, Fig. 7.2 shows the fuzzy solutions in two cases $x>0$ and $x<0$.and for any $x\in R$ the solution is demonstrated as shown in Fig. 7.3.

Example. Consider the following heat equation:

$$\partial_{t,i-gH}u(x,t)\ominus_{gH}0.76\odot\partial_{xx,i-gH}u(x,t)=0,\ \ u(x,0)=\begin{cases}(0.6,2.2,4.7), & x<0\\ 0, & x>0\end{cases}$$

Since $u(x,t)$ is $ii-p-gH$ differentiable with respect to t, then for $x>0$ we have:

$$u(x,t,r)=\left[(1.6r+0.6)+\frac{1}{2}(-2.5r+4.7)\left(\operatorname{erf}\left(\frac{x}{\sqrt{\frac{19}{25}t}}\right)-1\right),\right.$$
$$\left.(-2.5r+4.7)+\frac{1}{2}(1.6r+0.6)\left(\operatorname{erf}\left(\frac{x}{\sqrt{\frac{19}{25}t}}\right)-1\right)\right]$$

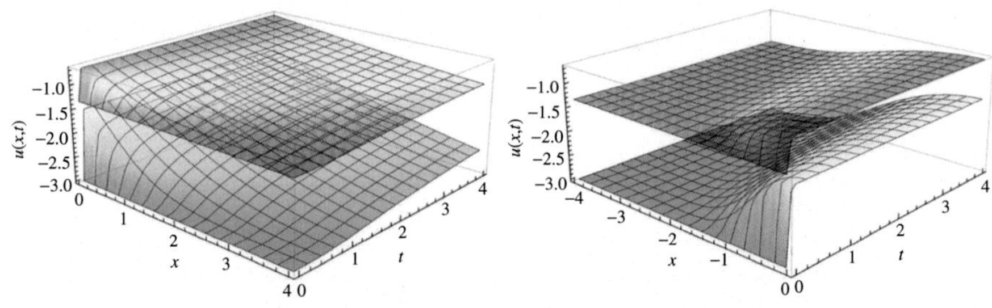

Fig. 7.2 The fuzzy solutions in two cases $x>0$ (*left*) and $x<0$ (*right*) for $r=\frac{1}{3}$.

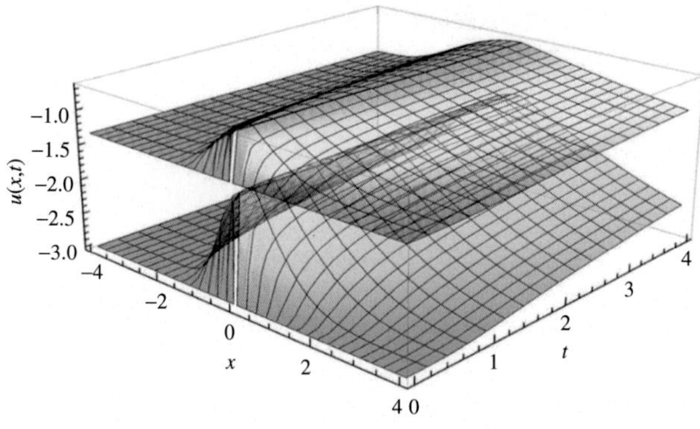

Fig. 7.3 The fuzzy solution for all $x \in R$.

If $x<0$:

$$u(x,t,r)=\left[\frac{1}{2}(1.6r+0.6)\left(\operatorname{erf}\left(\frac{x}{\sqrt{\frac{19}{25}t}}\right)+1\right),\frac{1}{2}(-2.5r+4.7)\left(\operatorname{erf}\left(\frac{x}{\sqrt{\frac{19}{25}t}}\right)+1\right)\right]$$

For $r=\frac{1}{3}$, Fig. 7.4 shows the fuzzy solutions in two cases $x>0$ and $x<0$.

7.3.1 The fundamental solution of the fuzzy heat equation

In this section, we are going to find the solution of a fuzzy heat equation based on the fuzzy Fourier transforms. These transforms have been discussed with more illustration in Chapter 3. Here are some concepts that we need in this section (Gouyandeha et al., 2017).

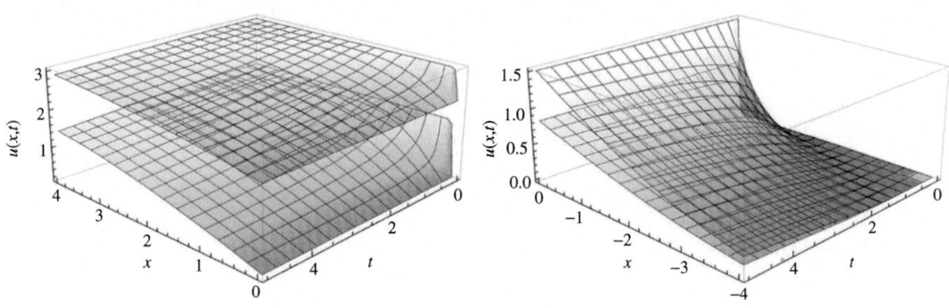

Fig. 7.4 The fuzzy solutions in two cases $x>0$ (*left*) and $x<0$ (*right*) for $r=\frac{1}{3}$.

7.3.2 Fuzzy Fourier transform

Consider the function $f: R \rightarrow \mathbb{F}_R$ is a fuzzy number valued function. The fuzzy Fourier transform of $f(x)$ denoted by $(\mathcal{F}\{f(x)\}: R \rightarrow \mathbb{F}_C)$ is given by the following integral:

$$\mathcal{F}\{f(x)\} = \frac{1}{\sqrt{2\pi}} \int_{-\infty}^{\infty} f(x) \odot e^{-iwx} dx = F(w)$$

Here $\mathbb{F}_C$ is the set of all fuzzy numbers on complex numbers.

7.3.3 Fuzzy inverse Fourier transform

If $F(w)$ is the fuzzy Fourier transform of $f(x)$, then the fuzzy inverse Fourier transform of $F(w)$ is defined as follows:

$$\mathcal{F}^{-1}\{F(w)\} = \frac{1}{\sqrt{2\pi}} \int_{-\infty}^{\infty} f(w) \odot e^{iwx} dw = f(x)$$

Also:

$$\mathcal{F}\{a \odot f(x) \oplus b \odot g(x)\} = a \odot \mathcal{F}\{f(x)\} \oplus b \odot \mathcal{F}\{g(x)\}$$

$$\mathcal{F}\left\{a \odot f(x) \ominus_{gH} b \odot g(x)\right\} = a \odot \mathcal{F}\{f(x)\} \ominus_{gH} b \odot \mathcal{F}\{g(x)\}$$

7.3.4 Fourier transform of *gH*-derivative

Let $f(x)$ be fuzzy continuous, fuzzy absolutely integrable, and converge to zero as $|x| \rightarrow \infty$. Furthermore, if $f_{gH}{}'(x)$ is fuzzy absolutely integrable on $(-\infty, \infty)$. Then:

$$\mathcal{F}\left\{f'_{gH}(x)\right\} = iw\mathcal{F}\{f(x)\}$$

Let $f(x)$ and $f'_{gH}(x)$ be fuzzy continuous on $(-\infty, +\infty)$ and $f_{gH}^{(k)} \rightarrow 0$ as $|x| \rightarrow \infty$, $k=0$, 1 and $f_{gH}^{(j)}$ is absolutely integrable in $(-\infty, +\infty)$, $j=0$, 1, 2, then:

$$\mathcal{F}\left\{f''_{gH}(x)\right\} = \ominus_{gH} w^2 \mathcal{F}\{f(x)\}$$

Consider the following fuzzy homogenous heat equation:

$$\begin{cases} \partial_{tgH} u(x,t) \ominus_{gH} \kappa \odot \partial_{xxgH} u(x,t) = 0, & -\infty < x < \infty, t \geq 0 \\ u(x,0) = f(x), \ \int_{-\infty}^{\infty} D_H(f(x), 0) dx < \infty, & -\infty < x < \infty \end{cases}$$

where $\kappa \in R^{\geq 0}$ is the constant heat conductivity coefficient and $f(x) \in \mathbb{F}_R$ is a fuzzy continuous function and the existence of the solution was discussed in Section 7.1.2.

For the fuzzy absolutely integrable function $u(x,t)$, the Fourier and its inverse transforms are defined as follow:

$$\mathcal{F}\{u(x,t)\} = \frac{1}{\sqrt{2\pi}} \int_{-\infty}^{\infty} u(x,t) \odot e^{-iwx} \mathrm{d}x = U(w,t) := \int_{-\infty}^{\infty} u(x,t) \odot e^{-iwx} \mathrm{d}x$$

$$\mathcal{F}^{-1}\{U(w,t)\} = \frac{1}{\sqrt{2\pi}} \int_{-\infty}^{\infty} U(w,t) \odot e^{iwx} \mathrm{d}w = u(x,t)$$

If $\partial_{tgH}u(x,t)$, $\partial_{xgH}u(x,t)$, $\partial_{xxgH}u(x,t)$ are fuzzy absolutely integrable on $-\infty < x < \infty$, then by using the following property:

$$\mathcal{F}\left\{\partial_{tgH}u(x,t) \ominus_{gH} \kappa \odot \partial_{xxgH}u(x,t)\right\} =$$

$$= \mathcal{F}\left\{\partial_{tgH}u(x,t)\right\} \ominus_{gH} \mathcal{F}\left\{\kappa \odot \partial_{xxgH}u(x,t)\right\} = 0$$

Since:

$$\mathcal{F}\left\{f''_{gH}(x)\right\} = \ominus_{gH} w^2 \mathcal{F}\{f(x)\}$$

then this relation can be rewritten for the $u(x,t)$ as follows:

$$\mathcal{F}\left\{\kappa \odot \partial_{xxgH}u(x,t)\right\} = \ominus_{gH} \kappa \odot w^2 U(w,t)$$

Moreover, since $\partial_{tgH}u(x,t)$ is a fuzzy absolutely integrable function, then we get:

$$D_H\left(\int_{-\infty}^{\infty} \partial_{tgH}u(x,t)\mathrm{d}x, 0\right) \le \int_{-\infty}^{\infty} D_H\left(\partial_{tgH}u(x,t), 0\right)\mathrm{d}x < \infty$$

then $\int_{-\infty}^{\infty} \partial_{tgH}u(x,t)\mathrm{d}x$ converges uniformly. Now we have, $u(x,t)$, $\partial_{tgH}u(x,t)$ are continuous and $\int_{-\infty}^{\infty} \partial_{tgH}u(x,t)\mathrm{d}x$ converges, then we conclude:

If we have:

$$\int_{-\infty}^{\infty} u(x,t) \odot e^{-iwx} \mathrm{d}x = U(w,t)$$

then:

$$\int_{-\infty}^{\infty} \partial_{tgH}u(x,t) e^{-iwx} \mathrm{d}x = \frac{\mathrm{d}U(w,t)}{\mathrm{d}t}$$

Based on the definition of the Fourier transforms:

$$\mathcal{F}\left\{\partial_{tgH}u(x,t)\right\} = \int_{-\infty}^{\infty} \partial_{tgH}u(x,t) \odot e^{-iwx} \mathrm{d}x = \frac{\mathrm{d}U(w,t)}{\mathrm{d}t}$$

On the other hand:

$$\mathcal{F}\{\partial_{tgH}u(x,t)\}\ominus_{gH}\mathcal{F}\{\kappa\odot\partial_{xxgH}u(x,t)\}=0,$$

$$\mathcal{F}\{\kappa\odot\partial_{xxgH}u(x,t)\}=\ominus_{gH}\kappa\odot w^2U(w,t)$$

By substituting:

$$\frac{dU(w,t)}{dt}\ominus_{gH}\ominus_{gH}\kappa\odot w^2U(w,t)=0\Longrightarrow\frac{dU(w,t)}{dt}\oplus\kappa\odot w^2U(w,t)=0$$

Multiplying both sides by $e^{\kappa w^2 t}$:

$$e^{\kappa w^2 t}\odot\frac{dU(w,t)}{dt}\oplus\kappa w^2e^{\kappa w^2 t}\odot U(w,t)=0$$

we have $\left(e^{\kappa w^2 t}\odot U(w,t)\right)'_{gH}=0$, then by integration:

$$\int_0^t\left(e^{\kappa w^2 s}U(w,s)\right)'_{gH}ds=e^{\kappa w^2 t}U(w,t)\ominus_{gH}U(w,0)=0$$

so:

$$U(w,t)=e^{-\kappa w^2 t}U(w,0)$$

where $U(w,0)$ is the fuzzy Fourier transform of the initial data, $u(x,0)=f(x)$:

$$U(w,0)=\frac{1}{\sqrt{2\pi}}\int_{-\infty}^{\infty}f(x)\odot e^{-iwx}dx$$

Since:

$$\mathcal{F}^{-1}\{U(w,t)\}=u(x,t)=\frac{1}{\sqrt{2\pi}}\int_{-\infty}^{\infty}U(w,t)\odot e^{iwx}dw$$

By substituting:

$$U(w,t)=e^{-\kappa w^2 t}U(w,0)$$

we have:

$$u(x,t)=\frac{1}{\sqrt{2\pi}}\int_{-\infty}^{\infty}U(w,0)\odot e^{-\kappa w^2 t}e^{iwx}dw=$$

$$=\frac{1}{\sqrt{2\pi}}\int_{-\infty}^{\infty}\left(\frac{1}{\sqrt{2\pi}}\int_{-\infty}^{\infty}f(\xi)\odot e^{-iw\xi}d\xi\right)\odot e^{-\kappa w^2 t}e^{iwx}dw$$

$$=\frac{1}{2\pi}\int_{-\infty}^{\infty}f(\xi)\int_{-\infty}^{\infty}e^{-\kappa w^2 t}e^{iw(x-\xi)}dwd\xi=\frac{1}{2\pi}\int_{-\infty}^{\infty}f(\xi)\odot\int_{-\infty}^{\infty}e^{-\kappa w^2 t+iw(x-\xi)}dwd\xi$$

The exponent can be rewritten in the following form:

$$-\kappa w^2 t + iw(x-\xi) = -t\kappa\left(w^2 - iw\frac{x-\xi}{\kappa t}\right) = -t\kappa\left[\left(w - i\frac{x-\xi}{2\kappa t}\right)^2 + \frac{(x-\xi)^2}{4\kappa^2 t^2}\right]$$

then:

$$\int_{-\infty}^{\infty} e^{-\kappa w^2 t + iw(x-\xi)}\mathrm{d}w = \int_{-\infty}^{\infty} e^{-t\kappa\left[\left(w-i\frac{x-\xi}{2\kappa t}\right)^2 + \frac{(x-\xi)^2}{4\kappa^2 t^2}\right]}\mathrm{d}w$$

Setting $w - i\frac{x-\xi}{2t} = \frac{s}{\sqrt{\kappa t}}$, we obtain $= \frac{\mathrm{d}s}{\sqrt{\kappa t}}$. Since $\int_{-\infty}^{\infty} e^{-s^2}\mathrm{d}s = \sqrt{\pi}$ thus:

$$\int_{-\infty}^{\infty} e^{-t\kappa\left[\left(w-i\frac{x-\xi}{2\kappa t}\right)^2 + \frac{(x-\xi)^2}{4\kappa^2 t^2}\right]}\mathrm{d}w = \int_{-\infty}^{\infty} e^{-s^2} e^{\left[-\frac{(x-\xi)^2}{\kappa t}\right]}\frac{\mathrm{d}s}{\sqrt{4\kappa t}} = \sqrt{\frac{\pi}{\kappa t}}e^{-\frac{(x-\xi)^2}{4\kappa t}}$$

Finally, we get:

$$\int_{-\infty}^{\infty} e^{-\kappa w^2 t + iw(x-\xi)}\mathrm{d}w = \sqrt{\frac{\pi}{\kappa t}}e^{-\frac{(x-\xi)^2}{4\kappa t}}$$

and:

$$u(x,t) = \frac{1}{2\pi}\int_{-\infty}^{\infty} f(\xi)\odot\int_{-\infty}^{\infty} e^{-\kappa w^2 t + iw(x-\xi)}\mathrm{d}w\mathrm{d}\xi = \frac{1}{2\pi}\int_{-\infty}^{\infty} f(\xi)\odot\sqrt{\frac{\pi}{\kappa t}}e^{-\frac{(x-\xi)^2}{4\kappa t}}\mathrm{d}\xi$$

$$= \frac{1}{2\pi}\sqrt{\frac{\pi}{\kappa t}}\int_{-\infty}^{\infty} f(\xi)\odot e^{-\frac{(x-\xi)^2}{4\kappa t}}\mathrm{d}\xi = \frac{1}{\sqrt{4\pi\kappa t}}\int_{-\infty}^{\infty} f(\xi)\odot e^{-\frac{(x-\xi)^2}{4\kappa t}}\mathrm{d}\xi$$

The fuzzy solution is obtained as:

$$u(x,t) = \frac{1}{\sqrt{4\pi\kappa t}}\int_{-\infty}^{\infty} f(\xi)\odot e^{-\frac{(x-\xi)^2}{4\kappa t}}\mathrm{d}\xi$$

We now discuss the type of differentiability of the solution $u(x,t)$. Consider the following relation:

$$\phi(x-\xi,t) = \frac{e^{-\frac{(x-\xi)^2}{4\kappa t}}}{\sqrt{4\pi\kappa t}} > 0$$

Then:

$$u(x,t) = \int_{-\infty}^{\infty}\phi(x-\xi,t)\odot f(\xi)\mathrm{d}\xi,\ \ \partial_{tgH}u(x,t) = \int_{-\infty}^{\infty}\partial_t\phi(x-\xi,t)\odot f(\xi)\mathrm{d}\xi$$

Now we can discuss $\partial_t\phi(x-\xi,t)$:

$$\partial_t\phi(x-\xi,t)=-\frac{e^{-\frac{(x-\xi)^2}{4\kappa t}}}{4(t\kappa)^{\frac{3}{2}}\sqrt{\pi}}+\frac{e^{-\frac{(x-\xi)^2}{4\kappa t}}(x-\xi)^2}{8t^2\kappa\sqrt{t\pi\kappa}}$$

Therefore:

$$\begin{cases}\partial_t\phi(x-\xi,t)\geq 0, & |\xi-x|\geq\sqrt{2\kappa t}\\ \partial_t\phi(x-\xi,t)<0, & |\xi-x|<\sqrt{2\kappa t}\end{cases}$$

If we suppose that:

$$K(x-\xi,t)=\phi(x-\xi,t)\odot f(\xi)\Longrightarrow\partial_{tgH}K(x-\xi,t)=\partial_t\phi(x-\xi,t)\odot f(\xi)$$

so:

$$\partial_{tgH}K(x-\xi,t)=\begin{cases}\partial_{t,i-gH}K(x-\xi,t)\geq 0, & |\xi-x|\geq\sqrt{2\kappa t}\\ \partial_{t,ii-gH}K(x-\xi,t)<0, & |\xi-x|<\sqrt{2\kappa t}\end{cases}$$

the derivative of the solution is:

$$\partial_{tgH}u(x,t)=\int_{-\infty}^{\infty}\partial_t\phi(x-\xi,t)\odot f(\xi)\mathrm{d}\xi=\int_{-\infty}^{\infty}\partial_{tgH}K(x-\xi,t)\odot f(\xi)\mathrm{d}\xi$$

In conclusion:

- $u(x,t)$ is $i-p-gH$ differentiable with respect to t in the intervals:

$$\left(-\infty,x-\sqrt{2\kappa t}\right],\left[x+\sqrt{2\kappa t},\infty\right)$$

- $u(x,t)$ is $ii-p-gH$ differentiable with respect to t in the intervals:

$$\left[x-\sqrt{2\kappa t},x+\sqrt{2\kappa t}\right]$$

Example. Consider the fuzzy heat equation:

$$\begin{cases}\partial_{tgH}u(x,t)\ominus_{gH}0.25\odot\partial_{xxgH}u(x,t)=0, & -\infty<x<\infty,t\geq 0\\ u(x,0)=(1,3,9)\odot e^{-x^2}\end{cases}$$

The level-wise form of initial value is:

$$u(x,0,r)=[1+2r,9-6r]e^{-x^2}=\left[(1+2r)e^{-x^2},(9-6r)e^{-x^2}\right]$$

$$u_l(x,0,r)=(1+2r)e^{-x^2}=f_l(x,r),u_u(x,0,r)=(9-6r)e^{-x^2}=f_u(x,r)$$

The fuzzy solution is obtained as follows:

$$u(x,t) = \frac{1}{\sqrt{4\pi\kappa t}} \int_{-\infty}^{\infty} f(\xi) \odot e^{-\frac{(x-\xi)^2}{4\kappa t}} \mathrm{d}\xi$$

In the level-wise form:

$$u(x,t,r) = \frac{1}{\sqrt{4\pi\kappa t}} \int_{-\infty}^{\infty} f(\xi,r) \odot e^{-\frac{(x-\xi)^2}{4\kappa t}} \mathrm{d}\xi$$

$$u_l(x,t,r) = \frac{1}{\sqrt{4\pi\kappa t}} \int_{-\infty}^{\infty} f_l(\xi,r) \odot e^{-\frac{(x-\xi)^2}{4\kappa t}} \mathrm{d}\xi = \frac{1}{\sqrt{4\pi\kappa t}} \int_{-\infty}^{\infty} (1+2r)e^{-\xi^2} \odot e^{-\frac{(x-\xi)^2}{4\kappa t}} \mathrm{d}\xi$$

$$u_u(x,t,r) = \frac{1}{\sqrt{4\pi\kappa t}} \int_{-\infty}^{\infty} f_u(\xi,r) \odot e^{-\frac{(x-\xi)^2}{4\kappa t}} \mathrm{d}\xi = \frac{1}{\sqrt{4\pi\kappa t}} \int_{-\infty}^{\infty} (9-6r)e^{-\xi^2} \odot e^{-\frac{(x-\xi)^2}{4\kappa t}} \mathrm{d}\xi$$

The solution in level-wise form is:

$$u(x,t,r) = [1+2r, 9-6r] \frac{e^{-\frac{x^2}{1+t}}}{(1+t)^{\frac{1}{2}}}$$

To check the type of differentiability, we need the $\partial_{tgH} u(x,t)$ and:

$$\partial_{tgH} u(x,t) = [1+2r, 9-6r] \int_{-\infty}^{\infty} \partial_t \left(\frac{e^{-\frac{(x-\xi)^2}{t}}}{\sqrt{\pi t}} \right) e^{-\xi^2} \mathrm{d}\xi$$

Then, for $|\xi - x| \geq \sqrt{0.5}t$:

$$\partial_{t,i-gH} u(x,t) = \left[(1+2r) \int_{-\infty}^{\infty} \frac{e^{-\frac{(x-\xi)^2}{t} - \xi^2} \left(2(x-\xi)^2 - t \right)}{2\sqrt{\pi} t^{\frac{5}{2}}} \mathrm{d}\xi, \right.$$

$$\left. (9-6r) \int_{-\infty}^{\infty} \frac{e^{-\frac{(x-\xi)^2}{t} - \xi^2} \left(2(x-\xi)^2 - t \right)}{2\sqrt{\pi} t^{\frac{5}{2}}} \mathrm{d}\xi \right]$$

Then, for $|\xi - x| < \sqrt{0.5t}$:

$$\partial_{t,ii-gH} u(x,t) = \left[(9-6r) \int_{-\infty}^{\infty} \frac{e^{-\frac{(x-\xi)^2}{t} - \xi^2} \left(2(x-\xi)^2 - t \right)}{2\sqrt{\pi} t^{\frac{5}{2}}} \mathrm{d}\xi \right],$$

$$\left. (1+2r) \int_{-\infty}^{\infty} \frac{e^{-\frac{(x-\xi)^2}{t} - \xi^2} \left(2(x-\xi)^2 - t \right)}{2\sqrt{\pi} t^{\frac{5}{2}}} \mathrm{d}\xi \right]$$

Indeed, the solution has the switching point type I with respect to $\left(-\frac{\sqrt{1+t}}{\sqrt{2}}, t\right)$ and type II with respect to $\left(\frac{\sqrt{1+t}}{\sqrt{2}}, t\right)$ (Fig. 7.5):

$$\partial_{tgH}u(x,t,r) =$$

$$= \begin{cases} \left[(1+2r)\dfrac{(1+t-2x^2)e^{-\frac{x^2}{1+t}}}{2(1+t)^{\frac{5}{2}}}, (9-6r)\dfrac{(1+t-2x^2)e^{-\frac{x^2}{1+t}}}{2(1+t)^{\frac{5}{2}}}\right], & |x| \geq \dfrac{\sqrt{1+t}}{\sqrt{2}} \\ \left[(9-6r)\dfrac{(1+t-2x^2)e^{-\frac{x^2}{1+t}}}{2(1+t)^{\frac{5}{2}}}, (1+2r)\dfrac{(1+t-2x^2)e^{-\frac{x^2}{1+t}}}{2(1+t)^{\frac{5}{2}}}\right], & |x| < \dfrac{\sqrt{1+t}}{\sqrt{2}} \end{cases}$$

Example. Consider the fuzzy heat equation:

$$\begin{cases} \partial_{tgH}u(x,t) \ominus_{gH} 2 \odot \partial_{xxgH}u(x,t) = 0, & -\infty < x < \infty, t \geq 0 \\ u(x,0) = (-10, 2, 10) \odot |x|e^{-x^2} \end{cases}$$

The level-wise form of the initial value is as follows:

$$u(x,0,r) = [12r-10, -8r+10]|x|e^{-x^2} = \left[(12r-10)|x|e^{-x^2}, (-8r+10)|x|e^{-x^2}\right]$$

$$u_l(x,0,r) = (12r-10)|x|e^{-x^2} = f_l(x,r), u_u(x,0,r) = (-8r+10)|x|e^{-x^2} = f_u(x,r)$$

According to the abovementioned description (Fig. 7.6):

$$u(x,t,r) = \frac{[12r-10, -8r+10]}{\sqrt{8\pi t}} \int_{-\infty}^{\infty} e^{-\frac{(x-\xi)^2}{8t}} \odot |\xi|e^{-\xi^2} =$$

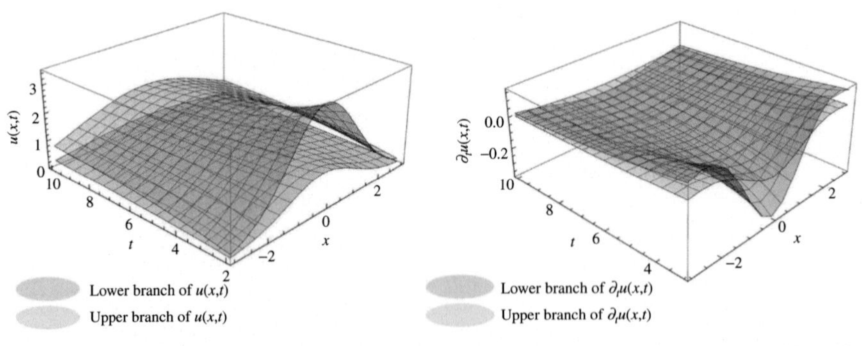

Fig. 7.5 The solution $u(x,t)$ (*left*) and $\partial_{tgH}u(x,t)$ (*right*), $r=\frac{1}{2}$.

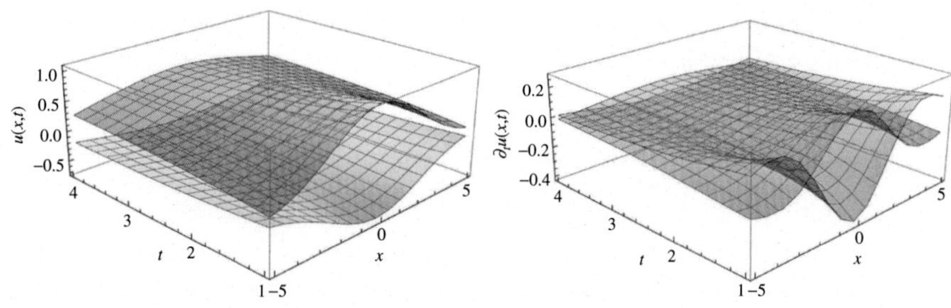

Fig. 7.6 The solution $u(x,t)$ (*left*) and $\partial_{tgH}u(x,t)$ (*right*), $r=\frac{1}{2}$.

$$=[12r-10,\ -8r+10]\left(\frac{2e^{\frac{-x^2}{4t}}t\left(4e^{\frac{x^2}{8t}}+e^{\frac{x^2+4tx^2}{4t+32t^2}}\sqrt{\frac{2\pi x^2}{t+8t^2}}\operatorname{erf}\left[\sqrt{\frac{x^2}{8t+64t^2}}\right]\right)}{2\sqrt{2\pi t}(1+8t)}\right)$$

7.4 Fuzzy finite difference method for solving the fuzzy Poisson's equation

In this section, first, the fuzzy Poisson's equation and the fuzzy finite difference method are introduced. Then, the fuzzy Poisson's equation is discretized by fuzzy finite difference method and it is solved as a linear system of equations. In addition, we discuss fuzzy Laplace equation as a special case of the fuzzy Poisson's equation. Finally, the convergence of method is considered and for more illustration, a numerical example is solved.

Numerous problems in industry have led to an equation with a fuzzy partial differential equation in the following form:

$$\Delta u(x,y)=f(x,y) \text{ in } \Omega$$

in which $\Omega=\{(x,y)|0\le x,y\le 1\}$ is regular area, and the operator Δ is defined as:

$$\Delta u(x,y)=\partial^2_{xx,gH}u(x,y)\oplus\partial^2_{yy,gH}u(x,y)$$

and $f(x,y)$ is a known fuzzy function and $u(x,y)$ is an unknown fuzzy function. First, we show that the equation has a unique solution.

7.4.1 Theorem—Uniqueness

The Poisson's equation:

$$\Delta u(x,y)=f(x,y) \text{ in } \Omega$$

with boundary conditions $u(x,y)=0$ in $\partial\Omega$ has a unique solution.

Proof. Suppose that the fuzzy solution is not unique and there are two different fuzzy solutions: u_1 and u_2. Consider $v = u_1 \ominus_H u_2$. Since $u_1(x,y) = u_2(x,y) = 0$ in $\partial\Omega$, and:

$$\Delta v(x,y) = \Delta u_1(x,y) \ominus_H \Delta u_2(x,y) = 0$$

then $v(x,y)$ satisfies the boundary condition and $v(x,y) = 0$ in $\partial\Omega$. So, $u_1 = u_2$.

To explain the finite difference method, first the intervals $0 \le x, y \le 1$ are divided into N equal subintervals with the length of $h = \frac{1}{N}$, then the points $x_i = ih$, $y_j = jh$ for i, $j = 0, 1, \ldots, N$ on the axis x, y are obtained. The purpose is to compute the fuzzy solution function $u(x,y)$ at the points (x_i, t_j), $i, j = 0, 1, \ldots, N$. For simplification, the values of the functions at the points are shown as:

$$u(x_i, y_j) := u_{ij}, \ f(x_i, y_j) := f_{ij}, \ i, j = 0, 1, \ldots, N$$

For the first derivative with respect to x, y, the approximate values are shown as the following equalities:

$$\partial_{x,gH} u|_{i,j} = \frac{1}{h}(u_{ij} \ominus_{gH} u_{i-1,j}), \ \partial_{y,gH} u|_{i,j} = \frac{1}{h}(u_{ij} \ominus_{gH} u_{i,j-1})$$

Considering the definition of gH-difference:

$$\partial_{x,i-gH} u|_{i,j} = \frac{1}{h}(u_{ij} \ominus_H u_{i-1,j}), \ \partial_{x,ii-gH} u|_{i,j} = \frac{1}{-h}(u_{i-1j} \ominus_H u_{i,j})$$

$$\partial_{y,i-gH} u|_{i,j} = \frac{1}{h}(u_{ij} \ominus_H u_{i,j-1}), \ \partial_{y,ii-gH} u|_{i,j} = \frac{1}{-h}(u_{ij-1} \ominus_H u_{i,j})$$

For the second order differential, we have combinations of two types of differentiability, because it may happen that the first derivative with respect to x is $i-gH$ differentiable and its second order differential might be $ii-gH$ differentiable and vice versa. Also, for differential with respect to y. In these combinations, several cases are the same and the results are in four cases that can be explained as follows.

Case 1. Both derivatives are $i-gH$ differentiable:

$$\partial_{x_{i-gH}, x_{i-gH}} u|_{i,j} = \frac{1}{h^2}(u_{i+1,j} \ominus_H 2 \odot u_{ij} \oplus u_{i-1,j})$$

Case 2. The first is $i-gH$ differentiable and the second is $ii-gH$ differentiable:

$$\partial_{x_{i-gH}, x_{ii-gH}} u|_{i,j} = \frac{1}{h^2}(u_{i+1,j} \ominus_H u_{ij} \ominus_H (-1)u_{i-1,j} \oplus (-1)u_{ij})$$

Case 3. The first is $ii-gH$ differentiable and the second is $i-gH$ differentiable:

$$\partial_{x_{ii-gH}, x_{i-gH}} u|_{i,j} = \frac{1}{h^2}((-1)u_{ij} \ominus_H (-1)u_{i+1,j} \ominus_H u_{i,j} \oplus u_{i-1,j})$$

Case 4. Both derivatives are $ii-gH$ differentiable:

$$\partial_{x_{ii-gH},x_{i-gH}} u|_{i,j} = \frac{1}{h^2}\left((-2)u_{ij} \ominus_H (-1)u_{i+1,j} \ominus_H (-1)u_{i-1,j}\right)$$

Similar cases occur for the derivatives with respect to y, and the results are listed as follows.

Case 5. Both derivatives are $i-gH$ differentiable:

$$\partial_{y_{i-gH},y_{i-gH}} u|_{i,j} = \frac{1}{h^2}\left(u_{i,j+1} \ominus_H 2 \odot u_{ij} \oplus u_{i,j-1}\right)$$

Case 6. The first is $i-gH$ differentiable and the second is $ii-gH$ differentiable:

$$\partial_{y_{i-gH},y_{ii-gH}} u|_{i,j} = \frac{1}{h^2}\left(u_{i,j+1} \ominus_H u_{ij} \ominus_H (-1)u_{i,j-1} \oplus (-1)u_{ij}\right)$$

Case 7. The first is $ii-gH$ differentiable and the second is $i-gH$ differentiable:

$$\partial_{y_{ii-gH},y_{i-gH}} u|_{i,j} = \frac{1}{h^2}\left((-1)u_{ij} \ominus_H (-1)u_{i,j+1} \ominus_H u_{i,j} \oplus u_{i,j-1}\right)$$

Case 8. Both derivatives are $ii-gH$ differentiable:

$$\partial_{y_{ii-gH},y_{i-gH}} u|_{i,j} = \frac{1}{h^2}\left((-2)u_{ij} \ominus_H (-1)u_{i,j+1} \ominus_H (-1)u_{i,j-1}\right)$$

In continuation, we assume that fuzzy finite difference method will be one of the several methods for solving fuzzy differential equations:

$$\partial^2_{xx,gH} u(x,y) \oplus \partial^2_{yy,gH} u(x,y) = f(x,y)$$

whose fundamental idea is based on replacing both sides of the mentioned equation with the obtained partial derivatives.

Cases 1 and 5. Both derivatives with respect to x and y are $i-gH$ differentiable:

$$\partial_{x_{i-gH},x_{i-gH}} u|_{i,j} = \frac{1}{h^2}\left(u_{i+1,j} \ominus_H 2 \odot u_{ij} \oplus u_{i-1,j}\right)$$

$$\partial_{y_{i-gH},y_{i-gH}} u|_{i,j} = \frac{1}{h^2}\left(u_{i,j+1} \ominus_H 2 \odot u_{ij} \oplus u_{i,j-1}\right)$$

By substituting in:

$$\partial_{x_{i-gH},x_{i-gH}} u|_{i,j} \oplus \partial_{y_{i-gH},y_{i-gH}} u|_{i,j} = f(x_i, y_j)$$

$$\frac{1}{h^2}\left(u_{i+1,j} \ominus_H 2 \odot u_{ij} \oplus u_{i-1,j}\right) \oplus \frac{1}{h^2}\left(u_{i,j+1} \ominus_H 2 \odot u_{ij} \oplus u_{i,j-1}\right) = f(x_i, y_j)$$

$$u_{i+1,j} \ominus_H 4 \odot u_{ij} \oplus u_{i-1,j} \oplus u_{i,j+1} \oplus u_{i,j-1} = h^2 f_{ij}, \quad i,j = 0,1,\ldots,N.$$

If $j=0$ is fixed and $i=0, 1, \ldots, N$, then:

$u_{i+1,0} \ominus_H 4 \odot u_{i,0} \oplus u_{i-1,0} \oplus u_{i,1} = h^2 f_{i,0},\ \ u_{i,-1} = u_{N+1,0} = 0,\ \ i,j = 0,1,\ldots,N.$

In level-wise form:

$$u_{i+1,0,l} - 4u_{i,0,l} + u_{i-1,0,l} + u_{i,1,l} = h^2 f_{i,0,l},$$

$$u_{i+1,0,u} - 4u_{i,0,u} + u_{i-1,0,u} + u_{i,1,u} = h^2 f_{i,0,u}$$

For $i=0, 1, \ldots, N$, we have:

$$\begin{cases} u_{1,0,l} - 4u_{0,0,l} + u_{0,1,l} = h^2 f_{0,0,l}, u_{-1,0,l} = 0 \\ u_{2,0,l} - 4u_{1,0,l} + u_{0,0,l} + u_{1,1,l} = h^2 f_{1,0,l} \\ \vdots \\ 4u_{N,0,l} + u_{N-1,0,l} + u_{N,1,l} = h^2 f_{N,0,l}, u_{N+1,0,l} = 0 \end{cases}$$

$$\begin{cases} u_{1,0,u} - 4u_{0,0,u} + u_{0,1,u} = h^2 f_{0,0,u}, u_{-1,0,u} = 0 \\ u_{2,0,u} - 4u_{1,0,u} + u_{0,0,u} + u_{1,1,u} = h^2 f_{1,0,u} \\ \vdots \\ 4u_{N,0,u} + u_{N-1,0,u} + u_{N,1,u} = h^2 f_{N,0,u}, u_{N+1,0,u} = 0 \end{cases}$$

If $j=1$ is fixed and $i=0, 1, \ldots, N$, then:

$$u_{i+1,1} \ominus_H 4 \odot u_{i,1} \oplus u_{i-1,1} \oplus u_{i,2} = h^2 f_{i,1},\ i,j = 0,1,\ldots,N.$$

In level-wise form:

$$u_{i+1,1,l} - 4u_{i,1,l} + u_{i-1,1,l} + u_{i,2,l} = h^2 f_{i,1,l}, \quad i,j = 0,1,\ldots,N.$$

$$u_{i+1,1,u} - 4u_{i,1,u} + u_{i-1,1,u} + u_{i,2,u} = h^2 f_{i,1,u}, \quad i,j = 0,1,\ldots,N.$$

For $i=0, 1, \ldots, N$, we have:

$$\begin{cases} u_{1,1,l} - 4u_{0,1,l} + u_{0,2,l} = h^2 f_{0,1,l}, u_{-1,1,l} = 0 \\ u_{2,1,l} - 4u_{1,1,l} + u_{0,1,l} + u_{1,2,l} = h^2 f_{1,1,l} \\ \vdots \\ 4u_{N,1,l} + u_{N-1,1,l} + u_{N,2,l} = h^2 f_{N,1,l}, u_{N+1,1,l} = 0 \end{cases}$$

$$\begin{cases} u_{1,1,u} - 4u_{0,1,u} + u_{0,2,u} = h^2 f_{0,1,u}, u_{-1,1,u} = 0 \\ u_{2,1,u} - 4u_{1,1,u} + u_{0,1,u} + u_{1,2,u} = h^2 f_{1,1,u} \\ \vdots \\ 4u_{N,1,u} + u_{N-1,1,u} + u_{N,2,u} = h^2 f_{N,1,u}, u_{N+1,1,u} = 0 \end{cases}$$

Finally, if $j=N$ is fixed and $i=0, 1, \ldots, N$, then:

$$u_{i+1,N} \ominus_H 4 \odot u_{i,N} \oplus u_{i-1,N} \oplus u_{i,N-1} = h^2 f_{i,N},\ \ u_{i,N+1} = 0,\ \ i,j = 0,1,\ldots,N.$$

In level-wise form:

$$u_{i+1,N,l} - 4u_{i,N,l} + u_{i-1,N,l} = h^2 f_{i,1,l}, \quad u_{i,N+1,l} = 0, \quad i,j = 0,1,\ldots,N.$$

$$u_{i+1,N,u} - 4u_{i,N,u} + u_{i-1,N,u} = h^2 f_{i,1,u}, \quad u_{i,N+1,u} = 0, \quad i,j = 0,1,\ldots,N.$$

For $i = 0, 1, \ldots, N$, we have:

$$\begin{cases} u_{1,N,l} - 4u_{0,N,l} = h^2 f_{0,1,l}, u_{0,N+1,l} = 0 \\ u_{2,N,l} - 4u_{1,N,l} + u_{0,N,l} + u_{1,N,l} = h^2 f_{1,N,l} \\ \vdots \\ 4u_{N,N,l} + u_{N-1,N,l} = h^2 f_{N,N,l}, u_{N+1,N,l} = u_{N,N+1,l} = 0 \end{cases}$$

$$\begin{cases} u_{1,N,u} - 4u_{0,N,u} = h^2 f_{0,1,u}, u_{0,N+1,u} = 0 \\ u_{2,N,u} - 4u_{1,N,u} + u_{0,N,u} + u_{1,N,u} = h^2 f_{1,N,u} \\ \vdots \\ 4u_{N,N,u} + u_{N-1,N,u} = h^2 f_{N,N,u}, u_{N+1,N,u} = u_{N,N+1,u} = 0 \end{cases}$$

In the compact form:

$$\begin{pmatrix} A_1 & O \\ O & A_1 \end{pmatrix} \begin{pmatrix} U_l \\ U_u \end{pmatrix} = h^2 \begin{pmatrix} F_l \\ F_u \end{pmatrix}$$

$$A_1 = \begin{pmatrix} A & O & O & O & \ldots & O \\ O & O & O & O & \ldots & O \\ \vdots & \vdots & \vdots & \vdots & \vdots & \vdots \\ O & O & \ldots & O & O & A \end{pmatrix}$$

where I is a specific and O is a zero matrix and:

$$A = \begin{pmatrix} -4 & 1 & 0 & 0 & 0 & \ldots & 0 \\ 1 & -4 & 1 & 0 & 0 & \ldots & 0 \\ 0 & 1 & -4 & 1 & 0 & \ldots & 0 \\ \vdots & \vdots & \vdots & \vdots & \vdots & \vdots & \vdots \\ 0 & 0 & 0 & \ldots & 0 & 1 & -4 \end{pmatrix}$$

$$U_l = \begin{pmatrix} u_{0,0,l} \\ u_{1,0,l} \\ \vdots \\ u_{N,0,l} \\ u_{0,1,l} \\ u_{1,1,l} \\ \vdots \\ u_{N,1,l} \\ \vdots \\ u_{0,N,l} \\ u_{1,N,l} \\ \vdots \\ u_{N,N,l} \end{pmatrix}, \quad U_u = \begin{pmatrix} u_{0,0,u} \\ u_{1,0,u} \\ \vdots \\ u_{N,0,u} \\ u_{0,1,u} \\ u_{1,1,u} \\ \vdots \\ u_{N,1,u} \\ \vdots \\ u_{0,N,u} \\ u_{1,N,u} \\ \vdots \\ u_{N,N,u} \end{pmatrix}, \quad F_l = \begin{pmatrix} f_{0,0,l} \\ f_{1,0,l} \\ \vdots \\ f_{N,0,l} \\ f_{0,1,l} \\ f_{1,1,l} \\ \vdots \\ f_{N,1,l} \\ \vdots \\ f_{0,N,l} \\ f_{1,N,l} \\ \vdots \\ f_{N,N,l} \end{pmatrix}, \quad F_u = \begin{pmatrix} f_{0,0,u} \\ f_{1,0,u} \\ \vdots \\ f_{N,0,u} \\ f_{0,1,u} \\ f_{1,1,u} \\ \vdots \\ f_{N,1,u} \\ \vdots \\ f_{0,N,u} \\ f_{1,N,u} \\ \vdots \\ f_{N,N,u} \end{pmatrix}$$

Cases 1 and 6. The derivatives with respect to x are $\partial_{x_{i-gH},\, x_{i-gH},}$ differentiable and with respect to y are $\partial_{y_{i-gH},\, y_{ii-gH}}$ differentiable:

$$\partial_{x_{i-gH},x_{i-gH}} u\big|_{i,j} = \frac{1}{h^2}\left(u_{i+1,j} \ominus_H 2 \odot u_{ij} \oplus u_{i-1,j}\right)$$

$$\partial_{y_{i-gH},y_{ii-gH}} u\big|_{i,j} = \frac{1}{h^2}\left(u_{i,j+1} \ominus_H u_{ij} \ominus_H (-1) u_{i,j-1} \oplus (-1) u_{ij}\right)$$

By substituting in:

$$\partial_{x_{i-gH},x_{i-gH}} u\big|_{i,j} \oplus \partial_{y_{i-gH},y_{ii-gH}} u\big|_{i,j} = f(x_i, y_j)$$

$$\frac{1}{h^2}\left(u_{i+1,j} \ominus_H 2 \odot u_{ij} \oplus u_{i-1,j}\right) \oplus \frac{1}{h^2}\left(u_{i,j+1} \ominus_H u_{ij} \ominus_H (-1) u_{i,j-1} \oplus (-1) u_{ij}\right) =$$

$$= f(x_i, y_j)$$

$$u_{i+1,j} \ominus_H 3 \odot u_{ij} \oplus (-1) u_{ij} \oplus u_{i-1,j} \oplus u_{i,j+1} \ominus_H (-1) u_{i,j-1} = h^2 f_{ij},$$

$$i, j = 0, 1, \ldots, N.$$

The level-wise form is:

$$u_{i+1,j,l} - 3u_{i,j,l} - u_{i,j,u} + u_{i-1,j,l} + u_{i,j+1,l} + u_{i,j-1,u} = h^2 f_{i,j,l}$$

$$u_{i+1,j,u} - 3u_{i,j,u} - u_{i,j,l} + u_{i-1,j,u} + u_{i,j+1,u} + u_{i,j-1,l} = h^2 f_{i,j,u}$$

By a similar procedure to that for Cases 1 and 5, the compact matrix form can be described as follows:

$$\begin{pmatrix} B_1 & B_2 \\ B_2 & B_1 \end{pmatrix} \begin{pmatrix} U_l \\ U_u \end{pmatrix} = h^2 \begin{pmatrix} F_l \\ F_u \end{pmatrix}$$

$$B_1 = \begin{pmatrix} B & O & O & O & \ldots & O \\ I & B & O & O & \ldots & O \\ \vdots & \vdots & \vdots & \vdots & \vdots & \vdots \\ O & O & \ldots & O & I & B \end{pmatrix}, \quad B_2 = \begin{pmatrix} -I & I & O & O & \ldots & O \\ O & -I & I & O & \ldots & O \\ \vdots & \vdots & \vdots & \vdots & \vdots & \vdots \\ O & O & \ldots & O & O & -I \end{pmatrix}$$

where I is a specific and O is a zero matrix and:

$$B = \begin{pmatrix} -3 & 1 & 0 & 0 & 0 & \ldots & 0 \\ 1 & -3 & 1 & 0 & 0 & \ldots & 0 \\ 0 & 1 & -3 & 1 & 0 & \ldots & 0 \\ \vdots & \vdots & \vdots & \vdots & \vdots & \vdots & \vdots \\ 0 & 0 & 0 & \ldots & 0 & 1 & -3 \end{pmatrix}$$

Cases 1 and 7. The derivatives with respect to x are $\partial_{x_{i-gH},\ x_{i-gH}}$ differentiable and with respect to y are $\partial_{y_{ii-gH},\ y_{i-gH}}$ differentiable:

$$\partial_{x_{i-gH},x_{i-gH}} u\big|_{i,j} = \frac{1}{h^2}\left(u_{i+1,j} \ominus_H 2 \odot u_{ij} \oplus u_{i-1,j}\right)$$

$$\partial_{y_{ii-gH},y_{i-gH}} u\big|_{i,j} = \frac{1}{h^2}\left((-1)u_{ij} \ominus_H (-1)u_{i,j+1} \ominus_H u_{i,j} \oplus u_{i,j-1}\right)$$

By substituting in:

$$\partial_{x_{i-gH},x_{i-gH}} u\big|_{i,j} \oplus \partial_{y_{ii-gH},y_{i-gH}} u\big|_{i,j} = f\left(x_i, y_j\right)$$

$$\frac{1}{h^2}\left(u_{i+1,j} \ominus_H 2 \odot u_{ij} \oplus u_{i-1,j}\right) \oplus \frac{1}{h^2}\left((-1)u_{ij} \ominus_H (-1)u_{i,j+1} \ominus_H u_{i,j} \oplus u_{i,j-1}\right) =$$

$$= f\left(x_i, y_j\right)$$

$$u_{i+1,j} \ominus_H 3 \odot u_{ij} \oplus (-1)u_{ij} \oplus u_{i-1,j} \ominus_H (-1)u_{i,j+1} \oplus u_{i,j-1} = h^2 f_{ij},$$

$$i,j = 0,1,\ldots,N.$$

The level-wise form is:

$$u_{i+1,j,l} - 3u_{i,j,l} - u_{i,j,u} + u_{i-1,j,l} + u_{i,j+1,u} + u_{i,j-1,l} = h^2 f_{i,j,l}$$

$$u_{i+1,j,u} - 3u_{i,j,u} - u_{i,j,l} + u_{i-1,j,u} + u_{i,j+1,l} + u_{i,j-1,u} = h^2 f_{i,j,u}$$

By a similar procedure to that for Cases 1 and 5, the compact matrix form can be described as follows:

$$\begin{pmatrix} B_1 & B_2 \\ B_2 & B_1 \end{pmatrix} \begin{pmatrix} U_l \\ U_u \end{pmatrix} = h^2 \begin{pmatrix} F_l \\ F_u \end{pmatrix}$$

$$B_1 = \begin{pmatrix} B & I & O & O & \ldots & O \\ O & B & I & O & \ldots & O \\ \vdots & \vdots & \vdots & \vdots & & \vdots \\ O & O & O & \ldots & O & B \end{pmatrix},\ B_2 = \begin{pmatrix} -I & O & O & \ldots & O & O \\ I & -I & O & \ldots & O & O \\ \vdots & \vdots & \vdots & & \vdots & \vdots \\ O & \ldots & O & 0 & I & -I \end{pmatrix}$$

with the same matrices and:

$$B = \begin{pmatrix} -3 & 1 & 0 & 0 & 0 & \ldots & 0 \\ 1 & -3 & 1 & 0 & 0 & \ldots & 0 \\ 0 & 1 & -3 & 1 & 0 & \ldots & 0 \\ \vdots & \vdots & \vdots & \vdots & \vdots & \vdots & \vdots \\ 0 & 0 & 0 & \ldots & 0 & 1 & -3 \end{pmatrix}$$

Cases 1 and 8. The derivatives with respect to x are $\partial_{x_{i-gH},\, x_{i-gH}}$ differentiable and with respect to y are $\partial_{y_{ii-gH},\, y_{ii-gH}}$ differentiable:

$$\partial_{x_{i-gH},x_{i-gH}} u\big|_{i,j} = \frac{1}{h^2}\left(u_{i+1,j} \ominus_H 2 \odot u_{ij} \oplus u_{i-1,j}\right)$$

$$\partial_{y_{ii-gH},y_{i-gH}} u\big|_{i,j} = \frac{1}{h^2}\left((-2)u_{ij} \ominus_H (-1)u_{i,j+1} \ominus_H (-1)u_{i,j-1}\right)$$

By substituting in:

$$\partial_{x_{i-gH},x_{i-gH}} u\big|_{i,j} \oplus \partial_{y_{ii-gH},y_{ii-gH}} u\big|_{i,j} = f(x_i, y_j)$$

$$\frac{1}{h^2}\left(u_{i+1,j} \ominus_H 2 \odot u_{ij} \oplus u_{i-1,j}\right) \oplus \frac{1}{h^2}\left((-2)u_{ij} \ominus_H (-1)u_{i,j+1} \ominus_H (-1)u_{i,j-1}\right) =$$

$$= f(x_i, y_j)$$

$$u_{i+1,j} \ominus_H 2 \odot u_{ij} \oplus (-2)u_{ij} \oplus u_{i-1,j} \ominus_H (-1)u_{i,j+1} \ominus_H (-1)u_{i,j-1} = h^2 f_{ij},$$

$$i, j = 0, 1, \ldots, N.$$

The level-wise form is:

$$u_{i+1,j,l} - 2u_{i,j,l} - 2u_{i,j,u} + u_{i-1,j,l} + u_{i,j+1,u} + u_{i,j-1,u} = h^2 f_{i,j,l}$$

$$u_{i+1,j,u} - 2u_{i,j,u} - 2u_{i,j,l} + u_{i-1,j,u} + u_{i,j+1,l} + u_{i,j-1,l} = h^2 f_{i,j,u}$$

By a similar procedure to that for Cases 1 and 5, the compact matrix form can be described as follows:

$$\begin{pmatrix} C_1 & C_2 \\ C_2 & C_1 \end{pmatrix} \begin{pmatrix} U_l \\ U_u \end{pmatrix} = h^2 \begin{pmatrix} F_l \\ F_u \end{pmatrix}$$

$$C_1 = \begin{pmatrix} C & O & O & O & \ldots & O \\ O & C & O & \ldots & O & O \\ \vdots & \vdots & \vdots & \vdots & \vdots & \vdots \\ O & O & \ldots & O & O & B \end{pmatrix}, \quad C_2 = \begin{pmatrix} -2I & I & O & \ldots & O & O \\ I & -2I & I & O & \ldots & O \\ \vdots & \vdots & \vdots & \vdots & \vdots & \vdots \\ O & \ldots & O & O & I & -2I \end{pmatrix}$$

where I is a specific and O is a zero matrix and the matrix C is as follows:

$$C = \begin{pmatrix} -2 & 1 & 0 & 0 & 0 & \ldots & 0 \\ 1 & -2 & 1 & 0 & 0 & \ldots & 0 \\ 0 & 1 & -2 & 1 & 0 & \ldots & 0 \\ \vdots & \vdots & \vdots & \vdots & \vdots & \vdots & \vdots \\ 0 & 0 & 0 & \ldots & 0 & 1 & -2 \end{pmatrix}$$

Cases 2 and 5. The derivatives with respect to x are $\partial_{x_{i-gH},\, x_{ii-gH}}$ differentiable and with respect to y are $\partial_{y_{i-gH},\, y_{i-gH}}$ differentiable:

$$\partial_{x_{i-gH},x_{ii-gH}} u\big|_{i,j} = \frac{1}{h^2}\left(u_{i+1,j} \ominus_H u_{ij} \ominus_H (-1)u_{i-1,j} \oplus (-1)u_{ij}\right)$$

$$\partial_{y_{i-gH},y_{i-gH}} u\big|_{i,j} = \frac{1}{h^2}\left(u_{i,j+1} \ominus_H 2 \odot u_{ij} \oplus u_{i,j-1}\right)$$

By substituting in:

$$\partial_{x_{i-gH},x_{ii-gH}} u\big|_{i,j} \oplus \partial_{y_{i-gH},y_{i-gH}} u\big|_{i,j} = f(x_i, y_j)$$

$$\frac{1}{h^2}\left(u_{i+1,j} \ominus_H u_{ij} \ominus_H (-1)u_{i-1,j} \oplus (-1)u_{ij}\right) \oplus \frac{1}{h^2}\left(u_{i,j+1} \ominus_H 2 \odot u_{ij} \oplus u_{i,j-1}\right)$$

$$= f(x_i, y_j)$$

$$u_{i+1,j} \ominus_H 3 \odot u_{ij} \oplus (-1)u_{ij} \ominus_H (-1)u_{i-1,j} \oplus u_{i,j+1} \oplus u_{i,j-1} = h^2 f_{ij}$$

$$i,j = 0,1,\ldots,N.$$

In level-wise form:

$$u_{i+1,j,l} - 3u_{i,j,l} - u_{i,j,u} + u_{i-1,j,u} + u_{i,j+1,l} + u_{i,j-1,l} = h^2 f_{i,j,l}$$

$$u_{i+1,j,u} - 3u_{i,j,u} - u_{i,j,l} + u_{i-1,j,l} + u_{i,j+1,u} + u_{i,j-1,u} = h^2 f_{i,j,u}$$

In the compact form:

$$\begin{pmatrix} D_1 & D_2 \\ D_2 & D_1 \end{pmatrix} \begin{pmatrix} U_l \\ U_u \end{pmatrix} = h^2 \begin{pmatrix} F_l \\ F_u \end{pmatrix}$$

$$D_1 = \begin{pmatrix} D & I & O & O & \ldots & O \\ I & D & I & \ldots & O & O \\ \vdots & \vdots & \vdots & \vdots & \vdots & \vdots \\ O & O & \ldots & O & I & D \end{pmatrix}, \quad D_2 = \begin{pmatrix} E & O & O & O & \ldots & O \\ O & E & O & \ldots & O & O \\ \vdots & \vdots & \vdots & \vdots & \vdots & \vdots \\ O & O & \ldots & O & O & E \end{pmatrix}$$

where I is a specific and O is a zero matrix and:

$$D = \begin{pmatrix} -3 & 1 & 0 & 0 & 0 & \ldots & 0 \\ 0 & -3 & 1 & 0 & 0 & \ldots & 0 \\ 0 & 0 & -3 & 1 & 0 & \ldots & 0 \\ \vdots & \vdots & \vdots & \vdots & \vdots & \vdots & \vdots \\ 0 & 0 & 0 & \ldots & 0 & 0 & -3 \end{pmatrix}, \quad E = \begin{pmatrix} -1 & 0 & 0 & \ldots & 0 \\ 1 & -1 & 0 & \ldots & 0 \\ \vdots & \vdots & \vdots & \vdots & \vdots \\ 0 & \ldots & 0 & 1 & -1 \end{pmatrix}$$

Cases 2 and 6. The derivatives with respect to x are $\partial_{x_{i-gH},\, x_{ii-gH}}$ differentiable and with respect to y are $\partial_{y_{i-gH},\, y_{ii-gH}}$ differentiable:

$$\partial_{x_{i-gH},x_{ii-gH}} u\big|_{i,j} = \frac{1}{h^2}\left(u_{i+1,j} \ominus_H u_{ij} \ominus_H (-1)u_{i-1,j} \oplus (-1)u_{ij}\right)$$

$$\partial_{y_{i-gH},y_{ii-gH}} u\big|_{i,j} = \frac{1}{h^2}\left(u_{i,j+1} \ominus_H u_{ij} \ominus_H (-1)u_{i,j-1} \oplus (-1)u_{ij}\right)$$

By substituting in:

$$\partial_{x_{i-gH},x_{ii-gH}} u\big|_{i,j} \oplus \partial_{y_{i-gH},y_{ii-gH}} u\big|_{i,j} = f\left(x_i, y_j\right)$$

$$\frac{1}{h^2}\left(u_{i+1,j} \ominus_H u_{i,j} \ominus_H (-1)u_{i-1,j} \oplus (-1)u_{i,j}\right)$$

$$\oplus \frac{1}{h^2}\left(u_{i,j+1} \ominus_H u_{i,j} \ominus_H (-1)u_{i,j-1} \oplus (-1)u_{i,j}\right) = f\left(x_i, y_j\right)$$

$$u_{i+1,j} \ominus_H 2 \odot u_{i,j} \oplus (-2)u_{i,j} \ominus_H (-1)u_{i-1,j} \oplus u_{i,j+1} \ominus_H (-1)u_{i,j-1} = h^2 f_{ij},$$

$$i,j = 0,1,\ldots,N.$$

The level-wise form is:

$$u_{i+1,j,l} - 2u_{i,j,l} - 2u_{i,j,u} + u_{i-1,j,u} + u_{i,j+1,l} + u_{i,j-1,u} = h^2 f_{i,j,l}$$

$$u_{i+1,j,u} - 2u_{i,j,u} - 2u_{i,j,l} + u_{i-1,j,l} + u_{i,j+1,u} + u_{i,j-1,l} = h^2 f_{i,j,u}$$

By a similar procedure to that for Cases 1 and 5, the compact matrix form can be described as follows:

$$\begin{pmatrix} F_1 & F_2 \\ F_2 & F_1 \end{pmatrix}\begin{pmatrix} U_l \\ U_u \end{pmatrix} = h^2 \begin{pmatrix} F_l \\ F_u \end{pmatrix}$$

$$F_1 = \begin{pmatrix} \boldsymbol{F} & I & O & O & \ldots & O \\ O & \boldsymbol{F} & I & O & \ldots & O \\ \vdots & \vdots & \vdots & \vdots & \vdots & \vdots \\ O & O & O & \ldots & O & \boldsymbol{F} \end{pmatrix}, \quad F_2 = \begin{pmatrix} \boldsymbol{F}^T & O & O & \ldots & O & O \\ I & \boldsymbol{F}^T & O & \ldots & O & O \\ \vdots & \vdots & \vdots & \vdots & \vdots & \vdots \\ O & \ldots & O & 0 & I & \boldsymbol{F}^T \end{pmatrix}$$

where I is a specific and O is a zero matrix and:

$$\boldsymbol{F} = \begin{pmatrix} -2 & 1 & 0 & 0 & 0 & \ldots & 0 \\ 0 & -2 & 1 & 0 & 0 & \ldots & 0 \\ 0 & 0 & -2 & 1 & 0 & \ldots & 0 \\ \vdots & \vdots & \vdots & \vdots & \vdots & \vdots & \vdots \\ 0 & 0 & 0 & \ldots & 0 & 0 & -2 \end{pmatrix}$$

Cases 2 and 7. The derivatives with respect to x is $\partial_{x_{i-gH},\ x_{ii-gH}}$ differentiable and with respect to y is $\partial_{y_{ii-gH},\ y_{i-gH}}$ differentiable.

$$\partial_{x_{i-gH},x_{ii-gH}} u\big|_{i,j} = \frac{1}{h^2}\left(u_{i+1,j} \ominus_H u_{ij} \ominus_H (-1)u_{i-1,j} \oplus (-1)u_{ij}\right)$$

$$\partial_{y_{ii-gH},y_{i-gH}} u\big|_{i,j} = \frac{1}{h^2}\left((-i1)u_{ij} \ominus_H (-1)u_{i,j+1} \ominus_H u_{i,j} \oplus u_{i,j-1}\right)$$

By substituting in:

$$\partial_{x_{i-gH},x_{ii-gH}} u\big|_{i,j} \oplus \partial_{y_{i-gH},y_{i-gH}} u\big|_{i,j} = f\left(x_i, y_j\right)$$

$$\frac{1}{h^2}\left(u_{i+1,j} \ominus_H u_{ij} \ominus_H (-1)u_{i-1,j} \oplus (-1)u_{ij}\right)$$

$$\oplus \frac{1}{h^2}\left((-1)u_{ij} \ominus_H (-1)u_{i,j+1} \ominus_H u_{i,j} \oplus u_{i,j-1}\right) = f\left(x_i, y_j\right)$$

$$u_{i+1,j} \ominus_H 2 \odot u_{ij} \oplus (-2)u_{ij} \ominus_H (-1)u_{i-1,j} \ominus_H (-1)u_{i,j+1} \oplus u_{i,j-1} = h^2 f_{ij},$$
$$i,j = 0,1,\ldots,N.$$

The level-wise form is:

$$u_{i+1,j,l} - 2u_{i,j,l} - 2u_{i,j,u} + u_{i-1,j,l} + u_{i,j+1,u} + u_{i,j-1,l} = h^2 f_{i,j,l}$$

$$u_{i+1,j,u} - 2u_{i,j,u} - 2u_{i,j,l} + u_{i-1,j,u} + u_{i,j+1,l} + u_{i,j-1,u} = h^2 f_{i,j,u}$$

By a similar procedure to that for Cases 1 and 5, the compact matrix form can be described as follows:

$$\begin{pmatrix} F_1 & F_2 \\ F_2 & F_1 \end{pmatrix}\begin{pmatrix} U_l \\ U_u \end{pmatrix} = h^2\begin{pmatrix} F_l \\ F_u \end{pmatrix}$$

$$F_1 = \begin{pmatrix} \boldsymbol{F} & O & O & \ldots & O & O \\ I & \boldsymbol{F} & O & \ldots & O & O \\ \vdots & \vdots & \vdots & & \vdots & \vdots \\ O & \ldots & O & & 0 \; I & \boldsymbol{F} \end{pmatrix},\ F_2 = \begin{pmatrix} \boldsymbol{F}^T & I & O & O & \ldots & O \\ O & \boldsymbol{F}^T & I & O & \ldots & O \\ \vdots & \vdots & \vdots & \vdots & & \vdots \\ O & O & O & \ldots & O & \boldsymbol{F}^T \end{pmatrix}$$

where I is a specific and O is a zero matrix and:

$$\boldsymbol{F} = \begin{pmatrix} -2 & 1 & 0 & 0 & 0 & \ldots & 0 \\ 0 & -2 & 1 & 0 & 0 & \ldots & 0 \\ 0 & 0 & -2 & 1 & 0 & \ldots & 0 \\ \vdots & \vdots & \vdots & \vdots & \vdots & \vdots & \vdots \\ 0 & 0 & 0 & \ldots & 0 & 0 & -2 \end{pmatrix}$$

Cases 2 and 8. The derivatives with respect to x are $\partial_{x_{i-gH},\, x_{ii-gH}}$ differentiable and with respect to y are $\partial_{y_{ii-gH},\, y_{ii-gH}}$ differentiable:

$$\partial_{x_{i-gH},x_{ii-gH}} u\big|_{i,j} = \frac{1}{h^2}\left(u_{i+1,j} \ominus_H u_{ij} \ominus_H (-1)u_{i-1,j} \oplus (-1)u_{ij}\right)$$

$$\partial_{y_{ii-gH},y_{i-gH}} u\big|_{i,j} = \frac{1}{h^2}\left((-2)u_{ij} \ominus_H (-1)u_{i,j+1} \ominus_H (-1)u_{i,j-1}\right)$$

By substituting in:

$$\partial_{x_{i-gH},x_{ii-gH}} u\big|_{i,j} \oplus \partial_{y_{i-gH},y_{i-gH}} u\big|_{i,j} = f(x_i, y_j)$$

$$\frac{1}{h^2}\left(u_{i+1,j} \ominus_H u_{ij} \ominus_H (-1)u_{i-1,j} \oplus (-1)u_{ij}\right)$$

$$\oplus \frac{1}{h^2}\left((-2)u_{ij} \ominus_H (-1)u_{i,j+1} \ominus_H (-1)u_{i,j-1}\right) = f(x_i, y_j)$$

$$u_{i+1,j} \ominus_H u_{ij} \oplus (-3)u_{ij} \ominus_H (-1)u_{i-1,j} \ominus_H (-1)u_{i,j+1} \ominus_H (-1)u_{i,j-1} = h^2 f_{ij},$$

$$i,j = 0,1,\ldots,N.$$

The level-wise form is:

$$u_{i+1,j,l} - u_{i,j,l} - 3u_{i,j,u} + u_{i-1,j,u} + u_{i,j+1,u} + u_{i,j-1,u} = h^2 f_{i,j,l}$$

$$u_{i+1,j,u} - u_{i,j,u} - 3u_{i,j,l} + u_{i-1,j,l} + u_{i,j+1,l} + u_{i,j-1,l} = h^2 f_{i,j,u}$$

By a similar procedure to that for Cases 1 and 5, the compact matrix form can be described as follows:

$$\begin{pmatrix} G_1 & G_2 \\ G_2 & G_1 \end{pmatrix}\begin{pmatrix} U_l \\ U_u \end{pmatrix} = h^2 \begin{pmatrix} F_l \\ F_u \end{pmatrix}$$

$$G_1 = \begin{pmatrix} G & O & O & O & \ldots & O \\ O & G & O & \ldots & O & O \\ \vdots & \vdots & \vdots & \vdots & \vdots & \vdots \\ O & O & \ldots & O & O & G \end{pmatrix}, \quad G_2 = \begin{pmatrix} D^T & I & O & \ldots & O & O \\ I & D^T & I & O & \ldots & O \\ \vdots & \vdots & \vdots & \vdots & \vdots & \vdots \\ O & \ldots & O & O & I & D^T \end{pmatrix}$$

where I is a specific and O is a zero matrix and the matrix G is as follows:

$$G = \begin{pmatrix} -1 & 1 & 0 & 0 & 0 & \ldots & 0 \\ 0 & -1 & 1 & 0 & 0 & \ldots & 0 \\ 0 & 0 & -1 & 1 & 0 & \ldots & 0 \\ \vdots & \vdots & \vdots & \vdots & \vdots & \vdots & \vdots \\ 0 & 0 & 0 & \ldots & 0 & 0 & -1 \end{pmatrix}, \quad D = \begin{pmatrix} -3 & 1 & 0 & 0 & 0 & \ldots & 0 \\ 0 & -3 & 1 & 0 & 0 & \ldots & 0 \\ 0 & 0 & -3 & 1 & 0 & \ldots & 0 \\ \vdots & \vdots & \vdots & \vdots & \vdots & \vdots & \vdots \\ 0 & 0 & 0 & \ldots & 0 & 0 & -3 \end{pmatrix}$$

Cases 3 and 5. The derivatives with respect to x are $\partial_{x_{ii-gH},\, x_{i-gH}}$ differentiable and with respect to y are $\partial_{y_{i-gH},\, y_{i-gH}}$ differentiable:

$$\partial_{x_{ii-gH},x_{i-gH}} u\big|_{i,j} = \frac{1}{h^2}\left((-1)u_{i,j} \ominus_H (-1)u_{i+1,j} \ominus_H u_{i,j} \oplus u_{i-1,j}\right)$$

$$\partial_{y_{i-gH},y_{i-gH}} u\big|_{i,j} = \frac{1}{h^2}\left(u_{i,j+1} \ominus_H 2 \odot u_{i,j} \oplus u_{i,j-1}\right)$$

By substituting in:

$$\partial_{x_{ii-gH},x_{i-gH}} u\big|_{i,j} \oplus \partial_{y_{i-gH},y_{i-gH}} u\big|_{i,j} = f(x_i, y_j)$$

$$\frac{1}{h^2}\left((-1)u_{i,j} \ominus_H (-1)u_{i+1,j} \ominus_H u_{i,j} \oplus u_{i-1,j}\right) \oplus \frac{1}{h^2}\left(u_{i,j+1} \ominus_H 2 \odot u_{i,j} \oplus u_{i,j-1}\right)$$

$$= f(x_i, y_j)$$

$$\ominus_H (-1)u_{i+1,j} \ominus_H 3 \odot u_{ij} \oplus (-1)u_{i,j} \oplus u_{i-1,j} \oplus u_{i,j+1} \oplus u_{i,j-1} = h^2 f_{ij}$$

$$i,j = 0,1,\ldots,N.$$

In level-wise form:

$$u_{i+1,j,u} - 3u_{i,j,l} - u_{i,j,u} + u_{i-1,j,l} + u_{i,j+1,l} + u_{i,j-1,l} = h^2 f_{i,j,l}$$

$$u_{i+1,j,l} - 3u_{i,j,u} - u_{i,j,l} + u_{i-1,j,u} + u_{i,j+1,u} + u_{i,j-1,u} = h^2 f_{i,j,u}$$

In the compact form:

$$\begin{pmatrix} G_1 & G_2 \\ G_2 & G_1 \end{pmatrix} \begin{pmatrix} U_l \\ U_u \end{pmatrix} = h^2 \begin{pmatrix} F_l \\ F_u \end{pmatrix}$$

$$G_1 = \begin{pmatrix} D^T & I & O & \ldots & O & O \\ I & D^T & I & O & \ldots & O \\ \vdots & \vdots & \vdots & \vdots & \vdots & \vdots \\ O & \ldots & O & O & I & D^T \end{pmatrix}, \quad G_2 = \begin{pmatrix} G & O & O & O & \ldots & O \\ O & G & O & \ldots & O & O \\ \vdots & \vdots & \vdots & \vdots & \vdots & \vdots \\ O & O & \ldots & O & O & G \end{pmatrix}$$

where I is a specific and O is a zero matrix and the matrix G is as follows:

$$G = \begin{pmatrix} -1 & 1 & 0 & 0 & 0 & \ldots & 0 \\ 0 & -1 & 1 & 0 & 0 & \ldots & 0 \\ 0 & 0 & -1 & 1 & 0 & \ldots & 0 \\ \vdots & \vdots & \vdots & \vdots & \vdots & \vdots & \vdots \\ 0 & 0 & 0 & \ldots & 0 & 0 & -1 \end{pmatrix}, \quad D = \begin{pmatrix} -3 & 1 & 0 & 0 & 0 & \ldots & 0 \\ 0 & -3 & 1 & 0 & 0 & \ldots & 0 \\ 0 & 0 & -3 & 1 & 0 & \ldots & 0 \\ \vdots & \vdots & \vdots & \vdots & \vdots & \vdots & \vdots \\ 0 & 0 & 0 & \ldots & 0 & 0 & -3 \end{pmatrix}$$

Cases 3 and 6. The derivatives with respect to x are $\partial_{x_{ii-gH},\, x_{i-gH}}$ differentiable and with respect to y are $\partial_{y_{i-gH},\, y_{ii-gH}}$ differentiable:

$$\partial_{x_{ii-gH},x_{i-gH}}u\big|_{i,j}=\frac{1}{h^2}\left((-1)u_{i,j}\ominus_H(-1)u_{i+1,j}\ominus_H u_{i,j}\oplus u_{i-1,j}\right)$$

$$\partial_{y_{i-gH},y_{ii-gH}}u\big|_{i,j}=\frac{1}{h^2}\left(u_{i,j+1}\ominus_H u_{i,j}\ominus_H(-1)u_{i,j-1}\oplus(-1)u_{i,j}\right)$$

By substituting in:

$$\partial_{x_{ii-gH},x_{i-gH}}u\big|_{i,j}\oplus\partial_{y_{i-gH},y_{ii-gH}}u\big|_{i,j}=f(x_i,y_j)$$

$$\frac{1}{h^2}\left((-1)u_{i,j}\ominus_H(-1)u_{i+1,j}\ominus_H u_{i,j}\oplus u_{i-1,j}\right)$$

$$\oplus\frac{1}{h^2}\left(u_{i,j+1}\ominus_H u_{i,j}\ominus_H(-1)u_{i,j-1}\oplus(-1)u_{i,j}\right)=f(x_i,y_j)$$

$$\ominus_H(-1)u_{i+1,j}\ominus_H 2\odot u_{i,j}\oplus(-2)u_{i,j}\oplus u_{i-1,j}\oplus u_{i,j+1}\ominus_H(-1)u_{i,j-1}=h^2 f_{ij},$$

$$i,j=0,1,\ldots,N.$$

The level-wise form is:

$$u_{i+1,j,u}-2u_{i,j,l}-2u_{i,j,u}+u_{i-1,j,l}+u_{i,j+1,l}+u_{i,j-1,u}=h^2 f_{i,j,l}$$

$$u_{i+1,j,l}-2u_{i,j,u}-2u_{i,j,l}+u_{i-1,j,u}+u_{i,j+1,u}+u_{i,j-1,l}=h^2 f_{i,j,u}$$

By a similar procedure to that for Cases 1 and 5, the compact matrix form can be described as follows:

$$\begin{pmatrix} C_1 & C_2 \\ C_2 & C_1 \end{pmatrix}\begin{pmatrix} U_l \\ U_u \end{pmatrix}=h^2\begin{pmatrix} F_l \\ F_u \end{pmatrix}$$

$$C_1=\begin{pmatrix} -2I & I & O & \ldots & O & O \\ I & -2I & I & O & \ldots & O \\ \vdots & \vdots & \vdots & \vdots & \vdots & \vdots \\ O & \ldots & O & O & I & -2I \end{pmatrix},\quad C_2=\begin{pmatrix} C & O & O & O & \ldots & O \\ O & C & O & \ldots & O & O \\ \vdots & \vdots & \vdots & \vdots & \vdots & \vdots \\ O & O & \ldots & O & O & B \end{pmatrix}$$

where I is a specific and O is a zero matrix and the matrix C is as follows:

$$C=\begin{pmatrix} -2 & 1 & 0 & 0 & 0 & \ldots & 0 \\ 1 & -2 & 1 & 0 & 0 & \ldots & 0 \\ 0 & 1 & -2 & 1 & 0 & \ldots & 0 \\ \vdots & \vdots & \vdots & \vdots & \vdots & \vdots & \vdots \\ 0 & 0 & 0 & \ldots & 0 & 1 & -2 \end{pmatrix}$$

Cases 3 and 7. The derivatives with respect to x are $\partial_{x_{ii-gH},\, x_{i-gH}}$ differentiable and with respect to y are $\partial_{y_{ii-gH},\, y_{i-gH}}$ differentiable:

$$\partial_{x_{ii-gH},x_{i-gH}} u\big|_{i,j} = \frac{1}{h^2}\left((-1)u_{i,j} \ominus_H (-1)u_{i+1,j} \ominus_H u_{i,j} \oplus u_{i-1,j}\right)$$

$$\partial_{y_{ii-gH},y_{i-gH}} u\big|_{i,j} = \frac{1}{h^2}\left((-1)u_{i,j} \ominus_H (-1)u_{i,j+1} \ominus_H u_{i,j} \oplus u_{i,j-1}\right)$$

By substituting in:

$$\partial_{x_{i-gH},x_{ii-gH}} u\big|_{i,j} \oplus \partial_{y_{i-gH},y_{ii-gH}} u\big|_{i,j} = f\left(x_i, y_j\right)$$

$$\frac{1}{h^2}\left((-1)u_{i,j} \ominus_H (-1)u_{i+1,j} \ominus_H u_{i,j} \oplus u_{i-1,j}\right)$$

$$\oplus \frac{1}{h^2}\left((-1)u_{i,j} \ominus_H (-1)u_{i,j+1} \ominus_H u_{i,j} \oplus u_{i,j-1}\right) = f\left(x_i, y_j\right)$$

$$\ominus_H (-1)u_{i+1,j} \ominus_H 2 \odot u_{ij} \oplus (-2)u_{ij} \oplus u_{i-1,j} \ominus_H (-1)u_{i,j+1} \oplus u_{i,j-1} = h^2 f_{ij},$$

$$i,j = 0,1,\ldots,N.$$

The level-wise form is:

$$u_{i+1,j,u} - 2u_{i,j,l} - 2u_{i,j,u} + u_{i-1,j,l} + u_{i,j+1,u} + u_{i,j-1,l} = h^2 f_{i,j,l}$$

$$u_{i+1,j,l} - 2u_{i,j,u} - 2u_{i,j,l} + u_{i-1,j,u} + u_{i,j+1,l} + u_{i,j-1,u} = h^2 f_{i,j,u}$$

By a similar procedure to that for Cases 1 and 5, the compact matrix form can be described as follows:

$$\begin{pmatrix} B_1 & B_2 \\ B_2 & B_1 \end{pmatrix} \begin{pmatrix} U_l \\ U_u \end{pmatrix} = h^2 \begin{pmatrix} F_l \\ F_u \end{pmatrix}$$

$$B_1 = \begin{pmatrix} -I & O & O & \ldots & O & O \\ I & -I & O & \ldots & O & O \\ \vdots & \vdots & \vdots & & \vdots & \vdots \\ O & \ldots & O & 0 & I & -I \end{pmatrix},\quad B_2 = \begin{pmatrix} B & I & O & O & \ldots & O \\ O & B & I & O & \ldots & O \\ \vdots & \vdots & \vdots & \vdots & & \vdots \\ O & O & O & \ldots & O & B \end{pmatrix}$$

with the same matrices and:

$$B = \begin{pmatrix} -3 & 1 & 0 & 0 & 0 & \ldots & 0 \\ 1 & -3 & 1 & 0 & 0 & \ldots & 0 \\ 0 & 1 & -3 & 1 & 0 & \ldots & 0 \\ \vdots & \vdots & \vdots & \vdots & \vdots & \vdots & \vdots \\ 0 & 0 & 0 & \ldots & 0 & 1 & -3 \end{pmatrix}$$

Cases 3 and 8. The derivatives with respect to x are $\partial_{x_{ii-gH},\,x_{i-gH}}$ differentiable and with respect to y are $\partial_{y_{ii-gH},\,y_{ii-gH}}$ differentiable:

$$\partial_{x_{ii-gH},x_{i-gH}}u\big|_{i,j}=\frac{1}{h^2}\left((-1)u_{i,j}\ominus_H(-1)u_{i+1,j}\ominus_H u_{i,j}\oplus u_{i-1,j}\right)$$

$$\partial_{y_{ii-gH},y_{i-gH}}u\big|_{i,j}=\frac{1}{h^2}\left((-2)u_{i,j}\ominus_H(-1)u_{i,j+1}\ominus_H(-1)u_{i,j-1}\right)$$

By substituting in:

$$\partial_{x_{i-gH},x_{ii-gH}}u\big|_{i,j}\oplus\partial_{y_{i-gH},y_{i-gH}}u\big|_{i,j}=f(x_i,y_j)$$

$$\frac{1}{h^2}\left((-1)u_{i,j}\ominus_H(-1)u_{i+1,j}\ominus_H u_{i,j}\oplus u_{i-1,j}\right)$$

$$\oplus\frac{1}{h^2}\left((-2)u_{i,j}\ominus_H(-1)u_{i,j+1}\ominus_H(-1)u_{i,j-1}\right)=f(x_i,y_j)$$

$$\ominus_H(-1)u_{i+1,j}\ominus_H u_{ij}\oplus(-3)u_{ij}\oplus u_{i-1,j}\ominus_H(-1)u_{i,j+1}\ominus_H(-1)u_{i,j-1}=h^2 f_{ij},$$

$$i,j=0,1,\ldots,N.$$

The level-wise form is:

$$u_{i+1,j,u}-u_{i,j,l}-3u_{i,j,u}+u_{i-1,j,l}+u_{i,j+1,u}+u_{i,j-1,u}=h^2 f_{i,j,l}$$

$$u_{i+1,j,l}-u_{i,j,u}-3u_{i,j,l}+u_{i-1,j,u}+u_{i,j+1,l}+u_{i,j-1,l}=h^2 f_{i,j,u}$$

By a similar procedure to that for Cases 1 and 5, the compact matrix form can be described as follows:

$$\begin{pmatrix}G_1 & G_2\\ G_2 & G_1\end{pmatrix}\begin{pmatrix}U_l\\ U_u\end{pmatrix}=h^2\begin{pmatrix}F_l\\ F_u\end{pmatrix}$$

$$G_1=\begin{pmatrix}G & O & O & O & \ldots & O\\ O & G & O & \ldots & O & O\\ \vdots & \vdots & \vdots & \vdots & \vdots & \vdots\\ O & O & \ldots & O & O & G\end{pmatrix},\quad G_2=\begin{pmatrix}D^T & I & O & \ldots & O & O\\ I & D^T & I & O & \ldots & O\\ \vdots & \vdots & \vdots & \vdots & \vdots & \vdots\\ O & \ldots & O & O & I & D^T\end{pmatrix}$$

where I is a specific and O is a zero matrix and the matrix G is as follows:

$$G=\begin{pmatrix}-1 & 1 & 0 & 0 & 0 & \ldots & 0\\ 0 & -1 & 1 & 0 & 0 & \ldots & 0\\ 0 & 0 & -1 & 1 & 0 & \ldots & 0\\ \vdots & \vdots & \vdots & \vdots & \vdots & \vdots & \vdots\\ 0 & 0 & 0 & \ldots & 0 & 0 & -1\end{pmatrix},\quad D=\begin{pmatrix}-3 & 1 & 0 & 0 & 0 & \ldots & 0\\ 0 & -3 & 1 & 0 & 0 & \ldots & 0\\ 0 & 0 & -3 & 1 & 0 & \ldots & 0\\ \vdots & \vdots & \vdots & \vdots & \vdots & \vdots & \vdots\\ 0 & 0 & 0 & \ldots & 0 & 0 & -3\end{pmatrix}$$

Note. The rest of the cases have a similar structure and the only difference is in the permutation of submatrices. Cases 4 and 8 are the symmetric cases of Cases 1 and 5:

$$\begin{pmatrix} O & A_1 \\ A_1 & O \end{pmatrix}\begin{pmatrix} U_l \\ U_u \end{pmatrix} = h^2\begin{pmatrix} F_l \\ F_u \end{pmatrix}$$

$$A_1 = \begin{pmatrix} A & O & O & O & \dots & O \\ O & O & O & O & \dots & O \\ \vdots & \vdots & \vdots & \vdots & \vdots & \vdots \\ O & O & \dots & O & O & A \end{pmatrix}$$

where I is a specific matrix and O is a zero matrix and:

$$A = \begin{pmatrix} -4 & 1 & 0 & 0 & 0 & \dots & 0 \\ 1 & -4 & 1 & 0 & 0 & \dots & 0 \\ 0 & 1 & -4 & 1 & 0 & \dots & 0 \\ \vdots & \vdots & \vdots & \vdots & \vdots & \vdots & \vdots \\ 0 & 0 & 0 & \dots & 0 & 1 & -4 \end{pmatrix}$$

As we know, the finite difference method needs error analysis or convergence investigation. In the following, we shall discuss the error analysis of the method (see Abdi & Allahviranloo, 2019).

7.4.1.1 Error analysis

Suppose that $U_{i,j}$ is the exact value and $u_{i,j} \approx U_{i,j}$ is the approximate value at the point (x_i, y_j), which is obtained by the difference method. Consider the error $e_{i,j} = u_{i,j} \ominus_H U_{i,j}$ at the same point and $u_{i,j} = U_{i,j} \oplus e_{i,j}$:

$$\partial^2_{xx,gH} u(x,y)|_{i,j} \oplus \partial^2_{yy,gH} u(x,y)|_{i,j} = f_{i,j}$$

Since $u(x,y) = U(x,y) \oplus e(x,y)$, then by substituting we have:

$$\partial^2_{xx,gH}(U(x,y) \oplus e(x,y)) \oplus \partial^2_{yy,gH}(U(x,y) \oplus e(x,y)) =$$

$$= \underbrace{\partial^2_{xx,gH} U(x,y) \oplus \partial^2_{yy,gH} U(x,y)}_{f(x,y)} \oplus \partial^2_{xx,gH} e(x,y) \oplus \partial^2_{yy,gH} e(x,y) = f(x,y) \oplus \hbar(x,y)$$

We assume that:

$$\partial^2_{xx,gH} e(x,y) \oplus \partial^2_{yy,gH} e(x,y) = h^2 \hbar(x,y)$$

where $\hbar(x,y)$ is called a reminder function and it is proportional to the fourth order derivative of $U(x,y)$. Indeed, our problem is now:

$$\partial^2_{xx,gH} e(x,y) \oplus \partial^2_{yy,gH} e(x,y) = h^2 \hbar(x,y)$$

It should be noted that $e(x,y)$ has the same properties of the solution function $u(x,t)$. Here we should show that the error function intends zero when the step size h intends zero. To this end, we show that the norm of error function at discretized points (as a vector) intends zero. In fact, we have:

$$\partial^2_{xx,gH} e(x,y)|_{i,j} \oplus \partial^2_{yy,gH} e(x,y)|_{i,j} = h^2 \hbar_{i,j}$$

$$\hbar_{i,j} \propto \frac{h^2}{12}\left(\frac{\partial^4}{\partial x^4}U(x,y) \oplus \frac{\partial^4}{\partial y^4}U(x,y)\right)_{i,j}$$

and considering:

$$M = \max\left\{\left|\frac{\partial^4}{\partial x^4}U(x,y)\right|_{i,j}, \left|\frac{\partial^4}{\partial y^4}U(x,y)\right|_{i,j}\right\}$$

then:

$$\hbar_{i,j} \propto \frac{Mh^2}{12}$$

As with the previously mentioned cases, eight cases happen here too. In each case, we have a system of linear equations, which are denoted in the following form, generally:

$$\begin{pmatrix} M_1 & M_2 \\ M_2 & M_1 \end{pmatrix}\begin{pmatrix} E_l \\ E_u \end{pmatrix} = h^2 \begin{pmatrix} H_l \\ H_u \end{pmatrix}$$

where M_1 and M_2 are three-diagonal sparse and block matrices. If the matrix $\begin{pmatrix} M_1 & M_2 \\ M_2 & M_1 \end{pmatrix}$ is nonsingular, then the vector solution $\begin{pmatrix} E_l \\ E_u \end{pmatrix}$ can be found easily. On the other hand:

$$\det\begin{pmatrix} M_1 & M_2 \\ M_2 & M_1 \end{pmatrix} = \det(M_1 - M_2)\cdot\det(M_1 + M_2)$$

and:

$$\det\begin{pmatrix} M_1 & M_2 \\ M_2 & M_1 \end{pmatrix} \neq 0 \Leftrightarrow \begin{pmatrix} E_l \\ E_u \end{pmatrix} = h^2 \begin{pmatrix} M_1 & M_2 \\ M_2 & M_1 \end{pmatrix}^{-1} \begin{pmatrix} H_l \\ H_u \end{pmatrix}$$

To show the convergence, it is enough that we show it under the infinity norm of the vectors and matrices:

$$\left\|\begin{pmatrix}E_l\\E_u\end{pmatrix}\right\|_\infty \le h^2\left\|\begin{pmatrix}M_1 & M_2\\M_2 & M_1\end{pmatrix}^{-1}\right\|_\infty\cdot\left\|\begin{pmatrix}H_l\\H_u\end{pmatrix}\right\|_\infty = h^2\left\|\begin{pmatrix}M_1 & M_2\\M_2 & M_1\end{pmatrix}^{-1}\right\|_\infty\cdot\frac{Mh^2}{12}$$

So, if $\left\|\begin{pmatrix}M_1 & M_2\\M_2 & M_1\end{pmatrix}^{-1}\right\|_\infty = \mathcal{M}$, then we have:

$$0<\left\|\begin{pmatrix}E_l\\E_u\end{pmatrix}\right\|_\infty \le \mathcal{M}\cdot\frac{Mh^4}{12}$$

which means that:

$$h\to 0 \Longrightarrow \left\|\begin{pmatrix}E_l\\E_u\end{pmatrix}\right\|_\infty \to 0$$

Example. Consider the following simple example:

$$\Delta u = y\odot \sin x, \Omega=\{(x,y)\,|\, 0\le x\le \pi, 0\le y\le 1\}$$

with the boundary condition $u=0\in\mathbb{F}_R$ in $\partial\Omega$, where 1 is noted as a fuzzy number.

For instance, if $h=\frac{1}{2}$ and in Cases 2 and 8, the derivatives with respect to x are $\partial_{x_{i-gH},\, x_{ii-gH}}$ differentiable and with respect to y are $\partial_{y_{ii-gH},\, y_{ii-gH}}$ differentiable:

$$\partial_{x_{i-gH},x_{ii-gH}} u|_{i,j} = \frac{1}{h^2}\left(u_{i+1,j}\ominus_H u_{ij}\ominus_H(-1)u_{i-1,j}\oplus(-1)u_{ij}\right)$$

$$\partial_{y_{ii-gH},y_{i-gH}} u|_{i,j} = \frac{1}{h^2}\left((-2)u_{ij}\ominus_H(-1)u_{i,j+1}\ominus_H(-1)u_{i,j-1}\right)$$

for $i, j=0, 1, 2$. The level-wise form is as follows:

$$u_{i+1,j,l}-u_{i,j,l}-3u_{i,j,u}+u_{i-1,j,u}+u_{i,j+1,u}+u_{i,j-1,u}=\frac{1}{4}y_j\sin x_i$$

$$u_{i+1,j,u}-u_{i,j,u}-3u_{i,j,l}+u_{i-1,j,l}+u_{i,j+1,l}+u_{i,j-1,l}=\frac{1}{4}y_j\sin x_i$$

$$i=0,1,2,\ j=0\begin{cases} u_{1,0,l}-u_{0,0,l}-3u_{0,0,u}+u_{0,1,u}=\frac{1}{4}y_0\sin x_0\\ u_{1,0,u}-u_{0,0,u}-3u_{0,0,l}+u_{0,1,l}=\frac{1}{4}y_0\sin x_0\\ u_{2,0,l}-u_{1,0,l}-3u_{1,0,u}+u_{0,0,u}+u_{1,1,u}=\frac{1}{4}y_0\sin x_1\\ u_{2,0,u}-u_{1,0,u}-3u_{1,0,l}+u_{0,0,l}+u_{1,1,l}=\frac{1}{4}y_0\sin x_1\\ u_{3,0,l}-u_{2,0,l}-3u_{2,0,u}+u_{1,0,u}+u_{2,1,u}=\frac{1}{4}y_0\sin x_2\\ u_{3,0,u}-u_{2,0,u}-3u_{2,0,l}+u_{1,0,l}+u_{2,1,l}=\frac{1}{4}y_0\sin x_2 \end{cases}$$

$$i=0,1,2,\ j=1\begin{cases} u_{1,1,l}-u_{0,1,l}-3u_{0,1,u}+u_{0,2,u}+u_{0,0,u}=\frac{1}{4}y_1\sin x_0 \\ u_{1,1,u}-u_{0,1,u}-3u_{0,1,l}+u_{0,2,l}+u_{0,0,l}=\frac{1}{4}y_1\sin x_0 \\ u_{2,1,l}-u_{1,1,l}-3u_{1,1,u}+u_{0,1,u}+u_{1,2,u}+u_{1,0,u}=\frac{1}{4}y_1\sin x_1 \\ u_{2,1,u}-u_{1,1,u}-3u_{1,1,l}+u_{0,1,l}+u_{1,2,l}+u_{1,0,l}=\frac{1}{4}y_1\sin x_1 \\ u_{3,1,l}-u_{2,1,l}-3u_{2,1,u}+u_{1,1,u}+u_{2,2,u}+u_{2,0,u}=\frac{1}{4}y_1\sin x_2 \\ u_{3,1,u}-u_{2,1,u}-3u_{2,1,l}+u_{1,1,l}+u_{2,2,l}+u_{2,0,l}=\frac{1}{4}y_1\sin x_2 \end{cases}$$

$$i=0,1,2,\ j=2\begin{cases} u_{1,2,l}-u_{0,2,l}-3u_{0,2,u}+u_{0,1,u}=\frac{1}{4}y_2\sin x_0 \\ u_{1,2,u}-u_{0,2,u}-3u_{0,2,l}+u_{0,1,l}=\frac{1}{4}y_2\sin x_0 \\ u_{2,2,l}-u_{1,2,l}-3u_{1,2,u}+u_{0,2,u}+u_{1,1,u}=\frac{1}{4}y_2\sin x_1 \\ u_{2,2,u}-u_{1,2,u}-3u_{1,2,l}+u_{0,2,l}+u_{1,1,l}=\frac{1}{4}y_2\sin x_1 \\ u_{3,2,l}-u_{2,2,l}-3u_{2,2,u}+u_{1,2,u}+u_{2,1,u}=\frac{1}{4}y_2\sin x_2 \\ u_{3,2,u}-u_{2,2,u}-3u_{2,2,l}+u_{1,2,l}+u_{2,1,l}=\frac{1}{4}y_2\sin x_2 \end{cases}$$

where $u_{-1,\cdot}=u_{\cdot,3}=0$, and $u_{0,j}$, $u_{i,0}$, $i,j=0,1,2$ are known. After solving the linear systems, the results are obtained as the following triangular fuzzy numbers at several points. For instance, assume that:

$$u_{0,0}=\left(\frac{-37r}{128},\frac{35r}{128}\right),\quad u_{1,0}=\left(\frac{-5r}{64},\frac{3r}{64}\right),\quad u_{2,0}=\left(\frac{-61r}{128},\frac{59r}{128}\right)$$

$$u_{0,1}=\left(\frac{-25r}{64},\frac{23r}{64}\right),\quad u_{1,1}=\left(\frac{-7r}{64},\frac{r}{64}\right),\quad u_{2,1}=\left(\frac{-41r}{64},\frac{39r}{64}\right)$$

$$u_{0,2}=\left(\frac{-37r}{128},\frac{35r}{128}\right),\quad u_{1,2}=\left(\frac{-5r}{64},\frac{3r}{64}\right),\quad u_{2,2}=\left(\frac{-61r}{128},\frac{59r}{128}\right)$$

Now, in Cases 3 and 8, the derivatives with respect to x are $\partial_{x_{ii-gH},\, x_{i-gH}}$ differentiable and with respect to y are $\partial_{y_{ii-gH},\, y_{ii-gH}}$ differentiable:

$$u_{0,0}=\left(\frac{-61r}{128},\frac{59r}{128}\right),\quad u_{1,0}=\left(\frac{-5r}{64},\frac{3r}{64}\right),\quad u_{2,0}=\left(\frac{-37r}{128},\frac{35r}{128}\right)$$

$$u_{0,1}=\left(\frac{-41r}{64},\frac{39r}{64}\right),\ u_{1,1}=\left(\frac{-7r}{64},\frac{r}{64}\right),\ u_{2,1}=\left(\frac{-25r}{64},\frac{23r}{64}\right)$$

$$u_{0,2}=\left(\frac{-61r}{128},\frac{59r}{128}\right),\ u_{1,2}=\left(\frac{-5r}{64},\frac{3r}{64}\right),\ u_{2,2}=\left(\frac{-37r}{128},\frac{35r}{128}\right)$$

Now, the derivatives with respect to x are $\partial_{x_{ii-gH},\ x_{ii-gH}}$ differentiable and with respect to y are $\partial_{y_{ii-gH},\ y_{i-gH}}$ differentiable:

$$u_{0,0}=\left(\frac{-61r}{128},\frac{59r}{128}\right),\ u_{1,0}=\left(\frac{-41r}{64},\frac{39r}{64}\right),\ u_{2,0}=\left(\frac{-61r}{128},\frac{59r}{128}\right)$$

$$u_{0,1}=\left(\frac{-5r}{64},\frac{3r}{64}\right),\ u_{1,1}=\left(\frac{-7r}{64},\frac{r}{64}\right),\ u_{2,1}=\left(\frac{-5r}{64},\frac{3r}{64}\right)$$

$$u_{0,2}=\left(\frac{-37r}{128},\frac{35r}{128}\right),\ u_{1,2}=\left(\frac{-25r}{64},\frac{23r}{64}\right),\ u_{2,2}=\left(\frac{-37r}{128},\frac{35r}{128}\right)$$

Now, the derivatives with respect to x are $\partial_{x_{ii-gH},\ x_{ii-gH}}$ differentiable and with respect to y are $\partial_{y_{ii-gH},\ y_{ii-gH}}$ differentiable:

$$u_{0,0}=\left(\frac{11r}{64}-\frac{11}{64},\frac{11}{64}-\frac{11r}{64}\right),\ u_{1,0}=\left(\frac{7r}{32}-\frac{7}{32},\frac{7}{32}-\frac{7r}{32}\right),$$
$$u_{2,0}=\left(\frac{11r}{64}-\frac{11}{64},\frac{11}{64}-\frac{11r}{64}\right)$$

$$u_{0,0}=\left(\frac{7r}{32}-\frac{7}{32},\frac{7}{32}-\frac{7r}{32}\right),\ u_{1,0}=\left(\frac{9r}{32}-\frac{9}{32},\frac{9}{32}-\frac{9r}{32}\right),$$
$$u_{2,0}=\left(\frac{7r}{32}-\frac{7}{32},\frac{7}{32}-\frac{7r}{32}\right)$$

$$u_{0,0}=\left(\frac{11r}{64}-\frac{11}{64},\frac{11}{64}-\frac{11r}{64}\right),\ u_{1,0}=\left(\frac{7r}{32}-\frac{7}{32},\frac{7}{32}-\frac{7r}{32}\right),$$
$$u_{2,0}=\left(\frac{11r}{64}-\frac{11}{64},\frac{11}{64}-\frac{11r}{64}\right)$$

References

Abdi, M., Allahviranloo, T., 2019. Fuzzy finite difference method for solving Poisson's equation. J. Intell. Fuzzy Syst. 37 (3), 1–16.

Allahviranloo, T., 2020. Uncertain information and linear systems. In: Studies in Systems, Decision and Control. vol. 254. Springer.

Allahviranloo, T., Gouyandeh, Z., Armand, A., Hasanoglu, A., 2015. On fuzzy solutions for heat equation based on generalized Hukuhara differentiability. Fuzzy Set. Syst. 265, 1–23.

Armand, A., Allahviranloo, T., Abbasbandy, S., Gouyandeh, Z., 2019. The fuzzy generalized Taylor's expansion with application in fractional differential equations. Iran. J. Fuzzy Syst. 16 (2), 57–72.

Bede, B., Gal, S.G., 2005a. Generalizations of the differentiability of fuzzy-number-valued functions with applications to fuzzy differential equations. Fuzzy Set. Syst. 151, 581–599.

Bede, B., Gal, S.G., 2005b. Generalizations of the differentiability of fuzzy-number-valued functions with applications to fuzzy differential equations. Fuzzy Set. Syst. 151, 581–599.

Gouyandeha, Z., Allahviranloob, T., Abbasbandyb, S., Armand, A., 2017. A fuzzy solution of heat equation under generalized Hukuhara differentiability by fuzzy Fourier transform. Fuzzy Set. Syst. 309, 81–97.

Stefanini, L., Bede, B., 2009. Generalized Hukuhara differentiability of interval-valued functions and interval differential equations. Nonlinear Anal. 71, 1311–1328.

Index

Note: Page numbers followed by *f* indicate figures, and *t* indicate tables.

Printed in the United States
By Bookmasters